TANNENBERG

CLASH
OF
EMPIRES

Dennis E. Showalter

ARCHON BOOKS
1991

First published 1991 as an Archon Book,
an imprint of The Shoe String Press, Inc.,
Hamden, Connecticut 06514.

The paper used in this publication
meets the minimum requirements of
American National Standard for Information Sciences–Permanence of Paper
for Printed Library Materials,
ANSI Z39.48-1984 ∞

Library of Congress Cataloging-in-Publication Data

Showalter, Dennis E.
Tannenberg, clash of empires / Dennis E. Showalter.
p.   cm.
Includes bibliographical references (p. 407) and index.
1. Tannenberg, Battle of, 1914.
I. Title.
D552. T3S55   1990
940.4′22 — dc20   90-1088
ISBN 0-208-02252-X (alk. paper)

Printed in the United States of America

Contents

Acknowledgments   vii

Introduction   1

Order of Battle   5

PART I	THE FASHION TO MAKE WAR	11
1	The Circus Rider of Europe	13
2	The Center Fails to Hold	36
3	War Finds a Way	69

PART II	NOW THRIVE THE ARMOURERS	103
4	The Virgin Soldiers	105
5	Taking the Measure of Danger	139
6	First Contact: Gumbinnen	172

PART III	THE BLOOD-SWOLLEN GOD	211
7	The Province of Uncertainty	213
8	The Province of Chance	249
9	The Province of Victory	286

PART IV	THE BITTER FRUITS OF VICTORY	321
10	Opportunities and Illusions	323

Epilogue   347

Notes   355

Bibliographical Essay   407

Index   411

Index to Military Formations   417

Acknowledgments

A book eight years in the making accumulates a corresponding structure of personal and intellectual debts. Clara Anne, Clara Kathleen, and John bore with good grace the regular disappearances of their husband and father into the arcanae of an era long past. Colleagues and students at Colorado College accepted the highs and lows accompanying the project with no more than an occasional, "Aren't you finished *yet?*" College President Gresham Riley, Deans Glenn Brooks and David Finley, and successive research committees were more than generous with financial support and released time. History department chairs Robert McJimsey and Susan Ashley earned my repeated gratitude for their empathy in discussing course schedules and administrative demands.

The reference staff of Colorado College's Tutt Library, in particular interlibrary loan librarians Susan Connolly, Kim Miklofsky, and Diane Burgner, once again did wonders in unearthing obscure works from unlikely locations. Sheila Fuller's typing of the final manuscript relieved much of the last-stage anxieties accompanying authorship. At the publishing level, Jim Thorpe demonstrated once again why he is among the Atlantic world's best editors of military history. His questions, comments, advice, and encouragement have been crucial from start to finish of this project. I owe special thanks as well to someone I have never met: Pamela Chergotis, the copy editor who saved me from serious professional embarrassment by catching numerous lapses in argument and consistency.

I owe particular debts to three people. Louis Geiger, my first department chairman, showed me that scholarship is a necessary element in the liberal arts college. Denys Volan of the University of Colorado, Colorado Springs, exemplified learning brought alive in the classroom.

Acknowledgments

History department secretary Judy McClow typed early drafts, provided valuable stylistic suggestions, and helped bring perspective to a complex enterprise. *Tannenberg* is dedicated to them, with affection and admiration.

Introduction

Why a book about Tannenberg? Can anything useful possibly be said about a battle which began a war but did not end it, a battle whose very place names are lost to geography and history alike? Tannenberg in fact offers material for analysis on three levels. It is a significant case study of the problems facing armies in the initial stages of a major war. First battles tend to be neglected, except as examples of how not to proceed.[1] Students of men in war, like John Keegan and Richard Holmes, tend to focus on armies that have a spectrum of experiences behind them. Agincourt, Waterloo, the Somme—none were fought by greenhorns on either side. Even the British New Armies had well over a year's experience in uniform. But all wars have a beginning, and performance in a first battle can often mean that there will be no second chance. France in 1940 is only the most obvious example of that particular truism.[2]

The opening rounds of a come-as-you-are war highlight the relative success—or failure—of armies in preparing for their primary task. The opening days and weeks of war test a nation's military system and its military institutions in ways far greater than in later stages, when experience begins taking over and soldiers at all levels learn when and how to break the rules. Europe's greatest military powers in the twentieth century have been Germany and Russia. Both had forty years to prepare for the first round in East Prussia. The details of their successes and failures remain correspondingly relevant to students of war and society.

Readers will note that the operational chapters of this work are presented from a German perspective. The Russian army of World War I is the subject of an increasing number of major monographs. Bruce Menning discusses its doctrinal antecedents, David Jones its operational

1

performance, Allan Wildman its collapse. William Fuller is completing a major work, based on previously unavailable archival sources, on the history of Russian strategic planning. The army of the Second Reich, however, is more often studied in its political or social contexts than as a military instrument. One of the major reasons for undertaking this study was a desire to evaluate the kaiser's fighting men as they made the transition from peace to war. The scale of the Tannenberg campaign offers opportunities to integrate case studies at the tactical, operational, and strategic levels into a framework small enough to be more readily comprehensible by non-specialists than the amorphous fighting on the western front.

Tannenberg had mythic properties as well. The victory in East Prussia stood comparison with Verdun as the most familiar battle of World War I in German public opinion. The legends and hopes clustering around it helped shape attitudes until the very end of World War II. Even today a remnant of the tale lives on. Poland, a country which did not exist when Tannenberg was fought, remembers well that the battle borrowed its name from a centuries-earlier encounter of Germans and Slavs—one with a far different ending.[3]

Tannenberg was, finally, a clash of empires. Recent discussions of the origins of World War I have taken two forms. One emphasizes the war's accidental nature. It postulates, with an obvious eye on the present, the existence of mutually antagonistic alliance systems whose rivalries are largely generated by internal stresses of the states involved. Essentially artificial, the hostilities are all the more inflexible because of that fact. Eventually a small event on the periphery sets in motion a chain reaction, drawing the great powers and their clients alike into a war no one wants or expects.[4]

This approach, the political science or crisis-management model, is balanced by an historical interpretation presenting World War I as the product of rational calculation. In this argument Imperial Germany is described as believing that a bid for continental hegemony and world empire had a good chance of success in the circumstances of 1914. Her behavior generated entente calculations that Germany must be stopped, and could be stopped at acceptable cost. The result was Clausewitzian: war became the continuance of policy by other means.[5]

Neither of these interpretations has much room for "evil empires." Where that role exists, it is almost universally assigned to Kaiser William's Germany. Paul Schroeder has aptly pointed out that German foreign policy after Bismarck was dominated by a contradiction. Her vital interests on the continent were best served by preserving the status quo. Yet the dreams of *Weltpolitik* pursued by William II and his advisors increasingly led the Second Reich into adventures provoking challenges from her rivals and neighbors—challenges from which Germany, for all its warlike rhetoric, was frequently constrained to withdraw because of her own greater need for stability in Europe.[6] This *Weltpolitik* in turn becomes a manifes-

Introduction

tation of Imperial Germany's structural malaise. A defensive coalition of capitalists, landowners, and bureaucrats, more or less influenced by grassroots imperialists and militarist pressure groups, is presented as uniting in an uneasy compromise to preserve existing anomalous socio-economic relations by an outward projection of power, whatever the costs to Europe and the world.[7]

Scholars who do not dismiss out of hand German fears for her geopolitical position as groundless smokescreens usually focus on Anglo-German relations. The British Empire is presented as Germany's ultimate objective rival for wealth and status, with Germany cast in the role of the challenger—the aggressor.[8] The Second Reich's repeated claims of being faced with a formidable threat on the other side of the continent is usually dismissed. *"Die russische Gefahr"* becomes either a figment of generals' and politicians' imaginations, or a deliberate invention fostered even by the Weimar Republic as a means of denying Germany's guilt for the outbreak of war in 1914.[9] A government like Russia's, which collapsed into revolution; an economy like Russia's, in the early stages of development; a society like Russia's, lacking in skills and sophistication, surely posed no real danger to the mighty German Empire.[10]

This interpretation has a contemporary aspect as well. It reinforces a significant body of literature stressing the weaknesses and shortcomings of Soviet Russia, and attributing those deficiencies to long-term factors that deny eradication by any political system. Well before the political upheavals that began in 1989, German anxieties in 1914 invited comparison with those of the United States and the NATO alliance as the products of exaggeration, when not malice. The USSR inherited Tsarist Russia's role as a more or less unwitting victim of her neighbors' paranoia.[11]

In such contexts the details of nineteenth-century Russo-German relations seem obsolescent—the stuff at best of doctoral dissertations likely to remain forever unpublished. Yet Germany's Russian connections lay at the heart of Germany's foreign policy prior to 1914 in a way wider and more fashionable issues did not. The Gorbachev era has generated increasing discussion of a Russo-German *quid pro quo* involving a partnership modernizing eastern Europe in return for Germany's distancing herself from the Atlantic world. This hypothesis frequently incorporates an historical dimension alleging long-standing harmony between Russia and Germany—a harmony fostering willingness to stand together against a West whose values are essentially alien to both of them.

Tannenberg suggests an alternate set of possibilities by demonstrating the growth and flourishing of Russo-German antagonism over a significantly long period of time. It has been said that nations have neither eternal friends nor eternal enemies—only interests. Certainly in the half-century before 1914 the empires of tsar and kaiser developed interests whose conflict cannot be dismissed as the product of false consciousness or specific misjudgments.

The association of the two great eastern empires illustrates the

3

Introduction

growing complexity of power relationships in an industrial, technological era that made international relations increasingly an affair of everyman, everyday. Tannenberg was in good part a product of increased anxieties and diminished alternatives. In particular, an evaluation of perceptions and realities as they developed in Berlin suggests that Germany's decision for war in 1914 was undertaken in a far more negative context than conventional academic and popular wisdom accept. It is with that development that our story begins.

Outline Order of Battle German 8th Army

I CORPS

1st Infantry Division
    1st Brigade—1st Grenadiers, 41st Infantry
    2nd Brigade—3rd Grenadiers, 43rd Infantry
    1st Field Artillery Brigade—16th, 52nd Field Artillery
        8th Uhlans

2nd Infantry Division
    3rd Brigade—4th Grenadiers, 44th Infantry
    4th Brigade—33rd Fusiliers, 45th Infantry
    2nd Field Artillery Brigade—1st, 37th Field Artillery
        10th *Jäger zu Pferde*

XVII CORPS

35th Infantry Division
    70th Brigade—21st, 61st Infantry
    87th Brigade—174th, 176th Infantry
    35th Field Artillery Brigade—36th, 72nd Field Artillery
        4th *Jäger zu Pferde*

36th Infantry Division
    69th Brigade—129th, 175th Infantry
    71st Brigade—5th Grenadiers, 128th Infantry
    36th Field Artillery Brigade—36th, 72nd Field Artillery
        5th Hussars

XX CORPS

37th Infantry Division
    73rd Brigade—147th, 151st Infantry, 1st *Jäger* Bn.
    75th Brigade—146th, 150th Infantry
    37th Field Artillery Brigade—73rd, 82nd Field Artillery
        11th Dragoons

Order of Battle

41st Infantry Division
    72nd Brigade—18th, 59th Infantry
    74th Brigade—148th, 152nd Infantry
    41st Field Artillery Brigade—35th, 79th Field Artillery
                10th Dragoons

I RESERVE CORPS

1st Reserve Division
    1st Reserve Brigade—1st, 3rd Reserve Infantry
    72nd Reserve Brigade—18th, 59th Reserve Infantry, 1st Reserve
    Jäger Bn.
                1st Reserve Field Artillery
                1st Reserve Uhlans

36th Reserve Division
    69th Reserve Brigade—21st, 61st Reserve Infantry, 2nd Reserve
    Jäger Bn.
    70th Reserve Brigade—5th Reserve Infantry,
    54th Infantry (transferred from 3rd Division at outbreak of war)
                36th Reserve Field Artillery
                1st Reserve Hussars

3rd Reserve Division
    5th Reserve Brigade—2nd, 9th Reserve Infantry
    6th Reserve Brigade—34th, 49th Reserve Infantry
                3rd Reserve Field Artillery
                5th Reserve Dragoons

Höherer Landwehr-Kommando No. 1
    33rd *Landwehr* Brigade—75th, 76th *Landwehr* Infantry
    34th *Landwehr* Brigade—31st, 84th *Landwehr* Infantry
                Landwehr Cavalry Rgt.

1st Cavalry Division
    1st Cavalry Brigade—3d Cuirassers, 1st Dragoons
    2nd Cavalry Brigade—12th Uhlans, 9th *Jäger zu Pferde*
    41st Cavalry Brigade—4th Uhlans, 5th Cuirassers

PRINCIPAL GARRISON AND LANDWEHR FORCES
MENTIONED IN TEXT

Hauptreserve Graudenz
    69th Provisional Brigade—Ersatz Bns. of 5th Grenadiers,
    34th Fusiliers, 59th, 129th, 141st, 175th Infantry

Order of Battle

Hauptreserve Thorn
    35th Reserve Division
    5th *Landwehr* Brigade—2nd, 9th *Landwehr* Infantry
    20th *Landwehr* Brigade—19th, 107th *Landwehr* Infantry
        3rd Reserve Heavy Cavalry

6th Landwehr Brigade—34th, 49th *Landwehr* Infantry

70th Landwehr Brigade—5th, 18th *Landwehr* Infantry

Hauptreserve Königsberg (engaged at Gumbinnen)
    Ersatz Brigade—1st, 2nd *Ersatz* Rgts. (*Ersatz* bns. of 4th
      Grenadiers, 33rd Fusiliers, 41st, 44th, 45th Infantry)
    9th *Landwehr* Brigade—24th, 48th *Landwehr* Infantry
    1st Reserve Dragoons

Outline Order of Battle
Russian Northwest Front

1ST ARMY

II Corps—26th, 43rd Infantry Divisions
III Corps—25th, 27th Infantry Divisions
IV Corps—30th, 40th Infantry Divisions
XX Corps—28th, 29th Infantry Divisions
56th Infantry Division
1st Guard Cavalry Division
2nd Guard Cavalry Division
1st Cavalry Division
2nd Cavalry Division
5th Rifle Brigade
1st Independent Cavalry Brigade
1st Heavy Artillery Brigade

2ND ARMY

I Corps—22nd, 24th Infantry Divisions
VI Corps—4th, 16th Infantry Divisions
XIII Corps—1st, 36th Infantry Divisions
XV Corps—6th, 8th Infantry Divisions
XXIII Corps—3rd Guard, 2nd Infantry Divisions
4th Cavalry Division
6th Cavalry Division
15th Cavalry Division
1st Rifle Brigade
2nd Heavy Artillery Brigade

Note: A Russian rifle brigade had four two-battalion rifle regiments.

PART I

THE FASHION TO MAKE WAR

1
The Circus Rider
of Europe

The relationship between Imperial Germany and Tsarist Russia before 1914 was a complex mixture of attraction and repulsion. Anarchist Michael Bakunin's statement that nothing united Slavs like their hatred of Germans can be balanced by the German impact on Russia's Westernization. France might provide inspiration, but it was a long road from Paris to St. Petersburg. German professors filled most of the posts at the University of Moscow and the Academy of Sciences. German pietism shaped Russian religious thought. German concepts of natural law and philosophy prepared Russian ground not for individualism and empiricism but for *Aufklärung*, with its sensibility, its religiosity, its collectivism.[1]

The assimilation of this quasi-German heritage was at best incomplete. Nevertheless in the aftermath of the Napoleonic Wars a bilingual, bicultural elite developed, an elite consciously seeking to fuse the best of Russian and German.[2] An emerging Russian intelligentsia, initially self-absorbed and isolated, turned eagerly to Germany for cultural and intellectual models. The philosophy of Hegel and the literature of the Romantics were uncritically imitated east of the Vistula. Students were regularly sent to Germany for advanced education even in the darkest days of Nicholas I. Under Nicholas, too, a system of secondary schools on the German model was established for the entire empire. German scholars and artists basked in the admiration of their Russian counterparts. In turn they praised the spiritual depths of the Slavic soul and the unlimited promise of the Russian people.[3]

The relationship was by no means one-sided. Restoration and *Vormärz* Prussia accepted the Russia of Alexander and Nicholas as a bulwark

13

against Austrian dominance, French revanchism, and popular revolution.[4] Militarily too the traditional positions of Prussia and Russia reversed themselves during the Napoleonic Era. Prussia's martial arrogance was humbled at Jena and Auerstädt. After 1813 the war-hardened Russian army, with its long-service peasant conscripts, compared all too favorably in all too many respects with the improvised Prussian forces. The shortcomings of the postwar Prussian army seemed even more glaring when compared with the situation in Russia. Officers facing limited budgets periodically turned longing eyes to Russia, where the soldier-tsar Nicholas I appeared to stint his military establishment of nothing, where elaborate maneuvers were staged regardless of cost, where developments in weapons, organization, and tactics could be tested on an army-corps scale.[5]

The Prussian foreign office recognized that Russia's diplomatic position in Europe, particularly after 1849, was less solid than it seemed. It also recognized Prussia's geographic, economic, and military weaknesses vis-à-vis both Western and Eastern Europe. Commitment to Russia meant the corresponding risk of becoming the Tsar's battering ram against liberalism in general and France in particular. Prussia's "active neutrality" during the Crimean crisis of 1853–55 was deliberately designed to sustain good relations with Russia at the lowest possible price. The policy's initial success is indicated by Russian foreign minister K. R. Nesselrode's belief that the Prussian connection must become the cornerstone of Russia's relations with France in the aftermath of the Crimean War. Ultimately, however, Russia remained more concerned until 1866 with mending French fences than with supporting the aims of a Prussia whose good will was often taken for granted and whose capacities to implement an independent foreign policy seemed derisory.[6]

The Seven Weeks' War of 1866 came as a corresponding surprise. Austria's unexpected collapse confronted Russia with a *fait accompli*. Should she intervene, it would be not to preserve a structure but to restore one—with proportionately increased risks. Four years later, on October 31, 1870, Russia collected a price for her abstention by unilaterally repudiating those clauses of the Crimean settlement that provided for neutralization of the Black Sea.

Bismarck was long in forgetting the minicrisis this generated. With Germany's armies too deeply stuck in the French tar baby to give him much freedom of action, the furious protests of Austria and Britain against Russia's action bade fair to escalate into an European war. It took all of the chancellor's skill to get the involved powers to a conference table, where Russia's action was eventually legitimated—at significant cost to Bismarck's nerves and with significant impact on his subsequent policies.[7]

The new German empire inherited other liabilities in relating to its Tsarist neighbor. A rising generation of Russian intellectuals blamed fifty years of playing safe, of hiding behind piles of paper, on Teutonic influences that stifled Slavic warmth and spontaneity. Pedantry and pettifogging were common hallmarks of the German in Russian literature. Among the least sympathetic minor characters of *War and Peace* is Captain

Berg, who knows the army regulations better than the Lord's Prayer, yet sees nothing beyond them. Goncharov's *Oblomov* depends essentially for its comic effect on the contrast between Oblomov, the lazy, slovenly, ultimately lovable Russian and the dignified, efficient, ultimately sterile German Stoltz.

Literary Germanophobia was reinforced by economic changes. In a Russia historically lacking a middle class, opportunities for emigrants and migrants of all ethnic backgrounds had been extensive. The upper levels of the economy and the higher ranks of the bureaucracy were by no means dominated numerically by men of German ancestry. Germans, however, particularly from the Baltic lands, constituted a highly visible element, one perceived as having a strong group identity. The Russian author who dubbed the Baltic Germans "the Mamelukes of the Empire" did not intend to pay them a compliment.[8]

Russian nationalism in midcentury was also acquiring a sharp edge. A growing band of zealots, soldiers and bureaucrats, journalists and academicians, was developing a reasonably coherent set of visions conveniently grouped under the concept of Panslavism. These Panslavs increasingly agreed on Russia's natural fitness for leadership of the Slavic communities. Works like Yuri Samarin's *Borderlands of Russia*, published in 1868, went farther and demanded the Russification of frontier minorities: Balts, Jews, and especially Germans.[9]

Germany provided a focus for other anxieties as well. Even the limited constitutionalism of Bismarck's Reich seemed revolution incarnate to conservatives east of the Vistula. Russian liberals, on the other hand, saw a Germany abandoning her traditional role of mentor and model, falling prey instead to a militarism that threatened every form of human progress.

The impact of these attitudes was enhanced by a growing perception in the foreign office of a relative decline in Russian power and status. Paul Schroeder has argued that within nineteenth-century Europe's diplomatic structure Russia was restrained less by any internal moderate impulses than by the behavior of her friends and allies. Hostile coalitions, on the other hand, merely encouraged Russia to strike back by applying pressure in one of the many areas vulnerable to her.[10] The point is reasonable as far as it goes. No successful statesman can afford to forget the fable of the wager between the north wind and the sun on who could first convince a man to remove his coat. But as George Lichtheim observes, Russians, never converted to Protestantism or liberalism, find it difficult to divorce politics from either ethics or metaphysics.[11] The geopolitics of Peter the Great and the metapolitics of Alexander I had left a heritage—a sense of mission, of destiny, of purpose that generated in Russian statesmen a determination at least as great as Bismarck's to conduct Europe's orchestra, if not necessarily to drown out the other players.

Any theoretical propositions on how best to contain Russia had therefore to be balanced by consideration of the diplomatic and political prices she set on her friendship. Russia might hypothetically have responded positively to a systematic German policy that was conciliatory, self-effacing, and deferential. Such behavior corresponded neither to political and economic realities nor to the personality of Otto von Bismarck. The "white revolutionary" may have regarded Germany as a sated power whose interests were best served by maintaining the status quo. He saw that process, however, as dynamic rather than static, achieved only by constant, positive action initiated from Berlin.

In particular, Bismarck's policy of "balanced tension" reflected his increasing concern with Russia's dynamism, the pattern of Russian challenges to the European structure that he saw developing in the aftermath of the Peace of Frankfurt. Even the limited Three Emperors' League of 1873 with Germany and Austria-Hungary, an agreement for mutual consultation rather than a formal treaty, was described as a threat to Russia's security and a brake on Russia's mission by diplomats who made no secret of their conviction that Germany was not being properly appreciative of Russia's moderation. From St. Petersburg's perspective, the Congress of Berlin in 1878 was ultimate proof of German perfidy. Bismarck's self-appointed role of "honest broker" seemed a mere mask for his real intention: the isolation and humiliation of Russia. A massive outburst of hostility in the press was accompanied by significant increases in the military establishment. The latter process survived the immediate crisis. It also confirmed and focussed a broad structure of anti-Russian suspicions and hostilities in Germany.[12]

German Russophobia existed on two levels. Throughout the nineteenth century the Left was hostile to its neighbor's form of government. After 1815, liberals and democrats saw Russia as a principal bulwark of reaction. Herder's nationalist disciples sympathized with the Poles rather than their Russian conquerors. Romantic poets and essayists described the coming conflict of West and East. In the Prussian Landtag and the German Reichstag alike, Russia was a familiar symbol of benighted oppression. *Zentrum* deputies expressing solidarity with Catholic Poles, Progressives and National Liberals disgusted by increasingly overt anti-Semitism, contributed their voices to a negative chorus that maintained strong intellectual links to the Russian opposition.[13]

German socialism's stand on Russia was strongly influenced by the views of its founders. Karl Marx's implacable hostility to tsarist despotism was matched by his attacks on a Russian character allegedly molded by centuries of subservience to oriental tyranny. Friedrich Engels, while usually exempting the Russian people from his general characterizations of Slavs as dogs, gypsies, bandits, and brigands, was even more critical than Marx of the aggressive behavior of a Russian government he described as dominated by alien adventurers.[14]

To theorists like Karl Kautsky or Eduard Bernstein, the Russian Marxists were intellectual country cousins, approaching the master's doctrine with the sophistication of a locomotive, unable to grasp its subtleties, yet correspondingly concerned with provincial hair-splitting. To practical politicians, the Wilhelm Liebknechts and the August Bebels,

16

their Russian comrades were poor relations, eating the bread of charity in exile or sustaining a hole-and-corner existence one step ahead of the *Okhrana*. Russia's masses of unlettered peasants, her small number of brutalized factory workers, were at best the remotest kind of raw material for socialism, particularly when compared to the increasingly literate, increasingly politically conscious proletariat of a Germany whose urbanization and industrialization seemed to be fulfilling the essence of Marx's predictions.[15]

Where the tsarist political order was concerned, patronization gave way to implacable hostility. Social Democrats lost no opportunity in or out of the Reichstag to attack the tsarist system's legitimacy—an approach culminating in 1905, when the news of Bloody Sunday vitalized activists throughout Germany. With *Vorwärts* running a front-page box score of events, with local party groups collecting and dispatching funds for the revolution, Russian conservatives might well be pardoned for entertaining however briefly the suspicion that, for all the intimacy of the Willy-Nicky letters, Germany's true feelings were best expressed by its political opposition.[16]

Russia also faced increasing thunder from the German Right. As early as 1853 Paul de Lagarde advocated colonization of the East, with Germans as an aristocracy of talent among brutish or degenerate Slavs.[17] Under the empire an expanding historical profession generated learned articles and journals devoted to Germany's eastward expansion. Gymnasium textbooks and university lecturers hammered home the point to generations of students. The Second Reich's best-known and most visible scholar of Russian history was Professor Theodor Schiemann. A Baltic German who emigrated at the relatively mature age of forty, he insisted on the inferiority of Slavic Russian culture, presenting the Russians as primitive, indifferent to beauty, lacking a sense of law. He described the need to destroy as part of the Russian nature, and argued that only force held the empire together.[18]

In 1892, Schiemann edited *De moribus Ruthenorum*, a collection of diary entries made at midcentury by Victor Hehn, a Baltic German scientist. Its 250 misanthropic pages amount to one long indictment of a people with neither pride nor conscience, destroying itself through vodka and syphilis. The Slavic national animal, according to Hehn, was the louse. A cultivated Russian was a contradiction in terms. Their intelligentsia used Western ideas to destroy rather than construct. The lesser types were able to do nothing, whether make a watch, bake a cake, or drive a locomotive, without German models. Among prostitutes it was a known fact that the most famous were Baltic Germans; Russian ladies of the evening lacked the endurance, the inner nobility, to sustain such an unconventional life. Russian men could not even use modern plumbing correctly—a point made clear to anyone unfortunate enough to have recourse to public toilets in the tsar's empire.[19]

The impact of such ideas was exacerbated by the ambiguous nature of nationalism in the new German Empire. Its roots at best were shallow, its symbols meager—a flag without a history, a monarchy without a heritage, an army without a common identity. The chauvinism that so offended Germany's neighbors in good part reflected deliberate government efforts to legitimate itself by creating a national self-consciousness.[20] At the same time, exponential improvements in transportation and communication were shrinking the map of Europe. Space and spatial relationships grew correspondingly important. Time itself seemed to grow more compact. In this context the new Reich seemed for all its surface strength to be "a mollusc without a shell," vulnerable physically and psychically from all directions.[21]

From this perspective it was a short step to visions of stabilization by expansion. Certain liberals, Friedrich Naumann, Lujo Brentano, and Gustav Schmoller, saw a partial solution to Germany's social problems in terms of a *Mitteleuropa*. Dominated culturally, politically, and economically by Germans, this entity would also secure the traditional heartland of the West against the threat posed by the emerging world empires: America, Britain, and above all Russia. The concept was, in the minds of its creators, a defensive reaction. Its advocates staunchly denied any interest in an *Ostimperium* of Slavic helots under German rule. In this they stood in sharp contrast to those nationalists whose praise for the Germanizing of Slavic territory in the Middle Ages increasingly combined with fear of Panslavic expansionism to generate advocacy of a *Drang nach Osten*—the eastward expansion of German power.

Benign considerations of this process described Russia's quick defeat and permanent withdrawal into the wastes of Asia, then hurried on to discuss how the Danube and Vistula basins would become Edens under German hands. Other writers dwelt more lovingly on the prospect of Russian troops fleeing before German bayonets, of villages razed and peasants deported to make room for the younger, fitter race. Yet it seems worth noting that even the most extreme ideologues of the Pan-German League focussed before 1914 on "internal colonization"—the resettlement of German peasants on German soil misused by Poles or Junkers. Their visions of conquest and resettlement were presented as reactions: consequences of Russia's unfortunate policies of aggression.[22]

Even a fire-eater like Heinrich Class denied as late as 1912 any real grounds for war between Russia and Germany. Should the tsar be foolish enough to start trouble, Germany would fight. But her war aims would involve no more than territorial adjustments to create a more defensible frontier and some room for colonization. Class conceded that the latter process would involve displacing the present inhabitants. But at least before 1914, he expressed himself in such a circumlocutory passive construction that the point is almost lost—"woher die Evakuierung sich nicht umgehen lassen wird."[23]

The increasing anxiety Germans of all ranks and classes felt toward Russia and her ultimate intentions was reinforced during the 1890s from a previously unlikely source. In 1879, Bismarck's growing hostility to domestic supporters of free trade had resulted in a new and comprehensive structure of tariffs including a schedule of duties on imported Russian grain.

Retaliation was swift and enduring. In the eleven years after Bismarck's initiative, Russia's import duties on manufactured goods, already high, were increased four times. The direct economic impact of this escalation on German industry must not be exaggerated. As Walther Kirchner argues, we should expect to find industrialists complaining of high customs duties whenever they deal with their governments. Practical men proceeded to find ways around the barriers—improving production or marketing techniques, securing Russian patents, seeking purchase contracts from state agencies. These, however, were second-best solutions in a German business community regarding Russia as a virtually inexhaustible reservoir of potential customers, private and official, all the more attractive for being difficult of access. By the time Leo von Caprivi succeeded Bismarck as chancellor, the chorus of grievances encouraged the negotiation of a new set of commercial agreements with Russia—agreements the German chamber of commerce described as incorporating "unprecedented" reductions in tariffs on manufactured goods in return for significantly lower taxes on grain. A wave of protest from the agricultural East, including many letters from peasants and small farmers, was not enough to keep the Reichstag from approving the treaty on March 10, 1894.[24]

This change in government policy contributed significantly to increase Russophobia on the agrarian right. Where businessmen saw markets, farmers saw competitors: a golden tide of cheap foodstuffs that would bankrupt estate owners and peasants alike. The anxieties generated by the Treaty of 1894 were further exacerbated as Russia embarked on a major program of railway construction. Its principal sponsor, Sergei Witte, made no secret of the fact that one of the main purposes of the improved transportation network was to enhance the marketability of Russian grain by reducing its delivery costs. The landowners of Germany's eastern provinces historically tended to identify with Russia's social and political order. But as more and more acres in previously isolated regions began contributing to the export pool, even the least imaginative of Junkers found no difficulty in seeing an economic threat from the East that could not be indefinitely conjured away by manipulating votes in the Reichstag.[25]

The old order was changing. Nevertheless the impact of popular antagonisms must not be overstated. The proverbial lieutenant and ten men could not really have closed the Reichstag, but parliament's role in German foreign policy involved far more pointing with pride and viewing with alarm than systematic participation in decision making. Russia's foreign affairs were even more firmly in the hands of an elite—an elite not necessarily susceptible to journalistic attacks on German intentions and literary suspicions of German good will.

This was demonstrated in the aftermath of the Congress of Berlin. Tsar Alexander III, who succeeded his assassinated father in 1881, viscerally distrusted the bumptious industrial empire on his western border, a distrust in no way diminished by his love match with a Danish princess brought up on memories of 1864. But his choice as foreign minister was N. I. Giers, who argued that Russia had too many internal problems to sustain overt antagonism with any of her neighbors. Bismarck for his part wished as far as possible to reknit the Russian connection. His Dual Alliance of 1879 was intended more to strengthen Germany's position vis-à-vis Russia than to underwrite either Austria's place among the great powers or any ambitions she might entertain in the Balkans.

The Second Three Emperors' League of 1881, renewed in 1884, marked on one level a triumph of common sense. The league linked the eastern powers in an agreement to remain "benevolently neutral" should any of them go to war with a fourth power. It secured Russia's European flank. It precluded the possibility of a Franco-Russian alliance and of Russo-Austrian rapprochement at Germany's expense. The league, however, also encouraged the bureaucratization of tension. Its very existence combined with Germany's insistence on playing a mediator's role to make Russia and Austria-Hungary aware on an ongoing basis of the problems in their relationship, and their fundamental insolubility within existing parameters.

For Bismarck this temporary stability was enough. He was confident of his ability to solve the tactical problems of diplomacy as they arose—a confidence exacerbated by his often-expressed contempt for the skills of his Russian and Austrian counterparts. But if Metternich had been the coachman of Europe, Bismarck was fast becoming its circus rider, standing with one foot on each of two galloping horses, hoping somehow to keep them moving in the same direction at the same pace. And the focus of tension between them, the Balkan Peninsula, was far too tempting a hunting ground for diplomats with delusions of genius, soldiers with illusions of glory, and businessmen with hopes of profit.

In periodically advocating a division of the peninsula into spheres of influence, Bismarck was by no means naive enough to assume that either Russia or Austria would be permanently satisfied with a half share. But such a division would buy time, and as Bismarck grew older even short periods of time became ever more important to him. The chancellor had no desire to see Russia expand her influence anywhere in Europe. Such aggrandizement would mean both a direct threat to Germany and Austria and a significant disturbance of the territorial status quo Bismarck was committed to preserving. At the same time he had no will even to risk war with the tsar's empire. Apart from the golden opportunities this would offer France, Russia's very size mitigated against anything like the kind of total victory won against France in 1871—a victory which itself seemed increasingly anomalous.[26]

From the inception of the German Empire, its military plans for the East were formulated in the context of a worst-case contingency: a two-front war against France and Russia. In such circumstances, Chief of Staff Helmuth von Moltke strongly favored seeking an operational decision in the east. While Russia was not likely to be overthrown in a brief campaign, the chances of knocking her out of a general war in a relatively short time were good—if the war was conceived as one of limited aims. A battle of annihilation was not a reasonable possibility. However, a series of theater-level victories might well disorganize her war effort to the point where the government would be amenable to negotiations if Germany offered reasonable terms.[27]

The alternatives were hardly promising. In 1885 a general staff exercise projected a two-front war against France and Russia, with Austria initially remaining neutral and the bulk of Germany's army concentrated in the West. Four active corps, supported by a mixed bag of reserve and garrison troops, were left to hold the eastern theater against twenty Russian divisions—a reasonable evaluation of Russia's capacities in the context of the problem. The best the Germans could manage was a fighting retreat across the Vistula. Four corps, Moltke sourly observed, could not hold East Prussia or protect Berlin against ten Russian corps no matter how cleverly they were maneuvered.[28]

On the other hand, the long, open frontier between Germany and Russia offered correspondingly wide scope for offensive operations. The East Prussian salient might be threatened with immediate strangulation by a Russian blow at its base, but it provided an excellent sally-port against a Russian concentration in Poland. Moltke believed the best way for the Dual Alliance to defend the Eastern frontier was to attack, with Germans from the north and Austrians from the south meeting somewhere on enemy soil. This conviction, tested successfully in a staff exercise of 1886, was strong enough to lead the chief of staff increasingly to consider the possibility of a preventive war—a first strike, in cooperation with Austria, against the Russian garrisons in Poland and Galicia.[29]

But what could Germany hope to gain from such a conflict? Intellectuals might dream of population shifts on a scale unseen since Genghis Khan. Bismarck was a practical statesman. The annexation of Alsace-Lorraine could be justified on the grounds of generating national identity while securing natural resources defended by Metz and the line of the Vosges. No such geographic barriers existed in the East. As for an economic equivalent to the iron mines of Lorraine, German agriculture was already alarmed at the prospects of competition from Russian grain. Territorial gains in the east would only mean an increase in the number of Poles, Balts, and Russians under German rule. Bismarck's distaste for the Poles of Posen and Silesia was already too marked for him to welcome that possibility.

Bismarck was, in short, not enthusiastic about challenging Russia for any reason, much less for the sake of Austria-Hungary's *beaux yeux*. He was unsympathetic alike to Cisleithanian businessmen's dreams of Balkan markets and to the Hungarian parliament's Russophobic rhodomontade. He spent much effort after 1878 warning Austria that Germany would not support her directly in the Balkans, particularly when it came to defending economic interests.[30] The exact degree of Bismarck's accep-

21

tance of specific Russian claims and positions in the Near East remains debatable. In general, however, he seems to have regarded Russia's territorial ambitions as part of that stream of time human beings could neither create nor, ultimately, direct. His frequent references to Russia as an elemental force, no more to be changed than bad weather, strengthen images of inevitability subject, perhaps, to judicious guidance, but beyond anyone's power to terminate or modify.

This perception was reinforced as Russia's suspicion of Bismarck's good will reached new peaks during the Bulgarian crisis of 1885. Russia's position in the state it had helped establish only seven years earlier virtually collapsed from Russian heavy-handedness. Nevertheless Bismarck emerged as the villain, the wire-puller and manipulator. He was presented in St. Petersburg as simultaneously obstructing Russia's legitimate Balkan claims and encouraging her further involvement in the swamp of Bulgarian politics.[31]

In this context golden bullets began acquiring new importance. Since the 1850s, Russia's domestic problems had been increasingly coalescing into what modern economic theory describes as a crisis of development. Costly foreign wars and territorial expansion in central Asia, combined with expensive programs of railroad building and industrialization, put unheard-of strains on the imperial treasury. The actual and potential supplies of private capital in Russia were limited. A political system neither strong enough nor autocratic enough to practice the forced bootstrapping common in the twentieth century turned logically to external sources.

German bankers and investors had been funding Russian economic enterprises for decades. Bismarck's own banker, Gerson Bleichröder, was deeply involved in the marketing of Russian securities, selling some of the paper to Bismarck himself.

The recipients of this German largesse were anything but suitably grateful. Nationalists argued that the interest rates were too high and the terms too short: Imperial Russia was being treated like a deadbeat gambler. Financiers were concerned with the growing complexity of a public debt contracted without any systematic planning. Panslavs took alarm at the threats posed by German involvement in Russia's economic life. Businessmen demanded higher tariffs, protecting their infant industries from German competition.[32]

By the mid-1880s the German foreign office was also questioning the success of Bismarck's embryonic economic diplomacy. Germany seemed to have benefitted little from official and private efforts to sustain Russia's development. The Cobdenite argument that, properly understood, a state's economic and diplomatic interests must coincide had never been widely accepted even in German liberal circles, much less among the group of young diplomatic Turks whose spokesman was Friedrich von Holstein.

Holstein's critics then and now have considered him a man of limited vision, blinded to the value of Germany's Russian connection by his hostility towards Bismarck, his sympathy for the ramshackle Habsburg Empire, and his identification with the saber-rattling militants urging a war of conquest in the east. Holstein was, however, by no means a blind Russophobe. Since joining the foreign office in 1876 he had observed and participated in Bismarck's increasingly desperate efforts to integrate Russia into a stable European network. The process had convinced him that the chancellor was making a fundamental error. Not France, but Russia, Holstein reasoned, was the greatest ultimate threat to Germany's security. France might be the clearer and more present danger, but a good big man can be expected to whip a good little man. Should France try conclusions with the German Empire, what happened in 1870–71 would happen again.

Russia, on the other hand, combined tremendous economic and military potential with the power of an idea. Her Alsace-Lorraine was the entire Balkan peninsula, if not Central Europe itself. In Holstein's view Russia's geopolitical ambitions threatened—or promised—not merely to bring all southeastern Europe under her sway, but to generate what later diplomatic generations would describe as Austria's Finlandization, if not her complete disappearance.[33] In the aftermath of the Bulgarian crisis, Holstein worked in tandem with the chancellor to foster an anti-Russian coalition of the great powers. The Mediterranean Agreements of 1887, linking Britain, Italy, and Austria in defense of a regional status quo, gratified him at least as much as they did Bismarck. But the fundamental dichotomy between the foreign policy positions of the two men remained. Bismarck wanted to keep Germany in the middle, holding the balance between Russia on one hand, Austria and the other Mediterranean powers on the other. For Holstein and the increasing number of his supporters, the new treaties merely cleared the ground for a confrontation that would show Russia her place at the international table once more—a place she had to date been unwilling to accept by peaceful persuasion.[34]

In a Russia already suspicious of German good will and German intentions, Panslavs and nationalists put increasing, and ultimately successful, pressure on Alexander to abandon the Three Emperors' League. An increasing number of voices suggested the virtues of a French connection. Bismarck responded by negotiating the Reinsurance Treaty of June, 1887. Its key was a mutual guarantee of neutrality except in case of a German attack on France or a Russian attack on Austria. But the belligerence and antagonism shown by the Russian press and the Russian foreign office during the negotiations boded ill for a long-term German-Russian entente. Should Germany's western front explode, was any piece of paper strong enough to bind Russia to its terms?[35]

Economic tension exacerbated diplomatic suspicions. Before the Reinsurance Treaty was negotiated, Bismarck was under pressure from both market agriculture and heavy industry to respond to a recent round of Russian tariff increases. In May, 1887, the tsar's government introduced new restrictions on foreign ownership of property in Russia, generating corresponding anxiety among actual and prospective German investors.

Russian securities began to diminish in attractiveness and drop in value on the Berlin bourse. The German press, partly with Bismarck's encouragement, began to raise alarms. The Reichstag debated the wisdom, political and economic, of continuing to accept Russian commercial paper. On November 10, Bismarck issued the *Lombardverbot*.

The order's scope should not be exaggerated. It simply forbade the German state bank to accept Russian securities as collateral. Russia did begin transferring securities out of Germany after November 10. Some went to France, some back home for purchase by private banks, some to other European capitals. This, however, was not a politically motivated reaction to a diplomatic initiative. Russia's government still had no real cabinet structure. Ministries worked in separate compartments, often virtually unaware of each other's problems. Attempting to influence Russian foreign policy directly by financial pressure correspondingly resembled attracting the attention of a dinosaur by giving the beast a hotfoot. By the time the message reached its intended goal, any response was likely to be irrelevant to the current situation.[36]

Austria for her part had reacted to the nonrenewal of the Three Emperors' League with a burst of anxiety. Russian troop concentrations in Poland and the Ukraine generated Habsburg demands for clarification of the Dual Alliance of 1879. Specifically, the Austrian generals pressed their German counterparts to accept clear Russian preparations for war as a *casus belli*. Their concerns found support in Germany. Moltke's deputy and designated successor, Quartermaster-General Alfred von Waldersee, shared with Holstein an ultimately pessimistic view of the prospects for retaining Russia's good will. By November, he and his aged superior were agreed on the military advantages of a preventive war, to be launched during the winter of 1887.[37]

Bismarck rejected this concept out of hand. He insisted that provoking a war was directly contradictory to German policy. More to the point, he was unwilling to surrender the making of that policy to military considerations. Nor was he standing alone. Bernhard von Bülow, the future chancellor, at the time secretary in the German embassy to Russia, spoke during the winter for common sense. Should war be fought, Bülow declared, it must be a war to the finish, a war which would cripple Russia for at least a quarter-century. He described the Russians as more fanatical, more capable of sacrifice, and more patriotic than the French. For victory to be permanent, for Russia to be incapable of taking revenge, her black-earth provinces must be devastated, her coastal towns bombarded, her commerce and industry crippled. She must be driven from the Black and Baltic Seas. Ultimately, she must be deprived of her western provinces. To do that would require a sequence of victories carrying German troops to the Volga—an eerie prefiguring of events in 1942. Given the obvious difficulties of winning such victories, Germany was far better advised to get along with her eastern neighbor.

And there lay the rub. It took two to agree, but only one to quarrel. Bülow went on to castigate the weakness and stupidity of Russian government circles, the systematic poisoning of public and political opinions against Germany. Should Germany ever stand alone, Russian would immediately join with the French against her. Any promises to the contrary would be swept away by the tides of Panslavism and Germanophobia. The real guarantees of peace were armed force and alliances, particularly the alliance with Austria. Germany could expect favorable results only from a policy of mistrust expressed in the most determined terms.[38]

Like other war scares before and since, that of 1887 blew over almost as rapidly as it emerged. But Bülow's letter reflected a changing attitude in German politics. Even those refusing to follow Holstein in regarding the tsar's empire as an implacable foe were beginning to concede a level of inevitability in Russo-German tensions that was foreign to Bismarck's argument that only interests, not friends or enemies, were eternal.

Military considerations sharpened the anxiety, especially for Waldersee, who finally succeeded Moltke in 1888. The new chief of staff's image as a Russophobic political general should not obscure the reasonable questions of strategy and operations that influenced his views on broader issues. The East, Waldersee had declared in 1884, was a far more dangerous theater for Germany than the West. Not only was the road to Berlin virtually without natural obstacles, but every yard of ground abandoned meant the loss of historic Prussian territory to an all-destroying enemy.[39]

The existing war plans developed by Moltke depended on Russian cooperation: specifically, Russian readiness to deploy substantial forces in the Polish salient, exposed to an Austro-German pincers. Since the 1880s, in an effort to counterbalance Germany's advantage of rapid mobilization, almost half the Russian army had been concentrated in the empire's western military districts. A British war office report circulated in January, 1893, highlighted the fact that in the previous decade the garrisons of those military districts not on the European land frontier had remained almost the same size. In Kiev, Vilna, and Warsaw, on the other hand, the garrisons had been augmented by 124 battalions, 148 squadrons, and 61 field batteries.[40]

These formidable forces were not projected to remain obligingly in place. The Russians had become sufficiently aware of German intentions to have altered their own. Rather than holding forward positions, their main armies now expected to retreat eastward, drawing their enemies after them. Waldersee's initial response was a strategy of hot pursuit, with one German army attacking south into Russian Poland towards the Narew River, and another, smaller force advancing east across the Niemen River, on towards Kovno and Vilna. The new plan was risky at best, involving as it did movement in diverging directions against superior forces. It left almost no margin for human error or acts of God. In particular, Waldersee fretted about the possible impact of weather conditions on his projected offensive. Mud would slow the German infantry. It would immobilize the artillery whose firepower was regarded as an indispensable counterweight to Russian numerical superiority. By the end of his term in offfice Waldersee was even suggesting that should war begin during the wet season, Germany might be better advised to reduce its forces in the east in favor of the west until the weather changed. The rain clouds on the chief of staff's horizon foreshadowed a basic change in Germany's plans for the contingency of a two-front war.[41]

Meanwhile, Russian relations with France steadily improved in the financial and military spheres. French bankers, eager to take Germany's place exploiting the Russian market, negotiated in the summer and fall of 1888 a major conversion loan giving Russian credit a much-needed boost. The respective general staffs were also beginning a series of systematic exchanges. Widely publicized improvements in French organization, armament, and training during the 1880s did not go unnoticed in a Russia increasingly dubious of Germany's probable attitudes in any European conflict. French generals for their part were all too aware of the enduring weaknesses of even their revamped military system. A Russian connection seemed to promise a quick fix, as opposed to dreary efforts to overhaul the army in the face of successive governments unable to pursue any policy over a long term.[42]

Bismarck's resignation on March 18, 1890, marked a watershed in German-Russian relations. The Reinsurance Treaty expired in June. Kaiser William II, logically enough, turned over the negotiations for its renewal to his new chancellor. Leo von Caprivi had no experience in foreign affairs. He had never even seen the texts of the treaty—hardly the best preparation for dealing with Holstein and his allies in the foreign office, who immediately sought to change the kaiser's mind. They described the Reinsurance Treaty as conflicting with Germany's other agreements, above all the Austrian alliance. Bismarck, the critics asserted, had been able to keep his complicated diplomacy alive because he was Bismarck. His reputation was such that even his follies were taken for wisdom. No successor could expect to have anything like the same status— or if it came to that, the same mind-set, with its enthusiasm for keeping a half-dozen balls in the air simultaneously. Clear-cut, unmistakable policies were preferable for a new administration under a young ruler.

Caprivi knew his own limitations. He was reluctant to assume Bismarck's mantle and risk keeping apparently conflicting commitments to five powers at once—particularly in the context of the domestic conflicts that had been the immediate cause of Bismarck's downfall and now demanded prompt attention. Responding to the overwhelming advice of his counsellors, William informed Giers that the recent changes in the government impelled Germany to avoid far-reaching commitments, at least temporarily. The Reinsurance Treaty would therefore not be renewed, but Russia could remain assured of Germany's friendship and good offices.[43]

Giers, shocked and upset, did everything in his power to change William's mind. His desperation was enhanced by his isolation. Russia's current chief of staff argued that the Congress of Berlin should have been lesson enough that Russia's most dangerous enemy was not the one who fought her directly, but the one who awaited her weakening to dictate terms of peace.

A government's policy is not always best evaluated by the opinion of its generals. But in March, 1892, Tsar Alexander suggested to a shocked Giers that a major order of Russia's business in any future war would be to correct the error of German unification by breaking up the Reich into a number of small, weak states. Such attitudes, expressed not in journalistic or academic circles, but at the highest policy-making level, suggest that Germany was not exactly abandoning a willing partner—unless "willing" be interpreted as an equal desire to embrace or to annihilate the object of one's affections.[44]

Nonrenewal of the Reinsurance Treaty was not an overt step towards considering alliances in terms of their value in preparing for war, as opposed to sustaining peace.[45] Holstein warned consistently against fatally alienating Russia at the wrong time by challenging her too sharply in a specific situation. Better by far to contain her through a structure functioning without Germany's direct intervention. Rejection of the Reinsurance Treaty had been a necessary taste of the stick. Now, Holstein argued, it was time for carrots—trade agreements, political concessions, perhaps even a new treaty. But all must take place within the status quo.[46]

Russia was in no position to issue direct challenges to any of the great powers. Her sponsorship of the Hague disarmament conference of 1899 reflected more a general consensus of the state's military backwardness than an altruistic concern for international order. Russian military appropriations had the highest growth rate of any European power during the 1890s. After 1892 Russia consistently outspent France; after 1894 Germany too fell behind the tsar's empire. But though Russia did move increasingly toward self-sufficiency in arms production, on the whole the amount of security purchased did not match the actual outlay of rubles. This reflected less internal inefficiency and corruption than the sheer size of the Russian military establishment—almost a million men during the 1890s, as opposed to the half-million or so kept with the colors by France and Germany. Russia's extensive frontiers, the lengthy period of active service considered necessary to train peasant conscripts for modern war, and the slow mobilization imposed by an underdeveloped transportation network combined to generate a conviction that Russia needed the largest peacetime army she could possibly support. This in turn meant more money spent on maintaining the structure than improving it.[47]

It was scarcely surprising in this context that Russian relations with Germany remained if not consistently warm, at least generally harmonious. French capital might dominate the official money market, but German investment in railroads and industrial enterprises steadily increased. German consumer goods made headway everywhere in Russian markets. Periodic vitriolic outbursts from Moscow or St. Petersburg over the inequities of the economic relationship were by this time familiar enough to be overridden. Where it counted the governments were well able to cooperate.[48]

Nor was Holstein's conviction that Imperial Russia and Republican France could sustain anything but the most fragile relationship directly disproved by the course of events. The first official French references to an "alliance" with Russia were made only in 1895. Not until 1897 would a Russian tsar acknowledge the treaty in public—and then it was Nicholas II, who in 1894 succeeded a father never proud of his French connection.

The new Russo-German relationship represented a significant departure from the direct influence Bismarck consistently sought to exercise. But restraints can be no less binding for being relatively loose. The possibilities of integrating Russia into a flexible network of diplomatic relationships seemed enhanced as France's moderate attitude suggested the survival, or perhaps the rebirth, of that Concert of Europe Bismarck had done so much to demolish. Holstein and his colleagues in the foreign office were by no means hostile to the concept. A Europe subdivided into rigid alliance systems offered too little scope for the exercise of the diplomatic talents on which they prided themselves. Inflexibility bade fair to neutralize the economic and military strength, the geographic position, and not least the mixed form of government that, in the minds of Germany's leaders, gave her such advantages as mediator and pivot point of an open international order. As early as 1895 Holstein asserted that "the Russians will need us before we will need them."[49] Germany could safely afford to wait for her eastern neighbor while preserving as far as possible a free hand towards the rest of the world.

An important aspect of this freedom was the search for a British connection. Holstein's vision of such a relationship involved accord rather than alliance: specific action in common for common specific ends. Yet even this modest goal remained out of reach. Paul Kennedy has demonstrated that above all Germany's rapid economic growth created a fundamental antagonism between the two powers that would have been difficult to overcome given the most conciliatory diplomatic behavior on both sides. Gregor Schollgen speaks of "ignorance," of a young and inexperienced nation pursuing a tragic course in its relations with the older power, ultimately failing to recognize that its goals of *Weltpolitik* could best be achieved as Britain's junior partner. Peter Winzen is more critical. He accuses Bülow, who became secretary of state for foreign affairs in 1897, of consistent bad faith, of sabotaging Anglo-German relations for the sake of a grand design that would ally Russia to Germany in the course of an Anglo-Russian war Bülow regarded as inevitable.[50]

These approaches overlook the basic fact that Britain and Germany had no common enemy, no common concrete danger strong enough to bring them together. The enduring continental alliances, Austria and Germany, France and Russia, were essentially insurance policies against objective threats, geographic possibilities that remained constant whatever treaty relationships might exist. Britain and Germany had no equivalent situation. Without one their relationship was likely to remain at best alignment without alliance, connection without commitment.

Holstein was correct in reasoning that Britain's interests, like Germany's, were best served by sustaining the existing order. Where he failed was in overestimating the strength of the British Empire. Britain was not merely sated, but saturated. Appeasement seemed by far the wisest course. This approach is historically congenial to imperial powers in decline. It reflected as well the position of the bourgeois-conservative elites that dominated Britain, and demanded global grandeur with limited liability.[51]

Toward whom should that appeasement be directed? Keith Wilson exaggerates when he speaks of Germany as "invented" to suit the role Britain needed to play in order to sustain its policies.[52] Yet the weakness of the concrete points of friction, even the naval issue, between Britain and Germany does suggest that Britain's commitment against Germany was a secondary, rather than a primary, fact of twentieth-century international relations. It was a by-product of the French and Russian ententes Britain needed to sustain her position as a world power. As such, it lay farther outside of German control than successive German governments were willing to concede.[53]

In view of the continued failure of its British policies, German encouragement during the 1890s of Russia's expansion in central Asia and towards the Pacific appeared almost brilliant in the first years of the new century. Russian advances in Korea and Manchuria generated resistance from Japan and increasing opposition from Britain, Japan's ally since 1902.[54]

Bülow, promoted from the foreign office to the chancellorship in 1900, was enthusiastic over a situation he regarded as an inviting opportunity for creative diplomacy. Bülow viewed international relations in a traditional context of alliances, balances of power, and national security. His concept of *Weltpolitik* was anything but a coherent program of economic or political imperialism. Depending on perspective, it can be described negatively, as the constant search for cheap successes at low risk or, positively, as the flexible exploration of a spectrum of options to solve long-standing general problems of international relations. To date the Franco-Russian alliance had been essentially a free ride for both partners. What might happen if a price tag suddenly appeared on the relationship? In Bülow's opinion a German initiative, properly couched and timed, could mean re-establishing close relations with Russia at bargain-basement terms. The Russians seemed in no position to be selective. A Russo-German alliance might in turn draw France into its orbit—particularly in view of that country's recent initiatives in Morocco. Germany's interests there were significant, but not vital. They could be negotiated, even bartered. The Franco-Prussian War had been history for over three decades; times seemed propitious for dramatic changes in great-power relationships.[55]

Bülow's underlying attitude towards Russia had changed little since

1887. She was not a shambling giant with feet of clay—that status Bülow reserved for Austria—but a power whose attitudes and behavior held the keys to Europe's stability. His policy depended heavily on Russian support to bring France to terms. But far from acting as the sophisticated mediator of interests and attitudes, the Russian government behaved more like a *Luftmensch* from the empire's own *shtetls*. Themselves with nothing to trade, the Russian delegates to the First Moroccan Conference devoted all their energies to persuading Germany into concessions. The foreign ministry officially stated that Russia would stand by France should war over Morocco arise. With the French government firmly refusing to negotiate directly with Germany, with even Austria-Hungary pressing Germany to back down, Bülow faced a choice: fight or quit. Germany chose to quit, accepting one of the twentieth century's most complete diplomatic defeats rather than risk a war that suddenly very few Germans seemed to want, no matter how belligerent their previous rhetoric might have been. And in April, 1906, Russia collected its payment—a new French loan on unusually favorable terms.[56]

German restraint in 1905 is frequently described as at best a temporary reflection of current shortcomings in armament and equipment, an anomaly in a political-military strategy essentially offensive in nature. The strategy is in turn most often presented as reflecting both extensive geopolitical aims and an institutional bias in favor of the offensive, which was considered to express most fully the values at the heart of the German military system: courage, decisiveness, initiative, and similar caste-influenced attitudes. Germany's sudden backdown did owe much to the fact that her policy during the crisis had been no more than a set of diplomatic initiatives. Coordination and consultation between the foreign office and the general staff was minimal. Yet for all of his rhetoric about the desirability of war with France in the context of current Russian weakness, even Chief of Staff Alfred von Schlieffen seemed reluctant to push his arguments to the limit in 1905.[57]

This caution was not specific to the situation. Germany's mainstream military theorists had moved a long way from Waldersee's ebullient advocacy of preventive war. Since the turn of the century they had become increasingly dubious about their country's prospects. For all of Tirpitz's elaborate building programs, naval planning against likely combinations of enemies more and more assumed the nature of the Mad Hatter's tea party in *Alice in Wonderland*. The army's consideration of invading Denmark and Holland, Schlieffen's eventual decision to attack Belgium, reflected a sense of weakness rather than strength, a fear that these small states would become sally-ports for future enemies, and a corresponding search for compensating advantages however ephemeral and costly these might be in the long run. As late as November, 1909, the general staff asked the navy to evaluate which Dutch harbors would be suitable for a major British landing.[58]

This pessimism reflected Germany's increasingly unfavorable diplomatic situation. It responded to the domestic strains engendered by increased military preparation: the social consequences of enlarging the army and the financial burdens of expanding the navy. At the cutting edge, however, it was a function of professional anxiety at two levels. Schlieffen's growing commitment to an all-out offensive against France represented at least as much a turn away from the east as a focus on the west. In a quarter-century's alliance between Germany and Austria, the Habsburg army had developed an image and a self-image as a military Avis—not exactly a poor relation, but an attendant lord, suited to start a progress and swell a scene or two but able to do nothing the Germans could not do better. In Schlieffen's opinion the Austrian army could not even protect its own state from a determined Russian offensive.

His judgment is open to question. Unit for unit, in equipment, efficiency, and command, there was arguably little to choose between Habsburg and Romanov. Psychic reality, however, was more important than hindsight. In his early years as chief of staff Schlieffen believed that if the main German strength were not deployed in the east Austria might collapse completely. Much to Waldersee's chagrin, he therefore replaced Moltke's pincers movement with a side-by-side German-Austrian offensive from Silesia and Galicia into southern Poland.[59]

This new concept left East Prussia completely exposed to a Russian attack. It meant deploying almost a million men in an area where road and railway networks were poor on both sides of the frontier. Its only advantage was the possibility of providing direct German support for an inefficient ally. And Schlieffen increasingly doubted whether the advantages of this operation justified its risks. A large part of the active Russian army was stationed on the western frontier. To expedite the deployment of the remainder, railroads were being built in European Russia with all possible speed. Russian strategic concepts had correspondingly altered. Revised war plans now incorporated one offensive from the Niemen against the German left, and another against the Austrian right flank in southern Galicia. Each ally would therefore have to secure its own respective flank before any combined operations would be possible. This in turn encouraged a tendency to establish two separate secondary theaters of war, whose geographically diverging objectives were likely to absorb critical numbers of the available troops.[60]

The possibility of winning even the kind of limited victory Moltke originally projected was substantially reduced. And if the allies could cope with the new strategic situation, what would they have gained? Moltke's original hypothesis that victory would encourage negotiation in the east depended on at least a stable front in the west. Schlieffen's ultimate dream may have been a repetition of the victory of Cannae on a European scale. But that dream was the fruit of his nightmare: a series of meaningless victories in the east, drawing German armies even deeper into Russia while a rejuvenated France drove at the Vosges and the Rhine.[61]

For all its positive qualities, however, the French army was to Germany what the German navy was to Great Britain—a challenge that no one doubted could be matched. This by no means made the French a foe to be despised. But since 1870 the French military had essentially formed itself according to patterns set in Germany. Despite specific advantages in some areas, it continued to sustain the image of a blurred copy of its original.[62] Even without the advantage of a larger population, German military planners were convinced that France could be beaten both by sheer numerical superiority and man for man, corps for corps. The growing faith among Europe's military planners in the tactical and operational superiority of the offensive only strengthened the conviction that an all-out attack on France would remove not only an immediately dangerous enemy, but the one most vulnerable to a Germany herself in no position to sustain a long, drawn-out war.[63]

Schlieffen's concern for the eastern theater also provided him with the beginnings of a solution to his greatest practical anxiety: the fundamental imbalance in manpower between Germany on one hand and France and Russia on the other. Even by training every fit man, Germany could not hope to match her enemies numerically. In an age when all armies were trained, armed, and equipped essentially alike, the prospects for securing more than a marginal advantage in quality seemed severely limited.[64] These problems posed a corresponding challenge to professional skill. The window of vulnerability must become a door of opportunity. The general staff exercises of the 1890s indicated the possibilities even under modern conditions of a small force defeating a larger one by concentrating against an enemy's flank, then driving against its lines of retreat. Far from ignoring or denigrating the power of modern weapons, Schlieffen proposed to take advantage of them by reducing the strength of covering and screening forces to what seemed an unacceptable minimum to more conservative colleagues. Instead of playing to its enemies' strengths by a series of frontal encounter battles, the German army must seek to change the rules, to impose a plan so comprehensive, so cohesive, that the enemy whould be able to do nothing except react.[65]

Orthodox general staff wisdom held that Germany's long and exposed eastern frontier could only be defended by a strategic offensive, by thrusts into Russian territory.[66] This opinion was unchallenged by Bismarck and shared by his successors, Caprivi and Hohenloe. Schlieffen for his part was willing to test the hypothesis that the east and in particular its most vulnerable area, the province of East Prussia, could be held even against heavy odds by relatively weak forces. East Prussia's complex network of lakes, swamps, and woods offered excellent possibilities to well-trained, boldly commanded defenders. The geography of the area and the disposition of the Russian railroad network encouraged dividing invading Russian forces into two halves, one advancing westward from the Niemen, the other northwest from the Narew. And this in turn offered excellent prospects for operational ripostes that would overwhelm the invaders in detail.

The general staff exercise of 1891 featured a simultaneous Russian invasion of Posen and East Prussia, with Schlieffen's summary highlighting the probable moral impact if even one invading column was destroyed.

The problem for 1898 saw the East Prussian garrison threatened on three sides, with Schlieffen insisting the optimal response was to engage the nearest enemy force as quickly as possible, decisively defeat it, then turn against the other two adversaries. In 1899 the Germans again countered numerical inferiority by crushing one of the Russian flanks, then moving against their lines of communication.

By the turn of the century it had become a textbook solution: throw the entire German strength at whichever enemy first came within range, then concentrate against the other. Time and again the concept succeeded in war games. On one memorable occasion a general staff lieutenant-colonel charged with leading one of the "Russian" armies found himself so completely surrounded that the rules demanded a surrender. The officer insisted that no force he led would ever lay down its arms. Schlieffen, who was not without a sense of humor, amended the final report to read that the "Russian" commander, recognizing his hopeless situation, sought and found death in the front line!

Such an outcome was, however, considered an optimal result. Schlieffen had a healthy respect for the size of the Russian army, and a high regard for the uncertainties of battle. After 1901 the mobilization plan reduced Germany's eastern force to an average of three corps, four reserve divisions, and two to four cavalry divisions. Schlieffen did not expect miracles from such a weak instrument. He recognized the possibility that a well-coordinated Russian advance, or a German defeat in the opening rounds, might require drawing troops from the west. But he also warned that once the reinforcements were on the scene, nothing would prevent the Russians from withdrawing until French pressure constrained the Germans to send troops westward, then resuming the advance. This sort of counterpunching, Schlieffen roundly declared, would lead in the long run to the complete annihilation of the German army. Instead, *Ostheer* should expect to fight with what it had, do as much damage as possible, and wait for the decisive victory over France. If necessary, Schlieffen was prepared to return to the concept of the 1880s, abandoning most of East Prussia and making a stand on the Vistula River. By 1903 the railway section of the general staff felt able to guarantee the transportation of eleven corps eastward as soon as France should be overthrown. And this would be only the vanguard of a German army strong enough not merely to drive Russian invaders out of East Prussia, but to pin them there and destroy them.[67]

Schlieffen's strategic conceptions incorporated his reflections on the changing nature of war. Often derided for their shortsightedness in failing to predict a war of attrition, Europe's generals were if anything even less correct in evaluating the pace of destruction in modern war. Far from being technological illiterates, soldiers were well aware of what modern weapons, the rapid-firing field gun, the machine gun, and the magazine rifle, could do in theory. What they were expecting was not a gentlemen's war, not a repetition of 1866 or 1870, but an Armageddon in quick time, with events proceeding at the outer limits of comprehension and control.

I. S. Bloch's *La guerre future* was not only discounted because of its pessimistic predictions of indecisive mass war. More and more experts agreed that the rates of loss under modern conditions made a war of attrition on the Bloch model impossible.

Military planners prior to 1914 are often described as underestimating the resilience of their war machines and the societies sustaining them. What they actually did was to overestimate the rates at which men would be killed and machines destroyed. They saw vulnerabilities more clearly than durabilities—and it was the latter that gave Europe time to adjust to the initial casualty rates of 1914–15. Given the nature of prewar anticipations, it by no means indicated lack of faith in one's people to assume that countries facing such a catastrophe were likely to collapse from psychic shock and physical stress. Schlieffen was hardly isolated in his growing belief that the armed forces available to modern nations could be maintained for any length of time only at the expense of the economic, social, and political institutions they were supposed to sustain. And in this context Russia, combining tremendous reserves of human and material resources with a relatively primitive social structure, emerged as the most likely survivor of a protracted war.[68]

The essence of strategy is the calculating of relationships among ends, means, and will. Let the process of calculation obscure the values of the relationships, and the result is not bad strategy but no strategy.[69] Neither the German Empire's power nor the German Empire's finesse was sufficient to establish her as the focal point of European diplomacy during the Bülow years. Instead, Germany remained one power of several—at the very time when increasing concern for her military position generated a corresponding policy of *Flucht nach vorne*. The German army in the years before 1914 became increasingly concerned with processes, methods, and techniques. Arguably, Schlieffen's essential flaw as a strategist was his acceptance of Germany's international position as defined by civilian political authority. He responded with a desperation move: a staff college *tour de force*, but a military myth requiring everything to go impossibly right to have a real chance of succeeding.

"Everything" included political and diplomatic factors, which between 1905 and 1914 became increasingly subordinated to this gambler's gambit. The Schlieffen Plan, however, had one supreme psychological virtue. It offered hope through diligence. If everyone did his bit and played his part, the Empire might have a chance. The plan's rapid evolution into dogma owed much to the increasingly narrow perspective of German military thinking. But that development in turn represented in large part a response to a paradox. The Imperial army was given—and accepted—the task of planning for a war which its own calculations suggested might well be so destructive as to be unpredictable, uncontrollable, and ultimately unwinnable. In this context, a withdrawal into procedures, a concentration on mobilization schedules and corps-level tactics, was natural if not exactly inevitable. The Schlieffen Plan was a sophisticated security blanket. Had it not existed its equivalent would almost certainly have been designed.

The climate of anxiety in Germany was reinforced by a new set of public slanging matches with Russia. In the agonizing reappraisals that followed the Peace of Portsmouth, Germany bore the brunt of the blame in St. Petersburg for encouraging Russia's disastrous Far Eastern policies. Even Witte criticized Berlin for "forcing" Russia to pursue her arms in Manchuria rather than closer to home. Holstein was not being blindly Russophobic when he acidly described "Russia of the Russians, where the 'inevitable' war with Germany is discussed in every *Zemstvo* . . . even if a treaty actually existed between Russia and Germany, the popular prejudices of the Russian people would today probably override it."[70]

Russia's increasing and unexpected postwar rapprochement with Britain generated corresponding despondency in the German foreign office. Both powers had significant reasons for settling their imperial rivalries. Britain was unwilling to maintain the land forces necessary to project her power into the Middle East and central Asia in the face of Russian opposition. Russia for her part needed above all a period of stability in international affairs. These positive factors drew Britain and Russia together independent of anything Germany was able to do. With France as an enthusiastic go-between, the Anglo-Russian entente of 1907 quickly emerged as something more than just another paper agreement.[71]

Both powers were concerned to reassure Germany that their improved relationship was not aimed at her. In his annual reports for 1906 and 1907 Ambassador Sir Arthur Nicolson was impressed by the "intimate and cordial" relations between Russia and Germany's courts and governments—relations he ascribed both to the unusual skill with which Germany managed her Russian affairs, and by the absence of direct points of friction between the empires. In the European field, he declared, "there is a desire on the part of the Russian Government to live on the best possible terms with Germany."[72] Nevertheless, no interpretation of the entente as a "warning," a structure aimed at containing a provocative and insatiable German diplomacy, can deny the objective reality of encirclement. Even Fritz Fischer concedes that Germany after 1907 "lived permanently under the threat of a war on two fronts." The continued failure to negotiate a naval limitation treaty with Britain set the seal on Germany's isolation. The Bosnian Crisis of 1908 demonstrated its consequences.[73]

2
The Center Fails to Hold

I

Russo-Austrian cooperation in the Balkans was always more a matter of interest than principle. When Count Alois Aehrenthal became foreign minister of Austria-Hungary in 1906, he was concerned with what he considered the empire's negative approach to foreign policy. Austria, Aehrenthal argued, must begin to act instead of reacting—not least to maintain its credibility with her German ally and her Russian collaborator. Aehrenthal even entertained hopes of reviving the Three Emperors' League, this time with Austria as its pivot. His dreams, however, were fettered by Austria's economic and military weaknesses. Lacking the resources to back an overt forward policy, Aehrenthal sought instead an opportunity to achieve a triumph through negotiations. The most likely field for such negotiations appeared to involve confronting the Balkan problem, specifically, the increasingly hostile attitude of Serbia. The newly established Russophilic dynasty in Serbia was combining with increasingly vocal Slavic movements in Macedonia and Austria-Hungary itself to generate increasing concern for the Habsburg Empire's viability.

Russia could not ignore the fate of what had become the principal Slav state, and certainly the noisiest one, in the Balkans. Neoslavism, with its emphasis on creating a league of independent Slavic states under Russian protection, was at the peak of its short-lived influence in Russian liberal circles. Conservatives and patriots were hostile by reflex to anything that might extend Habsburg influence in southeast Europe. Realists were influenced by the fact that Russia's western and southern frontiers were overwhelmingly populated by non-Russians whose disaffection had been made all too plain in the revolts of 1905. From Finland to the Caucasus, this unstable border correspondingly encouraged the formation of buffer zones and client relationships wherever possible. And the tsar's new foreign minister, Baron A. P. Izvolsky, also appointed in 1906, was just the man to bring the kettle to a boil.

Izvolsky was a gambler. From his first days in office he favored a policy of diagonals: keeping Russia balanced between the German-Austrian and the Anglo-French ententes. He regarded neither partnership as inherently friendly to Russia's interests, and was correspondingly suspected of insincerity, if not duplicity, by everyone else. It was scarcely surprising that Izvolsky found attractive the prospects of a knight's move in the Balkans. It might put relations with Austria on a firmer, more positive basis. It could fix Izvolsky's place in history. And it would show the rest of Europe that Russia was not to be despised. It was Izvolsky who on July 2, 1908, suggested to Aehmenthal an exchange of favors. Russia would support Austria's direct annexation of Bosnia and Herzegovina, provinces she had ruled *de facto* since 1879. Austria would support Russia's claim to move her warships freely through the Dardanelles. This right, enjoyed by no other nation, would be useful in itself and was a potential stepping stone to further pressures on the Ottoman Empire. Executed over Serbia's head, the agreement would also demonstrate the will of the great powers most directly involved in the Balkans to control that situation themselves, and not resign it to secondary actors.

The negotiations incorporated an essential imbalance: territory against a promise, provinces against words. Aehrenthal was able to make the annexation of Bosnia-Herzegovina a *fait accompli*, while Izvolsky roamed the chanceries of Europe, vainly seeking international consent to a Russian move that had been unacceptable since before the Crimean War. Nor did he find support at home. From left to right, Russian public opinion interpreted the Bosnian annexation as a disaster. Izvolsky's aim of acquiring free passage through the straits by diplomacy was ridiculed in the newly created Duma by deputies of all political stripes indignant over the apparent betrayal of the racial cause involved in abandoning two Slavic-inhabited provinces to Teuton rule. Professors, editors, and generals seethed with indignation. Students in Moscow and St. Petersburg took to the streets in protest—a shock to authorities used to seeing them on the other side. Premier P. A. Stolypin, the man on whose shoulders rested the entire fragile framework of domestic reforms that was tsarism's response to the disasters of 1905, threatened openly to resign unless Nicholas denounced Izvolsky's bargain. To make matters worse, Serbia denounced the agreement, spoke openly of war unless somehow compensated for the annexation, and turned to Russia demanding support for this policy.

Much of the domestic criticism of Izvolsky reflected the Aesopian politics characteristic of Russia long after 1917, with parties and pressure groups using questions of foreign policy as lead-ins or stalking horses for the domestic issues that were their real concerns. Nevertheless, particularly in its weakened state, the autocracy could not afford to ignore entirely the legitimations conferred by public opinion. On the other hand, Russia in the aftermath of her defeat by Japan was militarily in no shape to confront anyone—even Austria. Faced with paying lost bets from an empty pocket, the best Izvolsky could do was to try to placate the Serbs on one hand while on the other demanding a European conference to discuss the entire issue.[1]

Then Germany moved into the driver's seat. The eruption of the long-quiet Balkans was anything but welcome in the context of her increasing economic and political involvement in southeastern Europe and the Ottoman Empire. Bismarck had been able to present himself as a disinterested mediator with at least some credibility. Wilhelmian *Weltpolitik* had led to an increasing suspicion of German intentions in the Near East by Austria as well as Russia. Germany was developing a different set of friends and enemies, encouraging an Italian connection Austria found increasingly unpalatable, fostering an arms race that Austria could not sustain, and competing with Austria for economic influence in the Near East. In rejecting Izvolsky's call for a conference, Aehrenthal was simultaneously challenging the German government's commitment to its Austrian alliance.[2]

From Austria's perspective, the results were positive —almost too positive. Fatalism, an acceptance of what Wolfgang Mommsen calls the *topos* of inevitable war, was an increasingly important rhetorical flourish among German policymakers. Yet it was less a faith than an attitude, a mixture of *Weltschmerz* and *fin de siècle* posturing. It might be fashionable in diaries and drawing rooms. It might be given a retrospective edge through postwar hindsight. But despair hardly dominated the working days of men who remained too completely the children of an age of progress to wait for disaster. Instead they did their best to avert the worst.[3]

German policy was significantly influenced by Izvolsky's apparent isolation in his own country. Tsar Nicholas took pains to assure the German military plenipotentiary, navy Captain Paul von Hintze, of his continued desire for good relations. Ferdinand von Monts, German ambassador to Rome, reported his Russian colleague's insistence that the mood in St. Petersburg was absolutely peaceful. The Russian had sharply criticized Izvolsky's behavior, even though he was a close relative. From the Petersburg embassy, Friedrich von Pourtalès quoted the Russian war minister: Serbia was completely powerless to start a war; France was too weak to think of anything but the defensive; and Russia wished no war with Germany over Serbia's pretensions.[4]

For Bülow this was an opportunity to recover ground lost in 1905. Rejecting encouragement from within his foreign office to mediate directly between Izvolsky and Aehrenthal, he instead instructed Hintze and Pourtalès to stress both Germany's current support for Austria and Russia's current isolation as the direct consequences of a "demonstrative" Russian rush into England's embrace. Why, Bülow asked, should *not* the kaiser be hurt at Russia's abandonment of a Germany that, under constant threat to her own security and constant pressure from Europe's radicals, had been such a faithful and unrequited supporter for so many years? And what were the probable results if Aehrenthal released the documents

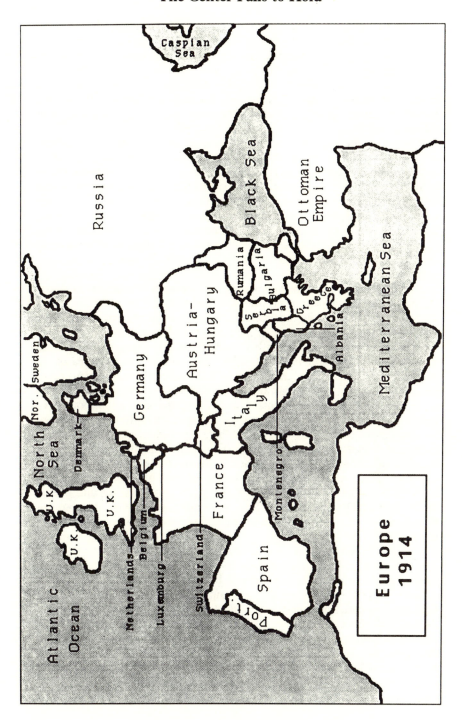

Europe
1914

showing Izvolsky's original encouraging of the annexation? What price then the rhetoric of Slavic unity and European solidarity?[5]

Aehrenthal had originally begun the annexation adventure to improve relations with Russia, not destroy them. Yet neither was he blind to the implications of Russia's continued waffling on the Serbian question. Russia, he insisted, must give up her "mad claim" to being Serbia's protector. Serbia was a local power, unentitled to compensation except as a concession.[6]

From a German perspective, Aehrenthal's position did no more than reflect the blind alley in which Russia found herself. The German consul in Moscow, for example, reported that the Russian government could hardly expect popular support for war on Serbia's behalf. Panslavism was a dead issue in central Russia. Domestic corruption and abuse of police power were far livelier themes. Witte too, in a long conversation with Pourtalès, began by stressing the centuries of tradition and the deep idealism behind the concept of Slavic brotherhood. But when pressed to declare if Russia had a real interest in helping the Serbs, Witte said decisively, "No."[7]

As early as December 11 Izvolsky had informed the German ambassador that he wanted war at no price. "What should I do now?" he asked despairingly. When told he needed only to reach an agreement with Austria-Hungary, the Russian foreign minister bristled that it was impossible to negotiate with Aehrenthal. Now, with February giving way to March, Bülow was convinced the crisis had gone on beyond reason or profit for anyone. With neither Russia nor Austria willing to move decisively, the risks of an accidental explosion were growing with each passing week. Sir Arthur Nicolson was among the firmest supporters of close Anglo-Russian cooperation. Yet even he observed the "strange inconsistency" of insisting that a rival "is not to advance beyond a certain point if it be not intended to prevent him doing so at all costs . . . I fear that Russia may some day find herself in the dilemma of having to decide either to afford material assistance to the victims of Austria . . . or to abdicate permanently her position as the great Slav protector and guardian."[8] The situation resembled nothing so much as a tightly covered pot of boiling water. Either the heat must be reduced or a safety valve introduced.

From Bülow's perspective, Russia's continued demands for an international conference only invited a repetition of the events of Algeciras: Germany and Austria could expect to be outvoted and humiliated. In a century shaped by two world wars and an ongoing threat of nuclear holocaust, negotiations tend to acquire talismanic significance lacking in earlier and simpler times. Bülow was familiar with the axiom that a diplomatic victory is best completed when the loser is allowed to save as much face as possible. But were Russia's aims really so innocent? It hardly represents a long-term triumph of statesmanship to talk an adversary initially intent on taking five of one's fingers into resting content with only two. On February 24, Hintze described the unspoken goal of Russia as being the master of the Balkan Peninsula and the Slavic world. The only thing keeping her from falling on Austria was German support.[9] This seemed too extreme to be accepted at full value. On the other hand, Russia had overbet her hand badly enough to make calling it a reasonable option on three levels. This might drive a wedge between Russia and her western partners—who had consistently shown their reluctance to underwrite Izvolsky's initiative. It might help teach Russia a lesson in great-power responsibility, a lesson recent events suggested was badly needed. Finally, by demonstrating to Aehrenthal and company how crisis management should be concluded, it would re-establish German ascendancy in that relationship.

Bülow's opportunity came in March, when Aehrenthal finally threatened to publish the documents conceding Austria's right to annex Bosnia and Herzegovina unless Russia cooperated in muzzling Serbia. A desperate Izvolsky appealed to Berlin. Bülow began by suggesting that Russia was attempting to play cards already beaten on the board. German good offices would depend on Russia's commitment to one thing: controlling Serbia by any means necessary for the sake of European peace. Otherwise Germany would, with deep regret, allow developments to take their course.

Given Russia's military weakness, domestic turmoil, and diplomatic isolation, any moderate response was welcome. Initial reactions in St. Petersburg were favorable. Then Izvolsky once again muddied the waters. Too much of his career was riding on the annexation issue to enable easy acceptance of what amounted to a clear-cut Austrian victory. Nor was he particularly happy about the possible results of pressuring Serbia to drop her protests. Might this not amount to abandoning permanently both Russia's Balkan position and the southern Slavs to the Dual Alliance? Izvolsky made his official reply opaque, hoping to negotiate better terms. Instead he strained Germany's already thin patience to the breaking point. William regarded Izvolsky's tone as insolent. Bülow felt the matter could be dragged out no longer. Nor did further delay seem necessary. On March 20 Hintze reported a conversation with an assistant to the Russian war minister. According to this official, Germany could be assured that Russia would not draw the sword for Serbia under any circumstances. Only liberals and revolutionaries wanted war. The next day Bülow insisted that Russia give an "unequivocal answer—yes or no" to the question of annexation. If no, then Germany would withdraw from the situation and—repeating a phrase used in the earlier dispatch—let developments take their course.[10]

This communication has been described as everything from a high-handed ultimatum to a courageous attempt at ending a dangerous situation by plain speaking. Interpretations have been complicated by German journalists and politicians who ranted about "*Nibelungen* loyalty" to Austria and the virtues of mailed-fist diplomacy. Technically, an ultimatum is a final opportunity for the receiving government to accept the stated terms or face direct coercion. This means that both involved parties must have a similar understanding of the diplomatic situation, and both must be aware that the communication has been submitted for the purpose of providing an either/or alternative. The German note did not meet the criteria because it contained no threat of positive actions. Announcing the intention of standing by in a crisis is no more than a statement of proposed behavior. The recipient of the statement remains free to act in his own perceived best interests. Russian finance minister V. N. Kokovtsov supported that position by telling the British ambassador that the German *démarche* "was not an ultimatum; it might perhaps even be admitted that it did not actually put any direct pressure on the Russian Government."[11]

From other perspectives, however, the distinction seemed irrelevant because Russia was in no position to give a negative answer. Her ministers agreed unanimously to accept the annexation—not least because Izvolsky's nerve broke and he insisted to all and sundry that failure to comply meant immediate and hopeless war. But "[i]n two, three, or four years," Stolypin declared privately, Russia "would be able to speak in European affairs with a very different voice from what was now the case."[12]

Russian grievances at having her hand thus forced were assiduously nurtured by France and Britain. Neither power, however, was ready to take concrete risks to support Russian aggrandizement in the Middle East. In the context of the intensifying naval race with Germany, the British foreign office in particular wanted a general settlement taking reasonable account of intensifying Balkan nationalisms.[13] This last was a significant point. Nationalism in the Balkan Peninsula was by now anything but an imported doctrine. It reflected the emergence of both strong popular elements and correspondingly strong local elites, intellectual and bureaucratic, able and willing to act independently in their own perceived interests, and requiring careful handling by any would-be ally or patron.[14] In this context Bülow could and did reasonably claim that he had done Russia a favor, extracting her from an impasse that was as dangerous as it was embarrassing.

The German foreign office spent the rest of 1909 working to diminish the impression of compulsion left by the March note. Six months after the crisis Izvolsky proclaimed Russo-German relations as back to normal. By February, 1910, Pourtalès was describing a renewed stress in conversations on Russia's "old traditional friendship" with Germany, but warned his government not to be deceived. The ambassador described recent Russian behavior as explainable only by the Slavic qualities of "sentimentality, passion, superficiality and illogic," which excluded any sober judgment of realities. The press continued to present the German *démarche* as a series of peremptory threats, and spoke of a "*coup de main*" and a "diplomatic Tsushima." Hintze too believed that whatever might be her temporary military weaknesses, Russia had psychological preparations for a war well under way. Even men like former war minister Alexi Kuropatkin, who described Russia as already large enough, needing rest after the revolutions of 1905, and wrong in her policies of reconciliation with Britain, had a way of punctuating their conversations with demands for the Bosporus and the Dardanelles. The best way of countering this attitude, Hintze argued, was to make Germany seem an enemy too formidable to tackle, either alone or in company with allies. Above all, Russia must fear Germany more than Britain.[15]

As if to confirm Hintze's position, the Russian army departed from precedent in using real states as "enemies" in its 1910 maneuvers. That year's mock war was declared against Germany and Sweden. More was involved here than a simple lack of tact. The elder Moltke had always argued that even a great power could prepare and organize for no more than one war. For Russia, that increasingly seemed to be a war with Germany and Austria. The continued strength of Slavic rhetoric in Russian policy making owed much to a sense that Teutonic dismissal of lesser Balkan breeds without the law implied denial of Russia's place among the truly civilized races. Though, Hintze argued, *German* policy makers might see no possible gains from a victory over Russia, war with Germany would be not only acceptable but popular in the tsar's empire.[16]

What would war with Russia mean in military terms for Germany? Above all it entailed improving her Austrian connection. Helmuth von Moltke "the Younger," nephew of the victor of 1866 and 1870, had succeeded Schlieffen as chief of the German general staff in 1906. He regarded the Austrian army as strong, its morale sound. But he was disturbed by the primary orientation of Austria's current strategic plans against Italy and the Balkans rather than Russia. Prudence might temporarily suggest a cautious Russian foreign policy. Nevertheless the state of the Russian army by no means compelled inactivity, particularly should Russia's entente partners join her in attacking the Central Powers. This seemed by far the most likely contingency, and by no means a pleasant one for a German army feeling itself so overcommitted it could not even provide troops to occupy Denmark should strategic or political decisions make it necessary.[17]

Even more than the army, the German navy at this period insisted on the necessity of worst-case planning. Its attitude was reinforced by its undeniable inferiority to its designated major opponent, the Royal Navy. Fleet spokesmen did not shrink from reminding the kaiser himself that the principle of seeking decisive battle at the first favorable opportunity must not become an endorsement of suicide against a stronger enemy. It might be desirable if continental states agreed to fight their wars only on land, leaving their fleets in reserve to face the enemy that threatened them all, Perfidious Albion! But since this was a utopian proposal the navy instead offered in March, 1909, a plan for cooperation with the army in the context of a general war. Its commitments were minimal, and oriented to the British threat. In the eastern theater German cruisers could make appearances in front of Russian ports. They could disrupt attempts to move troops and supplies by sea. They could stage mock landings to pin down Russian formations that would otherwise be available for an invasion of Germany. But even something as systematic as a blockade of the Russian coast was impossible in view of German naval weakness combined with the fact that many ships engaging in the Baltic trade possessed, or could easily obtain, neutral papers.[18]

The navy did not stand alone in its pessimism. Even more than Schlieffen, Moltke was dubious about prospects of a major German offensive in the east. An increasing weight of intelligence information indicated that faced with such a deployment, Russian war plans provided for withdrawal from the exposed frontier. Even should the Russians prove obliging enough to stand and fight on the border, Moltke regarded a major German offensive against the swampy bottomlands and fortified crossings of the Niemen and Narew Rivers as folly. The Russians could easily compensate for any local defeat by continuing to withdraw eastward while building up their own forces for counterattack. Nor was Moltke's reasoning based entirely on anxious readings of Caulaincourt. In 1904–05 the Russian army had blundered from disaster to disaster in Manchuria. But, Antaeuslike, it grew stronger with defeat. In terms of numbers and quality the Russians had arguably been more dangerous enemies after Mukden than before the Battle of the Yalu, particularly in the context of Japanese exhaustion. Foreign observers at the front, moreover, generally interpreted Russian deficiencies in terms of tactics, doctrine, and training—flaws that could be remedied with effort, as opposed to being inherent in the tsarist system.

Given the strenuous attempts the Russian army was making to assimilate the lessons of Manchuria, an eastern offensive seemed an increasingly risky option. The British military attaché was convinced that Russia in 1908 was "a most serious antagonist, and that a war against her would entail the greatest sacrifices of men and money." Particularly on the defensive the Russian army "would render a good account of itself even against a combination of its Western neighbours . . . any material successes gained by the attackers would involve the greatest effort and sacrifices." His American counterpart expressed similar opinions.[19]

Logistics problems also influenced German attitudes towards operations in the east. Since the days of Waldersee, staff officers had increasingly doubted the possibility of supporting a major offensive into either Poland or Lithuania. Converting the Russian railways to German gauges would take time even if the task were not complicated by enemy demolitions. Forward of the railheads the standard German horse-drawn supply wagons were heavy enough to make bogging down a constant risk. Replacing them with smaller, lighter vehicles, whether purpose-built or impressed from the countryside, in turn meant increasing the length of the supply columns and absorbing men and horses who might be more profitably utilized in combat units.

Yet the very factors handicapping the German army in a major eastern offensive strengthened Moltke's belief in the ability of relatively small forces to conduct a successful holding operation until relieved by troops from the western front. In contrast to the situation in Poland and Lithuania, the East Prussian road and railway networks were good enough to enable German units not merely to counter Russian moves, but to maintain the initiative locally. A general staff exercise for 1907 involved the defense of East Prussia in a two-front war by a force initially no stronger than two active corps, three reserve divisions, and some Landwehr brigades. In his evaluation Moltke, like Schlieffen, stressed the need of solving the problem offensively, concentrating first against one Russian army and then the other. Victory in the east, he argued, was possible even against markedly superior numbers. When asked by the admiralty staff whether he expected East Prussia to be cut off by amphibious operations, the chief of staff replied that by the time Russia could accomplish that feat, German operations in the interior would cancel it.[20]

Placed in the context of German plans and German force structures, the confusing correspondence between Moltke and his Austrian counterpart, Conrad von Hötzendorf, in the first months of 1909 acquires a new dimension. Conrad, a man of strong character, unshakeable will, and limited insight, was determined at any cost to secure the greatest possible initial German commitment against Russia in any future war. He was particularly conscious of the new threats to Austria that he perceived emerging in Italy and the Balkans. What would be the German response should Russia wait until Austria was engaged somewhere in the southeast, then attack her in overwhelming force? To encourage Moltke to pay more attention to the east, Conrad proposed a major Austrian offensive against Russia, directed between the Bug and the Vistula. While mounting this operation depended heavily on Serbian inactivity and Romanian cooperation, Conrad insisted that even if Austria became unexpectedly involved in the Balkans she could have approximately thirty divisions available against Russia within three weeks of mobilization. The heart of Conrad's argument, however, was his expressed hope for a strong and simultaneous German attack southeast, towards the Narew River. Failing that, Austria's safest course would be to withdraw her deployment areas behind the San and Dniester rivers, resigning the initiative with all the risks this entailed.

Moltke's quick response that Germany would not hesitate to support its ally by launching such an offense has puzzled soldiers and scholars ever since. He was certainly influenced by a desire to provide moral support for an Austria in the throes of the Bosnian Crisis. The exact nature of Conrad's proposed German attack may also have shaped Moltke's thinking. Neither general staff regarded direct cooperation between their main eastern armies as an immediate practical problem. The Polish salient worked against a united field command, much as the Ardennes salient was to do for the British and Americans in 1944. And instead of a *Grosse Ostaufmarsch*, the Austrian chief of staff initially suggested that the offensive against the Narew might be launched by as few as ten divisions— a number Moltke generously raised to thirteen. The latter figure was not arbitrary. In the 1907 exercise mentioned above, the Germans received a reinforcement of three active corps on mobilization. They were thus able to concentrate a dozen divisions against the Russians advancing from the Narew. This was hardly a force calculated to stagger the Russian Empire by itself. The most either chief of staff expected was that it would pin

45

down nineteen or twenty enemy divisions. But should Austria respect Conrad's commitment to a major offensive against Russia, this could be enough—just enough—to spell success in a high-risk environment.[21]

II

Germany's military position hardly inspired adventurism in its new chancellor. Theobald von Bethmann-Hollweg, who succeeded Bülow in July, 1909, assumed office in the context of *Weltpolitik*'s relative failure. Bülow had ultimately been unable to use global diplomacy to enhance Germany's continental position. Whatever might be the imperial root causes of Britain's commitments to her entente partners, the Anglo-German naval race had assumed a life of its own, poisoning relations between the two powers at all levels. The annexation crisis had generated increasing awareness that the continent could not any longer be safely neglected for the globe. Not only might future unrest in the Balkans spark a general war; Germany faced that prospect in a state of isolation. Encirclement, *Einkreisung*, began appearing more and more frequently alike in the public press and in official documents as a description of Germany's condition.

Bethmann's appointment marked the beginning of a return to a European approach to foreign policy. Bülow's hopes of a British alliance had proved illusory. Now, influenced by Britain's constant assertions that it maintained a "free hand" in European politics, the chancellor sought an exchange. British neutrality in any future continental war would be traded for limits on German naval construction.[22] Bethmann constantly encouraged his London representative to stress the openness of German offers in this area and German receptivity to any counterproposals.[23] At the same time he proposed to assert Germany's independence from Austria—not least because of Aehrenthal's continuing "gentle undertone" that the Habsburg Empire wanted to maintain a free hand in her dealings with Russia.[24]

Bethmann took particular notice when in September, 1910, Sergei Sazonov succeeded Izvolsky in the Russian foreign office. Sazonov, like his predecessor, was Russocentric, "a Russian of the genuine Moscow breed," as one German diplomat described him. He had been no happier than Izvolsky over the outcome of the annexation crisis, yet he had no desire to see Russia drawn into a committed anti-German network. For months before his appointment other voices in St. Petersburg had been asking whether Russia's estrangement from Germany was not a mistake. Had not Russia after all escaped with honor from a dead end in the Bosnian affair by following German advice?[25]

Sazonov did not have to accept the argument to perceive its utility. At least it offered an opportunity to signal Russia's entente partners that the tsar's empire must not be taken for granted. Bethmann for his part had been rapidly stalemated in his approaches to Britain, garnering little more than the overt hostility of domestic moralists and *Weltpolitiker*.

Britain's hands seemed free only to continue existing relations with France and Russia. Perhaps the way to London might be through St. Petersburg. If Russia broke ranks, Britain in turn might decide that a positive German connection was after all the best guarantee of her position in India and the Middle East.

It is a paradox that many of the same scholars who evaluate the pre-1914 alliance systems in general as poisonous medicine express what amounts to moral outrage at Germany's alleged efforts to "break" the Triple Entente after 1909. Great-power relations are seldom set in concrete, and in November, 1910, Bethmann and Sazonov successfully bear-led their respective and reluctant emperors through two days of conferences in Potsdam and Berlin. Russia withdrew opposition to Germany's long-cherished Berlin-to-Bagdad railway project in return for acceptance of a Russian sphere of influence in northern Persia. Closer to home, the two states agreed to pursue a policy of status quo and peaceful development in the Balkans, with Germany acting as mediator of any conflicts that Russia and Austria could not solve by direct negotiations. Bethmann assured Sazonov that Austria had no expansionist designs in that region, and had never asked Germany to support such designs. Sazonov for his part responded that no matter how he might strive for improved relations with Britain, Russia would never become part of a hostile combination directed against Germany.

Initial hopes were high. Aehrenthal said that as long as Russia remained "correct," the new orientation of her policies could only be greeted with joy. The Russian ambassador in Vienna spoke of new persons and new combinations on the horizon. Yet dreams faded quickly. Germany's investors were increasingly timid, her bureaucratized bankers unwilling to take risks without gilt-edged government guarantees. Her financial market could not match France in generating the capital still so important for Russia's economy. Russia's generals were reluctant to break a generation's habits in strategic planning. Russia's foreign office was correspondingly reluctant to commit itself to anything beyond comfortable generalizations. Bethmann offered drafts of the agreements and declarations, only to be met by the statement that verbal assurances made written ones unnecessary. Did not William trust the word of his imperial cousin?[26]

Not until August, 1911, was the document signed, and by then it had lost much of its value for a German government increasingly despairing of balancing Russia's words and Russia's policies. A paradigm of the confusion was the general staff report of February 21, 1911, on major changes in the Russian army during 1910. The army's peace strength was ostensibly unchanged, yet its order of battle had been increased by six corps headquarters and seven new divisions, most of them formed by converting reserve cadres and fortress garrisons to field troops. This enhanced immediate readiness for war at some expense to staying power. Several divisions had been also transferred from Russia's western frontier to the Volga region. This lessened the strain on the mobilization and replacement systems. It also gave Russia a strategic reserve, invulnerable

47

to any threat and able to be deployed quickly against either Germany or Austria along the railway network the empire was steadily in the process of improving. And, a possible straw in the wind, Russian maneuvers were becoming virtually impossible to observe as traditional professional courtesies gave way to systematic suspicion.[27]

Russia's capabilities to wage war seemed to be exponentially improving. What of her intentions? Malice or disorganization, a desire to lead Germany by the nose, an inability to coordinate decision making—the motives behind St. Petersburg's mixed signals seemed less and less important. Alfred von Kiderlin-Wächter was only the most coherent voice in the foreign office arguing for the particular necessity of speaking plainly and bluntly to Russia in times of crisis. Euphemisms and circumlocutions, not to say normal diplomatic good manners, lent themselves too readily to misinterpretation in the hothouse atmosphere of St. Petersburg. The question for Kiderlin, as for an increasing number of German diplomats and soldiers, was how far Russia's entente partners would be willing to underwrite Russia's behavior.[28]

German anxieties were further enhanced by Stolypin's assassination in September, 1911. Stolypin, Russia's premier since 1906, was no particular admirer of Germany. He had, however, accepted policies of peace and rapprochement as preconditions for the domestic reforms he considered necessary for the empire's survival. As much to the point, Stolypin tended to equate nationalist enthusiasms anywhere in Europe with revolutionary idealism, regarding them as dangerous, disruptive factors. His successor, V. N. Kokovtzov, was also convinced that Russia's vital interests demanded peace. He did not, however, have anything like Stolypin's influence over the tsar, the war ministry, or the foreign office—and least of all over a Duma and a journalistic community that had responded to the Potsdam negotiations with unconcealed and massive hostility.[29]

It was in these dubious international and domestic contexts that Russia took a step decisive in further estranging her from Germany. Since 1908, direct involvement in the Balkans had seemed less desirable to St. Petersburg than developing a network of proxy relationships. Influence exercised through Sofia or Belgrade offered a plausible excuse for France, and even more for Great Britain, to deny to their domestic critics that they were underwriting Russia's imperial ambitions. In the short run Russia was concerned less with fostering regional nationalism and nurturing Slavic unity than with establishing a diplomatic counterweight to what seemed heightened German and Austrian influence in the Near East.[30] Far from intending to encircle the central powers, fulfill historic missions of liberating the Slavs, or open the way to Constantinople, the Russian foreign office hoped for a league of states strong enough to provide a regional check on any expansionist aspirations entertained by Austria-Hungary. Some proposals even included Turkey as part of the league.

Hindsight indicates that had this initiative succeeded, it would have been a seismic shock to Europe's increasingly fragile power balance. Such a league could only function under Russian patronage, and would have represented a unilateral strengthening of Russia's position that Paris and London could hardly have swallowed whole, to say nothing of reactions in Berlin or Vienna. More pragmatically, policy in the Balkan kingdoms was increasingly being made by men with no commitment to Russia's visions. They dreamed instead of a regional offensive alliance strong enough to expel the Ottoman Empire from Europe and to secure its territory for themselves. Russia was viewed instrumentally: as an insurance policy against the consequences of defeat, and as a mediator with the great powers in case of victory.

Such aspirations were not likely to be modified by even subtle and forceful Russian diplomacy. Holstein had been uncomfortably accurate when he argued that a convoluted foreign policy in the style of Bismarck could only be administered by a Bismarck. Lesser talents must content themselves with simpler patterns. Sazonov was at best a mediocrity who hoped to thrust a hand into the Balkan wasps' nest and emerge with a fistful of honey. Instead, he proved once again that industry and dullness are a dangerous combination.[31]

Russia's approach to the Balkan question was also influenced by the pessimism of her generals. A constant in European diplomacy since the mid–nineteenth century had been the confidence of its soldiers that they could win, or at least draw, any war the statesmen initiated. Such warnings as they uttered were essentially self-serving admonitions that the situation would be even better were the military budgets increased as requested or current alliance relationships suitably adjusted. The Russo-Japanese War, however, had forced the Russian defense establishment into an agonizing reappraisal. As late as 1911, the Russian general staff bluntly informed the French that it would be two years at least before Russia would have any chance at all in a war with Germany.[32]

This was an attitude hardly calculated to inspire confidence in an ally. French generals, increasingly regarding a prompt and massive attack from the east as the Third Republic's only salvation against superior German numbers, responded by encouraging an increased orientation of tsarist strategy directly against Germany and Austria, with the implied threat of financial and diplomatic sanctions in case of refusal. At the same time, from a Russian perspective, the war ministry and the general staff of a great power could not indefinitely proclaim the impotence of their armed forces to their closest ally. The Franco-Russian alliance incorporated significant elements of interdependence, but was not quite a relationship of equals. The growing Russian acceptance of a necessity for putting early pressure on Germany was a useful way of reassuring the French, while at the same time meeting Russian perceptions of the current strategic situation.[33]

Even minimal compliance with French wishes forced Russia's Balkan and Caucasian frontiers to make do with leftovers. The Caucasus in particular tended to be a dumping ground for guards officers who had made Petersburg or Warsaw too hot to hold them. As a German observer put it, the Russians and the natives copied each others' bad habits; wine, women, and debts were the order of the day. On the other hand, in the aftermath of the 1908 Young Turk Rebellion Turkey had begun a significant overhaul of her long-moribund military establishment. German training missions and German arms salesmen had long been fixtures in Constantinople. In 1910 the Germans went a step farther by selling the Turks two old battleships. The next year the Turkish government contracted for two more warships, state-of-the-art superdreadnoughts, to be built in Britain. French and American promoters were negotiating the construction of railways in Asia Minor that if completed would significantly expedite the movement of troops along the Black Sea littoral, and to the Russian frontier. Should even some of these improvements succeed Russia's ability to exercise direct presssure on her southern neighbor would be significantly limited—so limited that good relations with the Slavic states of the Balkans seemed not desirable, but necessary from a military viewpoint.[34]

The destabilizing effects of these local power shifts on Europe as a whole became even plainer when, in the spring of 1911, France moved to consolidate its position in Morocco. The German government responded by forcing the issue. Domestic pressure played a role—pressure from Pan-Germans, industrialists, and assorted imperialists convinced either that Morocco represented too great an economic prize to abandon, or that it was a potential key to a future African empire. At the same time the foreign office desired to make a show of German power to a France that seemed all too confident of the strength of its alliances. Offensive diplomacy thus concealed a defensive stand. German policy did not take seriously the prospects of a conflict over North Africa. Neither the naval nor the military commands were consulted on anything more than a formal basis. At the height of the crisis the annual maneuvers, which made mobilization impossible for three weeks, were conducted as usual, and the reservists were discharged at their close.[35]

Some results of this policy of unsupported bluster were predictable. Britain and France drew even more closely together, congratulating each other on their solidarity in face of a threat that had proved ephemeral. Russia became correspondingly reluctant to risk becoming the odd state out in an entente. Far more serious, however, was an unexpected side effect. On December 16, 1900, France and Italy had agreed that should France extend her influence in Morocco, Italy could occupy Libya. At the time, it seemed to be one of those dead-letter, hypothetical-situation documents that clog the files of nineteenth-century foreign offices. But over the years Italy had sought and secured affirmation from Germany and Austria, her alliance partners. She had obtained Russian assent as well. Her way thus cleared, Italy went to war with the Ottoman Empire in September, 1911. The great powers, their hands tied by their own actions, stood by.[36]

This collective inaction during an overt attack on Turkey was carefully noted in the Balkan capitals. Since the Bosnian Crisis, St.

Petersburg had been under pressure to affirm its Slavic identity with more than words. Sazonov's hopes of a half-million Slav bayonets forever barring the Teuton from southeast Europe combined with his personal indecisiveness to encourage an increasing number of contradictory, mutually exclusive assurances to his Balkan negotiating partners. Russia's best and most forceful ambassador in the region, Nicholas Hartwig in Belgrade, was a committed Panslav and Austrophobe whose success in improving Serbo-Bulgarian relations made it correspondingly difficult for Sazonov to strike a balance between the Balkan states on one hand and the Dual Alliance on the other—not that Hartwig particularly cared. Ministers come and go, he was alleged to have said. Serbia should rely instead on a Russia that loved her, would always love her, and would not leave her in the lurch.[37]

By 1912 the Balkan tail was beginning to wag the Russian and European dogs. The network of alliances constituting the Balkan League, concluded between March and October, were negotiated independently of Russian ambassadors and the Russian foreign office. To Sazonov's anxious inquiry whether things were still as they had been in 1910 at Potsdam, Bethmann replied that Germany was as little interested as ever in encouraging a forward policy in the Balkans from any quarter. But when the Balkan League went to war with Turkey on October 17, Russia faced a choice that was no choice at all.[38]

As states in whose welfare she had expressed constant interest won victory after victory, Russia could not very well deny her approval. Yet from the war's first days Serbia's determination to secure an Adriatic outlet clashed with Austria's fear that a Serbian port might soon become a Russian one, and with Austria's determination to maintain her Balkan position in the face of the League's unexpected ascendancy. During a visit to Berlin a few days before the war's outbreak, Sazonov had suggested that if Austria were only patient she might eventually act as the powers' executor in limiting Serbian gains in the peninsula.[39] But in October, 1912, the Russian general staff ordered a practice call-up of reserves in Russian Poland. On November 10 the war ministry authorized the temporary retention with the colors of 400,000 men whose terms of active service were expiring. Since the entire Austro-Hungarian army had no more than 350,000 men under arms on a normal peace footing, the gesture could hardly be ignored in Vienna. Reinforcements were dispatched to the major eastern garrisons: Cracow, Lemberg, Przemsyl. The formations stationed in Bosnia-Herzegovina and Dalmatia were also put on a full war footing.[40]

Russia's decisions contrasted sharply with Germany's behavior during the Agadir crisis the previous year. Yet the entire process initially had a certain air of unreality as far as Germany was concerned. Reservist call-ups were common practice for all of Europe's conscript armies. This one was accompanied by reports of discontent and indiscipline amounting to mutiny in some cases—reservists allegedly assaulting officers and declaring that in case of a war they would know whom to shoot first.[41] When the

51

Austrian chief of staff made a quick trip to Berlin to consult his colleague, it was without the knowledge of the German government, which instructed its ambassador in Vienna to make it clear that *post facto* reports of such conferences were highly inappropriate.[42] In mid-November Pourtalès could still quote the Austrian military attaché in St. Petersburg as believing that Russia was not planning a mobilization. A "high general staff officer" expressed his preference for dealing with Austria in two years, but this was familiar rhetoric. The Austrians were even wondering whether they were not ahead of Russia in preparations for an eventual war. Then on November 22, Tsar Nicholas approved the ordering of mobilization in the military districts of Kiev, Odessa, and Warsaw.[43]

This decision, urged by the generals, was checked only by the impassioned pleas of Sazonov and Kokovtsov. Kokovtsov's account, the most detailed and the most familiar, is an exaggerated contrast of bloodthirsty soldiers to peace-loving statesmen. Ernest R. May interprets the incident as manifesting the structural weakness of Russia's decision-making process. May argues that bureaucratic infighting encouraged concealing information—in this case the information that no one at the meeting, civilian or military, actually wished or intended to start a war in support of Serbia's regional pretensions.[44] But the conference did not take place in a vacuum.

France had, on the whole, remained conciliatory in its direct relations with Germany after 1906. The republic's long-time ambassador to Berlin, Jules Cambon, consistently and successfully warned his government against overreacting to the kaiser's bluster. This, however, did not portend rapprochement. A reviving French nationalism was becoming an increasingly powerful force for anti-German sentiments and policies. Relations between the business and financial communities strained as they came into direct competition in the Near East. The French foreign office included a new generation of fire-eaters: young Germanophobes permanently convinced of Germany's ultimately evil intentions. Moreover, if the ententes of 1904 and 1907 had considerably improved France's diplomatic position, they were by no means ironclad guarantees. French diplomats recognized the instrumental character of their British connection. They retained enough respect for the German foreign office not to discount the possibility of Anglo-German rapprochement. The Franco-Russian relationship also seemed far more fragile in Paris than it appeared to Berlin, especially, in the minds of many professional diplomats, because it had to be defended against Radical politicians who dominated the cabinets after 1906, and tended to regard Tsarist Russia as morally and politically disgusting, an unreliable creditor and an ally from stark necessity. A major goal of French foreign policy in the three years before the outbreak of world war was to exercise a greater degree of control over her increasingly wayward eastern ally. This in turn meant maintaining, even enhancing, ties of friendship and good will[45]

This attitude was strengthened and supported by the evolution of the French army's strategic and tactical doctrines after Joseph Joffre's appointment as chief of staff in 1911. Joffre's commitment to the offensive as the only way to break an enemy's power and will was significant in view of the confidence he enjoyed in cabinet and parliament alike as a symbol of Republican virtue in uniform. Revised under his supervision, French strategy increasingly focussed on an all-out attack against Germany, an attack geographically limited to Lorraine only because Joffre's repeated proposals to include south Belgium were rejected as fatal to France's British connection.

Britain's insistence that a pre-emptive French move into Belgium would result in a British declaration of neutrality only highlighted France's concern for the military strength of the Dual Alliance. French prospects for success might not depend entirely upon the diversion of German troops to other theaters. They would, however, be significantly enhanced. This fact helps explain the optimism expressed by the French general staff in the summer of 1912 when considering the prospect of general war over the Balkans. With a good part of Austria's army presumably pinned down by the forces of the League, with the bulk of Germany's troops destined for the western theater, French experts reasoned that Russia should have excellent chances for victory in both Galicia and East Prussia—victories that would force Germany to reduce her strength on the French front and facilitate a decisive French breakthrough.[46]

France's premier and foreign minister, Raymond Poincaré, was hardly interested in giving Russia a free hand in the Balkans or anywhere else. But his fear of German intentions temporarily outweighed his fear of Russian behavior. Far from concealing the soldiers' potentially explosive vision, Poincaré not only circulated it to his ambassadors, but informed the Russian envoy in Paris. That man was Izvolsky, whose fall from office had been cushioned by comfortable exile to the Quai d'Orsay. Still smarting over his humiliation in 1908, he was hardly likely to refrain from passing the information to his successor.[47]

Lest the implication be mistaken in Berlin and Vienna, Russia's Grand Duke Nicholas was France's guest at her grand maneuvers in September. The duke's entourage, particularly his wife, a Montenegran princess, indulged in a spate of anti-German outbursts as extreme as anything heard at a French official function since the days of Boulanger. Senior Russian officers boasted to anyone within hearing that the military situation was highly favorable; all they needed to do was push the button—which they did in October and November. As late as December 26, War Minister V. A. Sukhomlinov described to the French military attaché's adjutant his intention to rub Germany's nose in Russia's readiness for war—ironically, during a forthcoming official visit to celebrate the Russo-Prussian victory over Napoleon a century earlier.[48]

The war minister may have been seeking to impress his allies. He many have been the temporary victim of his own enthusiasm. But even if Sukhomlinov saw Russia's partial mobilization as no more than a legitimate effort to take the current Balkan pot by raising the stakes, this kind of brinkmanship was fraught with risks against opponents who had put too much into the game not to call the bet.

III

Strategy did not yet determine policy in either France or Russia. By November, Poincaré was complaining that Izvolsky was misrepresenting his position, and insisting that France would support Russia militarily only should Austria and Germany attack her first.[49] Sazonov for his part dispatched a series of stern warnings to the Balkan capitals that Russia was not prepared to make war in defense of small-state pretensions. As much to the point, he was increasingly receptive to suggestions that a great-power conference discuss the Balkan question in general, and the Austro-Serbian dispute in particular.[50]

Sazanov's behavior was particularly welcome to Bethmann. It was clear that Germany could not afford simply to follow Austria's lead in the Balkans.[51] At the same time direct attempts at mediating between Russia and Austria were likely to do more harm than good. Austria's growing weakness relative to her eastern neighbor might force Germany to throw enough extra weight on the Habsburg side of the scale to make her objectivity suspect. On the other hand Russian indecisiveness might generate a repetition of conditions leading to the March, 1909, *démarche*. Given these undesirable alternatives, Bethmann turned to London, pressing for direct cooperation on the Balkan issue—cooperation in organizing an international conference.[52]

Britain was distant and dubious. Cooperation on specific issues, according to Foreign Secretary Sir Edward Grey, was welcome. It must not, however, become the first step in "a political understanding with Germany which would separate us from Russia and France, and leave us isolated while the rest of Europe would be obliged to look to Germany." In particular the foreign office feared that a Russia again overcommitted in the Balkans might this time abandon the entente for good and all.[53]

Despite these reservations, through the fall and early winter British and German diplomats cooperated more or less effectively in preparing for a Balkan peace conference. Then Bethmann played to another gallery. On December 2, he informed the Reichstag in ringing tones that should Austria be attacked by a third party, Germany would fight.

The reference to Russia was unmistakable, and in a German context hardly surprising. A little over a month earlier, on October 28, State Secretary Alfred von Kiderlin-Wächter had been even more open in a speech to the Bundesrat. Austria-Hungary, he declared, must be held responsible for defending her own interests in the Balkans. But should she be faced with a Russian attack, Germany had no choice but to provide assistance. This was not "fighting for Durazzo." Germany's ultimate purpose in the Dual Alliance was to sustain Austria's position as a great power. Otherwise the Reich would be isolated, trapped between France and Russia.[54]

Germany's position was by no means as obvious across the English Channel. The British government was both alarmed at what seemed unnecessary saber-rattling and concerned at the possibility of facing a continental war for which Britain was completely unprepared. In diplomacy as in poker, a good way of winning with a second-rate hand is to overbet it. On successive days Lord Chancellor Richard Haldane and Grey himself informed the German ambassador, Prince Lichnowsky, that Britain would not tolerate a single power dominating the continent. Should Austria invade Serbia, Britain would not remain neutral in any resulting continental war.[55] William flew into a rage. In October he had argued that hostilities in the Balkans were no bad thing even if they led to general war. Such a conflict was inevitable sooner or later, and Germany was in a favorable position relative to her potential enemies.[56] Now, on December 8, he summoned his military and naval advisors and demanded immediate consideration of the consequences of an Anglo-German war.

This crown council has become a key event in interpretations of Germany's foreign policy in the immediate prewar years. It has been presented as the beginning of the last stage of a coherent, goal-oriented policy designed to create favorable opportunities for a war of conquest that would destroy the status quo internationally while preserving it at home, giving Germany hegemony in Europe and a correspondingly strong basis for a drive to world power. It has also been described as no more than one of a series of limited responses to immediate situations, an opportunity for an incompetent kaiser and his feckless entourage to discharge their more juvenile emotions without addressing the real problems of a Germany so badly divided against itself that pursuit of any coherent foreign policy was ultimately impossible. In one case the appropriate imperial symbol is a vulture. In the other it becomes a turkey.[57]

The direct consequences of the December 8 meeting were marginal. The press was instructed to prepare public opinion for a possible war resulting from an Austro-Serbian conflict. Some general military and economic steps for mobilization were initiated, none of them on the level Russia had pursued in the previous two months. This behavior, however, suggests less about Germany's intentions than does Kiderlin-Wächter's memorandum of December 6 to the embassy in London. Its author insisted that no one in Germany was thinking of forcing Russia to retreat, to sacrifice her interests or prestige. Austria-Hungary's rights vis-à-vis Serbia, Kiderlin argued, were the same in essence as those of France in Algeria or Britain in Egypt. Had Russia committed herself to support Serbia's demands, one might be able to speak of a backdown, but Russia herself staunchly denied that that was the case.[58]

German hostility to south Slav aspirations is frequently described by its critics as an explosive mixture of economic imperialism and self-defeating paranoia. German industrialists and capitalists, according to this interpretation, saw southeastern Europe as both a source of increasingly scarce raw materials and a field for investment and exploitation. At the same time, German publicists and diplomats mistook Russia's emotional and intellectual sympathy towards fellow Slavs for a developed political position. Slavic identity was for Russia little more than a means of mobilizing and focussing domestic support in crisis situations. A German foreign policy sincerely oriented towards peace should have recognized and avoided the risks of igniting that particular tinder. Germany, however, had never really stabilized its own nationalist forces, much less developed any sympathy for self-determination on the part of peoples viewed as inferior in any case. Instead of getting behind this modern and progressive force, or at least standing out of its way, German policy makers chose to back reaction as embodied in Austria-Hungary, giving the high moral and political ground to Russia with predictable and tragic results.[59]

German and Austrian statesmen and opinion makers all too frequently demonstrated regrettable arrogance towards Slavs in general and Serbs in particular. *Simplicissimus*, that European model of a satiric journal, delighted in portraying the Balkan peoples as vermin-infested barbarians. Serbs never surrender, asserted one cartoon, because they can never find a white flag clean enough to be convincing. Moltke the Younger's comparison of Serbian aspirations to an abscess, threatening to poison the body of Europe and best cauterized with a red-hot iron, reflected an even more significant lack of empathy.[60]

Such insensitivities obscure, but do not negate, the argument that successive attempts to restructure eastern and central Europe along ethnic lines caused far more problems than they solved. The only stable order that unfortunate region has known in this century has been order imposed by outside forces, most recently the USSR. The Balkan Wars of 1912–13 set new standards for horror and violence, both on the battlefields and against noncombatants. An international commission surveying the conflict concluded that the fighting had been "as desperate as though extermination were the end sought."[61] As for Serbia's self-proclaimed role as liberator and integrator, growing Albanian resistance to Serb occupation was only the most obvious contemporary indication that Serbia was no less imperialistic than her larger contemporaries. She had merely lacked opportunity to indulge her ambitions.[62]

This perspective remains uncommon in an academic world that has tended since World War II to legitimate uncritically almost any political expression of nationalism. Joachim Remak, for all his sympathy to the Habsburg Empire, tacitly accepts a balance of rights between Austria's wish to survive and Serbia's desire to expand. The author of a distinguished general history of the Balkans describes the Serbian government before 1914 as having three options: a "greater Serbia" built largely on lands taken from the Habsburgs; a Balkan federation, again incorporating the Slavs of Austria-Hungary "should that state dissolve"; and a Yugoslav program incorporating "all" Serbs, Croats, and Slovenes in a single nation. It is noteworthy that a scholar of Barbara Jelavich's stature seems victimized by the tendency of Eastern European peoples to romanticize and aggrandize their national past. She does not even consider a fourth

56

possibility: renouncing these vaulting ambitions and living in relative peace with her neighbor, either willingly or under duress.[63]

National consciousness, particularly in the Balkans, has been to a significant degree the product of cultivation. The transformation of social groups into what Benedict Anderson aptly calls "imagined communities" depends heavily on intellectuals. Writers, academicians, and politicians set the style in which these communities are conceived. In practice this style has emphasized alleged genetically or, more recently, culturally based differences among peoples at the expense of historic ties, economic interests, and geopolitical realities.[64] Whatever the legitimate claims of national identity, they do not and cannot include an absolute right to secede and regroup at will. Self-determination remains subject to limitation by the claims of other rights and principles, including the principle of stability. Nor does self-determination confer moral or physical immunity from the consequences of acts committed in its name.

H.R. Trevor-Roper correctly observes that complete sovereignty for small states is a fiction, that "they are not free to conduct independent politics on a world scale." The concept of an international order based on a community of sovereign states whose borders are inviolable by unilateral military action no matter what the provocation owes much to the propaganda campaigns of World War I and more to the academic legalisms of Woodrow Wilson. In its pursuit, instead of Europeanizing the Balkans, politicians and intellectuals have in the long run Balkanized Europe and the world.[65]

It was this process of Balkanization that concerned Bethmann-Hollweg. Like Bülow, he sought to put Germany at the center of Europe's diplomacy, to restore that freedom of movement whose loss had been so painfully plain at Algeciras. In his approach to the Near East crisis, he hoped in the short run to dampen a crisis and in the long run to restore the Concert of Europe under German direction.[66]

In pursuing a policy of flexibility Bethmann recognized as clearly as Bismarck that a Europe divided into rigid alliance systems was both a second-best solution to the problem of national security, and a solution whose implications were becoming extremely dangerous for the continent as a whole. Statesmen whose academic training normally included firm grounding in the classics were hardly likely to have forgotten the Peloponnesian Wars, in which hostile leagues beggared each other at the expense of common civilization for over a century. And while German fire-eaters were fond of referring to Britain as the modern Carthage, to be eclipsed by the allegedly Roman virtues of the Second Reich, the Punic Wars also suggested a more somber analogy. These wars had, after all, so changed the internal structure of the Roman Republic that its victory had amounted to a defeat—a point stressed in the familiar works of Theodor Mommsen.

Alliances, in short, had their shortcomings as guarantees of order. At the same time the experience of the previous half-century, and of three hundred years of diplomacy, indicated that the great-power structure that had evolved since the Thirty Years' War was too complex and too dynamic to function without some form of guidance. Laissez-faire was no more viable as a principle of international relations than of domestic economics. On the other hand, any single power that attempted to be more than *primus inter pares* exhausted itself, either directly in fighting the enemies it generated or eventually by dissipating its power and influence in attempts to control a continent. The focus of German diplomacy since 1871 had been rather a desire to be at Europe's center, the principal force shaping and directing events. The German Empire's statesmen sought this pivot point with more system, and more consequence, than the Kehr/Wehler internal-crisis school of scholarship allows.

This desire cannot be directly equated with a search for hegemony. Woodrow Wilson, for example, was committed in a similar fashion in 1918 to directing the negotiations for ending the war and establishing the peace.[67] Maintaining a central position did, however, depend heavily on possession of armed forces strong enough to discourage any direct challenges to that position. It is appropriate in this context to recognize that 1914–18 marked the beginning of a significant inversion of vocabularies. Since those years, the use of force has been increasingly described in the verbiage of peace. War departments become departments of defense. Towns are destroyed in order to save them. Military occupation of a neighbor becomes a process of liberating that neighbor from oppression. In the era of Bülow and Bethmann, nationalism, Darwinism, and militarism combined to legitimate, sometimes to demand, a reverse process: the description of conciliatory behavior in belligerent terms. Private conversations and public correspondence alike tended towards rhetorical bloodthirstiness shocking to later sensibilities.[68]

In 1912 as in 1905, however, fear of war and its consequences continued to restrict the actual spectrum of acceptable initiatives. In the complicated game of snakes and ladders that was European international relations, to stand still was perceived as regression. Germany lacked the self-confidence to accept that risk. Yet her generals, statesmen, and diplomats continued to refrain from striking even when the immediate military advantage might lie with Germany.

Since 1908 the army had been steadily reasserting its position vis-à-vis the navy as the guarantor of the empire's power, the ultimate source of national existence in a Europe frantically preparing for the war everyone expected. Its continued acceptance of the "short-war illusion," the belief that future conflicts must be quick and decisive, has been frequently described by military historians as wishful thinking. To scholars emphasizing the primacy of domestic politics, it becomes a manifestation of the generals' unwillingness to risk destabilizing their society even further by overstraining national unity. It seems more accurate to suggest that the German army's growing concern with decisive victories and battles of annihilation in the years before 1914 manifested a corresponding reluctance to see war become an end in itself. Throughout the nineteenth century, Prussian-German military theorists had been concerned with retaming Bellona, with avoiding the unlimited wars of the Revolutionary-Napoleonic era, because they were ultimately indecisive. By the end of his tenure as chief of staff, Moltke the Elder was suggesting that the army's primary function lay in deterring wars rather than fighting them. Such contemporary prophets of total war as Friedrich von Bernhardi and Colmar von der Goltz were regarded as dreamers or extremists by their more sober contemporaries, the men who actually received the important staff and command appointments.[69]

The major challenge to both the diplomatic and the military aspects of German policy came from Russia. The tsar's empire was in a position simultaneously to threaten the existence of Austria-Hungary and the balance of Europe, either by direct initiative in the Balkans or indirectly by supporting the increasingly powerful Slavic states of the peninsula. Bethmann's overtures to Britain, while they certainly had the positive aim of enhancing Germany's position, incorporated a negative element as well: the hope of restraining Russia, whether by British actions or through collective diplomacy. In the final analysis, however, Germany must ultimately depend on her own resources. Bethmann's hopes for a reborn Concert of Europe were unlikely to bear fruit unless Germany should herself be capable of serving as its fulcrum. And in the context of the early Twentieth century, this meant developing and demonstrating the kind of military capacity that would make the risks of challenge too high to be undertaken except as a last, desperate resort.

Unfortunately for Bethmann's vision, most of the desperation seemed to be felt by Germany's soldiers. Schlieffen, in retirement the *éminence grise* of the general staff, had grown increasingly obsessed with the concept of a decisive battle in Belgium and northern France. His proposed modifications of the plan of 1905 developed corresponding tunnelvision, with schedules ever more rigid, with margins for error and friction reduced to the vanishing point. As chief of staff he had never felt able to ignore the Russian threat. As a theorist without responsibility, he was by 1913 advocating that the eastern theater be stripped of all save token garrison forces drawn primarily from the lowest categories of reservists. For support he turned no longer to the classical past, but to the campaigns of Frederick the Great. Frederick, he argued, could have crushed Austria in 1757 had he only possessed the moral courage to concentrate the Prussian army in Bohemia, instead of leaving detachments in Pomerania, East Prussia, and the Rhine provinces.[70]

Moltke the Younger was at once less sanguine and less abstract. In December, 1911, he observed that Germany's chances in a war against Britain and France were good—if Russia remained neutral. Britain's army was small. France lacked the manpower reserves to sustain a large-scale war. Russia, on the other hand, could use her vast spaces to prolong conflict indefinitely. Improved mobilization, new strategic railroads, and a revitalized officer corps combined to enhance Russia's military potential. The countryside was still not pacified. Non-Russian peoples smarted under Great Russian chauvinism. But Russia was well able to resume its expansionist policies at least in the Middle and Far East.[71]

In view of the actual course of events in the east between 1914 and 1917, a question of increasing interest is why Russia's power was so overrated in the years before 1914. Paul Kennedy suggests that Europe in general and Germany in particular were mesmerized by numbers in uniform. He goes on to demonstrate that despite the often-cited increases in Russia's armed forces, her productive capacity was actually decreasing relative to Germany's in the years before 1914. The military giant was an economic dwarf. Programs of military reform initiated after 1905 were frustrated by bureaucratic infighting and institutional inertia. The tsarist army's inefficiency, other critics argue, was the systemic product of centuries, not to be overcome by technical innovations, new drill regulations, or shuffling of officers' appointments. Russian generals themselves, when not speaking for public consumption, constantly questioned their army's readiness for war.[72]

In this context German concern for the Russian threat suggests incompetence on one hand, insincerity on the other. Was the general staff conjuring up a bogey to increase military budgets and enhance the acceptability of a future war? On a larger scale, did the new emphasis on Russia reflect a fundamental shift in German foreign policy from *Weltpolitik* to *Ostimperium*, either as an end in itself or an interim solution to domestic problems of encirclement and destabilization? Part of the answer lies in Germany's position in the first decade of the new century. Her population was expanding at a rate frightening to her continental neighbors. She had matched and surpassed Great Britain in a broad spectrum of industrial and business activities. Her socialist movement was a model for the world's organized labor. Her political system, with its synthesis of centralism and federalism, monarchy and populism, was an adventure widely respected beyond German borders. Culturally, intellectually, even sexually, Germany was a society open to experimentation, a society seeking new forms. Her *Einkreisung* was as much spiritual as political, a reaction to a world order imposed by French *civilisation* and the *Pax Britannica*. Yet this dynamism was balanced by a consciousness of weakness, of vulnerable geographic and military positions, of ideas subject to challenge by their very newness. The processes of change and growth at the heart of Germany's strength seemed at the same time a source of weakness, eroding society's all-too-fragile vital center.[73]

Germany was also developing a sense of her objective limitations. For all its emphasis on vitalism and the categorical imperative, the Second Reich was essentially a material empire whose superiority to her neighbors rested on an ability to mobilize domestic human and economic resources in a developed industrial system. An ethnically homogeneous Germany stood against a polyglot Austria-Hungary. Sixty million Germans outweighed forty million Frenchmen, as did an empire with a balanced national economy compared to a Britain depending for her existence, much less her prosperity, on a complex structure of imports. Yet even this powerful position was relative. Compared to the vast potential of the United States on one hand and Russia on the other, Germany was a dot on the map—a situation indicated, if not quite demonstrated, by her recent adventures in *Weltpolitik*.

As yet the New World could be discounted. Russia, however, was altogether another matter. While the United States was an uncertain participant in the game of power politics, Russia had a permanent seat at the table. Russian raw materials and Russian markets lured a Germany perceiving the limits of simple colonialism. But in the new century Russia's image was changing sharply. Tolstoy, Dostoyevsky, Chekhov, brought new life to a Western culture that seemed increasingly mannered, increasingly sterile. Russian music filled concert halls. Russian ballet drew superlatives from the most jaded critics. Russia was "discovered" as a land of simple peasant virtues by neo-Romantic intellectuals, and as a vital frontier by travellers eager to ride the newly completed Trans-Siberian Railway.

This process inspired respect and generated anxiety. The degenerated barbarians of *de moribus ruthenorum* posed less of a threat by far than a *Kulturvolk* with a million-man army and an economic system that bade fair in the coming decades finally to take advantage of a seemingly inexhaustible base of natural resources.

Attitudes towards Russia were also influenced by the actions of two specific pressure groups. The Baltic German community increasingly described itself as victims of Russification and revolution. Particularly in the aftermath of events in 1905-06, its image of Russia was of a colossus in its death throes, whose convulsions bade fair to bring down the rest of Europe as well. From a different perspective, an increasing number of Russian students and political exiles described a tyrannical autocracy determined to crush whatever sparks of freedom and dignity remained to its people in the aftermath of the Black Hundreds.

Neither the Balts nor the émigrés had anything like a general constituency in Germany. Liberals distrusted one, conservatives and anti-Semites the other. Both communities, however, contributed to a general sense that it was increasingly necessary to re-evaluate Germany's position, in particular her military position, relative to Russia.[74]

Historically, military intelligence work had been neglected in Germany, with officers avoiding it as a professional dead end. What intelligence efforts existed were primarily directed against France. For information about Russia the German army relied primarily on its attachés and military plenipotentiaries in St. Petersburg, and on Austrian sources. Efforts to build a modern intelligence network in the east encountered hostility from local civil authorities. The Prussian ministry of the interior disliked using royal officials for any kind of intelligence work. Corps commanders resented any interference with their authority. Schlieffen was relatively uninterested in the subject. As late as 1906, Prussian War Minister Karl von Einem insisted that no one could maintain relationships with spies, traitors, and similar disreputable characters without damaging his own character. Not until Moltke became chief did the intelligence branch of the general staff receive consistent support from the highest quarters.

Intelligence work in Russia was a challenge. The country's size and backwardness meant foreigners were relatively conspicuous. The archetypical nineteenth-century gentleman agent posing as a tourist or commercial traveller was correspondingly handicapped, particularly given the relatively rigid enforcement of passport and residence regulations in the tsar's empire. This meant developing and cultivating Russian sources. In 1906, Captain Walter Nicolai was assigned to Königsberg as senior intelligence officer of I Corps. He was thirty-three, bright, assertive, and a tireless worker. It was Nicolai's contention that good intelligence officers avoided isolated coups and bravura pieces, working instead to establish a total picture of their target's capabilities. After his routine reassignment in 1910, intelligence officers of the army corps on the eastern frontier followed the pattern he established, concentrating on collecting and processing large quantities of low-level information. But what did the data mean? Some reports described carelessness, incompetence, drunkenness. Others presented changes in doctrine, training, and command that suggested enhanced vitality in the Russian military system. Were the changes mere ephemera in a Russia ultimately unable to modernize? Could Germany risk that assumption? French behavior suggested that the scope of the Franco-Russian alliance had expanded significantly since 1908. The developing armed strength of the Balkan states, the shattering of Turkey's forces, and the continued weakness of Austria—all combined to enhance the danger of underestimating Russia.[75]

The Imperial German army was confident in its particular blend of human and material elements. It expected to defeat its enemies quickly and decisively. But in the first years of the new century military technology had not yet progressed so far that combat strength could not legitimately be reckoned in the traditional material form of sabers, bayonets, and guns. Nor had recent wars demonstrated beyond doubt just which intangible military virtues were most useful. Russian stolidity and endurance, German dash and initiative, might well cancel each other. Nor could German planners afford to forget a major lesson of the Russo-Japanese War. The Japanese, foreign observers generally agreed, were far superior man for man to their adversaries in enthusiasm, dash, tactical skill—all the qualities on which the German army prided itself. Yet the Japanese army bled itself white against the Russian colossus at Port Arthur, Liao-Yang, and Mukden. By war's end it was virtually crippled by its positive qualities.

The failure of Russia's military reforms are clearer by far from a half-century's hindsight than they appeared in 1912. Internal criticisms of the army's shortcomings can be taken as positive: the Russian military establishment was anything but complacent in the years between 1905 and 1914. British observers, with less of an axe to grind than their French counterparts, continued to be impressed with Russia's recovery after

1905.[76] Germany's generals, moreover, were not academic structuralists. Everything in their experience since the Wars of Liberation suggested that social organization, military efficiency, and victory in battle did not follow one another in anything resembling logical progression. On the contrary, armies had the potential to introduce significant reforms within existing institutional frameworks. Armies had the ability to make good the failings of the systems that committed them to battle. German soldiers were aware that the French and Austrians had come closer to altering the destiny of Nineteenth-century Europe on the battlefield than was generally realized. And even marginal improvements in Russia's military performance meant an exponential increase in the threat she posed. A skillful middleweight boxer's chances against a clumsy, untutored heavyweight diminish significantly once his opponent assimilates a few pointers on footwork and timing.

As for Russia's economic position, its weaknesses were hardly unfamiliar in a Germany whose businessmen and financiers were so heavily involved in her development. But no one of consequence anywhere in Europe expected any future war to last long enough for anything but the resources on hand to influence the outcome. The exponentially greater output of German farms and factories meant nothing if the tsar's armies delivered a knockout punch in the first round. Positive discrepancies between a state's armed force and the economic infrastructure sustaining it should generate anxiety among that state's neighbors. Fighting men can seize wealth easier than wealth can buy fighting men. The notion that economically limited states would spend themselves into bankruptcy competing with their neighbors proved an expensive delusion in the 1930s as Germany, Italy, and Japan demonstrated the military potential of unbalanced economies.

IV

The crisis of 1912 wound down, like so many of its predecessors, in a flurry of relieved correspondence. On December 17, the first session of the great powers' conference on the Balkans opened in London—a conference characterized by increasing cooperation between Britain and Germany. The mood in Moscow, according to the German consul, was by no means warlike. Everyone had expected things to go wrong with the mobilization, and they did. The Warsaw military district began discharging its time-expired men in March, 1913. The only overt sign of hostilities came from the frontier district of Taurowitz, where local officials reported suspicious lights and noises that could only come from a Russian airship. The Landrat responded by ordering the gendarmerie to try and force down the alien flying machine when next it appeared.[77]

As for the mobilization that triggered the anxiety, Sukhomlinov was at pains to tell the German military attaché that everything was Sazonov's fault. The war ministry, he declared, had informed the foreign office as early as May, 1912, of its plans to hold a practice mobilization and assumed the German government had been appropriately notified. His surprise at discovering the contrary appeared genuine enough to convince the attaché. The Russian ambassador to Berlin took meticulous pains to report to the German foreign office the dates of projected call-ups of reservists in the Kiev and Warsaw districts during 1913. By October of that year, the Warsaw consulate quoted General Alexei Brusilov, the military district's deputy commander, to the familiar effect that many senior Russian officers would welcome better relations with Germany. Only decrepit Austria would not be welcome in a new alliance.[78]

Rhetorical good will did not obscure objective military developments. In October, 1912, Germany's admiralty staff credited Russia with the capacity to transport, without special measures, a division-sized force from the Baltic ports of Riga and Libau to a Pomeranian coast German mobilization plans left stripped of all but token forces. Though Russia was not likely to run such a risk unless the Royal Navy first destroyed the German battle fleet, the potential nevertheless existed. It loomed even larger in the light of Russian proposals to build a modern Baltic fleet around new squadrons of dreadnoughts and battle cruisers.[79]

As for the Russian army, its very shortcomings were a paradoxical advantage. A less-prepared force could learn more from its mistakes than one at the peak of efficiency. The recent issuing of a set of regulations for the period *before* mobilization was strongly suggestive. Its measures and procedures could be an important guide to Russia's behavior in any future crises. Just as important, it indicated a commitment to overcoming Russia's most obvious weakness, her cumbersome mobilization.[80] In November, 1913, Moltke submitted a lengthy report to the foreign office insisting that practice mobilizations of the kind Russia regularly staged were extremely difficult to tell from the real thing. Should the diplomatic situation be at all tense, even if the call-up of reservists and the retention of time-expired men were routine exercises, Germany might be constrained to implement its own mobilization, with corresponding consequences.[81]

The Russian army was far from perfect. Its maneuvers in 1913 were "free," with commanders able to operate virtually at will within broad guidelines. The result was a series of bitter quarrels among the generals, requiring the frequent intervention of the maneuver directors. A significant number of favorable situations were missed through what the German attaché described as an "astonishing" lack of initiative. The Russians seemed embarrassed enough by the proceedings that they kept the French observers as far out of the way as possible. Yet at the same time the spirit and discipline of the troops appeared excellent. Even papers critical of the government were praising improvements in training. New French loans provided up to a half-million francs a year for the construction of strategic railway lines in western Russia. In October the authorized peacetime strength of the Russian army was raised by yet another half-million men. The Duma voted special grants to increase the artillery and enlarge the army's munitions reserve. The German foreign office was receiving reports of new cartridge factories designed to work twenty-four-hour shifts. The British military attaché calculated that Russia's defense expenditures had increased by 41.5 percent since 1908.[82]

The general staff's annual report on the major alterations in the Russian army during 1913 altered its internal structure. The section on finances, economics, and politics, placed at the end of earlier versions, headed this one. Russia, the document concluded, had emerged from the Balkan crisis without having to borrow money or increase taxes. Yet her budget had grown by 660 million marks, 230 million of them earmarked for defense. Russia currently seemed more involved in Persia and China than in the Balkans—a reasonable result of her disappointment with the League. But this was a political decision, and as such subject to reversal. A potential adversary's capacities are best judged independently of her probable intentions. And Russia's capacities were continuing to grow.[83] The war ministry had once again decided to retain its time-expired men for three additional months. The public explanation was that the continued shortage of noncommissioned officers required using the older soldiers to train the recruits. What would be next year's excuse?

Moltke was increasingly concerned at the freedom of strategic action Russia would have in any future war should Austria fail to mount the offensive promised by Conrad in 1909. The Russian army could advance with its whole strength against either one of its opponents, and the German sector would be by far the weakest. If the Russians crossed the Vistula and moved on Berlin, troops must be withdrawn from the west to meet the threat, whatever the risk of disaster on both fronts. Russia could also delay operations until her armies were fully mobilized, then advance against both allies at once in overwhelming force. The German general staff in the spring of 1914 estimated that Russia would be able to produce 50 active and 13 reserve divisions for the European front as early as the eighteenth day of mobilization. And when fully mobilized, the Russian army was expected to reach the awesome total of 59 active and 35 reserve divisions, 12 rifle brigades, and 35 cavalry divisions.[84]

In the face of these numbers Germany's eastern commitment remained unchanged. The wisdom of this policy was frequently challenged after 1918. No less an authority than Ludwig Beck, chief of staff of Hitler's Wehrmacht from 1933 to 1938, argued that German strategic planning should have allowed for only a defensive screen against France, directing the bulk of the Second Reich's forces against a Russia that in fact had proved so vulnerable. This line of argument has subsequently been repeated by scholars arguing that Germany planned and initiated in 1914 a war for European hegemony rather than a limited conflict.[85] From an alternate perspective, in the context of a generally accepted belief in the superiority of offensive operations, this vast Russian strength seemed to demand some kind of direct reaction. Otherwise, the war on the eastern front might well be lost in its first days. The German general staff under Schlieffen and Moltke had maintained after 1905 a contingency plan for a "Major Deployment East," the *Grosse Ostaufmarsch*. Its designers were, however, convinced that such an operation could only be implemented in the context of not merely British, but French neutrality. After 1909 it seemed increasingly clear that this was an unlikely possibility. And this forced the general staff to make a hard decision, one vital for Germany's security and existence. Which enemy offensive was likely to be the most immediately dangerous? Which opponent could be the most rapidly defeated? In 1912 the answers seemed the same as in 1905. Germany must above all maintain the initiative, mounting its offensive before a French attack that was as sure to come as the Russian one.

This in turn put increasing pressure on the corps headquarters, which were responsible for their own mobilizations, and on the railway section of the general staff, which had to move the armies as quickly and smoothly as possible. Maintaining two separate, up-to-date war plans aimed in opposite directions seemed a diffusion of effort not merely undesirable but dangerous. In early 1913 Moltke ordered not that the *Grosse Ostaufmarsch* be abandoned, but that it no longer be annually revised. Existing plans were to be preserved for implementation should circumstances change.[86]

Much ink has been spilled on the actual course of events in August, 1914: the brief moment when French neutrality appeared possible; the kaiser's enthusiastic suggestion that the German army could now be turned against Russia; Moltke's emotional collapse at the thought of abandoning the Schlieffen Plan. His argument that the troops would arrive at the eastern railheads as a disorganized and hungry mob was carefully refuted after the war by General von Staabs of the general staff's railway section.[81] Implementing the *Grosse Ostaufmarsch* would hardly have meant the removal of a generation's cobwebs. While the practical and emotional difficulties involved in executing such an emergency redeployment must not be underestimated, neither should they be regarded as insurmountable. Technical questions, plans or the absence of plans, were not the key issues. What counted was German professional opinion that an offensive of any scale against Russia was impossible in the context of even a potential French threat.

In March, 1913, the general staff played a war game in which the main force of eighteen army corps was concentrated in the east. By the thirty-fifth day of mobilization the Germans had occupied most of western Russia. They held Kiev in the south, Vilna in the north. But the Russian army was still undefeated, and the French were on the point of breaking through in the west. Ten days later they flanked the Metz fortress complex. The "Germans" were forced to retreat from an operational triumph that had become a strategic disaster.

The outcomes of such exercises have too frequently been adjusted to suit the demands of operational doctrine, state policy, or personal vanity to inspire absolute faith in any set of results. The Germans undertook this particular war game at the request of their Austrian allies, and might at least be suspected of trying to prove a preconception. The "French" commander, Hermann von Kühl, was one of the general staff's most brilliant young officers—a reputation he was to sustain and enhance in the coming war. But the "German" attack on Russia was entrusted to Karl von Bülow, a general considered good enough to command one of the armies on the Schlieffen Plan's vital right wing. His chief of staff would become quartermaster-general in 1914. These men too were part of the Imperial army's first team, and not likely to endanger their images and careers by doing less than their best.[88]

Adolf Tappen, one of Moltke's closest collaborators on the general staff, summarized the prevailing viewpoint fifteen years later. The Russians, he declared, always had the option of withdrawing from a decisive encounter until the situation in the west was decided to their advantage.[89] The best rider, the elder Moltke once observed, does not set his horse at an impossible obstacle. Pessimism about the prospects of a German strategic offensive into Russia extended to the attack discussed by Moltke and Conrad in 1909. Planners in Berlin and commanders in East Prussia increasingly agreed that given the projected strength of the Russian armies facing Germany, throwing a dozen divisions against the Narew meant feeding them into a meatgrinder for no purpose. The final staff study for the eastern theater, held in the winter of 1913, suggested that the most promising situation involved first stopping the Russian advance from the Niemen, then turning against those advancing from the Narew. It said nothing about an initial German attack in either direction. In its own collective mind the general staff increasingly doubted whether anything could save East Prussia from temporary occupation, even if *Ostheer* remained on the defensive and executed a fighting withdrawal towards the Vistula.[90]

The well-documented failure of the Germans to mount any kind of offensive in the east in 1914, combined with the disastrous Austrian defeat at Lemberg, raised prompt cries of betrayal from Conrad. Norman Stone and Oskar Regele are among the distinguished scholars taking pains to substantiate the Austrian chief of staff's self-image as something of a cat's-paw, who expected great results from a German attack and believed in it to the last minute. To accept this is to argue that Conrad could not evaluate his own correspondence, which consistently repeated the point that Germany's commitment to the east was limited to thirteen or fourteen divisions.[91] As early as March, 1909, moreover, Moltke had warned that "enemy action" might influence German operations. To call this blunt statement a "clever" escape clause or a mental reservation is surely to insult the intelligence of Moltke and Conrad alike.

Moltke had initially hoped that if he left enough troops in the east to carry out the proposed Narew offensive, the Austrians would in turn attack more vigorously and lessen the pressure on East Prussia. But the possibility of reassigning first-line units grew less each year, particularly since Italy's increasingly wavering commitment to the Triple Alliance made it likely that her previous promises of support on the western front would be fulfilled slowly, if at all. By late in 1912 the Italians talked openly of limiting their forces in that theater. The German naval attaché reported in November, 1913, that public feeling against Austria was so strong it could erupt in "the most unpleasant fashion" at any time.[92] It was not a good portent for future cooperation.

Revised German mobilization plans had made available an increasing number of *Ersatz* formations, composed primarily of men of military age who had received no peacetime training. Moltke believed that these second-line troops could be usefully employed guarding river crossings and providing garrisons in Posen and East Prussia.[93] In December, 1913, Germany proposed to cover the left flank of the promised Austrian attack by deploying an improvised force of thirty-two *Ersatz* and *Landwehr* battalions in Silesia. These additions to the order of battle were hardly calculated to frighten enemies or impress allies. Conrad was well aware of the difference between the Prussian Guard and an equivalent number of greenhorns and grandfathers. In May, 1914, he made a trip to Carlsbad, where Moltke was taking the waters. He began their conference by repeating his determination to attack in Galicia. He went on to emphasize the urgent need for more German troops in the east. It was "highly probable" that the main Russian attack would be directed against East Prussia. In this case, Conrad said, it would be to Germany's own advantage to be strong on the eastern front. What would happen if Austria were defeated? What if Germany failed to win an overwhelming victory in the west, and then found herself faced with a Russian invasion that *Ostheer* was unable to parry? Moltke answered only that the Vistula fortress would have to hold out long enough to enable reinforcements to arrive from France.

Just before Conrad left for Vienna, he asked Moltke how long it would be, in case of a two-front war, before German reinforcements could arrive in the east. Moltke's reply is significant: "We hope to be ready to turn our main strength against Russia six weeks after the beginning of operations."[94] This was a month later than the deadline he had mentioned in 1909! Yet even this additional thirty-day delay had no effect on Conrad's strategic visions. If the Austrian army's spine was broken in the first month of the war, it was not because German plans were even partly calculated to deceive or mislead her ally. The Austrians were victimized by the wishful thinking and overconfidence of their chief of staff, who continued down to the outbreak of hostilities to hear only what he wished to hear.

3
War Finds a Way

The generals were not Germany's only pessimists. Bethmann Hollweg's familiar suggestion that it was hardly worthwhile to plant new trees on his estate outside of Berlin since the Russians would be there in a few years anyway was in part a product of his trip to Russia in 1912. He returned deeply disturbed at his first-hand impressions of that empire's human and material resources. He was conscious, in a way many of his critics were not, of Russia's potential—a potential whose development lay essentially outside Germany's control, and which Russia's current allies seemed unwilling or unable to harness. Rational adjustments of political and economic conflicts between the two empires might be expected to reduce tensions. But could such fine tuning indefinitely avert conflict without significant changes in the international system?[1]

I

The chancellor's doubts reflected and reinforced the views of his confidential advisor, Kurt Riezler. Riezler is an outstanding early example of those terrible simplifiers who continue to stalk the twentieth century's corridors of power: system makers without any ultimate responsibility for implementation, and counsellors whose schemas can be dangerously refreshing and fatally attractive to superiors grappling with the concrete complexities of decision making. Riezler argued for an essential distinction between developing and stagnating powers. The former had time on their side. The latter were constrained to follow policies of bluff and calculated risk, trying to check and alter an ultimately unfavorable trend by short-term successes. Riezler was convinced that Russian power was

69

increasing steadily and objectively, almost in spite of the failures and blunders of her diplomacy. Austria, on the other hand, was at a level of stagnation that might well prove terminal. He therefore urged Bethmann to support at the first favorable opportunity a decisive Austrian initiative, specifically in the Balkans, one of the few remaining areas still allowing scope for such a move. The growing destructiveness of modern war, Riezler argued, made policies of brinkmanship potentially more effective than ever before. If Germany stood up and asserted herself, her adversaries would back down rather than risk actually going to war. Thus the cause of peace would ultimately be served by aggressiveness.

These theoretical formulations bear enough surface similarities to the events of 1914 to have given Riezler a certain status as the chancellor's evil genius. The days of think-tank intellectuals were, however, still far in the future. Bethmann was far too cautious to take his cues directly from the political metaphysics of an amanuensis. Instead he took pains in his public statements to deny the inevitability of a clash between the Slavic and Teutonic worlds. He hoped rather that reason would in time temper the strong Panslavic attitudes current in Russian political and diplomatic circles. But reason was most effective when backed by force; words unsupported by guns were an exercise in futility.[2]

Germany's perception of the Russian threat was a major motivator of the Army Bill of 1913, the largest in the history of the Second Reich. Like most German military legislation it was a compromise. The general staff had urged the creation of three new army corps—and not entirely for operational reasons. The army's strength had not been increased significantly since 1893. Rapid population growth in the intervening decades meant that military service was increasingly becoming a lottery, with as many as half the eligible men in a given year performing no active service at all.

To the war ministry the probable negative social results of continuing this process were balanced by other professional and political considerations. Creating new formations would further dilute officer and NCO corps already straining to fill their ranks with suitable men. More than simple social prejudice was involved in the objection. Much of Germany's militarism was skin deep and no more. A regular officer's career was by far less attractive to men with the necessary education than a reserve officer's commission; which provided social cachet at limited cost. The Russian army's recent expansion had required commissioning large numbers of marginally qualified candidates, with observed negative effects on efficiency. War Minister Josias von Heeringen and his subordinates argued the wisdom of concentrating instead on improving the quality of the existing system: increasing peacetime establishments, purchasing more machine guns and heavy artillery, recognizing the changes wrought by the internal-combustion engine by adding trucks and aircraft to the army's inventory.[3]

The debate was part of the beginning of that tension between numbers and technology, mass and quality, characteristic of twentieth-century military establishments throughout the world. But the bill ulti-mately presented to the Reichstag owed much to practical political consid-erations as well. From the beginning Bethmann feared the financial consequences of the general staff's demands. Nationalist public opinion overwhelmingly favored the increases—in principle. But Germany's con-servatives were openly hostile to a military budget whose funding would significantly change the nature and increase the amount of taxes they paid. On the other hand the Social Democrats, or at least some of their key leaders, seemed willing to modify their historic position of "not a man and not a penny for this system" if given reasonable justification.

In part this involved moving away from an increasingly sterile oppositionism. But it also reflected a growing concern among personalities as different as Edouard Bernstein and Kurt Eisner that Russia was in fact planning an attack on Germany. Germany's governments took the oppor-tunity to begin replacing walls with bridges. Bavarian authorities went so far as to share with SPD leaders intelligence information suggesting an imminent outbreak of hostilities. By March, 1913, Bernstein was writing to the editor of *The Nation*, Britain's leading radical weekly, that the new arms bill was completely justified in the context of Russian intentions. The legislation that ultimately passed the Reichstag left the army at its current size of twenty-five corps. But it provided for an increase of 120,000 men in the peacetime establishment, giving Germany an active army of 800,000. It also funded significant improvements in administration and armament, notably the addition of a machine-gun company to every infantry regiment.[3]

The Russian build-up that contributed so much to German defense politics reflected the tensions created by an assertive Balkan policy not underwritten by the force necessary to implement it. It reflected the alteration in election requirements for the Duma, which produced in the 1912 version of that body a nationalist, patriotic majority, frequently willing to make concessions on questions involving foreign and defense policy in order to improve leverage for domestically oriented programs.[4] It also reflected an increased level of French support, combined with lingering uncertainty about France's ultimate intentions. In August, 1913, it was Joffre's turn to be a guest at the Russian maneuvers. He pressed vigorously for immediate Russian participation in a combined offensive against Germany, promising that a million and a half Frenchmen would smite the Teuton foe no later than the eleventh day of mobilization. Nevertheless, as professionals the Russians were well aware that only in storybooks is the enemy always defeated. As soldiers they were uneasy about the probable behavior of civilian politicians, particularly French republicans.

Their anxiety seemed justified by the final version of the Franco-Russian military alliance, introduced in September, 1913. It prescribed that in case of "any act of war by the German army," both contracting parties were "free" to mobilize without consultation. Austrian or Italian mobilization, partial or general, made "concert . . . indispensable." In short, neither government was willing to give its generals anything like a free hand. This in turn indicated to Russian planners that they must prepare for a worst-case contingency, and field an army strong enough at least to check, if not to defeat, Germany and Austria combined.[5]

Enhanced military strength also seemed a necessary prop for a suddenly unravelling Balkan policy. States scrambling for territorial spoils in the aftermath of Turkey's collapse appealed to St. Petersburg for redress. Sazonov consistently promised to support everyone's claims—an approach made easier by the numerous marital connections between Russian and Balkan royalty. At no time did the foreign ministry try to assert systematically either Russia's interests or Russia's position. By the summer of 1913 Russia's credibility in the Balkan capitals was at an all-time low.[6] She was unable to prevent the League's collapse into the Second Balkan War. Six months later the German ambassador to Bulgaria informed Bethmann that Russia's attempts to establish a new Balkan League and to restore her influence in Bulgaria were still being frustrated by regional rivalries.[7]

Serbia emerged from the second conflict with her territory almost doubled and her population increased by half. Her prestige among the Dual Monarchy's Slavs was at a new height. And her propagandists continued to insist that the Bosnian annexation was anything but a settled issue.[8] Client-state management, even when that client is surrounded by rivals and enemies, is an exacting craft at best, one at which Imperial Russia had never manifested significant skill. Greece, Rumania, Bulgaria—all had turned more or less against St. Petersburg, largely as a consequence of Sazonov's failed balancing acts. From Russia's perspective in the last months of 1913, the question was whether she could afford to risk alienating Serbia as well by attempting to restrain Serbia's behavior towards Austria. Then Sazonov received another jolt from an unexpected direction. In November, 1913, Liman von Sanders, head of Germany's military mission in Turkey, was designated commander of the army corps stationed in Constantinople.

Russia's interests in that city and the straits it stood on were an explosive mixture of history and sentiment, strategy and economics. Her self-proclaimed status as the Third Rome, legitimate heir of Byzantium, combined with her image as protector of Slavic interests to render ideologically difficult accepting the legitimacy of a Constantinople either in Islamic hands or dominated by a non-Orthodox Christian power. From an economic perspective, between 1909 and 1913 Russian grain exports averaged eleven million metric tons annually—30 percent of the world's grain trade. By 1913 over a third of Russia's total exports, including three-fourths of these grain shipments, were going through the straits. And it was grain on which Russia's international credit largely depended. In direct contrast to the beliefs of optimistic economic determinists like Norman Angell, Russia's involvement in international economics only enhanced her desire to secure her trade routes.

Militarily, moreover, the Russo-Japanese War had been only the most recent demonstration of the fact that as long as control of the Bosporus remained outside Russia's hands, a large part of her fleet was useless except for coastal defense; while in the hands of an unfriendly state with a strong navy the straits were a gateway to Russia's back door. Complicating the picture was the growing conviction of Russian strategists that possession of Constantinople and the Dardanelles depended on dominating their hinterlands in Europe and Asia. A simple land grab would no longer suffice. Nor was subversion of the Ottoman Empire a desirable policy for a Russia not only plagued with its own revolutionaries, but uncertain of its ability to take quick advantage of a Turkish collapse. German-trained and German-led troops might well prove a significant barrier to any Russian attempts to seize the straits, then confront Europe with a *fait accompli*.[9]

In such a context it was hardly surprising that Kokovtsov expressed "deep sorrow" at the regrettable worsening of Russo-German relations generated by the Liman von Sanders appointment, or that Sazonov grew "extremely nervous" and was not to be reassured. The Russian foreign minister accused Germany of seeking simultaneously to undo the results of the Balkan wars of national liberation and to strangle south Russia's economy by gaining control of the straits herself. He recommended that the entente change Germany's mind by occupying selected Turkish ports as hostages![10]

The proposal was met with raised eyebrows by French and British officials on the spot in Constantinople. They argued the effect of Liman's appointment would be far less—even suspiciously less—than Sazonov seemed to expect. By this time, however, Russia's Turkish policy is best understood in terms of a running man who, feeling himself stumble, seeks to restore his balance by accelerating his pace. Sazonov insisted that concessions to either of the central powers would destroy Russia's credibility with foes and friends alike. When he proclaimed the Liman appointment a test of Russia's alliances, the French ambassador indicated that his government's support would be unequivocal and unstinting. Britain was less encouraging, but not discouraging.[11]

On January 13, 1914, an imperial council discussed the pros and cons of direct military action against Turkey. When asked if Russia could fight a war with Germany, the war minister and the chief of staff cheerfully agreed that Russia was perfectly prepared for such a conflict—with Austria thrown in. Kokovtsov's insistence that such a war would be the worst thing that could happen to Russia swayed just enough of the council just enough to the side of moderation that they accepted, at least provisionally, Bethmann's assurances that the entire affair was a misunderstanding.[12]

Did the chancellor's words mask darker intentions? Liman's appointment has been described as a major initiative in Germany's return to an aggressive continental strategy as a prelude to *Weltpolitik*. In this interpretation, Germany's leaders by 1914 were thinking in terms not of concert diplomacy, but of a Central European power bloc, with the

Ottoman Empire as its major sphere of direct influence. This meant the straits, the bridge to Asia Minor, must remain secure at all costs.[13]

Realities were a good deal more modest. German military missions had been "reforming" the Ottoman army at intervals for over twenty years with at best modest success. Given the results of Turkey's recent conflicts with Italy and the Balkan states, any improvements in her armed forces would amount to little more than restoring a regional balance. Turkish generals seemed for once willing to take advice—a welcome prospect after the frustrations of German soldiers and diplomats at the Porte in recent years. But Liman von Sanders, suspicious, petty both in public and private matters, was hardly the man single-handedly to bring Turkey into Germany's camp. He not only saw his task as narrowly professional; he was directly warned by the Kaiser to avoid involvement in local politics.

This admonition reflected the basic inconsistency of German policies towards Turkey. Specific issues of profit and loss, either economic or diplomatic, were less important than glowing visions of the future. Opinion was sharply divided on the importance and the possibility of establishing close links with a state needing at least a decade to recover from the effects of defeat and revolution. What success Germany did have was largely negative, a product of Britain's growing tendency to take Turkish good will for granted. As late as May, 1914, the grand vizier was insisting to the German ambassador that it was in Turkey's best interests to have no alliances with any of the powers. The only threat she faced was when one of the alliance networks was ready to start a world war.[14]

William's order to Liman to resign command of I Corps ended the crisis. It settled nothing more. From Berlin's point of view, Russia had significantly overreacted to a limited initiative, if indeed it could be called an initiative at all. Concert diplomacy was never meant to exclude self-interest—only to limit the parameters of its pursuit. Germany never denied direct and growing economic, political, and military interests in the Ottoman Empire. She was correspondingly unwilling to abandon that field to a Russia whose claims seemed increasingly designed to exclude everyone else.

In January, 1914, the Turkish military attaché in St. Petersburg expressed alarm at Russian troop movements in the Caucasus. His German colleague initially belittled the situation, saying that if Russia had designs on Turkey she would have implemented them during the Balkan Wars. But in April the Tiflis consulate confirmed extensive Russian military activity, including reports that a new army corps was to be raised on the Turkish border. In June the Russian government proposed that the Ottoman Empire's Armenian subjects be given virtual autonomy under what amounted to Russian protection. Farther to the east, Russia's continued pressure on Persia and in Central Asia was generating increasing concern about her ultimate intentions in a Britain for years at pains to appease her imperialist rival. In such a context Russia's vehement objections to the limited matter of a command appointment invited interpretation as part of a general campaign to renew the Great Game in Asia and complete the Balkan Wars by dismembering the Turkish Empire.[15]

Had Russia in fact decided to do herself what her purported clients had been unable to do after their recent falling-out? The evidence was ambiguous. Near East rivalries had been endemic among the powers for two centuries. Russian policy makers had accepted German economic interests in the Ottoman Empire. They understood the risks of war should Germany not be considered in any future reorganization of that troubled area. As late as 1912 the military attaché in Berlin warned that a Germany uncompensated for a Turkish collapse might well take "sword in hand."[16] Since the Bosnian Crisis, moreover, Russian diplomats had been at periodic pains to insist to their German colleagues that Austria was the real obstacle to peace in the Balkans and in Europe. Let Germany encourage her ally to be a bit more reasonable, to modify her aggressive responses to the development of south Slav autonomy under Russian auspices, and there was no reason why peace should be endangered. According to Sazonov the Russian government had no complaints about German behavior in the recent Balkan crises. Germany needed only to ignore the agitation of press and parliament, which meant nothing in an autocracy. As for Turkey, she was finished in any case. Why should Germany damage her relations with Russia by denying facts?[17]

Sazonov was not making these overtures in a vacuum. Since 1912 Austria had been under steadily increasing economic and diplomatic pressure in the Near East from her ostensible ally. Throughout the Balkans and Asia Minor the business interests of the two empires clashed noisily. For all the kaiser's rhetoric of fidelity and brotherhood, Bethmann-Hollweg's consistent advocacy of restraint and compromise seemed in Vienna only to bind Austria's hands in dealing with adversaries bent on her destruction. In Berlin, more and more policy makers were becoming more and more open in describing their Austrian connection as an alliance with a corpse. Bethmann-Hollweg's speculations on the Dual Monarchy's declining viability were paralleled by Foreign Secretary Gottlieb von Jagow's description of the Habsburg dynasty as a House of Atreus, stumbling from catastrophe to catastrophe.[18]

Austria's emerging role as the new Sick Man of Europe involved perceptions as well as realities. In an age still influenced by positivism, among men intellectually formed when scientific objectivity was gaining the status of a shibboleth, it was easy to accept diplomatic situations as given, unsusceptible to alteration by human efforts. In Britain, publicists like R. W. Seton-Watson and Henry Wickham Steed predicted glorious futures for the young and vigorous Slavic peoples of southeastern Europe, once the Habsburg Empire should disappear. French graduates of the *École Libre des Sciences Politiques*, considering Austria's demise imminent, were constructing alternate systems based on the soon-to-be-autonomous Czechs and Yugoslavs.

Arguments constantly repeated tend to acquire both a life of their own and a certain ascriptive credibility. Russia, France, and Britain individually were increasingly unwilling to run any significant risks to sustain Austria's existence as a participant in the great-power political system. None of the three states trusted the other two deeply enough to risk alienating them by advocating policies of restraint and support towards Austria. France, over the protests of her ambassador to Vienna, bowed to Russian pressure in refusing the Austro-Hungarian government access to the Paris Bourse in 1909–10. France was also increasingly ready to develop Greece as a bridgehead for the penetration of the Balkan Peninsula and the Ottoman Empire. British policies in principle recognized Austria's role as a counterweight to Russian ambitions in the Near East. In practice the foreign office followed a modification of the Fifth Commandment: Thou shalt not kill/ But need not strive/ Excessively to keep alive. Sir Edward Grey regarded British support for Austria as risking misinterpretation in Germany, as an attempt to detach her only ally. Proposed concessions to Austria were also carefully scrutinized for their possible impact in Paris and St. Petersburg—sometimes with a dose of cant gratuitously added. When in 1910 the foreign office thwarted the Hungarian government's negotiations for a loan in London, it justified its decision by explaining that the money might be spent on armaments.[19]

None of the entente governments gave serious consideration on a policy-making level to what might happen should Austria not choose to disappear quietly. Perhaps this was another manifestation of the Age of Science. If Austria's fate were objectively certain, she would disappear as the mastodon and the saber-tooth tiger had disappeared: without significantly disturbing the march of history.

But if other great powers might have little sympathy with Austria's increasingly strident claims that her vital interests were being neglected, Germany could not ignore them. Apart from the possible consequences of the Dual Monarchy's total collapse, Vienna's growing concentration on the Balkans was a serious danger sign. Should Austria in effect relinquish her great-power role, resigning herself to regional status and pursuing regional interests, Germany would be thrown on her own resources, no longer one of three, as in Bismarck's ideal, no longer even one of two, but one alone, too weak to stand for long, much less conduct a European concert.

Bethmann's increasing doubts of Austria's viability only encouraged his support for a policy of caution and circumspection in the Balkans, as opposed to forceful unilateral action the fragile empire might be unable to sustain. Germany's insistence that the will of the powers in that region was best exercised collectively, through the Concert of Europe, was correspondingly designed to serve two interlocking ends. The Concert would solidify Anglo-German détente, but also underwrite Austria's status and position. The Habsburg monarchy and the peace of Europe would be preserved; Germany's prospects for becoming Europe's new coachman would be correspondingly enhanced.

It can legitimately be argued that no system can long function if some of its great powers are in fact regional powers seeking to make the system resist change because their own weaknesses preclude flexibillity. But among the most serious gaps in entente diplomacy prior to 1914 was its failure to prepare consequently for Germany's reaction to the disappearance of her only reliable major ally—perhaps even by engaging her in the process. To states already concerned with the steady accretion of German power, to statesmen unwilling to see themselves as cold-blooded heirs of Machiavelli, such an approach seemed a potentially explosive reversion to an earlier and more savage era of international relations. In 1772, a Russian tsarina had recognized the necessity of involving a Prussian king in the destruction of a weak neighbor. The lessons of the Polish partition were, however, lost on Nicholas II and his advisors.

At the turn of the century, the French military attaché submitted several memoranda on the Russian army's planning for the contingency of a Habsburg collapse in the aftermath of Franz Josef's death. Apparently the general staff planners expected the empire's German provinces to seek admission to the Second Reich spontaneously—a development Russia would not oppose if suitably compensated with Galicia, a blank check in the Ottoman Empire, and possibly an independent Bohemia as well.[20] But these and similar projections remained the stuff of operational planning rather than state policy. In April, 1913, Tsar Nicholas, in an interview with the British ambassador, described Austria as "a source of weakness for Germany and a danger to peace" whose breakup was only a question of time. He went on to sketch a future situation in which Bohemia and Hungary would become independent kingdoms and the south Slavs absorbed by Serbia and Rumania, with Germany acquiring the "German provinces." Sir George Buchanan was one of the leading lights of the foreign office, with wide experience in both German and Slavic Europe. He had held his current post since 1910. He was highly regarded in London for his tact and skill. Yet he confessed himself "unable to follow the Emperor's train of thought, or to understand how he arrived at this conclusion." Buchanan was, however, perceptive enough to comment that such changes were not likely to be effected without a general war.[21]

In January, 1914, Sazonov echoed Buchanan, saying that the Austrian situation would end in either a federal solution along national lines, or a war for which Russia was in no way prepared. But on March 18, the nationalist and conservative St. Petersburg *Novoye Vremya* published the alleged comments of "a highly authoritative state official," probably Sukhomlinov. The article repeated Nicholas's line of argument almost verbatim, with the added provisions that Germany would sacrifice Alsace and Russia would annex Galicia. Sazonov was quick to deny that the war minister had anything at all to do with the story. The denial, however, becomes suspect in the context of Sukhomlinov's statement to the French ambassador in May that Russia intended to have Galicia after Franz Josef's death, and the tsar hoped Germany would accept this peacefully.[22]

These exchanges hardly count as *prima facie* evidence that Russia was ready to risk a general war to redraw Europe's map to her advantage. Russia was not the only state where politicians said one thing in public while generals said something else in private. Nor does every speculation on possible future contingencies necessarily represent a sinister hidden agenda. The scenario outlined by the tsar and his war minister was more than familiar; it could have been developed by anyone with a schoolboy's knowledge of central European ethnography. Dreams of natural future accretions to Russian power might well have been enhanced by the all-too-concrete failures of current Russian diplomacy. Nevertheless the evolution of the concept is not without interest: from Nicholas's omission of any direct gains for Russia, through the *Novoye Vremya*'s discussion of a general settlement with something for all the continental survivors including France, to Sukhomlinov's blunt statement of ultimate goals which Germany could like or lump as it pleased. The incidents illustrate the nature of the ideas unofficially discussed in St. Petersburg. They also demonstrate all too clearly Paul Schroeder's argument that while by 1914 every great power expected the European system to work for its benefit, none were willing to work for the system.[23]

II

A loosely-structured group of top officials and ex-officials did suggest that Russia was wrong to sacrifice Berlin for London. These men respected the German Empire as a more reasonable model for their own than the Western parliamentary systems. In particular, Sergei Witte and former interior minister Pavel Durnovo insisted that Germany and Russia had no differences that could not be negotiated. A Russo-German war, Durnovo argued, would bring revolution if it were lost, and a victory would be almost as disastrous. Russia would become financially and economically dependent on her allies, while having to cope with the anarchy sure to break out in the defeated states and likely to spread across their borders.[24]

Hindsight indicates the wisdom of the Witte-Durnovo forecasts. In the event Russia got the predicted negative effects of both winning and losing its German war—a fact arguably not lost on Stalin during the 1930s. At the time, however, this was a minority position. By 1913 Germany had captured almost 40 percent of Russia's foreign trade. Russian critics of existing commercial relations presented their country as a virtual colony of her economically dominant neighbor, a source of cheap raw materials and a dumping ground for even cheaper finished products. Russia, in the words of one group of merchants, must emancipate herself from this humiliating dependence, preferably by cultivating improved relations with countries willing to establish more equitable trade relationships. Industrialists too regarded Germany as the principal foreign obstacle to Russia's economic development, and decried their country's dependance on German techniques and German machines. While the manufacturers were not enthusiastic at the prospect of a war, they more than any other group saw clear benefits arising from a German defeat. As it was more and more German firms were losing Russian contracts to French and British suppliers submitting higher bids, despite years of cooperative relationships with local authorities. The navy minister went so far as to urge the German director of the Putilov armament works to consider becoming a Russian citizen. Something of the relationship between business and patriotism at this period is suggested by the latter's prompt willingness to make the change and his justification of it as making him better able to serve German industrial interests.[25]

By the spring of 1914 the German consul in Warsaw was reporting Polish students throwing rocks and bottles at his windows—a concrete affirmation of Slavic identity at sharp variance with the normal tensions between the nationalistic academicians and the heavy-handed Russian authorities.[26] The Duma increased duties on all imported grain: a direct blow at German agricultural interests, carefully described as such by its supporters concerned lest the point be missed. Military budgets passed uncriticized and unprotested save from the far Left. In the public sphere, veteran journalists and diplomats were taken aback by the depth and breadth of newspaper hostility to Germany and Austria alike. Not only nationalist and Panslav sheets, not only the colportage of the Right, but more respectable middle-of-the-road papers took up the patriotic chorus. Everywhere voices described the inevitable clash between Slav and Teuton, a clash in which divine favor would rest with the younger, more vigorous race.

At the highest levels of government Sazonov was increasingly convinced that Germany's ultimate goal was to bar Russia's way to the world's oceans not only in the south by establishing a *de facto* protectorate over Turkey, but in the north as well by extending her influence in Scandinavia. His views acquired new importance at the end of January when Kokovtsov was dismissed as premier. He had been less a friend of Germany and an advocate of peace than a pessimistic highlighter of military and economic shortcomings. Nicholas willingly sacrificed him to critics seeing no reason to be reminded of such things in their search for a great Russia.[27]

This assertiveness, paradoxically, was accompanied by a growing chorus from everywhere on Russia's political, social, and cultural/intellectual spectrums affirming that Russia society was in the throes of a profound crisis. The objective validity of this belief was less important for German statesmen than its existence. Russia's capacity to pursue anything like a coherent foreign policy had long seemed open to question. And if Russia was in fact only half as unstable an amalgam of conflicting forces as her own spokesmen insisted, she was a profoundly dangerous neighbor.

Unpredictability is the greatest single barrier to effective diplomacy. United with military power it will make even the calmest of neighboring governments uneasy. It can also affect journalists. The *Kölnische Zeitung*'s well-known "war in sight" article of March 2, 1914, was a think-piece rather than a reaction to specific events. Its assertion that Russia if left undisturbed would be ready for war by 1917 parallelled opinions in German military circles closely enough to support the assumption that the author had drawn some background information from at least the German embassy in St. Petersburg if not the general staff itself. The Russian press, the *Times*, and French and Scandinavian sources alike insisted that the article was officially inspired. The author was in fact a Pan-German sympathizer with extensive contacts among German officers. He had also been briefed by the German military attaché to Russia. Most of the information in his article was, however, available to a normally competent investigative reporter with a normal spectrum of Russian contacts. Nor did he invent his descriptions of extensive Russian military preparations combined with efflorescent public and official hostility to Germany. Finally, the alleged 1917 deadline for war was a product neither of German reasoning nor German imagination. In 1912 Russian officers had spoken of needing five years to complete their preparations for dealing with their enemies to the west and south. That period had ever since remained a familiar benchmark in informal conversations.[28]

Then Sukhomlinov entered the scene. On March 12 the Russian war minister published an article in a major St. Petersburg newspaper, denying the *Kölnische Zeitung*'s allegations and declaring that Russia wanted only peace, but was perfectly prepared for war, and would wage war offensively if it came.

In his memoirs Sukhomlinov disingenuously claimed that his only concern had been to pacify his fellow countrymen.[29] German reactions were less sanguine. Was there not an essential difference between an article written by a civilian journalist and one from the pen of a senior government official? Sazonov's transparent effort to deny the essay's authorship only encouraged a chain reaction. Newspaper after German newspaper picked up the subject, commenting as much on each other's reports and interpretations as on the original piece. The foreign office, anything but pleased at the prospect of a continued newspaper war, did its best to encourage countervailing materials. Pourtalès denounced the original article as pessimistic and trivial. Projecting Russia's behavior three or four years in the future was risky, he declared, if one did not have the gift of prophecy apparently possessed by the *Kölnische Zeitung*'s correspondent. As for Sukhomlinov's effusions, the ambassador recommended letting Russia off the hook with a sharp warning of the risks of this kind of careless talk.[30]

Arguments that the anti-Russian campaign was accepted, or even orchestrated, by either the Imperial German government or a set of variously defined "strategic elites" as a means of creating a war spirit overlook the proven value of international crises in improving circulation figures. When Bethmann attempted to modify the rhetoric of Germany's journalists, he encountered a press confident of its legal rights, and increasingly reluctant to submit to the manipulations of bureaucrats who made no secret of their intentions. These attempts to intervene arguably kept the issue alive longer than it might have survived on its own merits. No newspaper, Left or Right, was willing to look as though it was backing down in the face of government pressure.[31]

Anti-Russian agitation continued to grow, particularly among the nationalist, patriotic organizations. A new weekly, *Das grössere Deutschland*, began publication with the avowed purpose of preparing Germany for imminent war with a Russia it described as Europe's greatest threat to peace. Pamphlets compared the military and economic strengths of Russia and Germany, arguing that the time to strike was immediately.[32] The foreign office found itself involved in verifying the most ridiculous rumors. Bethmann, for example, was constrained to request the text of a Russian order allegedly giving a regiment red boot-tops in memory of wading in Prussian blood at the Battle of Kunersdorf. The reply was that the regiment in question had indeed waded knee-deep in blood at Kunersdorf—its own blood. The new ornaments were a modern version of the red stockings bestowed on the regiment by Tsarina Elizabeth in recognition of its heroism under Prussian fire.[33]

But journalists were not the only pessimists in Germany as spring gave way to summer. Apart from the domestic tensions endemic to German politics, the British connection on which Bethmann-Hollweg had placed such hopes increasingly seemed a vision, a manifestation of hope rather than calculation. French hostility had been a diplomatic constant for fifty years. Austria was a broken reed. In this context the French ambassador's report to Pourtalès that Sazonov and Sukhomlinov assured him Russia's increasingly-strong military establishment was no more than a necessary response to her long frontiers, and reflected no aggressive designs, bore the flavor of mockery. Even Pourtalès, generally a voice of phlegmatic common sense regarding Russian intentions, was increasingly concerned at the absence of coherent policies and firm guiding hands in the Russian ministries. If Russia had no leaders who could plan a war successfully, the ambasador declared, neither did she have any who inspired confidence that they could maintain the peace.[34]

In April a Berlin insurance company with an eye on the main chance issued a circular aimed at the officer corps. Since war with Russia was inevitable within a few years, officers should consider it a moral duty to prepare for a hero's death by insuring their lives. The carrot was a guarantee of no increased premiums during a war. The stick was that the policy could not be purchased once mobilization was declared! In the same month the German embassy in Rome reported a conversation with the Bulgarian envoy, a man with extensive Russian contacts. He quoted the current director of the Oriental department of Russia's foreign ministry to the effect that as soon as Russia's military reforms were completed, its foreign policy would have a different emphasis than was now the case. The lead time mentioned was three years—bringing the date to 1917.[35]

From a military perspective nothing spoke against that deadline. In February, 1914, Moltke submitted a report on Russia's readiness for war. The army's cadres, its noncommissioned officer corps, and its reserve system were alike significantly improved. The mobilization plans were more efficient, the preparations for concentration on the frontiers more systematic. In Moltke's eyes these were not marginal changes. The Russian military system was reaching unheard-of heights of effectiveness.

The next month the general staff submitted its report on the training of Russian troops. Based primarily on an evaluation of the 1913 maneuvers, it emphasized the continued existence of traditional problems: overcontrolling, with corresponding lack of initiative at subordinate levels; slowness in issuing and executing orders; waiting for developments instead of forcing the issue. But the Russian army was correspondingly aware of its own weaknesses, working hard and systematically to develop flexibility and enhance aggressiveness. One military district had gone so far as to order all solutions to tactical problems to incorporate the offensive spirit. Not only was acceptance of defeat and retreat forbidden; umpires were no longer allowed to order withdrawals during exercises.[36]

Twentieth-century developments in firepower make these alleged improvements read like a recipe for disaster. To Moltke, to the general staff, and to the German army as a whole, however, they were indicators that Russia was adding state-of-the-art skills to the historic strengths of her military system. And given Russia's distances, Russia's resources, and Russia's masses, even small improvements in efficiency could have exponential results.

On May 12 Moltke bluntly told Conrad that the central powers could not in future expect to compete with Russia's masses. A few days later he informed Jagow that once Russia completed her military preparations, in two or three years, the superiority of Germany's enemies would be such that Moltke did not know how the empire would cope. This meant there was no longer any alternative to a preventive war. Jagow energetically disagreed, stressing Germany's continuing economic growth as a compensating factor and arguing that Germany had no war aims that would justify the sacrifice. Yet on July 18 he informed the German ambassador in London that "according to all expert opinion," Russia would in a few years be in a position to crush Germany with her huge army, her modern Baltic fleet, and her new strategic railroads. On June 21 the kaiser had used almost the same phrasing in a conversation with banker Max Warburg, asking whether it might not be better to go to war than await the completion of Russia's new railways in 1916.[37]

Russia's sudden accretion of strength attracted attention everywhere. British General Sir Henry Wilson, no Teutonophile by any stretch of the imagination, nevertheless understood German anxieties for her future in the face of a Russian military build-up that was altering the entire balance of power in Europe. British diplomats thought Russia in a position to replace Germany as the continent's leading military power. From St. Petersburg, Buchanan asserted that "the days of German hegemony in Europe will be numbered" unless she drastically increased military spending. Sir Edward Grey believed that however great Germany's initial victories might be in a war with Russia, Russia's immense resources would ultimately exhaust Germany even without British aid.[38]

British perceptions were shared across the Atlantic. In May 1914, an anxious Woodrow Wilson dispatched his friend and confidant Colonel Edward House on a fact-finding mission to Europe. House was enough of an apostle of the strenuous life to boast of carrying a six-gun whenever he was with the president, and to believe himself a quicker and surer shot than any secret service man. He was not a particular admirer of the Second Reich. Writing from Berlin he described the atmosphere as "surcharged with war and warlike preparations . . . militarism run stark mad." But Germany's fears, according to House, were not entirely imaginary. England held her entente partners "like a cocked gun: whenever [she] consents, France and Russia will close in on Germany and Austria."[39]

House's efforts to defuse the tension, amateurish though they may have been, reflected his belief that Russia was ultimately the greatest menace to European order. Germany was the barrier between Europe and the Slavic hordes, and England did not want Germany crushed because this would leave her alone in Russia's path. By August 30, Wilson himself was musing to the colonel that eventually the world might be reduced to only two great powers: the United States and Russia.[40]

Russia's policy was not one of deliberate adventurism. Nor was it a consequent, reasoned reaction to a German threat. It reflected instead a growing sense of insecurity and confusion. From the first months of 1914 Sazonov had worked desperately to strengthen Russia's entente relationships. He argued for a clear, public Anglo-Russian alliance, a political impossibility for liberal England. He remained unreassured by the increasing weight of opinion in the British foreign office that Russia's rapidly expanding strength made her friendship worth retaining at any price—an attitude clearly manifested during the Anglo-Russian naval negotiations that took place in the summer of 1914.[41] Sazonov's alarm so disturbed French ambassador Maurice Paléologue that he informed his home government that France must retain the three years of active military service domestic critics argued were turning the country into a barracks and crippling the economy, because war could begin at any moment.[42]

It was in this tense environment that Sukhomlinov once again took pen in hand. On June 13 he published a long article asserting that "Russia is ready, France must be ready also." The Russian war minister's human and professional reputation has recently benefitted from some upward revision. From the warmongering incompetent described by Kokovtsov, Sazonov, and his other foes, Sukhomlinov has become a modernizing moderate, trying to move the Russian army into the twentieth century, rattling no more sabers than necessary to satisfy old-school officers and mistrustful allies, at worst no more than a bureaucrat devoted to the limited interests of his agency. But if Sukhomlinov was, in the words of the German military attaché, "energetic, methodical, and bold," too often the last of these qualities dominated his public pronouncements. The intended thrust of his latest outburst may have been to convince France to keep her army up to strength by maintaining the Three Years' Law. But Sukhomlinov reinforced his arguments with glowing, not to say lurid, descriptions of the massive power over which he presided as Russia's war minister. Two weeks later Russia's most prestigious daily, *Novoye Vremya*, urged Germany to abandon its warmongering Austrian ally rather than risk a century's achievements in an unwinnable war with the Triple Entente. In a still-tense Germany the effect of such pronouncements was of gasoline on a fire.[43]

Russia's ambivalent position was not lost on Serbia's shrewd premier, Nikola Pašić. Convinced for decades that the main threat to Serbia's independence came from Austria-Hungary, increasingly committed to the vision of a south Slav state unified under Serbian auspices, Pašić had journeyed personally to St. Petersburg in the spring of 1914 and obtained a grudging promise of protection in case of an unprovoked Austrian attack.[44] It was anything but a guarantee. It did not encourage Pašić to return home and begin plans for the assassination of Franz Ferdinand. But neither did it encourage him to risk his domestic position by proceeding directly and energetically against the south Slav revolutionaries and their contacts and sympathizers in the Serbian government. On June 28, a half-dozen of them assassinated the heir to the Habsburg throne in Sarajevo.

III

As the murder escalated into an international crisis, Pašić manifested the steadiest nerves of any of the gamblers. Through the month of July he counted on Russia's ultimate support—and in this context he read the minds of the tsar and his advisors better than they did themselves.

Or perhaps he read their souls. Certainly Austria's statesmen shared his perspective. The decline of Russian influence in the Balkans after 1912 had not been matched by a corresponding improvement in the Habsburg Empire's position. Rumania and Bulgaria were more interested in courting Berlin than Vienna, and increasingly concerned with St. Petersburg as well. In February, 1914, Franz Josef expressed fear of Russian military preparations in a conversation with the German ambassador. How, he asked, does Russia propose to use her increased strength? When answered by a homily on the importance of maintaining good relations, the old emperor grumbled, "but nothing more is to be done with the Russians." A month later, Foreign Minister Leopold von Berchtold, who had succeed Aehrenthal in 1912, expressed a similar opinion, this time to the German foreign ministry's representative to Franz Josef. Georg von Treutler suggested that overestimating Russia's strength and Russia's desire for war led to unnecessary alarm. No matter how highly the tsar's empire was rated it almost always failed when put to the test. Berchtold responded by saying that his years as ambassador to St. Petersburg had made him well aware of Russian bluster. But now the situation was different. Russia was making her intentions clear by her military buildup. Even should she not choose to act directly, her new strength would be a formidable prop to any revived alliance of the Balkan states. Conrad too insisted that Russian military preparations were designed to underwrite a major move in the near future, perhaps as early as the coming fall.

On the other hand, Conrad's alarmism was a minority position among Austria's soldiers in the first half of 1914. The general staff as a body put little credence in talk of war with Russia. Alertness was desirable; fear was grist for Russia's mill. The war minister suggested that Russia's vast practice mobilizations and similar saber-rattlings were designed to do no more than encourage Austria to waste her limited resources in equivalent efforts. This mind-set may have represented a self-conscious distancing from the current trends in Germany. It persisted, however, well after Franz Ferdinand's assassination. The German military attaché in Vienna reported as late as July 13 that his Austrian colleagues believed there was a fifty-fifty chance Russia would remain neutral in the face of military initiatives against Serbia.[45]

Whatever the soldiers' opinions, in the aftermath of Sarajevo the Austrian foreign office had no doubt that a direct Austro-Serbian confrontation would pose a significant challenge to Russia. An Austrian success would be more than an object lesson to the rest of the Balkan states. It would diminish Russia's diplomatic position in the region for years to come. Austria's insouciant unconcern for the possibility of Russian intervention in the July Crisis, has been interpreted as a reaction to German pressures and as a response to German guarantees of support too often absent in the recent history of the Dual Alliance. It has been presented as a failure of crisis management, as a psychological response to a "catalytic situation," and as a failure of judgment and imagination.[46] An alternate hypothesis involves Austria's recognition that Serbia was more than a stalking horse for Russian ambitions in the Near East. Russia at her most assertive still had general interests to defend and a general position to threaten. Serbia's focus was local. A regional power prepared to risk all to gain all can achieve much against a far stronger rival whose behavior is constrained by a broader spectrum of pressure points. And Vienna's decision makers were increasingly convinced that whatever might be her policies at a given moment, Serbia ultimately had no interest in a peaceful solution to the Balkan question.

Since 1912, Austria's Serbian policy had been steadily militarized— and not merely, as Samuel Williamson suggests, because mailed-fist diplomacy worked on specific occasions.[47] The Habsburg Empire was increasingly perceived, by its small neighbors and its own generals alike, as unable to assert itself militarily in the Balkan Peninsula without a significant effort. In April, 1914, the ambassador to Bucharest told his German colleague that in case of a European war, twelve of Austria's sixteen corps would be pinned in the Balkans to counter the combined armies of Rumania and Serbia. Four only would remain to stand by the side of the Second Reich.[48] These figures, though exaggerated, nevertheless reflected the Balkan states' development into formidable enemies on their home ground, able and willing to mobilize armies a quarter-million strong and larger in pursuit of their national interests. They were correspondingly unlikely to modify or abandon those interests for the sake of words alone.[49]

From an Austrian perspective Serbia in particular seemed responsive to nothing but force. Whatever the long-term limits to her economic development, in recent decades Serbia's rate of growth had been close to Europe's average. She no longer depended on Austrian credit or Austrian trading connections.[50] Economic sanctions had proved futile in the Pig War of 1906–09. Economic concessions in the commercial treaty of 1909 had brought no better result. Repeated pledges from Belgrade to end subversive propaganda had been shown to be so many scraps of paper. Great-power diplomacy as advocated by the Germans since 1912 appeared an even deader end. What remained to discuss with an adversary whose ultimate goal was nothing less than the dissolution of the Habsburg Empire itself? In November, 1913, Bechtold had moodily expressed belief that the solution to the Serbian problem would either leave only remnants of the present Serbian state or would shake Austria to its foundations. Eight months later it represented no obvious surrender to militarism to decide that Austria's hawks were being proved right by the course of events, that it was the conciliators, the peace advocates, the internationalists, who inhabited the airy empire of dreams.[51]

Austria's relative delay in acting against Serbia reflected neither domestic discords nor dependance on German behavior. It was rather a product of calculation based on experience. Had the Dual Monarchy moved promptly in the aftermath of the assassination, demanding redress, moving troops to the frontier, occupying Belgrade, would not an outraged chorus have been raised against trigger-happy Habsburgs endangering the common good by overreacting to what was, after all, an isolated incident whose ultiimate responsibility was uncertain? In England, for example, the virulently Austrophobic Wickham Steed of the London *Times* insisted from the beginning that all was not as it seemed, that the Habsburg warmongers might well use Sarajevo as a pretext to destroy Serbia, that perhaps the assassination itself might have been stage-managed.[52]

Better by far to take pains. Not until July 23 did Austria present its ultimatum to Serbia. There can be no questioning the nature of that document. Sir Edward Grey's characterization of it as "the most formidable . . . I had ever seen addressed from one State to another that was independent"[53] indicated the clarity of Austria's intentions: to establish beyond any chance of misunderstanding the difference between a great state and a minor one, almost certainly through force of arms. Yet by the summer of 1914 Austria had increasingly moved away from a great-power mentality and begun adopting *de facto* the position and attitude of a regional power.[54] If during the July Crisis Austria's policy makers acted virtually as if Russia did not exist, this reflected a fact too uncomfortable to be considered, let alone acknowledged: Austria could no longer function autonomously in an European context. She could no longer afford the luxury of balancing local sacrifices against maintaining a general order benefitting all the larger states in the European system. The Serbian boil must be lanced. The consequences of that action were tacitly accepted as being beyond Vienna's control. Russia's army had become as irrelevant as Germany's blank check.

War Finds a Way

The Serbian government was initially thrown into confusion by Austria's ultimatum. Coming a month after the assassination, from a state that for years had seemed able to do nothing but bluster, it seemed not merely anticlimactic but unfair. Pašić was away from Belgrade when the note was delivered. With his return tentative support for accepting Austria's demands in their entirety for the sake of peace faded. Serbia's final reply, delivered on July 25, was a model of injured dignity and studied moderation. Generally conciliatory, it nevertheless insisted that participation of Austro-Hungarian officials in the investigation of Franz Ferdinand's murder was incompatible with Serbia's position as a sovereign state. Since Austria had demanded complete acceptance, her ambassador to Belgrade declared the answer unsatisfactory and left for Vienna at 6:30 p.m. the same evening.

Serbia's hard-line attitude was a product less of confidence in Russia than of her history as an independent state. Since at least the 1840s Serbian foreign policy had been characterized by a strong irredentist streak. Whether as a Slavic Piedmont, as the nucleus of a Greater Serbia, or the matrix of a Yugoslav kingdom, Serbia's future transcended existing boundaries. Now Serbia's hour of destiny was upon her. The wine was drawn and must be drunk. It is no accident that the dates on the tomb of Yugoslavia's unknown soldier are 1912 and 1918; for Serbia World War I at least began as the Third Balkan War.[55]

Nor did Serbia's coming election encourage moderation. After so many years of uninterrupted nationalist enthusiasm, what politician wished to face his constituents with a record of showing the white feather to Austria's challenge? Pushing forward into the unknown offered grave risks but corresponding opportunities.

Rejection of Austria's demand to participate in the investigation was encouraged, finally, by a general sense of anxiety about what the foreigners might find. The tracks of the archduke's killers did not lead directly to Belgrade. A Serbian government exhausted by war and preoccupied with absorbing its newly acquired territories had no interest in specifically provoking any kind of quarrel with Austria in the summer of 1914, to say nothing of giving such spectacular offense as murdering the heir to its throne. The exact nature and extent of Serbian involvement in the assassination vanished in the labyrinth of intrigue and counterintrigue that marked the government's relationship with its intelligence service. There is evidence that some officials were aware before the Sarejevo murders that something involving clandestine operations in the Habsburg Empire was in the wind. Pašić himself sent a vaguely-worded caution to Vienna, which promptly got lost in the Habsburg bureaucracy. But confrontation, to say nothing of disclosure, had obvious risks. Given Serbia's long history of conspiratorial politics, could any cabinet minister or parliamentary deputy be sure exactly what all of his colleagues were doing? Might not an excessively rigorous inquiry into the activity of one's associates prove physically as well as politically dangerous? The patriotic secret societies had proved their ruthlessness time and time again. It seemed by far the better part of valor and prudence alike to play the role of innocence outraged, and hope for the best.[56]

Serbia's increasing regional pretentions and Austria's increasing regional focus put an unexpected strain on Germany's continental visions. Most analyses of the July Crisis present the German chancellor as either a pessimistic fatalist who allowed events to take their course, or a willing initiator of a war designed to stabilize German society, confirm German military superiority and expand German influence throughout the world. At best he emerges as a man running a calculated risk, pursuing defensive ends with offensive means, his claims of supporting Germany's last ally strongly contradicted by a dynamic, imperialist thrust towards European hegemony and eventual world domination.[57]

Without denying the existence of a strong will at official levels to extend Germany's influence by force of arms, support for such an extension was rather negative than positive. Bethmann himself had argued for years that even threats of war were criminal unless Germany's honor, security, and future were inextricably involved. On June 4 he informed the Bavarian minister in Berlin that a world war was not likely to improve Germany's domestic position, and that the time for a preventive war, if it ever existed, had passed in 1905.[58]

Such statements cannot be dismissed out of hand as window-dressing. For a state dominated by the rhetoric of belligerence, a state constantly in diplomatic conflict with her neighbors, Germany in 1914 was surprisingly unready for the contingency of a major war. A. J. P. Taylor's argument that the entente would have weakened over the next few years had war not occurred, that Germany in fact jumped the gun in 1914, is credible only in the context of the kind of cold, long-range calculations on general policy that were conspicuously absent in Berlin.[59] Like their counterparts elsewhere in Europe, the generals and diplomats of the Second Reich were a long way from being unreconstructed warmongers. They accepted Germany's capacity to win any future war. They accepted the fact that this victory would correspondingly enhance Germany's continental and global position. But the moral and physical risks and costs were far too great to be accepted voluntarily, much less sought out or planned for.

Wilhelm Groener's sarcastic postwar comment that national economics did not form part of the officers' training curriculum was only partially accurate.[60] That average stocks of raw materials were sufficient for no more than six months was also unimportant in the context of belief in a short war that would be decided in the enemy's country. Supplies could be imported through neutral states and third parties, replenished through conquest, or seized as part of the postwar settlement. What was significant was the attitude behind the preparations. Consultation between the government on one hand, the captains of industry and agriculture on the other, was minimal. Cooperation among public and private agencies involved little more than vague debates about the best ways of storing forage, or how Germany might best be fed in case of a British naval blockade. Administrative routine dominated the discussions. Memoranda were passed from bureaucrat to bureaucrat and office to office with no particular urgency. The army itself seemed hardly interested in front-loading for the off-the-shelf war it expected. In 1912 the general staff and the war ministry finally responded to the massive consumption of material by both sides in the Russo-Japanese War by instituting an expanded program of shell production. Two years later, business as usual had left the program still unfulfilled.[61]

Among German policy makers this dissonance was perhaps most pronounced in Moltke. Moltke's martial rhetoric in the context of his personality, the cello-playing dabbler in the occult, able to see four sides of every three-sided question, constantly doubting his fitness for the post he held, invites speculation along psychological lines: overcompensation through posturing.[62] It seems more correct to assert that Moltke, along with many of his uniformed counterparts, expected war, perhaps even desired war—but not tomorrow and not next week. For years everywhere in Europe the time had not been quite right. Better to wait for the next arms bill, for the next round of negotiations, for something else in the future. It was the way of sustaining a dream whose risks were great, yet whose prospects were just alluring enough to inhibit any desperate efforts to preserve a peace whose preservation seemed in any case essentially beyond Germany's control.

The nature of the July Crisis has also been obscured by the issue of British policies. Since 1911 Anglo-German relations had steadily improved. Cooperation in the Balkan crises of 1912–13 was only one in a series of events that led observers everywhere in Europe to talk of détente between states whose rivalries were as recent as they seemed artificial.[63] Fritz Fischer, Gerhard Ritter, and Egmont Zechlin, their students, their critics, and their *epigoni*, have devoted miles of typescript to discussing whether or not Bethmann in fact expected that Britain would stay out of a continental war, and whether Germany proposed to take advantage of that fact to keep the war localized in order to execute a planned program of continental conquest.

Would a clear, early statement of British intention to intervene have deterred Germany? In 1914, the question was secondary in Berlin. Bethmann-Hollweg has been described as embarking in July on a diplomatic offensive testing the entente's will for war. He interpreted his own actions as testing the entente's, and specifically Russia's, will for peace. Bethmann hoped for British cooperation in defusing the current Balkan crisis. He was shocked and upset when it failed to materialize. But ultimately he could not afford to depend on it.

In 1861 Abraham Lincoln carefully publicized his intention to send supplies to a beleaguered Fort Sumter, not so much to provoke the embryonic Confederacy into firing the first shot as to provide an opportunity for the displaying of its general intentions. Peace bought at the price of union, the president insisted, was meaningless.[64] Bethmann-Hollweg was no Lincoln. But in the minds of German policy makers one salient point distinguished the Sarajevo incident from all the other crises that failed to escalate beyond the pages of now-unread diplomatic histories. This time Austria was insisting that not merely her prestige, not merely her "vital interests" as a negotiating abstraction, but her very existence as a power was part of the stake. If Germany from the beginning encouraged decisive action against Serbia, she was not winding the Habsburg clock.[65] Bethmann had not abandoned hopes for the Concert of Europe. But to function effectively concert diplomacy required full participation by all its members. The politics of restraint are effective only when pursued from a position of strength; otherwise they impress no one. Given Austria's already shaky standing in the community of nations, given the increasing tensions within the Dual Monarchy, who would believe that unilateral efforts at conciliation showed anything but the absence of any consequent will to survive?

At least as much to the point, what were the concrete prospects of entente restraint in this situation? Sazonov's shocked response to the Austrian ultimatum, *"C'est la guerre européenne,"* reflected the position of a Russian government unable quite to believe what was happening. Hartwig, who died suddenly of a heart attack on July 10, and the Russian military attaché in Belgrade both had close and longstanding links with Serbia's intelligence service—the agency most often mentioned in connection with possible government complicity in the assassination. Whatever the exact degree of information may have been in Belgrade, no evidence indicates Russian officials at any higher level had any foreknowledge of the deed. Russia was involved nevertheless. On July 24 Regent Peter of Serbia appealed personally to Nicholas, saying that Austria's demands were unreasonable, and in any case Serbia could not defend herself against them. The tsar's "generous Slav heart" must speak to him in this time of crisis.

Sazonov was not deeply concerned at the moment with Slav hearts of any temper. Serbia, he mused, might even be well-advised to submit to military occupation without resistance while continuing to appeal to the great powers for redress. But diplomacy unsupported by guns is at best a credit operation, and Russia's international credit stood none too high in Sazonov's mind. At a crown council on July 24, the foreign minister requested the initiation of a partial mobilization. This meant what amounted to general mobilization in the four military districts closest to Austria. Believing that such a measured mobilization did not mean war, Sazonov described it to the tsar and his fellow ministers as a defensive measure.[66]

The council confirmed Sazonov's request. On the morning of July 26 the preliminary orders went out. On that same day, however, Sazonov described the Balkan Slavs as a burden to Russia. He expressed a willingness to see Serbia severely chastened—if only Austria would transfer the issue to a European stage. Sukhomlinov insisted "on his honor" that no mobilization order as such had been issued. Russia was taking preliminary measures, to be implemented only if Austria crossed the

Serbian border. Peace with Germany, moreover, was "earnestly desired," whatever Austria might do.[67]

What could be made of these mixed messages? In requesting action by the powers, Russia might be banking on her relations with France and Britain to bring the current crisis before a forum where Russia could expect a majority of sympathetic ears. She might simply be playing for time to complete her own military preparations. But Sazonov's insistence that Serbia's sovereignty not be infringed, that Russia would not tolerate her reduction to vassal status, was disquieting in itself. General wars are seldom a product of the automatic functioning of international systems. Instead they manifest disfunction: the breakdown of the agreements, implicit and implied, that hold an order together. If German ambitions before 1914 had contributed to this dysfunction, German policies at least incorporated some sense of Europe as a system. Could the same be said of Russia? The governments of the Balkan Peninsula had for years sustained an image as unstable and undeveloped, undeserving of a place at the head diplomatic table and certainly not worth a European war. If Russia now regarded the Serbian issue as a *casus belli*, if she could convince her allies to support her to the brink and beyond, this was virtually *prima facie* evidence that the gulf between the tsar's empire and its immediate neighbors had indeed grown too wide to sustain the existing international order.

The German military was anything but sanguine. On July 3, Moltke's deputy, Quartermaster-General Georg von Waldersee, son of the former chief of staff, had suggested to the Saxon military plenipotentiary that peace depended on Russia's behavior, not Austria's.[68] On July 5 the general staff submitted memoranda to the foreign office on the Russian railway network and on Russia's expanding military power. The latter report described a Russian army that proposed not only to increase its annual recruit contingent from 455,000 to 585,000 men, but to keep them with the colors three months longer during the spring. In three or four years, 2,300,000 Russians would be under arms during the winter months—a key time for individual training—and 1,800,000 the rest of the year. Three or four new corps were to be raised. The strength of the corps artillery was to be increased from 108 to 144 guns, including heavy howitzers with improved fire-control equipment.

This new-model army would be more than a human steamroller. The tactical training of officers had been greatly improved by war games and staff rides. The number and duration of maneuvers had been increased. In 1914 alone almost a half-million reservists would be recalled to the colors for six weeks of refresher training. Even more than the material improvements, these personnel changes threatened to render obsolete two generations of German military planning and a quarter-century of German diplomacy.[69]

The general staff's pessimism encouraged Bethmann to turn his thoughts again and again to Russia. Few accounts of the chancellor's behavior during this period make direct references to the death of his wife on May 11, after a long and painful illness. The couple had been married for twenty-five years in what was by all accounts a love match, and work had not proved a complete antidote to sorrow. Particularly in moments of letdown or relaxation, Bethmann was more prone than usual to slip into a *neiges d'antan* melancholy. As early as July 6 he mused to Kurt Riezler that this time things were worse than in the Balkan crisis of 1912. And the key to the crisis was Russia—the Russia that was underwriting Serbia, that was building its military power, that was negotiating a naval convention with England that would expose the north German coast to amphibious assault by Russian troops from British ships.[70]

Bethmann's anxiety on the latter point was in part a product of Sir John Fisher's long-standing enthusiasm for the Baltic Project—the movement of an invasion fleet into the Baltic, where it would embark Russian troops and land them on the German coast for a thrust into the Reich's presumably unprotected heart. The risks of such a proposal, obvious to cooler heads, had led Britain even before 1914 to abandon an active naval strategy in the area. Given the weakness of Russia's Baltic fleet, operational cooperation would be difficult to impossible while the German navy still commanded the inner line. From a British perspective, the negotiations were more important for their diplomatic than their military aspects.

The Russian government took the proceedings far more seriously. It was clear in St. Petersburg that a landing in Pomerania had prospects of success only at the victorious end of a war. Exactly that fact made an agreement attractive. It would help bind Britain to the entente to the bitter end—and be correspondingly useful as a means of applying diplomatic pressure on Germany.

In such a context it was scarcely remarkable that two weeks later Bethmann spoke again of Russia's "growing aspirations and monstrous disruptive power." In a few years, he said, she would be irresistible, particularly if the current alliance systems remained in existence. That very strength made her a correspondingly desirable ally. A permanent agreement with her was worth far more than even an English alliance, and Sazonov was supposed to have told Berlin banker Robert Mendelssohn that if Germany would drop Austria, Sazonov would promptly drop France. But in Bethmann's mind, any possibility that Russia still might turn from her allies if they failed to support her in the Serbian crisis was far outweighed by the military build-up and the diplomatic ingenuousness of the tsarist colossus. Bethmann, far more than Holstein had ever done, regarded Russia's behavior as a reaction to internal tensions. Panslavism was a counterweight to revolution. This, however, made it no less dangerous. Let Russia put her own house in order as need be, but not at her neighbors' expense.[71]

Germany's support and encouragement of Austria's stand on Serbia was thus ultimately a warning directed at St. Petersburg—a warning the Russian government, at least in German eyes, seemed deliberately to ignore. Austria's actions against Serbia, up to and including the declaration of war and the subsequent bombardment of Belgrade, had one major point in their favor. They were not directly taken against a great power. The fact is simple enough to be easily overlooked. The Concert of Europe may have been little more than a convenient fable even in its salad days. Yet at least since the Crimea, no major state had gone to war with another in the interests of a lesser power, even an avowed client. Nor had any great power defined its vital interests in the context of a lesser state's policies. The one arguable exception had been Russia's support of Rumania and Bulgaria in 1877. And if Austria had now replaced the Ottoman Empire in Russian policy making, this substitution was hardly reassuring in Berlin.

Bethmann's reiterated argument that Russia was betraying the monarchical principle, supporting revolutionaries and regicides in the company of liberal and republican allies, was more than a simple assertion of conservative principles of social order, and more than a crude effort to split the entente. It was also a reminder that Russia was risking the very basis of international relations for the sake of goals and principles she was either unable to define even to herself, or was camouflaging beneath rhetoric of self-determination for small states—a rhetoric that had never ultimately defined the behavior of great powers.

In 1772, during the course of another significant readjustment of Eastern European boundaries, a cynical Frederick the Great allegedly said of Maria Theresa's avowed reluctance to participate in the partition of Poland, "She weeps, but she eats." In 1914, Russia's tears seemed similarly crocodilian. As early as July 23 Bethmann declared privately that if Russia mobilized, Germany would go to war.[72]

He was expressing a mood of resignation rather than aggression. Appeasement, for all its negative connotations, remains the most basic measure of diplomacy in the sense of discovering and meeting each others' desires through negotiation. But if those desires are badly articulated, if they are expressed in vague or contradictory terms, then appeasement, like restraint, becomes an exercise in futility. Far from "unleashing" Austria-Hungary, far from using the Sarajevo incident as an excuse for initiating a long-prepared war of conquest, Germany was reacting to her eastern neighbors in a most un-Bismarckian way. The Second Empire did not slide into war in 1914 by accident or miscalculation. Instead it deliberately resigned the initiative to the game's other players. This was in sharp contrast to her by now traditional behavior in crisis situations. From San Stefano to Agadir, from Samoa to the Balkans, Germany had held center stage for a quarter-century, pointing with pride or viewing with alarm, demanding, threatening, or blustering—and always ultimately backing down. Suddenly her diplomats were taking a calm, almost fatalistic attitude. Her ambassadors were talking in terms of "if-then" in a way that bewildered their opposite numbers and continues to confuse historians, but made far too much sense to Bethmann-Hollweg.

Bethmann saw Germany as on the low side of a seesaw. Instead of being the fulcrum of European diplomacy, she found herself in a situation where the balance was in danger of being permanently upset in the wrong direction. Writing in later years in the contexts of stalemate and defeat, men with the vastly different political positions of Karl Lichnoswky and Philipp Eulenberg argued for the stupidity of their country's policy in the summer of 1914. The erstwhile ambassador to England and the one-time imperial favorite agreed that no vital interest justified Germany's anti-Serbian position, that Russia had made plain her support for Serbia's integrity, and that it was nonsense to risk a war that offered even the possibility of global involvement.[73] Bethmann interpreted the situation differently. The Serbian issue was a litmus test. If Russia and her allies took it to the brink successfully, this would be only the beginning. There would be another crisis, and another, in a pattern later generations would describe as salami slicing. In Bethmann's opinion, if Russia meant to have a war, let it begin now.

By this time Bethmann had little confidence in England's restraint. He considered the Anglo-Russian naval negotiations, successful or not, as a particular sign that Britain regarded war with Germany as not much more than a question of time and place. Nevertheless, throughout July he continued to urge the island empire to remain neutral. Without her support, he argued, Russia would back down from a position morally untenable and dangerous to Europe's stability. Should Russia fail to see reason, why should Britain underwrite her folly?

These efforts to limit the conflict did not exclude considerations of how Germany might profit from the victory she expected to win. If Bethmann's exact goals were relatively vague, his concepts of colonial compensation and enhanced political and economic influence in Europe and the Near East were clear enough.[74] Wars, however, are not necessarily fought for their causes; war aims are not a logical indicator of prewar goals. No state in history had fought a war to restore the exact *status quo ante bellum*, if for no better reason than that was the situation generating war in the first place. If the result of present events was a Europe under German hegemony, then that would be a by-product of a series of incorrect decisions—all of them ultimately made outside Berlin.

Nor was Bethmann under massive internal pressure to begin a war. For men so often described as trembling with eagerness for battle, Germany's senior officers reacted to Franz Ferdinand's assassination with remarkable insouciance. Moltke, taking a cure at Karlsbad, was told by the chancellor to stay there and saw no reason to challenge his instructions. Lieutenant-Colonel Wilhelm Groener, head of the all-important railway section of the general staff, was visiting Bad Kissingen for his health. In the aftermath of his warning to the Saxon plenipotentiary, Waldersee had been given compassionate leave because of a death in his family. On July 8 Bethmann's office advised him to spend some additional time on his father-in-law's estate in Mecklenburg, restoring health shaken by recent surgery. Waldersee would not return to Berlin until July 23, and did little during his holiday to keep himself abreast of the deepening crisis.

Was the absence of so many key officers part of an elaborate plan to lure the rest of Europe into a false security regarding Germany's intentions? Waldersee's comment on July 8 that he was "ready to jump" and that the general staff was so well prepared "there is nothing for us to do" deserves interpreting with a grain of salt.[75] Given the military's concern with maintaining its place in Germany's power structure, a rhetoric of confidence in the presence of civilians was predictable. On the other hand, it is difficult to imagine warmongers so confident that they completely ignore intelligence, if only to ensure that the prospective target remains safely in the dark. But not until July 16 were the intelligence officers of the eastern corps informally instructed to pay more than routine attention to developments in Russia. Not until July 23 were these men officially informed that Berlin had a special interest in keeping abreast of events in the tsar's empire. And not until July 25 did the head of military intelligence explain to his subordinates that a war was likely, and that their agency was expected to concentrate on finding out whether military preparations were in fact taking place in France and Russia.

To the men on the spot in eastern Germany, Berlin was merely seeking confirmation of what everyone already knew. Since early July, every train passing through Danzig or Königsberg into Russia seemed to bear its quota of officers and their ladies returning ahead of schedule from the watering places of Western Europe. Every contact, personal or official, with Russians of any social standing seemed to be accompanied by a recommendation to stock up on caviar, or a suggestion not to put too much hope in the coming autumn's hunting season. The men's handshakes were firmer than usual; the women's tears more public.

Technology reinforced personal impressions. From the beginning of their alliance both France and Russia had been concerned with the problem of maintaining direct, secure communications during a crisis. Everything from cables to carrier pigeons had been considered, tested, and rejected as too slow, or too random, or too vulnerable. The development of radio appeared to solve the problem. In 1907 and again in 1909 the French pushed for the establishment of radio links. By 1912 the Russians had constructed a major—for the times—communications station in the White Russian town of Bobruisk. From there daily communications were possible to Paris, where the practical French utilized the Eiffel Tower for transmission and reception.

The Germans were reasonably quick to respond. By 1913 the senior intelligence officer of I Corps in Königsberg was utilizing the garrison's own powerful radios to intercept Russian dispatches. By calling on reserve officers and utilizing civilian professors from the university who were experts in Russian language and culture or skilled mathematicians, he had made significant progress deciphering codes and understanding transmission patterns. The traffic had been growing steadily and ominously heavier when, during the night of July 24/25, Königsberg's operations picked up a lengthy coded exchange between Bobriusk and the Eiffel Tower. Its import seemed all too clear the next day, with the news of Russia's projected partial mobilization.[76]

95

IV

Sazonov had forty-eight hours' time between Serbia's rejection of the ultimatum and Austria's declaration of war. As the sands ran out he found it easier to continue a long tradition of Habsburg-bashing, easier to accuse Austria of deliberately setting Europe on fire, easier to boast of the Austrian ambassador being "gentle as a lamb" in discussing the crisis than to appraise Russia's interests and opportunities, much less Serbia's guilt or Austria's determination. On July 28, as Austrian warships and artillery opened fire on Belgrade, Sazonov implemented the partial mobilization approved four days earlier.

The foreign minister continued to insist that this mobilization did not mean war, that Russia did not have to attack Austria and had no intention of attacking Germany. But Berlin was not the only European capital where it was legitimate to ask whether the politicians or the generals ruled. Chief of staff N. N. Yanushkevitch informed not merely the four districts Sazonov authorized, but every military district in the empire, that July 30 was to be the first day of a general mobilization.[77]

Russia's alleged inability to risk partial mobilization in view of the clumsiness of her military system has by this time been thoroughly exposed as a red herring. Russia was in fact better able than any of the continental powers to call up only part of her huge forces. Her general staff, however, had never taken this alternative seriously. In operational terms Russian generals had no faith in Serbia's ability to withstand unaided the army of a great power. As early as November, 1912, a conference of chiefs of staff of the military districts had warned of the risks should Russia delay entry into an Austro-Serbian conflict and recommended mobilization as soon as Austria acted. The size of the Russian Empire, its low population density, its inefficient bureaucracy, continued to make mobilization a difficult process even after the recent reforms. It was further complicated by the fact that, unlike circumstances elsewhere in Europe, a large number of the army's active formations were stationed away from major population centers. Nor could the Russian railway network support the heavy traffic of its French or German counterparts. Individual lines were often lightly built and poorly maintained. Water tanks, fuel supplies, and maintenance facilities were calculated for limited traffic. So were repair gangs and train crews. It was neither insouciance nor warmongering that led the chief of the general staff's mobilization section to describe a general war as "settled" as early as July 26. From his perspective, anything else was an unconscionable risk.[78]

On the same day the French military attaché, General Laguiche, informed his war ministry that Sukhomlinov, while repeating Russia's intention to avoid overt measures that might be interpreted as directed against Germany, confirmed the mobilization of the four southern districts. At the same time the military districts of Moscow, Kiev, and St. Petersburg—those closest to the German frontier—had been secretly put under orders to prepare for the contingency of war.

The possibility of French intervention to stop the process was diminished by continuing domestic pressure to modify the Three Years' Law. The government was correspondingly unwilling to weaken its Russian alliance. To get along it seemed desirable to go along. At the prompting of Joffre, War Minister Adolphe Messimy instructed Laguiche on July 27 to urge an invasion of East Prussia as soon as possible. The next day, Joffre and Messimy insisted to the Russian military attaché that France was fully prepared to fulfill her alliance obligations. In St. Petersburg, French Ambassador Maurice Paléologue made the same point to Sazonov, and to anyone else willing to listen. His encouragement was unofficial, but in the current supercharged atmosphere no one was asking awkward questions.[79]

Russian premobilization measures were reported to Berlin almost as soon as they began. German intelligence officers sought the whereabouts of any Russian units observed away from their normal stations. They increased the number of "tension travellers," civilians and reserve officers legally dispatched across the border under various pretenses to observe possible war preparations. Königsberg described empty freight trains being transferred to the interior out of harm's way, and troops moving by rail in the direction of a major junction. Other Russian units were leaving their maneuver grounds with unusual haste. Franco-Russian radio traffic, all in code, remained heavy. By the afternoon of the 27th, intelligence officers in Berlin were convinced that Russia had implemented, not merely announced, her premobilization program.

Through the next day reports of troop movements, of concentrations of rolling stock, of security guards posted on railway lines, bridges, and water towers, continued to pour in. The paramilitary frontier guard was in some areas being reinforced by army troops. Agents in place were reporting the calling up of reservists and the purchasing of horses. Radio traffic between Paris and Bobriusk was increasing. Everything known to date fit German information and German assumptions about Russia's war plans.[80]

The relatively weak forces allotted to Germany's eastern theater could not have been far from Moltke's thoughts when he compiled his "Evaluation of the Political Situation" on July 28. The memorandum is dominated by fear of a Russia the chief of staff saw as pursuing the politics of brinkmanship. She was advancing her own preparations to the point where her armies could cross the frontier within a few days of mobilization, but stopping short of issuing the final orders in an effort to force her enemies, Germany and Austria, into mobilizing first. This in turn would act as a *casus foederis* for France, perhaps for England as well.[81]

Intelligence reports, submitted through August 29 and summarized at 4:00 p.m., described the Russian preparations to date as "passive." The deployment of troops on the frontier and along the railways had been followed neither by a general call-up of reservists, even in the border districts, nor by mobilization orders. At 5:25 p.m., however, a telegram from the German consul in Moscow quoted "a very good source" that

97

Russian mobilization was set for the next day.[82] From a military perspective Germany seemed to face a choice between abandoning the Schlieffen Plan with its western focus and exposing Germany's eastern provinces fully to the Russian steamroller. Even the most pessimistic general staff calculations of the prospects for a successful delaying action in the east had not been based on the kinds of hammer blows the Russians could throw if allowed to mobilize and concentrate undisturbed.

Yet neither Moltke's alarm nor the demands of Prussian war minister Erich von Falkenhayn for preliminary mobilization were enough to move Bethmann. The chancellor's reluctance reflected mixed motives—hope that at the eleventh hour a miracle might happen; desire to bring the Social Democrats into line behind a war waged against tsarist autocracy; and determination to make Russia cut her own diplomatic throat. As early as July 26, Bethmann had reacted to a demonstration before the Russian embassy by insisting that such behavior merely gave Russia an excuse to claim that Germany wanted war. This would be premature as long as Russia had made no aggressive moves. Whatever happened, Bethmann insisted, Russia must be put in the wrong before Germany and the world.[83] When he met with Moltke, Falkenhayn, and Jagow on the evening of July 29, he responded to the generals' urging by stressing the risks of sacrificing public opinion at home and in Great Britain. England, Bethmann argued, would not stand by her ally should Russia unleash a general war by attacking Austria.

Bethmann's position was reflected in the conference between Sazonov and the German ambassador, held sometime between 5:00 and 7:00 p.m. the same day. Pourtalès insisted that if Russia continued her mobilization measures, Germany would be forced in her turn to mobilize and a European war would be almost impossible to stop. Sazonov regarded the communication as a virtual ultimatum in the worst traditions of 1909. As soon as Pourtalès left, Sazonov contacted the war minister and the chief of staff. Like their German counterparts, they insisted on immediate general mobilization. Unlike Bethmann, Sazonov agreed.

The foreign minister was not well equipped to respond to the kind of if/then situation apparently presented by Pourtalès. In common with civilian heads of state everywhere in Europe, he was essentially ignorant of military matters. The days of the soldier-kings, even relatively pedestrian ones like Napoleon III or William I, were long past. The evolution of professionalism in the nineteenth century had generated a corresponding climate of specialization—particularly in Russia, whose administrative ethos was anything but friendly to the military virtues. Wearing a bemedalled uniform on state occasions hardly conferred expertise. Nor did a major crisis provide a favorable environment for challenging the men who claimed to know what they were doing, even if they were part of the system that had most recently produced Tsushima and Mukden. Since the question had first been raised, Russia's generals had insisted that a partial mobilization would significantly interfere with a general mobilization. And Germany's attitude in the context of Austria's attack on Serbia seemed to render general mobilization inevitable.

The orders were on the point of being dispatched when Nicholas suspended them. A conciliatory telegram from William had led the tsar to hope Germany might yet back down. Sazonov was not directly informed of the imperial decision, but the war minister lost no time in letting him know the new turn of events. By that time it was close to midnight and Sazonov, understandably exhausted, went to bed. At 1:00 a.m. on July 30, Pourtalès asked to see him once more. The dishevelled foreign minister heard Bethmann's latest proposal: Germany would do its best to get Austria to renounce territorial claims against Serbia. Sazonov replied that this was no longer enough. Under pressure he finally agreed that if Austria would remove from her ultimatum the clauses attacking Serbian sovereignty, Russia would halt her own military preparations.[84]

In making this offer Sazonov may have wished for no more than a chance to go back to bed. In any case his mind had changed when he met with the French and British ambassadors during the morning of July 30. Germany's latest proposal, Sazonov declared, was unsatisfactory. Under its terms, even if Serbia's territorial integrity were respected, she would eventually become a vassal of Austria, "just as Bokhara . . . was a vassal of Russia."[85]

Sazonov's conclusion that Russia would face internal revolution by accepting this possibility is less significant than his choice of comparisons. Insisting on an essential identity in terms of foreign policy between central Asia and southeastern Europe was a major contribution to the outbreak of world war and the end of the Russian Empire. It was also a significant vindication of Holstein's position on Russia's ultimate intentions in the Balkans.

At 11:00 a.m. Sazonov had another meeting, this one with the war minister and the chief of staff. Both once again urged immediate general mobilization, arguing that war was inevitable and German mobilization was much further advanced than anyone supposed. This convinced Sazonov once more—if further convincing was, in fact, needed. Unable to persuade the tsar by telephone to take this step, Sazonov made a personal appointment for 3:00 p.m. For almost an hour he used his considerable eloquence to persuade a still-wavering Nicholas to order general mobilization, "as it was clear to everybody that Germany had decided to bring about a collision." When the tsar finally agreed Sazonov telephoned the chief of staff, transmitted the authorization, and told the officer that the decision was final. He could smash his telephone.[86]

Once again, Sazonov chose an illustration that was a metaphor. The telephone and the telegraph had done much to shape events in the past month, both by overwhelming statesmen with more material than they could process and by accelerating the pace of events. Modern communications technology was a double-edged sword. It enabled a much finer tuning of crisis management than had been possible in earlier generations. Sir Charles Napier's conquest of Sind, Marchand's and Kitchener's clash at Fashoda, were anachronisms by 1914. No longer could general wars begin inadvertently on Europe's peripheries. But once a crisis began frightening the participants, the ready availability of information tended to destabilize the situation even further.[87]

The impact of broken sleep, interrupted meals, and ruined digestions has seldom been considered in evaluating the outcome of the July Crisis. Such factors were not likely to be stressed in the memoirs of men raised in atmospheres of Victorian reticence. Who would dare suggest he had contributed to starting a war that slaughtered millions of men because bowel disturbances affected his judgment? Yet most of the key decisions in every European capital were being made by men in their fifties and sixties, accustomed to eating and drinking well in an era when geriatric medicine was based principally on admonitions to lead a regular life with limited stress.

Anything less like the situation in Berlin can scarcely be imagined. Fritz Fischer, Immanuel Geiss, and their imitators present a picture of Germany's decision makers insouciantly playing Russia as a matador plays the bull, waiting patiently for the final decision that would make her the villain of the drama at home and abroad. As late as August 25, senior officials of the foreign office reassured *Berliner Tageblatt* editor Theodor Wolff that "neither Russia, nor France, nor England" wanted war. Russia in particular would find "everything stolen . . . and no ammunition." But Wolff remarked on Jagow's shuffling gait and stopped posture. Kurt Riezler noted that after the news of Russia's partial mobilization the work "day" began extending to 5:00 or 6:00 a.m.[88] Moltke continued to warn of the risks Germany was running by not ordering her own general mobilization—particularly in view of Britain's repeated statements that she would not remain neutral in a Russo-German conflict. And as Bethmann faced the collapse of his strategy, his aplomb collapsed along with it.

Like every other politician in Europe Theobald von Bethmann-Hollweg had spent his career talking of war, considering it, evaluating its prospects. Morocco, Durazzo, or Armenia—the obscure places of the globe had repeatedly inspired speculations of Armageddon. But at the eleventh hour, with reality on his doorstep, Bethmann sought to withdraw from the brink. He turned eastward, not to St. Petersburg, but to Vienna, encouraging Austria at least to consider the prospects of mediation. Germany, he declared, refused "to be drawn lightly into a world conflagration by Vienna." A second dispatch, reflecting Pourtalès' conversations with Sazonov, suggested that if Austria now declined to bend it would scarcely be possible to blame Russia for the outbreak of a war.[89]

Metaphorically at least, Bethmann was speaking into a wire deader than Yanushkevich's demolished telephone. Berchtold did agree to discuss views with St. Petersburg, but remained adamant in his insistence that this time the great powers would have to accept Serbia's reduction to vassalage. Apart from Austria's particular circumstances, the risks to

100

Europe as a whole of allowing this petty state a continued free hand were entirely too high.[90]

In this context, the final agreement between Bethmann and Moltke to proclaim Germany's State of Imminent War (*drohende Kriegsgefahrzustand*) no later than the morning of July 31 reflected more desperation than affirmation. The initial decision was taken around 9:00 p.m. on July 30 at the end of another long, exhausting day of waiting for words from Vienna or St. Petersburg that never came. Unlike the Russian, the German system had no built-in grace periods. Implementing the *drohende Kriegsgefahrzustand* meant automatic mobilization and war. The first rumors of a Russian general mobilization reached Berlin around 11:00 p.m. This was probably enough for Bethmann. His long-term forebodings about Russia's aims and intentions could scarcely have led him to put much faith in any last-minute changes in St. Petersburg's course. There was still time—twelve or fifteen hours—for something to happen, even if no one quite knew what. But one final corroboration, one final scrap of paper, remained important.[91]

The stream of reports to Berlin that Russia had ordered general mobilization steadily increased. At 8:00 a.m. on the 31st the intelligence officer of XX Corps at Allenstein sent a coded message. His agents had seen at several points along the Russian frontier red posters proclaiming general mobilization. Moltke was initially skeptical. Perhaps the poster announced no more than a practice mobilization, or a recall of reservists. When confronted with corroborating accounts from XVII Corps at Danzig and VI Corps at Breslau, Moltke breathed deeply and said that Germany now had no choice but to mobilize. His next step was to telephone XX Corps headquarters, insist he needed solid proof of Russia's mobilization, and instruct that an actual notice be obtained by any means necessary.

Perhaps the chief of staff wanted physical evidence in case Bethmann changed his mind. Perhaps after a month of ephemera, of telegrams and conversations and phone messages, he just wanted to have something tangible in his possession. But any lingering thoughts that the red posters were phantoms of overheated imaginations, that this crisis would fade away as had so many others, vanished when the intelligence officer of XX Corps took the risk of telephoning over an open line to report that a copy of the Russian announcement was in German hands.[92]

German intelligence in the east depended heavily for low-level information on Polish and Lithuanian Jews. Cattle dealers and small-scale merchants, occasionally smugglers, they were constantly moving back and forth across the border. Few of them had any cause to feel loyalty towards a tsarist government that had systematically and brutally persecuted Jews for generations. Fewer still cared much about the high politics of the *goyim* except as it influenced their lives, threatening their sons with conscription or offering the chance to turn a profit. Selling grain to a commissary, horses to a remount officer, or information to an intelligence bureau—all were part of the same process of making a living on the margins of societies whose official representatives despised and distrusted them.[93]

Pincus Urwicz was a merchant in the Russian town of Kolno—a high-flown designation for a horse-and-cart trader in general merchandise who had a small sideline in military information. To date he had hardly been a Scarlet Pimpernel. The bits and pieces of news he delivered to Allenstein were so unimportant, the documents he obtained so routine, that he had never felt constrained to take security precautions more profound than carrying the material out of plain sight. Though German records are silent on this point, it is probable that Urwicz was a low-grade double agent, providing similar information to the Russians on his return trips. But on July 30 he noticed something unusual. Large placards in the Russian language were being posted all over Kolno. Like many of his coreligionists, Urwicz read no Russian. But talk of mobilization and war was as common in the marketplaces and synagogues along the border as it was in barracks or offices. Urwicz waited until dark, slipped out of his house, made his way to the city hall, and removed one of the posters. Then, with a coolness surprising under the circumstances, he returned home and went to sleep. After a few hours he harnessed his horse and started for the border, the poster carefully sewn into his coat.

Urwicz was both a familiar figure and a potential firsthand source of information on what the Germans might be doing. The Russian guards passed him through without question, and he promptly reported to the German customs office. When his contact officer, Captain von Röder, received a telephone call that a Jew with a Russian mobilization poster was on the German side of the frontier, he had no trouble securing a car to take him at the breakneck speed of thirty-five miles an hour to a rendezvous with Urwicz.[94]

The ironic implications of a Prussian aristocrat dashing off to meet a despised *Ostjude* are exceeded by the greater irony that made the whole event a footnote. At 11:45 a.m., only a few minutes after Röder confirmed to Berlin the fact of Russian mobilization, official notification arrived from St. Petersburg. At 1:00 p.m. Germany declared its own *drohende Kriegsgefahrzustand*. At 3:30 p.m., Bethmann telegraphed Pourtalès to inform Sazonov that mobilization must follow unless Russia stood down her military preparations and clearly notified Germany of that fact within twelve hours.[95] Pincus Urwicz slipped out of history's pages. How might postwar anti-Semites have coped with the story had Urwicz crossed the border a few hours earlier, or had the Russians announced their intentions a few hours later? It would have been a challenge to deny the deed of a little man who, whatever his motives, risked his life to bring Germany its first proof that, at last, the Cossacks were coming.

PART II

NOW THRIVE THE ARMOURERS

4
The Virgin Soldiers

I

In the German army, high summer was a pause for breath. Officers contemplated long leaves and cures. Time-expiring NCOs thought of pensions and prospective civil-service posts. Privates in their last weeks of active duty invested in beer mugs, pipes, and photos commemorating their service. Regimental and brigade exercises were over. Next on the training schedule would be the autumn maneuvers, which, rumor had it, were this year expected to be more realistic than ever. In the garrison towns of East Prussia, parade grounds and barracks stood temporarily empty as the regiments turned to help bring in a bumper crop, one of the best in years.

Farmers, chronically short of help, disliking and distrusting the gangs of Polish and Russian seasonal workers that crossed the border at harvest time, welcomed the soldiers. Not only were they honest Germans; they cost nothing but bread and cheese, a little sausage, and plenty of beer. For the officers, harvest duty was reciprocity for an autumn's hunting and a winter's dancing, an insurance policy against the next year's round of rural social activities. For countrymen among the rank and file, harvesting could be a pleasant reminder of their own home villages, particularly if the women were friendly. City boys from Hamburg or Dortmund, marked as aliens by their accents, sweating over unfamiliar implements and unfamiliar tasks, might at least rejoice in a change from the endless routines of drill and spit-and-polish.

The use of soldiers as harvest help symbolized conditions in the German east. In an empire increasingly developing along lines of regional specialization, this area had been left behind. Limited resources, limited capital, and limited markets retarded the growth of industrialization. The

105

agrarian conservatives insisted on maintaining an agricultural system increasingly uncompetitive on a European market. In 1914 the average personal income in the province was about the same as the average for the entire kingdom of Prussia in 1892.

Underdevelopment generated massive emigration westward, to Berlin and the Ruhr, in search of work and opportunities. Almost the entire natural population increase of the Reich's eastern provinces from 1870 to 1914 was absorbed by this internal migration. By no means was all of it to the factories. Few German villages did not have a native son or two who had made his career as a NCO. Prussian farm boys were highly desired by colonels of regiments in Alsace, the Ruhr, and the Rhineland as sources and models of old Prussian virtues. Enlisted men could expect to be correspondingly well treated on maneuvers or detached service east of the Oder. Clean straw at worst, feather beds at best; good tobacco and better schnapps; an occasional slap-and-tickle with a maid, perhaps a smile from the daughter of the house; and all for the price of listening to the *paterfamilias* describe his days in uniform, show off his souvenirs, and boast of his sons on the far side of the Reich.[1]

The army's position in the east was also influenced by a German-Polish struggle that by the twentieth century politicized the entire region at the grass roots. National conflict enhanced mythologies based on national and religious differences dating back to the Middle Ages. The stakes were small and the issues marginal. Nevertheless the electoral process affirmed and intensified cleavages that seemed to defy political solutions. If no East Elbian politician rose in the Prussian Landtag or the German Reichstag to denounce the projected abandonment of his homeland to Slavic hordes as a result of the Schlieffen Plan, a sense of the eastern provinces as an ethnic and cultural battleground was nevertheless too pervasive to ignore. Social democracy, that bugbear of respectable opinion in the Reich proper, was just visible enough in East Prussia's home towns to provide a sense of danger for the patriotic societies to exploit at their meetings. But ethnic chauvinism had been comprehensively fostered in recent years by the work of anti-Slav, anti-Polish propagandists for the H-K-T Society and similar groups. While the cutting edge of their work was in Posen and West Prussia, their speakers and pamphlets were familiar in this trans-Vistula province as well.

Nor was this attitude entirely a product of propaganda. The border districts boasted some of the highest crime rates in Germany. Neidenburg, Heydekrug, Niederung—three East Prussian *Landkreise* were in the top ten of the entire Reich for the years 1903-12. Their common denominator was the possession of significant minorities, Polish for Neidenburg, Lithuanian for the other two. Urbanization and modernization, those often-cited harbingers of disorder, were less significant on the frontier than old-fashioned poverty combined with discrimination. And while efficient municipal police forces and an ever-present *gendarmerie* could be counted on to keep the lesser breeds in good order under most circumstances,

German nationals considered a strong military presence a welcome insurance policy.[2]

Rather than being stationed in the countryside by squadrons and companies, like British troops in eighteenth-century Ireland or their Austrian counterparts in Galicia, most of the German regiments in West and East Prussia were concentrated. The principal garrisons of XVII Corps were the old fortress cities strung along the Vistula: Thorn, Graudenz, Danzig. Across the river, most of the men of I and XX Corps were stationed in the small- and medium-sized market towns dotting the East Prussian landscape at thirty- or forty-mile intervals: Allenstein, Insterburg, Rastenburg, Lyck. Some could trace a heritage to the days of the Teutonic knights. Others owed their modern existence to the colonization programs of Frederick William I. All sought and welcomed garrisons. In depressed agricultural areas, soldiers were a major source of income. Almost a third of the male wage earners in Graudenz, for example, wore uniforms. Food and forage, construction and maintenance, could be important items in the ledgers of any local business fortunate enough to get army contracts. Generals and colonels were usually politically astute enough to see that the benefits were reasonably widely distributed, even to Polish landowners and contractors with the right patriotic spirit.

The army also offered social variety. In West Prussia, ethnic, economic, and historical factors combined to isolate the towns from the countryside. East of the Vistula, most of the towns were just large enough to make monotony a scourge for their residents. In both cases a garrison's bands and parades provided public entertainment, while the officers were a welcome addition to circles impossibly narrow in terms of the brighter lights to the west.

The officers themselves frequently had other ideas. At the end of the nineteenth century, service on the frontier was to many *officiers moyens sensuels* a career-threatening mixture of professional stress and soul-killing boredom. Commanding generals were likely to be fire-eaters who took seriously their task of defending the Reich's outposts and were correspondingly quick to ensure the premature retirement of anyone failing to measure up to their exacting standards. Gottlieb Haeseler, for years commander of XVI Corps in Metz and the Reich's most familiar military eccentric, had an equally fearsome counterpart in August Lentze, who from 1890 to 1902 made service in Danzig's XVII Corps an exercise in anxiety for any officer above the rank of captain. As a familiar Kasino rhyme enjoined:

Gott behüt mich vor der Grenze
Gottlieb Häseler, August Lentze.[3]

Assignment to a frontier province meant isolation from both the increasingly attractive civilian social scene and the mainstreams of professional development and professional advancement. It meant years in endlessly monotonous small towns with their one good restaurant, their two or three respectable *Gasthäuser*, their choral groups and gymnastic associations so difficult for any outsider to penetrate. The universal appellation for these places was *Drecknester*, "shitholes." Few officers were convinced by the argument that civilian officials, doctors, and lawyers managed to make quite comfortable lives in such communities. Drinking and gambling, often financed by borrowed money, flourished. Unmarried lieutenants consorted with women of questionable reputation. Married captains seduced each others' wives. Personal antagonisms bred quarrels, duels, and courtmartials. In the hothouse atmosphere of provincial Germany, the stories lost nothing in the repetition among outraged and titillated civilians. In Gumbinnen, when an officer murdered his unfaithful wife, the scandal kept tongues wagging for years.

In 1904, a disgusted lieutenant published *Life in a Garrison Town*, a *roman à clef* describing scandalous goings-on among the officers in Forbach in Alsace. Coming on the heels of Franz-Adam Beyerlein's *Jena oder Sedan*, with its exposé of the alleged dry rot in the German army, this work earned the author the rewards critics expected of Imperial Germany: a sentence for libel accompanied by impassioned denials that anything serious was amiss. In fact, the German officer was the victim of a double bind. The army's pretensions as the school of the nation and the embodiment of its highest ideals generated correspondingly high expectations of its officers. Like Caesar's wife, they were to be above suspicion—mature, circumspect, and discreet; reflective in judgment and wise in counsel. In such a context even youth's predictable lapses were unlikely to be ignored. Nor were critics willing to make distinctions between private behavior and that involving matters of public trust. German subalterns were never allowed the license their British contemporaries took for granted.[4]

Yet the army's well-documented reluctance to stamp out antisocial exuberance was not entirely a crude manifestation of militarism. It is easy to forget just how thoroughly domesticated was the German soldier of the early twentieth century. In his unpublished memoirs General Otto von Below described his first courtesy call as a brigadier on his division commander. As he approached the door he overheard an outburst of scolding. When he rang the bell he found his superior deep in a "discussion" with his teenage daughter. As she flounced out of the house with a final "Oh, *Daddy!*" the general explosively vented his frustration, while his wife expressed her hope that Below's own daughter would be a calming influence on their uncontrollable offspring. Both of these family men would take army corps into action in 1914. A few years later Below, in full uniform, found himself stranded in a small rural *Gasthaus* late in the evening. When he requested a meal the landlady informed him that she had no time; she needed to help her son with his schoolwork. The general promptly and gallantly mounted the breach and earned his dinner by taking the youngster through his Latin exercises.

Apart from their modification of the image of Imperial Germany as a militarized and patriarchal society, such anecdotes suggest a real problem within the officer corps. Combat leadership, particularly at junior levels, involves a mixture of forceful character and a certain indifference to consequences. Lieutenants and captains are never expected to have long life spans once the shooting starts. No army can contemplate with equanimity the thought of stable, settled, emotionally middle-aged men leading platoons into enemy fire. The German army had to walk a consistently fine line between the Scylla of emasculating its junior leaders by converting them into bureaucratized good citizens and the Charybdis of allowing panache and enthusiasm to degenerate into publicity-generating hooliganism.[5]

The war ministry and the general staff agreed that idle hands were mischief-prone. The expansion of the Prussian garrison, from one corps in 1889 to three after 1912, generated a critical mass that fostered efficiency by emulation and competition. Living conditions improved. New formations received new barracks, solidly built, comfortable structures with storage rooms, running water, accommodations for married NCOs, and separate quarters for the bachelor NCOs—the last a minor development that improved discipline and morale by giving the rank and file and their junior leaders mutual privacy off duty. The officers were not always so fortunate. As late as 1913, one major had to content himself with two tiny apartments, ten minutes' walk apart. To go from his sitting room to his bedroom required the use of a lantern. In bad weather the journey was a nightly adventure. The storyteller leaves the sanitary arrangements to our imaginations.[6]

As the army in East Prussia increased in size it became more public. Old regiments like the 4th Grenadiers displayed their silver, their portraits of retired colonels, their trophies from past victories. Newer ones like the 141st Infantry showcased marksmanship prizes. Wise colonels made their regimental bands available for concerts, and regularly distributed invitations to the officers' club among locally prominent citizens. For everybody else parades, target practice, and route marches offered welcome breaks in daily routines. In Ortelsburg, the lieutenants of the 1st *Jäger* Battalion occasionally ended a particularly relaxing session in the officers' mess with an improvised midnight parade through the small town. At least one good citizen, far from deploring his interrupted sleep, complained instead that the merry pranksters never passed by his house. The oversight was remedied at the earliest opportunity.[7] The incident, typical of many, suggests that the posturing, monocled caricature of *Ulk, Simplicissimus,* and the Social Democratic press was to a degree the product of perception and expectation. Particularly outside the big cities, a bit of good will accompanied by some concessions to immaturity was likely to give a garrison town the junior officers it deserved.[8]

The German soldier of 1914 was the product of a deferential society. Even the Social Democrats had an articulated, hierarchic organization rigid enough to be frequently described by contemporaries as directly borrowed from the military. At the same time the Second Empire's was a society sufficiently open to diffuse and defuse a good deal of class antagonism and hostility. In particular the development of a large lower middle class, and the growing complexity of that class, contributed to a general perception of choice as a factor in class identity. The pride of the white-collar worker, so often described in negative terms by academic critics, had a positive side as well: a sense of achievement and a promise of better things to come. Even the socialist movement drew its essential strength from affirmative identities. The ideal party member was class-conscious as well as class-determined—committed to the triumph of socialism because he wished to be so committed.[9]

These attitudes were part of the army. The negative aspects of Germany's military have been so stressed that it sometimes seems every officer from the chief of staff to the newest lieutenant must have had as his first thought on arising, "What can I personally do today to fix the yoke of decaying Junker feudalism on the necks of the emerging proletariat?"[10] The army of Imperial Germany was in fact much more than a collection of sullen conscripts marking time till their discharge, destined to shoot down their brothers or be sacrificed in pursuit of militaristic dreams. It was also a significant instrument for integrating and legitimizing the Second Reich.

The process of legitimation began with the officer corps. Its role was significantly enhanced by the relative confusion of Imperial Germany's status network. No class, caste, or social group perceived itself as clearly dominant. In this climate an officer's commission, active or reserve, easily became generally negotiable social currency. To consider it a symbol of bourgeois insecurity or an instrument for co-opting the middle class is to apply models irrelevant to most of the principals in the situation.[11] The institution of the one-year volunteer, allowing young men with specific kinds and levels of education to serve a year in the ranks and then apply for a reserve commission, was not democratic. It was in a significant sense liberal in its encouragement of individual development, and correspondingly appealing to the ambitious. Acquiring a commission amounted to gaining membership in a club. The process was just difficult enough to make the goal desirable. But, at least for gentile Christians, it involved no extraordinary humiliations—nothing beyond the normal frustrations of entering a new environment, combined with the kinds of judicious log-rolling and compromising that were increasingly the norms of a plural society. Engaging in this process was seen less as selling out than as buying in.

Even before 1871, the number of Prussian noblemen willing to spend their active lives in military service could not meet the demand for officers. The expanding army of a united Germany presented an increasing spectrum of opportunities to commoners, or to men whose patents of gentility were only a generation old. William II's rhetoric about the necessity of preserving the aristocratic spirit in the officer corps fell more and more on the ears of aristocrats by ascription.[12] The system of commissioning officers definitely excluded social and political undesirables as defined by the establishment. The key to the process of stratification was the right of each regiment's officer corps to approve candidates for active and reserve commissions into its ranks—an approval that had to be unanimous. Even the kaiser was reluctant to influence the process, and would rarely approve the commission of a man who did not have his future comrades' assent. Anyone without the right pieces of paper, the right connections, or the right recommendations, found himself on the outside looking in.

The defects of this selection process have so often been stressed that they hardly require further comment here. The kaiser's officer corps was, however, neither retrograde nor unique in its approach. Characteristic of secondary institutions in modern societies is their tendency to maintain significant nonprofessional criteria for judging and advancing their members. Board rooms, city rooms, even college faculties, have their own ways of deciding just who qualifies for admission, and just who reaches the inner circle. Subjective qualities valued by the collective—gender, ethnicity, politics, behavior—can count for far more than objective qualifications. A Thatcherite in a British university of the 1980s, a Berkeley professor who voted for Reagan, was likely to know the same kind of loneliness as a closet liberal in the Prussian Guard.

Contemporary critics of the German officer corps tended to regard the principle of exclusivity as more important than any actual career opportunities that might be generated by its removal. To Walter Rathenau, denying him as a Jew the chance to become a reserve lieutenant reflected the empire's failure to use its elites properly. It did not mean he was unable to pursue an eagerly sought career as a professional officer.[13] The German army, moreover, softened the system's edges by maintaining within general limits a kind of free-market system of application. The very requirement of unanimity tended to make a candidate's final approval something of a formal process. The real weeding had been done earlier, frequently on the basis of common sense exercised by would-be officers and their families. The makeup and the attitude of a given regiment's officer corps were hardly secret. A candidate *prima facie* unsuitable in one regiment might be acceptable, or even welcome, in another. Thus while seven of the army's line cuirassier regiments had images as aristocratic strongholds, the 8th, stationed in Köln, was hospitable to the sons of bourgeois industrialists. Formations with undesirable garrisons or reputations often were in the embarrassing position of finding it difficult to attract candidates of any kind. The 44th Infantry, in the isolated town of Goldap on the Russian frontier, included 79 active officers in its ranks between 1905 and 1914. Fifty-four were transfers from other regiments. Of the 25 commissioned into the 44th, only 9 joined voluntarily. The other 16 were assigned from various cadet schools.[14]

The army's institutional structure paralleled that of society in that its pecking order was determined by such a complex combination of branch prejudices, family connections, traditions, and garrison locations that it is almost impossible to untangle from the perspective of another century. William II complicated the process by a general fondness for bestowing elaborate titles on his regiments. Formations that had for decades contented themselves with a simple number could suddenly sprout references to incidents and generals in Germany's remote military past. Nor was the gap between guard and line by any means as absolute as in Britain or Russia. Many smaller German counts maintained their own household regiments. Officers of Bavaria's *Leib-Regiment*, Württemberg's Queen Olga Grenadiers, or the Grand Duchy of Hesse's Bodyguard Infantry were no less proud of their service than the subalterns of "Christianity's Most Elegant Regiment," the 1st Foot Guards of Prussia. Within the Prussian Guard itself regiments looked down on some, swore drinking brotherhood with others. Thus in the 1880s the 1st Guard Dragoons considered themselves the finest of the cavalry regiments, and described their sister 2nd Guard Dragoons as representing the barrooms. The Guard Cuirassiers dismissed the 1st Dragoons as carpet-knights and dance floor heroes. The Uhlans, whose barracks were at some distance from the other three regiments, were excluded from this Morris dance of status.[15]

And so it went. Assignment to a tradition-encrusted formation garrisoned in rural Posen might or might not overbalance the advantages of a commission in a newly created regiment with a "high house number" stationed in or near a large city. The cavalry's pecking order of lancers, cuirassiers, hussars and dragoons involved such subtle permutations of respective dates of raising and respective feats of arms that everyone was comfortably able to feel superior to everyone else. While the artillery is frequently described as being socially beneath the other combat arms, the exact balance of status and career opportunities between a nonnoble lieutenant of Berlin's 3rd Brandenburg Artillery and an aristocrat assigned to the 172nd Infantry and stationed in the Alsatian market town of Neubreisach would have been by no means obvious to contemporaries.

For the mass of men in the ranks, the Imperial army played a major role in certifying and affirming male adulthood. The drastic changes in German society since the 1780s had invalidated many traditional male rites of passage. For women, menstruation and marriage remained the keys to adult status. Males had no equivalent generally acceptable ways of defining themselves as men. The peasant youth waiting to inherit a farm, the teenaged unskilled laborer living at home and contributing his paycheck to his parents, the junior clerk in a department store—all faced a similar problem. Their own in-group might have rituals, like the student *Mensur*, separating the men from the boys. These rituals, however, were likely to be meaningless or irrelevant to anyone else. At the same time, the young German man was part of a society laying significant stress on sex-role stereotypes and divisions. Nicolaus Sombart describes a *Männergesellschaft*, a rigid, militaristic, patriarchal social structure—but one with just enough fundamental doubts about its masculinity to give rise to an efflorescent homosexual movement, and to what Sombart calls *Männerbünder*: societies in which the feminine component in men found legitimate expression in male relationships.[16] One need not accept this argument entirely to see how in such a context military service could offer a useful psychological testing ground for males uncertain of their sexual identities.

Once in uniform the recruit found himself part of an institution whose challenges and rewards could provide balm for the wounds of modernization. The myths of both modern liberalism and traditional society asserted a direct, perceptible connection between endeavor and achievement. A man made his way through his own efforts, individually or in a group context—a contradiction more apparent to contemporary sociologists than real in the home towns and farming villages of Biedermeyer Germany. In the course of the nineteenth century, however, industrialization and agribusiness diminished to the vanishing point any links betwen those myths and everyday reality. The alienation of labor in mines and factories was paralleled by the resentments of clerks, postmen, and the rest of an emerging white-collar world, by the frustrations of independent peasants whose economic position was visibly declining, and even by the anger of farm laborers undercut by competition from the Russian Empire. The prizes, tangible and intangible, of the new Germany seemed either completely out of reach or bestowed by criteria incomprehensible to the average man. Hard work now pitted a man either against machines that wore him down and broke his spirit directly, or against a system impossible to comprehend, much less master.[17]

The army was different. It was ultimately designed to promote success instead of failure. No military organization can function if a significant percentage of its members cannot live up to its standards. The demands of the parallel bars, the rifle range, and the drill ground might be high, but they could be met—and not only by a chosen, exceptional few. One reason why so many Germans spoke so favorably of their military service is that they experienced there the kind of triumphs, visible and recognized, that would be denied them the rest of their working lives in an industrial society. A cigar or a mark piece from the captain, a chance to win one of the kaiser's medals, perhaps even promotion to *Gefreiter* towards the end of one's second or third year, might seem trifles to the opulent bourgeoisie of the late twentieth century. But such trifles, and the implications behind them, can often do far more to motivate behavior than the most high-flown abstract principles.

Once completed, military service came increasingly to be a gateway to the adult world. Marriage, permament employment, a place at the men's table in the local *Gasthaus*—all were associated, directly or indirectly, with a certificate of demobilization. Among adolescents and young adults, military service became a major demarcation line. This in turn tended to modify, if not entirely remove, resistance to the annual conscription. The way in which the process was conducted, with an entire age group inducted simultaneously, frequently in a festive environment, generated a collective spirit encouraging potential dissenters to keep their questions to themselves.

Nor was the prospective recruit entirely a pawn of fate. If he was willing to volunteer for conscription, he had the opportunity of exercising some choice of branch of service and formation. Popular regiments had waiting lists. Some senior officers grumbled that this led to an uneven distribution of high-quality manpower, with only the unambitious and the unqualified remaining to be allocated by the recruiting authorities.[18] The sense of participation more than balanced this disadvantage. Regimental commanders, moreover, frequently permitted their recruits to express a preference for a certain battery or company—a preference usually allowing some possibility of improving specific circumstances. Perhaps an older brother had served in Number 6. Perhaps the *Feldwebel* of Number 4 came from one's neighborhood. Perhaps the corporals of Number 10 were known not exactly to accept bribes, but to be suitably grateful for hospitality freely offered. Small choices can often appear more liberating than great ones. And anyone still wondering if his experience was really necessary could comfort himself with the observable and verifiable fact that he would return two or three years later a full-fledged adult by the standards of his peer group, his community, society in general-and probably in his own eyes as well.

The Prussian/German army's treatment of its conscript rank and file is generally presented in terms of a coherent attempt to socialize them into the existing order: to generate enthusiastic acceptance of capitalism and Christianity, to inspire support for monarchy and aristocracy and contempt for businessmen and politicians. It is not necessary to deny this interpretation in order to suggest another dimension. Between 1871 and 1914 it grew increasingly apparent to the military that the virtues of the modern soldier were so intertwined with those of the citizen that it was impossible either to separate them, or to tell where one set began and the other ended. The army's task was to emphasize their military aspects. Discipline imposed from above no longer enabled men to function on a modern battlefield. They needed instead what F. Scott Fitzgerald was later to describe as a "whole-souled sentimental equipment"—an equipment easier to describe than to develop in the context of an increasingly skeptical age.

Training the modern German soldier thus required a significant evolution in the army's concept of obedience. Formal discipline, the often-criticized *Kadavergehorsamkeit* of barracks and drill field, was a means to an end. It was not a structure for limiting human rights, or creating obedient citizens uninterested in demanding social changes. Formal discipline was rather the first step in maintaining control on the battlefield—in making patriotism and enthusiasm into military rather than martial virtues. The killing zones and the killing power of modern weapons made rapid movement and rapid decision essential. There would be no time for debate or reflection. Men had to be conditioned to respond promptly under extreme stress, stress having no civilian equivalent. A conscript, citizen army after a long period of peace would have no combat veterans able to inculcate by osmosis the necessity of automatic response in battle. The conditioning process must therefore be theoretical, and preferably involve something disagreeable enough to generate initial resistance. This was the real purpose of the German army's particularly rigorous close-order drill, despite constant abuse by officers afflicted by a fondness for precision as a military absolute, and despite the certainty of criticism by civilians and enlisted men who saw the whole process as anachronistic.

Emphasis on conditioned obedience was also designed to help soldiers cope with the emptiness of the modern battlefield. Theory and experience alike indicated that even the bravest of men could be shocked into incoherence by modern firepower. Even the most willing could become lost or confused, drop behind cover, straggle to the rear, or appear on the objective after the fighting was safely over. Casualties and confusion were certain to play havoc with command structures. No modern soldier could count on remaining part of a familiar group, or receiving orders from a familiar leader. He must learn to respond to ranks, not men—to accept as a rule of thumb that his superior was better fitted to cope with a military situation because he was a better soldier.[19]

The lessons of 1866 and 1870/71 suggested that only conscious commitment to a collective brought favorable results in modern war. The military system's negative sanctions posed a real threat to this commitment. Here the scholar encounters a paradox. On one hand, the empire's records are replete with horror stories indicating tolerance, indeed acceptance, of harsh treatment escalating into obscene brutality. On the other, most of those same records were generated by the army's efforts to solve the problem of mistreatment of enlisted men. The issue was a natural focus for interest group conflict. For socialists and liberals, tales of oppression illustrated the essential corruption of the military system. In an open society increasingly interested in scandal and exposé, human-interest anecdotes of suffering while in uniform sold books and newspapers.

The army's claim to be a training school of the citizen made it correspondingly sensitive to charges of failure in that area. Official spokesmen tended to respond with a mixture of denial and unctuous boys-will-be-boys declarations that a barracks was not a young ladies' seminary—not an approach calculated to enhance credibility. Specific cases, however, frequently had two sides. One might, for example, sympathize with a battery commander when some of his reservists undergoing a refresher course took the opportunity to get blind drunk. His description of the culprits as *Luder* and *Schweinigels* was not exactly refined. But his punishment of the drunks with a day's arrest appears positively mild even by modern standards. Even his initial desire to put the whole battery through extra drill hardly seems sadistic, particularly since he dropped the idea on reflection. And the account of the incident in the Socialist *Dresdner Volkszeitung* bears every sign of a manufactured scandal.[20]

Institutionally the army refused to whitewash mistreatment. Bad NCOs, declared the Prussian war minister in 1908, did more for social democracy than political agitators. Officers and NCOs were regularly reminded in their professional literature that men brutalized on the drill field could hardly be expected to follow their tormentors into battle. Orders urged fair treatment of recruits. Investigations produced a high rate of court-martials and convictions. Administrative discipline separated other flagrant offenders from the service quietly but permanently—and without pensions or civil service employment.[21]

Despite this apparent commitment to abolishing brutality, it remained a persistent thorn in the army's side. One explanation is simple: to dismiss the orders and exhortations as window-dressing. A more fruitful approach involves examining the army's ambiguous structural position in Imperial Germany. On one hand it assumed the role of a primary social institution, demanding ultimate loyalty from and control over its personnel while on active duty—a state within a state long before Hans von Seeckt. But the army was also a secondary institution, in that its primary justifying function was instrumental. It existed not to guarantee the welfare of its members but to *do* something. In secondary institutions, whether armies, corporations, or universities, abstract claims of justice tend to be balanced against a pragmatic need for results. The ultimate question becomes not "What is right?" but "What is required to complete most efficiently the task for which we are here?" A boxed ear, a kicked backside, or a series of imaginative comments on a soldier's ancestry and character deserve consideration in that context, as well as more familiar ones.

The German military establishment can hardly be exonerated from treating its draftees harshly. Officers and sergeants did not regard themselves as psychiatrists in uniform. A favorite contemporary joke involved a recruit asked by his regimental commander, "Who are the father and mother of your company?" He gave the expected answer: "The captain and the *Feldwebel*." When asked what he would like to become in the service, the new private promptly replied, "An orphan." Court-martial proceedings, civil trials, and orders from generals, kings, and emperors demonstrated that the army was no easy rite of passage. But an easy rite of passage is a contradiction in terms. In Western societies since at least the Renaissance, if not the Age of Pericles, males in particular have been conditioned against accepting the verdict of Lewis Carroll's Caucus Race: everyone has won and all must receive prizes. The fathers, uncles, and older brothers of Imperial Germany may have enjoyed telling horror stories about their time "with the Prussians," but they did not significantly discourage new generations of conscripts. Nor were men in their second and third years of service likely to be sympathetic to freshly shorn recruits undergoing their initial weeks of torment.

While it might be possible to apply Erich Fromm's concept of a sado-masochistic German bourgeoisie to the workers and peasants who made up the bulk of the army's rank and file, it seems more reasonable to conclude that on the whole, the everyday routine of peacetime service between 1871 and 1914 was not regarded as an unbearable strain on the average man in his early twenties. Exceptions were seen as just that— exceptions. If company offices were not crowded with men anxious to make the army their career, neither were guardhouses and military prisons filled with rebellious conscripts. The average German soldier of the empire was willing enough to put in his time. Negative sanctions, direct and indirect, combined with positive rewards of compliance to produce an annual intake of tractable recruits. Perhaps they deserved their nickname of *Hammel* in more ways than one. They were also useful raw material for any military establishment that understood its avowed task of preparing for war.

II

How well did the German army perform that task? Recent analyses present a military anachronism, dominated by an establishment unwilling to risk losing its social place by opening its professional eyes. Twentieth-century war demanded the radicalization of an institution committed to sustaining itself as part of a traditional, autocratic state structure. Faced with this choice, the German army preferred to place its strategic faith in a short, decisive war based on the gambler's gambit of the Schlieffen Plan. Its approaches to tactics were similarly retrogressive. Taking counsel from neither the lessons of contemporary wars nor the comments of foreign critics, the German army emphasized formal discipline and parade-ground drill, denied the effects of firepower, and ultimately drove massed formations of human cattle into the slaughter-pits of 1914.[22]

On both human and doctrinal levels, reality was more complex. S. L. A. Marshall once declared that when a soldier is known to those around him, he has reason to fear losing the one thing he is likely to value more than life: his reputation as a man among men. The structure of the German army was designed to foster this mutual knowledge. Administratively, operationally, emotionally, its focus was the army corps. Its recruiting district coincided wherever possible with provincial boundaries or historic regions. Its triumphs were the source of loyalties and traditions; Brandenburgers of III Corps, Pomeranians of II, Württembergers of XIII, all boasted their own histories and their own heroes. The corps was the largest, most prestigious military formation existing in peacetime. Command of one was the accepted capstone of a normally successful career. Beyond lay only the shadowy ephemera of army inspections, or the even less likely prize of chief of the general staff. Even these might seem mere baubles when compared to the power and the status a corps commander possessed in his own district.

The German army of 1914 had twenty-five active corps. They resembled the modern division in combining an essential mixture of the principal combat arms. Their strength had been originally calculated at the number of men that could come into action from a single road in a single day: about 30,000 fighting men. Additions, particularly of artillery and the ammunition columns needed to keep modern quick-firing guns in action, had increased both the numbers and the transport of a German corps substantially beyond that, to over 40,000 in 1914. Since such a force was far too large to move comfortably on one road, the primary operational unit tended more and more to become the division, a practice systematized in 1915 to compensate for a shortage of strategic reserves.

In many ways this was a second-best solution. In World War I a combat division was seldom able to operate without the support of arms and services pooled at corps level. As much to the point, morale and efficiency were fostered when divisions were familiar with their neighbors, and with the higher headquarters under which they operated. Until 1918 most French divisions were permanently assigned to a specific army corps. In the British Expeditionary Force, the vaunted efficiency of the Australian and Canadian divisions owed much to their concentration in the separate army corps of the respective dominions. The commander of a German active corps in 1914 was supposed to fight his formation as a single entity, not two divisions side by side. He controlled a major source of intelligence: a squadron of six aircraft. He had at his disposal one of the single strongest element of fire support in any of Europe's armies: a battalion of sixteen 150-millimeter howitzers, the best medium guns in the world. And he had his personality. His eccentricities, real or calculated, were familiar to his subordinates. Unlike his modern counterparts, shadowy figures to the divisions shuttling in and out of their control, a German corps commander expected to be known and recognized throughout his formation.

A German division commander's task was in some ways more complex than his superior's. Like most continental armies, Germany organized its higher formations by twos: two divisions to a corps, two brigades to a division, two regiments to a brigade. The four regiments were not a problem. A division with four regiments could simultaneously perform a principal and a secondary mission while retaining a reserve. This capacity was desirable during maneuvers, where seldom more than a corps or two were involved on either side and where formations did not have to worry so much about getting in each others' way. The brigade, however, seemed by 1914 an increasingly unnecessary link. The telephone and the automobile enabled a division commander to control his four regiments directly. On the other hand, abolishing the brigade would mean eliminating a large number of command positions for general officers in an army already concerned about the limitations of promotion to senior ranks. It was not quite an accident that such a widely respected military theorist as Friedrich von Bernhardi, when proposing an internal reorganization of the army corps, left the brigade structure intact. The high command's desire to create a strategic reserve quickly, rather than any obvious tactical considerations, motivated Germany's move to a three-regiment division in 1915. Even then, one brigade headquarters remained in each division, usually performing the role of a combat command.[23]

The two infantry brigades were supported by a regiment of cavalry—four squadrons, each around 170 "sabers" in official parlance. Since 1916 it has been militarily and academically fashionable to deride the cult of the horse. Critics overlook the fact that before World War I, cavalry was the only operationally mobile arm in existence. The internal-combustion engine was unreliable under operational conditions. The spectacular success of individual reconnaissance and combat operations by improvised mechanized units in 1914 should not obscure the fact that the early armored cars were essentially roadbound. Properly used in the kind of open warfare made possible by the geography of Eastern Europe, cavalry was seen as vital for successful offensive operations. The German army, however, was relatively weak in this arm, particularly when compared to the Russians. The military budget, despite its size, could not be stretched to accommodate larger mounted forces without sacrificing even more important elements.

This tended to foster caution among both the formers of German cavalry doctrine and the officers who implemented it. Cavalry could not be improvised. As both the Union's experience in the American Civil War and Great Britain's in South Africa indicated, it took upwards of three years to turn a man on a horse into a fighting trooper. Given the general expectations of a short war, it is hardly surprising that the cavalry regarded itself as a one-shot instrument, to be used and expended only at the decisive moment of a campaign. This attitude had at least as much to do with the arm's continued acceptance of shock tactics as did any nostalgic longings for the glory days of the *arme blanche*. For all their swagger, few German troopers really believed their arm could operate effectively against infantry or artillery under modern conditions. Instead they perceived their combat role as fighting other cavalry: the military equivalent of an exchange of knights in a chess game.

This mind-set had an unfortunate effect on those regiments unlucky enough—from their perspective—to be assigned as divisional cavalry instead of being massed in the mounted divisions and corps. Their principal mission of close-range reconnaissance, tended to be at best indifferently performed by horsemen seeking opportunities for mounted action even on a troop or squadron level. Nor did the divisional cavalry seek to develop its potential as a mobile reserve of firepower.[24]

Far more important to a German divisional commander was his artillery brigade. It had two regiments, each with two eighteen-gun battalions: a total of seventy-two pieces. Fifty-four of them, three battalions, were flat-trajectory 77-millimeter cannon. Their design represented one of the major examples of premature rearmament in the modern era. The German field artillery of the early 1890s was equipped with a gun whose basic design dated back to 1873, so clearly obsolete that the war ministry ignored the protests of technicians and introduced the C/96 field gun just a year before France revolutionized field artillery with the famous French 75. Its steel shield, long range, and hydropneumatic recoil rendered all existing guns obsolescent. Russia in 1902 and Great Britain in 1904 introduced their own version of the quick-firing cannon. Germany was unable to afford the cost of two complete rearmaments in less than a decade. While pundits found fault with the 75, technicians fussed over the C/96, giving it a shield, an improved recoil mechanism, better sights, and redesigned ammunition. The resulting FK 96 nA (Modified Field

Gun 96), introduced after 1905, had neither the range, the accuracy, nor the rate of fire of its entente counterparts. Its high wheels gave it a vaguely antique appearance compared to the sleek, deadly *soixante-quinze* or the businesslike 18-pounder. The German gun had one advantage that would prove useful in the eastern theater: it was mobile. Its light weight and large wheels made it less likely than any of its rivals to bog down in mud or sand, or to exhaust horses pulling it on short rations. But when it came to fighting, professionalism would have to compensate for material in three-fourths of Germany's field artillery.

The division's fourth artillery battalion was far better off. Since the Franco-Prussian War, German gunners had been committed to support a doctrine of the offensive. This involved developing a capacity to shoot over the hill, to search out trenches and covered positions with high explosive. Around the turn of the century the German army had adopted a 105-millimeter field howitzer, a state-of-the-art design unsurpassed by anything in Europe. By 1914 each division had a full battalion of them. So while one artillery regiment had two battalions of conventional 77-millimeter field guns, the other had one gun and one howitzer battalion. The problems this posed for both decentralized and direct fire support are obvious. Assigning a howitzer battery to each gun battalion was rejected as diminishing the effect of their high-angle fire. Kept in the chain of command, the howitzer battalion had a deplorable tendency never to be where it was needed. Placing it under the direct control of the division commander, on the other hand, left one artillery colonel with nothing to do except supervise his remaining battalion—a waste of a senior officer and his staff. But shortcomings in the artillery's command structure were more than balanced by the multiple uses of howitzers in a war that even in the east tended almost immediately to become a war of entrenchments.[25]

For all of the emphasis on World War I as a war of machines, the dirty work was still done by the foot soldier. A German infantry regiment included just over three thousand of them, distributed among three four-company battalions. The regiment was likely to be the highest formation of which the soldier was directly aware. It was the regimental flag before which he swore his oaths of loyalty. It was the regiment's number painted on the canvas cover of his helmet. It was the regiment's history he heard in the rainy-day lectures. But as a cult object the regiment was more likely to engage the identities of the officers. For the rank and file, loyalty was more likely to be developed at the levels British sociologist Anthony Sampson describes as the "pack" and the "tribe." The German soldier's "pack" in 1914 was his squad or *Gruppe*: eight men and a lance-corporal. Still more of an administrative unit and an affinity group than the tactical formation of later years, the squad was correspondingly less significant than the individual's "tribe," his company. The company was the private soldier's primary source of promotions and punishments, reprimands and soft jobs. It was also something more. In theory the battalion had long been considered the basic tactical unit, the largest formation a single officer can control in combat. In practice, modern firepower meant prior to 1914 that role devolved on the company, with its 250 rifles commanded by a captain. Within weeks in the field even platoons of eighty men proved far too large for one man to command as a unit; the German infantry began that articulation into squads and sections under NCOs with independent responsibilities that contributed so much to its combat efficiency in both world wars.[26]

The German infantryman went to war carrying a rifle that was just a cut below the best available. The *Gewehr 98* was a Mauser design. Sturdy and reliable enough, it was bulkier and clumsier than the British Lee-Enfield and the U.S. M1903 Springfield, neither as rapid firing as the British weapon nor as accurate as the American. These points were, however, less significant in an army much less interested in individual aimed shots than in producing concentrated, controlled bursts at the right time. This was not merely a manifestation of skepticism at the prospect of turning the average German conscript into a Daniel Boone. Field tests, even under artificial peacetime conditions, demonstrated time after time that an exaggerated emphasis on individual marksmanship, the approach fostered by imperial awards to the army's best shots, was less important than volume of fire, with the first round placed somewhere near the target and the rest more or less in the same place.[27]

Another clear indication of the German army's appreciation of the potential of massed small-caliber fire was the new organization most German regiments were taking into the field: a thirteenth company, manning six water-cooled Maxim automatic machine guns. The German army had introduced this weapon not for its defensive potential, but for its perceived uses in preparing and supporting the offensive. After the turn of the century an increasing number of voices suggested that this "concentrated essence of infantry" be massed as a reserve of firepower at the disposal of higher commanders, either to enable riflemen to be massed for an attack or to support that attack by concentrated fire on selected positions. They particularly stressed the value of the extremely accurate Maxim-model guns once the artillery had to cease fire for fear of destroying its own men. Given suitable enfilade positions, machine guns could play on an objective until the very moment an assault was pushed home. Other military futurologists foreshadowed the use of machine guns for offensive barrages in the way best developed in the British army of 1917/18: firing indirectly on ranged lines, borrowing techniques of observation and control from the artillery.[28]

Emphasis on the tactical offensive was in no sense an unconsidered decision. The difficulties accompanying attack under modern conditions were recognized and accepted in Germany long before the first rounds were fired from the guns of August. But no army, however confident in its generals' abilities, could afford to base its doctrines on the assumption that enemies would be obliging enough to dash themselves to pieces on one's own rifles, artillery, and machine guns. Some time, somehow, it would be necessary to go forward—to go through.

The generals of Imperial Germany were not particularly bloodthirsty. They perceived that the best way for them to maintain and enhance their class position was to win any future war decisively, while sacrificing as few German lives as possible. The best way to do this was to produce infantrymen able and willing to advance on the modern battlefield. Since the seventeenth century a concept of battle had been developing in Europe and in Germany—a concept too often submerged under vitalist rhetoric about battles of annihilation and the mystique of cold steel. The deficiencies of drawing up masses of men to mow each other down had been plain since the days of Gustavus Adolphus. Even at its most effective the process resembled a duel at ten paces with submachine guns. Victory was meaningless if its price became too high; even Napoleon's conscripts were not an infinitely self-renewing force.

Instead of killing an enemy in place, the essential craft of war involved convincing him to run and *then* killing him. To achieve this, it was necessary to concentrate superior force at one point. "Force" in this context meant to the German army a combination of firepower, numbers, and moral superiority. Experience indicated that all three were required. Fire action by itself was not decisive. Infantry skirmishes could wear down an enemy but were as a rule unable to do more for a very human reason. Once an advance stopped and men spread out to fire their weapons, it was difficult if not impossible to get them moving again. Yet move they would have to. A line of skirmishers doing no more than blazing away at defenders increasingly likely to be concealed behind improvised fieldworks, was an open invitation to attrition on the wrong side of the balance sheet—and to the drawn-out, murderous, indecisive battles characteristic of the Napoleonic Era or the American Civil War. The problem was exacerbated as improved weapons made traditional maneuvers like the cavalry charge, or the concentration of masses of guns to blow apart an enemy's front at close range, less and less feasible alternatives to the forward movement of the infantryman.[29]

That movement posed a comprehensive challenge to all levels, from commanding general to rear-rank private. It required preparation: precisely coordinating infantry movements and artillery support, timing attacks to the minute, providing adequate reserves to exploit success. But the attack demanded above all striking an exact balance between dispersion and control in order to maintain momentum.

The industrial revolution, with its unique challenges to human flexibility, offered grounds for optimism in all of these areas. If the sons of men conditioned for generations to the peasant's plow or the artisan's bench could be socialized by the hundreds of thousands into mills and factories, then surely civilians could be taught in two or three years of peacetime active service how to use terrain, act independently, and respond to orders even on the empty modern battlefield. Images of the nineteenth-century industrial worker frequently suggest or imply that factory routine itself dulled the mind. The reverse was far more likely to be the case. Participation in a modern industrial plant demanded degrees of alertness and cooperation that were mentally and physically exhausting.

The miner, the mill hand, the iron worker, could rarely afford the luxury of detaching his mind from what his hands did, or from what his workmates were doing.[30]

What civilian employers could do, the German army saw itself able to do even better. Far from being stagnant or retrograde, the German army recognized more clearly than most of its critics the single most difficult problem of modern warfare: getting soldiers not only to advance under fire, but to accomplish something by advancing. In war, as in so many other human endeavors, the necessary tends to become the possible. But in fact nothing in the small wars of the twentieth century indicated that infantrymen could no longer attack successfully against modern firepower. No one in Germany argued that the process of advancing was easy—only that it was still feasible under the right conditions. The revised drill regulations of 1906 recommended in paragraph after paragraph the need to develop "inner assertiveness," a compulsion to reach the objective before one's neighbors, to charge to the music of bugles and to shouts of "Hurrah!" But German tactics also reflected growing appreciation of the lessons of the Boer War, the Russo-Japanese War, and the two Balkan Wars. Inadequate preparation, clumsy formations, and one-sided reliance on enthusiasm brought defeat to British and Japanese, to Bulgars, Serbs, and Greeks indiscriminately.[31]

The craft of war in the twentieth century, at least as practiced in the Western world, has increasingly focussed on substituting the internal-combustion engine for men's muscles and will power. In the absence of such technology it was not romanticism but hard, practical considerations that led the kaiser's army to concentrate as heavily as it did on human factors.

These were particularly important in an army of mobilized civilians. Almost half the men in every active infantry regiment at war strength were reservists; the proportion in the artillery was only slightly lower. Entire regiments, divisions, and army corps were composed of these hostilities-only soldiers. The German army is frequently credited with being far ahead of its continental contemporaries in recognizing the martial virtues of the citizen in uniform. Unlike the French and Russians, who treated their reserve formations as second-line troops suited only for garrison duty or subsidiary missions, the Germans used their reserve units alongside the active ones, giving them the same tasks and assuming the same levels of proficiency.

A military system increasingly committed to the concept of a short war, sandwiched between two powerful and determined enemies, saw little advantage in maintaining a large pool of individual replacements. Keeping combat units up to strength was not seen as a significant problem by German planners in the years before 1914. What was important was putting the largest possible organized force in the field in the shortest possible time. From the 1890s, the German army earmarked an increasing number of reservists for separate formations. These, unlike the *Honvéd* and *Landwehr* of Austria, or the Russian reserve units before the Russo-

Japanese War, existed entirely on paper, with no peacetime cadre. A small number of active officers would be transferred to them on mobilization, primarily as staff officers or company and battalion commanders. The rest of the command positions would be filled by men from civilian life: NCOs who had completed their twelve years of service, officers retired into the reserve, or commissioned and promoted as reservists. For them, and even more for the men they led, faith in the system as a whole and confidence in its component parts were all-important, particularly in the first days of war.[32]

The German army's morale was more than a temporary creation of blaring bands and cheering civilians. It was more as well than the belligerence of ignorance. Most accounts of World War I stress the naïvete with which Europe's youth rushed to arms—a mixture of generational awareness, belligerent rhetoric, and a commitment to abstract ideals of heroism at best obsolescent in an age of industrial war. Germany is a particularly fruitful source of supporting images. Trainloads of young men gaily sing "Die Wacht am Rhein" on their way to be slaughtered; others even younger scream the "Deutschandlied" as they charge into British rifles at Langemarck. Stefan Zweig, Erich Maria Remarque, even the fire-eaters like Werner Beumelberg or Ernst Jünger, fill their pages with tales of innocence sacrificed at Verdun or on the Somme, with the resulting emotional discord contributing to a postwar generation at once terribly lost and tragically vulnerable.[33]

This process of disillusionment must not be exaggerated. Unlike their counterparts in the English-speaking countries, German men were part of a society with a long tradition of compulsory military service. Those who took the field in August were not the schoolboys whose dying lent such poignance to the *Langemarck-Mythos* on one hand and *Im Westen nichts Neues* on the other. They were overwhelmingly either serving soldiers or men who had worn uniforms earlier in their lives. This generated a high level of cultural familiarity with the army. The men who marched to the sound of the guns of August had a broad spectrum of concrete expectations—but these concerned what might be called their working conditions, rather than the nature of the war itself. The German soldier, whether serving conscript or long-discharged reservist, saw himself as part of an institution incorporating both the rectitude of certitude and a significant technical competence. Much of the content of British or American military reminiscences in the twentieth century involves the superiority of the individual soldier, particularly the narrator, to an insensitive, indifferent, essentially inefficient system. German soldiers, on the other hand, not only went to war in an atmosphere of patriotic enthusiasm, but had their enthusiasm reinforced by the army's capacity to give at least the appearance of knowing what it was doing.

The German army of 1914 was by no means as good as its press releases. It had, however, kept steady pace with developments in material and doctrine. It had paid close attention to the lessons of the world's recent battlefields. The kaiser's army had not gone down to the operational dead end of the French in 1940, or the United States in Vietnam. It clearly recognized an uncomfortable ultimate: victory in war depends on advancing. Unlike the British, with their suspicion of any kind of theory, unlike republican France, whose soldiers were expected to replace skill at arms with patriotic zeal, the Germans attempted to respond to the problem by producing men with both the psychological and the professional equipment to survive on the modern battlefield. Emphasis in principle on dispersion and articulation put the German army on the right tactical track, even if that emphasis was not sufficiently developed to antedate directly the infiltration and stormtroop methods of the world war.

While questions of initiative and flexibility are more difficult to resolve, the evidence suggests that discipline did not drive independence out of German heads, nor did the German rank and file have to be led everywhere. German snipers and German patrols were respected by their western front adversaries, including the Canadians and the Australians. As in any mass army, some formations were excellent and others were a liability. In the course of four years, the same company might on one occasion collapse without its officers and sergeants, and another time carry on to the last man under the senior surviving private.

Yet if Germany's direct preparation for war was not necessarily impractical, it was theoretical. Relevant battle experience was virtually nonexistent at all levels. Some of the senior generals had been subalterns in 1870. A few adventurous company officers had served against the Herero in Southwest Africa—too few to be a major source of wisdom and advice on what to do when the ammunition was live. The German army of 1914, in short, was a brittle instrument. The first shocks of war might temper it, but they might just as possibly break it. No one could in his heart really be sure what was going to happen—particularly in the context of the eastern front.

III

Germany had gone to war in good part from fear of Russia—specifically, fear of a massive Russian invasion. How real had the anxiety been? With hindsight sharpened by exile, Russia's military memoirists described their 1914 offensive as a sacrificial gambit made to fulfil a moral obligation to their French ally by relieving the German pressure in the west. Soviet scholars too present the relationship between France and Russia in terms similar to George and Lenny in John Steinbeck's *Of Mice and Men*: the weak-minded, good-hearted giant, more or less controlled by his smaller and smarter comrade. In fact, an offensive into East Prussia made strategic sense in its own right. The alternate possibility of a direct attack westward into Silesia from Russian Poland looked promising on maps—especially French maps. Russia's ally had repeatedly urged such a blow in the years before 1914. Launching it, however, would expose the force involved to counterattacks from north and south against increasingly long flanks. A Napoleon, facing Napoleon's opponents, might have taken the risk. Russian planners had too much respect for the German army not to seek an easier solution, one exploiting advantages bestowed by geography and history. The salient was Germany's most obvious geographic weak point. Apart from this, East Prussia's assumed cultural and political importance in the Second Empire seemed to guarantee that the German army—or at least that part of it left in the east—would stand, fight, and be crushed.

The operational plans for that happy contingency were the product of a series of ambiguities. The size and hererogeneity of the Rusian officer corps combined with the army's broad spectrum of missions to enhance professional diversity. More than any of their European counterparts, Russian officers differed strikingly from each other in status, education, and attitudes. In the face of its unpopularity among the intelligentsia and the middle classes, in the face of aristocratic contempt for a military career except within strictly limited parameters, the Russian army tended to accept and retain what it could get. Unlike their German colleagues, Russian officers also developed a broad spectrum of professional orientations based on alternate forms of experience. Service in the Caucasus or Siberia could generate perspectives on the empire's military needs that were quite different from those cultivated in St. Petersburg, or on the western border. Unlike the situation in France, such officers were not encapsulated as "colonials." A more legitimate comparison might be to the U.S. army of the post-Vietnam era, with its ongoing debate between those officers advocating a focus on the "real soldiering" of NATO's central front and those insisting that the coming threats to vital U.S. interests would be posed in Latin America, Africa, or other regions demanding low-intensity and unconventional war-fighting capacities.

The growing institutional rivalry between the war ministry and the general staff after 1905 was the tip of a structural iceberg. Neither the army's professionalism nor its corporate spirit were strong enough to create an integrated officer corps from variegated material. More and more officers, particularly in the field grades, considered their career to depend less on competence than on an interlocking network of favors and patronage whose distribution depended on both sponsorship by and identification with a major power group. Administrative decisions, command appointments, and operational policies alike reflected increasingly bitter, increasingly complicated power struggles by men who saw not only their own futures but the destiny of the state as depending on the "right" decision in each case.[34]

Russian military thought, particularly after 1905, correspondingly tended to be centrifugal rather than cohesive. The work of the uniformed intellectuals documented attitudes as opposed to inspiring analysis. While this kind of solipsism was no more prevalent in Russia than anywhere else in Europe, the bases of the various arguments were far enough apart to ensure an army divided against itself doctrinally as well as institutionally. The major fault line lay between Westernizers and nativists: those who favored deliberate, conscious adjustment to the demands of industrial technology, following models developed in France and Germany, and those who emphasized Russian experiences with an eye to strengthening the internal cohesion and moral force of the Russian army. This was by no means a simple division between reformers and traditionalists, materialists and vitalists. Both factions were concerned with Russia's response to the demands of modern war. Would it be short or long? Should the state plan for total mobilization, or prepare to fight and win with the resources on hand? What was the proper balance between moral and material factors?

Whatever their specific perspectives, since the 1870s Russia's generals, like their German counterparts, had focussed on the worst-case contingency: Russia alone in a war with Germany and Austria. The strategic policies developed against this background by no means reflected unrelieved belligerence. Much professional literature stressed the dual historical mission of the Tsarist empire: transmitting European culture to the peoples of Asia while defending the West from Oriental barbarians. In this context, even offensive war against one or more Western powers was considered "military," as oppposed to "political," in nature, a temporary manifestation of maladjusted diplomacy.

In the 1870s Russia's first modern war minister, D. I. Miliutin, had consistently argued against risking any conflict with a coalition of the Western states. This initial support for a cautious strategy of building up strong forces behind the frontiers and awaiting the enemy's attacks gave way during the 1880s to a policy of preparing active operations against Austria combined with a passive, defensive posture towards Germany. The new approach combined military and political considerations. The Habsburg Empire was both Russia's obvious diplomatic adversary and an enemy Russia's generals were confident of defeating. Germany was a dangerous military opponent, but also a potential mediator of armed conflict between her eastern neighbors as she so often mediated diplomatic disputes. Common sense suggested the wisdom of antagonizing her as little as possible, particularly given the risks of forcing battle with the finest army in Europe.

Feelings of admiration, envy, and inferiority generated an attitude of deference reinforced by the relative failure of Russian intelligence to provide much inside information on the German military. On the other hand, a series of extremely successful intelligence operations against Austria not only resulted in an imbalance of material on the Central Powers, but encouraged a tendency to exaggerate both Austrian weaknesses and German strengths.

Russia was by no means ill-informed of the general outlines of prospective German moves. As early as 1891, the Russian chief of staff explained to his French counterpart his plans for checking a German attack towards the Niemen while delaying the armies of the Dual Alliance in Poland until reinforcements arrived from the interior. His description of the Central Powers' probable strategy and force structures fit the German and Austrian intentions at the time almost exactly.

Discussions of striking first, of mounting a spoiling offensive into East Prussia from the Niemen line, gave way to a more cautious approach during the 1890s. This reflected Russia's increasing concentration on central Asia and the Far East. It also reflected the unacceptable financial and diplomatic costs of preparing in peacetime an infrastructure for an immediate, full-strength onslaught against Germany. Some general staff officers argued, particularly in the company of the French attachés, the moral advantages of beginning the next war with a decisive victory over Germany. Nevertheless the policy of concentrating against Austria continued to prevail. When pressed for specifics, its advocates said the Russian army would take the offensive on the twenty-fifth day of mobilization and crush the Austrians no more than ten days later. Within another ten days Russia would be ready to strike for Berlin.

This optimism was unconvincing to the French general staff. Between 1900 and 1905 it continued to press for a Russian strategy designed to draw German troops from the western theater by striking at the vulnerable East Prussian salient. Russia's generals continued to temporize. Despite an increasing weight of evidence that the Germans proposed to remain on the defensive in the east, the tsarist high command never quite abandoned belief that their country might after all be the target of the main German attack. Their anxieties were enhanced by the Russo-Japanese War. In the minds of Russian planners, defeat exposed Russia's weaknesses in a way that invited exploitation. Nor were they certain after 1905 that France could be relied on, particularly if the *casus belli* turned out to be a Russo-Austrian dispute focused on Eastern Europe. In the annual meetings of the French and Russian general staffs, Russian generals repeatedly stressed the difficulties of mounting an offensive with an army that in Manchuria had proved so deficient in training and endurance. Yet they also remained aware that France needed Russia far too badly to terminate the relationship because of a dispute over the timing of an offensive. And it was in this context of confidence that the general staff began preparing and implementing an alternative strategy taking advantage of Russia's historic strengths.[35]

Part of the planning for war with Japan had involved questioning what to do in case of a surprise attack by the Central Powers while Russia was occupied in Asia. The solution was obvious and traditional: mobilize and concentrate in the heart of Russia, abandon the Polish salient and the western fortresses, and allow the enemy to exhaust itself in endless marches and debilitating siege operations. This approach was brought out of the sphere of emergency procedures in the writings of General N. P. Mikhnevich, professor at the general staff Academy from 1904 to 1907. Mikhnevich was more than a spokesman for Russia's past as a guide to future operations. He was the closest thing to a grand strategist produced in the empire's final years. Accepting the familiar argument that developed, industrial economies could not sustain long wars, Mikhnevich argued that Russia should adopt a defensive strategic posture, accompanied by a comprehensive plan for developing the national economy along lines favorable to national security. Denied a chance to win the quick victories demanded by their socio-economic systems, Russia's future opponents would face domestic chaos at the same time their armies were bearing the brunt of Russia's fully mobilized forces.[36]

Mikhnevich's proposals made a strong initial impression on Sukhomlinov. They blended well both with the need to buy time to complete the post-1905 reform programs, and with such manifestations of reform as increased territorialization of recruitment and more money for the field army at the expense of the fortress network. By 1910 the revised Russian war plan proposed not only to abandon the Polish salient and the Narew River line, but to concentrate a maximum of fifty-three divisions against Germany and only nineteen against Austria. Its principal sponsors, Sukhomlinov in the war ministry and Yuri Danilov in the general staff, were not acting from pessimism. Danilov was a worst-case planner, conscious of the limits of Russia's power and accepting a corresponding need for caution in war and politics. He also regarded Russia's initial defensive orientation to be merely the prelude to a massive counterattack into East Prussia and Silesia. Sukhomlinov for his part argued that fixed fortifications encouraged committing field armies in all the wrong places. Troops concentrated in the interior provinces, on the other hand, could quickly be brought to war strength with reliable reservists, then sent forward on a railway network whose efficiency was rapidly improving thanks to recent and projected French loans. Like Danilov, Sukhomlinov insisted to the French at every opportunity that Russia's war plans were essentially offensive. It made no sense, he asserted, to concentrate masses of troops in an exposed salient like Russian Poland. Nor were fortifications being razed haphazardly. Those which could not be improved were being abandoned, not destroyed. Russia would not advance prematurely, but her strategy was sound in providing for concentrating against and defeating the strongest enemy first, at minimum risk to either coalition partner.[37]

From the beginning this plan generated a broad spectrum of opposition. Westernizers saw its defensive aspects as violating the principles of war as understood everywhere across the Vistula. Nationalists and traditionalists cited Russia's centuries of experience against Turkey, Prussia, and France to prove their case that the best way of fighting a war is on someone else's territory. As early as 1898 a comprehensive history of Russia at war proudly asserted that thirty-six of the empire's thirty-eight campaigns since 1700 had been offensive.[38] Operational commanders criticized abandoning or downgrading the fortresses, and questioned the tactical wisdom of concentrating so far in Russia's interior. Diplomats argued that French good will was being sacrificed to unnecessary caution. And from all points of the spectrum, Danilov's and Sukhomlinov's critics argued that Russia's new strategy was aimed at the wrong enemy. It reflected expectations of a massive German offensive, twenty-five divisions or more. An overwhelming weight of evidence, including maneuvers, staff rides, and similar relatively public events, indicated instead that Germany would initially deploy no more than token forces in the east, and would pursue a correspondingly defensive strategy.

This made Austria Russia's strongest immediate enemy in case of a war between the alliance systems. Events in the Balkans since 1908 suggested, moreover, that France was not to be relied on to support Russia's interests there—which made unilateral Russian action against Austria-Hungary at least a thinkable possibility. In either case, an invasion of Galicia was likely to have significant impact on the attitudes of the Balkan states and the Dual Monarchy's Slavs. Finally, it was significantly risky for a great power to resign so completely the strategic initiative. If Russia waited for a German offensive that never came, and if things went badly for the French, Russia might well face a German-Austrian coalition by herself. Did it not make better sense to concentrate against and eliminate Austria at the start of the next war, then deal, militarily or politically, with a Germany which even in the worst-case contingency was virtually sure to be bled white by her struggle with France?[39]

Eighteen months of debate fueled by personal as well as professional disagreements resulted in a compromise. In May, 1912, Russian plans were changed again, this time to provide for two possible concentrations. Case G was based on facing the main armies of both Germany and Austria. It provided for forty-three divisions to be sent against Germany and thirty-one against Austria. Case A presumed that Russia would face the full strength of Austria, plus whatever forces Germany could spare after completing its concentration against France. It provided for the commitment of forty-five divisions in an all-out blow against Austria, leaving approximately thirty divisions for the German theater.

The question was what those thirty divisions were to do. At its most insouciant the Russian general staff never envisioned dividing their forces into roughly equal parts, then mounting two major offensives along divergent lines of advance, west into Germany and southwest into Austria. Case G initially projected three Russian armies driving into East Prussia along interior lines to cut off and destroy German forces in the province, while the Austrian sector remained passive. Though this might be the less likely strategic contingency, it continued to engage a certain undercurrent of pessimism regarding Russia's actual prospects in a war with the Central Powers.

Russian military planners, whatever their other differences, agreed that under no circumstances could Russia successfully fight Germany and Austria by herself. They were correspondingly dubious regarding the capacity of Russia's foreign office to keep Germany out of any Russo-Austrian conflict. Under these circumstances, might not Russia's most prudent course be to accept risks at the beginning of a conflict in order to ensure that France would not be crippled or overrun? Like its counterparts everywhere in Europe, the Russian army accepted the offensive as the strongest form of war at all levels, strategic, operational, and tactical. Particularly against the Germans, with their powerful, flexible army, losing the initiative anywhere could be the first step to disaster. A war game held in April, 1914, even evaluated the possibility of a partially mobilized Russian army attacking a superior German force. But this was presented as the result of a German pre-emptive strike into Russia—a response, in other words, to the kind of contingency that Plans G and A were supposed to avoid.

The distribution of forces under Case A in the 1912 plan also enhanced pressure for an offensive in the north. While the latter plan officially provided for no more than a holding action against Germany, the most pessimistic general staffer was reluctant to act on the assumption that thirty divisions, almost five hundred battalions, with full complements of cavalry and artillery, could not be risked against what amounted to Germany's military leftovers, particularly in the context of a mobilization plan and a railway system sufficiently improved by 1913 to provide eight or nine corps facing Prussia by the fifteenth day of mobilization, and the impressive total of twenty-four corps ready for deployment against the Central Powers by $M + 20$.

Russia's promise, made in August, 1913, of an offensive against Germany beginning on $M + 15$, and the tsar's accompanying assurance that France could have absolute confidence in the Russian army, were ultimately the product of internal decisions rather than external pressure whatever its reasons.[40] French encouragement, moral and financial, to improve the strategic railway network was incorporated into Russia's own changing war plans. The government cheerfully used French loans to build tracks and sidings on the Austrian frontier as well as the German. French military and political leaders, increasingly convinced of the likelihood of war in the years before 1914, were aware of this, but convinced of the need to maintain Russian good will at virtually any cost—as long as the tsar's army crossed the German frontier at the outbreak of war.

In August, 1914, the Germans in East Prussia faced many fewer battalions than the five hundred originally projected. Three active corps were diverted on mobilization to Warsaw as the core of an improvised army, which was to make a direct attack into Silesia once the victories on the flanks, in Galicia and East Prussia, were secured. Russian commanders also left large garrisons in fortresses far behind the frontier. Most of these were reserve formations, but in their absence the Russian active corps were forced to shed an ever-increasing number of companies and battalions for local security duties as they moved towards the frontier.[41]

This attrition of first-line combat strength was not unjustified. The Russians were concentrating in an area whose dominant civil populations, Poles, Lithuanians, and Jews, might well prove hostile given the opportunity. Strong guards on bridges, railroad junctions, and power stations were an insurance policy rather than an indulgence.[42] Russian reserve formations in 1914, unlike their German counterparts, were not particularly efficient. Limiting them to garrison roles was more a recognition of fact than an exercise in fecklessness. Several reserve divisions intended to take over security in the field armies' rear were being formed in the interior of Russia. Their arrival in the theater of operations would, however, take time—and time was something the Russians did not have.

Russia's performance in the Tannenberg campaign has been so universally excoriated that it is easy to forget that Russia's front and army commanders were not deliberately trying to lose. The senior officers assigned to the northern theater of operations were familiar enough with their adversary's probable behavior. Apart from the logic suggested by the terrain, twenty years of German maneuvers and war games had played variations on the same scenario of defeating the Russians in detail. This made the Russians' task significantly easier. Reasonable perception of an enemy's intentions is the first step in their frustration, and there appeared no reason why the newly formed Northwest Front should not have an excellent chance to win a set of victors' laurels.

As early as August 3, when it was plain that Germany's main effort was in fact being made in the west, the Russian high command, the Stavka, began debating whether more troops should be sent against East Prussia. But even with detachments and shortages, the theater seemed to have all the men and guns it needed. Only four active German corps, the three in East Prussia and V Corps from Posen, remained in the east, and V Corps was expected—accurately—to leave within days. Against them the Russian 1st Army, six active infantry divisions, a rifle brigade, and five and a half cavalry divisions, would advance westward from the Niemen. The 2nd Army, with an initial assigned strength of eight and a half active divisions, a rifle brigade, and four divisions of cavalry, would move northwest from the Warsaw salient and the Narew River.

The Russian plan depended more on finesse and less on brute force than is generally conceded. The two armies were expected to coordinate their movements, one moving north of the Masurian Lakes, the other south and west of them. The Northwest Front's optimal strategic goal was a double envelopment, with one army pinning the Germans in place and extending around their flank while the other struck their rear. Should the Germans stand and fight anywhere, a single envelopment seemed certain given the Russian numbers. And should they retreat towards the Vistula, a vastly superior Russian cavalry would have its chance to turn the movement into a rout.[43]

The Russian army, like all of its European counterparts, had spent a century grappling with the challenge of institutionalizing competence. Through the Napoleonic Era the craft of war had been mastered, particularly at the higher levels, by apprenticeship. Every campaign involved a process of shaking loose the generals who had exceeded their level of ability and replacing them with men better able to learn from experience. A scientifically minded nineteenth century encouraged the alternate approach of forming leaders by a process of continuing training, schooling, and tests. Birth and connections were still vitally important, particularly in Russia. They were, however, no longer the *ne plus ultra* of major command and staff assignments.

In this context Yakov Zhilinski, commanding the Northwest Front, was in many ways the model of a modern Russian general. Commissioned into the cavalry, he later attended the staff academy, graduating in 1883. Most of his duty over the next twenty years was in staff and liaison assignments. During the Russo-Japanese War, his efficient service as chief of staff in Manchuria marked him as a comer. A series of escalating staff and command responsibilities brought him to the post of chief of staff of the whole army in 1911. He established a reputation as a firm Francophile—at least to his French opposite numbers. He also became identified as a supporter of Sukhomlinov by his acceptance of the latter's drive to assert the war ministry's control over the general staff.

Zhilinski's assignment in 1914 to command the Warsaw military district was not a routine transfer, but neither was it a demotion. Given the chronically disturbed state of Russo-Polish relations, the Warsaw assignment had a significant domestic political dimension. The previous incumbent, appointed during the revolution of 1905, had been reasonably effective in conciliating the Poles but was not highly regarded as a soldier. His sudden death cleared the way for a new emphasis. Rumor in St. Petersburg even had Sukhomlinov taking that post, with Zhilinski succeeding him as war minister—a miscalculation of the balance of power between the two men that nevertheless indicated Warsaw's importance.

Mobilization plans designated the Warsaw district's commander as commander of the Northwest Front, Russia's main effort against Germany. Zhilinski's appointment made excellent sense in terms of coalition politics. As chief of staff he had repeatedly promised the French that Russia would undertake a prompt offensive against Germany. His presence in Warsaw was a reassurance that Russia would in fact turn words to deeds should war break out. In professional terms Zhilinski was clearly identified as a soldier, as opposed to an administrator in uniform. His extensive staff experience was expected to be vital in coordinating the movements of his two armies in executing a complex plan. It was true that he had shown no signs of possessing a great commander's talents. On the other hand, neither did his career indicate that he did *not* possess such talents. It did reflect a reasonable capacity for rising to occasions, and this was about as much as any army making the transition to a general war could expect from its senior leaders.

Zhilinski's principal subordinates were slightly better-known quantities. Pavel Rennenkampf became chief of the 1st Army when his Vilna Military District mobilized. A Baltic German by birth, he was a staff academy graduate who had made his reputation in the cavalry, seeing action in China in 1900, commanding a division in Manchuria in 1904–05, and most recently suppressing revolutionaries in Russia itself. Rennenkampf was socially well-connected and a known figure at court, but he did not owe his command entirely to favoritism. His performance in Manchuria had been steady rather than brilliant, but he had established himself as a man with at least some sense of how to conduct mobile operations under modern conditions. He was acquainted personally with many of his prospective opponents, having represented his government at official functions in East Prussia—most recently, ironically, at celebrations of the Russo-German Convention of Tauroggen against Napoleon in 1812.

Rennenkampf's counterpart with the Russian 2nd Army was also a cavalryman. Like Rennenkampf, Alexander Vasilevich Samsonov was a staff academy graduate who had done reasonably well in the field—notably commanding a cavalry division during the Russo-Japanese War. Since 1909 he had been governor-general of Turkestan and commander of the Turkestan military district. The distance, physical and mental, between this post and Samsonov's assignment on mobilization, has been described as symbolizing the insouciance with which Russia went to war in 1914. In fact Samsonov was by no means an unconsidered choice. The 2nd Army's logical commander would have been the peacetime head of the Warsaw military district, but that officer, as we have seen, was designated for front command. Samsonov, for his part, had also been chief of staff of the Warsaw district, from 1905 to 1907. In difficult revolutionary and postrevolutionary circumstances he had been calm and successful—so successful, indeed, that in early 1914 he too was considered a viable candidate for the district command that eventually went to Zhilinski. As a soldier, the German military attaché had declared, Samsonov certainly appeared to be well qualified for the post. There is no indication that the Germans believed he had gone into a decline in the intervening six months. There is, indeed, no indication that the Germans regarded any of their principal Russian adversaries as obvious military lightweights.[44]

A persistent legend of 1914 is that of bitter personal enmity between Rennenkampf and Samsonov—a feud beginning during the Russo-Japanese War and culminating in a physical altercation between the two generals in a Mukden railway station. The anecdote's viability reflects its usefulness as a symbol of prewar Russia's structural inefficiency. What other system could entrust to two men who hated each other a campaign depending upon close cooperation for its success? The only flaw in the scenario is that the incident never occurred. Rennenkampf's principal biographer takes pains to demonstrate that his protagonist was hospitalized with a wound at the time of the alleged scuffle. To reach the railway station, he would need to have been carried on a stretcher. Alternative possibilities for encounters generating personal antagonism between the generals are even more far-fetched. In any case, Jean Savant asks, why should Rennenkampf, with his brilliant prospects and his network of connections in high places, under any provocation engage in undignified fisticuffs with a relative nobody like Samsonov?[45]

Savant's common sense question highlights the fact, mentioned earlier in this text, that the Russian army was clique- and faction-ridden. On August 9, the French ambassador described the rivalries of court and drawing room over command appointments as resembling a chapter of *War and Peace*.[46] Senior command and staff assignments to the Northwest Front did reflect a balance among interests and viewpoints. Thus Samsonov was considered Sukhomlinov's man, while Rennenkampf was identified with the opposition to the war ministry headed by the Grand Duke

Nicholas. In turn Samsonov's own chief of staff was an anti-Sukhomlinov-ite, while Rennenkampf's supported the war minister.[47]

Taken at face value, this becomes a recipe for disaster before the first shots were fired. Yet no peacetime officer corps ever remotely resembles a band of brothers. Personal and professional antagonisms, networks of sponsorship and protection, patterns of political influence, are norms, not exceptions. The Royal Navy's "Fishpond," George C. Marshall's lists of promising officers, the interlocking directorate of paratroop generals in the U.S. army of the 1950s and 1960s—examples can be multiplied indefinitely. Victory tends to soften, or at least to blur, the existence of these divisions. And the Russian army expected to win.

The image of the Russian soldier of World War I as a uniformed primitive is so strongly established that challenging it seems an act of perversity. Yet the army which took the field in 1914 was by no means ignorant of reading and writing. This in large part reflected collective wisdom that "among the soldiers the illiterate is a doomed man." Until 1906, a school certificate had meant four instead of five years' active service. Literacy remained of obvious and increasing value in learning regulations, performing ordinary duties, and, last but hardly least, competing for soft assignments in orderly rooms and offices. Sixty-eight percent of the conscript class of 1913 met government standards of literacy. A significant number of the rest were likely to acquire at least its rudiments during their first months of service, if for no better reason than to avoid being victimized by the system and their fellow soldiers.

These points hardly suggest the Russian private took the field with a copy of Dostoyevsky in his knapsack. Official definitions of literacy were generous; recruits able to do more than sign their names and spell their way through a chapbook were likely to be assigned to one of the technical arms rather than the infantry. But it is worth noting that when the United States raised a conscript army from scratch during World War II, its manpower allocation programs also sent a disproportionate number of men in the lowest two categories of "usable" intelligence to the infantry. An infantry division was held to require fewer leaders and specialists than other, more technically oriented formations, and many of those they did receive were eventually transferred to special programs.[48]

Most accounts of Russia's initial defeat stress material, rather than human, factors. N. N. Golovine published in 1926 the first edition of the most familiar general book on Tannenberg from a Russian perspective. In this and later works he devotes paragraph after paragraph to demonstrating Russia's inferiority at the point of contact—in shells, in guns, even in riflemen. He inspired a virtual cottage industry of affirmation and refutation, to the point where number crunching has seriously obscured the presentation of events.[49] The following pages accept the risks of omission by eschewing precise calculation of formations and gun barrels except when they appear actually to influence the course of events—an occurrence that proved far less usual than the author expected.

A Russian army corps essentially resembled its German counterpart.

The infantry was organized into two divisions, each of two brigades and four regiments. The regiments had four battalions instead of three and were numbered sequentially within their divisions. The 1st Division included the 1st-4th Regiments, the 36th, the 141st-144th, and so on. Regiments, however, were far more frequently known by their titles, usually geographic: Reval, Viborg, Orel. Like the Germans, the Russian army stressed the regiment as the focal point of loyalty, using religious as well as patriotic exhortations to bind the men to their colors. But under conditions of modern war morale was likely to depend heavily on material factors. The Russian infantryman carried the Mosin-Nagant rifle, a sturdy and simple design whose five-shot magazine was often considered less important than the wicked thirty-inch bayonet always carried fixed on active service. He was supported at regimental level by a company of eight heavy machine guns whose modified Maxim design survived through two world wars and continued to soldier on in other hands on the other side of the world, in Korea and Indochina.

If the Russian soldier was well served by his small arms, the same could not be said of his artillery. Each Russian division included a brigade of 48 field guns, organized in six eight-gun batteries. The gun itself, a Putilov design reflecting strong Krupp influences, was markedly superior to its German rival in range and muzzle velocity, good enough to serve in modified form through World War II in the Red Army and the Wehrmacht alike. The ratio of guns to rifles was three to a thousand—25 percent lower than the Germans' figure, but not a crucial weakness in an era when artillery's real strength lay not in the number of barrels, but in ammunition supply and fire control. The Russian artillery had shells enough, at least for the war's first stages. However, its command and communications structures were significantly below the standards of Western Europe. These shortcomings were exacerbated by branch-of-service arrogance generating a sense of superiority great enough to make artillery officers reluctant to take orders from their superiors in the infantry or the cavalry.

At least as serious was the absence from Russia's order of battle of any equivalent to the German howitzers. Debate over the use and cost of this weapon had retarded its adoption. Compared to the forty-eight light and sixteen heavy howitzers of a German corps, in 1914 each Russian corps had only twelve 122-millimeter howitzers, throwing a heavier shell than the German 105-millimeter piece but significantly less mobile. All heavier artillery was concentrated at the army level—a good way of being reasonably sure of its unavailability in an emergency.

The Russian army put great faith in its cavalry, mobilizing the equivalent of over thirty divisions plus a large number of independent regiments and squadrons. A Russian cavalry or Cossack regiment included six squadrons, around a thousand men, and was correspondingly difficult to control in battle. Four of them made up a division which, with twelve guns and some small supporting units, consisted of around 4,500 men. This gave Rennenkampf over 20,000 of the best horsemen in the Russian army.

The Virgin Soldiers

In early August, the Stavka was increasingly concerned with the news from the west. The fall of Liège and the massive German sweep through Belgium, seemed to be confirming the pessimists' worst fears of having to cope singly with the victorious Central Powers. German behavior in the east, on the other hand, was so passive as to be almost comforting. Discussions of starting uprisings behind Russian lines, in Poland or Lithuania, came to nothing. Suggestions of spreading misinformation, such as rumors of amphibious landings in the Baltic, were squelched by an order from Berlin on August 10 forbidding giving false information to the enemy except of the local variety—an order probably inspired by a belief that one's own intelligence might become more confused than the enemy's.[50]

On August 10, Stavka also decided that the advance toward East Prussia should begin on August 13. On the next day Rennenkampf's leading elements crossed the German border.

In addition to its mass of cavalry, the 1st Army included three infantry corps. They advanced in line abreast. On the right, closest to the Baltic and to Königsberg, was XX Corps, commanded by Lieutenant-General Smirnov. An infantryman, he was at sixty-five the army's patriarch, whose last field experience had been in the Russo-Turkish War. He had commanded XX Corps since 1908, establishing a reputation for phlegmatic calm rather than energy, with no signs of being above average in ability. In the center, III Corps took the field under another infantryman, Lieutenant-General Yepantschin. Like Rennenkampf, he moved in high circles. Commissioned into the Preobrazhenski Guards, he had directed the Imperial School of Pages and served as professor of military history at the War Academy before returning to troop duty in 1907, first as a division commander, then succeeding Rennenkampf in III Corps. His reputation was similar to that of General Charles Lanrezac, commanding France's 5th Army in the developing Battle of the Frontiers. Lanrezac, a difficult personality but a brilliant theoretician, was widely expected to make up for his human shortcomings by his operational performance. Yepantschin too was disliked cordially enough to generate hopes that he might be an undiscovered talent.

The commander of IV Corps on Rennenkampf's left was potentially a far more interesting character than either of his counterparts. Lieutenant-General Eris Khan Alieuv was a Caucasian Muslim, a descendant of princes, and an artilleryman by specialization. He had served under Rennenkampf in Manchuria, commanded the II Siberian Corps from 1908 to 1912, and transferred back to his old chief in 1912. In contrast to Yepantschin, his reputation was that of a driving field soldier whose strategic skills were correspondingly limited.

In terms of backgrounds and careers these men were a reasonable cross-section of the Russian army's high command: the routinier, the theoretician, and the thruster; the linesmen and the guardsman; the

Europeans and the Asian. None stood out as a Napoleon in embryo; none was an obvious disaster waiting to happen. How they would fare depended on an interlocking network of unknowns—not the least of them being the Germans to their front.[51]

5
Taking the Measure of Danger

I

On August 1, 1914, the headquarters of the 8th German Army began forming in Königsberg. Its commander, General Max von Prittwitz und Gaffron, has had a consistently bad press. Critics described him as an imperial favorite, self-indulgent and coarse, who held his post over the general staff's protests because War Minister Erich von Falkenhayn wanted him out of Berlin.[1] This judgment incorporates a deal of hindsight. Prittwitz's was a typical successful military career of the late empire. Scion of one of Prussia's oldest noble families, he had made an excellent peacetime reputation as a trainer and commander. He was promoted to colonel at the age of forty-four, and to brigadier-general three years later. In 1906, at the relatively young age of fifty-seven, he took over XVI Corps at Metz. Exposed as it was to the first shock of any war with France, this was one of the most demanding and prestigious posts in the peacetime army. Its holder could reasonably expect higher things. In 1913 Prittwitz was promoted to Colonel-General and assigned to command the Königsberg army inspection.

On the surface the transfer seemed a waste of his expertise. The waste seemed compounded when I Corps's long-time commander, Alexander von Kluck, a man with extensive knowledge of the East Prussian theater, was also promoted and transferred to Berlin.[2] Kluck's new post was the army inspection destined on mobilization to form the army that would sweep through Belgium and northern France on the right wing of the Schlieffen Plan. Both assignments reflected the German army's long-standing concern with providing a broad spectrum of professional experience for its upwardly mobile officers. A regimental commander in Posen was likely to be assigned on promotion to command a brigade in Kassel or Frankfurt, to move from there to a division in Pomerania or East Prussia, and then back to an army corps in Magdeburg or Schleswig-Holstein. Any temporary sacrifice of specialized knowledge was an acceptable risk in an army that may have accepted the next war as a given, but never expected it to break out next year.

Had the 1912 crown council, or any of its later successors, actually implemented the sinister plans subsequently attributed to them, one excellent and unobtrusive measure would have been to alter these transfer patterns by leaving Kluck in place. In fact, no reason existed to modify standard procedure in 1913 when the assignments were made. Nor did there seem any reason to consider any drastic changes as the July Crisis developed. Despite a collection of nicknames attesting to his corpulence, Prittwitz was a man of marked self-confidence and apparent physical and emotional vigor. His reputation for harshness, while in sharp contrast to Kluck's more easy-going image, was hardly unique in the German army and was likely to be a help in getting the last possible exertions from officers and men in the demanding situation facing his army. His staff was first-rate. Its chief, Brigadier-General Georg von Waldersee, was one of the general staff's bright young men, a favorite of incumbent chief Helmuth von Moltke. He had been quartermaster-general until mobilization, a post generally and legitimately regarded as giving its occupant an inside track to become chief of the general staff itself. Waldersee had undergone major surgery earlier in the year, but he had performed effectively on returning to duty in July. He insisted on his fitness. There seemed no reason to deprive him of his mobilization appointment, particularly since conventional wisdom suggested that simple animal vitality would be far less important for senior commanders in modern war than had been the case when generals led their troops in person from horseback.[3]

Of Waldersee's two principal subordinates, the quartermaster, Colonel Grünert, gave the lie to jokes about the cavalry officer who was so stupid all the other cavalry officers noticed it. Grünert's last peacetime assignment had been commanding a cavalry brigade, but he was also a highly regarded administrator, a man who understood that logistics and traffic problems had become major elements of modern war. The army's First General Staff Officer (G.S.O.I.), responsible for intelligence, plans, and operations, was a more complex character. In his photographs Lieutenant-Colonel Max Hoffmann appears a caricature of the typical Prussian officer: a stern face set in a close-cropped bullet head with almost no neck separating it from a barrel-shaped body. In point of fact he was Hessian by birth, the son of a county court judge. Though the German army never made quite as much of field sports and physical fitness as its British counterpart, Hoffmann was remarkable for his indifference to exercise. At forty-five, he was equally familiar in general staff circles for his brilliant mind, his caustic wit, and his immense appetite.

The fat around Hoffmann's middle did not extend above his ears. Widely regarded as the best man in the general staff's Russian section, he

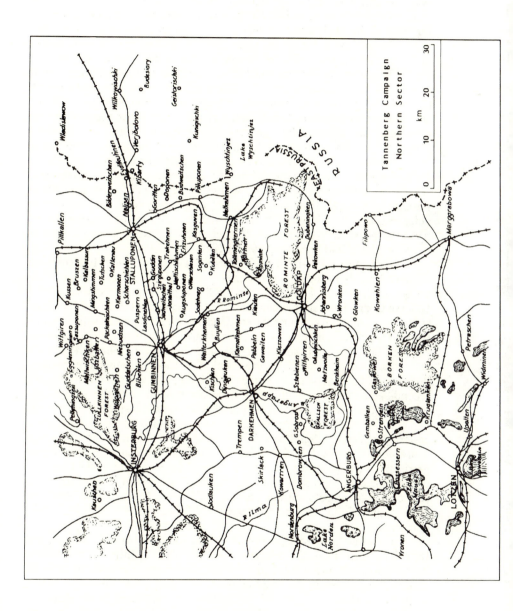

had travelled extensively in that country. He knew the language and the military system. As military attaché to Japan during the Russo-Japanese War, he had had ample opportunity to study the tsar's army in action from an enemy's perspective. Hoffmann, in sum, was a logical candidate for the post he held, a man of whom great things could be expected, but at the same time a bit of an eccentric, the sort of man whose proper utilization might put serious strains on a commander's patience.[4]

The importance of the staff in the German army of August, 1914, should not be exaggerated. The image of command exercised for all practical purposes by general staff officers, with some elderly excellency as a convenient figurehead, is at best a product of the war's later years. In peacetime the commanding generals of Germany's corps districts and army inspections exercised a broad spectrum of authority. They were jealous of their prerogatives, and correspondingly suspicious of the "demigods" who wore the carmine stripes of the general staff on their trousers. After over forty years of peace, these men had enough of an image as penpushers and paper-shufflers that they would not command automatic deference in a field headquarters, particularly since most senior generals had themselves served terms on the general staff. Respect would have to be earned, as it had been in 1866 and 1870–71.[5]

When fully mobilized, the German 8th Army was hardly a cohesive body of neighbors fighting for homes and firesides. At its core were the six active divisions of I, XVII, and XX Corps. The two divisions of I Reserve Corps were supplemented by the independent 3rd Reserve Division from Pomerania, whose parent II Corps was assigned to the western front. There was one cavalry division—hardly a comfort when balanced against the clouds of horsemen available in Russia. The 8th Army's commander could also call on the rough equivalent of four more infantry divisions, for what they might be worth. These were a mixed bag of second- and third-line battalions, some composed of middle-aged *Landwehr* with their active service far behind them, others formed from surplus personnel at regimental depots. Most were intended as garrisons for the eastern fortresses. Königsberg, Thorn, and Posen each had approximately a division; Graudenz and Breslau had a mixed brigade apiece. These garrisons were relatively strong in heavy artillery, but lacked almost everything else. Kitchens, communications equipment, trains, medical services, field maps were not part of their normal equipment. And the guns frequently lacked enough teams and vehicles to be useful for field operations.

In theory each active army corps was expected to draw its recruits from its assigned district. However, the population shifts accompanying industrialization had combined with the demands of frontier security to modify this pattern in the years between 1871 and 1914. Five of the eight corps raised after the Franco-Prussian War were stationed on the empire's borders, three in the west and two, XVII and XX, in the east. Even in peacetime large numbers of men from more heavily populated areas were drafted to their ranks. Over two-thirds of the men in I Corps came from

Westphalia and Brandenburg. The 5th Grenadiers of XVII Corps drew a third of its recruits from northeast Germany: industrial Westphalia and the Hanseatic cities. The active regiments thus depended heavily on the prompt arrival of reservists from Berlin and points farther west at a time when most German trains were moving in the opposite directions. In Germany proper, most active corps were able to duplicate themselves on mobilization, or at least furnish a reserve division. The three eastern corps districts combined could produce only a single reserve corps, and many of its regiments too had to fill their ranks with men from elsewhere in the Reich. The 3rd Reserve Infantry, mobilizing in the regional metropolis of Königsberg, drew half of its enlisted men from Berlin and Hanover. The 36th Reserve Field Artillery incorporated a similar mix—a core of East Prussians completed by Berliners, Westphalians, and Hanoverians.[6]

Shortly before the outbreak of war, Prittwitz was summoned to Berlin for a verbal briefing. He came away convinced that the chief of staff wished him to maintain contact with the Vistula River at all costs. But Moltke refused to concede that the situation would ever become that serious. Superior leadership, spirit, and tactics should enable the 8th Army to keep the Russians at bay for a long time. In fact, he insisted that the 8th Army should by no means conduct merely a passive defense. "When the Russians come," he wrote to Waldersee, "not defense only, but offensive, offensive, offensive."[7]

Moltke was thinking in tactical and operational, rather than strategic, terms. On August 1, the German military attaché in Vienna telegraphed Waldersee, still acting in his capacity as quartermaster-general, and appealed for coordinated plans to be developed as soon as possible. Everyone, declared this frustrated officer, assumed that the chiefs of staff had personally worked out appropriate agreements that only needed removing from appropriate pigeonholes.[8] Instead the allies behaved like a long-married couple embarking on a vacation with each assuming the other has turned off the stove.

German confidence in Habsburg security and Habsburg judgment had most recently been shaken by the Redl scandal of 1913, involving the exposure of one of Austria's principal intelligence officers as a homosexual who had concealed and supported his life-style by hawking the Dual Monarchy's military secrets all over the continent. Austrian intelligence services for their part knew enough about Russia's mobilization plans to be well aware of the strong forces earmarked for the East Prussian theater, and the correspondingly limited prospects of a German offensive in support of Austria.[9] But the Austrian general staff saw no reason to depend on Germany's behavior. Its revised war plan of March, 1914, continued to be based on an immediate attack northwards from Galicia, aimed at overrunning and destroying a substantial part of the Russian forces in that sector before they could complete their concentration. Hypotheses that a more Fabian approach would have better suited both the general nature of modern war and Austria's specific circumstances are in good part the product of hindsight. Given Russia's immense potential numerical superiority, combined with the steady improvements in the speed and efficiency of her mobilization, a defensive strategy seemed an open invitation to disaster—particularly on the open plains of Galicia. To resign the initiative to Russia, to allow her armies to complete their concentration and choose their axis of advance, meant a risk approaching certainty of being overrun in the field or trapped in the fortress complexes of Lemberg or Przemysl.

The Austro-Hungarian army's very shortcomings invited a motto of *toujours l'audace*. Taking a blow, then attempting to counterpunch, had brought disaster to France in 1870 and, on a smaller scale, to Spain in 1898. The Japanese experience in Manchuria, on the other hand, suggested that Russia was a foe best beaten early. If Austria successfully maintained the initiative, she could reasonably expect support from an ally victorious in the west before her own limited military resources were exhausted. Direct German participation in this strategy would be welcome. It was neither essential nor at bottom expected, at least in the campaign's initial period.[10]

Moltke for his part believed that Austria's offensive could best be supported not by charging blindly into the Russian wasteland, but by drawing as many Russian troops as possible into East Prussia. Every Russian on Prittwitz's front was one less to check the Austrian drive. At the same time, the 8th Army must be preserved as a nucleus for future operations. Under no circumstances was Prittwitz either to risk its destruction in the open field or to let himself be besieged in the fortress of Königsberg in the pattern of Bazaine at Metz in 1870. As a last alternative, Moltke authorized Prittwitz instead to retreat behind the Vistula River and there await reinforcements from the west.[11]

Max Hoffmann describes these orders as providing serious dangers for a weak or pessimistic character.[12] They are more appropriately considered mission tactics with a vengeance. Prittwitz was responsible for using his best judgment to keep his army intact, yet he was expected to give battle even at long odds. He was authorized to abandon East Prussia in an emergency, but at the same time warned that such a decision would be little short of disastrous. He was supposed to secure German territory, yet his orders emphasized and re-emphasized the need for close cooperation with Austria. The chief of staff had covered himself by anticipating all contingencies. No matter what Prittwitz did, it was likely to violate, or at least seriously challenge, at least part of 8th Army's assigned mission.

Prittwitz and Waldersee were well aware that Moltke was expecting them to square the circle. Waldersee's initial directive of August 6 was a cautious document. Corps commanders were told that until future notice 8th Army's was to be a posture of watchful waiting. It would concentrate only when reconnaissance and intelligence reports provided specific information on Russian movements. This decision also reflected common-sense awareness that 8th Army's ranks were filled by men and animals unused to the rigors of active campaigning. Such a force could not be moved around the map haphazardly in the manner of the good old Duke of York.

Confusion and exhaustion might prove deadlier enemies than the Russians, particularly in the context of terrain features and transport capacities in the theater of operations.[13]

East Prussia in 1914 was a maze of irregular hills covered with wild and uncultivated areas of barren, sandy soil, alternating with an intricate network of swamps, lakes, and forests. Strategically it could be divided into four zones. The first was the Königsberg region, extending east and west from Labiau to Tapiau. The Deime River, barely fordable and with few bridges, provided a natural first line of defense. Small fieldworks had been established along the Tapiau-Pillau line just before the war, and Königsberg itself was an up-to-date fortress, impregnable to anything short of heavy artillery. It could easily be reinforced by sea, and, properly defended, it offered a major threat to the flank of any force attempting to bypass it.

The second strategic zone ran north and south: the forty-three-mile Insterburg Gap from Tapiau to Angerburg. Here the country was generally open, dotted with large farms and small villages, but containing forest areas that offered serious obstacles to the movement of large forces. The most important terrain feature in the gap was the Angerapp River. It was fordable, but the west bank was higher than the east and so provided a useful defensive position. The river line itself had been carefully reconnoitered by the Germans before the war.

South of the Insterburg Gap came the fifty-mile region of the Masurian Lakes, extending from Angerburg to the Russian frontier south of Johannesburg. Taken as a whole, the chain of lakes presented an almost impregnable barrier to the movement of large forces: a nightmare of soft ground, water obstacles, and paths leading nowhere in particular. The only major road was barred by Fort Boyen. This nineteenth-century work might be technically obsolete, but an attempt to capture it by direct assault would almost certainly involve heavy casualties. In particular the fort's glacis was completely exposed, and could not easily be stormed in the face of machine gun fire.

The fourth strategic zone extended east and west from Johannesburg to Soldau, a distance of of seventy-five miles. The roads here were good, but the country was rugged and densely wooded. A number of long, shallow lakes with their axis extending north-south made lateral communications extremely difficult for any force advancing north.

The Germans had strengthened nature by artifice—but only to a point. The state's willingness and ability to construct railway lines exclusively for military purposes has frequently been exaggerated. The Prussian government evaluated proposed railway routes on the basis of existing movements of goods and people. Lines were built where current effective demands were heaviest, and correspondingly likely to generate profits. Eastern Germany was far from the Reich's population centers. Since the 1880s it had been separated from potential Russian markets by tariff barriers. However impressive the region's railway network may have been compared to the Russian side of the frontier, it was second-rate relative to the rest of the empire. Little money had been spent on sidings to expedite the loading and unloading of troops and equipment. Even less had been spent on spurs leading to nowhere except the Russian border.

The province's highway network was correspondingly thin, reflecting low population densities, limited local incomes, and a regional market system. The main roads and many secondary ones were paved. This would prove a boon to the horse-drawn guns, wagons, and ambulances that provided the 8th Army's logistics. Motorization, however, had made far less progress in the German east than around Berlin, Hamburg, or Hanover. This meant that relatively few civilian trucks were available to supplement supply columns or provide emergency transportation for men. Far more than their comrades in the west, the Germans of 8th Army would fight a horse and rail campaign in the old style.[14]

German regiments spent the first days of mobilization shaking down: absorbing reservists, staging practice marches, sending detachments in their new field gray uniforms to cover beaches, bridges, and roads against expected Russian raids. Hair was cut short or completely shaved in the interests of hygiene. Pastors announced God's blessing on the war in open-air services, and all but the most committed Socialists or agnostics could be pardoned for joining in the hymns more enthusiastically than usual. In Danzig and Königsberg, in Allenstein, Lyck, and a dozen smaller towns, troops marched to the railway stations under flying colors, headed by their regimental bands, forcing their way through cheering crowds of well-wishers. Cigars, candy, and enthusiastic embraces from women of all ages helped submerge any lingering qualms in the ranks and among the spectators.

On departing from their garrisons, the regiments of I Corps concentrated around Gumbinnen and Insterburg, with I Reserve Corps in support around Nordenburg and Angerburg. The XX Corps, from its home station of Allenstein, covered the southeast frontier. The XVII Corps moved southwest from Danzig to the area of Soldau. The 3rd Reserve Division was unloaded in the fortress of Thorn. This cordon deployment invited comparison to that allegedly criticized by Napoleon as perfect if a high command wanted to stop smuggling. But it possessed two complementary virtues. To a degree, it camouflaged numerical weakness. It also expedited concentration once the Russian threat developed: a covering force would be at hand.

The Russians offered few signs of life. In 1910 the Königsberg intelligence office had obtained information that Russia would begin the war with a series of massive cavalry raids into East Prussia—a logical maneuver given her vast superiority in horsemen. In 1914 the Russian cavalry confined itself to patrol- and squadron-level skirmishes. The contrast between expectation and reality was so great that the Germans subsequently wondered if they had not been deliberately fed false information.[15]

The answer was by no means so sophisticated. Deep-penetration mobile operations had a long tradition in the Russian armies, and Sukhomlinov was particularly impressed by the Civil War exploits of the Confederacy's Jeb Stuart. The mobilization plan deployed eight of the best mounted divisions in the Russian army on the East Prussian border. But the Russian cavalry at its best moved slowly. Unaccompanied by infantry or artillery, its average rate of march were calculated at 3.3 miles per hour at a walk and 4.6 miles per hour at a mixed walk and trot.[16] Neither speed would have impressed James Harrison Wilson or Nathan Bedford Forrest; neither gave great hopes for deep penetration behind German lines.

Nor was Russian cavalry organized and trained to operate in masses. Russia had no peacetime cavalry formation higher than the division, and too many of those were led by men too old or too frail to spend days in the saddle and make quick decisions after two or three sleepless nights. The commander of the 1st Army's improvised cavalry corps, the sixty-one-year-old Hussein Khan Nakhitchevanski, had reached the limits of his ability commanding a brigade in Manchuria. This unhappy descendant of the Tatars was hardly likely to obtain maximum results from even the boldest warriors. Brave enough personally, he had neither the vision nor the energy required of a senior commander of mobile troops. Apart from the physical problems to be expected of a man his age, the Khan suffered so badly from hemorrhoids that it was almost impossible for him to mount a horse.

The Russians were also suffering as badly as the Germans from mobilization jitters. When reconnaissance patrols did cross the border, their reports showed more creative anxiety than scouting ability. Lurid descriptions of German soldiers disguised as peasants and women, interpretations of curious adolescents as enemy intelligence agents, increased the level of jumpy trigger-happiness among Russian rank and file, but contributed little towards finding and fixing the enemy. Lieutenant Adam Bennigsen of the elite horse guards described a night alarm: "General quarreling in the darkness, swearing, complete ignorance as to where to go or what to do, anxious waiting—a usual picture of a night move."

Nor did the cavalry's doctrine and training prove particularly useful in overcoming initial insecurities. Unlike their counterparts in Western Europe, Russia's horsemen had a strong tradition of dismounted fighting. The enemies confronted on the empire's southern and eastern frontiers were often less vulnerable to massed charges than to mobile firepower. Between 1872 and 1910, the army's entire line cavalry had been baptized "dragoons" and trained extensively to fight on foot. But while this might safeguard against Balaklavas or Mars-la-Tours, it proved a positive handicap in patrolling and scouting. The concept of cavalry spirit, so often derided by critics of nineteenth-century armies, was by no means a pure atavism. Russian squadrons confronted by a detachment of snipers were less likely to press forward and test the enemy's strength than to dismount and trade shots at long range with their adversaries. This early version of "reconnaissance by fire" seldom brought results more significant than a dead horse or two, a handful of empty cartridge cases in an abandoned position, and a growing sense of frustration. Wait for the real offensive, regimental wisdom counseled. Then the Russian troopers would show what they could do while pursuing a defeated enemy.[17]

The German troops on the border were also learning some of the differences between a military campaign and a youth group hike. They went to war in uniforms whose color was the product of years of study and debate. In 1910 the Imperial army had relegated its traditional bright colors to the garrison and the parade ground, introducing for active service the color known as *feldgrau* (field grey). Its greenish tint set it apart from the *hechtgrau* (pike grey) of the Austrian field uniform. Particularly with a bit of wear, the color blended well with smoke, with mud, and—not least in importance—with the late-fall foliage of central Europe. The impression of a German column on the march in 1914 was of a drab flood, highlighted only by the scarlet regimental numbers painted on helmet covers and embroidered on shoulder straps. Throughout the war it would be shoulder straps, taken from prisoners or ripped from corpses, that provided basic hard intelligence on the location of German units.

Color had been the army's principal concession to modernity. The new field uniforms retained the style and cut of their predecessors, especially in the cavalry. They were correspondingly constricting. For the infantryman, however, tradition had even greater impact on his feet and at his head. Where the French and British armies had introduced shoes and puttees, the Germans retained calf-length boots. Boots, their advocates insisted, provided protection and support. They were less likely to impede circulation in a marching man's leg than were puttees or leggings. The risks of loss in mud or snow could be limited by reasonably careful attention to fitting. While German storm troops and mountain formations adopted puttees later in the war, the army's boots seemed on the whole to have justified their retention.

Far less could be said for World War I's single most prized souvenir, the spiked helment, or *Pickelhaube*. The initial version of this leather helmet, introduced in 1842, was high-crowned to provide its wearer with some protection against sword cuts. The elaborate pattern of metal trim on the more familiar, smaller version, adopted later, was only partly for decorative purposes. The chains and ribbing served to reinforce the leather and retard wear—an important point for an army having to watch its peacetime pennies. They added nothing to the helmet's utility. On the march, its weight was not compensated by any protection from the sun. The leather and the metal acted instead as heat conductors. On peacetime firing ranges, the large neckpiece constantly tipped the visor into the shooter's face. The addition of a canvas cover for field service did little to modify the headgear's deficiences. But if no German soldier or politician was willing to assert *"Die Pickelhaube ist Deutschland"* with the same intensity their French counterparts proclaimed *"Le pantalon garance, c'est la France,"* the spiked helmet continued to defy replacement by anything more practical or comfortable.

The rest of the German soldier's equipment was heavy but practical. He carried up to seventy pounds, most of it in a square knapsack nicknamed "monkey"—a term introduced to American slang first by drug addicts, then by any troubled person carrying "a monkey on his back." Six ammunition pouches, bayonet and entrenching tool, haversack and mess kit, were suspended from a harness of belts and straps—leather instead of the more up-to-date webbing favored by the British—designed to distribute the weight as evenly as possible over the upper body with a minimum of handles or straps dangling below the waist to impede movement.[18]

Not even German structural engineering could keep a fully equipped infantry private from resembling the proverbial Christmas tree. The process of lightening packs by abandoning gear, an art form in the less formal armies of the American Civil War, was a court-martial offense under the kaiser. The German soldier was, however, fortunate in belonging to an army that, though many of its veterans would dispute the point, in the field did not emphasize spit and polish for its own sake. The German private had less freedom than the French *poilu* to leave everything unbuttoned except his fly, but by comparison to his British counterpart, he was allowed to look positively scruffy.

Other things—particularly diet—were perceived as more important, even by the regimental officers. In the 1870s, army doctors had evaluated the merits of the coca leaf as a source of quick energy on the march, a possible miracle cure for colic, constipation, and hypochondria.[19] In 1914 soldiers continued to depend, at least officially, on more conventional stimulants: alcohol, tobacco, and above all hot food and drink. The German soldier was not expected to feed himself from the contents of his haversack. That contained emergency rations: tinned meat and preserved vegetables, biscuits, coffee, and salt, to be touched only on an officer's orders. Under normal circumstances meals were prepared from bread baked by more or less stationary field bakeries, beef killed and seasoned at more or less stationary field butcheries, and vegetables and condiments obtained locally or sent from the interior, all of it distributed by corps supply columns.

In the field, the state of these provisions on reception could hardly be guaranteed. Rock-hard loaves of bread and cuts of meat still quivering were common grievances even on maneuvers. Just before the war, however, the German army had introduced kitchens on wheels, able to boil coffee or cook stew on the move and issue it at any convenient halt. They made it possible for men to begin and end the day with something hot in their stomachs, without the effort involved in doing for themselves or erecting the old type of kitchens. This was particularly important for men new to active service and likely to end a day too exhausted to take any pains for their own well-being.

War is described as being composed of two elements: mud and dust. The summer of 1914 had been dry and as hot as any in recent memory. After two or three days on the roads of East Prussia, few German footsloggers would not have welcomed mud as a change from their present miseries. Throats and nostrils clogged. Faces and hands turned as gray as uniforms. Feet burned in their new boots. Men complained it was like walking on hot coals. Reservists fresh from office desks and workshops, enervated from several days in trains, strained to keep in ranks. A medical officer furnished his regiment with a welcome laugh when, never having ridden a horse in his life, he inadvertently used his spurs to improve his seat. His normally phlegmatic charger raced through the column at a dead gallop, with the unfortunate doctor sinking his spurs in deeper and deeper, until he was rescued by a comrade better versed in horse management.[20] But most of the Germans found enough triumph in being able to put one foot in front of the other until the "halt" sounded at day's end.

II

For the Germans to concentrate, they needed at least some idea of what the Russians were doing. Initially Prittwitz expected great things from Germany's espionage networks, but the reports from field agents rapidly declined in number and value as Russian security measures tightened. The German civil police, who often acted as contacts, could no longer take peacetime risks along the frontier. Border guards who knew when to look the other way were reinforced by Cossacks inclined to shoot first and ask questions later. The outbreak of war cut off another useful source of information: German train crews on the international runs. Russian counterintelligence handicapped the Germans still further by the simple device of stopping the mails to Germany.

Particularly in the operational zones, where information was most urgently sought, the Germans depended heavily on small fry: peasants and peddlers, customs personnel, an occasional middle-grade official. These men worked for money, and war increased the risks of their activities beyond any reasonable hope of profit from a German intelligence service with a history of tightfistedness. A typical "success" involved a Russian reservist who brought in one final report from Vilna, then answered his own mobilization notice like a good citizen.

Nor were the Germans particularly sophisticated in protecting their agents. In the spring of 1914 an insurance salesman in Poltava was recruited by unspecified means. His normal peacetime contacts were in Berlin and East Prussia and explainable as business connections. Then on July 26, the agent was ordered to send his reports to "Mademoiselle Robert" in Copenhagen. In a small city deep in Russia, it was hardly likely to escape notice when a man with a record of business relationships in Germany, but none in Denmark, suddenly began corresponding with a lady in Copenhagen at a time of acute international crisis! To make things worse, the unfortunate spy was sent on August 26 or 27 two hundred rubles through a Königsberg bank. Under the circumstances it is hardly surprising that the Germans heard nothing further from their Poltava connection.

Taking the Measure of Danger

In an attempt to answer the increasingly pointed questions from Berlin about Russian dispositions, 8th Army issued on August 13 a general order that anyone declaring they had any kind of information was to be brought before designated intelligence officers. But the German intelligence structure had been badly disrupted by mobilization. An experienced captain in Königsberg was ordered to his regiment on mobilization; his replacement got the job because he was seen reading a Russian newspaper. The 8th Army's senior intelligence officer, Captain Frantz, was assigned from Berlin and viewed as the high command's spy by the rest of the army staff. Wherever possible he was ignored or overlooked, to the point of being deliberately kept away from situation maps. Frantz's situation was even worse because he was junior in rank to the corps intelligence officers. Frustrated by the lack of useful information, they responded by dismissing Frantz as incompetent.[21]

Intelligence was not the only possible source of military information. Strategic reconnaissance had historically been a major responsibility of the cavalry, but the 8th Army's horsemen were inhibited by a mix of doctrinal and practical considerations. Odds of one division against ten encouraged keeping the German troopers under wraps. Aggressive leadership might have compensated for numerical weakness, but Major-General Brecht, 1st Cavalry Division's commander, was no Murat.

Experience indicated that more than any combat arm, cavalry depended on youthful leaders, men able to make and seize the fleeting opportunities that were all that remained for cavalry in modern war. Napoleon's horsemen knew their greatest days with leaders in their early thirties. The cavalry of the American Civil War by 1865 was serving under generals a decade younger than that. The Imperial German Army's pensions were not enticing enough, the civilian second-career opportunities not sufficiently attractive, to encourage general officers to retire while they could still sit a saddle. Brecht had entered the Prussian army in 1867, and his primary extra-regimental duty had been in various riding schools—hardly an indication of unusual professional gifts. Two of his brigadiers were well into their fifties.

The German cavalry of 1914 was primarily trained to function as a screen for offensive operations.[22] On the defensive, it was not quite certain whether its mission was to fight for information or keep the Russians at bay. It had difficulty doing either, at least from horseback. For forty years cavalrymen everywhere in Europe had debated the deadliest form of the *arme blanche*. Germany had settled on the lance. It might be cumbersome, but it was long enough to reach even a prone man. In mounted combat, moreover, the lancer was able to deliver only a thrust, which was much deadlier than a cut with a saber. Every trooper in the German army had spent hours in peacetime practicing with the weapon. But once in the field, excitement tended to overcome instruction. The lance was attached to the trooper's shoulder by a sling—useful in preventing the weapon's loss, but also restricting the arc of a thrust. When the initial shock was past, the Germans found themselves jabbing at their opponents with no more force than that generated by arms and torsos, and with accuracy impaired by excited horses. One lucky Cossack of Rennenkampf's army survived eleven lance wounds and won the George Cross. His horse was successfully treated for no fewer than twenty-one stabs.

This was a far cry from prewar expectations that a single lance thrust would be enough to decide most man-to-man combats. Responding to the limitations of cold steel, patrol and troop leaders increasingly dismounted their men to engage Russian scouting parties. German troopers were by no means helpless with firearms. A corporal of the 1st Dragoons, cut off and surrounded by forty Russians, used his dead horse as cover and by his own account at least, shot eight of them out of their saddles before the rest drew off. He rejoined his squadron afoot and unhurt, proudly showing the bullet holes in his helmet and cartridge pouch.[23]

Such scenes from a Frederick Remington painting did little to enhance specific knowledge of Russian movements and intentions. The shortcomings of the intelligence service and the cavalry threw by default an increasing responsibility for securing information on the newest branch of the kaiser's army. Prussian technical agencies and the German general staff had paid increasing attention to balloons and airships since the 1890s, and to aircraft development since the Wright Brothers' first flight. The initial purchase of airplanes in 1911 was followed by the establishment of a provisional, then a permanent, air service. By 1913 this had been elevated to its own inspectorate, organized in four battalions. Germany's eastern frontier was the home of *Flieger-Bataillon* 2, with companies in Posen, Graudenz, and Königsberg. There were no Red Barons in its ranks, and few barons of any sort. The battalion was a mix of enthusiasts, dilettantes, and a few hard cases, drinkers or womanizers encouraged by their previous commanders to volunteer for the new branch of service.

Prior to 1914, the development of air reconnaissance was handicapped by problems of terrain recognition and information transmission. Critics suggested even the limited successes achieved in peacetime were gained when air crews were able to familiarize themselves with the exercise areas. Aircraft had participated in maneuvers in East Prussia for the first time in August, 1913. They attracted a proportionate amount of military and journalistic attention. But they proved significantly unsuccessful in actually finding troops on the march, much less identifying the side to which they belonged. One unfortunate pilot even mistook the Russian town of Tilsit for the German town of Tauroggen, discovering his error only when Cossack bullets began whistling past his wings.

On the outbreak of war the 2nd Battalion, like its counterparts, was divided into detachments. Each active corps and 8th Army headquarters was assigned a six-plane *Feld Flieger Abteilung*. The fortresses of Königsberg, Thorn, Graudenz, and Posen each received a separate detachment of four aircraft. They were equipped with a mixed bag of monoplanes—the famous *Tauben*, or doves, so called from the shape of their wings—and biplanes manufactured by a half-dozen firms. A three-hour flight at speeds from fifty to eighty miles per hour when tail winds were obliging was reckoned as a good performance from a new machine. A particularly belligerent crew might take a rifle aloft to supplement their service pistols. Occasionally light bombs or hand grenades would be added, to be tossed over the side in the hopes of frightening a few horses. But aircraft were supposed to provide information—a task so important that the observer, not the pilot, was in command of the two-seater aircraft equipping the detachments.[24]

By the standards of 1916, to say nothing of later years, it was an unpromising matrix. But the German pilots and observers were eager to show what they could do. By August 2 and 3, aircraft from XVII and XX Corps were taking advantage of the good weather to cross the frontier. A week of random missions ended when Prittwitz's staff gave each field and fortress squadron a specific zone to patrol. By August 9, German airmen had observed and photographed as far east as Kovno, Novogeorgievsk, and Lodz. In particular, observers of I Corps's *Flieger Abteilung* 14 reported brigade-strength camps, long columns of wagons and massive troop movements between Suwalki and the frontier. On the other hand reports described the area from Warsaw to the border as free of any large Russian forces.

Zeppelin flights confirmed the information. The fortresses of Posen and Königsberg each had one of these awkward gasbags, slow, vulnerable to a wide variety of threats, but with a long range which made them invaluable for strategic reconnaissance. The Z V took off from Posen on the evening of August 7 and spent the night cruising over Russian territory and throwing out propaganda leaflets. The crew reported no sign of troop movements or concentrations. Three days later Königsberg's Z IV flew south to the Russian border town of Mlawa, deposited a few bombs, but saw no large camps or any significant movement on the railways in the area.[25]

Balancing the information from the two sectors, army command made its decision. In his August 9 report to OHL, Waldersee declared that the checks administered to Russian cavalry patrols on the southern frontier, combined with the damage done by German screening forces to the railroads and bridges in this area, made a rapid advance from the Narew unlikely. The 8th Army would therefore concentrate along the Angerapp with the equivalent of nine divisions and a cavalry division and prepare to meet an attack from the Niemen. The XX Corps, reinforced by garrison and *Landwehr* troops, would remain in position against any surprise movements from the south.

Prittwitz and Waldersee were taking a calculated risk. By waiting for the Russian 1st Army to approach the Angerapp line, they virtually committed 8th Army to winning a decisive victory in the north. If the 1st Army was only checked, it would be difficult or impossible to bring forces against any Russian offensive from the Narew without in turn risking exposure to an overwhelming blow from the rear—a Königgrätz in reverse, with Germany playing Austria's role.[26]

The anxieties accompanying such a decision were suddenly exacerbated by the same force that encouraged making the decision in the first place. A stream of reports from I Corps's pilots continued to confirm the Russians' forward movement from the Niemen. Whole divisions and corps were on their way to the border. Then on August 13, Prittwitz's airmen also began reporting the roads and railroads to the southeast full of Russian troops—the vanguards of the advance from the Narew.[27]

Since the dawn of time, commanders have bewailed their inability to see what lies on the other side of the hill. After leading an army-sized force in the maneuvers of 1911, Colmar Freiherr von der Goltz mused that developments in communications technology had made possible a much looser deployment of large forces than had been the case forty years earlier. Reports on the enemy situation that once took days and hours to arrive now could reach higher headquarters in minutes. This fact, Goltz argued, gave the modern commander much more freedom to maneuver against an enemy's constantly changing weaknesses.[28]

Theory and practice did not quite overlap. Intelligence information can readily become a two-edged sword. It is possible to know too much, to be so aware of an enemy's circumstances that command decisions are postponed indefinitely or implemented halfheartedly. Even in the days of the helicopter and the communications satellite, operational plans can be modified into confusion as troops are shifted here and there to counter an adversary's moves as presented by one's own intelligence sources, human or technical.

This problem was even more acute in the military circumstances of 1914. Generals and staff officers were psychologically unprepared to deal with the instant intelligence provided by air reconnaissance and, as will be shown later, radio interception. Being able to read the enemy's dispatches, receiving information from hundreds of miles behind his lines in a matter of hours, as opposed to the days required by cavalry scouts and messengers, could generate stress as well as comfort because of a technological paradox. Tactical mobility had if anything declined since the Napoleonic era. A modern field army, or even an army corps, with its masses of artillery and its long supply trains, was unable to respond quickly to either challenges or opportunities. Once committed to an axis of advance it could not easily be switched to another. Strategic mobility was limited by the time it took to load and unload trains under operational conditions. Below division levels communications and control tended towards the haphazard, even in the German army. The risks of "order, counter-order, disorder" were drummed into officers from their subaltern days. Ignorance may not be bliss, but the gap between knowledge of a situation and ability to influence responses certainly was an unexpected addition to an already high stress level. Even Max Hoffmann, who prided himself on his imperturbability, confided to his diary on August 13 that the responsibility was "gigantic, and more of a strain on the nerves than I expected," and informed his wife that "if things go well, Prittwitz will be a great captain; if things do not go well, they will blame us."[29]

An alternative strategy had been loudly proposed by the commander of I Corps. At 58, Lieutenant-General Hermann von François was another Prussian officer who fit only some of the usual stereotypes. Descended from a Huguenot family, emigrants to Prussia in the seventeenth century, he began his service in the Prussian Guard in 1874, graduated from the War Academy, and reached the apparent peak of his career in September, 1913, when he was assigned to command I Corps. In the course of his service François, like Hoffmann, had established something of a reputation as a maverick, but on professional rather than personal grounds. He was considered a difficult subordinate, a man who liked to go his own way in making and executing decisions. This trait had limited his usefulness during his periodic staff assignments. It also plagued him as a commander. François's predecessor at I Corps, von Kluck, was the kind of popular, respected general who is always a difficult act to follow. François compounded the inevitable difficulties of his position by overreaching himself, seeking to be everywhere at once, supervising his subordinates too closely for their comfort. The question was whether I Corps's prickly commander would be able to justify his temperament by his performance in the field.[30]

This in turn involved the question of I Corps's role in the German battle plans. On evaluating the mobilization mission of his new command, François was disturbed to find that the corps was expected to withdraw towards the Angerapp no matter what the Russians did. From a general staff perspective this made sense. The I Corps was more useful as part of an army concentrated in the middle of East Prussia than as an isolated force extended along the border. François disagreed, but his unwillingness to abandon even temporarily half of his corps district reflected more than a single officer's personal vanity or professional pride. A major element of nineteenth-century social contracts implied the protection of civilians by the state—not their exposure to war's horrors. The concept of populations as hostages and targets awaited a later era. Nevertheless the days when merchants would remain in their stores and peasants in their fields while armies marched and countermarched were long past, particularly in an area increasingly terrorized at the expected behavior of an invader so often described in their newspapers as Asiatic barbarians.

In November, 1913, the general staff had requested François's opinion on the prospects of a more aggressive local defense of East Prussia. By using improved reconnaissance methods, Zeppelins and aircraft, by taking advantage of the clumsy Russian command structure, might not a series of limited, spoiling attacks across the border preserve large areas of the province from invasion? François liked the idea, and replied by asking permission to deploy more infantry and machine guns closer to the frontier. The general staff authorized assignment of an extra battalion and a machine-gun company to the garrison of Goldap, directly on the frontier. This was not a large force, but it was enough of a concession to encourage François to develop in peacetime his own plans for striking across the border as soon as the I Corps mobilization should be completed. Boldly handled, he reasoned, even a single corps might disrupt the Russian concentrations.

When ordered instead to concentrate his corps on the Angerapp line, leaving the screening of the area east of the river to the cavalry, François strongly protested. A chance existed, he argued, for a major success against the assembling Russians if I Corps attacked immediately and was supported by the rest of the 8th Army.[31]

Given the encouragement he had previously received from the general staff for a forward policy, François was not without grounds for wondering if the army's right hand quite knew what its left was doing. Prittwitz and Waldersee for their parts reasoned that François's proposed attack would risk I Corps losing contact with the rest of the army. The maneuver might even mean that the entire army would be drawn into a battle on the "wrong" side of the Masurian Lakes. Fighting far to the east was the last thing that Prittwitz wanted. If the risks attending battle on the Angerapp were obvious, those accompanying even a decisive victory on the frontier were greater. Given ordinarily competent leadership, under such circumstances the Russian 2nd Army could be expected to drive hard past the lakes, to strike the German lines of communication and catch 8th Army on the flank and rear before it could redeploy.

François remained unconvinced. Fighting on the Angerapp to him meant surrendering too much German territory. As days passed without any major Russian initiative, François began pushing forward in the way General Patton would later describe as "making rock soup"—a reconnaissance in force supported first with a battalion, then a regiment, then the whole corps. By August 13, most of I Corps had reached the line Goldap-Stallupönon, about twenty miles east of the Angerapp River.[32]

Prittwitz was concerned by now with his ally as well as his subordinates. Conrad's optimism of August 3 had been modified by ten days of reality. Austria's final mobilization plan had divided the army into three sections. Eight divisions were designated for the Balkans; twenty-eight would move into Galicia. The remaining twelve were, depending on one's perspective, a swing force or a strategic reserve. Should Russia remain neutral, they would move against Serbia. Should Russia enter the war, they would reinforce the troops in Galicia. Unless Austria's enemies were unusually obliging, or Austria's diplomats unusually gifted, chances were good that they would be nowhere at the right time.

This was in fact what happened. Initially, Conrad's determination to deal once and for all with Serbia combined with public and political pressures to send the twelve uncommitted divisions towards the Balkans. This led to significant modifications of plans for the Galician offensive— modifications reflected most clearly by changing the debarkation points of the Austrian forward units, pulling them back as much as two hundred miles behind the frontier. Then Conrad changed his mind again. Protests from the Germans and complaints from the politicians reinforced his own common-sense judgment that there was limited logic in sending almost half of Austria's army into a secondary campaign while the Russians kicked in the Dual Monarchy's front door. When Conrad asked the general staff's railway section if the swing divisions could after all be sent eastward, he was informed that it would cost less time to allow them to go on to Serbia, then turn them around. But his real problem was that the troops already moving into Galicia were being unloaded much farther from the frontier than the original war plan intended. This meant wearying foot marches into the intended theater of operations. When this fact was combined with the unexpected speed of Russia's mobilization, a German offensive in the east suddenly assumed an importance unexpected in prewar Habsburg planning.

On August 3 Conrad attacked on two fronts. He sent Moltke a letter explaining, not to say whitewashing, his sending twelve divisions to Serbia and reassuring his ally that Austria did intend to fight its decisive battle in Galicia. He accompanied this with a telegram announcing his intention to launch a general offensive on August 20. To support it, Conrad requested that a German attack of nine divisions—the first-line field strength of *Ostheer*—be made southeast into Russian Poland, in the direction of the town of Siedlice, as soon as possible.

Moltke's reaction is unrecorded. Perhaps there flashed through his mind some version of the epigram that Austria was always an idea, an army, and a century too late. Perhaps he was too preoccupied with the execution of the Schlieffen Plan to spare energy for one more Austrian fiasco. His reply of August 5 said nothing about a German offensive against the Narew, in the direction of Siedlice, or in any other direction except towards Paris. It expressed hopes for victory, vague theories about starting a Polish insurrection, and vaguer rumors about Russian troop movements. Its only positive content was its insistence on the necessity of gaining a decisive victory in the west as soon as possible.[33]

Conrad spent a week hoping for the best. But his cavalry was unable to penetrate the Russian screen long enough to locate the enemy's areas of concentration. His infantry was reporting heavy losses from straggling and heat exhaustion as the corps moved forward on foot from their distant unloading points. An uncomfortable number of Russians was out there somewhere, and Conrad continued to insist on the need for a German offensive against Siedlice to relieve the pressure on the Austrians in Galicia. He received his answer on August 15 from his own liaison officer with the 8th Army, Captain Fleischmann. The telegram said that "a decisive blow" was about to be struck, not south but east against the Russian Niemen army. Within a few days this thrust should succeed, but an attack in Conrad's proposed direction could only be contemplated afterwards. Thus expired, with barely a whimper, the final remnant of a quarter-century's plans for a concentric German-Austrian offensive into Poland.[34]

On August 14 Prittwitz implemented Waldersee's dispatch of the 9th by ordering XVII Corps, I Reserve Corps, and the 3rd Reserve Division to the Angerapp River as reinforcements for the corps he believed to be already there. A general of an earlier era would have been constrained by lack of information to do one of two things: commit himself fully to defeating one enemy and then take his chances with the other, or fall back and launch a series of ripostes against both. Prittwitz, however, knew just enough to make him nervous. While continuing his original plan to concentrate on the Angerapp, he continued to send his airmen south, patrolling towards the Narew as a tongue explores a hollow tooth, reinforcing XX Corps's aircraft with those of the army reconnaissance squadron, *Flieger Abteilung* 16. The pressure at army headquarters increased one more notch when the weather suddenly broke. As clouds and summer storms hindered observation, the few reports that did arrive from the airmen indicated that the Russian 2nd Army was reaching its concentration areas far more rapidly than Prittwitz and Waldersee found comfortable.[35]

Eighth Army headquarters was in for yet another rude surprise. Prittwitz may have intended to fight on the Angerapp, but François proposed to await attack where he stood. He was confident that his corps, which he regarded as the best in Germany, could defeat any number of Russians—or at least hold them in check until Prittwitz was forced to move the rest of the army forward to its support. He found justification in precedent as well as strategy. The Prussian/German command system stressed allowing subordinates maximum liberty within the limits of a mission. An officer who stuck too closely to textbook solutions in war games or maneuvers was likely to be informed that His Majesty the King of Prussia and German Emperor needed neither parrots nor phonographs.[36] The difficulty of maintaining contact with the far-flung units of a modern army made such initiative more important than ever. In 1866 and again in 1870/71, corps commanders had acted on their perceptions of the operational situation, bringing on general actions at times and places not expected by the high command. Victory had been their justisfication. François expected no less, and no desk general was going to interfere, whether at army levels or in I Corps itself.

François's chief of staff, Colonel Schmidt von Schmidtseck, was shocked by his chief's blithe disregard for plans and orders. Schmidtseck, a holdover from the Kluck years, had not been particularly impressed by François's frenetic and splenetic behavior in peacetime. He had no intention of risking his own career and the 8th Army's fate by underwriting his mercurial chief now. General staff officers had the right and the duty to submit independent reports to their superiors—the familiar *Generalstabsdienstweg*. Intended more as a backup system than secret chain of command, the structure depended for effective functioning on a reasonable degree of harmony between a commanding general and his chief of staff. François, however, did not propose to be bypassed. Instead he developed a solution that seems in retrospect to have been almost tongue-in-cheek. He maintained his official corps headquarters at its peacetime station of Insterburg, on the Angerapp River. He left his chief of staff there, miles behind the troops but in a good position to sustain the deception by his presence. To prevent any awkward revelations, François came as close as he dared to confining Schmidtseck to his quarters and forbidding him access to a telephone or telegraph. Reports were doctored to conceal the limits of I Corps's advance. François himself took pains to be out of touch whenever direct questions might be raised about the location of his troops. Hints dropped at army headquarters by young staff officers with an idea of what was happening were not enough to generate serious investigation of the situation.[37]

The I Corps had a good opinion of itself. It included some of the oldest regiments of the Prussian army, survivors of the debacle of 1806, victors on a dozen fields of battle from Leipzig in 1813 to Paris in 1871. After ten days in the field the war seemed like nothing so much as maneuvers with live ammunition. Foot soldiers lanced their blisters and overhauled their uniforms, dulling their buttons, sewing plain gray cloth on the braided cuffs and shoulder straps. Gunners instructed reservists in the mysteries of new optical equipment. Only the reports of German victories in the west and the eerie emptiness of the villages set the days apart from the familiar fall maneuvers.

Not all was peaceful. The I Corps's cavalry squadrons scattered unwary Russian scouting parties, now and then even raiding across the frontier. Infantry detachments exchanged shots with Cossacks. Improvised motor and cyclist patrols, often composed of local reservists familiar with the countryside, scoured the roads. Volunteers eager for action brought back lurid tales of burned houses and plundered farms, accounts substantiated by the clouds of smoke that rose daily along the frontier. Other horror stories also began circulating in I Corps's bivouacs: stories of women raped, mutilated, and murdered or left to die; stories that lost nothing in the telling, yet always seemed to come from another company or battalion.[38]

This was the beginning of the myth of East Prussia's harrowing at the hands of Cossack hordes—a myth kept alive during and long after the war for political, ethnic, and ideological reasons. Reality was significantly less dramatic. A committee despatched to East Prussia in the aftermath of Tannenberg began its work primed with stories of gang rapes and severed organs. It was ultimately constrained to report that descriptions of the occupation's horrors had been greatly exaggerated. The large-scale destruction of towns and villages owed more to artillery fire than arson. Several *Landräte* weighed in with the information that much of the looting attributed to Russians in their districts was in fact the work of German civilians—a point consistent with the relatively high peacetime crime rate in the border districts. The haphazard nature of evacuation in many communities enhanced the possibilities of loss and destruction. Abandoned stoves started fires. Open doors attracted the greedy and the malicious. Geese and chickens left unpenned were not likely to be found once their owners returned.[39]

The invading Russians pursued an official policy of common sense. Only in October would the chief of staff order the expulsion of all men of working age from occupied German territory, with women, children, and old men remaining as hostages against partisan activity. Centuries of experience had shown Europe's armies the necessity of living at least in part from the countryside. Even in an age of railroads, horse-drawn wagons could not move an army's complete requirements of food and forage from railheads to nose bags and haversacks. This meant not plunder but systematic requisitioning with payments made, in hard cash whenever possible, to willing providers. In the first days of the invasion, Rennenkampf issued a series of orders and proclamations promising ample compensation for services rendered. Russian officers regarded themselves as men of honor, not common thieves. They paid for food and forage out of their own pockets when regimental funds were unavailable. German civilians for their part were often so relieved at not being shot, raped, or dispossessed out of hand that they did their utmost to please. Lieutenant Bennigsen described one hostess who was not only willing to sell her uninvited guests everything they needed, but who made coffee and cooked eggs for the young officers before they rode on.

This state of affairs rapidly deteriorated. Small-scale plundering of abandoned property was difficult to control in an army whose NCOs were often reluctant to enforce regulations to the letter, and whose company officers seldom commanded the respect given to their German counterparts. Was it really worth testing already shaky authority for the sake of some straw, a chicken or two, or a few trinkets taken from an empty house—particularly when those swine from the rear echelon were sure to help themselves in any case. And if a carelessly lit cigarette or an overturned lamp meant fires that spread quickly in the August heat, who could spare time and energy to extinguish them? There was still a war to fight. So trophies were thrust into knapsacks or stowed in baggage wagons, as clouds of smoke on the East Prussian horizon suggested that the war was beginning to turn serious.

The Russian army too had its rumors. On August 11, Bennigsen uneasily noted that men of another regiment had responded to a sniping incident by driving the inhabitants of the guilty village into their houses and burning them alive "in a most terrible and merciless manner." Five days later he described villages blazing in the distance—all set on fire by regiments other than his own. By August 17 he wrote of the necessity for carrying a pistol in hand while riding through the streets of a town rendered dangerous by snipers. It is no coincidence that this town was the first place where Bennigsen and his comrades took what they wanted without paying for it. By August 23, Benningsen's squadron was camping in the open to restrict looting. "We are expected," the lieutenant wrote with an old soldier's insouciance, "to behave like gentlemen and pay for everything. It is doubtful if we do."[40]

As the armies groped towards each other, patrol actions became sharper. The wild firing of the first encounters gave way to cooler heads and better aim. Here and there uneasy young men in spiked helmets clustered around the corpse of a Russian trooper before carrying his carbine, saber, or saddle back to their companies as trophies. The occasional Russian airplane was greeted with volleys of rifle fire, even if the airplane turned out to be a soaring bird. Russian artillery observers gave the men of one German company a laugh when they mistook a field kitchen for a machine-gun wagon, took it under fire, and sent it on a wild ride to the rear, the cook and his mate desperately lashing their horses as shrapnel burst around them. Number 1 Company of the 1st Grenadiers was green enough to appreciate the joke even when its noon meal was delayed until late into the night.

More seriously, Russian gunners were showing an uncanny ability to range even the best-concealed German position and bring it under accurate fire in two or three salvos—a fruit of the Manchurian campaign the Germans had not expected. German artillerymen who pushed their guns forward in an effort to compete found themselves under fire from sharpshooters who seemed able to disappear into the ground at will. One venturesome battery of the 52nd Field Artillery came near to being overrun by an assault from trenches no one saw until the Russians were almost on their gun positions. Point-blank rapid fire, with fuses set at zero, saved the day, but the lesson remained vivid: tactically, the Russians were an opponent not to be taken lightly.[41]

Prittwitz was of the same opinion. When he finally learned on August 15 that part of I Corps was east of Gumbinnen, he faced a decision. Rather than ordering François to retreat to the Angerapp, he instructed him instead to concentrate at Gumbinnen, leaving only detachments at Goldap, Stallupönen, and Tollmingkehmen. This was more than simple reluctance to overrule the man on the spot. Air reconnaissance reports and information obtained from prisoners and deserters had created the impression at army headquarters that the main thrust of the Russian advance was coming south of François's presumed position, directly against the line of the Masurian Lakes. Were this true, I Corps might well be able to roll up the enemy right flank in a day or two.

On August 16, another set of fragmentary intelligence reports led Prittwitz and Waldersee to the tentative conclusion that the Russian 1st Army was in fact extended farther north than the lakes—perhaps even far enough to envelop I Corps's left flank. Prittwitz, however, was reluctant to act on the conclusion. Ordering François to change position against a threat that was still vague meant the risk of overcontrolling. The I Corps, the army commander reasoned, should be secure enough around Gumbinnen until the situation became clearer.[42]

Even before Prittwitz's order, François had begun withdrawing his forward elements under Russian pressure. This was more than an operational decision to men like Lance-Corporal Schwadtlo of the 16th Field Artillery. His gun crew helped to destroy his home town of Eydtkuhnen, occupied by the Russian advance guard. Anti-Semites in the same regiment may have found something to think about when Corporal Cohn and his gun team covered the retreat of the 3rd Battery by successfully duelling a Russian machine gun at four hundred meters—a task akin to shooting mice with a rifle, one for which the 77-millimeter field gun had never been designed. In the rifle companies, war diarists marvelled over the ostensible coolness of soldiers who fell asleep in the midst of the heaviest shelling—

161

a stress response still unfamiliar to this inexperienced army. NCOs were learning that a rough tongue and a heavy boot were worth any amount of patriotic exhortation in keeping men in position under fire.[43]

But François had no intention of falling back as far as Gumbinnen. By August 16, instead of the detachments authorized by Prittwitz, I Corps had a brigade of the 2nd Division at Goldap and another at Tollmingkehmen, with the entire 1st Division around Stallupönen. The Germans were extended like beads on a string. A rapid, coordinated Russian advance might well break through François's cordon and strike for the Angerapp, then the Vistula, without opposition. The stakes were higher than François expected when on August 17 he finally found the large-scale trouble he had been seeking.

III

The corps commander was inspecting advanced positions of the 1st Division when he learned that the Russians were on the move. He went immediately to division headquarters in Stallupönen, and learned from Major General Richard von Conta that the 1st Division was being attacked along its entire front. François, concerned with covering as broad a sector as possible, had kept none of his infantry in corps reserve. All that he had available was his battalion of sixteen heavy howitzers, still in Gumbinnen. He ordered them forward to support Conta's division. At the same time he sent a dispatch to the brigade at Tollmingkehmen, ordering it to advance north and attack the Russian left flank. Able to do nothing else at the moment, François and his personal staff went up to the tower of the church at Stallupönen to follow the course of the battle, only to have eardrums and composures temporarily shaken when some overzealous civilians decided to ring the alarm.[44]

The bell tower was far from the noisiest place in the area. German regimental histories are fond of describing the heroic enthusiasm accompanying the baptism of fire—a tendency best described by Mark Twain as "half lie and half forget." Yet even with due allowance for retrospective pieties, morale in Conta's front line was initially high. To the euphoria that can accompany individual recognition of the fact that one is actually surviving under fire was joined the observation that peacetime battle drills seemed to be working in roughly the way that the officers had said they would. Companies taking the trouble to entrench found Russian shrapnel fire more an exhilarating nuisance than a paralyzing danger. One reservist described cheering with his men like children on a playground as the short rounds and duds missed their marks.

From Conta's perspective, the situation offered little encouragement for schoolboy analogies. As the morning progressed more and more Russians entered the battle, until the 1st Division was fighting elements of three Russian divisions. That the Russians attacked piecemeal instead of mounting a coordinated blow is hardly surprising. Their tactical doctrine stressed the importance of engaging from the line of march, deploying as soon as possible after making contact. But war is the province of delay and confusion. Fifteen minutes here, an hour there, and soon enough one is talking about entire days.

There was a deeper question as well, one that involves time measurement. The development of cheap, dependable watches around the middle of the nineteenth century encouraged the diffusion in armies of a knowledge of measured time. The Waltham Watch Company first began showing a profit by selling its bottom-line models to Union soldiers during the American Civil War. At least one Russian colonel subsequently ordered over two hundred watches for his regiment, but rural Russian society in 1914 was still essentially clockless. Peasants caught trains by arriving at stations hours ahead of time, then waiting. Religious and secular officials drew crowds for their ceremonies in the same fashion. Time, like land, was not seen as an individual's property.[45] In such a context, a NCO's or subaltern's possession of a watch did not mean that he comprehended, much less internalized, the value system accompanying the timepiece. At company and battalion levels, particularly in the infantry, a time sense was likely to be an artificial product of training and exhortation, rather than the virtually automatic reflex of an industrialized society.

Whatever the reason, Conta's division never received the one hammer blow that might have finished it. The I Corps's heavy howitzers reached the field around noon. Their ninety-pound shells were a welcome supplement to the lighter pieces of the divisional artillery, but they could not prevent the Russians from working around both of Conta's exposed flanks and probing for gaps in his forward positions. The 43rd Infantry was especially hard pressed. By 11:30 a.m. its last reserves had been engaged; an hour later it was reporting Russians in front, flank, and rear. If the regiment held its ground, it was in good part because no one could think of anywhere safe to run.

Writing fifteen years later, Conta indignantly denied that he held a council of war with his staff to discuss ways of coping with the threat.[46] The vehemence of his protest suggests that something like that probably did take place. It would have been a logical move for a man who had been commanding a division less than a year, and whose appointment reflected the fact that he was junior to François as much as any specific professional qualifications.

Around midday François found an opportunity to visit his hardpressed subordinate. The result of the conference was a decision to follow prewar doctrine. The 1st Division was engaged too closely to retreat; it was therefore necessary to buy space by counterattacking. Two battalions of the 3rd Grenadiers went forward, but were stopped in their tracks within minutes by superior Russian forces. They were able to do no more than hold their ground against repeated counterattacks by enemy infantry who once again showed themselves masters of concealment in apparently open terrain.

Unable to go back or forward, with all four of his regiments in line, Conta by early afternoon was borrowing companies and battalions from everywhere in his sector to shore up weak spots. Trying to protect his flanks, he opened a five-kilometer-wide gap in his center. That the Russians did not turn opportunity to disaster owed something to their failure to spot the opportunity quickly. It owed more to two rifle companies of the 41st Infantry, less than five hundred men. Thrown into the gap like the 20th Maine at Little Round Top, they held their ground against fivefold odds, bought time for the rest of the division to reform its lines, and were completely forgotten by everyone but themselves as the day wore on.[47]

Their isolation was not unique. Everywhere on the field orders failed to arrive, or were garbled beyond recognition in transmission. The German army's inclusion of buglers in its ranks was by no means an anachronistic dream involving heroic attacks to the sound of regimental bands. The musicians were expected to transmit simple situation reports and pass on orders by sounding or repeating the appropriate short calls. It worked well enough in maneuvers, and in the small-scale fire fights on the border. But in the front lines of a modern battle, any bugler foolhardy enough to expose himself was likely to be shot down before the first notes left his instrument. If by chance he did complete a call it was often drowned out, or went unheard by officers whose attention was far more distracted than they had ever expected.

This put much of the burden of communication on runners. The peacetime army had generated amusement and anger by insisting that soldiers addressed by a superior should give loud, clear, short replies, looking the man they were addressing straight in the eye. For critics of the system, this "military expression" was a means of subordination, an expression of spirit-crushing militarism that reduced the private soldier to the status of a trained animal. Combat quickly demonstrated that the indoctrination had a functional purpose as well as a social one. At platoon or company level, messages and orders were often verbal. If written, they were likely to be cryptic, scrawled on any handy piece of paper, often unsigned. The recipient seldom had time to question carefully a man who might well have delivered the information at substantial risk of his own life. Nor could a platoon commander afford the luxury of meaningful dialogue with his squad leaders while under fire. In the area of personal communications, at least, the Prussian drillmasters knew well what they had been doing.

The Germans were feeling the limits of peacetime doctrine and peacetime training in other ways. The local counterattacks demanded in the manuals produced limited results, but generated heavy straggling as men were shocked out of the fighting line or became lost in the confusion. Ammunition ran low. Chains of command broke as companies and battalions plugged holes in strange formations. Conta was too good a soldier not to be aware that his division was being squeezed into a pocket. There was still plenty of daylight for the Russians to complete the process; and François's cheerful assurances that support was on its way from

Tollmingkehmen was no substitute for more rifles in the firing line. Then the high command of the 8th Army made a long-distance appearance.

Early on the morning of August 17, a supply requisition was brought to the army commander's attention. It came from I Corps, and requested replenishing of ammunition used in skirmishes on August 15—skirmishes whose locations were far east of where the corps was supposed to be. Full generals do not normally concern themselves with routine supply matters. The incident leaves a suspicion that some of Prittwitz's staff officers used the situation as an excuse to discuss with their chief the rumors about François's behavior. The army commander telephoned Insterburg, still the official corps headquarters, to demand specific information on I Corps's positions. Further dissembling was impossible. For the first time Prittwitz discovered that François had posted most of his corps far forward of his assigned position at Gumbinnen, that he was in fact forty kilometers in front of the Angerapp. Eighth Army's other units had not even reached their assigned positions along the river. If I Corps became heavily engaged, there was no possible way to support it.

The horrified Prittwitz immediately ordered François to retire at once on Gumbinnen, avoiding battle if possible. To ensure that this order, at least, was delivered, Prittwitz instructed that an officer be sent forward from Insterburg. According to François, the man found him in the bell tower at Stallupönen and shouted, "The commanding general orders you to break off the battle at once and retire on Gumbinnen." François replied, "Tell General von Prittwitz that General von François will break off the battle when the Russians are beaten."

Whether or not François really expressed himself so dramatically matters little. A diplomatic junior staff officer softened the dispatch in transit to read that François was "not at the time able to break off the combat." In any case it was after 3:00 p.m. before the reply reached Insterburg and was telephoned to Prittwitz. It was the first direct communication of any kind from François in several days. To say that Prittwitz was shocked by it is an understatement. His only reasonable choice at the moment was to hope that I Corps could hold on, and settle accounts with its commander at day's end.[48]

But if army command could do nothing, help was on the way from the south. Major-General von Falk had commanded François's 2nd Division only since mobilization, replacing an officer promoted to one of the new reserve corps. His last peacetime assignment had been behind a desk, commanding the small arms school. But he knew how a field soldier of the German army was supposed to act in a crisis. From his headquarters at Tollmingkehmen he heard the sound of gunfire in Conta's sector early in the morning. Without waiting for François's orders he decided at once to join the battle.

Falk had six battalions and thirty-six guns available. He left two battalions and six guns at Tollmingkehmen with orders to hold at all costs. By 11:30 a.m., the rest of his brigade was on its march north; by 2:00 p.m. it had reached the village of Todszuhnen, just south of Conta's line.

Falk deployed his riflemen off the line of march and began advancing northeast. The Russians had been probing for an open flank all day; it was the Germans who found one. Suddenly the men of the Russian 27th Division found themselves under German fire from two directions. They saw long lines of men in field grey, elements of Falk's 33rd Fusiliers and 45th Infantry, moving towards them from the south. Simultaneously Conta's 3rd Grenadiers and part of the 43rd Infantry launched one last counterattack to their front. For men thirsty and bewildered, already stunned by a day's hard fighting, the combined pressure was too much to withstand. The 27th Division dissolved in panic; the Russians fell back all along the line. Over three thousand of them remained as prisoners in German hands. At least as many were dead or wounded.

The neat local success owed much to the initiative of von Falk. His march to the sound of the guns was in the best textbook traditions of the German army—a calculated risk to restore a dangerous situation. Three German brigades had fought three Russian divisions to a standstill, holding the field both materially and morally. This was war the way it was supposed to be: victory at the end of a day's hard fighting, with the enemy in full retreat, prisoners on their way to the rear, colonels and majors shaking hands in the midst of a stricken field. But it was an empty triumph. Strong Russian forces were advancing on both sides of the immediate battlefield. To the north, Russian cavalry patrols had been reported around Pilkallen. To the south, a full division was pressing towards Goldap. Another division was threatening Falk's original position, and that the two battalions left there suffered only two fatal casualties all afternoon did not diminish the imminent danger of a breakthrough in that sector.

François had decided to retreat even before he arrived at his corps headquarters and found both a direct order to withdraw to Gumbinnen and a sharp demand for an explanation of his reasons for advancing and engaging the enemy in defiance of Prittwitz's plans. François immediately telephoned army headquarters. With understandable exaggeration he informed his chief that "two enemy corps" had been decisively defeated and forced back over the frontier.[49]

More important to Prittwitz was the information Stallupönen gave about the overall enemy deployment. The strong forces engaged there indicated that the main Russian axis of advance was significantly farther north than he had believed—a useful confirmation of his decision to concentrate 8th Army along the Angerapp. A general made of sterner stuff or flushed with the rectitude of certitude might have relieved, or at least severely reprimanded, I Corps's unruly commander. But by that evening Hermann von François possessed more direct experience of modern war than anyone of his rank in the 8th Army. Who, moreover, would take his place? Conta and Falk were new in their current assignments; no spare senior officers were in the theater. And once his corps was safely back on the Angerapp, François would be under Prittwitz's direct supervision. The army commander decided, *faute de mieux*, to overlook the circumstances.

François used up a career's worth of luck on August 17. His sovereign contempt for the enemy may have been justified by events, but it was not a good spirit with which to begin operations against superior numbers. The fact that he escaped disaster—and even won a striking little victory—cannot conceal the danger of the premises underlying his "rock soup" deployment. It can be readily admitted, particularly in view of later events, that his military ability was superior to that of Prittwitz. It is possible to justify his concept of attacking the Russians as far to the east as possible. But deliberately jeopardizing a corps to prove a point is quite another matter. As it was, François escaped unscathed, justified in his own mind by events, and firmly convinced that he alone was able to conduct the campaign in East Prussia. His pride was to play a major role in the subsequent development of events.

Yepantschin, whose III Corps did most of the Russian fighting at Stallupönen, originally proposed to renew the attack all along the line at 4:00 a.m. on August 18. During the night, however, his patrols discovered that the Germans were gone. Only the two companies of the 41st Infantry, who had held the center of the line by themselves for so much of the day, remained in their hastily dug trenches in front of the village of Bilderweitschen. It grew darker and darker. Strawstacks were set on fire to provide improvised illumination. Nothing was visible far and wide but Russians, some dead and too many very much alive. The senior German captain insisted that he had no orders to retreat, and as a soldier he was accustomed to fight where he was put. When the Russians sent forward a white flag and a request to surrender, he reacted by ordering his men to resume firing their scarce ammunition at invisible targets. The other company commander responded to a subaltern's hint that such heroics were misplaced by declaring that he could not leave a comrade in the lurch, and had promised to fight to the finish.

As the Germans fixed bayonets for a last stand, the Russians worked around their main positions and into Bilderweitschen. Not until their reserve platoons reported house-to-house fighting did the fire-eating captains agree that it was time to go. And once again peacetime discipline proved its value. The men of the 41st not only succeeded in withdrawing through Bilderweitschen in pitch darkness with almost no straggling, they brought with them thirty prisoners when they rejoined a regiment by this time convinced their comrades were well on their way to Siberia.[50]

The incident did nothing to encourage vigorous pursuit. Not until late in the afternoon of August 18 did the Russians resume their advance. The ferocity of Falk's counterattack had concealed its weakness. Its direction, south to north, suggested to Rennenkampf that the main German concentration was somewhere south of Stallupönen. This in turn meant the enemy's contact with Königsberg was correspondingly weak. For an army commander with no desire to bog down in a siege of that strong fortress the next logical move seemed to be a right hook, moving between the 8th Army and Königsberg to drive the Germans south and west. They might stand and fight on the Angerapp; they might keep going towards the Vistula. The Russian advance continued on August 19, and met no resistance severe enough to change the army commander's mind about German intentions.

Rennenkampf decided to give his infantry a day of rest on August 20. This decision reflected both logistic and operational considerations. The 1st Army had been moving forward for six days. Its first march had been forced; all the others had been accompanied by fighting. Straggling was becoming endemic. Supply columns lagged far behind the troops they were supposed to be feeding. The East Prussian countryside offered limited possibilities for inexperienced foragers. By a combination of design and accident most large stores of grain and fodder had been set on fire as the Russians advanced. In a deeper sense the Russian army's strength lay in its steadiness, not its glitter. Brilliant operational strokes were not the empire's forte. To attempt them, Rennenkampf reasoned, was to compete with the Germans at their strongest point. Wherever it might be fought, the next battle was more likely to be lost through excessive haste, and the resulting disorder, than by taking a bit of time to restore his army's balance.

His commanders obeyed the order to halt with more alacrity than expected. Before the war German observers at Russian maneuvers had noted the cavalry's inability to keep touch with a moving enemy even under peacetime conditions. Now the Cavalry Corps went into bivouac after a few skirmishes with German *Landwehr*. All along the 1st Army's front troopers stacked their lances, unsaddled their horses, and stoked their campfires. The Germans were allowed to disappear into the middle distance. This loss of contact was to cost the Russians dearly the next day.[51]

In the aftermath of Stallupönen, Prittwitz had feared an immediate Russian pursuit of I Corps. On learning that the Russians were not following François closely, however, the army commander decided to await the Russians behind the Angerapp. But he also ordered I Corps to remain concentrated around Gumbinnen, somewhat in advance of the main position.[52] Why Prittwitz still left this corps in such an isolated position is not clear. Perhaps he simply disliked giving François another order to retreat.[53] It is more probable that Prittwitz still underestimated the northward extension of the 1st Army's right flank. He expected that the Russians could not avoid attacking the line of the Angerapp head-on. By the evening of August 18 the position was strongly held by XVII Corps, I Reserve Corps, and the independent 3rd Reserve Division. These formations should be well able to hold their ground while François struck the Russian right and rear. But just in case the Russians might after all be in a position to do the outflanking, just in case their line extended farther north than expected, François was authorized to move his southern division, the 2nd, into reserve behind his left flank. To fill the resulting gap in his line, he was assigned the field reserve of the fortress of

Königsberg, a division's worth of *Landwehr* and Ersatz troops with thirty-six guns and a dozen heavy howitzers. They might not be able to take ground; they could reasonably be expected to hold it.[54]

The relatively limited intelligence on Russian movements in good part reflected the problems faced by 8th Army's airmen. Flying in 1914 was enough of a risk to strain the least sensitive nerves. Improvised airstrips, bad weather, and the embryonic antiaircraft defense of several thousand Russians shooting into the air at random had reduced the efficiency of the air crews even further. The Russians were also improving their camouflage discipline. At the beginning of the campaign the German airmen had had an almost free hand against an enemy apparently making no effort to conceal his movements. Now, particularly as they advanced into the thick forests along the frontier, the Russians became increasingly difficult to see and count. Add to this the risk, magnified tenfold by rumor, of being massacred by Cossacks should one be forced to land in Russian-held territory, and the increasing vagueness of reconnaissance reports is readily explained. [55]

The army's *Flieger Abteilungen* nevertheless braved overcast skies and Russian rifle fire throughout August 18 to report that the Russian 1st Army was still advancing slowly, and that a wide gap existed between its left flank and the right flank of the force coming from the Narew. Then at 10:45 a.m. on the 19th, 8th Army headquarters received three separate reports that the Russian Narew army had definitely begun to move. That fact made a quick victory over the 1st Army more urgent than ever, but by this time German radio operators had picked up Rennenkampf's orders for a halt on the 20th.

Virtually every account of the Tannenberg campaign mentions the Russian practice of sending radio messages in the clear, and suggests it as another paradigm for the weaknesses of the Tsarist empire. It seems almost a shame to diminish the legend by mentioning that the Germans did not always code their messages either. Like their Russian counterparts, German military codes were simple substitution ciphers—childish by modern standards. Yet German communications officers feared loss of the code books, and were under constant pressure to balance security against speed and accuracy. These concerns were even more significant on the Russian side. Coordinating an advance in enemy country depended heavily on efficient communications. Telephone or telegraph lines were easily tapped. The ether was free, and the danger of using codes their intended recipients might be unable to decipher appeared greater than the possibility that the Germans would monitor every possible frequency. It was a calculated risk, and not an unreasonable one.

In theory the large permanent stations at places like Posen or Königsberg, manned by well-trained cadres of operators, should have found little difficulty in picking up and passing on the Russian messages. Reality was less impressive. German fortresses were officially responsible for monitoring their neighbors' broadcasts. Their successes had been mixed, and depended heavily on the availability of interpreters and knowledge of whether or not the broadcasts were in code or clear. From the start of mobilization, moreover, the fortresses and the field signal units had a multiplying number of higher-priority missions. Neither instruments nor operators could be spared to scan empty air. Interception of Rennenkampf's order was a corresponding piece of luck.[56]

The interception may have been a significant intelligence coup. Nevertheless twentieth-century communications technology, the airplane and the radio, had combined to put Prittwitz in a quandary. Dared the Germans continue to wait for the Russian advance to reach the Angerapp? Or was it now necessary to force the issue in the north, abandoning prepared field positions and attacking possibly superior numbers before the Russians from the Narew came within striking range? Prittwitz and Waldersee temporized until once again François made the army commander's decision for him.

Around 4:00 p.m. on August 19 François telephoned Prittwitz to inform him that he expected to be attacked in force either that evening or early on the 20th. The corps commander's proposed countermove reflected his faith both in technology and in the young officers of his reconnaissance squadron. Their reports repeated again and again that the Russians in I Corps's sector were advancing in force but carelessly, without much apparent regard for march discipline or flank security. François was sure that a spoiling attack, delivered before the Russian deployment could begin, would have an excellent chance of success. He proposed to move Falk's 2nd Division not into reserve, as Prittwitz had authorized, but right around the corps's main line, to strike the Russian right flank from the north as it came within range. To support the attack, François begged Prittwitz to order XVII Corps and I Reserve Corps forward.[57]

Prittwitz initially said that he could decide only when he had a better view of the situation farther south. But by the evening of the 19th, that view was rapidly taking shape. The Russian 2nd Army's vanguards were across the border and advancing on Ortelsburg. As for the Russian 1st Army, air reconnaissance reported no enemy anywhere near the Angerapp. Instead, up to two divisions were advancing from the south and east towards Darkehmen, a few miles south of Gumbinnen. This combined with François's earlier report to convince Prittwitz that his subordinate had been right: the Russians *were* advancing in force on I Corps's position. At 4:50 p.m. Prittwitz informed François that XVII Corps would attack the next morning in support of I Corps's offensive. François said that "this joyful message took a weight from my soul." He summoned his division commanders immediately and began issuing orders for his own attack.[58]

Once again François's determination overcame the caution of his superior. This time, however, he had received assistance from the Russian advance in the south. Prittwitz saw that if he waited much longer, the 2nd Army might be in his rear before he could even attack the 1st Army, much less destroy it. Whether he perceived the coming action as a decisive battle is debatable. One of his aides referred to a *Gefecht*, or combat, in German military terminology an action of lesser magnitude.[59] Prittwitz's orders, moreover, did not allow for the simultaneous use of his entire available force. Instead the 8th Army would enter battle in echelon from the left, with I Corps opening the battle against the Russians around Gumbinnen. The XVII Corps would then advance against the left and rear of an enemy facing, and, pinned in place by François, Prittwitz believed a single corps alone was strong enough to force a decision in that sector. The rest of the 8th Army would have to do no more than act as a flank guard. The I Reserve Corps would attack and fix any Russians to its front; the 3rd Reserve Division, on the army's far right, was in turn to cover I Reserve Corps.[60]

Engaging the enemy a corps at a time was not taught in the War Academy, or anywhere else. *Klotzen, nicht Kleckern*, "kick, don't tickle," was a German army rule of thumb long before Heinz Guderian. Perhaps unconsciously, Prittwitz and Waldersee had set the stage for François. If I Corps's commander had correctly read the situation, if his troops could do what he expected, the next day's prospects were good. Otherwise, Germany's main force in the east ran the risk of being defeated in detail and rolled up like a rug.

6
First Contact: Gumbinnen

I

François' plan mixed pragmatism and audacity. The increasing size of armies in the latter nineteenth century had made flank attacks increasingly difficult to deliver even in maneuvers. Some German generals had adjusted their thinking towards the concept of breakthrough. For François, however, war's tactical challenge continued to be in creating flanks where none existed. At Stallupönen he had come close to being enveloped from the north. Now he proposed to turn the tables by pulling Falk's 2nd Division out of its position on I Corps's right and sending it on a night march across the rear of the 1st Division and around the open Russian flank. Falk was to attack at 4:00 a.m. and drive the Russians onto the 1st Division's guns.

The prospect of a fifteen-kilometer night march ending in a dawn attack against a superior enemy did little to soothe anyone's nerves. No sooner were his men on the move than Falk received a report that the Russians had broken through the 1st Division. Falk promptly halted his men to meet the supposed threat. What had happened was one of those incidents which generals in any war usually de-emphasize or omit from their memoirs. With dusk turning to night, someone in the wagon lines of the 1st Division had shouted that the Russians were coming. Given the marches and countermarches of the past few days, anything seemed possible. Tired men groped for rifles and packs. Others started from the half-sleep of exhaustion and began to run. Equally tired officers sought to bring some order out of confusion slipping into chaos. By the time discipline was restored, I Corps's rumor mill had spread the story of the supposed breakthrough everywhere in the sector.

When Falk learned that the Russian threat was imaginary, he took

172

advantage of a peacetime amenity, the excellent and still-functioning East Prussian telephone network, to ask François directly if the planned movement was still possible. His division had lost over two vital hours forming a front against nightmares. François replied with a direct order to move immediately. Falk knew better than to argue. At 10:00 p.m. he reported that his division would be in position to attack by the assigned time. He had six hours to make good his assurances.[1]

The 2nd Division's deployment was complicated by fog heavy enough to cause a thirty-minute delay in the attack. Nevertheless the first rush caught the men of Smirnov's XX Corps in their blankets. As Falk's artillery poured shrapnel into the Russian bivouac areas, his infantry stormed forward. The village of Mallwischken fell to the first charge of the 33rd Fusiliers. A squad of the 4th Grenadiers was able to get close enough to the Russian gun lines to shoot a field battery out of its position, taking two guns and fifty dazed prisoners. Everywhere men in flat caps and brown uniforms seemed to be throwing down their rifles and calling for quarter: "We are Christians too, brothers!" Then almost in minutes the situation changed. As the German infantry outran their supporting batteries, Russian rifles and machine guns took toll of the advancing troops. Losses were almost absurdly light by the standards of 1916 or 1918, but as men began to drop, their comrades went to earth and stayed there for two hours.

Around 8:00 a.m. two battalion commanders of the 45th Infantry tried to mount a bayonet charge. The relatively low casualty lists of their formations for the day indicate that their soldiers melted away behind them. Not until German artillery worked forward and apparently silenced the last of the machine-gun nests did German bugles get any response when they sounded the advance.

As the German riflemen stood hesitantly upright they learned another harsh lesson of twentieth-century war: some defenders always survive. A battalion of the 45th Infantry was stopped in its tracks by fire from a barn as yet unnoticed by the artillery observers. Lance Corporal Otto Reusteck rushed the barn, reached the dead ground beneath the wall, and took out his matches. He needed only moments to ignite the dry wood of a building full of ripe grain. The barn burst into flames. Its Russian occupants, unable to find a way out or unwilling to face the German rifles, burned alive. Reusteck's good fortune ran out on the way back to his company. He was killed—probably by a shot from the burning barn.

These were not the same Russians who had been so easily scattered by the flank attack at Stallupönen. Their artillery ranged German batteries and German skirmish lines with equal facility. Once over the initial surprise their infantry fought desperately from improvised trenches and foxholes, shooting at everything that moved, fighting to the last man against Germans who were as confused as their enemies. Not until 11:30 a.m. were men of the 45th Infantry able to rush what had become the key to the Russian position, the strongly defended village of Uszballen.

Since the introduction of firearms, Europe's armies had utilized farms and villages to anchor defensive positions, nightmares to the attacker. For every Blenheim, with a garrison massed too closely either to move or to shoot, there were a dozen Hougoumonts or Le Bourgets to act as bones in the throat of a regiment, a division, sometimes an army corps. Clearing them usually meant street-by-street, house-by-house brawling that could leave the victors as disorganized as the vanquished, and correspondingly vulnerable to counterattack.

Logic suggests that street fighting should have formed a major element of any European army's peacetime training—particularly one as offensive-minded as Germany's. Yet while Europe grew more densely settled after 1871, maneuvers were held on open ground. No annual budgets included money to construct dummy villages, or to purchase farmsteads for practice assaults. Instead doctrine prescribed avoiding built-up areas wherever possible, bypassing them and leaving their neutralization to the artillery.[2]

However sound might be the principle, its execution proved impossible on the 2nd Division's front. There were enough Russians in Uszballen to pin down any clever flanking movements, and no time to wait for the guns. Lieutenants took their platoons into the village outskirts, a subaltern of the 45th's 9th Company showing the way by capturing two dug-in machine guns one after the other. By the time the fighting reached the center of town, sergeants and corporals were setting the pace. As yet the German infantry had no grenades, that subsequently indispensable weapon in house-to-house fighting. The magazines of their rifles held only five rounds. Not all of the peacetime training in gymnastics and bayonet drill had been wasted. Cold steel and rifle butts took the men of the 45th forward against desperate resistance. It was noon when the Russians broke, the few survivors seeking shelter in the basements and outbuildings of a village ablaze from end to end.

As the firing died down Uszballen's conquerors became suddenly and uncomfortably conscious of the stench of charring bodies, the screams of trapped Russians suffocating or burning alive. For not a few of the 2nd Division's young men the taste of victory was a mouthful of vomit as company officers and NCOs tried to collect prisoners and organize rescue parties. Majors and colonels, more concerned than their juniors with pursuing a beaten enemy, ordered bugles sounded and colors unfurled as rallying points, but it took a half hour to round up enough exhausted, nauseated rank and file to launch a halfhearted movement forward towards the next cluster of villages.[3]

At 5:30 a.m. Conta had ordered the 1st Division forward into a nightmarish network of fortified farms and villages, connected by hastily dug trenches. Conta deployed his four regiments abreast, retaining only local reserves. The front-line battalions advanced under flying colors, to the beat of drums and the sound of bugles. Almost immediately they began taking heavy casualties from sharpshooters concealed in the trees or firing from roofs and cellars. A lieutenant of the 1st Grenadiers kept

First Contact: Gumbinnen

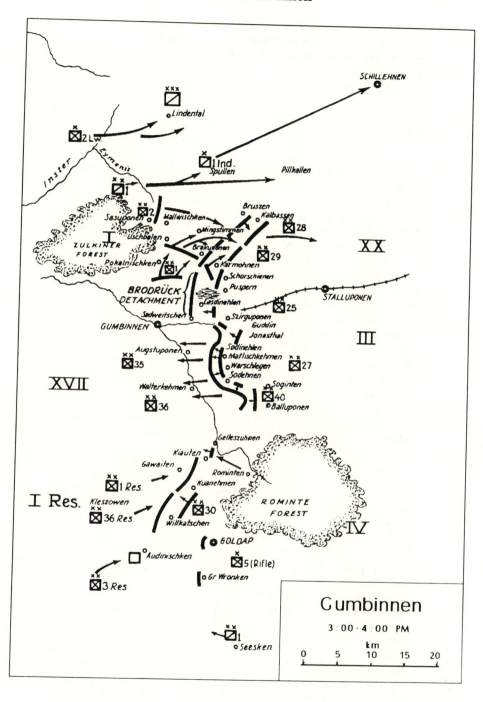

SCHILLEHNEN

Lindental

XXX

2 L.W.

Inster

Eymenis

1 Ind.
Spullen

Pillkallen

1

Bruszen

Kalbassen

2

Mallwischken

Sasupanen

28

Uschbalen

Mingslimmen

Brakupanen

ZULKINER
FOREST

Pokalnischken

29

XX

Karmohnen

Schorschienen

Puspern

STALLUPONEN

BRODRÜCK
DETACHMENT

Lasdinehlen

25

Sadweitschen

Szirguponen

GUMBINNEN

Guddin

Jonasthal

Sodinehlen

Augstuponen

Matlischkehmen

35

Warschlegen

27

Sodehnen

Walterkehmen

Soginten

40

36

Balluponen

Gelleszuphen

Kiauten

Gawaiten

Romniten

1 Res.

Kuanehmen

ROMINTE
FOREST

Kleszowen

30

36 Res.

Willkatschen

Audirischken

GOLDAP

5 (Rifle)

3 Res.

Gr Wronken

XVII

I Res.

III

IV

XX

Gumbinnen

3:00 - 4:00 PM

km

| 0 | 5 | 10 | 15 | 20 |

1

Seesken

175

shouting that the Russians could hit nothing until he dropped with a bullet in his chest. The same regiment's fusilier battalion worked to within a hundred meters of another Russian position to be confronted with white flags, shirt-tails, and handkerchiefs. The unwary who moved forward to take the presumed surrender were met with a burst of fire at point-blank range.

Time after time in the early days of World War I, combatants accused each other of deliberate misuse of the white flag. Apart from the obvious chances of confusion, with troops unaware of the flag's presence responding to an apparent enemy advance, German junior officers and enlisted men seem to have been generally ignorant of two facts about a white flag. It signifies no more than a desire to parley, and it is not necessarily a sign of surrender. Moreover, the hoister of the flag is expected to take the initiative in making contact. The Germans were not required to expose themselves in response to the Russian gesture; they did so at their own risk. But few rifle platoons contained experts in the fine points of the laws of war. The Grenadiers overran the trenches and shot or bayonetted every man in them. Their regimental history records the deed with pride.

Like Falk's 2nd Division, Conta's men fell into increasing confusion as they pushed forward. For every enemy position cleared, every trench rushed, two more seemed to appear. Regimental and battalion staffs discovered that remaining mounted within range of the Russian rifles was suicidal; even led horses offered too inviting a target. This in turn reduced the speed of order transmission to the strength of a man's legs and the soundness of his lungs. In peacetime adjutants and orderly officers, well rested and well mounted, carried fresh instructions to rifle companies advancing against blank cartridges or marked enemies. Now they ran desperately from place to place, cursing every glass of beer and every cigar consumed so casually before August 1.

By 11:00 a.m. the village of Brakupönen, key to the Russian position on Conta's front, fell in another vicious seesaw dogfight. The 28th Division, which had thus far provided most of the opposition to François's corps, began to crumble. Its men retreated in all directions, one regimental color party getting as far as the fortress of Kovno almost fifty miles inside Russia, where it turned over its symbolic burden to a bemused commandant. But the division's seven thousand casualties, half its infantry strength, gave proof of its hard fight. Five thousand were prisoners, but most of them had been too closely engaged for retreat to be practical. When they surrendered it was with their rifles in their hands, and every German account from the fighting line pays tribute to their valor and endurance.[4]

Any chance for François to achieve his mini-Cannae ended shortly after noon.[5] Conta's men were already overmarched and underfed by the standards of peacetime maneuvers. The 28th Division might be broken, but its sister formations were mounting fierce local counterattacks. Then Falk's artillery took a hand. The 2nd Division's batteries, out of a

176

generalized sense that something must be done to stop the Russian attacks, began blasting the landscape in front of them almost at random. They found their targets in the ranks of Conta's infantry. Men stood upright in a hail of shrapnel, waving their arms, swinging helmets on the points of their bayonets. One colonel ordered his bugles to sound the signal to cease fire, in the desperate hope that the gunners might hear. Two months later at Langemarck, uniformed adolescents would sing patriotic songs to identify themselves to their equally raw comrades of the artillery. The men of I Corps took the direct approach and ran for their lives.

Most of the 1st Division and part of the 2nd streamed off the battlefield in disorder. But the Russians had been too badly shaken to take real advantage of the German discomfiture. Once out of the zone of their own artillery, most of the running men stopped to catch their breath, then milled around until their officers and NCOs began sorting them into companies and platoons. Messengers on bicycles finally reached the gunners and informed them of their error. Between 1:30 and 2:30 p.m. the Germans began moving forward again. Around 3:00 p.m. they reached the Gumbinnen-Kussen road. There they stopped.

Straggling and heat exhaustion by now were felling more men than Russian bullets. Officers, themselves tired and stunned from a day's hard fighting, could no longer galvanize their staggering riflemen. The I Corps had no reserves left to exploit its success. There was no sign of XVII Corps, supposed to be advancing from the south. At 4:00 p.m. François reluctantly gave the order: halt for the day.

What had become of XVII Corps's attack? Its commander, August von Mackensen, is most familiar as a background member of Adolf Hitler's entourage in the 1930s: a hawk-faced, fiercely mustached old man, eyes deep-set under the fur busby with the skull-and-crossbones insignia of his old regiment, the 2nd Hussars. But Mackensen's symbolic role in fusing the old and new Germanies began far earlier. Born in 1849, the son of a nonnoble estate manager, he served as a one-year volunteer in 1869 and spent two years at the University of Halle. Recalled to active duty for the Franco-Prussian War, he earned a field commission as a reserve officer, then after a brief return to the university, transferred to the active army and made a successful career as soldier and courtier. One of the new empire's finest horsemen, he first attracted notice for his performances on the amateur turf. Detached to tutor the future Kaiser William in military history, Mackensen did much to establish the young Prince's image of an ideal officer. But it was his skills as an administrator, unusual for a cavalryman, that earned him assignment to the general staff without the usual background of War Academy training, and subsequent appointment as Schlieffen's adjutant in 1891. William II not only named Mackensen an imperial adjutant—a status giving him the continuing privilege of direct access to the kaiser—he sent his eldest son to serve under Mackensen's command in the 2nd Hussars.

By this time the commoner's boy had become almost too polished for some of his contemporaries. His elegant manners, especially a predilection for kissing the imperial hand, evoked hostility. But his six-foot good looks aroused enough open, and reciprocated, admiration from the court's ladies to stifle any snide remarks about Mackensen's sexual proclivities. The kaiser's favor continued to bring tangible rewards: promotion to colonel, advancement to the ranks of the nobility, assignment in 1903 to command the 30th Division in Alsace. Five years later, as *General der Kavallerie*, he took over XVII Corps. In 1914 he was Prittwitz's senior subordinate.[6]

Mackensen was also part of one of the Edwardian era's more intriguing legends. In 1903 British Major-General Sir Hector Macdonald, a public hero of the empire's little wars, committed suicide in a Paris hotel in the wake of charges of homosexual behavior with adolescent boys. The event generated a broad spectrum of rumors, including one that Macdonald had been a victim of blackmail by the German secret service. On the point of exposure, he and his employers staged a suicide. Macdonald defected to Germany and took the place of a senior officer dying of cancer. That officer was August von Mackensen.[7]

The difficulties involved in making such a switch—not the least of them being the four inches' difference in height between the two men—did not scotch the stories, which surfaced again as recently as 1962. Perhaps Mackensen's subordinates might not have regarded the exchange as a dead loss. Macdonald was a combat-experienced infantryman. As for Mackensen, it was generally conceded that he was a hard driver and a fierce disciplinarian. His tactical abilities were more dubious, particularly among infantry generals critical on principle of cavalry officers in corps commands. In the 1910 maneuvers I Corps, then commanded by von Kluck, had made XVII Corps look ridiculous by erecting camouflage screens and dummy wood lots, so changing the appearance of the terrain that Mackensen's officers lost confidence in their own maps. It was the kind of fiasco that terminated many a career. Though Mackensen's imperial connections helped him to survive, the story remained good for a laugh over drinks in the *Kasinos* of eastern Germany—those, that is, outside the XVII Corps district.

Whatever Mackensen's professional shortcomings, he knew his subordinates well; he was proud of his corps and eager to show his mettle in the field. At sixty-five he was not likely to have many more chances. To him the war was a welcome alternative to imminent retirement in some sleepy garrison town. He received Prittwitz's order to advance at 4:40 p.m. on the 19th. Fifty minutes later XVII Corps, less one regiment, was on the move.

Mackensen's men faced a twenty-five-kilometer night march from their original concentration area on the Angerapp before reaching the assigned line of departure on the Rominte River. The XVII Corps had had several days of rest; peacetime experience indicated that the march was well within the capacity of the active soldiers and young reservists who filled its ranks. Advancing to a first battle, however, imposed a different set of stresses than the most difficult peacetime exercises. The roads were crowded with civilians fleeing their homes in the face of lurid stories of Russian atrocities. Bellowing cattle and bleating sheep, lost children seeking their parents, women and old men seeking to save what they could in the absence of husbands and sons called to arms—it was a discouraging montage to the green German infantrymen. Rumors shot through the marching columns. Cossacks had occupied the Angerapp crossings. The Russian Guards were ready to enter the battle. The roads ahead were mined. By daylight gossip might have been laughed away. In the darkness men thrown on their own resources found it easy to take counsel of the little, formless fears that made Napoleon describe two-o'clock-in-the-morning courage as among the rarest of military commodities.[8]

Circumstances tried nerves still further. Time and again the streams of refugees forced the marching columns to detour from main roads onto rough, unpaved tracks. Field kitchens and supply wagons tipped over in the fading light or bogged down in sand. Unexpected halts, a half-dozen in an hour, broke the marching rhythm. Muscles cramped and limbs stiffened during pauses too short to provide real rest. The German army put much store on singing in the ranks—not merely as a gesture of high morale to please the officers, but as a means of keeping men moving, providing a distraction from the boots and the knapsack of the man in front. By twilight the voices of XVII Corps were muted. The leading squads in a company might sustain a song out of respect for or fear of the captain riding at their head. No one else was feeling musical.

As the sound of gunfire from François's sector grew louder, anxious officers forced the pace. It began to rain—a cold, steady drizzle whose sharp contrast to the day's heat enhanced the misery of the men in the ranks. Under all but the strictest discipline, any long marching column tends to suffer from an accordion effect: it stretches out until the men at the rear have to double-time to close the formation. Platoons and companies lost touch in the rain, attaching themselves to other formations and straggling back to their parent units as best they might. Mackensen's regiments were playing crack-the-whip by the time they reached their bivouac areas.

Another problem, one generally overlooked even in the biologically obsessed literature of a later era, involved calls of nature. In the German army men were expected to relieve themselves during the regulation halts of five or ten minutes in the hour. But the emotions accompanying a trying night march, with a battle certain to follow, had an inevitable effect on bowels and bladders. At least one company commander ordered that all short-taken privates be accompanied by a corporal who was responsible for seeing his charges back into the ranks by the next halt. The same captain detailed his senior lieutenant and the company *Feldwebel* to march in the rear and make certain that no one fell out of ranks without permission.[9] Other officers were less cautious. More and more stragglers exchanged relief for anxiety as they vainly sought their place in the ranks.

It was almost dawn when XVII Corps finally halted. Artillery batteries pushed forward to their improvised gun lines. Staff officers galloped here and there seeking to avoid giving the impression of confusion. Infantrymen threw themselves down on the damp ground for whatever rest they could catch. Pitching shelter halves in the wet darkness seemed a useless exercise for the few hours remaining before dawn. There were no friendly farmers to provide bundles of straw to soften the ground. And why waste the hour necessary to unpack, then repack, heavily laden knapsacks? Here and there an ambitious *Landser* scraped a shallow hole to protect himself from the night winds. Most slept where they first dropped, knots of men along the road or scattered in the fields tossing and turning from cold and exhaustion, muttering in their uneasy sleep, giving at least one platoon commander a grisly shock when he awoke to a command that seemed to consist of corpses.[10] Fortunate was the company whose field kitchens had kept pace with the march, and whose cooks could supply their comrades with a cup of hot coffee to ease the shock of the morning.

Mackensen was almost as bewildered as his men. Initially he had been told that the Russians were advancing against I Corps, and that their left was open. At 8:00 p.m. a telephone message from I Corps informed him that only weak Russian forces were south of the corps's sector. Reports sent later spoke of Russian advances in strength against I Corps's positions. No orders arrived from army headquarters to coordinate the movements of I and XVII Corps.[11]

Mackensen, thrown on his own, concluded from the available intelligence that the Russians were concentrating against I Corps, with XVII Corps facing no more than flank guards.

Surprisingly, neither the old hussar nor his division commanders used their cavalry to reconnoiter ahead of the likely corps line of advance.[12] The corps air detachment sent out patrols at first light, but the reports were only of abandoned camp sites and columns of supply wagons. Mackensen, convinced he had reached a favorable position unobserved, saw no reason to delay his attack. As the noise of battle from I Corps's front grew ever louder, the commander of XVII Corps issued his orders. Both divisions would attack northeast. The 35th Division on the left was to go through the village of Todszühnen; the 36th would take Walterkehmen and secure the corps's right flank.

At 4:15 a.m., a message from army headquarters informed Mackensen that the corps's detached regiment, the 129th Infantry, was on its way to reinforce him, and that I Reserve Corps would cover his southern flank. The dispatch confirmed Mackensen's decision to attack at once. The XVII Corps deployed its seven available regiments side by side in line—a disposition reflecting the breadth of the corps sector and limiting the formation of all but local reserves. At 4:30 a.m. the forward battalions advanced. The rank and file had had at most an hour's rest, but adrenalin kept them moving against light opposition. By 9:00 a.m. the 35th Division's left brigade, the 87th, was just north of Todszühnen. And there its commandant received a visitor.

First Contact: Gumbinnen

At 8:30 a.m. François sent a liaison officer south with a message for Mackensen. It stated that I Corps had been successfully advancing since dawn, and it promised a great victory if XVII Corps would only swing north and take the enemy in the rear. Brigadier-General von Hahn responded by shifting the direction of his attack on his own responsibility. Mackensen was not pleased at this unauthorized adjustment of his front. He was even less pleased when the 87th Brigade came under fire on three sides from Russian artillery, and found itself pinned down. The 35th Division's right brigade, the 70th, was similarly stopped in its tracks within a few minutes of its sister formation.[13]

Mackensen's other division, the 36th, was faring even worse. Like the 35th, it initially advanced into a vacuum. At 7:35 a.m. the division commander, Major General von Heineccius, reported optimistically that he expected to "block the retreat" of the Russians on his front. He was unaware that his men were facing two full Russian divisions, the 27th and 40th, well entrenched among a maze of hills and small woods offering poor observation at best. Mackensen and Heineccius might believe that the Russians were withdrawing. Mackensen's airmen might continue to report the area clear of enemy formations. By 8:00 a.m., however, regimental officers, company and battalion commanders, were increasingly aware that they were facing the prospect of a breakthrough battle against an invisible enemy. One frustrated colonel assumed a subaltern's role, riding ahead of his deployed battalions to see for himself where the Russians were. Five hundred meters north of Walterkehmen he found out. A burst of rifle fire at point-blank range sent him back to his own lines with undignified haste.[14]

German tactical doctrine called for frontal attacks to be made by lines of skirmishers strong enough to keep the enemy pinned by their own fire action, yet flexible enough to work forward in small groups to within a half- or quarter-mile of the position. The skirmish line—perhaps better called an assault line—would establish fire superiority, then close to about a hundred yards and mount a final, all-in attack with the bayonet, drums beating and bugles sounding. The whole operation was to be prepared and supported by artillery.[15] But this morning the officers of XVII Corps were unwilling to lose time by following the book. Reluctance to risk being considered laggards outweighed the years of training and the suggestions of common sense. Instead, three regiments of the 36th Division stormed heedlessly forward against everything the Russians could throw at them.

Within minutes the Germans began learning that command from the front as practiced in the kaiser's army had military disadvantages. In peacetime regimental messes, a familiar cliché was that a company officer's duty was to lead his men forward at the double. What became of him afterwards was irrelevant. This attitude might have merit when applied to the climactic charge of a decisive battle. Modern war, however, offered few such high points. Everywhere on the front of XVII Corps's attack, captains and lieutenants were among the first to drop. Some sacrificed their lives inspiring the men they were supposed to command. But where in earlier centuries a thousand men might be galvanized by a single act of courage, rapid-firing weapons tended to restrict the audience for such feats to a half-dozen or so—and they were more likely to curse the would-be hero for drawing fire than they were to emulate his self-immolation. Too often the successors to these casualties could not be found amid the growing confusion, or were themselves hit before learning of their changed status. Emotions also intervened. The German private, like his counterparts everywhere in Europe, was strictly forbidden to leave the ranks to tend casualties. The same principle applied to officers—but in practice it could prove difficult to abandon a comrade without the incentive of threats from an NCO. The result was a collection of suitably edifying death scenes eloquently recorded in letters or diaries, and a corresponding contribution to breakdown in the chain of command.[16]

Live officers did not guarantee progress and control. Companies overran Russian trenches, then stood waiting for orders instead of pursuing or consolidating. A lieutenant of the 5th Grenadiers, sent to notify the artillery of his regiment's position, encountered his division commander, who asked how things stood in the fighting line. When told of the confusion and casualties, the general shouted, "Dig in the way the Russians did!" But too many field and company officers shared the opinion of the Grenadier captain who insisted that "Prussian infantry does not entrench!" Doctrine and regulations accepted the desirability, even the necessity, of field fortifications.[17] Every infantryman carried his own entrenching tool. In peacetime, however, few regiments taught their men to use these clumsy implements. The Germans dug like amateurs. Those who concentrated on deepening their foxholes risked the wrath of superiors who wanted to know why they were not firing on the Russians. At least one captain who asked that question had it promptly answered by a bullet through his head—an event duly reported to the next in command by the company *Feldwebel*, whose own sense of soldierly honor did not prevent him from taking cover in a handy potato field.[18]

Some riflemen took revenge for comrades struck down by enemies who seemed invisible until they stood up almost in the midst of their attackers and tried to surrender. A lieutenant of the 141st Infantry wrote of Russians shot down at point-blank range until he intervened to stop the slaughter. Far from being proud of his behavior, the officer described himself in a subsequent letter as a sentimental fool.[19] But at least his men were still in ranks. Others ran for their lives, throwing away rifles, shedding helmets and belts in their single-minded desire to get away— anywhere that the bullets were not flying. A lieutenant of the 5th Grenadiers picked up a rifle and fired at a group of fugitives. A few stopped, throwing themselves to the ground in desperation. The rest kept running. A single marksman was nothing compared to what they had faced earlier in the day.[20]

Those Germans who kept trying to move forward found confusion compounded by adherence to another peacetime cliche: building up the firing line. The experience of decades of maneuvers, long embalmed in various infantry drill regulations, dictated that when an advance stalled, fresh troops should be brought forward as quickly as possible to restore momentum. Regiment and battalion commanders committed their own reserves, then began commandeering other troops wherever they could be found. The too-frequent result was that, as at Stallupönen, detachments of different regiments found themselves next to each other in the same sector, fighting under leaders they did not know against a foe they could not see.

Around noon Mackensen had become aware that his battle plan was based on a series of singularly ill-favored guesses. Both of his divisions were stalled in front of a defense network no one could see, much less break. Any movement, whether to advance or to entrench, drew fire. A high proportion of the casualties were hit in the head or upper body—wounds demoralizingly likely to be fatal without prompt evacuation and treatment. Isolated rushes toward the Russian trenches continued throughout the early afternoon, motivated as much by junior leaders' desperation or desire to die while attempting something as by any orders from higher headquarters. They were repulsed every time. One hard-charging lieutenant of the 128th Infantry entered the battle leading a platoon of seventy-two men. Three remained to follow him at day's end.[21]

One hope remained: find a Russian flank and turn it. Mackensen still had one of his eight regiments uncommitted. The 36th Division's 129th Infantry reached the field late in the morning. At 12:49 p.m. it received orders to go forward on the right of its parent division and roll up the Russian positions from the left. The 129th was well commanded and well trained, as good a regiment as any in the army. It had literally gone to war from the maneuver grounds, and had had ample time since then to integrate its reservists into their platoons and companies. Its fate on August 20 can stand as a case study of the tactical problems of the offensive in the early days of World War I.

Almost as soon as the Germans deployed they came under heavy rifle and artillery fire. The Russians seemed to have turned every farm and every copse into a fortress, and to have fortified every piece of high ground. The 129th's attack broke down into a series of isolated struggles for buildings or clumps of trees. Once one was cleared, the ostensible victors promptly came under fire from two or three others which in their turn had to be masked or rushed. It was a platoon commanders' battle that rapidly absorbed battalion, then regimental reserves in fights for tactical objectives that led nowhere. By late afternoon the 129th had dissolved into four separate, unconnected groups. The colonel and his staff had changed their positions so often that they had completely lost touch with all the higher headquarters. The Russian flank remained invisible and inviolate.[22]

As infantry attacks stalled all along Mackensen's line, shouts went up: "Machine guns forward!" The evolution of the machine gun as the psychologically dominant weapon of World War I is usually taken for granted, presented as an inevitable consequence of its high firepower. Human factors were also involved in the process. The modern military rifle had become almost too easy to operate. Loading and firing it were such simple processes that they did not engage the infantryman's attention in the way that the more complicated muzzle-loader had done. He had correspondingly greater opportunities to be aware of his surroundings. And on a modern battlefield, the results of that awareness could readily become some form of shock reaction. He might exhaust his ammunition blazing away at nothing. Or he might simply go to ground. Regulations proclaimed that a good field of fire was more important to the infantryman than shelter from enemy bullets. But these were mere words on a field where any movement seemed to make one a specific target.

The machine gun, on the other hand, involved for its crew total participation in specific tasks—tasks whose performance followed familiar paths. Unlike a rifle, a machine gun was complicated enough to absorb attention, particularly in situations where such absorption was psychologically welcome. The water jacket must be kept full. Cartridge belts must be checked for irregularities that might result in a jam. When the gun did cease firing it could be for any one of dozens of causes, each with its own prescribed remedy demanding precise execution. Machine gunners were no braver than their relatively isolated comrades in the rifle platoons. They were more distracted from their environments and more involved in their immediate jobs. The gunner was not necessarily firing on specific human targets. His usual task was to spray an area with lead, to contribute to creating a beaten zone in which movement was difficult or impossible. He was preoccupied with controlling the length of his bursts, lest the gun barrel overheat. He was preoccupied with controlling the gun's arc of fire—what the British called the "two-inch tap." Killing was a by-product of other, essentially technical responsibilities.[23]

German machine gunners also benefitted from administrative factors. Their companies were less than half the size of a rifle company, yet had almost the same complement of officers. The German army's failure to adopt machine guns at a regimental level until 1913 meant that there had been no time to train many reserve officers on the weapons. The interchange of command personnel with reserve units, universal in the rifle companies, was far less common in the machine-gun companies simply because there were too few lieutenants or NCOs on the regimental rolls even nominally qualified to lead a machine-gun platoon. An active machine-gun company was likely to take most of its peacetime cadre into the field, with corresponding benefits to morale and stability.

By companies, platoons, and single guns, XVII Corps's machine gunners worked their clumsy weapons forward to take Russian positions under fire. Even if they did no more than blast away at trench parapets, they were welcome enough that riflemen emptied their own ammunition pouches to keep the Maxims in action. But instead of supplementing infantry fire, the machine guns replaced it. They became an excuse for more and more riflemen to keep their heads down. In turn, with their bunched crews and bulky mounts, they became unchallenged targets for Russian sharpshooters and Russian artillery. One by one they fell silent, gunners dead or wounded, water jackets pierced, actions hopelessly jammed.

As for the artillery, Mackensen's gunners proved consistently unable to find the range of the Russian positions. The flat-trajectory 77-millimeter pieces did little more than spray shrapnel over the enemy trenches. The field howitzers were more useful, but there were not enough of them to protect their own infantry by counterbattery fire, let alone prepare an attack. To the infantry it seemed that the artillery was simply shelling the landscape at random. The German gunners found it no easier to keep touch with the men they were supposed to support. Brigadier-General Hahndorff, commanding the 36th Division's artillery, exploded in despair that if the infantry persisted in storming forward like madmen, they could hardly expect the guns to follow. Messengers were hit or got lost. The few forward observers who survived were as helpless as the infantry among whom they lay. Around 2:00 p.m., the corps's heavy howitzers finally reached the field and took a hand on the 36th Division's front. The first salvo of shells hit between the firing lines. Instead of "walking" forward towards the Russian trenches, the second and the third landed directly on the positions held by the 5th Grenadiers. In the still heat of an August afternoon, officers could hear clearly the sound of the guns to their rear and trace the flight of the shells overhead as they added the last, unbearable touch to the Germans' plight.[24]

Desperate circumstances inspired desperate gestures. A battery of the 81st Field Artillery galloped into the open in a frantic attempt to support the infantry at close range. Within minutes it was shot to pieces, men and horses heaped in ghastly piles around the gun positions. The vaunted splinter-proof shields, fitted after much controversy to all German field guns before the war, were limited protection against high-powered, small-caliber bullets. The 2nd Battery, 36th Field Artillery, took position a few hundred yards away, only to have its range-finding equipment knocked out and its commander knocked senseless by Russian shrapnel. One caisson, then another, exploded. A reserve lieutenant and a cannoneer kept a single gun in action until its limber was empty. Crews of the other guns dropped so rapidly that the pieces could not be manned long enough to fire the few rounds left. Saving the guns was not an heroic option. Too few men remained in the firing positions to hitch them up, even had it not been suicidal to send the limbers forward.[25]

The sacrifice of these batteries was XVII Corps's final gesture. Most of Mackensen's infantry had gone over twenty hours without sleep. Ammunition was so low that some men were using Russian rifles and cartridges. Water bottles were empty. Mangled comrades had screamed themselves into exhaustion and were beginning to die. Like all European armies, the Germans had carefully prepared for the evacuation of casualties. Wounded men were to receive first aid from their own stretcher-bearers, who would then carry the victims to the battalion aid station.

After primary treatment by the battalion surgeon they would be evacuated by litter or ambulance to field hospitals out of artillery range, yet close enough to the front lines to keep the stretcher-bearers from exhausting themselves.[26]

In peacetime all had worked splendidly. The test of battle showed flaws in every step of the process. Company officers were not likely to detail their best men for a task which had seemed through years of maneuvers little more than an exercise in shadow-boxing. It was a job for mothers' boys with hollow chests, for slow learners unable or unwilling to distinguish left from right, for misfits of all sorts. It was no accident that the German army's 1914 equivalent of World War II's Sad Sack was "Hospital Orderly Neumann"—a proverbial *schlemiel*, a well-intentioned maladroit, an antihero of bawdy songs and obscene jokes. It was not the kind of image making it a point of honor to answer at any risk the cry of "*Sani*," "medic."[27] That came later.

Once out of the killing zone the plight of the wounded improved only marginally. Germany's army surgeons, most of them reservists recalled from civilian life, were unprepared to cope with hundreds of major traumas simultaneously. Years of peacetime practice had conditioned them to regard serious injury cases as the exception to a routine of broken bones, tumors, and pregnancies. Even men with experience in a mining town or a big city emergency room were shocked by the effect of high explosives, shrapnel balls, and shell fragments on the human body. Triage, the sorting of casualties by the seriousness of their wounds and the prospects for their recovery, with those likely to die left to die, and those likely to live without medical assistance given no assistance, was still to most doctors a theoretical concept. True to their medical oaths and their peacetime experience, they sought to help all. Too often they ended by helping none, dashing aimlessly from stretcher to stretcher as the numbers mounted.[28]

At his headquarters Mackensen was finally beginning to doubt that his corps could break the Russian line unassisted when his men made the same decision. Flight in modern war is frequently an unfeasible option. Apart from the pressures of discipline and comradeship, the battlefield is swept by such a heavy volume of fire that staying put, even in an unfavorable position, may reasonably seem a lesser risk. Situations combining obvious danger and limited possibilities of escape encourage a kind of passivity that can become furious defense when the enemy shows itself.[29] But the Russians, instead of obliging, stayed under cover and held their ground. Around 3:00 p.m. individual soldiers of XVII Corps began to stand up and run for the rear. Whether from indifference, humanity, or a sense of opportunity knocking, the Russians held their fire. Within minutes, rout began spreading along the firing lines of the hard-hammered 35th Division. Major-General Hennig's orders to hold on at all costs went as unheeded as his promises that fresh troops were advancing on the flanks.

A major of the 5th Grenadiers carried his battalion's flag forward against the tide, yelling that any man who abandoned his colors was a bastard. Two colonels went forward, collecting stragglers with a mixture of personality and official authority, organizing them into squads and platoons and sending them back into the line. An occasional captain kept most of his company in hand. An occasional ditch sheltered a line of men too exhausted or frightened to run any more. Two privates of the 141st Infantry stood back to back in a shallow trench, covering the retreat of a half-dozen of their comrades. German soldiers were not known for their marksmanship, but these men picked off so many Russians that finally none were willing to risk exposing themselves. Instead they thrust their rifles over the parapet and fired blindly. One German dropped, a bullet through his head. The other fixed his bayonet and waited. It took twenty Russians to bring him down, desperately wounded. He survived to become a prisoner of war and meet the lieutenant who witnessed and reported his valor in a camp north of Vladivostok.[30]

Courage born of desperation was not enough. German records are silent on the use of force to stop the rout, but the most eager lieutenant or the most liverish major might have entertained second thoughts about the probable personal consequences of emptying a Luger into his own men. By 4:00 p.m. the retreating infantry had reached the artillery positions. Batteries were overwhelmed by wounded begging for water, bandages, and above all a ride to the rear. With and without orders, the guns began limbering up. By 5:00 p.m., XVII Corps was in full flight. Mackensen left his command post to rally his troops, and promptly became just an elderly man borne along on a gray-green flood. Badly shaken physically and emotionally, he ordered a general retreat behind the Rominte River.[31]

Like many another general between 1914 and 1918, Mackensen attacked into a void, under a complete misconception of the situation, without attempting any kind of systematic reconnaissance to verify his hasty conclusions. He kept pressing his attack long after his mistake should have been apparent. Mackensen had learned a lesson, but his fighting men had paid the tuition. In round numbers, 30,000 men had gone into action that morning in the rifle companies and field batteries of XVII Corps. Over eight thousand had been killed or wounded, had surrendered to the Russians, or were wandering dazed through 8th Army's rear areas. Temporarily at least, XVII Corps was finished as a fighting unit.

Some fugitives from the broken regiments just kept going; a few got as far as the Angerapp before being stopped by the military police. Once the initial shock passed, however, the vast majority of the runaways were in the position of Stephen Crane's Henry Fleming: they had nowhere to go. Desertion in the context of August, 1914, was an unfeasible option even if one briefly entertained the thought, and most of Mackensen's men were still willing soldiers. They had been overmarched, underfed, and badly defeated—but tomorrow was another day.

Traditional symbols had not yet lost their power to move men. A sergeant of the 141st Infantry, badly wounded, staggered up to a section of the 71st Field Artillery and begged its officer to take care of the flag he had carried through the fighting. The lieutenant delivered the colors as requested.[32] But neither the threat of being shot by military police nor the inspiration of regimental standards were as important in rallying XVII Corps as the humble field kitchen. The smells of cooking, the hearty stew of meat, vegetables, and potatoes that was the army's staple evening meal, drew stragglers like moths to candle flames. Most company cooks had prepared full portions, unaware of the day's casualties. A man, even one from another regiment, could count on two or three full mess tins, washed down with all the coffee he could drink. It was as good a way as most to prove he was still alive.[33]

On the 8th Army's right, Otto von Below's I Reserve Corps received the order to advance with a mixture of trepidation and enthusiasm. Its regiments had been stamped out of the ground since August 1, with no more than a week's time to enroll, equip, and assign officers and men before being shipped towards the borders. Most of the officers had been trained by the regional regiments, but the rank and file of the infantry regiments seldom included more than half local residents. The rest were Berliners and Westphalians, Hanoverian farmers and industrial workers from the Ruhr. The 3rd Reserve Infantry even incorporated a large number of undergraduates from the University of Göttingen.

Like its active counterparts, I Reserve Corps went to war with jokes and slogans chalked on its boxcars: "If the weather is unfavorable, the war will be held indoors." Colonels issued orders of the day in the best heroic style, urging their men to emulate the heroism of their forefathers and earn the admiration of their contemporaries. In practice the corps divided its first days of existence between digging trenches and refreshing more or less rusty martial skills. Nights were spent in uneasy anticipation of Russian surprise attacks. And, however eager the reservists might have been to come to grips with the foe under the midday sun, their jittery sentries blazed away so much ammunition firing at shadows and each other that they were finally ordered to stand guard with empty rifles.[34]

Below was what the Germans call an *alter Hase*. A regimental soldier with minimal staff experience, he had served in every corner of Germany during a forty-year career culminating in assignment to I Corps's 2nd Division. The army's senior division commander in 1914, he found serving under François an experience trying enough to lead him to consider retiring rather than await the next selections for corps command.[35] Now he had his first chance to show his skill in the field—but at the head of a formation hitherto unknown to the German army: a full corps of reservists.

Below had little notion of what he might expect from his officers and men. Himself anticipating a Russian attack, he was surprised on the afternoon of August 19 to receive Prittwitz's orders to advance. His corps was to move forward towards Goldap and cover the right of Mackensen's attack by engaging the Russians presumed to be in the area. On a map the idea was sound. In the field it meant a long night march with unseasoned troops, over unimproved roads, through mobs of refugees. As the columns struggled forward, old jokes about "knapsack sickness" seemed less and less funny. Around midnight bullets began whistling around the ears of the vanguard. Orders rang into the night: "Deploy at the double! Fix bayonets! Charge!" Then came the anticlimax: the shots had been fired by one of Mackensen's outposts. There was no time to check for losses. The reservists fell back into ranks and pushed forward over roads that suddenly and ominously seemed almost empty. At 3:30 a.m. Below ordered a halt. With no concrete information on the nature or positions of the enemy he expected to face, it seemed the better part of wisdom to give his men a few hours' sleep. Within minutes I Reserve Corps's positions were marked by motionless blanket- or overcoat-wrapped knots of men snoring loudly enough to generate concern that any Russians in the area need only follow their ears to victory.

At 6:30 a.m. the reservists were on the road once more, most of them with at least a cup or two of hot coffee in their stomachs. In the meantime Below's orders had been changed. Instead of attacking, I Reserve Corps was now merely to "observe" the Russians until it could be reinforced.[36] Unlike Mackensen, however, I Reserve Corps had sent its cavalry forward. Patrols found no sign of any Russians ten kilometers in any direction from Goldap. On the basis of that information, Below concluded that his immediate front was clear. He could best contribute to the day's fighting by turning northeast and joining Mackensen's battle, already clearly audible. At 7:30 a.m. he issued the appropriate orders.

Modifying, even ignoring, commands irrelevant to circumstances was accepted practice in the Imperial army. Below may have had visions of the *Pour le Mérite* before his eyes as he altered his line of march. But he had overlooked another accepted element of German military wisdom. This one was negative: never trust the reconnaissance reports of reserve cavalrymen. Below's troopers may have seen no Russians around Goldap, but when Below informed Prittwitz of his on-the-spot initiative, he was informed that air reconnaissance reported two Russian corps on the move north from Goldap—Russians the cavalry had somehow missed.

Nor were the cavalry the only unobservant ones. The 1st Reserve Division on Below's right, strung out in a single line of march along eleven kilometers, had just halted for lunch when it was attacked in flank by the 30th Russian Division of Alieuv's IV Corps. Shimmering heat and dust clouds so obscured the uniforms that at first the Germans feared a repetition of the previous night's misunderstanding on a larger scale. Finally an infantry colonel rounded up a few of the division's cavalry and ordered them to ride towards the advancing columns until they were either cheered or shot at. The colonel might well have been pardoned for thinking that this was one way to get some use out of the "frog-stickers" who had so obviously failed to do their jobs earlier. Within minutes the whole division was engaged. Within a few minutes more the German reservists experienced the Russians' use of terrain and their professional coordination of infantry and artillery. Whole skirmish lines seemed to disappear in the broken ground in front of the division, probing with a surgeon's skill for exposed flanks and weak spots in the firing lines. Batteries that pushed forward to support the hard-pressed infantry were overpowered and silenced by Russian shrapnel, increasingly supplemented by heavy howitzers from IV Corps reserve. Not until the arrival of the 36th Reserve Division were the Germans able to mount a successful series of counterattacks.

German tactical doctrine stressed maintaining or recovering the initiative, and reserve officers were more likely than their active counterparts to operate by the book. Battalion and company commanders drove their men forward, often without orders, pushing from one farm or set of outbuildings to another with more enthusiasm than coordination. More than doctrine inspired this aggressive behavior. A German reserve division had only half the number of guns of its active counterpart—thirty-six instead of seventy-two, all of them flat-trajectory pieces. To make up for their lack of firepower, the German gunners had blasted away most of their ready ammunition. They had also changed position under fire so often that they had lost touch with their supply wagons. By midafternoon the German infantry was fighting on its own in many parts of the field, and their eagerness to close with their enemy was being enhanced by two related discoveries. Since the Russian infantrymen tended to shoot too high, the closer one advanced to their positions the safer one was likely to be. And the efficient Russian artillery was unwilling to inflict losses on its own men by shelling too close to their reported positions.

By nightfall I Reserve Corps was master of its field. Below's men had held the Russians in place, keeping them from turning north against Mackensen. But the corps's divisions had advanced in such different directions that they were virtually out of touch with each other. The loss of contact boded more ill for the next day than Below wished to concede.[37]

II

The German 8th Army fought three separate battles on August 20. Each of its corps found all the fighting it wanted against an enemy in no way as obliging as those found at maneuvers or in war games. The result had been incomplete victories on the flanks, defeat in the center. What was to be made of the total? European military mythology stressed the role of the supreme commander—the guiding genius who surveys the maps and demonstrates to his less-gifted subordinates the order underlying apparent chaos. Reality, even during the Wars of German Unification, had been significantly different. A quarter-century later, in Manchuria, neither Japanese nor Russian generalissimos had shown any particular skill in directing, as opposed to reacting to, the movements of their subordinates.

To a significant degree this was recognized as an inevitable result of the extended fronts created by the size of modern armies and the empty battlefields created by the destructiveness of modern weapons. Controlling a battle in the Napoleonic sense of the concept had become impossible. In 1909 the British military writer Ernest Swinton published a short story set in a higher headquarters during "the next great war." While staff officers strain their nerves, while telephones ring and messengers rush to and fro, the commanding general spends the day fishing. He wanders into headquarters at twilight, carrying a two-pound trout. Then, with clear eyes and unimpaired vitality, he studies the map and issues orders for the next day.[38]

The story's moral was the necessity for senior officers to avoid becoming overinvolved in details which they had no power to influence. Prittwitz began his first battle as though he accepted the principle. He established his headquarters in the town of Nordenburg. It was thirty miles behind the fighting lines. It was also a regional communications center with excellent telephone and telegraph connections. In theory this location enabled Prittwitz to keep in touch with his entire front, rather than the section under his immediate eye. The 8th Army's commander, however, lacked the self-confidence to pursue ad hoc field sports. Instead he spent the morning waiting for phone calls and telegrams.

Around 10 a.m. Prittwitz made an appearance to tell some of his staff officers that things were going very well, and to receive congratulations from the more optimistic and the more sycophantic of them. But the atmosphere of victory created by the early successes of François and Mackensen evaporated rapidly during the afternoon. On the left, I Corps was not advancing. In the center, it seemed increasingly doubtful if XVII Corps would be able to hold its ground, much less continue its attack. On the right, I Reserve Corps seemed to be facing superior forces. Air reconnaissance also reported masses of Russian cavalry to the north of the main armies.

None of this was news to inspire optimism. Then at 2:00 p.m. more intelligence information arrived from an unexpected quarter. The long-range radio station in the fortress of Posen reported intercepting a Russian dispatch giving the strength of their 2nd Army as five corps and a cavalry division. Since Prittwitz had left only a reinforced corps to screen his southern flank, it was scarcely a panic reaction when thirty minutes later he telephoned the headquarters of that corps to ask what was happening in its sector. He received a cheerful reply from Chief of Staff Colonel Emil Hell. Since daylight, Hell reported, the corps aircraft had been patrolling south and east, bringing back reports that the Russians were indeed advancing in force. At least six divisions had almost reached the frontier. When Prittwitz warned that he could spare no reinforcements, Hell confidently answered that XX Corps needed none, and could hold its positions until victory was won around Gumbinnen.[39]

The army commander remained unconvinced. At 5:00 p.m., just about the time XVII Corps's tactical retreat was becoming an operational rout, Prittwitz telephoned François. He declared that in view of the news from the south and the failure of XVII Corps to advance, he would "probably" have to retreat across the Vistula. In reply he received another burst of effervescent good spirits. The Russians in I Corps's sector were defeated, François declared. He could easily roll them up from the north and ease the pressure on Mackensen. His corps had inflicted heavy casualties on the enemy. It had taken thousands of prisoners. Success depended only on one more attack. Prittwitz answered that he wanted to "think through the situation." Then he hung up.[40]

The difference between thinking and fretting can be a fine one. The XX Corps was likely to be fighting for its life within thirty-six hours. Gumbinnen was apparently neither a clear-cut defeat nor a textbook victory. What to do? Prittwitz had as yet issued no orders when at 7:00 p.m. he received another technological jolt. Brigadier-General von Unger commanded the grandiloquently titled "Field Reserve of the Fortress of Graudenz," a collection of reservists and depot battalions removed from its comfortable garrison to cover as best it might the right flank of XX Corps. Unger also commanded the services of the Graudenz air detachment. Around 2:30 p.m. one of its four planes had made a routine flight south across the border. Its crew discovered a strong column of infantry, cavalry, and artillery advancing towards the Russian town of Mlawa— miles to the west of even Unger's position. Clouds of dust further south on the Warsaw road indicated that this was only a vanguard. The plane took two and a half hours to return to its improvised base. It required two more hours for the report to reach Prittwitz.[41]

It was suddenly clear to a shocked army staff that the Russian 2nd Army was not only advancing in force, but that it was extended much further west than Prittwitz had expected or feared. Any lingering doubts about the accuracy of the dispatch were dismissed when one of XX Corps's planes reported seeing a large dust cloud about five kilometers northeast of Mlawa around 4:55 p.m.—just about the right distance for the column seen by the other air crew to have advanced in three hours on a hot day.[42]

Max Hoffmann subsequently declared that he reacted to the arrival of one of these messages by suggesting to Grünert that the contents be withheld until 8th Army ended its battle in the north.[43] His words have the ring of retrospective bravado. Enough information had reached army headquarters about Russian movements in the south to make anyone question previous judgments—even Hoffmann, and certainly Prittwitz. Suddenly the 8th Army seemed in mortal danger. In view of the apparent wide sweep of the Russian advance, the Germans were at significant risk of being cut off from their Vistula bases and driven into Königsberg, or against the Baltic coast. The specter of a new Sedan suddenly seemed all too real. But it would be a Sedan in reverse.

Much was subsequently said and written about Prittwitz's behavior on the night of August 20. Most of it was critical; all of it enjoyed the benefit of hindsight; all of it tended to simplify the issue. A detailed examination of events on the night of August 20 suggests more than mere failure of nerve was involved. The process of confusion began when

First Contact: Gumbinnen

Prittwitz, presumably after some consultation with Waldersee, called Hoffmann and Grünert into his office. The 8th Army, he declared, would break off the action at Gumbinnen and retreat immediately to the Vistula River. Both junior officers challenged the decision. Grünert in particular urged continuing the attack against Rennenkampf, arguing that it would take at the most two or three days to defeat him and turn on the other Russian army. Until then, he said, XX Corps and its attached units should certainly be able to hold on in the south. Prittwitz cut him off, saying angrily that the army was to retreat at once. He and his chief of staff were responsible for the decision—not the quartermaster or the G.S.O.I.[44]

It was easy to marshal powerful arguments in favor of continuing the attack against Rennenkampf. Schlieffen had consistently emphasized that the only way to defend East Prussia was to take advantage of the division of the enemy's forces caused by the Masurian Lakes, to strike and destroy whichever enemy first came within reach. Withdrawal in the face of an enemy with the Russians' immense superiority in cavalry was perceived as an extreme risk by generals as yet unconvinced of the defensive power of modern weapons. And while the Russian 2nd Army might advance toward the Vistula while the battle against Rennenkampf was in progress, it would increasingly expose its right flank and lines of communication to a German attack from the north.

Victories of this scope are easiest won in retrospect. Whether a German attack on the 21st, made without the advantage of surprise, could have broken through the Russian positions under the tactical conditions of 1914 is at least questionable. At the same time, howevers, Waldersee was apparently unconvinced that retreating to the Vistula was the best response to the 8th Army's operational dilemma. Certainly the chief of staff was unwilling to prepare orders mentioning the river as a possible destination.[45] Prittwitz was an elderly man at the end of a long and trying day. This was neither the first, the second, nor the hundredth time that a commander had made a snap judgment, then lost his temper when challenged. Given an hour or two to calm down, given a word or two of concrete advice, and the chief would be fine. The telephone and the telegraph, after all, made it unnecessary to issue next day's orders immediately.

Fulfilling the cynic's definition of autobiography as the life of a hero by one who knows, Max Hoffmann presents himself as convincing Waldersee that since the Russians at Mlawa were closer to the Vistula than was the main body of the 8th Army, a general retreat would be impossible. Even if it degenerated into an every-man-for-himself flight for the river, there was every chance the Russians would get there first. If fighting it out at Gumbinnen was no longer a feasible alternative, the only remaining solution was a concentration to the south, against the Russian 2nd Army.

Other staff officers described the G.S.O.I. as bursting into fits of tears and rage, tearing off his decorations in despair, and sitting silently while Grünert and Waldersee did the actual work of changing Prittwitz's mind. To the extent the latter accounts are correct, they suggest behavior motivated by frustration rather than panic. Writing to his wife on August 21, Hoffmann called the previous day the most difficult of his military life. Until noon he had firmly believed in a great victory. He considered retreat from Gumbinnen a major error. "I am," he declared, "so boundlessly sorrowful that you cannot imagine."[46]

Whatever Hoffmann did or did not do, no extraordinary persuasive gifts were required to move Prittwitz once he made himself available for consultation. A switch from one front to the other had been so often discussed, so often described as necessary in prewar plans, that thoughts of its implementation came naturally to tired men late in the evening. An even more mundane explanation involved saving face. Prittwitz had announced his intention to retreat from Gumbinnen too openly and too loudly to reverse himself completely without appearing a weakling or a fool. Concentrating to the south was in some ways an even riskier maneuver, yet it was the kind of compromise that enabled Prittwitz to retain at least part of his authority. With no more than token objections, he approved orders to I Corps and the 3rd Reserve Division to move southwest, eventually deploying on the right flank of XX Corps against the threat from Mlawa. The I Reserve Corps would remain facing Rennenkampf on the Angerapp. The XVII Corps would retreat westward and reorganize as a general reserve. Walter Elze accurately observes that these orders resembled only in a general way the actual concentrations for the battle of Tannenberg. Nevertheless they suggest that Prittwitz and his staff were beginning to cope with the new situation by 9:00 p.m., when the first of them was issued.[47]

Prittwitz, however, had not simply gone off to cool down in his own company. *Oberste Heeresleitung* (OHL), the army supreme command in Koblenz, was concerned about the situation in East Prussia. It responded to Prittwitz's initial report of François's insubordination with repeated requests for information on 8th Army's "intentions and measures." Prittwitz obliged. At noon on the 20th, his headquarters informed OHL by phone that the army was engaged in a "promising" battle at Gumbinnen, and that spirits were "tremendous."[48] That evening Prittwitz picked up the phone once more. He began, according to Moltke, by describing 8th Army's situation as desperate, with eight enemy cavalry divisions on its flanks and with XVII Corps "as good as finished." "If still possible," he proposed to disengage and retreat. When Moltke advised him to pull himself together and rally southward on XX Corps, Prittwitz declared the maneuver impossible and asked for reinforcements. Moltke replied that at least the Vistula must be held at all costs. Prittwitz by this time resembled a bull harassed to its limits by *banderilleros*. He asked how he could defend a river line against superior forces with his "handful of men" when the river was so low it could be forded anywhere. Moltke answered that that was Prittwitz's problem. He could hardly expect the chief of the general staff to plan his campaign in detail from Koblenz.[49] It was hardly a reassuring exchange. Prittwitz may not have played the role of a storybook

194

hero, but Moltke's generalized carping was hardly calculated to restore anyone's equilibrium.

Nor was Prittwitz finished for the day with modern communications. At 9:00 p.m., Mackensen telephoned to explain what had happened to his corps. Prittwitz interrupted him to say that the army was going to retreat across the Vistula.[50] Shortly after 9:00 p.m. François received a phone call from army headquarters ordering the artillery and trains of the Königsberg division back to the fortress. About 11:30 a.m. he received a telegram declaring that the army was withdrawing in the face of the Russian advance from the south. François, as might be expected, was outraged. But nowhere in his memoirs did he say or imply that either the conversation or the telegram mentioned the Vistula as 8th Army's destination, though he continued to insist that he had received verbal orders to retreat across the river.[51]

Max Hoffmann later suggested that while Prittwitz was out of the office he informed both his superiors and his subordinates that he was going to withdraw beyond the Vistula. He forgot—or perhaps was too embarrassed—to tell any of his staff what he had said. Then when he changed his mind, he neglected to inform OHL of the fact.[52] This explanation ignores the timing of the various conversations. A more reasonable reconstruction of events is that when Prittwitz left Hoffmann and Grünert he was convinced that retreat across the Vistula was necessary. His exchange with Moltke began the process of jolting him back to reality—at least the reality that ordering such a maneuver would almost certainly cost him his command. He returned to consult with his staff, and approved the orders designed to begin moving the army southward. At 8:23 p.m. army headquarters also sent a dispatch to OHL, briefly declaring that in view of the strong Russian concentration in the south, the army was withdrawing to West Prussia (*nach Westpreussen*).[53]

By design or accident, this was an interesting mental reservation. The Vistula River was not mentioned—but much of West Prussia lay behind this river. Perhaps Prittwitz was not quite as convinced by his staff's calculations as he seemed and was readier to share his anxieties with Mackensen, whose corps had been so badly shaken, than with the aggressive and unsympathetic François. Or just perhaps the staff officers were not quite as confident as they sought to appear for posterity. It had been two busy hours at the end of a long day and a longer three weeks. A little geographic vagueness was a reasonable price for enough surface consensus to keep the headquarters functioning. Time enough now for a night's sleep and hopes for a better tomorrow.

The news from East Prussia had a shattering effect at OHL, not least because it arrived in the context of wildly optimistic reports of a complete German victory at Gumbinnen dispatched independently from Königsberg.[54] General Ritter von Wenninger, the Bavarian military plenipotentiary, described the gloomy depression that settled over all the officers—especially Moltke—as they learned of it.[55] Many of the officers at OHL had relatives, many had their own homes, in the suddenly

195

threatened region. The campaign in the west was by no means progressing as smoothly as planned. Stubborn Belgian resistance in the north and a determined French attack in Lorraine were combining to alter the timetable of the Schlieffen Plan. The attention of the high command was focussed on the developing Battle of the Frontiers, the battle expected to decide Europe's fate for a century. Now from the east came these confused reports of defeat and withdrawal.

Eighth Army headquarters awoke on August 21 with a collectively uneasy conscience. At 7:45 a.m., OHL received a long-distance call offering a whitewashed explanation of the previous day's events, ending with the statement that Prittwitz had decided "initially" to withdraw "behind the Angerapp." At 9:30 a.m. an angry Moltke was on the telephone. Was Prittwitz planning a general retreat? Did he now propose to use part of his force to hold the Russians on the Angerapp while moving the rest around Prussia like a manic chess player? Attempts to explain via long distance only enraged Moltke further. Nor was the mood at supreme headquarters improved when during the morning François took advantage of his peacetime rights as a corps commander to bypass the chain of command and report the situation in the east—or his interpretation of it—directly to the kaiser.

Moltke grew increasingly convinced that not only was the army in full retreat to the Vistula, but that Prittwitz was foolishly planning to divide his forces in the face of a superior enemy. Even if this should be interpreted as one of those "grave situations" in which the 8th Army was authorized to withdraw to the river, such a movement was feasible only if strong reinforcements could be sent east to cover the retreat and help hold the Vistula line. On August 21 OHL had no troops immediately available.[56]

While Moltke stewed, 8th Army Headquarters began recovering its equilibrium. Gumbinnen, mused Max Hoffmann, had evidently hurt the Russians more than expected. Rennenkampf was not moving; 8th Army seemed on the way to gaining a day's march on its enemies. Hoffmann contacted the chief of staff of XX Corps, and probably of I Corps as well, to discuss the prospects of an attack on the Russian 2nd Army. Waldersee was more specific in cautioning XX Corps to avoid those frontal attacks that had cost so many lives at Gumbinnen. Hold your position, he instructed Scholtz, until I Corps takes position on your right and XVII Corps and I Reserve Corps come up on the left.[57]

OHL remained unaware of the changing mood. During the day, junior officers in its operations section, acting on their own initiative, also contacted 8th Army's corps by phone, bypassing Prittwitz's headquarters. None of the corps commanders felt themselves defeated or considered the outlook hopeless.[58] Most probably, none would have risked expressing any doubts under the unusual circumstances. Openly ignoring the chain of command in this fashion was hardly routine in the German army. The sound of axes being sharpened was audible even across the miles separating Koblenz from East Prussia.

196

First Contact: Gumbinnen

During the afternoon Waldersee too received a private call. His came from Quartermaster General Hermann von Stein, urging that the 8th Army concentrate west of the Masurian Lakes and attack the right, rather than the left, flank of the Russians coming from the Narew. Waldersee temporized, repeating Prittwitz's intention to concentrate in West Prussia and aim at the Russian left. Stein let the matter pass, but the conversation only confirmed impressions that Waldersee's nerve was also gone. A chief of staff who allowed his commander to manifest unchecked the panic-stricken pessimism Prittwitz had shown the night before was a dubious quantity at best. Even in daylight, Waldersee seemed to have at least one eye fixed over his shoulder. Army headquarters had moved west, not south. Lines of communication troops were falling back with what seemed in Koblenz indecent haste. Rhetoric about concentrating against the left flank of the Russian advance from the Narew appeared little more than an attempt at camouflaging incipient disaster.[59]

On the evening of August 21, Prittwitz and Moltke talked once more. In 1859, Moltke's uncle had declared no commander to be more unfortunate than one having in his headquarters someone who could call him to account every day and every hour, subjecting his plans and decisions to criticism, offering advice without responsibility.[60] The telephone, making possible instant communication over hundreds of miles, bid fair to turn a gloomy theory into uncomfortable reality. Moltke had been anxiously pressing Prittwitz for information about the eastern front well before the day of Gumbinnen, and the telephone left impressions that were as strong as they were limited. For men from a generation accustomed to visual contact on one hand and the detachment of the written word on the other, the telephone's reliability as a means of judging states of mind was questionable. It was impossible to evaluate any intangibles except voice tones, and this was difficult enough given the shaky connections. But did it make sense to risk catastrophe in the name of sustaining command responsibility?

Evidence indicates that Moltke had made up his mind to relieve Prittwitz before he talked to 8th Army's commander on the evening of the 21st. The actual course of events, however, involves a problem of reconstruction more familiar to the medievalist than to the student of modern history, who is more likely to be embarrassed by a plethora of documents than baffled by their absence. It begins with internal contradictions in Moltke's account of the conversation. He describes it as having taken place on the 20th—a date substantiated by the lurid circumstantial account of Prittwitz's behavior discussed above, and in Max Hoffmann's memoir. Most British and American histories accept that date without further ado. Yet Moltke also refers to an event that could only have occurred late on the 21st: Prittwitz declaring his 1st Cavalry Division out of touch and presumably annihilated, then a few minutes later reporting its reappearance with five hundred Russian prisoners.[61] This in turn justifies the German official account, Walter Elze's detailed narrative, and most German works derived from them, in attributing the whole conversation to the 21st—particularly since there were no independent records of a similar conversation on the 20th.[62]

More than a simple question of timing is involved. To partisans of Hindenburg and Ludendorff and critics of Max Hoffmann, the later date proves the case that Prittwitz was still panic-stricken beyond all reason, and that his G.S.O.I. was not quite the gray eminence that he described himself as being. Until his death in 1919 Prittwitz staunchly denied entertaining any serious intention to retreat behind the Vistula.[63] Nothing in his behavior during the day inspired his subordinates or staff officers to suggest that the chief continued to be disproportionately anxious. But even if his fears had not subsided, why, on the night of August 21, should Prittwitz refer to XVII Corps as "finished" when his headquarters was well aware that most of Mackensen's men were back in the ranks and the corps was responding to orders? By what stretch of imagination might he describe his army as "surrounded" by Russian cavalry when he was aware that the Russians had barely moved from their position all day? His concerns were correspondingly likely to fix on negative interpretations of the current day's events—such as the missing 1st Cavalry Division.

Other accounts from OHL are of little direct help. One possible straw in the wind is Wenninger's report of August 21. It describes concern with the unfortunate leadership of Prittwitz and Waldersee, and talk of "hurried retreat behind the Vistula"—but it is dated 10:00 p.m.[64] Two and a half hours is a relatively short time for any event to become the stuff of general gossip in a body as large as OHL. Wenninger was not a particular confidant of Stein or Moltke. His primary concerns involved the Bavarian troops in Lorraine; events in the east played a marginal role in his correspondence. On the other hand, OHL had enough contacts with the eastern theater during the course of the 21st to produce by nightfall a general sense that something was going wrong.

Two possibilities seem likely. The simplest is that Moltke, who in any case had much on his mind, confused two successive evening conversations when he wrote his report. Alternatively Moltke may have confronted Prittwitz on the 21st with his own fears and suspicions, and the two men became involved in a long-distance shouting match. Moltke was high-strung and Prittwitz high-tempered: not the best combination for a meeting of minds under stress. The army commander might well have lost control of his tongue from a mixture of tension and embarrassment. It is worth noting that Prittwitz believed Moltke never quite understood what he planned to do with the 8th Army—a point whose accuracy need not be diminished by any lingering suspicions that Prittwitz was himself not too sure what to do next.

The ultimate importance of the conversation of August 21 was not whether Prittwitz stated or repeated an intent to retreat to the Vistula. It was his inability to alter Moltke's conviction that the situation in East Prussia was out of control, that the army commander had lost his head. No small part of Moltke's frustration was the product of his own ignorance of circumstances combined with Prittwitz's inability to communicate anything but a generalized sense of disaster. Whatever his private reservations, Moltke had chosen the Prittwitz-Waldersee team for the eastern theater. Already too many voices in OHL were suggesting that the chief of staff was not the man his uncle had been, that he needed to be propped up like a sick horse. Immediate action seemed necessary for Moltke to maintain his own position.[65]

III

None of these points made reorganizing the 8th Army's command structure any easier. It was the first case of its kind since the war began, the first in the modern history of the German army. Even that prickly incompetent Karl von Steinmetz had been eased out of his command during the Franco-Prussian War, rather than being summarily dismissed. Nor would Prittwitz be the only one relieved. Any chief of staff unable to check the panic-stricken pessimism Moltke associated with Prittwitz was also superfluous. At 9:00 a.m. on August 22nd, Major General Erich Ludendorff received two messages, one from the chief of staff and one from the quartermaster-general. Moltke's informed him:

> A new and difficult task is entrusted to you. . . . I know of no other man in whom I have such absolute trust. You may yet be able to save the situation in the East. . . . Of course you will not be made responsible for what has already happened, but with your energy you can prevent the worst from happening.

Von Stein's letter was written in a similar vein; it concluded by saying, "Your task is a difficult one, but you are equal to it."[66]

The decision had not been made in a vacuum. Ludendorff has frequently been described as representing everything negative in the rising generation of German staff officers: bourgeois by birth, specialist by training, philistine by temperament, an archetypical militarist with no vestiges of humanitarian impulse and no sensitivities beyond a Biedermeyer attachment to his immediate family.[67] But he had made a peacetime reputation as an intelligent, hard-working staff officer, one of Moltke's most able subordinates and a leading candidate for the post of chief of operations on mobilization. His thorny personality and his deep belief that Germany's peacetime military establishment must be increased whatever the social, economic, or political costs made him numerous enemies inside and outside of the army. His premature transfer in 1913 from the general staff to the command of an infantry regiment went beyond the standard procedure intended to keep general staff officers *au courant* with troop duty. Ludendorff and most of his counterparts regarded his particular assignment, to an undistinguished regiment in the industrial city of Düsseldorf, as punitive. In the corridors of power he was considered to be well under a cloud. Then at the outbreak of war, he was assigned to the improvised task force sent against the key Belgian fortress of Liège. When an assault column faltered, Ludendorff rallied the men, led them into the city, and became an instant hero by demanding single-handedly the surrender of its citadel.

It is scarcely surprising that he came quickly to Moltke's mind as Waldersee's successor. The German general staff had historically forgiven boldness far more readily than inaction. Ludendorff had proved in front of Liège that he was not a man to sit and wait for orders. As far as his personality was concerned, no one at OHL assumed that the situation on the eastern front in any way resembled a popularity contest. A hard-driving kicker of hindquarters seemed to be just what was needed at 8th Army headquarters. Ludendorff was ordered to report to Coblenz immediately. At noon on the 22nd, while he was still *en route*, his appointment as chief of staff of the 8th Army was confirmed by the kaiser.

At 6:00 p.m., Ludendorff arrived at Koblenz and reported to OHL. There Moltke informed him the 8th Army had been defeated at Gumbinnen and was in full retreat, with Prittwitz planning to withdraw across the Vistula. In his memoirs Ludendorff says he viewed the situation as "serious but not impossible." Interestingly, he agreed with at least part of Prittwitz's judgment. Ludendorff too believed the Vistula line could not hold without reinforcements as yet unavailable—to say nothing of the effect a withdrawal to the river was likely to have on the developing Austrian offensive in Galicia. Based on the sketchy information he had been given, he ordered I Reserve Corps and XVII Corps to rest on the 23rd. The I Corps was to detrain around Deutsch Eylau, close to von Scholtz's position. Army headquarters would meet him in Marienburg.[68]

Ludendorff was unaware of the orders issued in East Prussia on the 20th and the 21st. That he arrived at almost the same conclusions as the men on the spot is frequently cited as proof of the high level of German staff training and the comprehensive nature of German doctrine. On the other hand, the concept of maneuvering between the two Russian armies was so familiar that it hardly required genius to consider it the most logical solution—particularly since 8th Army was already on the move west and south.

The value of strategic insight is easily exaggerated. Any cadet, and many civilians, can plan brilliant campaigns on a map. The test comes in matching plans to the capacities of troops and commanders, in coordinating combat and logistics, and above all, in dealing with the friction endemic in that mixture of organization and confusion called war. Ludendorff deserved credit for instantly realizing the situation with only sketchy information, and for the courage to issue orders at long range on his own responsibility. Whether he could oversee the implementation of these orders remained to be determined.

Ludendorff left Koblenz at 9:00 p.m. by special train, with orders to pick up the new army commander on the way east. The selection of this man had also been a difficult task. Good knowledge of human nature was necessary to form a team under the German command system. Ludendorff was not an easy man to work with. He was arrogant, touchy, and humorless; his service in the general staff had made him more admirers than friends. He was almost certain to regard himself as responsible for salvaging a desperate situation at the last minute, and correspondingly disinclined to self-effacement. Prittwitz was no less stubborn. Even if OHL had not lost confidence in him, a pairing of these men would probably have proven unfortunate.

At the least someone calm and steady, a man able to get along with almost anyone, would be required at 8th Army's helm. The officers chiefly responsible for nominating the new commander, Major General von Lyncker and Colonel Freiherr von Marschall of the military cabinet, began by considering Colmar Freiherr von der Goltz. He knew East Prussia intimately, and had a substantial reputation as a theorist of war. But his very intelligence and strength of character suggested that he might find it difficult to cooperate closely with Ludendorff. Two sets of good ideas at the same headquarters could prove as disastrous as one bad set.[69] Then Colonel von Fabeck suggested an acquaintance. Paul Beneckendorff und Hindenburg had the necessary seniority. He wanted an active assignment; on August 12 he had petitioned Berlin to be considered if a higher commander were needed. He was also living in Hanover, on the direct route to East Prussia from Koblenz—a useful plus when haste seemed imperative.

According to Wilhelm Groener, while the choice of Ludendorff was universally welcomed, Hindenburg was "a blank page for most of us" at OHL.[70] Yet Hindenburg was by no means the elderly and simple-minded dolt, the designated figurehead, of some legends. His was an old military family, though not an extensive and well-connected clan like the Kleists or the Bülows. Commissioned in the Prussian guards, he had served as a subaltern in the Wars of Unification, graduated from the war academy, and held the alternating succession of command and staff appointments that was the normal path to high command in the kaiser's army. His reputation was in no way that of a blockhead. Julius Verdy du Vernois, one of the elder Moltke's original demigods, was not a man with a weakness for flattery. In a letter of 1884 to Waldersee, he described Hindenburg as a man on whom the general staff could set great hopes.[71]

If Hindenburg's star did not shine brilliantly over the next two decades, neither was it dimmed by false steps. In 1898, as chief of staff of VIII Corps, he was given the assignment of preparing a contingency plan for the defense of the east. His study followed in detail Schieffen's developing conventional wisdom of an "offensive defense" by weak forces. He was conventionally critical of spending money on fortifications, insisting that Germany's best defense was an army fighting on enemy territory. It was not entirely surprising that in 1903 Hindenburg was asked by the chief of the military cabinet if he was interested in becoming the next chief of staff. Hindenburg replied that he would not fit in at court. Six years later he was also briefly considered for the post of Prussian war minister.

These trial balloons reflected the favorable impression Hindenburg made as a man of force and integrity—the latter mixed with a shrewd sense of the line between honor and intransigence. One anecdote in particular clung to Hindenburg's name. During his last years of command, a captain justified the punishment of a private soldier by describing the man as *dickfällig* (thick-skinned). The battalion commander refused to accept this vulgarism. The colonel upheld the captain. The brigadier and the division commander took sides. The whole matter finally landed on Hindenburg's desk, when he settled the affair by correcting the spelling of *dickfellig*.[72] The story's validity is less important than its double-meaning credibility. It reflects a general opinion that Hindenburg did not possess the kind of subtle, imaginative mind needed in appointments demanding a certain degree of intellectual sophistication and a certain skill in people management. But it also suggests a degree of native shrewdness not to be lightly dismissed.

Hindenburg finished his active career commanding IV Corps in Magdeburg, retiring in 1911, as he put it, to make way for younger men. He was neither promoted on retirement nor assigned as an army inspector. But he had not come so near to the top of his profession by accident. In 1912 the military cabinet had considered him as a possible field army commander in war. Once his name emerged from the discussion at OHL, more and more points in his favor came to light. His health was good. He was famous for his imperturbability. He was a big man, well over six feet tall, bulky without being fat—the kind of imposing physical presence that can convey authority without words. While he had never served with Ludendorff, von François had at one time been his chief of staff, an experience that should presumably give him some advantages controlling a man known throughout the army as headstrong.[73]

At 3:00 p.m. on August 22, Hindenburg received a telegram from Koblenz asking if he were prepared for immediate employment. He answered simply, "I am ready." OHL seems to have been sure of this, at least. Even before his wire could have reached Koblenz he received three more in succession. These informed him that Ludendorff was to be assigned as his chief of staff, that he was to command the 8th Army, and that a special train would pick him up at 3:00 a.m. on the 23rd. The new army commander had no time even to acquire a field uniform. He went to the station wearing the traditional Prussian blue.[74]

The kaiser was not particularly happy with either choice. He regarded Hindenburg as not merely simple, but simple-minded, lacking the *panache* William so admired in his generals. Army rumor had it that the conflict of personalities had been exacerbated during the imperial maneuvers of 1908, when Hindenburg refused to cooperate in one of the elaborate military set-pieces his master so loved. As for Ludendorff, he was in the kaiser's eyes a mucker, a jumped-up technician lacking in social graces.

More than personal judgments were involved here. From the beginning of his reign William had sought to govern Germany himself, to concentrate key decisions in his hands. He had been markedly successful in this process, creating an entourage of yes-men and an administrative structure increasingly reluctant to act without first determining the kaiser's will. The outbreak of war had changed that utterly, at least on the part of the army. For all William's martial posturing, for all of his determination to exercise military command personally, even the most sycophantic generals found it difficult to take him literally as a war lord. The kaiser's penchant for interfering with the conduct of maneuvers, taking command of one side or the other, was compounded by a tendency to treat the exercises as a contest in which victory or its trappings had the same meaning as a successful coup at the gaming tables. The results were uniformly negative. William was exposed to professional criticism from the umpires—a process artificial at best and risky at worst, depending on the state of the kaiser's temper. Or the maneuvers themselves were distorted to allow the war lord his spectacles. Or William was politely but firmly sidetracked, a craft at which Moltke was far more skilled than his predecessors.

Staff officers took pains to defend their guild from the charge of taking William's generalship seriously. Everyone knew that the kaiser was a hopeless tactician, and at best an amateur strategist. If men like Schlieffen were content to humor him, to tickle his vanity, this was only another version of a process virtually universal in the modern world: flattering politicians into thinking they know more than they actually do, or ever can, know about complex technical specialties. To agree with Wilhelm Deist that this process encouraged "Byzantinism" and "corrupted the intellectual development" of senior officers is to accept an exaggeration.[75] What William's military behavior encouraged was less Byzantinism than cynicism. His consistent ignoring of the adage that it is better to keep one's mouth shut and be thought a fool than to speak and confirm the suspicion was poor preparation for his taking the field with OHL.

Isabel Hull describes a kaiser seriously depressed by the strain of the July Crisis, sleeping late in the morning, alarming even his wife by his despondency. His mood could hardly have been improved by his sense of being a fifth wheel in what he initially regarded as his own field headquarters. Suddenly under the stress of a real war, no one of importance had time to play with William, to soothe his ego or lift his spirits. He learned of the crisis in East Prussia only in the course of the 21st, and the news sent him into a tailspin. He invited his two cabinet chiefs—the only officers who could be spared—to take a walk with him. After several hours of aimless rambling, he seated himself on a bench and invited his companions to join him. Deeming the bench too small to hold three portly men, one of the officers brought another. William asked if he was already so despised that none would sit beside him.[76]

The chief of the naval cabinet thought the kaiser was grieving over German territory in enemy hands. He might well also have mourned for lost illusions. He was not consulted on the new appointments for the east; he was given names for approval. Given William's self-image and his recent frustrations, he would probably have balked at Napoleon and Clausewitz. But the situation was too urgent for even Moltke to worry about ruffled imperial feathers. Hindenburg and Ludendorff received official confirmation in the face of William's grumbling. And the kaiser sealed his capitulation by summoning Ludendorff to his presence and personally investing him with Germany's highest decoration, the *Pour le Mérite*, for his role in the capture of Liège. It was the first of many gestures of submission William would make in the next four years.

At 4:00 a.m. on the 23rd the special train arrived in Hanover—one hour late—and one of the great partnerships of military history began. For about thirty minutes Ludendorff briefed Hindenburg on the general situation and on the orders that he had already issued. "Before long," Hindenburg says, "we were at one in our view of the situation." Specifically, both men agreed the important thing was to keep the 8th Army east of the Vistula. To help ensure that, I Corps must not be brought too far west but instead directed south towards the XX Corps sector. The rest would be left for decision at army headquarters. Then, since there seemed nothing to be done beyond unprofitable speculation, the two generals went to bed. Neither mentioned how long he required to fall asleep.[77]

The relationship between Hindenburg and Ludendorff at this early stage remains difficult to determine. Subsequent personal, professional, and political developments have invited hindsight by soldiers and academicians alike. Winston Churchill regarded the two men as a symbiosis so complete he referred to them by their joined initials, as HL. Ludendorff in his memoirs says that "for many years Hindenburg and I worked together like one man in the most perfect harmony. . . . our . . . views were in complete agreement and harmonious cooperation was the result." Hindenburg speaks of "a happy marriage. . . . In such a relationship, how can a third party clearly distinguish the merits of the individuals. . . . They are one in thought and action."[78]

Hindenburg's metaphor is the most suggestive for the Tannenberg campaign. Hindenburg's and Ludendorff's was a marriage—a marriage of convenience. Neither the general bypassed for higher command nor the staff officer whose career was still under a cloud were fools. Each was well aware that he had been given the professional opportunity of a lifetime, accompanied by a corresponding challenge. Both knew that they would be arriving as outsiders in a headquarters apparently unable thus far to produce anything but disaster, and presumably likely to be correspondingly hostile and suspicious. If the newcomers did not watch each other's backs no one could be expected to do it for them.

Overwhelming practical considerations, then, indicated deliberate efforts by both men to establish harmony from the first hours of their acquaintance. If Ludendorff expected to be the brains of the combination, Hindenburg was never reluctant "to give scope to the intellectual powers, the almost superhuman capacity for work, and the untiring resolution of my chief of staff."[79] Far more than Ludendorff, Hindenburg had been through the Imperial army's mill. He knew that the degree of cooperation between a commander and his chief of staff was largely a matter of personalities. He also knew his own qualities and limitations: he could provide a base and framework for a man more brilliant than himself. Ludendorff for his part could drive ahead and be supported, knowing that if he slipped he had the base to fall back on.

It was correspondingly important to establish the new team's presence immediately, even if that required some conscious posturing. In the days to come Hindenburg and Ludendorff would play roles—one the abrasive genius, the other the imperturbable father figure. Both were calculated projections of aspects of their personalities. In time it would become difficult, if not impossible, to separate the men from their self-generated legends. But the great days of the Hindenburg/Ludendorff myth were far in the future as their train crossed Germany in the early hours of August 23, 1914.

By a fluke of communications I Corps was the first formation in 8th Army to learn of the change in command, late in the afternoon of August 22.[80] When Max Hoffmann called the chief of staff of I Corps to check on Russian movements in the corps's front, Schmidtseck asked Hoffmann if he knew what had happened. Hoffmann said no. Schmidtseck replied that he did not feel called upon to enlighten him; he would learn soon enough. A few minutes later a junior officer brought in a telegram announcing the arrival of a special train with a new commander and chief of staff. The official telegram superseding Prittwitz and Waldersee arrived a half-hour later.

Hoffmann accurately suggested that the manner of disposing of these two previously highly regarded officers was "a bit abrupt." Hindenburg was relatively unknown outside his old corps district; few officers of the 8th Army staff were even casually acquainted with him. Ludendorff was a more familiar quantity. Hoffmann had served with him. They had been stationed at Posen together; from 1909 to 1913 they had lived in the same house in Berlin. Writing his wife next day, the G.S.O.I. informed her that the army's new chief of staff—"hold onto your hat"—was Ludendorff. The interjection suggests that Hoffmann, for one, did not regard Ludendorff as a savior from afar—an interpretation supported by Hoffmann's grudging concession that the new chief at least had earned his *Pour le Mérite*.[81]

There was little time for anyone to study the personalities of the new commanders. By the afternoon of the 23rd the situation in the south appeared increasingly serious. The Austrian offensive in Galicia, begun with high hopes a week earlier, had promptly run into difficulties. On the 21st Conrad had contacted both OHL and the 8th Army and expressed an urgent request for a German offensive to support his own.[82] This was obviously impossible. The mass of the Russian 2nd Army was advancing on a sixty-kilometer front from Soldau to Ortelsburg. Strong cavalry forces were believed moving forward on its right. On the 22nd Colonel Hell had countered his earlier breezy optimism and telephoned his anxiety about the left flank of XX Corps. It was possible, Hell said, that the

Russians might envelop it before I Corps arrived. To prevent this he requested that the 3rd Reserve Division detrain at Allenstein and move to the left of XX Corps, instead of to its right as originally ordered. The Russians were by this time so close, Hell declared, that XX Corps expected a battle by the 24th at the latest.[83]

It was with this prospect in mind that the army staff arrived in Marienburg. Hoffmann reported depression and discouragement as a natural consequences of the change in command. Ludendorff described the initial mood as "anything but cheerful." According to Hoffmann the new chief of staff was very surprised" to find that most of the preliminary orders for a concentration against the 2nd Army had been issued. Hoffmann told his new superiors not to be impressed by Russian numerical superiority; their army seemed unimproved since Manchuria. Moreover, a set of notes found on the body of a Russian officer revealed that the 2nd Army was extended so far west that the Germans would be attacking a scattered enemy. If the notes were accurate, any Russian blow through the center, the Masurian Lakes, was correspondingly impossible. Ludendorff was less optimistic. Should Rennenkampf follow up his victory at Gumbinnen XVII Corps and I Reserve Corps were likely to be unavailable for use against the Russian 2nd Army. In this case, the chief of staff declared, the balance of 8th Army would do what it could. If the attack failed the survivors would try to establish a defensive line east of the Vistula, holding the bridgeheads until reinforcements could arrive from the western front.[84]

Ludendorff's anxieties become clearer in the context of the German army's lack of doctrine for fighting a delaying action against superior numbers. The regulations spoke instead of attack and defense, with the latter a temporary phenomenon. In all cases the implication that the Germans would retain the initiative was almost illogically strong. Collective unofficial wisdom went no farther than advising removing oneself as soon as possible from the enemy's immediate reach—limited help in the context of the current situation.[85] Yet despite Ludendorff's concern, the Russian 1st Army was not advancing. Even its cavalry had remained inactive.

Max Hoffmann described this tardiness as the last act of the feud with Samsonov discussed in a previous chapter. In his later years he was prone to say that if the battle of Waterloo had been won on the playing fields of Eton, the battle of Tannenberg was lost on the railway platform at Mukden where the two generals came to blows.[86] Hoffmann told the story with such confidence that one standard reference work even describes him as having witnessed the fight—a remarkable feat for an officer attached at the time to the Japanese army.[87] But this particular legend had an immediate, instrumental purpose. Given Ludendorff's concerns about the possible threat from Rennenkampf's sector, what was more logical for a man like Hoffmann than to search his memory for any scraps and tags of information that might calm the new chief? What was more likely than the fusion of vague rumors based on the Russian generals' membership in different military cliques with a bit of poetic license to produce a story that even its author came to believe—particularly since it was not directly discredited by Rennenkampf's behavior?

IV

The 1st Army's failure to pursue its enemy reflected Rennenkampf's perception of its condition. Before the Battle of Gumbinnen some of his staff officers had argued that a retreat was essential. The army's supplies of food and forage were almost gone. Straggling was becoming epidemic. The ferocity of the German attack on August 20 had shocked veterans of Liaoyang and Mukden. Russian casualties were heavy; ammunition had been used at a staggering rate. Then for no apparent reason the Germans had begun to withdraw. Why? One explanation was both reasonable and comforting: they had been beaten, soundly and unexpectedly. One of Rennenkampf's staff officers, detailed to interrogate prisoners, was impressed in spite of himself by the respect amounting to terror all ranks showed for Russian firepower. "We have many things to learn from you," one wounded officer declared. "The Russian army is not at all what we thought it was." It was not entirely wishful thinking to argue that the Germans were perhaps a bit too civilized for the modern battlefield. Lacking Russian staying power they were retiring as fast as possible, preserving their forces for a major battle further west. It was little wonder that Rennenkampf ended the day by telling one of his staff officers that he could safely take off his clothes and go to bed.

The sense of relief at 1st Army headquarters may have been inappropriate. It was also understandable. No European army was unaware of the inertia tending to strike troops and headquarters alike in the aftermath of a victory. The need for pursuit to physical and emotional limits had been inculcated into Russian generals as well as their German counterparts. But peacetime theory was of little help to a headquarters commanding hungry, tired men, confronting an enemy with a high reputation for wiliness in adversity. The retreat might be an elaborate deception. Even if it were genuine, attempting to follow the Germans too closely in the 1st Army's current state of disorganization might well have the approximate effect of throwing boiled peas at a windowpane.

Nor was Rennenkampf likely to be galvanized into action from above. Zhilinski, cautious by temperament, was not anxious to see 1st Army exhaust itself prematurely, particularly since he expected Rennenkampf's men to have to besiege or blockade the strong fortress of Königsberg. If the Germans were too hard-pressed in the north, moreover, they might retreat fast enough to outrun the 2nd Army's pincer from the south. Zhilinski was not a strategist subtle enough to encourage Rennenkampf to halt in the hopes of holding the Germans in place. On the other hand, he saw no immediate need to drive his army commander faster than he chose to go. Probably fatigue and overconfidence played equal roles in Rennenkampf's decision to halt—but his delay gave the Germans a golden chance to disengage and move south. In their dream of decisive victory, the Russians set the stage for their crushing defeat.[88]

Meanwhile, the German I Corps was beginning its redeployment. François was for once in complete accord with his orders. At 6:00 p.m. on August 22, OHL asked him for a situation report. He replied that since the retreat had been in progress for two days, the chance of a successful attack against Rennenkampf was gone. The best possible course of action was therefore to concentrate in the south. By nightfall of the 23rd, I Corps was loaded and on its way. The Königsberg Division covered the entraining of François's men, then fell back on its base and began entrenching along the Deime River.[89]

The next formation to move south was the 3rd Reserve Division. Its commander, Major-General Curt von Morgen, was in German army slang an "iron-eater," eager to show what he and his uniformed civilians could do, eager for distinction and promotion. He had been too late for Gumbinnen, but he drove his men forward during the evening of August 20, expecting to attack the Russian left flank at first light on the next day. He had no radio station and no telephone connections. An anxious army staff telephoned the fortress of Lötzen, requesting the commandant there to get in touch with Morgen at all costs. Not until midnight did a motorcyclist finally reach the elusive general. Morgen faced temptation. To turn Nelson's blind eye to the dispatch and open battle as he planned, expecting the rest of the army to march to his guns in the manner of 1870, was to risk all to gain much: victory, acclaim, perhaps the *Pour le Mérite* itself, the much-coveted Blue Max.

But Morgen's stars did not sit quite firmly enough either in his eyes or on his shoulders to encourage him to stake his career on his judgment. The 3rd Reserve Division remained in place until daylight on August 21, then marched to the rear and boarded trains for Allenstein. Loading and unloading their reservists proved a complex challenge for inexperienced officers. By the night of the 22nd, Morgen's combat elements had arrived at the assigned detraining areas. It took over forty-eight hours to move the rest of the division.[90]

Mackensen's corps was well on its westward way by noon on August 21, when a brief eclipse obscured the sun. In the eyes of those whose romantic visions survived Gumbinnen, it was nature's own memorial to the dead. By evening of the 22nd the lost field was forty miles away. Most of the stragglers had by this time found their way back to their companies, and few awkward questions were asked by superiors themselves trying to make peace with their experience and their behavior. August 23 was officially a day of rest—for the lucky, a chance to clean clothes and equipment, to shave, to bathe in one of the small streams on the line of march, to write a field post card affirming survival, above all to sleep.

On August 24, XVII Corps started to move south in earnest. By that night it reached Friedland. By the 25th it was in the region of Gross Schwansfeld. The West Prussians had fought a battle, then marched over a hundred miles in six days of ninety-degree heat—an impressive first view of the elephant by any standards. As his men left the field of Gumbinnen behind them, Mackensen's spirits rose. By the 24th he was describing the situation as "interesting but difficult," and expressing confidence that "we will succeed in mastering it"—a far cry from his gloomy report of the 20th.[91]

But XVII Corps was marching through endless columns of refugees, forcing them off the roads and into the fields, upsetting wagons, throwing abandoned household goods aside like the rubbish they had suddenly become. To citizen-soldiers indoctrinated with their responsibility to defend the people they were now brutalizing, it was a heavy burden. Ambulances filled with the wounded from Gumbinnen were bypassed, despite the despairing appeals of men who feared being left behind for the Cossacks.

Mackensen rode up and down the regiments telling his men that they were not retreating, only attacking in a different direction. His credibility in the ranks during those days was questionable. More important than the general's rhetoric was an occasional loaf of bread commandeered from a passing supply column to supplement raw bacon scavenged from the bottoms of almost-empty haversacks and turnips dug from an abandoned field during one of the all-too-brief halts. Most of the kitchens had fallen behind, or had nothing left to cook.

The moral recovery of XVII Corps was also fostered by the German army's "book." Whatever might be the mood of the fire-eating lieuten-tants, the captains, majors, and colonels were professionals who knew that only in storybooks is the enemy always defeated. Doctrine and experience since 1870 had stressed that a frontal attack against prepared positions with haphazard artillery support was unlikely to achieve much by itself. At best such a maneuver would hold an enemy in place and divert his strength from other sectors. In that sense XVII Corps's middle-ranking officers could rationalize that they had done their job, and the real failures were the units on their flanks. It might be Dutch comfort, but it would carry the corps into its next fight.[92]

The I Reserve Corps was the last to move. Below's men were even more hindered than Mackensen's by the refugees crossing their lines of march, not least because his officers seem to have been less ruthless than Mackensen's in clearing the roads. Particularly at road junctions the tangle of wagons and animals so challenged the best efforts of the military police that detours seemed the better part of wisdom. More than the other corps commanders, Below was aware of the physical limitations of his reservists. He and his staff took pains to provide water, hot food, and regular brief halts. Regimental officers were more willing than their counterparts of the active corps to overlook the chickens, geese, and ducks from abandoned farmyards that volunteered for special duty in the haversacks of the rank and file. Better that than leaving them for the Russians. More than his counterparts, too, Below was willing to take citizens in uniform into his confidence. His order of the day for August 21 not only expressed the usual appreciation for the troops' performance at Gumbinnen, but regretted that the fruits of victory had been rejected because of Prittwitz's insistence on retreat.[93]

By August 23, only the 1st Cavalry Division remained facing Rennenkampf. It had done well at Gumbinnen, not only keeping its Russian counterparts in check but riding behind enemy lines as far as Pilkallen, sowing panic in Rennenkampf's headquarters and returning to its own lines, as mentioned with a sizeable bag of prisoners. A few more men, a bit more firepower, and a bit more aggressiveness might have enabled the writing of a last, heroic chapter in the mounted arm's history. But the German squadrons had been constantly on the alert since mobilization. Some had been reduced to less than half their assigned strength. Casualties had played a less significant role in that process than exhausted horses. German cavalry were on the whole better horsemasters than their French or Russian counterparts. Nevertheless forced marches and night alarms, short rations and hasty saddling combined in an epidemic of cast shoes, sore backs, and injured legs. Senior officers, despairing requests for a day's rest, and their even more despairing demands that the civil authorities do something to control the refugees blocking the roads, did not suggest a sudden return to the dashing days of Napoleon.[94]

The weakness of the cavalry enhanced the problem facing 8th Army command. For its proposed concentration to have any effect the Russian 2nd Army had to be stopped as close to the German border as possible. Every mile it advanced meant that the Germans had to concentrate further to their rear, giving Rennenkampf even more time to move into the gap opened as XVII Corps and I Reserve Corps moved south. Somehow the Germans facing Samsonov had to hold out; a reinforced corps had to stop an army. The burden of the campaign now rested on XX Corps, and on its commander, Lieutenant-General von Scholtz.

PART III

THE BLOOD-SWOLLEN GOD

7
The Province of Uncertainty

On a map, the advance of the Russian 2nd Army was a deadly thrust. An attack northwest towards the Vistula, if successful, would render impossible any German plans for switching troops from sector to sector behind the line of the Masurian Lakes. It would cut the German lines of communication into East Prussia. It would hopelessly trap every German soldier in the province. *Ostheer* would be forced either to fight at a disadvantage or to let itself be shut up in Königsberg. This bold conception was the product of evolution. Zhilinski, initially mindful of the risks of dividing his forces, had originally planned only a tactical envelopment on the 2nd Army's front, with two of its corps advancing directly west towards the line Lyck-Johannesburg, and two more executing a short left hook around the Masurian Lakes. Then on August 10 the Russian high command "suggested" instead that the major axis of the 2nd Army's advance should be south of the Lakes. Zhilinski took the recommendation as an order. On August 13 he informed Samsonov that the 2nd Army was to shift its lines of march westward. From right to left, VI, XIII, and XV Corps, and a division of XXIII Corps would advance to the line Rudczanny-Passenheim, then swing north to Seeburg-Rastenburg. Only II Corps would advance directly against the Masurian Lakes, while maintaining contact between the 1st and 2nd Armies. To cover his left, which would be more exposed by this change in plans, Samsonov was assigned three more divisions, I Corps, the 3rd Guard Division, and the other division of XXIII Corps.

Samsonov himself made a third set of changes in his march orders. His Directive Number 1, issued on August 16, extended the front of his advance by a further twenty-five miles. On paper the objective remained

213

that set by Zhilinski: the line Rudczanny-Passenheim. But the 2nd Army's three center corps would now begin by marching northwest. Only after crossing the frontier would they begin swinging northward as originally instructed.

When Zhilinski protested sharply, Samsonov answered that the new lines of advance were necessary if he was to have sufficient freedom to maneuver. His alteration offered the chance of enveloping the Germans, avoiding the costs and risks of a head-on encounter. It also required two days' extra marching for the corps involved. It increased the risk of losing communication with the 1st Army. It set back the time when the Russian forces could unite. It created the possibility of a dangerous overextension of the 2nd Army's front. And it demanded from the start extremely rapid movements.[1]

Complaints from higher authorities received the unvarnished reply that the troops were moving as fast as they could but were being delayed by "sand." More than sand was involved. To reach Samsonov's revised line of departure from their original concentration areas, XV, XIII, and VI Corps had to average between sixteen and eighteen miles a day for five days. Even more than on Rennenkampf's front the strategic situation indicated prospects for what the Soviets now call an operational maneuver group: a strong advance guard of cavalry supported by enough infantry and artillery to give it a reasonable degree of firepower.[2] But however often the Russians had used such a force in their military history, Samsonov and his staff regarded the risks as unacceptable. They preferred an alternate set.

"Freedom to maneuver" was a shibboleth of peacetime wargaming. Considered in the abstract, long marches might seem a reasonable trade-off, a Napoleonic decision to make war with soldiers' legs. But men, not painted wooden blocks, were executing the new orders. They were moving not on a smooth map, but over roads little more than dirt tracks, often deliberately left unimproved to slow a potential German invasion. Nor were they all peacetime soldiers hardened to forced marches. As many as 60 percent of the men in some battalions were newly mobilized reservists, no more accustomed than their German counterparts to the feel of army boots and the weight of a full pack. Temperatures in the eighties and nineties added to the misery of clouds of dust kicked up by thousands of blistered feet. It was not mere superstition that led Samsonov's men to curse the solar eclipse of August 21 as a bad omen. Their luck seemed hardly capable of getting worse.

Efficient logistics could have done much to ease the strain of the Russian advance. Most of the infantrymen who lurched toward the frontier were young and healthy. Peasants or townsmen, they were inured to physical exertion. Ample food, regular supplies of water, and the opportunity for one or two nights of uninterrupted sleep were familiar restoratives of energy and morale.

But the Russian army's supply services were disorganized to the point of confusion. A new system of centralized administration had been

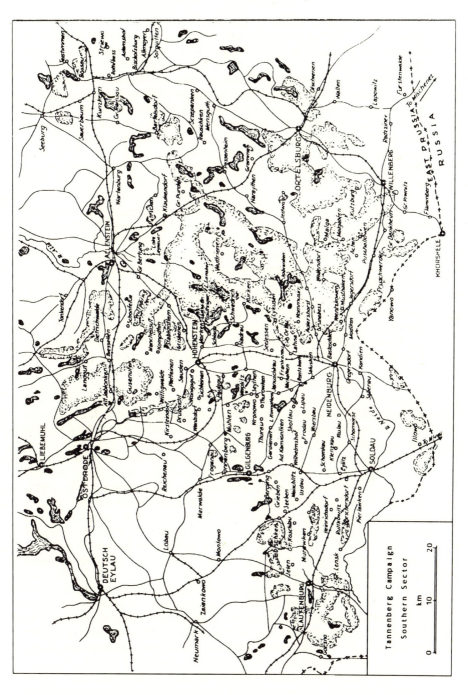

Tannenberg Campaign

Southern Sector

introduced just before the war. As a result front, army, and corps quartermasters spent more time debating jurisdictions than moving rations forward or keeping roads clear. Supply columns frequently lacked their authorized number of wagons. Requisitioned civilian vehicles broke down under their loads. Heavy government wagons stuck in the sand. Using double teams restored mobility temporarily, but at the price of further exhausting horses unaccustomed to being worked such long hours on so little forage. The end result was rations not reaching their destinations at all, or arriving at odd times of the day and night, disrupting meal and sleep schedules accordingly. Water discipline collapsed as thirsty men broke ranks to empty wells in the villages through which they passed, then fell out with stomach cramps. Straggling grew from a problem to a plague as hungry, footsore men lagged behind the marching columns to nurse their galls and seek something to eat. Complaints from company and battalion commanders were discounted by senior officers who sententiously proclaimed that active service demanded energy and sacrifice from all ranks.

The 2nd Army had more to worry it than an epidemic of blisters or an outbreak of empty stomachs. Its corps, in contrast to Rennenkampf's homogeneous force, came from three different military districts and were correspondingly unused to working together. Its staff had been drawn from the Warsaw Military District, which had also formed the staff of the Northwest Front. The best and most ambitious officers naturally went to the higher formation. The 2nd Army inherited the remnants, a hastily assembled group of self-defined rejects unused to working together. The British military attaché, Major-General Alfred Knox, acidly criticized its inclusion of an "eccentric youth" whose appointment depended on his ability to draw caricatures. This degree of professional purism is acceptable only in terms of hindsight. Most higher headquarters include a few drones whose real function is to keep their harder-working compatriots relaxed and amused—an important function given the stresses of modern war. Questions of temperament and personality were far more relevant. Samsonov was identified with Sukhomlinov; his chief of staff, General Postovsky, was one of the war minister's biting critics. At least as serious from an operational perspective, Samsonov was phlegmatic to the point of indifference; Postovsky was so nervous that his irreverent subordinates nicknamed him "The Mad Mullah." A calm commander and a highly strung chief were regarded in all armies as a potentially fruitful combination. Too broad a gap in temperaments, however, could split a headquarters down the middle quite independently of questions of patronage or protection.

Personal problems of command were rapidly overshadowed by technical ones. The 2nd Army depended for communications less on its own resources than on peacetime telegraph and telephone networks. Each corps was responsible for establishing links with army headquarters and with each of its subordinate divisions. But the available wire soon proved insufficient for both missions. Lines constantly went out of commission.

The Province of Uncertainty

Ill-trained repair crews stumbling thorugh heavily wooded, unfamiliar terrain took hours to find the breaks, and more hours to repair them. The Russians complained of sabotage on both sides of the frontiers. German stragglers or patriotic adolescents probably cut an occasional wire in defiance of the risk of being shot out of hand. But the alleged saboteurs were too consistently successful in evading Samsonov's patrols to be much more than a symbol of Russian frustration.

The unreliability of its electronic nervous system was a particular shock to the 2nd Army, because its corps were too widely extended for mounted dispatch riders to be of much use. The army's establishment of automobiles and motorcycles was low. The vehicles available were regarded as best used for transportation and short-range liaison, as opposed to long-distance communication among scattered headquarters. Nor were they were so mechanically reliable that using them on unfamiliar roads, in a hostile country, with drivers guided by maps at best inadequate, was likely to improve connections.

In this context, the decision of Samsonov's staff to make extensive use of radio was hardly irresponsible. Over the preceding quarter-century high commands everywhere in Europe, even in Russia, had become dependent on modern communications technology to transmit orders and information. In 1904/05, Russian radio operators had discovered that they could pick up transmissions from Japanese warships, and that the intensity of those transmissions often prefigured movements and concentrations. In 1914, therefore, the Russians clearly understood the possibility of German interception—not least because their own operators were regularly able to pick up German messages, some in clear, others whose coding kept them a mystery. The 2nd Army headquarters was also well aware of the risk of sending dispatches in clear. Like its counterpart to the north, however, it perceived a choice between two evils: interception on one hand, incomprehensibility on the other. Samsonov's staff could only guess at the qualifications of the German signal personnel, but knew all too well the weaknesses of their own. Sending messages in plain Russian while juggling lines and frequencies seemed an acceptable risk in the context of the alternatives.[3]

An even more pressing problem for the 2nd Army involved finding the enemy it was supposed to fight. The Russians were bedevilled by confused and contradictory reports of German concentrations and advances. The few aircraft at Samsonov's disposal failed to coordinate their reconnaissance flights; their crews seemed unable even to find their way around East Prussia. His independent cavalry divisions were fully occupied securing the flanks of the advance. The mounted regiments allotted directly to his corps and divisions were not active units, but Cossack reserves. In 1914 this too often meant semitrained plowboys mounted on requisitioned farm horses. Reconnaissance demanded a set of skills not exactly complex, but also not capable of being imparted by osmosis. Too many patrols rode forward uncertain of what to look for and unwilling to get too far from their own supporting infantry.

By August 21, however, the cavalry had at least determined that there were some Germans in Neidenburg and Ortelsburg. With an enemy at last in reach, Samsonov's orders for the next day were simple enough. The VI Corps, on his army's immediate right, was to take Ortelsburg. Its left-flank neighbor, XIII Corps, would remain in support, ready to attack either Neidenburg or Ortelsburg as the situation required. On the army's left I and XV Corps would advance to the line Neidenburg-Soldau, while the 2nd Division of XXIII Corps moved to Mlawa and made ready to strike the German rear.

Zhilinski was not pleased. To ease Samsonov's command burden, Zhilinski had on the 21st transferred II Corps to the 1st Army. Now he telegraphed Samsonov to complain about the "lack of resolution" in 2nd Army's operations. Samsonov pointed out in reply that his units were too depleted, his men too tired, to take both presumed German positions simultaneously by a single frontal blow. It made better sense to outflank them.

Samsonov was more accurate in his evaluation than even he knew. As his corps crossed the German border they found deserted villages and uncut crops. Commanders inculcated in peacetime with a horror of looting and a corresponding respect for private property found it difficult to organize systematic requisitions. Despite the better-paved roads of East Prussia, straggling increased as men stayed hungry. Staff work at division and corps level deteriorated as tired, anxious officers began snapping at each other. Despite these handicaps, XV Corps reached and occupied Neidenburg on the afternoon of August 22.[4]

Neidenburg's experiences are as illustrative as they appear old-fashioned to a generation reared on the horrors of modern, ideologically based conflicts. Neidenburg in 1914 was a market town and county seat. Too small to have its own garrison, it had used its schools, churches, and the town's one synagogue to quarter troops during mobilization. The town even provided free coffee—an initiative of Mayor Andreas Kuhn. He was forty-one years old, a career civil servant whose initial dreams of high office and distinction had been tempered by the realities of administrative routine in the provinces, but who remained as yet unsoured by his limitations. If Imperial Germany was largely ruled by its administrators, men like Kuhn were the bearings on which the machinery turned. His photo shows a man whose square face, short haircut, and bristling kaiser mustache combine to create an impression of energy uncorrupted by imagination—a bureaucratic and sympathetic version of Heinrich Mann's Diederich Hessling.

Kuhn needed all of his phlegm as word of the Russian advance generated panic. On the morning of the 22nd, civilians began crowding the roads to the north and west burdened with whatever mix of personal and household goods they were able to seize and carry. Rabbit hutches and sewing machines, babies and grandparents, a cow or a few milk goats—Neidenburg was not too far from its days as an enlarged village. A patrol of Cossacks rode into the fast-emptying town from the south, exchanged shots with some German stragglers, and rode out again, leaving behind a half-dozen civilians wounded by random bullets. The next Russian probe was in squadron strength, and it ran into an unexpected surprise.

The armies of Europe had been debating the military potential of the bicycle for a quarter-century. Since 1913 each German *Jäger* battalion included a cyclist company in its order of battle, but their commanders were not quite sure how to use them. In Germany the uniformed cyclist fell between two stools. To the cavalry he was a road-bound object of pity as he puffed along in his vain efforts to keep up with horsemen. To the infantry he was a monkey on a stick, a man without a place in the serried ranks of the line.

Mobilization brought enlightenment. Theoretically, reconnaissance of all kinds was the cavalry's responsibility. Cavalry colonels, however, were reluctant to split their proud commands into troops and squadrons for attachment to and probable misuse by mud-crunching infantrymen. The infantry turned to self-help. Not a battalion in 8th Army but counted its share of men who owned, rode, and loved bicycles. Volunteers were easily found for improvised cyclist detachments, which found plenty to do scouting and patrolling the East Prussian countryside.

Nor were all of these men civilian reservists. The 151st Infantry Regiment rejoiced in a lieutenant with the indisputably aristocratic name of Burscher von Saher zum Weissenstein, who in peacetime alternately shocked and amused his superiors by risking his neck on a motorcycle in his off-duty hours. He was a logical choice to command the regiment's wheelmen, and on August 22 he was on a one-man patrol when he met four farmers on the road a few kilometers from Neidenburg. The civilians painted a vivid picture: a horde of Cossacks spreading terror to all points of the compass. The lieutenant reversed his direction, assembled his cyclists, and at the head of twenty-nine men started back towards Neidenburg. A kilometer outside the town he halted his column and went forward alone on foot. Pistol in hand, Lieutenant von Saher climbed a small hill to find himself almost face to face with a Russian scout on a similar errand. A frightened youngster in a spiked helmet fired a wild shot. Another frightened youngster in a flat cap turned and ran—only to be dropped in his tracks by a German rifleman with a steadier hand.

The shooting brought more Russians. A squadron of Cossacks advanced to carbine range, fired a volley from horseback, and charged. It was a drill book maneuver with predictable results. The Germans, by this time well under cover, emptied saddle after saddle. With half their men down the Russians rode back into the town, followed at a discreet distance by the Germans. The cyclists found no snipers, no machine guns hidden in carefully contrived ambushes—only empty streets and one old lady who marvelled at their willingness to take on such superior numbers. The patrol traversed the whole town before it discovered an enemy: a squadron peacefully preparing its noon meal in the Neidenburg *Bahnhofsplatz*, unaware of any danger until the Germans opened fire. Cossacks and horses scattered in all directions. When the shooting stopped the Germans counted their booty. Two hundred lances, stacked according to regulations. Discarded sabers. A single unwounded horse. And, most useful of all, a map taken from the body of the squadron commander, with the Russian advance positions carefully marked. Before departing with this important piece of intelligence, the lieutenant and his men took time to eat the Russians' lunch.[5]

The Cossacks reported their discomfiture with suitable embellishments. Whether from ignorance, or understandable reluctance to admit they had been routed by a handful of *Landser*, their surviving officers insisted that they had been ambushed by *franc-tireurs*, armed civilians. The commander of the Russian XV Corps, Lieutenant-General Martos, responded by ordering his artillery to open fire on Neidenburg. Martos, while far from atrocity prone, was apparently motivated by a desire to scare off uniformed stragglers, while at the same time providing an object lesson to any belligerent citizens. His gunners had no specific targets, and the shelling was a bagatelle by later standards. To the Germans remaining in Neidenburg it seemed the end of the world. Over three hundred rounds hit and exploded, most of them in the center of town—a natural focus for batteries still developing their skills in observation and range taking. Of Neidenburg's 470 buildings, 193 were destroyed. Many more were damaged by fires defying the best efforts of the Russians to put them out after they entered the town.

For the next eight days Neidenburg was under Russian military occupation. Kuhn sent his family to safety but stuck to his post and kept his records. Initially the Russians lived down to the worst expectations of anti-Slav racists. Trees, fences, and sheds disappeared into their bivouac fires. Houses left locked by refugees were broken into, their furniture destroyed or vandalized. Stores were stripped of their goods, honey and syrup poured over what was not carried away. Every safe in Neidenburg was forced open and its contents requisitioned. Enterprising enlisted men, prefiguring the behavior of their sons three decades later, "collected" watches from those *Neidenbürger* foolhardy enough to appear on the streets.

The Germans rapidly learned to temper their indignation in the presence of armed foreigners who tended to be slightly trigger happy. The Russians had had ample time to develop and circulate their own rumors about civilians who poisoned wells, put pieces of wire in forage, or carried concealed weapons. One civilian was shot when he threw a stone at a horseman. A farm laborer met the same fate for not responding quickly enough to a Cossack NCO's demand for oats. And—arguably even more shocking to respectable German sensibilities—Russian officers systematically spat all over the bust of William II that was a prominent feature of the lobby decor in Neidenburg's best hotel!

But this was only one side of the story. Martos picked up lost children in his own car. Some of his privates shared their bread with a poor civilian reading his Bible in lieu of the dinner he could not afford.

The Province of Uncertainty

Even Mayor Kuhn conceded that the ordinary Russian behaved well enough when met with "tact and energy." The town commandant, a Colonel Dovator, cooperated with German technicians to get water and sewer services back into operation. He issued orders to stop looting by soldiers or civilians. He threatened to shoot any Russian caught accosting or propositioning women. During the eight days of Neidenburg's occupation a half-dozen executions were actually carried out, and as many lesser offenders were knouted in the public square. The form of punishment, with the victim held on the ground by his hands and feet while a Cossack plied his *nagaika*, generated "all respect" among the civilian onlookers—not least because the normal sentence was fifty lashes. Would-be resisters and potential saboteurs were at least as thoroughly deterred as prospective military miscreants.[6]

The relatively bloodless occupation of Neidenburg also convinced Samsonov that the Germans had withdrawn faster and farther than either the Northwest Front or his own headquarters had anticipated. Since there no longer seemed any possibility of pinning his enemy against the Masurian Lakes, Samsonov proposed to shift his axis of advance even farther westward. His orders for the 23rd held VI Corps in position around Ortelsburg. The XIII Corps would swing westward towards Jedwabno while XV Corps moved through the towns of Orlau and Frankenau. The I Corps would take position around Soldau as the army's left-flank guard; and the 2nd Division would fill the resulting gap between I and XV Corps.

Samsonov and his staff were aware that this new line of march would increase the distance between his army and Rennkampf's. The risk, however, seemed acceptable. Russian plans called for strategic, rather than tactical, coordination of the armies. By advancing westward instead of north, Samsonov argued to Zhilinski, the 2nd Army could cut the German line of retreat and eventually advance into the heart of Germany itself. More immediately, the army could use the Soldau-Mlawa railroad to move badly needed supplies forward.

Zhilinski was initially hostile to Samsonov's concept. Not only did it represent a departure from northwest front's original orders, it exposed both of the 2nd Army's flanks. Almost half of Samsonov's force, I and VI Corps, would be reduced to a security role, guarding the flanks of the five divisions in the center. In the course of the day, however, reports from Rennenkampf describing a headlong German retreat in the north led Zhilinski to reconsider. Ultimately he was more attracted by the possibility of preventing a German escape across the Vistula than concerned with the risks of a German concentration against the 2nd Army. Samsonov, moreover, was the commander on the spot, and presumably knew what he was about. Zhilinski finally instructed his subordinate to do at least part of what Samsonov proposed to do in any case: reach the line Sensburg-Allenstein with three and a half corps by August 26, while leaving I Corps in position at Soldau as a flank guard. At 7:30 p.m. on August 23, Samsonov issued the appropriate orders. They differed only in detail from those he had drawn up earlier.[7]

The Germans had not been idle in the face of Samsonov's advance. Scholtz had his own XX Corps, reinforced by the 20th *Landwehr* brigade, the 70th *Landwehr* Brigade from Thorn, and the 69th Provisional Brigade from Graudenz—a total of eighteen improvised battalions. They were short of transport but well supported by artillery and machine guns, and the corps commander expected them to fight instead of march. Scholtz was a pathbreaker. Despite the growing importance of artillery in modern war, a combination of seniority regulations and caste prejudices had restricted the gunners' access to higher commands before 1914. The military cabinet considered them in general unsuitable to lead combined arms formations because their training and experience was excessively specialized. This image of artillerymen as technicians was applied with far more vigor to the anonymous regiments of the line than to the Prussian Guard. Scholtz was the first line gunner to be promoted lieutenant-general in peacetime while still young enough to take command of a corps.

He had earned the appointment. Born in Schleswig-Holstein, he entered the 9th Artillery as a student volunteer in 1870, making a solid reputation as an administrator and establishing a sufficiently visible image of ambition that his biographer is at some pains to defend him from the charge of careerism. Perhaps what saved him was his easy-going charm. He was a bachelor; in contrast to British army mythology, bachelor senior officers, with fewer domestic problems to irritate them, were seen as preferable to married men. But Scholtz's behavior was a matter of principle as well as character. More than François or Mackensen, Scholtz believed in a calm, steady approach. He considered "discussion" a better word than "critique" for the process of evaluating exercises. Well-known for a puckish sense of humor, Scholtz liked making jokes. Among his favorite ways of dealing with minor complaints was making the participants write reports on the issue until everyone gave up in disgust or laughter.

Scholtz's assignment in October, 1912, to form and lead XX Corps was a sound matching of ability with mission. The bourgeois specialist would not be put into an existing command structure, with its risks of friction and tension. He could give the new corps his own stamp. And Scholtz's chief of staff complemented, rather than challenged, his commander's abilities. Colonel Emil Hell was also a gunner, a foot artillery-man whose early career had been spent in a role regarded by the infantry and cavalry as little more martial than driving wagons. Like Scholtz, Hell was a hard driver with a reputation for cast-iron nerves and imperturbable good cheer. He was also a local man who had ridden or hunted over every inch of the ground XX Corps was expected to defend. His home was near Gross-Grieben, directly in the path of the Russian invasion.

Within months of his appointment, at a time when administrative responsibilities might be assumed to absorb all of his energy, Scholtz was bombarding the kaiser, the war ministry, and the general staff with his ideas for the defense of East Prussia. Germany must, Scholtz argued, reckon with a Russian breakthrough in the frontier provinces. Russia must invade, not merely raid; otherwise she would forfeit all international credibility. And XX Corps lay directly in the path of one of the likeliest axes of advance. Schlieffen, in one of his last interviews before his death, grumbled to the new corps commander that the Russians were not coming at all, and that he had left three active corps in the east only until the first railway lines were free to move them west. He dismissed Scholtz with the sarcastic suggestion to "go play with your frontier security."

Scholtz took the advice. The regiments of XX Corps were much like their commander. Most of them had no glorious histories. They were high-numbered workaday units, organized in 1905 or 1912 or 1913, given a provincial title, and told to make their own traditions. But they had marched and maneuvered over the ground they were now defending. The corps's peacetime headquarters was at Allenstein. Two of its infantry regiments were also stationed there. The 18th Infantry garrisoned Oster-ode; the 59th had a detachment at Soldau. More than other corps commanders, Scholtz encouraged close ties between the military and the civilian populations. Whatever the garrison, participation in local feasts and holidays was encouraged, bands and honor guards made freely available. Scholtz himself demonstrated enough talent as a public speaker to be in high demand on the regional banquet circuit.[8]

Initially he took a similarly aggressive approach to his assignment of screening the 8th Army's right flank. In the war's first weeks his two divisional cavalry regiments, the 10th and 11th Dragoons, took the measure of the Russians to their own satisfaction in a series of swirling fights along the border. A corporal and six men scattered two dozen Cossacks by a bold mounted charge. A reserve lieutenant and sixteen troopers, reconnoitering across the frontier into Russia, cut their way home through a full enemy squadron. The stories multiplied and spread, losing nothing in the telling.

As his men's confidence soared, Scholtz briefly considered concentrating against the 2nd Army's left and attacking it without waiting for support. Scouting reports soon forced him to abandon the idea. The Russians were too strong; it was impossible to mass against part of their front without risking being enveloped by the rest of the army. Instead Scholtz withdrew his forward units gradually; by August 22, his force was in position on an east-west line from Gilgenburg to Lahna. Scholtz's headquarters were in Mühlen, behind the center of his line. On the right, around Gilgenburg, were stationed ten battalions of fortress troops drawn from the Vistula garrisons. Next to them came the 41st Division, reinforced by a regiment of the 70th *Landwehr* Brigade. The corps's left flank, from Frankenau and Lahna to Orlau, was held by the other half of the *Landwehr* brigade and the active troops of the 37th Division. It was in this sector that the Russians, the 8th Division of XV Corps, struck on August 23 the forward positions of the 37th Division around the villages of Lahna and Orlau.[9]

For a little while it was war the way schoolbooks and pulp novels described it. "We'll have another game after this little bit," a lieutenant laughed as he tossed away a *skat* hand. An hour later he and his partners lay dead, victims of the furious seesaw fighting as Germans and Russians, galvanized by the valor of inexperience, swept back and forth across the high ground in front of Orlau. Instead of waiting for the Russians to come to them, the Germans charged with bands playing and colors flying. Postwar memories credited some formations with singing the *Deutschland-lied* as they stormed forward. A battalion commander too badly wounded to walk had himself carried by two of his men—whose opinions on the assignment remain unrecorded. Another major cheered his men forward until a shrapnel ball smashed his skull like a watermelon and spattered brain tissue over his horrified staff. A lieutenant of the 1st *Jäger* jumped into a Russian trench, sword in hand. A Russian officer rushed forward with his own sword ready. Steel clashed on steel in a scene reminiscent of the eighteenth century. A quick thrust and the Russian sank gurgling to the bottom of the trench. At the same moment the German took a bullet through his head. "Like friends who have fallen asleep after a day's outing," the two young men lay side by side as those still alive climbed over their comrades' corpses in their eagerness to kill each other.

An added horror was provided by a field of lupines that stretched across part of the front. Even in the midst of battle the bright colors and sweet fragrance attracted notice. But those who fell wounded there found the lupines so tall and thick that stretcher-bearers often failed to see their huddled bodies. Days after the battle, dead men were being recovered from among the flowers.

Hysteria mixed with low comedy. A sergeant shouted at a hobbling comrade to take cover. The private replied, "But I've been wounded already." Not until reminded that this fact did not confer permanent immunity did he seek the nearest trench. A machine gunner had to be forcibly restrained from firing on a company of his own regiment whom he insisted were retreating Russians. An even uglier incident was narrowly averted as a detachment of the 151st Infantry rounded up and disarmed prisoners. A German *Feldwebel* stalked purposefully towards the group, shortening his grip on his bayonetted rifle. "You murdered my father," he shouted, "and I'm going to pay you for it!" The Russo-German frontier was a semipermeable barrier. Smugglers, poachers, line-crossers of every type, made such posts as gamekeeper and customs guard high-risk assignments. The *Feldwebel's* father, a forester, had recently been slain by parties unknown. The son, battle madness on him, wanted blood in return, and was only dissuaded when soberer comrades reminded him that he would be butchering helpless men in cold blood. As an added irony, the prisoners were not Russians, but Poles. The bereaved NCO was named Kontratowitz.[10]

Like murderous schoolboys, Germans and Russians on another part of the field fought for possession of the 29th Russian Regiment's battle flag. At the end rifle butts, fists and teeth settled the issue. The staff fell into German hands; the colors, torn away in the melee, disappeared. A German burial party later discovered them wound around the body of a

Russian officer, who had saved his flag before crawling away to die of his wounds.[11]

At Orlau the point-blank dogfight continued into the evening. German staff officers were exchanging their binoculars for rifles by the time a final desperate German rush drove the Russians out of the village. Around Lahna the fighting was even grimmer and dirtier. If glory can ever be found in battle, the riflemen of the 1st East Prussian *Jäger* Battalion "Yorck von Wartenburg" trod its blood-stained road that day. The *Jäger* of the line were the closest thing to an elite infantry the kaiser's army possessed. They were recruited from professional hunters and foresters, from men whose civil occupations involved an open-air life, and from "suitable" volunteers—which usually meant twenty-year-olds bemused by the shakos, the green tunics, and the mystique surrounding these dashing warriors. Since 1871 the *Jägers'* worth as separate formations had been sharply questioned. Their relationship with public and private forest agencies, who valued the *Jäger* as a steady source of employees, had as much to do with their continued existence as any perceived operational utility. But the riflemen continued to go their own way, cherishing their image as crack shots and bold adventurers, using hunters' calls like "*Horrido*" or "*Waidmannsheil*" in place of conventional commands, and putting in extra hours on the rifles ranges while bemoaning the growth of impersonal means of killing enemies en masse.

Two companies of these green-coats, five hundred men, were under orders to hold the village of Lahna. Like most of its counterparts in that part of East Prussia, Lahna's origins went back to the final wave of German colonization in the fourteenth century. Its three hundred inhabitants were German to the marrow; the 1920 plebiscite would result in unanimous rejection of the new state of Poland. Its layout was equally German. Most of Lahna's houses fronted on the two or three main streets, giving the village a straggling, extended character and making the organization of a coherent defense correspondingly difficult. Each house with its sheds and outbuildings was on its own, to stand or fall with its handful of riflemen.

The *Jäger* profited, at least temporarily, by the Russians' attempt to carry Lahna in one quick rush—mass over finesse. Against the best marksmen in Germany, attack after attack collapsed. The officers and NCOs who led the charges were the first to fall; their surviving privates massed in knots the rawest recruit could hardly miss. The *Jäger* kept up their fire as the Russians closed to seventy-five, then to fifty yards, until there were too many Russians to shoot and they began pouring into the village from all sides. Captain Bergmann, the senior surviving officer, rallied fifteen or twenty men for a counterattack. He got as far along the main street as the village smithy before being mortally wounded. His last words were, "Don't worry about me! Hold Lahna!" By then the fighting had come down to bayonets and rifle butts, fists and furniture. A knot of Russians waved white flags. It may have been an offer to surrender. More likely it was a request to negotiate a German capitulation. In either case the few *Jäger* foolish enough to respond by standing up became targets for every belligerent or opportunistic Russian within range.

Were their deaths a misunderstanding, or a signal of "no quarter"? No one wanted to find out. By this time much of the village was in flames. Breathless, his tunic singed and torn, the 2nd Company's *Feldwebel* ran from group to group of riflemen, looking for an officer. Among a half-dozen dead men he found someone able to point out his platoon leader's position. It was occupied by a corpse already beginning to stiffen. Whatever the original orders might have been, remaining in Lahna could serve no useful purpose. In a twilight deepening into darkness, the *Feldwebel* collected all the survivors he could find. With twenty or thirty men, many of them wounded, he made his way back to the main German line, while behind him the Russians mopped up stragglers and shot each other in mutual confusion.[11]

As small arms and artillery fire died down the first thing that struck the Germans of XX Corps was the eerie silence. But it was a relative silence. Instead of bursting shells and rattling machine guns came calls for stretcher-bearers; orders and warnings shouted in delirium; screams for a mercy shot as the torment of wounds untended finally grew too much to bear in silence. In the years before the war, medical and military experts had projected a coming era of clean wounds made by high-velocity, small-caliber rounds punching such neat holes on entry and exit that the victims might well feel next to nothing. Theoretical wisdom paled before the realities of bullets that fishhooked on striking bone, tearing holes that made an earlier century's thumb-sized musket balls look almost humane. It vanished entirely when confronted with the effects of artillery fire on unprotected bodies. The opposing guns had fired mostly shrapnel on August 23, and the balls of a shrapnel round could shred a man into raw meat yet leave him alive.

Unwounded Germans were little less disoriented. Losses had been high, particularly among company officers and NCOs. Individually and in small groups men straggled back through the darkness, looking for their parent formations, for someone to tell them what to do next, for hot food and coffee. Here and there searchlights were brought forward to illuminate the scene in hopes of preventing a panic. One enterprising lieutenant had his bugler sound *"Das Ganze Halt."* Others took up the call. As the familiar notes sounded over the battlefield, men remembered the war games of peacetime, where that call meant a night's sleep, a sing-song around the bivouac fire, perhaps a rendezvous with a willing or curious local woman. It seemed years away instead of weeks. Officers who had spent years training a company, who knew almost every man in its ranks by name and reputation, counted losses of 60 or 70 percent. Friends and brothers had fallen, been carried away by stretcher-bearers, or just disappeared. Surviving officers of the 1st *Jäger* sat in the dining room of an abandoned farmhouse, observing the burning down of the candles "as though it was an experiment of indescribable importance." A captain of another regiment shared with one of his sergeants his fear that Lahna and

Orlau would go down in history with Jena and Auerstädt as a German disaster.[12]

Scholtz too was a worried man. As late as 7:00 p.m. he had proposed to counterattack the Russians at dawn. But in the hours before midnight his subordinates made plain that their units were so disorganized that it would be well into the next morning before they would be sorted out. Then at midnight Scholtz received a message from army headquarters: since I Corps would not be able to reach his sector until noon on the August 26. Scholtz was instructed to conserve his strength. After two hours' deliberation, he and his staff decided that the best course was to withdraw at least the left flank of the corps, the units engaged at Orlau and Lahna, before the Russians could attack again.

Colonel Hell for one seriously doubted if retreat was possible. Dawn was at best two hours away and a daylight withdrawal in face of a superior enemy was a dangerous undertaking. Hell was overruled; the order was issued. Implementation was more difficult. Companies remained unaccounted for throughout the night. Orders vanished with messengers lost in the confusion or shot by Russian stragglers and infiltrators. During the short hours of darkness the Russians worked closer and closer to the German positions. Around 3:45 a.m. they opened fire everywhere along the line, less by intention than by imitation. The popping of individual rifles gave way to a steady roar of small arms fire, joined within minutes by artillery. Some batteries fired blindly into the fog. Others engaged targets located the previous day. From the perspective of hindsight it was little more than a waste of ammunition. For the Germans it seemed to prefigure another Russian attack—one that this time would catch XX Corps off balance.

The 150th Infantry Regiment's first and second battalions were particularly exposed. Not until 5:20 a.m. did orders to retreat finally reach these men, who had spent the night preparing for a fight to the finish. In one machine gun position alone, an enterprising *Feldwebel* had brought up 300,000 rounds of ammunition. Now they had to withdraw, with Russians on top of the forward trenches and swarming through the rear areas in fog so thick that it was impossible to see more than twenty paces in any direction. As the riflemen fell back they masked the fire of the two machine guns supporting the 2nd Battalion. The Russians closed in. Lieutenant Höhne stood up with a Lüger in each hand, emptying them into the Russians as they rushed his gun pits. His one-man stand could not prevent the capture of both guns.[13]

The nighttime activity of the Russians on his front did nothing to restore Scholtz's peace of mind. Around 5:00 a.m. he ordered Morgen's 3rd Reserve Division forward to Hohenstein, where it would be able to cover the 37th Division's retreat. Shortly afterwards he moved his corps headquarters northward to the village of Tannenberg, the better to deal directly with any Russian threat to his now exposed left wing. The wisdom of the decision seemed confirmed when around 8:00 a.m. the Königsberg radio station intercepted another Russian dispatch ordering XIII Corps to advance north and west in order to envelop the German left flank.[14] But Martos's corps had been hammered too badly to encourage another frontal attack. The Russians failed to pursue their advantage.

The 37th Division was able to spend most of August 24 sorting itself out in its new positions. Morale, so badly shaken the previous evening, took a sharp upswing. Regimental histories of all the armies of World War I frequently stress the rapid recuperative powers of youth as yet unshaken by the drawn-out horrors of the trenches. A more pragmatic explanation involves the return to the ranks of large numbers of men—including not a few officers—shaken loose in the course of the day's fighting. The II/ 150th Infantry, for example, listed in its report 106 dead, only 21 wounded, and 507 missing. Two hundred of these lost sheep were collected by staff officers and military police, placed under the senior officer, a regular first lieutenant, and sent posthaste after their parent regiment. Instead they were commandeered by another colonel, who insisted his regiment needed every rifle. As in XVII Corps, those who did manage to find their own colors and campfires within the next two or three days found few majors or *Feldwebels* in a mood to ask awkward questions. Even the sternest of superiors was often humanly glad to see familiar faces he had written off as lost.[15]

II

Around noon Scholtz received visitors. Eighth Army Headquarters had moved south from Marienburg, arriving at Rastenburg on the morning of August 24th. Hindenburg and Ludendorff promptly went forward by auto for a conference with Scholtz and Hell. These officers, their outlooks none the better for a lost night's sleep, described their situation as serious. The XX Corps was outnumbered on its front and threatened on its left. Scholtz proposed that his entire force withdraw further to Gilgenburg-Mühlen. Should the Russians try to flank this line, they must extend themselves far enough to the north to expose their own flank and rear to Below's and Mackensen's corps marching south.

Hindenburg and Ludendorff were aware, as Scholtz was not, that under the best of circumstances these latter troops could not arrive in the battle area for several days. They accepted Scholtz's opinion that a general Russian attack along the front front of XX corps was imminent. But any further withdrawal by Scholtz meant that neither François nor Mackensen would have the maneuvering room they needed to deploy against the 2nd Army.

Hindenburg, the imperturbable, liked what he saw at Scholtz's headquarters. The commander and his staff seemed in control of the situation; the spirit of the troops seemed good. Ludendorff was less sanguine. He promised reinforcements from I Corps as soon as possible, but he insisted to Hell that XX Corps must hold its position "to the last man."[16]

Ludendorff's melodramatic rhetoric was in good part a product of railway timetables and march schedules. François had arrived in Deutsch-Eylau by auto about 5:00 p.m. on the 24th, but he was well ahead of most of his men. The German railway system was not friction-proof. Most of the rolling stock needed to move I Corps had to come from beyond the Vistula. Troops had been kept waiting until 1:00 p.m. on the 23rd because a minor flood delayed the arrival of trains from Danzig. Some station personnel had been withdrawn to Königsberg; some had simply fled in the aftermath of Gumbinnen. As a result units suffered up to four-hour delays in loading. Moving at right angles to the 8th Army's main east-west lines of communication, troop trains were frequently slowed or sidetracked by other traffic. Ludendorff had hoped to complete the detraining of I Corps by the evening of August 25. Now even the hard-driving François argued that his corps would not be ready for action as a unit before noon of August 26.[17]

Ludendorff had received equally disquieting news from the other end of his newly forming front. Civilians, using the intact telephone lines in their village post offices, were reporting a Russian advance in force northward from Ortelsburg. Eighth Army headquarters interpreted this as a movement designed to link up with Rennenkampf. It was also, however, an opportunity: for once the Germans had a chance to achieve local superiority against an apparently isolated enemy. The nearest German unit, I Reserve Corps, was ordered to push south and attack the Russians where it found them. The XVII Corps would support Below's men, at the same time keeping an eye cocked over one shoulder for a sudden advance by Rennenkampf in the German rear.[18]

The influence of Schlieffen's turn-of-the-century studies of the classic battle of Cannae on German military thinking can easily be exaggerated. A double envelopment may be theoretically among the most decisive battlefield maneuvers, but the risks of setting the stage can also resemble a boxer's attempt to punch his adversary on both ears simultaneously while leaving his own torso exposed. Ludendorff's concern that Scholtz's corps hold its position as far forward as possible, and his belief that its retreat would be the same as a defeat, were far cries from Hannibal's deliberate refusing of his center to draw the Roman legions deeper into his tactical ambush. Ludendorff's hopes may have been high on the night of August 24. His expectations probably did not extend beyond successful operations against the Russian flanks. He certainly made no promises in his evening telephone report to OHL. The mood of the army, he declared, was determined, but a bad outcome of events could not be excluded.[19]

The night remained quiet. Daylight increased the confidence at army headquarters as every hour saw more of François's corps arrive and detrain. During the morning of August 25 Hindenburg decided to go to François's headquarters and coordinate final plans for the attack he intended to make next day. Before he left, an intercepted Russian wireless message came in from Königsberg. It was a complete army order of the 1st Army, sent in clear at 2:30 a.m. It embodied detailed instructions for the 1st Army's advance—instructions setting the limits of that advance only as far as the line Gerdauen-Allenburg-Wehlau by August 26.[20] This meant Rennenkampf had almost no chance of reaching the new battle area in time to support the 2nd Army directly—*if* the order was genuine, and not a Russian plant.

Eighth Army received another welcome message early on the 25th. OHL informed Hindenburg that a *Landwehr* Division, previously on guard duty in north Schleswig, was being assigned to 8th Army and would arrive on August 27. Mindful of the still-vague situation on its left flank, army command decided to set the detraining areas well out of the zone of operations.[21] A division of German *Landwehr* was small change against an army of Russian regulars. Nevertheless, the new division might provide some security against a surprise move by Rennenkampf.

François established his field headquarters on a hill southeast of the village of Montowo at 8:00 a.m. on the 25th. Hindenburg and Ludendorff found him there and informed him I Corps was to attack towards the village of Usdau at 5:00 a.m. the next day. François immediately began to raise objections. His corps, he declared, had only half its complement of field artillery. Its heavy howitzers and ammunition columns were still en route; their trains were behind schedule. Fire support was more important than peacetime doctrines suggested to infantry regiments whose casualties of Gumbinnen and Stallupönen had not yet been replaced. "If it is ordered," he said sarcastically, "naturally the attack will be made; of course the men must fight with bayonets."[22]

François's objections had a hidden agenda. Mackensen's repulse on August 20 had shown, if it needed to be redemonstrated, the danger of a frontal attack against even improvised positions. Moreover, by attacking Usdau directly, I Corps would expose its own right flank to the Russians François's air reconnaissance reported around Soldau. Gumbinnen and Stallupönen had suggested that the Russians were extremely vulnerable to a flank attack, and François wanted to swing south towards Soldau and attack northeast.

Ludendorff disagreed sharply. Probing for a flank would give Rennenkampf more time to change his mind about his rate of advance. It would hand Samsonov another day to mount a coordinated frontal attack on Scholtz in the German center. And the same airmen who gave François his information had also reported strong Russian forces even further south, in the Mlawa area. Logically, then, the proposed German flanking movement would have to extend its own flank guard south of Mlawa. This in turn would stretch I Corps beyond acceptable limits and leave it too weak to attack anywhere.

The debate over tactics was merely the tip of an iceberg. François had met the new command team at Marienburg. He professed to be shocked at how much Hindenburg appeared to have aged since his retirement, at how little he conveyed the image of an inspired captain. Ludenforff and Hindenburg for their part had been thoroughly briefed by the 8th Army staff on François's behavior since the outbreak of war.

Ludendorff was aware of François's peacetime career, and did not regard him highly. But whatever the talents of I Corps's commanding general, it seemed clear that François was once again trying to force his plans on higher headquarters. It was correspondingly necessary to show him that the new commanders intended their orders to be obeyed. The discussion grew more and more heated, until Ludendorff finally said that if François was unwilling to attack he would ask Hindenburg to appoint a new corps commander. Hindenburg said nothing. But François remembered his former chief well, and interpreted Hindenburg's silence as indicating that I Corps would attack with or without François at its head. Deciding that discretion was the best course, François stopped arguing.[23]

Hindenburg and Ludendorff sweetened the pill by insisting that everything possible would be done to strengthen I Corps by the 26th. Army headquarters would try to speed up the arrival of its missing artillery. The XX Corps would also support the operation by attacking Usdau from the north, and by sending a strong detachment to reinforce I Corps directly. François, his face suitably saved, issued preliminary orders for an advance at 11:30 a.m.—under the eyes of his superiors.

After this stormy conference Hindenburg, Ludendorff, and most of their staff officers returned to Löbau by car. On the way they stopped in Montowo, where Max Hoffmann telephoned army headquarters to see if any new reports had arrived—another indication of the increasing pace of the modern battlefield. Prewar theories had emphasized the need for peace and quiet in higher headquarters, creating an environment that would sustain the generals' energies for the crucial plans and decisions they must make. Realities in East Prussia involved dashing from point to point to impose one's will on situations, using automobiles as Frederick the Great's generals used horses, but with periodic halts to call the office and inquire after important messages.

This mixture of the heroic and the bureaucratic, characteristic of military leadership throughout the twentieth century, influenced even a sober staff officer like Hoffmann. In his conversation he learned that German radio intelligence had intercepted another Russian message in clear. Sent to XIII Corps by Samsonov himself, it was an order projecting the dispositions of the 2nd Army for August 25. This overview of what was on the other side of the hill so excited Hoffmann that he drove furiously after his superiors, who had gone on ahead, and handed them the message from a moving car—a maneuver more appropriate for a rodeo cowboy than a middle-aged staff colonel with a weight problem.[24]

The order originated in Samsonov's earlier reports to Zhilinski. By this time Russian battlefield intelligence was worse than ever. On August 23 XV Corps had captured a bagful of unsent personal letters. Not for thirty-six hours did anyone think to look through the mail. Even then the initial examination was the work of an underemployed aide rather than an intelligence officer. When General Knox acidly suggested that a more systematic evaluation of this material might prove useful, no one literate in German was on hand.[25]

Yet, despite lack of specific corroborating information, Samsonov interpreted the withdrawal of Scholtz's left wing on August 24 as a general German retreat. In consequence he proposed to shift his own axis of advance even further westward, marching on Allenstein-Osterode instead of Allenstein-Seeburg. Zhilinski agreed with Samsonov that a wider sweep than originally calculated would be necessary to gather 8th Army into the Russian net. The front commander, however, made one modification. He had received information from Rennenkampf's sector that German troops had been seen retreating directly south from the field of Gumbinnen. Zhilinski therefore ordered Samsonov to protect his right flank by sending his VI Corps and a cavalry division north, towards Bischofsburg, fifteen miles from its presently assigned positions around Ortelsburg.

This was making war by map with a vengeance. If the Germans were retreating in disorder, they were unlikely to be going anywhere except towards the Vistula. There was certainly no reason for them to retreat across their enemy's line of advance in numbers strong enough to demand the attention of a full corps. And if the German movement instead was offensive, the Russian flank guard was at significant risk of becoming a military appetizer, devoured before it could be supported. Sending VI Corps to Bischofsburg also further dispersed Russian forces already suffering seriously from wastage. Casualties had been heavy in XV Corps. Straggling had become sufficiently visible for Knox to remark on it to Samsonov. The Russian commander's reply that the shirkers were over-whelmingly Jews seeking to avoid the firing line convinced neither man. Samsonov, nonetheless, continued to believe "God helps the brave." As developed, dispatched, and intercepted, his orders for August 25 were for 2nd Army's center, XIII and XV Corps and the 2nd Division, to advance northwest on Allenstein-Osterode. As ordered by Zhilinski, VI Corps would move due north to Bischofsburg. The I Corps would continue to support the army's left.[26]

A few minutes of reflection and evaluation by the side of the road showed Hindenburg, Ludendorff, and Hoffmann that the Russians were preparing no major operational surprises. Almost certainly the 8th Army would have to face neither major frontal attack on the 25th nor a tactical envelopment from 2nd Army's left flank corps. Operationally the German plans could stand as written. But no one had ever expected subtle strategy from the tsar's generals, and the fighting capacity of the Russian soldier could never be discounted. The 2nd Army still had to be defeated in the field.

Certainly General von Scholtz was not ready to consider victory in his hands. Before Hindenburg and Ludendorff left Löbau they sent Grünert by car to inform Scholtz of the Russian intercept and the army's plans for the following day. When he arrived at XX Corps headquarters he found Scholtz and Hell full of good cheer, since the attack they had expected had failed to materialize. Samsonov's orders spoiled their mood. Whether VI Corps remained at Ortelsburg or moved further north was at the moment less relevant than the threat posed to XX Corps's left flank by the as-yet unengaged and presumably full-strength XIII Corps.

Scholtz proposed to transfer the garrison troops that had been holding down his extreme right to his left, forming a new defensive flank behind the Drewenz River. Army command agreed. By nightfall the 41st Division was alone on XX Corps's right. The 37th Division, reinforced to eighteen battalions by the attachment of some fortress units, held the center, its left covering the high road west of Mühlen. North of Mühlen were stationed the 70th *Landwehr* Brigade and the by-now footsore garrison troops of Unger's command, a total of eleven battalions and four batteries. The 3rd Reserve Division remained behind them in corps and sector reserve. Well fed and well dug in, with fields of fire cleared and batteries ranged, Scholtz's East Prussians would be a tough nut to crack at any odds the Russians were likely to generate.[27]

Higher levels of command had their concerns as well. On the evening of the 25th Hindenburg informed his staff: "Gentlemen, our preparations are so well in hand that we can sleep soundly tonight."[28] But he knew air reconnaissance was continuing to report Russian troop trains on the way to the stations at Mlawa. The possibility of a major thrust from the south against I Corps by fresh Russian forces made Hindenburg and Ludendorff even more determined to seize the initiative in François's sector. Final army orders were issued at 8:30 p.m. The I Corps would attack the Seeben Heights "around" 4:30 a.m. From there the corps was to advance to Usdau by 10:00 a.m. at the latest, while keeping its forward units deeply echeloned to the right against a possible threat from Mlawa or Soldau.[29]

A venerable German proverb warns against adding up the bill without consulting the waiter. By the night of the 25th, the arrival and concentration of François's corps from the west was increasingly apparent to the Russian cavalry in that sector. Even Samsonov was concerned. His original intention for August 26 had been for his I Corps to move northwest from Soldau, supporting and conforming to the movements of the two center corps. With Germans reported in strength on his army's left, Samsonov considered the wisdom of halting his advance and redeploying to meet this possible threat. The I Corps was stationed in St. Petersburg in peacetime and had a high proportion of reservists from the city's factories. Their fighting spirit was at least questionable. Their commander, Lieutenant-General Artamonov, was considered neither one of the army's brighter intellectual lights nor one of its better combat leaders. Samsonov's men were tired and hungry. Hard marches and short rations were by now swelling the sick list, especially with reservists who had had no time to harden themselves. But the 2nd Army's logistical crisis is easy to exaggerate in the light of the disaster that overtook it in the coming days. Of Samsonov's troops, only XV Corps had been seriously engaged, and the Russian soldier was historically accustomed to privation. To go over to the defensive now would be to give in to ghosts and shadows—those formless fears that stalk the corridors of all higher headquarters, and whose mastering is a prerequisite of effective command.

Instead of halting his army Samsonov decided to reinforce his menaced flank. The I Corps was assigned XXIII Corps's other division, the elite 3rd Guard from Warsaw, some of whose trains the German airmen arriving had seen at Mlawa. It was given the 1st Rifle Brigade, eight good active battalions, and the 6th and 15th Cavalry Divisions. Added to I Corps's two organic divisions this force appeared strong enough on paper both to make up for any of Artamonov's shortcomings as a general and to secure the 2nd Army's left flank against almost any opposition.

Critics accurately insist there was little chance of concentrating these troops except on paper. The guardsmen and the rifles were too far away to reach I Corps's positions in less than forty-eight hours. Both cavalry divisions were badly scattered. Samsonov's rhetorical flourishes ordering the corps to hold at all costs were merely a counterpoint to his generalship by map.[30] Yet with no more than its own resources, I Russian Corps was intimidating François. Like Scholtz, he had received a copy of Samsonov's intercepted order. Like Scholtz, he found it cold comfort. The Russian forward positions in his sector were based on high ground around the village of Seeben. To reach them I Corps would have to advance over broken country, ford a river, and then cross open fields in the face of an entrenched enemy. Most of I Corps's infantry had arrived on August 25, but much of the artillery and, even more important in the era of rapid-firing guns, most of the ammunition columns were still en route. François's staff doubted if these deficiencies could be made good during the night. Even if the guns and wagons could be unloaded, they could hardly be deployed in time for a dawn attack.

François continued to hope army command would adopt his plan of a flank movement. Though he verbally agreed to advance after his argument with Ludendorff, he did not prepare formal orders until the written army order reached him at 11:45 p.m.—twelve hours later. The corps order went out only at 12:30 a.m. on August 26. The 1st Division was to advance at 4:00 a.m., capture the Seeben Heights, then at 10:00 a.m. advance towards Usdau. The 2nd Division and the 5th *Landwehr* Brigade, which had just arrived from Thorn, were to advance in support at 7:00 a.m., echeloned to the south.

While the instructions certainly conformed to the sense of the army orders, François's real intentions are not so plain. Given the march distances involved it was impossible for the 1st Division to reach its assigned line of departure by 4:00 a.m. unless it was ready to move as soon as it received the orders. But François had not informed Conta of Hindenburg's and Ludendorff's insistence on an early attack. As a result Conta had settled his division for the night, with no thought of having to advance until sometime into the next morning.[31] The attack order came as a corresponding surprise to all ranks—even Conta, who by this time had grown used to the unpredictable behavior of his corps chief. The 1st Division shook itself out of its blankets, fell into ranks, and struggled slowly forward in the dark over unfamiliar roads.

The Province of Uncertainty

At 5:30 a.m. François telephoned army headquarters and reported the attack "in progress," though he could not answer for its outcome. Hindenburg and his staff assumed this was just another of François's complaints.[32] Actually, the advance had not yet begun. Conta's regiments neither pushed nor were driven. Not until 8:00 a.m. did they reach the Russian outposts in front of Seeben. François arrived at Conta's headquarters shortly afterward, and both commanders agreed that continuing under existing circumstances was risky. Conta had only eight battalions and four light batteries on hand. He had no ammunition columns, which meant empty caissons and cartridge pouches within minutes of engaging. François promptly contacted army headquarters and requested permission to set the time of attack himself. He was just as promptly informed that this was impossible. At 9:00 a.m. François was instructed by phone that the attack on Usdau would have to start at noon. At 10:30 a.m. written orders to this effect arrived at I Corps headquarters. At 11:15 a.m. army headquarters received a message that Seeben still remained in Russian hands. It answered with a sharp request for an explanation why the position had not been carried seven hours earlier, as ordered. François replied that his men had been fighting for Seeben since 4:00 a.m., but so far without success. Infantry alone, he implied, could not be expected to carry modern defenses even against Russians.[33]

Ludendorff flew into a frustrated rage—a rage exacerbated by its causes. The days when a Marlborough or a Wellington could survey the battlefield and control the actions of his subordinates by messenger had ended a century earlier. Even Napoleon had been unable to direct his campaigns effectively by keeping his corps and army commanders on a short leash. Necessity had led the Prussian army and its imperial successor to develop the conception of mission performance. An officer given an assignment was expected to execute that assignment on the basis of the situation he faced. Evading responsibility by awaiting orders was a sure ticket to civilian clothes, even in peacetime.

The system functioned well enough by default in 1866 and 1870. The increasing frontages of modern battles made it virtually impossible for higher headquarters to keep abreast of operational situations as long as information was supplied by horsepower. But the introduction of the telephone altered circumstances substantially. Unlike some of his superiors, Ludendorff was at home with the instrument's use. He was doubly eager to make good in directing his first battle. Saving East Prussia meant that his own career would be back on the main track. He was correspondingly reluctant to submit his fate to an unruly subordinate like François. But what exactly was he to do? Ludendorff could hardly repeat his behavior at Liège and risk the disruption of his general plan while personally supervising the execution of one of its parts. As for relieving François on the spot, aside from the risks of changing I Corps's commander in the midst of battle, who would replace him? Nothing indicated that either Falk or Conta would drive the corps any harder than its present commander.

The chief of staff contented himself with a curt order to François that he report as soon as Seeben was captured.[34] François's response was to set back army command's timing even further. His final orders, issued at 11:30 a.m., sent the 1st Division "from" a still-uncaptured Seeben against Usdau. The time of the advance, however, was given at 1:00 p.m.; the troops were to be given a chance to eat before going forward.[35]

As François bought time in half-hour increments, Prussia's railway staffs gave their best to bring up the balance of I Corps. Conductors and stationmasters abandoned lifetimes of adherence to regulations to push along open stretches of track as fast as possible. Derailment or brake failure could have sent trains piling into each other in a chain reaction of disaster. But in the cliché of one junior staff officer, nothing ventured meant nothing gained. Peacetime schedules allowing up to two hours for unloading were cut back to twenty-five minutes and less. One engineer saved ninety minutes by taking his train forward into the combat zone. Only when Russian shells began exploding around the locomotive did the battalion he was carrying abandon its boxcars, form skirmish lines, and advance on foot towards the front.[36]

By noon, all but two of I Corps's twenty-four infantry battalions were on the ground. Most of the artillery was also in position. As patrols reported Russian defenses lightly held, battalion and regiment commanders tested their sectors more seriously. By 12:30 p.m. Seeben was in flames and the Russians in retreat, with Conta's infantry rounding up diehards and stragglers.

Following up initial success was a skill that required practice in all the armies of 1914. Even with Seeben firmly in German hands it took two hours to concentrate the 1st Division for the next move on Usdau. Then it was Conta who balked. His men had been advancing since the early morning of a day that had turned blindingly hot. Their water bottles were empty. Cases of heat exhaustion were mounting. To reach Usdau meant an advance of seven kilometers over open fields in the hottest part of the day, against positions that were sure to be stronger than the outposts around Seeben. The Germans might be able to work up to the Russian defenses, but their ability to carry them before dark without becoming seriously disorganized was questionable.

In taking this position Conta was following generally approved procedures. In the later stages of the Russo-Japanese War the Japanese army had tended increasingly to make its attacks under cover of darkness. The method, intensively considered in all Western armies prior to 1914, did provide some security from the effects of modern firepower. It also sacrificed any advantages of command, coordination, and flexibility. Night combat tended to dissolve almost immediately into an all-out brawl, with victory going to the more ferocious or the more fortunate. German military theorists might admire the Japanese, but unit commanders were soberly aware that the men they led were not samurai *manqué*. Fighting at night against the Russians was to test the enemy at his strongest points: imperturbability and brute strength. The experience of XX Corps on

August 24 had hardly been an encouraging practical test of the German army's capability to operate even under twilight contitions. There might be enough remaining daylight to go for Usdau, but in Conta's judgment a night's rest, full stomachs, full ammunition pouches, and full caissons were more likely ingredients of success than a series of regimental or battalion-scale blows that were likely only to improve the defenders' morale. Conta was also well aware that his immediate superior did not consider the situation to require extreme measures. François solemnly deferred to the commander on the spot. At 3:45 p.m. he decided to break off I Corps's attack for the day.[37]

François did not have his tongue entirely in his cheek. Falk's 2nd Division, advancing on the corps's right, had become badly stuck in the woods south of Usdau. Though the Germans faced only detachments, broken terrain combined with memories of Gumbinnen to make everyone in the front line more than a little cautious. Company-level rumor credited the Russians with mounting machine guns in trees, the better to catch attackers by surprise. The difficulties of finding a tree large enough to support a plaform stable enough to sustain a water-cooled machine gun's recoil are exceeded only by the difficulties of building that platform and camouflaging it. The Russian army's machine gun was so heavy that it was mounted on a small two-wheeled carriage to facilitate its movement. Yet to men and officers raised on Karl May's novels, arboreal automatic weapons seemed a reasonable explanation for the bursts of bullets, seeming to come from every direction, that stopped the 2nd Division in its tracks by midafternoon.

As with Conta, François made no effort to get Falk moving again.[38] The day-long inactivity of a man who had demonstrated such an aggressive spirit in earlier operations, and who was to demonstrate it again in the coming days, is usually explained in terms of his defiance of the 8th Army staff. B. H. Liddell-Hart describes Ludendorff as more concerned with time than tactical realities.[39] Max Hoffmann, not one of François's admirers, comments that an attack against a prepared position without artillery support could be justified had XX Corps been in serious danger of being overrun.[40] During the night of the 25th, however, François had contacted Colonel Hell at XX Corps Headquarters. Hell informed him that the situation in his sector was not serious enough to require a premature attack.[41] Ultimately Ludendorff himself not only declared that the attack was postponed because I Corps had been unable to concentrate in time, he agreed that François was correct in his actions. Hoffmann went even further, asserting that had I Corps attacked with only the units available on the 26th the attack would probably have been defeated. Had it failed, the approach of I Reserve Corps and XVII Corps would only have forced a Russian retreat. The encirclement could not have succeeded.[42]

These commentators on the strategic implications of François's decisions overlook another significant point. The generals of World War I are commonly described as indifferent to man management, believers in the power of élan to overcome the most extreme physical obstacles.

Realities at the operational level could often be quite different. In 1927, François engaged in an acrimonious debate with Lieutenant-Colonel Theobald von Schäfer of the *Reichsarchiv*. Schäfer had been responsible for the official history's volume on the East Prussian campaign, and contributed an excellent narrative volume on Tannenberg to the popular German series, *Battles of the World War*. He was convinced Hindenburg and Ludendorff were right to order François to attack on August 26. The I Corps's halfheartedness, he argued, reflected unnecessary caution. François's reply was uncharacteristically reflective. The situation, he declared, was not as clear on the battlefield as it might seem in a library. Even in peacetime, 8th Army's new chief of staff had shown no sense of the importance of cooperation between infantry and artillery, and no sense of the limits of will on the battlefield.

François was a Prussian aristocrat to his fingertips, with none of that common touch so dear to reporters and correspondents in the contemporary West. But he had a thoroughly modern sense of what his still-unhardened infantry could and could not do under twentieth-century conditions of warfare. To treat every operation as an emergency was to risk neglecting war's physical side: the importance for combat efficiency of full canteens and full stomachs. The Germans, moreover, had no idea of the main location of the main Russian artillery positions. François sent his son, a gunner officer serving on his staff, to climb a tree and look for muzzle flashes, but in vain. François had not quite internalized the postwar French aphorism that the artillery conquers while the infantry only occupies. But two weeks of campaigning had shown him that enthusiasm was no substitute for a well-prepared fire plan, and that aggressiveness could be significantly enhanced by following up a properly executed bombardment.[43]

III

In the German center, Scholtz and Hell had learned through their conversation with François that I Corps would probably not require a supporting advance immediately. Scholtz therefore decided to hold his position on the 26th. He was less concerned with his role in a possible Cannae than with maintaining his lines against steady Russian pressure. The manor house dominating Mühlen village collapsed under Russian artillery fire, its lord abandoning his home hell for leather in an elegant landau to the amusement of the watching soldiers. Colonel Hell's well-known imperturbability passed a test when he turned XX Corps's artillery on his own house in Gross-Grieben on learning that it was in enemy hands. In the 1st *Jäger* a company commander discussed with one of his lieutenants the respective mathematical probabilities of being hit by a bullet, a shell splinter, or a shrapnel ball.[44]

During the morning 8th Army headquarters received several reports of a gap between the left flank of the Russians opposing XX Corps and the right flank of the Russians in front of François. At 1:00 p.m.

Hindenburg and Ludendorff decided to order Scholtz to test the opportunity.[45] At 2:45 p.m. the commanding general ordered the 41st Division and the 75th Brigade of the 37th Division forward. In the first attack in the corps's history, the East Prussians did well across the board. Scholtz's infantry moved out at 3:45 p.m. after a fifteen-minute artillery preparation that caught the Russian 2nd Division completely by surprise. Carelessness in reconnaissance and flank security cost the Russians even more dearly. The 41st Division enveloped the Russian left and drove it south of Lake Kownatken. A brigade of the 37th Division found a gap between the 2nd Division's two brigades, struck the left flank of the 1st Brigade, and forced it back on the north side of the lake.

Large-scale histories make the process sound easy. The 41st Division's infantry advanced with the enthusiasm of inexperience, taking heavy casualties because of their reluctance to lie down between rushes. One colonel went so far as to inform his officers that he would have prohibited such eagerness in a peacetime exercise. For the men of one regiment the jest had little humor. The 59th Infantry's first and second battalions suddenly came under fire from their own guns. Unable to establish contact with the erring batteries, company officers led their men forward away from the shelling, only to fall dead or wounded in front of Russian rifle pits no one saw. Command from the front against a determined enemy compounded the results of failure. The surviving captains and lieutenants, commanding mixed bags of anyone willing to rally to their voices and whistles, lacked the opportunity to consider alternative plans. Probing for a flank or waiting for neighboring units to put pressure on the Russians were dismissed as insults to the regiment's dead. At 6:00 p.m., what remained of the 59th finally carried the Russian positions to their front. Five hundred fifty men, including twenty-three officers, lay in the tracks of the advance.

German casualties elsewhere on the field might have been correspondingly heavy but for the artillery. The broken terrain and the speed of the advance put scientific gunnery at a discount. Instead battery and battalion commanders pushed their guns almost into the infantry's skirmish lines, taking Russian positions under point-blank fire, then moving before enemy artillery had time to register. The only major Russian counterattack was shattered by the 150th Infantry's machine gun company. Six Maxims firing as a unit smashed an embryonic charge into piles of corpses within minutes. In one part of the front a Russian NCO systematically shot down any of his own men who showed signs of wanting to abandon the fight or surrender. Once this man's position was discovered and blasted with machine-gun fire, the collapse continued unabated.[46] By nightfall the 2nd Russian Division was temporarily finished as a combat unit. Its 7th Reval Regiment alone had suffered over 2,900 casualties; the survivors were so scattered and demoralized as to be almost out of control.

On Scholtz's left, the 3rd Reserve Division had been initially ordered to move to Hohenstein. Its commander had other ideas. These, Morgen declared in his memoirs, were still wonderful times for a senior officer. He could stand on a hill, survey the situation, and give orders without being bound to a telephone line. Morgen was convinced that advancing as ordered would bring him into frontal collision with the Russian XV Corps, and perhaps expose his left flank to their XIII Corps. On his own reponsibility Morgen therefore decided to remain in position until the enemy was committed to the attack on XX Corps. Only then did he intend to move his division south and strike the Russian right flank. Unfortunately—and deliberately—Morgen failed to inform either the 8th Army or XX Corps of his decision. As late as 6:00 p.m. both headquarters still firmly believed the 3rd Reserve Division was advancing as ordered.

This episode again reveals the advantages and the disadvantages of the German insistence on individual initiative. Max Hoffmann was convinced that if the division had gone forward it would have enveloped the right flank of XV Corps without interference from XIII Corps. Walter Elze similarly blames Morgen for thwarting Hindenburg's offensive designs in the north as François had in the south.[47] On the other hand, by late afternoon of August 26, XIII Corps had reached Stabigotten and Allenstein. XV Corps extended its right as far as Grieslienen and Hohenstein.[48] Had the 3rd Reserve Division followed orders it might indeed have walked into a trap. Under the best circumstances an encounter battle against superior forces in the broken, wooded country around Hohenstein would have been a risky business. Morgen preferred a solid shoulder to a broken neck. His decision, like François', would be justified in the next twenty-four hours.

By the end of August 26 8th Army's staff, Ludendorff in particular, was badly on edge. The army's command post had been established east of Löbau, but its communications center remained in the larger town of Rastenburg. This reflected a problem that would recur time and again during World War I. Communications networks were just sufficiently developed to be frustrating. Like its Russian adversary, 8th Army was still heavily dependant on the ordinary peacetime telephone network, kept operating by civilian officials. Air reconnaissance and radio intelligence provided more strain than reassurance. A pilot from the army's air detachment had reported around noon that strong Russian reinforcements were still detraining in Soldau and Mlawa. An intercepted radio message from that sector mentioned the arrival of a regiment of the Russian Guard. Perhaps this was the 3rd Guard Division, the other half of XXIII Corps. But perhaps it was the vanguard of the Russian Guard Corps, reported by German agents to have been sent to the Warsaw area. Not only had I Corps gained no ground, it seemed entirely possible that François's delay had given the Russians a chance to start a flank attack of their own with some of the best troops in their army. The advance of XX Corps had gone well enough, but its units were badly mixed up and the men were tired. No reports at all had been received from the 3rd Reserve Division. Of XVII Corps and I Reserve Corps, army headquarters knew only that they were engaged in battle, and that Rennenkampf's forward units had reached Gerdauen and Drengfurth in their rear—too close for comfort.[49]

The staff ate its evening meal in dead silence. Ludendorff had a habit of rolling bread crumbs at the table when he was concentrating or worrying. That night his hands never stopped. Suddenly he stood up and asked to speak privately with Hindenburg. The men left the room to a sudden buzz of speculation. All available intelligence indicated that Russians were advancing against the rear of both of 8th Army's flanks. Two-o-clock-in-the-morning courage might be important for a field commander. For the 8th Army's staff, the crucial time was early evening, when orders for the next day had to be issued. Should the army strengthen its rear against Rennenkampf and turn a flank guard towards Soldau? Should it abandon the hope of destroying the 2nd Army in order to save itself from possible destruction?

As Hindenburg's memoirs grandiloquently put it, "Misgivings fill every heart; firm resolution yields to vacillation; doubts creep in where clear vision had hitherto prevailed." It was generally accepted among the staff and command of 8th Army that these words were an oblique reference to Ludendorff's temporary loss of confidence, leading to his urging that François's attack, at least, be abandoned. Ludendorff's reminiscences are silent on the subject. Hindenburg says only, "We overcame the inward crisis, adhered to our original intention, and turned in full strength to effect its realization." Whether in public or in private, Hindenburg to the end of his life insisted that the commitment to continue the operations as they were originally conceived was a joint decision.[50]

This stand was complicated by the appearance in 1928 of Walter Elze's *Tannenberg*. Elze, professor of military history at the University of Berlin, was a distinguished civilian scholar of operational history. His account of events at army headquarters implied that the chief of staff virtually collapsed in panic on the night of the 26th and had to be brought to reality by a stiff dose of Hindenburg's common sense. Elze's statement that Hindenburg had affirmed the accuracy of his interpretation in a personal conversation is credible given the close relationship between them, but was only written four months after Hindenburg's death, and remains correspondingly unverifiable.[51]

Ludendorff reacted by denouncing Elze, Hindenburg, and anyone else remotely connected with the issue. Writing to Friedrich Wilhelm Förster, director of the Military Archives, he insisted that Elze's book showed that the "establishment" was out to destroy his reputation. Ludendorff dismissed Förster's explanation that Elze had no official standing as "the most unheard-of calumnies under the mask of good will," and accused Elze of falsifying history under the influence of "Freemasons and unknown sources."[52]

The best that can be ascertained from the tangle of charges and countercharges is that the original plan was left intact. It strains no possibilities to suggest that Ludendorff, a nervous and highly strung man, may have been temporarily overcome by stress. It is equally logical that

Hindenburg was able to talk him out of it with limited effort. That, after all, was one of his functions as army commander. But at 8:30 a.m. an even better nerve tonic arrived at army headquarters—the day's first message from *Ostgruppe*, the name given to the operational grouping of XVII and I Reserve Corps.

On August 25th Mackensen, senior officer of the two corps, had telegraphed Ludendorff requesting clarification of his mission. At 5:00 p.m. Ludendorff telephoned that a Russian corps was advancing on Bischofsburg. *Ostgruppe* was to attack at once.[53] But it was first necessary to get to Bischofsburg. Both of Mackensen's corps had been faced with increasing numbers of frightened civilians—too many to halt; too many to avoid. I Reserve Corps marched thirty kilometers on the 25th, much of it on sandy side roads. Its horses were beginning to drop in the traces from sickness and overwork. On the same day XVII Corps's 36th Division had been forced by detours into a fifty-kilometer march over secondary roads in burning heat. The 35th Division had had an even longer march; both units were almost exhausted by nightfall. The German army's company officers, like their counterparts everywhere in Europe, were expected to inspect their men's feet regularly. This, however, was the kind of task all too easily neglected, whether by haughty Junkers contemptuous of such tasks or, more prosaically, by tired young men in shoulder straps overwhelmed with more obviously urgent burdens of command. The results could be seen limping along far into the night, trying to overtake their units while avoiding the field police.

In the 1st Battalion of the 36th Division's 175th Infantry, three companies suffered an average loss of between one hundred and 120 stragglers—well over 50 percent of the men who began the march. The fourth did not report a single man falling out of ranks. This feat was credited to its captain, who manifested an unaristocratic concern for such mundane problems as blisters and soft corns.[54]

In the course of the 25th Mackensen and Below had arranged to cooperate in dealing with any Russians to their front. While Mackensen struck the enemy right, I Reserve Corps and the 6th *Landwehr* Brigade, which had joined *Ostgruppe* during the march south, would attack the left. Lake Dadey and Gross-Lautern Lake formed an effective geographic boundary between the corps sectors.

At 11:45 p.m. Mackensen issued his orders for August 26. The XVII Corps would advance against Bischofsburg in a single column, with the 36th Division leading. It was imperative, Mackensen asserted, to drive forward as rapidly as possible. The success of the entire operation depended on the corps's marching ability. Shortly afterwards Mackensen received an army order, issued at noon on the 25th, which said that a division should be left to secure *Ostgruppe*'s rear against any sudden moves by Rennenkampf. He considered this order superseded by his phone conversation with Ludendorff, and decided to disregard it. For the success of his plan he would need his whole corps.[55]

Below had received Ludendorff's noon order before Mackensen did.

Responding to it, he proposed to advance with his divisions abreast on a broad front in order to contain the Russians in case they should try to evade Mackensen by moving west. He ordered that advance to begin at 10:00 a.m., a relatively late departure time. Below, an infantryman and an experienced field soldier, consistently stressed the relationship between his reservists' combat performance and the ability of their officers to see that the men had hot food and the chance to wash and clean their clothes. The administration of these improvised formations could hardly be free of friction. A bit of extra time at the beginning of what promised to be several strenuous days was likely to pay disproportionate dividends in improved spirit and efficiency.

Below's formal corps order, issued at 9:50 p.m. on August 25, did not reach XVII Corps until noon the next day. Mackensen, however, based his times of departure on the assumption that I Reserve Corps would advance around 7:00 a.m. This meant that instead of both corps attacking simultaneously, XVII Corps would strike the Russians first. Such sacrifice of *Ostgruppe*'s local numerical superiority gave the Russians a good chance to defeat the Germans in detail, or at least check their advance.[56]

Both chances proved theoretical. The Russian VI Corps, with the 4th Cavalry Division attached, had originally been instructed to advance from Ortelsburg to occupy Bischofsburg. Europe's experiences since 1866 indicated that given some time to prepare positions, even an isolated army corps could give an excellent account of itself. But during the day of August 25, Samsonov changed the corps's mission once more. A telegram from 2nd Army instructed VI Corps to advance to Allenstein with the bulk of its force in order to participate in the developing attack on the German center, leaving only a screen at Bischofsburg. This order was received at VI Corps headquarters late on the 25th. Preparations were immediately made to execute it. Then early on the 26th Samsonov thought better of exposing his flank so completely, and revised his revision. Now VI Corps was to remain at, or return to, Bischofsburg as a flank guard for the advancing 2nd Army. This order, however, was not received at all.[57]

Order and counterorder prefigure, but do not inevitably spell, disorder. Lieutenant-General Blagoveschensky was operating in a vacuum. The East Prussian theater, unlike the western front, was characterized by a low ratio of force to space. In France and Belgium one usually knew where the enemy was: everywhere. Opportunities for tactical and operational reconnaissance were correspondingly limited. In the east at this stage of the war, cavalry was just as necessary as in the days of Napoleon or Genghis Khan. But instead of scouting for VI Corps or screening its movements the 4th Cavalry Division remained concentrated. The divisional cavalry squadrons brought in no reports of German activity in the area. Airmen had reported troops moving southwest, but these were thought to be Russians, from Rennenkampf's 1st Army! Blagoveschensky therefore proposed to move three-fourths of his corps west on the 26th, leaving a single brigade of the 4th Division at Bischofsburg. His plans were abruptly changed when at dawn Mackensen's 36th Division, which had been marching since 4:15 after only a short night's rest, ran into the Russians deployed around Lautern village.

General von Heineccius was an artilleryman who had spent most of his career following the guns. Commissioned into the 1st Guard Field Artillery in 1877, he had risen by 1911 to command the Guard's 1st Field Artillery Brigade and had taken over the 36th Division only in 1913. Gumbinnen had been for him an unpleasant lesson in the limitations of the cavalry spirit; he was determined not to attack a second time without adequate artillery preparation. Mackensen arrived at Heineccius's headquarters a few minutes later and confirmed his intention to wait for the guns. The corps commander also decided to bring the 35th Division forward on the left of the 36th, to support the attack and to guard the corps flank against Russian cavalry that had been reported maneuvering to the east.

Mackensen issued the appropriate orders at 8:00 a.m. An hour later he was informed the 35th Division was too tired to march without rest. Nor were the 36th Division's infantrymen proving especially eager to repeat their behavior at Gumbinnen. Instead of storming forward at the head of their men, colonels and majors sent out patrols to test the Russian strength. Some disappeared into the dawn fog, dying under the bayonets of a waiting enemy. Others were pinned down by machine gun and rifle fire. Officers bunching to study their maps became targets of opportunity for Russian guns. Others were picked off by snipers concealed in the tall pine trees that covered most of the division's front. Mackensen's airmen soon brought confirmation of what the men on the firing line knew: the Russians were on the ground in force. Observers reported a division in front of Bischofsburg and another farther south at Ortelsburg.

The latter formation was probably VI Corps's supply trains, but the misidentification intimidated the Germans. Around 10:00 a.m. the 71st Brigade's commander ordered his men to "dig in to the eyebrows." Passed down the line by word of mouth, it generated no suggestions about the incompatibility of entrenchments with Prussian military honor. The Germans had learned other things as well at Gumbinnen. Field kitchens were brought close enough to the forward positions to distribute hot food and coffee to the infantry—a KP detail that became a defaulter's nightmare when the Russians mistook the "goulash cannons" for artillery pieces. As their own guns continued to shell the Russian positions, some Germans dozed off in their foxholes, succumbing to tension, fatigue, and suddenly full stomachs.

These moments of martial domesticity did not obscure a potentially dangerous situation. The 36th Division had gone, as inexperienced troops are prone to do, from one extreme to the other. Its men were well content to improve their positions and await developments, but the Russian 4th Division was aggressively commanded at all levels. In Manchuria Russian officers had too often reacted to Japanese initiatives. Postwar wisdom in the tsar's army correspondingly stressed the necessity of seizing opportunities as they appeared. Counterattacking skirmish lines, extending east-ward into the sector still unoccupied by the 35th Division, rapidly threatened the German left. An infantry lieutenant spotted the maneuver and managed to get word to the gun positions. This was the kind of situation for which the 77-millimeter gun had been designed. German field batteries checked the advance with shrapnel as Mackensen and Heiniccius fumed over the continued absence of the 35th Division.

That formation for its part appeared on the point of disintegrating under the pressures of a forced march. Its men were discarding their knapsacks in defiance of orders. Some companies were down to sixty rifles. There seemed more wagons and field kitchens than infantry on the line of advance. The division commander finally ordered a halt and informed Mackensen not to expect his troops until around 4:00 p.m. Should the Russians attack in force, it was an open question whether the 36th Division could maintain itself until either its sister formation or I Reserve Corps relieved the pressure.[58]

Hearing the guns on Mackensen's front, Below proposed to swing the bulk of his corps around the south end of Lake Dadey and take the Russians in the rear. The 6th *Landwehr* Brigade, attached to *Ostgruppe* after Gumbinnen, and part of the 36th Reserve Division would screen this movement by attacking the Russian positions around Gross-Bössau. This time Below's reservists were well served by their cavalry. The 1st Reserve Uhlans in particular stayed in close touch with Russian movements; the regiment's messengers kept corps headquarters well informed of enemy positions. By 12:30 p.m. I Reserve Corps reached its intended line of departure without having fired a shot.

The Russians made the corps's task even easier. The 36th Division's halfhearted attack had convinced the 4th Division's commander that he was facing only flank guards thrown out by Germans retreating towards the Vistula. Blagoveschensky felt justified in sending the 16th Division westward towards Allenstein around noon, in obedience to the last set of orders he had received. The 4th Division remained with one brigade facing Mackensen, the other in position south of Gross-Lautern Lake. Without a German in sight, Major-General Komarov ordered that brigade forward to support the attack that had so discomfited the 36th Division. While on the march to its new sector the brigade ran into the 36th Reserve Division and the *Landwehr*.

In a textbook encounter battle, the Russians held their ground well. Below's 69th Reserve Brigade was initially shelled into immobility by the corps's own artillery. By the time the gunners were informed of their mistake Russian machine guns, dug in to the point of invisibility, were cutting swaths through the ranks of the reservists and their older comrades of the *Landwehr*. Most of the latter were married men with families, correspondingly unsusceptible to heroic inspiration, advancing at their own pace when they went forward at all. In one sector the tide turned almost by accident. Two *Landsturm* batteries, whose middle-aged gunners and officers had served in the days before indirect fire was a part of the training manuals, closed to point-blank range to blast Russians out of a gravel pit. Even then an infantry battalion commander had to ask his men if they expected him to win the war alone before they followed the guns. With night falling, the Germans played their last cards. Generals and colonels dismounted and drew their swords; bugles sounded the charge all along the line. The 69th Reserve Brigade's commander was wounded leading the final rush. The Russians abandoned their positions; the Germans bivouacked on the field. Here and there around their fires a few enthusiasts even raised the Leuthen Chorale, "Now thank we all our God."

The German victory was also a Russian defeat. As the afternoon wore on it became increasingly apparent to Blagoveschensky that he faced something much more dangerous than the flank guard of a retreating enemy. He ordered the 16th Division to turn around and return to support the 4th. Since the division was advancing on a single main road, the order was easier issued than executed. Once the Russians straightened themselves out, their attention was focussed on the battle they were marching towards. Flank security and rear guards were neglected. Around the southern end of Lake Dadey the division was overtaken by the vanguard of the 1st Reserve Division. German artillery firing over open sights wreaked havoc among the unsuspecting Russians. By 4:00 p.m. the 16th Division had been driven completely out of the battle area.[59]

In the meantime, Mackensen's corps had not been totally idle. Around 6:00 p.m., as the reservists were clearing Gross-Bössau, the 36th Division's artillery opened a hurricane bombardment on the Russian positions to the division's front. The Russians, isolated, under attack from two sides, exhausted by a stubborn, day-long defense, collapsed. When the 36th Division's infantry advanced—cautiously behind a screen of fighting patrols—they found only abandoned positions, corpses, and stragglers anxious to give themselves up.

Total Russian casualties for the day were about 5,300 officers and men, with the Germans taking over 1,700 prisoners. But VI Corps had lost more than men. It had advanced to Bischofsburg confidently, expecting to deal with nothing more threatening than a defeated enemy retreating across its front. Its generals conducted no systematic reconnaissance. No one in a responsible position tried to verify preconceptions of the German situation. As a result one division was surprised and defeated in detail by a superior enemy while the other was moving beyond effective supporting range. Then the second division was overrun from the rear. The VI Corps was so demoralized it retreated thirty kilometers without being pursued. Blagoveschensky's nerves collapsed even more thoroughly than his corps. Like a schoolboy caught in mischief, he waited until 2:00 a.m. on August 27 to inform his superior what had happened, using the intervening time to issue a series of confused and contradictory orders that contributed nothing to rallying his shaken troops.[60]

Out of this day's battle grew something else—the story of thousands of Russians being driven into the swamps of Masuria and left to die. A part of the 4th Division actually was thrown back against Lake Gross-Bössau, and a few men did drown there. At 8:30 that night, I Reserve Corps reported that "many Russians" had been driven into the lake. Eighth Army in turn repeated the information, suitably embellished, in a later army order that François and Max Hoffmann agree was the probable basis of the legend.[61]

Hindsight makes the German victory over VI Corps look easier than it appeared to the men on the spot. Blagoveschensky and his subordinates may have offered opportunities; the Germans had to take advantage of them. Below and Mackensen ordered tired, footsore men, three-fourths of whom had been wearing civilian clothes a month earlier, into broken terrain against an enemy whose tenacity in defense was proverbial. Mackensen's men in particular still showed the effects of Gumbinnen in their sudden reliance on artillery to destroy the Russians instead of merely suppressing their fire. Despite their triumph, moreover, both German commanders expected to be attacked from somewhere the next day. The II Russian Corps, its advance through the Masurian Lakes barred by Fort Boyen, had been ordered to swing north of the lakes, then turn south and establish contact with Samsonov's army. Air reconnaissance reported prepared Russian positions south of Bischofsburg. Other airmen reported Russian troops in Gerdauen—which an intercepted order had described as being on the line of advance of Rennenkampf's IV Corps.[62]

Knowledge can generate anxiety as well as power. Since Gumbinnen Mackensen's headquarters had strong images of Rennenkampf's energy and ability—not least because he had beaten them so badly. Current information about Russian movements was hardly comforting. Air reconnaissance still depended heavily on the skill of individual observers and the daring of individual pilots. One team might mistake a few squadrons of cavalry for an army corps; another could confuse an infantry division with a wagon train. The question facing commanders on the ground was always just how much salt to sprinkle on the information. A day earlier Mackensen's chief of staff had grumbled to one of his subordinates that XVII Corps was in more danger than Blücher had been after Ligny a century earlier. Making worst-case assumptions, the Germans now risked being sandwiched between II and IV Corps coming south and the bulk of the 2nd Army moving north towards Allenstein.

Mackensen's response was determined by tactical rather than strategic, local rather than general, concerns. On the principle of "in for a penny, in for a pound," he decided that the only feasible option was to continue the attack against the Russians to his front with every man able to march and shoot. The 6th Landwehr Brigade had neither field kitchens nor machine guns. Its men were exhausted. Mackensen ordered it out of the battle zone. The XVII Corps would drive straight ahead; I Reserve Corps would seek to turn the Russian left flank. All that remained to screen the Germans from II Corps, and perhaps the rest of Rennenkampf's army, was the 1st Cavalry Division. Small wonder that the XVII Corps staff gave up their supply trains for lost and abandoned hope of seeing their personal baggage again.[63] That was far from the worst that might happen.

8
The Province of Chance

Any weakness in Ludendorff's nerves during the early evening of August 26 was not reflected in the orders he issued at 9:00 p.m. Eighth Army was to destroy the Russian XV Corps and anything remaining of the 2nd Division before XIII Corps could come to their aid. The decisive sector would be in the south, with François taking Usdau, then advancing eastward on Neidenburg to roll up the Russians facing Scholtz. Since I Corps would have to guard its own right flank against the Russians around Soldau, Ludendorff ordered Scholtz both to detach a half-dozen battalions to reinforce François and to mount a "strong" secondary attack towards Usdau, while at the same time continuing the frontal attack begun on August 26. The 3rd Reserve Division and the garrison troops would remain in position on Scholtz's left, holding a line extending from Hohenstein to Waplitz.[1]

Ludendorff's orders suggest that he continued to think less in terms of an idealized Cannae than of a more conventional victory. Here again were no subtle operational combinations, no deliberate refusing of the center to lure the Russians deeper into a trap before springing it. Ludendorff was too much the practical soldier not to be aware that an army still depending on muscle power for mobility, with a communications system as shaky as 8th Army's had proven, was not likely to be successfully brilliant. What was required instead was hard fighting all along the line in the hopes that somewhere the enemy would crack.

At 10:50 p.m. on the 26th Ludendorff boasted to OHL over the telephone that the success of his attack was as certain as human calculation could make it, even in the face of five enemy corps. He may have been talking as much for his own benefit as Moltke's. At 10:30 p.m. 8th Army headquarters had finally learned that the 3rd Reserve Division was nowhere near its assigned position. Informed of Morgen's failure to advance, Scholtz and Hell were relieved. They still expected an attack on their left flank the next day—an attack delivered by the combined strength of XIII and XV Corps. While the main body of XX Corps was attacking towards Usdau, Scholtz, rather than see the 3rd Reserve Division as far north as Hohenstein, wanted it moved south behind the Drewenz to serve as his flank guard. Army command, deferring once more to the commander on the spot, finally accepted this disposition, but only under protest. It seemed the virtual end of any hopes of executing a tactical envelopment against the 2nd Army from the north. Now everything depended on the operational flanks: François around Usdau and Mackensen at Bischofsburg.[2]

I

The night of August 26 remained quiet on I Corps's front. François had issued his orders at 8:30 p.m. The 1st Division would attack Usdau from the northwest. The 2nd would strike from the south with one brigade, while the 3rd Brigade covered its right flank. The 5th *Landwehr* Brigade would screen the entire operation against any advance by the Russians around Soldau. In reserve, ready to exploit any success, was the detachment from XX Corps: six battalions, a squadron of cavalry, and a battalion of field artillery. The artillery preparation would begin at 4:00 a.m., with the infantry advancing an hour later.[3]

The I Corps was ready. Its infantry had a full night's sleep; most of them also received a hot breakfast. The corps artillery and the ammunition columns were finally in position. But the Russian position was naturally strong. It offered good fields of fire to front and flanks and ample room to conceal artillery close to the front line. It had been improved by several days of digging. Conta initially held his infantry on the lines of departure to give the guns more time to do their work. Falk's 2nd Division, which had worked closer to the Russian positions during the previous evening, advanced on schedule. Both divisions were nervous—so nervous that François's headquarters received a report of Usdau's capture around 5:00 a.m. He learned the report was false only when his headquarters convoy drove into heavy rifle and machine gun fire along the Usdau road. An enthusiastic junior officer had mistaken an isolated farm west of Usdau for the beginning of the village itself.[4]

The arrival of I Corps on his front initially caught François's Russian counterpart completely by surprise. Artamonov had not used his two cavalry divisions for anything but flank security. Neither of his infantry division commanders bothered to send out patrols to their front. Artamonov regarded himself as a soldier's general, a front-line commander impatient of modern restraints. Instead of coordinating what little intelligence reached his headquarters, he kept popping up in forward positions, interfering with company officers and "inspiring" enlisted men by asking

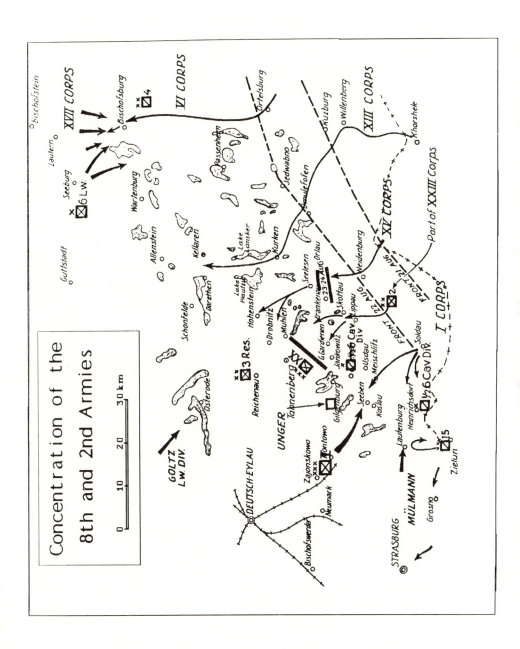

Concentration of the 8th and 2nd Armies

inane questions about their home lives while an entire German corps detrained within a day's march of his positions.

Artamonov might have been taken unaware; he had no intention of merely holding his ground. On the night of the 25th/26th he reported to Samsonov that he expected to be attacked by superior forces from the northwest. But to Artamonov, as to most of his contemporaries everywhere in Europe, the best defense was a determined offense. The Russian corps commander decided that he could best fulfil his role as flank guard by attacking the only enemy whose position he definitely knew: the 5th *Landwehr* Brigade at Lautenberg. To get the strength to do this he withdrew a brigade from his right, thereby increasing the already wide gap between I Russian Corps and the 2nd Division in Samsonov's center. A first result of this unfortunate maneuver came on August 26, when Scholtz was able to outflank and scatter the 2nd Division without interference. Yet the next morning Artamonov had no thoughts beyond overwhelming the Germans at Lautenberg.[5]

For all its shortcomings, Artamonov's plan appears more feckless in retrospect than it might have been with better luck or better execution. The Russian advance collided head-on with the *Landwehr*, who had been advancing since early morning and were feeling quite pleased with themselves. The forward elements of the brigade came under Russian fire just west of Skurpien and suffered heavy casualties in the first few minutes, some of them from German artillery, which once again fired too short. At the same time the brigade was flanked from the south by a strong force of Russian cavalry. Word swept through the ranks that they had been ordered to halt. Officers who tried to get the lines moving again were shot down by Russian sharpshooters. The situation seemed serious enough to justify a prompt retreat and an immediate appeal to François for reinforcements.

The *Landwehr* were well off compared to the 2nd Division. Falk's 4th Brigade reached the Usdau road by 5:00 a.m., but its commander was a tidy-minded officer who preferred to keep his casualties low and his flanks well covered while other units did the dirty work. Not until 11:15 a.m. did the 33rd Fusiliers occupy the high ground behind Usdau, and by that time the town was already in the hands of the 1st Division. The 3rd Brigade had worse fortune. Reinforced for its role as flank guard by two battalions of the 45th Infantry, it was ordered toward the village of Gross-Tauersee. Though one colonel with a taste for melodrama ordered his men to "advance towards the rising sun," early-morning fog combined with broken ground to disorganize the forward elements before they encountered the first Russian positions. The line of advance had not been reconnoitered during the night, nor was it well screened by skirmishers. Two kilometers short of its objective, the brigade was advancing across open ground when it came under rifle and machine-gun fire from what seemed every point of the compass. Within minutes Russian artillery joined in—first the field guns, then the 122-millimeter howitzers of I Corps artillery, which found Falk's men a welcome target of opportunity.

The transition from peace to war is a never-ending process of adjusting doctrine and practice to technology and methods. Strategic studies of the Tannenberg campaign frequently criticize both the Germans and the Russians for their apparently exaggerated concern with flank security. Time and again during World War I a few automatic weapons proved able to defeat or delay attacks from any direction, particularly in the crowded conditions of the western front, with its high ratio of bodies to space. But in August, 1914, neither troop commanders nor the men in the ranks had any way of knowing precisely how effective firepower was. The 45th Infantry's machine-gun company, detached from its parent regiment to support the 3rd Brigade, dug its six Maxims into a gravel pit. For awhile they anchored part of the line. But decades of prewar training had deeply inculcated sensitivity to one's flanks in officers. The rank-and-file infantryman of 1914 also needed time and experience before he would accept the rattle of his own machine guns as security for an exposed flank or a threatened rear. Even for veteran troops a sudden burst of fire from an unexpected direction can be disconcerting.

Even more disconcerting can be finding empty space in an ammunition pouch when reaching for a fresh clip of cartridges. The reluctance of nineteenth-century armies to adopt rapid-firing weapons on the grounds that they used too much ammunition has also been the subject of decades of ridicule. The men of the 3rd Brigade were not laughing. Under the impact of surprise, fire discipline vanished. Within minutes men, companies, and battalions were running out of ammunition, seeking supply wagons that had lost their way in the confusion, trying to borrow from more timorous or more provident neighbors. Orderly officers, sent forward now laden not with dispatches but with cartridges, often lost their way. A battalion of field howitzers from the 37th Artillery attempted to silence the Russian guns, but was itself outshot and overpowered. The regiment's other battalion was pushed almost into the firing lines as a visible support and rallying point for the infantry. One battery became stuck in the boggy ground. The other two fired off their ammunition and then discovered the impossibility of bringing caissons forward across soft ground that the Russians by this time had perfectly ranged.

Shouts of "We're surrounded!" and "Let's get out!" drowned the orders and the whistles of the company officers. The brigadier rode forward to rally his command, found himself invisible and inaudible, and promptly rode back out of the melee. In the American Civil War it might have been called a skedaddle. Korean veterans would have spoken of bugout. German histories describe an "orderly retrograde movement." In fact the 4th Grenadiers and the 44th Infantry fled for their lives to the woods north and east of Heinrichsdorf—a good mile from the first point of contact with the Russians. A good half of Falk's division was temporarily out of action.[6]

The 3rd Brigade's behavior on the morning of August 27 invites discussion of a more general point. Throughout the Tannenberg campaign, an unexpected fact recurred: active German formations, not reservists, did most of the serious running. This seems a paradox. While not composed of long-service professionals, the active regiments incorporated the cream of the German army: its youngest, fittest, best-trained rank and file. They were virgin soldiers, but so were the volunteer regiments of Dixmude and Langemarck or the British at the Somme. None of François's regiments faced a challenge as stern as the 235th Reserve Infantry Regiment on October 21, 1914, or the Tyneside Irish Brigade on July 1, 1916. They broke under for lighter losses and far less immediate threats.

Part of the answer lies in the irrationality, at least in materialist terms, of the factors that make soldiers fight. War is essentially a network of conventionally defined actions. Even if human aggression is genetically determined, there is nothing natural about organized violence. The commitment of any soldier correspondingly depends on standards and attitudes that are cultivated and inculcated. Discipline, patriotism, comradeship, fear of alternatives—all involve arbitrary belief systems. All involve behavior undertaken for its own reasons. That behavior incorporates an implied contract. Military institutions stress the importance of honor, not for archaic, caste-determined reasons, but because ultimately any soldier will perform only to the point where his personal honor is satisfied. That point in turn depends heavily on his sense of the rules of the game, on his expectations. Completely inexperienced men, with no frame of reference for their situation, could and often did fight harder and longer than veterans because of their ignorance. Men with peacetime military service, on the other hand, had some idea of what they would be doing, which contributed to a sense of what they should be doing. When that sense was exceeded, the contract was broken and the soldiers went on strike.[7]

The 1st Division benefited from better luck and better management, despite the German artillery's by now familiar tendency to drop shells on any likely looking target. One battalion escaped heavy casualties only when a bugler stood upright and walked forward into Russian rifle fire to signal the batteries of their mistake. He survived to wear his Iron Cross. Initially Russian small arms fire was heavy enough that the men in the German ranks nervously reminded each other that not every round finds a target. But Conta's guns and the corps heavy howitzers, reinforced by an additional battalion from Thorn, made such good practice against the Russian trenches around Usdau that the infantry tended to hang back and let the gunners.

As the Germans slowly closed in on Usdau from the north and west, more and more Russian batteries, anxious for their own local security, limbered up and withdrew. The infantry followed—those who did not wave handkerchiefs or stick their bayonetted rifles in the sand as token of surrender. When the Germans entered Usdau around 11:00 a.m., they found only dead and dying Russians heaped in trenches destroyed by howitzer shells. The village was in flames, its streets littered with corpses of men and horses, their eyes bulging, then bursting from the heat. Anyone questioning the fate of Russian stragglers found his answer as the wind spread the smell of burning flesh from collapsed walls and blocked cellars.[8]

François's pleasure at his victory was marred when at 10:55 p.m. he received a report of the 3rd Brigade's retreat—a report that had been exaggerated into a rout of the whole 2nd Division. Simultaneously, the 5th *Landwehr* Brigade's request for support arrived at corps headquarters. It seemed impossible to advance on Neidenburg until his flank was cleared. At 11:20 a.m., François informed 8th Army of his decision to turn the weight of his attack south and southeast. Ten minutes later Hindenburg and Ludendorff confirmed his decision.[9]

Conta had already begun responding to the new threat by swinging his division south. The 2nd Division also rallied and pushed forward, without one battalion that was pursuing its own as yet unnoticed odyssey to the German rear. François's coordinating orders, issued at 3:45 p.m., proposed to secure by nightfall a position from which I Corps could on the 28th cut off the Russian line of retreat entirely by a wide flanking move. The 1st Division was to take Fylitz. The detachment from XX Corps, called Schmettau's Force after its commander, was to advance south of Klentzkau. The 2nd Division would occupy the heights south of Gross-Tauersee. All available cavalry would pursue as opportunity offered.[10]

The Russians were not there to be attacked. I Corps had begun falling back immediately after routing the 3rd Brigade. Its presence on the field surprised the Russians even more than the Russians surprised the Germans. A series of contradictory orders from Artamonov's headquarters combined with the increasingly heavy fire of the German artillery around Usdau to turn what began as an orderly withdrawal into a rout. Instead of retreating eastward toward Samsonov's main body, the Russians followed their original line of advance, now become the line of least resistance, and fell back beyond Soldau. By nightfall all of I Corps that remained in the battle zone was a weak rear guard, fragments of a half-dozen regiments, strung out along the railway north of Soldau. Not only had the Russians lost any contact with the rest of the 2nd Army; they seemed to have small chance of stopping the Germans should they choose to push south instead of east the next day.[11]

In XX Corps's sector Scholtz's preparations were influenced by experience. On the 26th he had received verbal orders to delay his attack until I Corps's movements were well under way. Given the course of events that day, Scholtz felt he had been put in a potentially dangerous position operationally and professionally by I Corps's failure to advance. He was determined to avoid a repetition of the situation. When the army order of 9:00 p.m., August 27, specified an attack "with the greatest energy," Scholtz and his staff turned to the telephone. A brief conversation with army headquarters settled the matter. Scholtz issued his corps orders at 11:00 p.m. The 3rd Reserve Division, now definitely committed to Scholtz's left, was to make a feint to draw Russian strength from the south. In the center the garrison and *Landwehr* troops would hold their positions along the Drewenz River. The XX Corps's two active divisions were to attack south, but Scholtz's orders conveyed the impression of an advance in support of I Corps, rather than of a vigorous attack pursued independently. François's reputation as a general who went his own way did nothing to encourage Scholtz to take extreme risks in aiding his hard-headed associate.

This was also the case for the 41st Division on the right of Scholtz's line. Its riflemen were reluctant to repeat the dashing advances of their first day's combat, despite an almost complete initial lack of opposition. One company even captured the abandoned instruments of a Russian regimental band, but the division commander became unnerved by his very success. Though gunfire was audible from the direction of Usdau, there were no other signs of I Corps. Nor was there any word from the 37th Division on his left. Rather than risk isolation, Brigadier-General Sontag ordered a halt to await developments.

Staabs's 37th Division was having its own troubles. Its four strongest battalions had been sent south with Schmettau's Force. Its commander was, if anything, more concerned than Scholtz about the possibility of a Russian breakthrough on the corps's left flank—particularly since no one in Staabs's headquarters was sure whether the 3rd Reserve Division had received or obeyed XX Corps' orders to support the threatened northern sector. Staabs therefore hedged his bet. He left his 73rd Brigade in position to cover his rear and attacked only with the 75th. That formation made good progress against little opposition until around 9:00 a.m. Then Brigadier-General Böckmann ordered a thirty-minute halt to rest his forward elements and give stragglers time to rejoin.[12]

Had anyone at any of the responsible headquarters known it, Sontag's and Staabs's three brigades initially encountered only what remained of the Russian 2nd Division. These were the same units that had been so roughly handled the previous day. A Russian staff officer later reported them as "exhausted, with only a few rounds left, three days without bread or sugar." They broke as soon as the Germans attacked. One brigade streamed back to Neidenburg, where it was reformed around noon by the army staff. The other held its position a bit longer, until the division commander ordered a retreat, which turned into a rout. The brigade fled even further to the rear than its sister unit. It could only be rallied at Frankenau.[13]

The scattering of the 2nd Division temporarily exposed both the flank of XV Corps and the rear of 2nd Army. But the woods were too thick for German cavalry patrols or German air reconnaissance to discover and report the opportunity. Scholtz, moreover, had other worries. At 4:30 a.m. Russian artillery had begun shelling Mühlen—a systematic, heavy barrage, in sharp contrast to the more or less ineffective bombardments of the last two days. Scholtz also received a radio intercept ordering XV Corps to attack around Mühlen. The thick woods in front of the German position in that sector offered the opportunity to deploy a strong force with little danger of observation, and Scholtz had a healthy respect for the Russians' ability to utilize terrain. No matter what success his active divisions gained on the right, Scholtz by midmorning was far more concerned with his left flank, held by second-line troops and supported by a division whose commander had demonstrated a Françoislike capacity to turn a blind eye to orders he considered inappropriate.[14] On a smaller and more immediate scale than army headquarters, he feared being caught in a revolving door, with Russians smashing into his rear while he tried to find theirs.

Scholtz's problems were compounded when Hindenburg and Ludendorff established a forward command post just south of the Gross-Damerau Lake. Just before the staff left Löbau a report arrived that Usdau had fallen to I Corps. This seemed to fulfill everyone's highest hopes. Even Ludendorff said that on learning this news he considered the battle won. Once in the field, however, it soon became apparent that a mistake had been made—Hindenburg was able to see through a stereo-telescope that German artillery was still firing on Usdau. When Hindenburg and Ludendorff learned that XX Corps's attack south had also halted they were even less pleased, though the overall situation still did not seem to require direct interference with Scholtz's orders.

This opinion changed around 11:00 a.m., when confirmed reports of Usdau's capture arrived simultaneously with news of the Russian advance on Muühlen. It seemed clear that François no longer needed support from XX Corps. It seemed equally clear—at least on a map—that the Russian attack on Mühlen offered a chance to envelop the attackers with a short right hook. This was the kind of opportunity that had made reputations in 1866 and 1870. At 11:30 a.m. Scholtz was directed to switch the axis of advance of his active divisions almost 180 degrees from due south to north and east, in order to roll up the flank of the Russians engaged at Mühlen.[15]

The corps staff was still assimilating the new orders when around noon it received an excited telephone call. A lieutenant commanding a telephone platoon in the Mühlen sector declared that the German line had broken and Russians were pouring into the gap. Scholtz promptly directed Staabs's 75th Brigade to turn in its tracks and march towards Mühlen "as rapidly as possible" to restore the front. This left only the 41st Division to continue the enveloping maneuver ordered by Hindenburg and Ludendorff. At 12:15 p.m. Sontag was ordered by telephone to advance at once on the village of Waplitz. About the same time Colonel Grünert arrived at his headquarters, sent by Hindenburg to make sure the division moved in the new direction.

Sontag was less than happy with the situation. Patrols from his divisional cavalry regiment reported Russians everywhere in his sector, with Waplitz held in particular strength. He was not reassured by Grünert's dismissal of this enemy as mere "fragments" of previously defeated forces. The 41st Division turned itself around by 1:30 p.m., but its advance was delayed by a combination of heat, sandy roads, few wells, and delayed rations. Instead of driving his tired men forward Sontag decided around 5:00 p.m. to dig in along a line from the south end of Lake Mühlen to the village of Januschkow. A corps order to take Waplitz before halting arrived at 6:00 p.m. but was rejected as impossible to execute in the few hours of daylight remaining.

Sontag was not one of the Imperial army's obvious success stories. He was a mobilization appointment, coming to the 41st Division from command of the 10th Infantry Brigade in III Corps. He does not appear to have been the kind of forceful personality who made an immediate impression on his new subordinates. He finished the war in an undistinguished administrative post, as governor of Kalisch. At the same time nothing in his prewar record suggests that he received his job in the absence of anyone better qualified. Sontag was simply a good, ordinary general, the kind of solid professional every army taking the field after a long peace must accept on trust and hope. It was one thing to send a division forward against a visible enemy with colors flying and drums beating. It was quite another to advance into tangled forests one's own scouts insisted were teeming with Russians. And those Russians had a peacetime image that did not encourage expecting whole divisions of them to dissolve after a few days' fighting, no matter how confident the army's liaison officer might be on that subject.[16]

Sontag's lack of aggressiveness was far less important to XX Corps headquarters than the continuing threat from the north. As the afternoon wore on it became apparent that the initial report of a Russian breakthrough at Mühlen had been greatly exaggerated. Some men of the 69th Garrison Brigade, ersatz reservists with no peacetime training, broke under the Russian artillery, but their company officers brought them back to their positions. Brigadier-General Unger inspected his lines at the gallop and was able to report not only that his infantry were holding their ground, but that his *Ersatz* and *Landsturm* batteries were actually silencing some of the Russian guns to their front. The only major assault, made about 4:00 p.m., was rapidly checked, with over a thousand men of XV Corps surrendering rather than risk a run back to their own lines through the German fire.[17]

This local triumph was, however, almost lost in the growing number of reports that strong Russian forces were advancing far beyond XX Corps's left flank. They belonged to XIII Corps, whose commander had spent most of August 26th on the horns of a dilemma. He had been ordered to advance on Allenstein, yet he could also hear the noise of battle to the south where XV Corps was engaged with Scholtz. Like every European general properly schooled in the campaigns of the elder Moltke, Kluyev proposed to march to the sound of the guns. Unlike some of his German opposite numbers, he did his superior the courtesy of notifying him. But almost simultaneously he received direct orders to continue advancing on Allenstein.

Major-General Kluyev was in a quandary. His new orders mentioned that VI Corps was also to advance to Allenstein and cooperate with XIII and XV Corps against the German left flank. But efforts to establish direct communications with Samsonov had been frustrated by line-cutting German civilians and incompetent Russian repair gangs. Radio communications with Blagoveschensky were initially and inadvertently jammed by the powerful Russian transmitter across the border at Novogeorgievsk. When contact was finally made VI Corps's reply could not be deciphered, as XIII Corps's signallers had no code key. Kluyev's final decision to keep moving towards Allenstein reflected in part a reluctance to risk leaving VI Corps—which presumably was marching there too—in the lurch. His men, moreover, were hungry. Even their emergency rations had been eaten. Presumably Allenstein's granaries and bakeries could feed XIII Corps at least one solid meal. Presumably, too, Samsonov knew what he was doing when he issued the order.

Kluyev almost changed his mind on the morning of August 27 when he received a telegram from XV Corps asking for support. But when this was followed by another wire specifying that only a brigade be sent, Kluyev decided that given his lack of specific information, he was still best advised to start his corps on the road to Allenstein.[18] By late afternoon the undefended town was in Russian hands. Their first demand was for bread—120,000 kilograms of it, to be delivered within ten hours. This meant 60,000 standard loaves, and with only six bakeries available, Mayor Zülch was correspondingly worried about exactly what would happen when the deadline was not met.[19]

The occupation provided a different challenge to First Lieutenant Walther von Stephani of the 8th Army Staff. He had been ordered to make arrangements for the arrival and unloading in Allenstein of the *Landwehr* from Schleswig-Holstein, and for transferring army headquarters to the town of Osterode. Promptly on the morning of August 27, Stephani drove to Osterode to commandeer a locomotive. The station was overflowing with refugees; no train was immediately available even for a carmine-striped demigod from the general staff. Stephani spent the interval convincing the proprietor of the town's principal hotel to abandon his own plans for flight in favor of grilling a steak for a hungry lieutenant and making rooms available for the rest of the army staff, scheduled to arrive in Osterode that evening.

The hotelier had never heard of either Hindenburg or Ludendorff, and had no very high opinion of generals who appeared incapable of protecting German territory against invaders. Appeals to his patriotism brought no more result than suggestions of the profit to be made by lodging and feeding all those high-ranking officers. Stephani finally closed the issue by insisting that no more civilian trains would be leaving Osterode in any direction until the fighting was over. With necessity become a virtue, Stephani was able to set out for Allenstein secure in the knowledge that his commanding general would have a reasonably comfortable bed for the night.

Osterode did not possess elaborate switching facilities. The only engine available had just arrived from Allenstein and had to retrace its route in reverse. Stephani, more or less comfortably ensconced in the coal car, felt the effects of his full stomach and promptly fell asleep. As the locomotive neared the outskirts of Allenstein he was awakened by one of the train crew, who pointed out what looked to him like a column of troops on the road paralleling the tracks. Stephani, confident of his professional judgment, said that they were only refugees. Then he decided to use his field glasses. What had looked to the naked eye from a half-mile's distance like farm wagons suddenly turned into field kitchens and machine-gun carts. The Russians seemed to be eating their noon meal, but there was no reasonable doubt that Allenstein was in enemy hands.

What to do next? This was not the kind of emergency discussed in the war college. The only logical action was to reverse course, if possible before arousing suspicion. But a heavy engine could not simply be brought to a dead stop. While the engineer was applying the brakes, Stephani saw a half-company of Russians marching along the right-of-way. The Russians, naturally enough, scattered out of the locomotive's way. Stephani, perched on top of the coal pile, drew his pistol with all the aplomb of a cat at a dog show. German officer and Russian soldiers stared at each other for split seconds. Then the spell was broken. Friendly hands dragged Stephani to the bottom of the tender as Russians unslung their rifles. Bullets began whistling around the engine, thudding into the coal and pinging off the boiler. The engineer replied with the official emergency signal: three short blasts on the whistle. Finally, after what seemed endless minutes, the brakes took hold. The train stopped, reversed, then began moving faster and faster in the opposite direction, through a small defile, out of sight, then out of range of the Russians.

With Allenstein out of the question as a destination for the *Landwehr*, Stephani, once he recovered from his shock, arranged for the division to be diverted to the nearest station with a network of sidings. Within two hours, the first trains from Schleswig began disembarking their cargoes of leg-stiffened reservists at Biessellen.[20]

The Russian occupation of Allenstein confirmed Scholtz's belief that XX Corps faced a major Russian threat to its left flank. He decided to respond by pulling the entire 37th Division out of the line and sending it north, to deploy behind the left flank of the 3rd Reserve Division. This was a risk on two accounts. It would diminish by half the ability of XX Corps to attack eastward as Hindenburg and Ludendorff had ordered. Given the day's heat, the dust, and the disorganization still plaguing Staabs's formations, the 37th Division also might reach its new positions too exhausted or too demoralized to fight. Some of Staabs's battalions had to countermarch to pick up knapsacks temporarily abandoned. Others barely settled into their bivouac areas when they were awakened for still another night march. Rumors of a new disaster, of a German retreat across the Vistula, began passing through the stumbling ranks despite all efforts of the officers. They were not the best omens for the new mission.[21]

II

Army headquarters had its own problems with erratic troop movements. *Ostgruppe*'s victory on the 26th had raised hopes at headquarters that XVII Corps and I Reserve Corps could march undisturbed against the Russian 2nd Army's flank and rear. At 7:30 a.m. on August 27, Below and Mackensen were told to advance south with every available man as soon as the enemy at Bischofsburg was disposed of.[22] These orders, transmitted by messenger rather than telephone for security reasons, reached Below's headquarters at 12:30 p.m. Fifteen minutes later the army liaison officer with Below responded. Below's cavalry patrols had found that the Russians had abandoned their positions south of Bischofsburg without a fight, and I Reserve Corps was moving south as ordered. But Below wanted to know how the fighting was going on Scholtz's front. He also wanted to know the exact whereabouts of Rennenkampf's army. An excited telephone call from Allenstein had said Russians were in the town. A staff officer sent to investigate confirmed the report by backing his car down the road into Allenstein until he saw Russian sentries. Before the surprised soldiers could react, he changed gears and vanished towards his own lines in a cloud of dust and exhaust fumes.[23]

But where had this new enemy come from? Were they Rennenkampf's men or part of the 2nd Army? Hindenburg and Ludendorff as yet did not know themselves. They responded by ordering Below to send only a detachment south, to Passenheim. The bulk of his corps was now to face west, ready either to advance on Allenstein should the Russians be there in force or to turn southward as originally ordered.[24]

No matter which Russian army was mounting it, the possibility of a concrete threat from the north led Hindenburg and Ludendorff to leave their command post during the afternoon of the 27th and drive to Scholtz's headquarters at Frögenau. Their announced intention was to discuss plans for the next day's operations. Almost certainly they also hoped to put some vigor into a headquarters apparently more concerned with holding positions than with driving forward. They were especially disturbed at the way the 41st Division's attack had been allowed to fade away. Hindenburg and Ludendorff reasoned that both flanks of the 2nd Army, at Bischofsburg and Usdau, had been driven back. According to the best available reports on the main enemy forces, the Russian 2nd Division was broken and in retreat. The XV Corps was in position along the Drewenz. On the immediate Russian right, if Scholtz's and Below's intelligence was correct, XIII Corps had turned west to support XV Corps and was somewhere around Allenstein.

In a war game, 8th Army might have been willing enough to let the two latter corps concentrate. The more deeply the Russians committed themselves against Scholtz the less chance they would have of retreating successfully—*if* all went well in the field. In fact, the situation as perceived at 8th army headquarters by late afternoon of the 27th bore an uncanny resemblance to that existing around noon on July 3, 1866. At Königgrätz the 1st Prussian Army held its ground all morning against superior Austrian numbers. Its left flank, however, was in serious jeopardy until relieved by the 2nd Army, which emerged from the north to crush the Austrian right at the same time the Elbe Army's three divisions drove in the enemy's left. Though no memoirs mention the similarities, perhaps they crossed a few minds as the army staff prepared orders for the 28th. In the German center, the Goltz *Landwehr* Division, which had been detraining during the day, the 3rd Reserve Division, and XX Corps would attack the Russian XIII and XV Corps, pinning them in position. On the left I Reserve Corps would move against the Russian flank and rear, while XVII Corps pushed south and cut their line of retreat. François' corps would close the ring from the south.

But Königgrätz had been near run. Had the 1st Army broken under the Austrian attacks, the 2nd Army might well have arrived only in time to cover a Prussian retreat. Should Scholtz be right about the extent of the Russian threat from the north, the 8th Army might find itself facing an analogous situation, with its fate depending heavily on the fighting power and the military know-how of the uniformed civilians under Goltz, Morgen, and Below.[25]

Ludendorff was anything but complacent as the army staff drove back to Löbau in the late afternoon. When the officers reached the town they found the streets blocked by a disorderly stream of army wagons headed north. They were from the supply train of I Corps, and their senior officer knew no more than that he had been ordered to prepare for a general retreat. Wild rumors were circulating that I Corps had been routed and overrun, that its remnants had withdrawn to Montowo in the army's rear. In light of the day's events as reported the stories made no sense. Max Hoffmann promptly made a phone call to the railway station commandant at Montowo. That officer declared that earlier in the afternoon a badly disorganized battalion of the 2nd Division, the II/4th Grenadiers, had arrived in the town. The major in command said that the entire I Corps had been completely defeated; his battalion had only been saved by a rapid retreat. He then ordered the supply troops in Montowo to prepare to evacuate to the north. Some units had already started without orders, and their wagons were those blocking the road.

Hoffmann was unwilling to believe that this was anything but a manifestation of the fog of war. Still, it *was* just possible that the Russians around Soldau had given François more than he had been able to handle. Hoffmann, never a man to minimize his own exploits or abandon a good story, described calling the errant battalion commander to the phone and peremptorily ordering him to turn his men around and advance until he found an enemy to engage. Then he instructed an aide to take a staff car, drive towards Montowo until he found either Russians or Germans, and report the actual situation.[26]

The explanation was not long in coming. When the 3rd Brigade had deployed that morning its commander kept the battalion in question in brigade reserve. Its commander had been marked before the war as having "bad nerves," which might mean anything from an unfair efficiency report through a slightly overactive imagination to acute dipsomania. Brigadier-General Mengelbier was neither the first nor the last commander to cope with a weak link by putting him in a position where he could be directly supervised. This time everything went wrong. Mengelbier had proposed to establish his command post with the battalion, but was unable to find the unit in the fog. The anxious major for his part lost touch with his regiment, his brigade, and his division. The few reports he received from stragglers and fugitives were of Russians everywhere. In a kind of homing instinct he marched his men back to Montowo, picking up most of two machine-gun companies and part of a cavalry regiment along the way. By the time he reached the town he had apparently convinced himself of the truth of the story of disaster that was his sole protection against disgrace unthinkable to a German regular officer. Then the telephone caught up with him.[27]

If confusion ended as farce in the south, it threatened to become tragedy in the north. Below's and Mackensen's corps had spent an uneasy night after their victory on the 26th. Instead of merely bivouacking in the field they were ordered to dig in—a task easier outlined on a staff map than executed in pitch darkness. Trenches and rifle pits wound up facing every point of the compass. Guns painfully positioned at midnight were revealed at dawn to be targeted on their own rear areas. Company officers were not particularly sorry when orders came to abandon the area before their superiors had time to inspect the scene. The men were even more pleased to find the Russians running faster than the Germans were chasing them. Dismounted cavalry scattered the few stragglers remaining in Bischofsburg. Airmen reported a corps's worth of Russians on the road south. Civilians described the enemy's flight in lurid terms.

In XVII Corps headquarters, the previous day's misgivings gave way to a euphoria sanctioned by higher authority around 12:30 p.m., when the army order to march south finally reached Mackensen. Below, arguing that his men were too fatigued to get very far, had asked Mackensen to assume full responsibility for the pursuit.[28] By their own accounts at least, the regimental officers were overwhelmed with volunteers. The corps's two cavalry regiments, the 5th Hussars and the 4th Mounted Rifles, began the chase, followed by machine guns, artillery, and infantry riding trucks borrowed from the supply columns or bicycles commandeered from civilians. When the cavalry, its horses blown, bivouacked for the night, the infantry kept moving. At 2:15 a.m. on August 28 an improvised flying column consisting of a battalion of the 175th Infantry supported by the regimental machine gun company, a battery of field guns, and two troops of cavalry reached Passenheim. The village had been ransacked by the retreating Russians, who left behind an entire ammunition column and a war chest containing 200,000 rubles.[29]

Thus far, so good. But at 9:00 p.m. on August 27, Ludendorff's evening was disturbed by a phone call from I Reserve Corps. One of its cavalry patrols had just arrived with information. Strong Russian forces, estimated as at least a division, had in fact occupied Allenstein. When the troopers left at 4:00 p.m. to report, Russians were still marching in. Apparently the enemy in that sector was much stronger than anyone had thought. Possibly, moreover, XIII Corps, instead of turning against

Scholtz as expected, was trying to extend north and east to join Rennen-kampf's II Corps, which according to the best German information had reached Rastenburg by 11:00 a.m. on the 27th. If this happened the rearward communications of XVII Corps and I Reserve Corps would be well and truly severed. Below therefore proposed that the full strength of both his and Mackensen's corps be turned against Allenstein the next morning in order to drive the Russians there south onto the guns of Scholtz, Morgen, and Goltz.

Army command approved the change in plans. The I Reserve Corps and elements of XVII Corps were ordered to attack Allenstein the next day. The two corps must strive to mount a joint attack by noon, but I Reserve Corps was definitely to be in action at that time. To ensure that contingency, Below was to move out without waiting for Mackensen. August 28, declared Ludendorff, must be the day of decision.[30]

Mackensen's headquarters still had not established a direct telephone link with army headquarters in Löbau. With Allenstein in Russian hands, even a fast car would have to make elaborate detours over questionable roads to maintain contact. The army staff therefore expected Below to pass the revised orders along to Mackensen. He did not—at least not in the form intended. Instead Colonel Posadowsky, chief of staff of I Reserve Corps, drove to Mackensen's headquarters in person and informed him that the entire XVII Corps, including the detachment at Passenheim, was to move on Allenstein, extending only security detachments south towards Jedwabno and Ortelsburg.

After the war Mackensen wrote that this turn against Allenstein was so much opposed to his view of the situation that at first he hesitated to execute the operation. Army headquarters only noted that Below's headquarters "misunderstood" the new orders.[31] The confusion is not hard to understand. The general army order issued at 10:00 p.m. said that "elements" of XVII Corps would cooperate with I Reserve Corps around Allenstein. "In addition," the former corps was to drive south "in the direction of Willenburg."[32] However, the specific orders sent to I Reserve Corps stated that on August 28 XVII Corps was to advance on Ortelsburg while attacking Allenstein. The two towns were in opposite directions from the corps's current position. The missions were not exactly mutually contradictory. But in the face of an enemy whose strength and positions remained uncertain, pursuing them simultaneously might put Macken-sen's corps in the position of the proverbial chameleon on a plaid shirt. Instead of striking a concentrated blow, it risked the fate of being too weak everywhere, and too tired from overmarching, to accomplish anything.

In his study of the Tannenberg campaign, N. N. Golovine argues that the German orders were intended to provide a barrier against Rennen-kampf, rather than to expedite the annihilation of Samsonov. According to his interpretation, Ludendorff intended *Ostgruppe* to remain more or less in position while XX Corps and I Corps pursued the 2nd Army and drove it north. These latter corps would then deploy on the right flank of

Ostgruppe, with the Goltz Division and the 3rd Reserve Division in reserve, to face Rennenkampf should he move south. Golovine asserts that the orders to march on Allenstein did not reach Mackensen directly because "some calmer person" at army headquarters intervened to prevent this. Posadowsky was sent to XVII Corps Headquarters by mistake, because Below did not understand either the situation or his orders.[33]

The thesis, though provocative, does not appear tenable in light of the German records. Fatigue played a significant role in the mix-up. Mackensen was sixty-five, Below fifty-seven. Their principal staff officers were men in late middle age. While they were collectively fit enough none was as yet accustomed to, or indeed fully aware of, the constant stress of campaigning under conditions of modern war. These were not the circumstances of 1916 or 1917, when staffs spent months at a time in the same comfortable surroundings. The corps of *Ostgruppe* had been on the move since the start of the campaign. Questions of interpretation that seem obvious in a scholar's study or the academic precincts of a war college can loom much larger late at night in a field headquarters to men whose lifetime routines of eating, sleeping, and moving their bowels have been rudely and systematically shattered.

Other human factors were at work as well. The obvious course for Below, requesting clarification from army headquarters, incorporated two less-obvious risks. The first was looking like a fool in the eyes of a new set of superiors. The second was hearing what one did not wish to hear. While I Reserve Corps had done well in limited actions with a solid block of active troops close at hand, Otto von Below might well have been pardoned for feeling uneasy at the prospect of taking his civilian soldiers into Allenstein against a strong concentration of Russians while XVII Corps marched in the opposite direction. Instead Below and his staff, after consulting with the army liaison officer with I Reserve Corps,[34] apparently put together the two orders in their possession and developed an interpretation performing three functions. It fulfilled their understanding of the letter of army headquarters' directives. It preserved XVII Corps as a concentrated striking force. And it allayed the unspoken, perhaps unconscious, fears of what might happen were I Reserve Corps to be left on its own at Allenstein.

That Below was uneasy about his solution is indicated by Posadowsky's appearance at Mackensen's headquarters. Using a corps chief of staff as a liaison officer was hardly common practice in the German army, but its wisdom in this case was plain. According to Mackensen, only the respect he had for Posadowsky's reliability kept him from disregarding the orders he bore. With many misgivings, Mackensen finally prepared to march west in support of Below.[35]

Had it been necessary, the 8th Army could probably have taken up the positions Golovine suggests. Perhaps Ludendorff had this in the back of his mind. But the army orders of the night of the 27th, based on the information available at the time and taking into account Scholtz's constant concern for his northern flank, reflected a firm decision to continue the attack against the 2nd Army as long as possible. If they were flexible enough to be well adapted to a defense against an unexpected onslaught from Kennenkampf, this reflected the professional skill of the staff officers responsible for developing them under such pressure.

The Germans had more than a well-drawn operations order in their favor. Martos had decided on the night of August 26 that he could not safely advance on Osterode as ordered without clearing his left flank of the threat posed by Scholtz's corps. After checking the 41st Division's halfhearted attack, at 4:00 p.m. Martos committed XV Corps to the counterattack around Mühlen whose limited results have been described earlier. An hour later he was summoned to the telephone by Samsonov's chief of staff. Throughout the day Martos had been begging army headquarters to order XIII Corps to cooperate with him. Now he was informed instead that Samsonov wanted XV Corps to advance to Allenstein on August 28 to "cooperate" with Kluyev and Blagoveschensky.

Martos exploded. He shouted that it was impossible to disengage his corps from the fighting in progress, and insane to march it north leaving behind an undefeated enemy. Rather than attempt such follies, Martos declared, he would prefer to be relieved of his command on the spot. Whatever its mixture of conscious bluff and simple bad temper, the challenge worked. Postovsky temporized, informing Martos that he would call again in an hour.

By this time Second Army headquarters was a scene of confusion dominated by impressions. Learning of I Corps's defeat and retreat was a shock. So was becoming aware of the scope of the disaster that had overtaken the 2nd Division. In the light of these events and Martos's report, Samsonov seems to have decided by early evening that the main German strength was on his left, facing XV Corps, I Corps, and what remained of the 2nd Division. His mind and his plans changed accordingly. The formal orders for August 28 were that the latter formations hold at all costs. Instead of Martos joining Kluyev, XIII Corps would march south from Allenstein and, under Martos's tactical command, combine with XV Corps in an "energetic offensive" against the presumed flank and rear of the German position. The VI Corps would move west to the area of Passenheim and cover the 2nd Army's right.[36]

It was these orders, intended to concentrate the Russian center corps against the Germans in the southern sector, that set the actual stage for what so many later general accounts described as a Cannae, or at least the possibility of one. Neither Ludendorff's directives nor the gratuitous coups of the radio interceptions were nearly as significant for the developing Russian disaster as the command decision taken at 2nd Army headquarters during the evening of August 27—a decision made for a most logical set of reasons.

Max Hoffmann suggests that if nothing else the length of the German line, extending as it did from Usdau to Mühlen, should have convinced Samsonov that he was facing a larger force than he thought.[37] But Samsonov's orders reflected more than careless thinking or blind stubbornness. He had received no concrete information from either Rennenkampf or Zhilinski about the whereabouts of the German troops who had fought at Gumbinnen. As the situation on the 2nd Army's own front grew more complex, Samsonov and his staff had enough to occupy their minds. Unless otherwise informed, it was logical to assume that Rennenkampf had remained in touch with a force retreating westward, or into Königsberg. In any case Samsonov had no immediate fear of an attack from the north. The VI Corps's fragmentary reports did not indicate the scope of that formation's collapse. As for XIII Corps, its staff and commander had settled in for the night at Allenstein convinced that there were no Germans anywhere in the vicinity!

The process of reaching this remarkable conclusion illustrates once again the problems of assimilating tactical intelligence information at the operational level. Kluyev, after two days on scraps of reconnaissance, decided to see for himself at least by proxy. He sent out two airplanes, one to check the positions of XV Corps, the other to scout the roads to the east over which VI Corps was supposed to be advancing. The latter observer reported a corps-strength force marching westward. Though he had been unable to determine if the troops were German or Russian, XIII Corps's staff was firmly convinced that the airman had spotted VI Corps advancing as ordered. The time and place were right. No one at XIII Corps headquarters had received any information encouraging even a suspicion that German troops might be that far south. Kluyev promptly sent the pilot back with a message for Blagoveschensky and orders to land beside one of the columns and see that the dispatch was forwarded.

Around 5:00 p.m. a Russian plane, flying low as ordered, was brought down by a fusillade of small arms fire. Though the pilot said nothing about the origin or purpose of his flight, presumably he was one of the more surprised men in either army—not because he had been shot down, but that his captors were Germans. His failure to return generated no alarm at corps headquarters. Those new-fangled contraptions were always breaking down. And when a cavalry patrol of Kluyev's 36th Division reported that it had been fired on by a column advancing westward, the division commander assumed his men had simply mistaken a trigger-happy advance guard of VI Corps for Germans! He neither attempted to verify the information nor passed it on to corps and army headquarters. The troops in question in fact belonged to I Reserve Corps, which had halted for the night only ten kilometers northeast of Allenstein.[38]

Kluyev's behavior cannot be dismissed as simple incompetence. Defeat is a possibility in every military operation, and can be produced by a broad variety of circumstances. No commander can afford to reflect too deeply on potential failure. Taking counsel of possibilities can bring on fears that paralyze the will to act. For Kluyev, starting at ghosts was less important than imposing his will, and the will of his superiors, on the Germans in the next day's fighting.

Second Army headquarters was operating from the same matrix. In the context of the information—or lack of it—provided by XIII Corps, Samsonov's decision to push forward in the center seemed the best way of alleviating what he saw as the major, indeed the only, immediate German threat: the growing pressure on his left flank. Like Prittwitz, Hindenburg, and Ludendorff, Samsonov was a nineteenth-century general trying to cope with a twentieth-century problem: the gap between communications and mobility. The generals of World War I faced in greater measure than any of their predecessors the test of knowing at least in outline what was going wrong, without a corresponding possibility of adjusting the situation. Railroads might have enhanced strategic mobility, but the tactical and operational pace was still determined by the muscles of men and horses. The wars of the nineteenth century had increasingly shown that an army commander holding a corps or two out of action in the manner of Napoleon was simply depriving himself of that many troops. Modern battlefields were too large to permit the ready shifting of large reserves either to shore up weak spots or to turn stalemate into success. Samsonov was able to do nothing directly to support his left except relieve Artamonov of command and hope his successor could straighten out the mess. But it seemed reasonable to hope, particularly in view of Martos's reports during the day, that XV and XIII Corps acting together might give the Germans something to worry about on *their* left flank. As late as 11:30 p.m. on the 27th, Samsonov informed Zhiliski that Mühlen was in Russian hands, and that German troops had been observed retreating southwest. If all went well the next day, Kluyev and Martos might overrun their immediate opponents and decide the battle, or at least one part of it, favorably.

This consideration almost certainly influenced Samsonov's next decision. At 7:15 a.m. on August 28, he told Zhilinski that he was going forward to XV Corps headquarters in order to take control of the attack in the center. He and his staff left Neidenburg at 8:00 a.m. and drove northeast along the road to Jedwabno.

Critics generally agree that this was the final step in the 2nd Army's destruction, that Samsonov ceased from that time effectively to command anything. At best the move has been interpreted as a brave but limited man's desire to influence events slipping out of his grasp, a despairing gesture of personal courage in the face of disaster. It was both less and more. Since crossing the frontier, the exigencies of maintaining communications with its far-flung units had forced Samsonov's headquarters further and further behind its subordinate formations. The point had been sharply and repeatedly noted by Zhilinski. Samsonov's pride was wounded by his superior's observations, but vanity alone did not impel him to leave Neidenburg. He was going to reinforce what seemed like success, a maxim taught in every military school in Europe. At least his presence should remove some of the strain from the commanders on the spot, and ease cooperation between XV and XIII Corps. Samsonov's detractors tend to overlook the fact that on the other side of the line Hindenburg and Ludendorff spent most of their days not at headquarters, but with subordinate formations believed in need of guidance or encouragement. Samsonov's announcement that he was temporarily closing down the 2nd Army's signal station was not a gesture of resignation but an example of bad staff work. Samsonov expected to restore communications once he re-established his headquarters farther up the line.

At 9:30 a.m., however, Samsonov's hopes received a severe jolt when a messenger from VI Corps finally reached him along the Jedwabno road. For the first time Samsonov discovered the dimensions of the defeat that corps had suffered around Bischofsburg. It was hardly remarkable that he described the situation as "serious" when overtaken shortly afterwards by Major-General Knox, the British military attaché. According to that officer, whose acerbic memoirs remain the most familiar summary source of information on the 2nd Army's fate, Samsonov told him that I Corps was retreating on the left, VI Corps had been defeated on the right, and Samsonov was going to XV Corps headquarters and collect what forces he could to drive the Germans back.

Writing with the advantage of hindsight, Knox expressed surprise at the relative calmness of Samsonov and his staff. "The enemy has luck one day; we will have luck another," Knox was told. What he and many subsequent critics interpreted as a mixture of inconsequent insouciance and "Russian fatalism" was probably an almost desperate desire to be rid of a nuisance—an hypothesis reinforced by Samsonov's suggestion to Knox that he turn back because in case the worst should happen he had the duty to send "valuable reports" to the government in London. Samsonov still hoped to avert the worst as he and his staff switched from autos to horses for the final ride to XV Corps headquarters.[39]

III

Samsonov's spirits might have lifted, at least temporarily, had he known exactly what was happening to the Germans opposing Martos. Scholtz and Hell prepared their orders for August 28 believing XX Corps faced three full divisions on the sector of its front from Mühlen northwards. But the Russian troops south of Mühlen were not thought to have much power of resistance after their hammering of the previous day. Scholtz decided to take corresponding advantage of what seemed a gap in the Russian line. He ordered the 41st Division to make a night march around Lake Mühlen, its geographic objective being Paulsgut in the enemy rear. As soon as the heights of Paulsgut were taken the *Landwehr* and reservists in what was now the center of the corps sector, placed for the day under the overall command of von Morgen, would attack to their front. The 37th Division, already on the march north, was to be ready to advance in support of Morgen by 4:00 a.m.

The actual timing of the latter movements depended on the progress of the 41st Division. Sontag's men were expected to be in position by 4:00 a.m. By 5:30 a.m., however, no firing was audible from the division's front. Hindenburg, wanting to get a closer view of the battle, again moved

269

forward to Frögenau. He arrived there about 7:00 a.m. and set up field headquarters in the creamery on Frögenau's outskirts. Scholtz had previously established his own command post in the village. The only direct communication to 8th Army's other formations was a field telephone line to I Corps—not too much different from Samsonov's situation. Scholtz arrived within minutes to explain that fog had delayed Sontag's advance and was making observation impossible. Fog also played tricks with sounds, but according to Scholtz gunfire had been heard in Frögenau since around 6:00 a.m. That meant the 41st Division was attacking. Now there was nothing to do but wait.[40]

The corps orders had been issued late the preceding night, at 10:40 p.m. The 41st Division had not received them until 11:20 p.m.; its own orders reached the forward regiments shortly after midnight. Fresh troops, careful preparation, and aggressive leadership were reasonable prerequisites for infiltrating the lines of an enemy army corps. Sontag's division lacked all three. Its men were tired. They had spent most of the evening of August 27 entrenching themselves in expectation of Russian counterattacks. At this stage of the war few company or battalion commanders sent out patrols as a matter of course. Reconnaissance was assumed to be the cavalry's task, and cavalry considered itself next to useless in the dark. By the time the orders to advance reached the division's forward units, it was the middle of the night—too late to dispatch scouts who would probably do little more than alert the Russians by stumbling around in the woods. Sontag himself questioned the attack's prospects. He had only nine of his twelve battalions available. Two more were with Schmettau's Force. A third was cleaning up the battlefield of the 26th, collecting wounded and salvaging equipment. But Sontag's objections to the attack on Waplitz the day before and his apparent lack of grip during the afternoon had already cost him a sharp reprimand from Scholtz. Rather than risk losing his reputation or his command by another protest, the division commander decided to keep silent and hope for the best.

Sontag's attack orders reflected a preference for finesse over force. He divided his attenuated division into three of what a later generation would call battle groups: two or three infantry battalions reinforced by a battalion of field artillery and a detachment of cavalry. He proposed to slip these task forces one after the other in a single column between the Russian positions, cut the high road, swing left and break through Waplitz to the Paulsgut heights. Then the battle groups would take separate positions to block the Russian retreat.

The plan's flaws lay less in conception than in execution. The night march to the lines of departure was made in increasingly thick fog. Platoons and companies lost their way time and again. Whole battalions scattered out of control, regrouped, and scattered once more. For security reasons the infantry marched with unloaded rifles, a command decision that did nothing to enhance feelings of confidence in the face of episodic bursts of fire from Russian stragglers and pickets.

The Province of Chance

As the German advance guard passed through the abandoned village of Adamsheide it was greeted by the crowing of a solitary rooster. It was as though the bird gave a signal. By 3:45 a.m. the banging of individual Russian rifles had become a steady rattle. Sontag's leading regiment, the 59th Infantry, deployed blindly in the fog, overran Russian outposts, and drove forward in what the officers hoped was the general direction of Waplitz. The regiment's vanguard, its third battalion, was pinned down in minutes by what seemed random firing. In the damp air, every shot sounded as though it came from every direction. The 59th's heavy loss of officers on August 26 took quick effect. One or two casualties left entire companies leaderless. No one of any rank knew what was happening. Patrols sent into the fog never returned, their men shot, bayoneted, or simply lost in the confusion.

By 4:15 a.m. the regiment's second battalion joined the fighting line, its squads and platoons advancing as best they could on their own initiative. Waplitz, a large village rather than a small town, straggled for a kilometer along both sides of the shallow Maranse River. Captain Benecke, commanding the 59th's 8th Company, led a rush across the bridge west of the village. A Russian officer and a few enlisted men, up to their knees in water, waved handkerchiefs in token of surrender. In Scholtz's corps, as in Mackensen's before Gumbinnen, tales were rife of enemy abuses of the white flag. A few shots, a few hoarse screams, and a half-dozen brown-uniformed corpses were left bobbing in the slow-flowing water. But the Germans were unable to advance farther across the open, boggy ground in the face of Russian fire to their front and flank. What began as a bridgehead within minutes became a pocket.

With his casualties mounting almost faster than his confusion, the colonel of the 59th committed his reserve battalion. By this time, even if the Russian infantry could see no more clearly than the Germans, their artillery was finding the range. Elements of four German companies pushed into Waplitz house by house, seeking cover as much as victory. There the attack stalled. Nowhere in the 59th's sector could reinforcements or ammunition be brought forward. Every man still on his feet and every round still available must be husbanded, at least until the fog lifted enough to determine who was where.

As they came up on the 59th's right flank, the battle groups based on the 148th and the 152nd Infantry stuck fast in their turns. Once the fog began to clear between 6:00 and 7:00 a.m., it was the Russians who took advantage of the changed situation. Batteries of XV Corps opened an increasingly accurate fire from the east. The 2nd Division's guns, which had survived the previous day's rout of their infantry, joined in from around Frankenau. German counterbattery fire was ineffective, at least in the eyes of infantrymen who already felt all too thoroughly mishandled by their superiors. Instead Waplitz, the most obvious target in the area, came under fire from the 41st Division's guns.

As he saw more and more German shells burst in the village Captain Benecke, still holding his bridgehead with a handful of men, decided the situation was serious enough to justify leaving his position to make a personal report. For almost an hour he stumbled blindly in fog and smoke until he found not the poorly directed artillery, not the 59th's regimental headquarters, but the colonel of the neighboring 148th Infantry. That officer promised to do all he could to help if Benecke was willing to attack. Benecke's optimism soared further on the way back to his own men when he encountered and commandeered a detachment of pioneers commanded by an *Offizierstellvertreter*. Within minutes elements of the 148th also reached the Maranse, using the ditches alongside the road as protection from the Russian fire. But they were still on the wrong side of the river. With the fog lifting minute by minute, the young lieutenant commanding the 148th's leading platoon refused to take his men across a bridge that had become a magnet for concentrated Russian fire. And thereby hung a tale of arms and men.

The pioneers of the Imperial German Army were specialist troops, whose primary mission of building and overcoming field fortifications set them apart from ordinary infantry. Yet more than Britain's Royal Engineer field companies or France's sappers, they were considered a combat arm. On many occasions in their history, particularly in their versions of it, pioneer companies had served as emergency reserves and assault troops. Peacetime maneuver experience had reinforced by default the pioneers' infantry role. Time and costs forbade much direct practice in construction and demolition. Rather than pay compensation for destroyed fields to angry landowners, troops in field exercises usually marked their entrenchments with flags. Corps commanders correspondingly tended to regard their pioneer battalion as an extra source of manpower. That as much as anything had determined Sontag's assignment of Company 3, Pioneer Battalion 26, to the 59th Infantry's combat group. Even if they found nothing technical to do, their 250 rifles would be useful. Now some of them were staring more or less nervously at the fire-swept planks in front of them.

Their commander was also something of an anomaly. The German army had long recognized in peacetime that it would not have enough commissioned officers to fill all the positions that would open upon mobilization. Expanding the reserve officer corps was unacceptable partly on the familiar social grounds, but also for financial reasons. Instead, as so often, the army turned to its NCOs—specifically its *Vizefeldwebels*. Best translated as staff sergeant or platoon sergeant, this grade was held in the active army by men promoted beyond ordinary squad and section responsibilities, yet too junior to be considered for *Feldwebel* or unable to find a vacancy in that grade. In 1866 and 1870/71, *Vizefeldwebels* frequently and successfully served as platoon commanders in the field. In the intervening forty years, the grade was also increasingly given to those one-year volunteers who for one reason or another, social, economic, or professional, failed to qualify for a reserve officer's commission.

Recognizing that some of these men would from the beginning of mobilization be performing officers' duties, the army created for them the rank of deputy officer (*Offizierstellvertreter*). The concept was not unique to Germany. During World War II the British army experimented with something similar, the warrant rank of platoon sergeant major, to remedy a shortage of lieutenants. More recently, the U.S. army spared itself the institutional and economic costs of a permanently expanded officer corps by deciding to have most of its helicopters flown by warrant officers.

In a short war the German compromise might have worked. Most of the OSV's would have been returned to civilian life too quickly for serious friction to develop with the career officer corps. Discrepancies in benefits and status would have been obscured by common enthusiasm for the national cause. The actual result during World War I was to create a class of men whose status and problems were similar to enlisted pilots in the U.S. navy or Britain's Royal Air Force three decades later: neither fish nor fowl, with harmony depending so heavily on mutual good will and mutual common sense that both the latter services ultimately ended the anomaly by commissioning all their pilots. But if in August, 1914, a lieutenant of infantry would not lead his men across a bridge under fire, an *Offizierstellvertreter* of pioneers had two reasons for doing so: the honor of his rank and the honor of his branch of service.

The men of Company 3 rose to their leader's whistle and charged. No one got more than halfway across. As bodies piled up on the road and the planking, even the fire-eating Benecke conceded that any more attempts with the resources at hand would be an irresponsible waste of life. With no reinforcements in sight more and more of the Germans in Waplitz abandoned the fighting line, seeking shelter from artillery and snipers in cellars or in the rubble of destroyed buildings. The explanation of being out of ammunition was so commonly offered and accepted that it suggests a more or less unconscious collusion. If no one had anything left to shoot, everyone was spared from making a heroic last stand. Around noon, as Russian patrols drew closer, the Germans smashed their rifles, broke their swords, and hoisted the white flag. A private committed suicide with one of the few remaining cartridges in Waplitz. Over three hundred of his comrades marched into Russian captivity.

The 148th and 152nd also began to dissolve. Men shouted that they were out of ammunition. Others sought the chance to assist slightly wounded comrades out of the line. One officer rallied a batch of stragglers, put them through a few minutes of close-order drill, then led them back to the front. Sontag, however, did not regard the situation as salvageable by Frederician heroics. Instead of shoving open the door to the Russian rear as intended, his battalions were being squeezed into a pocket. Russian company and battalion commanders were mounting increasingly aggressive local counterattacks into the gaps between Sontag's units. The 41st Division seemed uncomfortably on the point of being trapped, faced with the task of turning about and cutting its way out. Rather than accept the risk, Sontag ordered his men back to their original lines of departure.[41]

This meant squeezing through a two-and-a-half-kilometer gap between the Maranse Lake and the Russians—a gap that narrowed as more and more Russian infantry learned what was happening, a gap that threatened to become a killing ground. Before 1914 Europe's artillerymen had hotly debated the relative advantages of covered and open firing positions. The British, responding to their experiences against Boer marksmen, tended to favor concealment. The French advocated seeking the best field of fire and silencing any opposition with *rafales* from *Mademoiselle Soixante-Quinze*. The Germans, as was so often the case, were somewhere in the middle. Germany's artillery theorists recognized that dead gunners and knocked-out pieces could support nothing, but they also accepted the argument that at certain crucial points, even in a modern battle, the infantry needed tangible proof that it was not fighting alone. Whether to support the last stages of an attack, to screen the beginning of a retreat, or just to attract enemy attention, the guns would sometimes have to break cover.[42]

Now, as the Germans fell back from Waplitz, the batteries of Sontag's 35th Field Artillery offered themselves as an alternative target. Taking positions in the open, they drew Russian fire while intimidating Russian infantry with their own shrapnel. Their sacrifice enabled the infantry to survive as a more or less organized force. In only three hours the 41st Division had lost over 2,400 men as casualties or stragglers.

At first neither XX Corps nor army headquarters knew anything about this defeat. The sounds of heavy firing from around Waplitz were not accompanied by the kind of movement in the Russian positions, suggesting a German breakthrough in the south. Sontag, however, was in no hurry to report the details of his embarrassing situation. Then at 8:00 a.m. Scholtz received an unexpected message. The Germans around Mühlen were attacking on their own initiative.[43]

Kurt von Morgen was another of 8th Army's atypical generals. A picture taken four years later shows a thick-set, jowly man, the ribbon of the Iron Cross in his buttonhole and the *Pour le Mérite* at his throat, staring into the middle distance with an expression more determined than sympathetic. Born in 1858, his peacetime career suggested a taste for the exotic. He had varied routine garrison duty with a period as chief of a research expedition to the Cameroons, and also served briefly as a military attaché in Turkey. Ennobled only in 1904, he was eager for further honors and confident in the men he led—the equivalent by now of over two divisions. The 70th *Landwehr* Brigade was deployed east of Mühlen. Two active battalions of the 37th Division held the town itself; the 69th Garrison Brigade extended the line to the north. Morgen's own 3rd Reserve Division was echeloned north and west behind the main front.

Since 4:00 a.m. the whole force had been standing to arms. Hours passed, yet no news arrived of Sontag's advance. Morgen's impatience was heightened by the rapid lifting of the fog he hoped would mask his attack. Finally he decided to go forward on his own. On his left the 6th Reserve Brigade was sent forward through the Jablonken forest to find the Russian right flank and roll it up. The other three brigades would attack the Russians frontally, holding them in place for the blow. It was a textbook solution, not particularly original or imaginative, but presumably well within the capacities of Morgen's men and their recycled officers to execute. At 7:00 a.m., Morgen's guns opened on the Russian positions; his infantry advanced thirty minutes later.

Morgen, aware that he was ignoring his orders, waited until the movement was well under way before notifying corps headquarters. Scholtz and his staff were unwilling to run the risk of disorganizing a sector they saw as threatened by calling Morgen back. But neither could they send troops to support him, and within an hour Morgen needed all the help he could get. His reservists were fighting from memories of active service during profound peace. They had none of the field howitzers whose fire was so useful in silencing Russian guns on other parts of the front. The 69th and 70th Brigades did little more than stab at their assigned objectives east of Mühlen. The 5th Reserve Brigade paid a stiff price to capture the village of Dröbnitz from Russian defenders that fought almost to the last man. One battalion lost all four of its company commanders and over two hundred men—casualties reflecting the reservists' lack of skill at mopping-up operations. Under heavy fire from bypassed positions, the brigade was painfully slow to reorganize and continue advancing towards its next objectives.

As for the flanking force, the 6th Reserve Brigade, it advanced through the Jablonken woods in closed columns, with so little regard for security that its vanguard was scattered by a Russian ambush. Its over-eager commander then deployed his main body and pushed forward without waiting for artillery support. Instead the reservists' machine guns, a company in each regiment, acted as units to provide bases of fire, keeping Russian heads down while the infantry worked forward in short rushes. But machine guns or not, the Germans found themselves in an all-morning, stand-up, tree-to-tree fight against the Narva and Korpor Regiments of XIII Corps. These men of the Russian active army had not read the foreigners' prewar reports of their shortcomings. Not until 12:30 p.m. did the 6th Reserve Brigade force its way into Hohenstein—one house at a time. Of over six hundred Russians buried in this sector after the battle, almost all bore bullet wounds, as opposed to shrapnel or splinter marks, a fact suggesting the closeness of the fighting. All along Morgen's front, hopes of a decisive breakthrough were translating into a rapidly escalating casualty list.[44]

Another ambitious general of an improvised formation had also received his orders to advance the night before. Major General Freiherr von der Goltz's "Higher *Landwehr* Command 1" had been formed on the outbreak of war to guard the coasts of Schleswig-Holstein against a possible British invasion. The force—more commonly and euphoniously dubbed the Goltz *Landwehr* Division—had been ordered east to reinforce the 8th Army on August 26.

The *Landwehr* was the German army's third line. Most of its men were in their thirties, with terms in the active army and its reserves well behind them. Their principal reminder of their days in uniform was the annually updated notice telling them where and when to report should general mobilization be ordered. In theory the officers and administrative NCOs were to report a day early, check preparations, and have all in readiness for the arrival of the rank and file. In practice things went far less smoothly, at least in the Hanseatic cities of Hamburg and Altona, Lübeck and Bremen, which mobilized most of the battalions now serving under Goltz. Officers were assigned and reassigned with bewildering rapidity. Those recalled from civilian life had lost much of their capacity for compelling instant obedience. Those transferred from administrative jobs were still caught up in the mystique of peacetime routines. Active and first-line reserve formations, concerned with expediting their own mobilizations, took first pick of available material. Questions of physical fitness, on the other hand, were met with initial indifference. "We're all healthy, we all want to go," shouted one anonymous private in broadest Hamburg dialect when his company fell in for its initial medical examination. A few days in barracks, perhaps accompanied by a bit of sober reflection, generated a significant turnover of men to the depots. But there were dozens more eager for a place in the ranks. By mid-August the *Landwehr* companies and regiments were beginning to shake down, testing their organization and equipment in field exercises and assuming local security responsibilities on the coast and in the harbors. Then came orders to move east.

At first it did not seem much of a war. The north Germans of the Goltz Division were oriented westward, to the great struggle against France and Britain. Who cared for the potato farmers east of the Elbe? But as the *Landwehr*'s trains moved slowly eastward they had ample opportunity to observe trainloads of wounded and columns of refugees going in the other direction. They had an even better chance to be cheered as saviors once their trains began rolling through the towns of East Prussia.

The *Landwehr* would need all of their morale. By the morning of August 27 only seven of the division's twelve battalions, and one lone artillery battery, had been able to detrain. The arrival of the rest had been delayed indefinitely because of a collision on the line. Goltz knew a Russian division was supposed to be in Allenstein, east of his position. Despite this possible threat to his flank he started southward in the direction of Hohenstein at first light with the troops he had on hand, leaving the balance of the division to follow as best it might. After a sixteen-kilometer march, his advance guard reached the area south of the *Kämmerei-Wald* when at 9:00 a.m. it encountered Russian outposts. The night before, Max Hoffmann had suggested that the *Landwehr* avoid unnecessary risks. "We'll bring them to you," he declared. Instead Goltz, riding at the head of his column, deployed six battalions and attacked the Russian position across the Hohenstein-Mörken road, leaving only two companies at the south edge of the woods to guard against a possible advance from Allenstein.

The *Landwehr* advanced with enthusiasm but without artillery. Like Morgen's men they were unable to make much progress after the initial contact. Then at 9:20 a.m. a cavalry patrol brought Goltz the disturbing information that Russians had been reported advancing from Allenstein in his direction since 4:30 a.m. As if on cue, enemy skirmishers appeared in the German rear.[45]

They were part of the vanguard of XIII Russian Corps. Kluyev had received neither direct orders nor direct information from 2nd Army during the night of the 27th/28th. His only link with the outside world was a message transmitted through one of Martos's divisions. This, reflecting Samsonov's army order for August 28, put Kluyev under Martos's command and ordered XIII Corps to turn southward to cooperate with XV Corps in attacking the German left. It corroborated both Kluyev's own view of the situation and the impressions of the staff officer who had acted as observer for the reconnaissance flight over Martos's positions on the afternoon of August 27. But Kluyev's corps was almost twenty miles away from Martos—a good day's march even for fresh troops. To turn out exhausted men for a night move seemed an exercise in futility, especially since Kluyev believed XIII Corps could not reach the expected battle area until the evening of the 28th. The corps therefore started south only at dawn on that day.

Kluyev's decision was sound enough given the information available. Yet it remains one of the unconsidered might-have-beens of a battle that invited so much speculation on both sides. What were the potential effects of an army corps debouching even an hour or two earlier in the rear of inexperienced *Landwehr* already engaged to their front?[46]

Things as they stood were discouraging enough. Goltz's officers knew how to lead and how to die, but they were unable to move their men forward against even the limited opposition offered by elements of the same brigade that was giving Morgen's reservists such difficulties further south. Lieutenants found themselves leading twenty men instead of eighty as overweight family fathers collapsed from heatstroke. One of Goltz's brigadiers galloped forward shouting to a bugler: "Sound the charge with everything you've got! I'll give you a *taler!*" But this appeal to Hanseatic business sense could not sustain the Germans' momentum. Not until part of Morgen's 6th Reserve Brigade came up on the *Landwehr*'s right flank did the outnumbered Russians finally pull back. They had bought the 2nd Army a morning's time. And they could still bite hard in the face of a pursuit characterized by more disorganization than enthusiasm—a combination reflecting heavy loss of officers and NCOs, a particular problem in *Landwehr* formations that often had no more than two officers in a company to begin with.[47]

At 8th Army headquarters, the situation became increasingly opaque as the morning progressed. Where was Rennenkampf? What would happen when he found that he had almost no Germans in front of him? Where were the reports from the 41st Division? No information had arrived from Morgen since 8:00 a.m. Why were the garrison troops north of Lake Mühlen not yet advancing? What were the Russians in Allenstein doing? At 8:15 a.m. the governor of the Fortress of Thorn made that last question especially vital by forwarding an intercepted radio message. In it Kluyev informed Martos he was moving south to support XV Corps and intended to be in Grieslienen at the head of his vanguard "around noon." Grieslienen was across Goltz's and Morgen's lines of advance! The flank and rear of 8th Army's poorest troops might well be open to a major Russian counterattack. Uncertainty was an increasing torment.[48]

Later reports did nothing to alleviate the tension. At 8:00 a.m. Sontag finally notified Scholtz of his defeat, concluding his dispatch by saying that he was unsure whether the 41st Division could hold its position, much less resume the advance. Army headquarters only learned of this situation an hour later—a significant lapse of time given the relative proximity of the headquarters. Ludendorff immediately sent an officer by car to investigate. His report "was not encouraging."[49]

The mood of the high command was improved significantly by the first reports from 8th Army's problem child. Hermann von François had brought his share of the battle into full swing well before dawn. The initial corps orders, issued at 7:30 p.m. on August 27, reflected an expectation of strong Russian resistance around Soldau. François assigned his air squadron the special responsibility of reconnoitering that area. "For the solution of artillery problems" he organized a force of eight heavy and fifteen light batteries, a mass of 120 guns, the largest concentration yet seen in the Tannenberg campaign. The infantry would only advance at 6:00 a.m., presumably after the Russian guns were silenced. Every available battalion from I Corps's organic divisions, Schmettau's Force, and the 5th *Landwehr* Brigade, would cooperate in the attack.

During the night, however, François's anxieties diminished—perhaps once again with the assistance of technology. At 5:30 p.m. on August 27, an aircraft patrolling from Graudenz reported to the fortress commandant that the Russians around Soldau, far from entrenching or massing for a counterattack, were retreating south in apparent disorder. The information did not reach army headquarters until 1:35 a.m. on the 28th. The copy of the observers's report sent to I Corps was not mentioned by François, nor did it exist in the archives by the mid-1920s. On the other hand, François acted as if he had received it. Certainly he changed his mind about needing his entire corps to overrun Soldau. Around 6:20 a.m. the corps commander ordered Lieutenant-Colonel Schäffer von Bernstein to take his own 8th Uhlans from the 1st Division plus the two cavalry squadrons of Schmettau's Force, an improvised cyclist company formed by the 43rd Infantry, and a battery of field guns, and ride east to cut the Neidenburg road. Just how this mixed bag by itself was supposed to sever the main line of retreat of two Russian corps was left unanswered. But at 6:40 a.m. François also ordered the 2nd Division to remain in reserve instead of advancing on Soldau. In the absence of positive confirmation of enemy movements by his own scouts or aircraft, François was not going to split his force and attack in two directions at once. But if the airmen were right he would have a full and fresh division ready to march on Neidenburg in support of his mobile group.[50]

The Province of Chance

The German advance on Soldau in the event met little resistance. The reports had been correct. Most of the Russian had left during the night; those remaining were battered into inaction by the German artillery. The Germans halted only when air reconnaissance reported that the Russian main body was far out of reach, beyond Mlawa. By 8:00 a.m. François was confident enough to start the 2nd Division toward Neidenburg.

Hindenburg and Ludendorff initially responded to this initiative by confirming it, ordering François to occupy the town as soon as possible and send his cavalry toward Willenburg, deeper into the Russian rear. But the news of Sontag's defeat changed minds in a hurry. At 9:10 a.m., François was told instead to divert both the 2nd Division and Schmettau's Force northeast to deal with the supposed Russian breakthrough in the 41st Division's sector. Army command took no chances dealing with its unruly subordinate. He was ordered to begin this movement at once, and to report as soon as he issued the orders. At 10:10 a.m. a phone message to 8th Army confirmed that the 2nd Division was on its way in the new direction.[51].

As XX Corps and army headquarters continued to receive alarmist reports from Sontag's sector,[52] Hindenburg and Ludendorff decided around noon to turn the whole of I Corps not east against Neidenburg, but northeast in the direction of Lahna. This movement would both relieve the direct pressure on Sontag and bar once more the Russian lines of retreat left open by his defeat. It seemed safe enough since François had reported at 11:45 a.m. that Soldau was firmly in German hands. By this time the staff knew François too well for comfort. The new order ended with a statement that "everything depended on I Corps." A junior officer telephoned I Corps headquarters a half-hour later with the solemn adjuration that the corps could render "the greatest possible service" to the army by carrying out its mission exactly.[53]

François regarded the changed orders as unsound to the point of folly, reflecting Ludendorff's inexperience in commanding large formations. The chief of staff wanted I Corps to cover the reteat of the 41st Division and to cut off the Russian lines of withdrawal. François was convinced that both missions could best be fulfilled by advancing not on Lahna, but on Neidenburg as originally planned. The only major road to Lahna ran through thick woods, where I Corps's maneuverability would be useless. Nor could its artillery expect to do much more there than shell trees more or less at random. With Neidenburg in German hands, however, the Russians would be trapped and presumably too concerned for their own position to pursue the 41st Division in any direction. François, never a man to let a superior's judgment overrule his own, decided to disobey once more. He hedged his bets only by instructing Conta to halt and feed the 1st Division, in effect giving I Corps a reserve. But he issued no new orders to the rest of his troops. As long as Hermann von François was commanding, I Corps would fight its battles his own way.[54]

François's behavior in this situation highlights once again the ambiguities created in practice by the German principle of "mission orders," leadership by directive. François is a man easy to admire—from a distance. Among the military virtues initiative is the one most overrated, by soldiers and scholars alike. The general who wins the battle the wrong way when his superiors are losing it the right way appeals to the iconoclast lurking in every academic. The role organizational shortcomings play in turning military misfortune into military catastrophe has been most recently demonstrated by Eliot Cohen and John Gooch. These authors stress the role of generals in correcting organizational flaws, even at high risk.[55] Yet there is another side to the question. How is it possible to direct a complicated battle when a principal subordinate with a crucial mission insists on total independence?

Hindenburg and Ludendorff had no immediate answer. But by 1:00 p.m. it was clear to them that François either had an instinct for the dynamics of this particular battle, or possessed what the French colonial army called "baraka"—fighting man's luck. The 41st Division had been badly shaken, but the Russians were not pursuing it. On the other hand reports of success were arriving from Goltz and Morgen. These were significantly exaggerated. They did, however, convince 8th Army command that François's attack should be executed as originally planned. At 1:30 p.m. army command assumed its hope and announced to François that the Russians were in retreat to the southeast. The I Corps was to cut off their combat formations, sweep through their rear elements, and disrupt their lines of communication. The 1st Division was ordered to reach Neidenburg and Muschaken and the 2nd Grünfliess by nightfall. Cavalry and cyclists were to advance to Willenberg; the main body of I Corps would resume pursuit as soon as possible the next day.[56]

François received this order at 2:30 p.m. Fifteen minutes later he started the 1st Division and Schmettau's Force on the road to Neidenburg. Conta's men were rested enough to be able to execute their mission with limited straggling—particularly when a corps staff officer drove along the column shouting that the Russians had been beaten and were on the run for the border. It was a textbook advance against light opposition, with artillery driving the Russians out of the few strong points they were able to organize before the infantry closed in. One battery even took thirty prisoners, who asked the gunners for an escort to protect them against further shelling! By midafternoon Conta's 8th Uhlans had swung south of Neidenburg; the cavalry of the 2nd Division, the 10th *Jäger zu Pferde*, was advancing on the town from the west.

Around 4:00 p.m. François, hearing from one of his pilots that Neidenburg had been evacuated, drove forward with his staff to see for himself. Outside the town the caravan halted. Peering through his binoculars, François noticed "a few brown spots" in a nearby potato field. Then bullets started whistling past his ears. The officers took cover, but as the Russian fire grew heavier a passive defense seemed insufficient. Cars were ransacked for rifles. Majors and captains whose days on the small arms range were long behind them formed a skirmish line and tried to remember how to estimate ranges and set sights. Their world was turned right side up again when a cavalry detachment arrived on the scene, dismounted, and drove the Russians off. François, zeal undiminished, ordered his rescuers to bypass Neidenburg to the south and head for Willenburg and the Russian supply trains. He agreed to wait for his own infantry before entering the town.

The first foot soldiers on the scene were the men of Schmettau's Force. His battalions had helped take Soldau early in the morning, then had covered the twenty-five kilometers to Neidenburg without a halt. But instead of allowing the East Prussians to spend the night in Neidenburg François told Schmettau to move through the city, bivouac at Muschaken, and advance on Willenberg as early as possible the next day.[57] Around 7:00 p.m. the German vanguard entered Neidenburg after exchanging a few shots with Russian stragglers. Schmettau's *Landser* turned their march into a victory parade, cheered to the echo by the civilians remaining in the town. During the day some unknown patriots had hoisted two huge German flags on the municipal fire house. When ordered to remove them Mayor Kuhn refused, saying that he had not put them there. Kuhn abandoned his schoolboy defiance in the face of a drawn pistol. He now had the satisfaction of seeing the erstwhile Russian town commandant a crestfallen prisoner. The 1st *Jäger* Battalion occupied the municipal hospital, one of the few principal buildings undamaged and unlooted. They found a large number of German wounded, including some of their own comrades captured at Orlau and Lahna. These men were loud in praise of the treatment they had received from the Russians. One young lieutenant, his face cruelly mutilated, had even had a sentry posted at the door of his room to ward off the curious and the ghoulish.

François, finally able to set up his corps headquarters at Neidenburg, received an unexpected reinforcement at 7:30 p.m. when I Corps's own Lost Battalion, the II/4th Grenadiers, arrived on the last lap of its erratic odyssey and was put to work rounding up stragglers. Its commander faced the task of reporting and explaining himself to an unsympathetic François. About the same time, Mayor Kuhn, body and spirit alike tried by his recent experiences, stopped to rest in the hotel housing François's staff when his eye was taken by a sight unseen for nine full days in Neidenburg: a keg of beer, prominently displayed at the bar. Kuhn promptly ordered a glass, and was just as promptly stopped from drinking it by a carmine-striped major. "How did you get the beer?" asked that gentleman. "The general staff brought it for itself. You'll have to forego the pleasure." The officer took the glass from Kuhn's hand and walked into the hotel dining room. The incident tells more about the social dynamics of Imperial Germany than many a learned and footnoted volume—not only by itself, but because Andreas Kuhn described and recorded it with neither indignation nor irony.[58]

Meanwhile the war went on for other men to whom beer had long been a memory. Schmettau's riflemen finally bivouacked at 3:00 a.m. on

August 29 in and around the village of Muschaken. The 1st Division's 2nd Brigade reached Neidenburg around midnight. The 1st Brigade halted south of the town, its men exhausted from up to eight hours of stop-and-go marching on secondary roads and tracks.

Falk's 2nd Division had spent a day less spectacular and less successful. It was opposed only by the Keksgolmski Regiment of the 3rd Russian Guard Division, three batteries, and a depleted brigade of the 6th Cavalry Division. But for once the Russian cavalry provided an effective screen, keeping the Germans from discovering how weak the enemy in front of them really was. The Keksgolmski Regiment, which had been detached from its parent formation to support the hard-hammered 2nd Division, put up a stout fight against superior numbers in its first action of the war. The guardsmen had dug individual foxholes and small rifle pits instead of trenches. Their officers knew enough to ensure the positions were well-sited for mutual support. The 2nd Division emptied its cartridge pouches firing at shadows, neither reaching its assigned objective of Grünfliess nor making contact with the 41st Division.[59]

Russian resistance in Falk's sector was facilitated by German inactivity further north. The army order issued at 1:30 p.m. ordered XX Corps to attack "in the direction of Lahna-Kurken." Seven minutes later Scholtz instructed the 41st Division to advance on Orlau and the 3rd Reserve Division on Kurken. The Goltz Division and the 37th were to secure the corps left flank against the Russians presumably coming from Allenstein. Sontag demurred. He informed the staff officer who deliverd Scholtz's order that his troops were physically and emotionally exhausted, that the Russians in his sector were well dug in, and that he had no intention of ordering or leading another attack that day. Everywhere his men lay asleep, rousing only to laugh skeptically at reports of victory in other sectors. The staff was more exhausted than the line. Too many nights spent redrafting orders had finally taken their toll. The 41st Division stayed in place until evening. Then, far from advancing, it withdrew to bivouacs up to five kilometers behind the front line.

In Scholtz's center, Unger's garrison troops and elements of the 3rd Reserve Division made slow but steady progress against Russian resistance that softened with the waning day. Martos's corps was almost fought out. Not even local reserves remained to plug gaps in the fighting line. As water bottles, haversacks, and cartridge pouches emptied, hands went up. Almost two thousand Russians surrendered to the 70th *Landwehr* Brigade. Unger proudly looked on as his middle-aged warriors marched off their prisoners. The Russians on Morgen's front were also showing signs of wavering. Galloping forward, Morgen grandiloquently informed a cavalry major that he was getting a true cavalryman's mission. "Do you see those retreating Russians? Follow them!" The orders were worthy of a Murat, but the troops obeying them were saddle-sore peacetime soldiers, *Landwehr* men and ersatz reservists. The major in command was dubious at the prospects of achieving anything before nightfall. The cavalry boldly charged through one Russian bivouac area, then lost its way in the growing darkness and began stumbling into ambushes.

At around 6:00 p.m. the infantry took over. With the 41st Division unwilling to move, Scholtz gave its assignment to Morgen. Instead of going east towards Kurken the 3rd Reserve Division was turned southeast towards Orlau. The 5th Reserve Brigade advanced almost without opposition, bivouacking for the night on the ground over which the 59th Infantry had fought in the morning and liberating around two hundred German wounded left behind in the 41st Division's collapse. But in this sector the Germans had, in the final analysis, pushed their enemy back rather than broken through.[60]

The men of the 37th Division had spent most of the forenoon battling bad roads and leg weariness rather than Russians. Staabs had no idea where the enemy was—only vague orders to advance east against what was "probably" no more than a weak force. He took correspondingly few chances. Unlike Morgen, Staabs moved his brigades forward in deployed lines covered by unlimbered guns. Then at 11:20 a.m., a messenger arrived from Morgen stating that the 3rd Reserve Division was heavily engaged and the 37th Division's line of advance was clear. Staabs suddenly became aware not only that he was missing a major battle, but that the brunt of the action was being borne by reservists. He shook his men into column and started them down the road to Hohenstein at the fastest pace they could sustain—or that their general assumed they could sustain. Men marched open-mouthed in the heat, gasping for air as their tongues swelled and their mouths filled with dust. At every halt men fought for a chance to drink the cloudy water of roadside ditches. Men asked each other, where were the water carts? Where were the rations? The German army was a citizen army, for all its vaunted iron discipline. As Staabs rode past the columns of the 150th Infantry he was greeted by shouts of "*Kohldampf! Kohldampf!*" ("We're starving! We're starving!") from the ranks. He was soldier enough to know when to hear nothing.

The division's vanguard reached the high ground west of Hohenstein around 3:00 p.m. The 37th Field Artillery Brigade formed a gun line and opened fire on the landscape to its front as the infantry struggled through the heat and dust, to deploy as skirmishers. Joined by two stray batteries from the 70th *Landwehr* Brigade and a battery of 150-millimeter howitzers, the German guns drew Russian fire from everywhere in the sector. Some infantrymen fell so sound asleep that their snoring seemed to drown out the sound of bursting shrapnel. Those still conscious began digging themselves in with an eagerness foreign to maneuvers. The 150th Infantry's colonel was inspecting his forward positions when he was greeted by a salvo of 122-millimeter Russian shells. He seized a spade, shoveled like a badger after each series of explosions, and popped into his fast-deepening hole at the whistle of the next incoming rounds. Everyone else was too busy or too frightened to laugh.

Compared to the Russians, the German artillery's target acquisition left much to be desired. Within minutes Goltz sent a staff officer to report that the 37th Division was firing on his *Landwehr*, and would Staabs please desist. Major-General von Staabs was one of the Imperial army's educated soldiers, with extensive service in the general staff and in the war ministry. He had spent his life preparing for these days, only to see his division repeatedly split up and marched to exhaustion in response to threats that had proved mostly imaginary. Now he bade fair to miss the climactic battle of the campaign. By the time Goltz's liaison officer reached him, Staabs was on the edge of explosion. The unfortunate captain compounded the problem because he was not wearing the staff officer's uniform that lent weight to critical messages. Staabs "suggested" that the *Landwehr* was blocking the advance of *his* division, then demanded that Goltz move his men out of the way so the 37th could attack.

After the war Staabs professed not to remember the incident—a memory lapse perhaps assisted by his division's failure to support the Goltz Division more effectively during the afternoon of August 28. Goltz had originally intended to attack south with the bulk of his force. Instead he found himself facing east as well, feeding companies and battalions into the *Kämmerei-Wald* to protect his flank against growing Russian pressure from the forward elements of XIII Corps.

Goltz, a cool head and a solid professional, kept at least his staff calm by cracking jokes, but morale was no substitute for rifles in the fighting line. A *Landwehr* battery advanced at the gallop to the south end of the *Kömmerei-Wald*, unlimbered in the open, and blasted the Russians back into the forest. But the gunners, whose experience was seldom less than a decade old, were less successful when it came to hitting targets they could not see. Fighting from tree to tree, the *Landwehr* infantry kept contact by singing and shouting to each other. Time and again the familiar Hamburg rallying cry, "*Hummel, Hummel*," and the equally familiar obscene response, served as password and countersign for men blinded by smoke and sweat. But the Germans steadily lost ground to their younger and fitter adversaries. When Goltz rode forward to rally his men, his personal staff was scattered to the points of the compass by a sudden Russian charge. Unlike their comrades of the active reserve, the *Landwehr* had no machine guns to provide close fire support. They fell back, leaving not only the Kämmerei-Wald but the village of Mörken in the hands of XIII Corps. Goltz's division was cut in half, its companies and battalions scattered almost at random across the sector, when darkness ended the fighting.[61]

Goltz's downcast staff officers settled for the night with the sense of having taken a beating. Ludendorff, with the advantage of hindsight, could afford to be more generous. The *Landwehr* had performed a mission prewar planners regarded as appropriate only for active troops or first-line reservists. They held off an army corps and barred its road to the south. Yet a fresh Russian brigade might have given Goltz's division, and by extension the whole German position in that sector, much more than a sense of guilt. As things stood on the night of August 28, the 2nd Army's center had not broken. Its flanks had been shaken. It had been pushed back. But disaster was to overtake it only on the next day, and only through the efforts of troops other than those on its immediate front.

9
The Province of Victory

I

At 1:20 a.m. on August 28, one of Mackensen's staff officers telephoned army headquarters to report the Russian VI Corps in full retreat. Over two thousand prisoners and two complete batteries of artillery were in German hands. Fifty more Russian guns were reported bogged down and abandoned. Mackensen hoped this information would convince Hindenburg and Ludendorff to allow XVII Corps to continue its pursuit south instead of marching on Allenstein. "I do not believe it possible," he declared, "that we will go still further back tomorrow." But this ambiguous, not to say incoherent, statement was as far as he went in questioning what he believed were his orders.

Army headquarters responded with no more than a question mark in the margin of the message's written version. The lateness of the hour probably had as much to do with the confusion as did Mackensen's diffidence. The results were the same. Mackensen ordered his divisions to turn towards Allenstein. Even the detachments which had gone south ahead of the main body were called back—all except for one advancing on Ortelsburg, as directly prescribed by orders.[1]

Eighth Army command had insisted that I Reserve Corps attack Allenstein as soon as possible on August 28—at least, no later than noon. Below, however, put his own gloss on the requirement. Over the protests of the army liaison officer Below decided, as he had done on the 26th, to wait for Mackensen and give his own men an extra bit of rest. The I Reserve Corps left its bivouac areas only around 10:00 a.m., its divisions one behind the other on a single road. This meant they were not likely to reach Allenstein much before 2:00 p.m. The reservists were edgy; an unfortunate Russian pilot overflying their line of march attracted the

286

attention of what seemed to be every rifle in the corps. At 10:30 a.m., however, a cavalry patrol reported that Allenstein was only lightly held. From that Below concluded that the Russians had gone south and decided to follow them, hoping to overtake them from the rear.

Hindenburg and Ludendorff had the same idea. Responding to Kluyev's intercepted radio message stating his intent to be in Grieslienen around noon, 8th Army at 9:45 a.m. ordered Below to pursue the Russians by the shortest possible route "at all costs." This time Ludendorff took no chances. A phone call sent a plane from Air Detachment 16 northeast. Its crew, guiding on the spiked helmets, tossed out copies of the new order over the marching columns. Instead of waiting on the chain of command, the commander of Below's leading division informed the corps commander of the change in orders and promptly turned his men south. By that time, 11:30 a.m., Below had received the orders himself, by both aircraft and phone. "Just like a war game" he commented as he and his staff determined the new lines of march.[2]

One element of a successful war game was missing: completeness. The revised orders made no reference to XVII Corps. Hindenburg believed only part of the corps was with Below. His staff was sure, for reasons unknown, that all but "elements" of Mackensen's men were on the march south and that in any case Below would promptly inform Mackensen of the new situation.[3] Both assumptions were unfounded. Mackensen remained ignorant; XVII Corps remained on the way to Allenstein. Not until noon did Below communicate with Mackensen, and then it was only to suggest that, in view of the "changed situation," XVII Corps march south once more to cut the Russians' escape routes eastward.

Mackensen, whose temper was proverbial, flew into a rage. Against his better judgment he had abandoned the pursuit of a beaten enemy—at Below's urging. Now he was being asked by the same man to reverse his direction again. Mackensen was tired of marching hither and thither on the recommendations of the commander of a mere reserve corps, a man his junior in years, seniority, and influence. He was determined to fight somebody that day, and by this time he was not overly concerned about who it was. The nearest target seemed to be somewhere around Allenstein. Senior officer Mackensen ordered Below to clear the main road. Then, as Below's troops and wagons slowly made way, Mackensen had second thoughts. Halting his corps for a brief rest, he decided to send Captain Bartenwerfer of his staff by airplane to army headquarters to inform them of his decision and to request specific orders.

Meanwhile, at 2:00 p.m. 8th Army finally established phone contact with the liaison officer attached to I Reserve Corps. Exactly what he reported remains uncertain. After the conversation his superiors definitely remained unaware that XVII Corps was not moving south as expected. They did, however, know that the Russians had left Allenstein. And a crew from the army's reconnaissance flight, Air Detachment 16, had just returned with a report that the Russian VI Corps had retreated so far out of the battle zone that it no longer posed an immediate threat to Mackensen. A sudden euphoria gripped the army staff. It seemed possible once more to use XVII Corps as the northern arm of an operational pincers, linking up with François's advance from the south to cut off any Russians that excaped XX Corps and its attached troops. Technology underwrote the dream at 2:35 p.m., when the army signallers opened a telephone connection with Mackensen's headquarters. The bemused commander of XVII Corps was promptly ordered to advance south with every man he could muster, pursing the Russians "to the last breath."[4]

About this time Bartenwerfer landed at 8th Army headquarters. Whether he arrived before or after the conversation with Mackensen is uncertain. Hoffmann says he came before XVII Corps had been contacted. Mackensen and the official history disagree. In any case, Bartenwerfer brought the first detailed news of the situation in the north—and he received "a correspondingly cool reception." The army staff saw Mackensen's ill-tempered and ill-judged orders for Below to clear the Allenstein road as at the least risking a monumental traffic jam that would render both corps useless. Bartenwerfer was ordered to fly back immediately and see that Mackensen understood and carried out his new mission.[5]

Bartenwerfer was also ordered to see that I Reserve Corps attacked that day. On his return flight at 4:30 p.m. he dropped a note to this effect on a column of the corps. The gesture was dashing but irrelevant. It was 8:30 in the evening before the message reached Below, and by then his corps had had a stomach full of fighting.[6]

Elements of the 36th Reserve Division marched into Allenstein to the cheers of a grateful populace. The Russians had already evacuated the town. The major challenge the victorious Germans faced involved removing a dud shell from the courtyard of the provincial mental hospital, where its effect on the staff apparently exceeded its impact on the patients. Once beyond Allenstein, however, the division was stopped in its tracks by Kluyev's rear guard. The rhetoric of war is replete with accounts of heroic resistance to the last man. Most of them are best described as exaggerations, but the Russians in this sector made the boast good. The colonel of one regiment died sword in hand, leading the remnants of his men in a bayonet charge. Five hundred Russians were buried in a single mass grave after the battle. Four hundred more fell prisoners into German hands. A few desperate stragglers swam to a small island in the middle of one of the lakes dotting the region. Not until August 31 did they finally surrender.

The other half of Below's corps, the 1st Reserve Division, began its afternoon more favorably by overrunning XIII Corps's baggage. Kluyev had sent his wagon trains along the highway southeast from Allenstein. Outside the village of Sasdrosz the Germans caught up with them. Here too the Russian rear guards set a high price on victory. Riflemen climbed the trees of the Allenstein Municipal Forest to pick off anyone bearing such signs of leadership as field glasses or a map case. Not until 3:00 p.m. was Sasdrosz in German hands. By that time every road and path was thoroughly blocked by dead horses and overturned wagons abandoned by

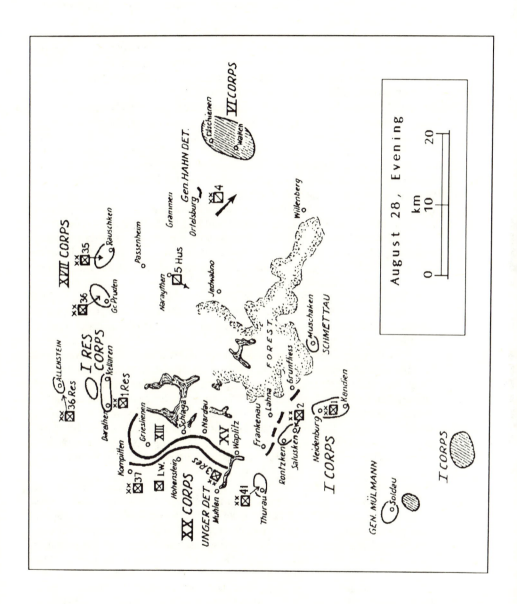

panic-stricken drivers. Equipment ranging from camp beds to field telephones to ladies' underwear looted in Allenstein lay strewn about the landscape. Amidst the lesser booty was Kluyev's corps war chest, whose contents were duly shared out among its captors after the fashion of the Thirty Years' War.

As the Germans cleared the highway and emptied the captured wagons, the Russians rallied around the villages of Darethen and Dorothowo. For Below's infantry, working their way across sand hills and through woods with by now empty canteens was initially a greater torment than enemy bullets. Optimism in the ranks briefly grew when patrols of the 1st Reserve Uhlans reported only weak enemy forces ahead: stragglers and survivors of the rear guard so roughly handled by the 36th Reserve Division. But the troops sent forward on that information ran into a buzz-saw. No one knew where the enemy was. "Flanks" and "rear" became concepts from a training manual. Guns were brought forward, but remained silent for lack of targets. Nor were the Russians in this sector passive opponents. Their local counterattacks threw the German advance into confusion time after time. One battalion of the 3rd Reserve Infantry lost all four of its company commanders in less than two hours of fighting.

Below had ordered his divisions to advance "as far as possible," and not until after midnight did the exhausted and hungry men of I Reserve Corps finally break contact. Kitchens were long since left behind. Emergency rations were long since consumed, with or without authorization. Men broke out of uneasy sleep to empty their rifles into the darkness. The cannoneers of at least one field battery spent the night under the partial protection of their gun shields, as spent and unspent bullets rang against the steel from all directions.[7]

XVII Corps had a no less trying afternoon and evening. Max Hoffmann supplemented his face-to-face conversation with Bartenwerfer by giving Major Schwerin of the corps staff a detailed briefing over the phone. Mackensen's first response was a long-distance call to Frögenau in which he expressed his views on the need for even senior officers to make up their minds. He then turned to—and on—his division commanders, informing them XVII Corps was to use everything resembling a road to reach Jedwabno and Ortelsburg as fast as possible and at any necessary cost.[8]

Mackensen might not have been the army's brightest intellectual light, but he was a driver and his men were ready to respond. Since midmorning rumors of great victories in the south had been spreading through the ranks of XVII Corps. Now staff officers rode from headquarters to headquarters with the information that the corps was marching in pursuit of a beaten enemy. Knapsacks were abandoned or thrown onto wagons. Infantry clung to gun carriages and stirrup leathers. But zeal was no substitute for system. The day was hot enough to produce mass sunstroke if everyone tried to march as long as he could move his legs. Infantry officers looked with speculative eyes on their supply trains. Typical was the experience of the 5th Grenadiers. Two companies and part of a third jammed themselves, their rifles and knapsacks into a mixture of army wagons and commandeered civilian vehicles. At the head of the column, burning with eagerness, Captain Lilie of the regiment's fusilier battalion gave the order: "Forward!" But he started his convoy in the wrong direction, towards Allenstein. In the confusion someone had failed to pass the word that XVII Corps was now headed the opposite way! Finally the matter was sorted out, and Lilie's task force moved south at a brisk trot. As long as the Germans remained on the high road all went well. But after a few kilometers their route led onto a sandy, rutted side road that seemed to go up and down the steepest part of every hill in East Prussia. Wagon after wagon got stuck or tipped over. The passengers spent so much time freeing or righting their transport that they were overtaken by the rest of the regiment and retransformed into workaday marching infantry.[9]

Local initiatives were supplemented by more orthodox flying columns—a squadron or two of cavalry, a battalion of artillery, and a hundred or so riflemen as local security, mounted on the gun limbers or riding in trucks commandeered from the supply trains. What these forces lacked in strength, they were expected to make up in speed. Horses dropped dead in their traces. Men collapsed from heat exhaustion beside them, or fell asleep on their feet, staggering forward until they collided with someone in the next rank. Unlimber and deploy, open fire, fall in, and push on until the cavalry reported another target, until a burst of Russian fire meant dispatching patrols to clear woods or farm buildings. Day gave way to a night that seemed bitterly cold to exhausted men drenched in sweat. But at 3:00 p.m. on August 29, a squadron of the 35th Division's 4th *Jäger zu Pferde* rode into an Ortelsburg only recently abandoned by the Russians. An hour later a ragtag group of men on foot, led by a detachment of gunners whose horses had long since given out, stumbled in to reinforce the troopers. The XVII Corps was at last moving in the right direction.[10]

Events on the German side of the line on August 28 were a microcosm of the World War I—an often random, almost antic mixture of old and new, of modern technology and traditional histrionics, of orders disregarded as irrelevant and orders obeyed too well. A general pushing forward aggressively by auto had to be rescued by horse cavalry. An airplane became an instrument of direct command in a manner prefiguring Vietnam while whole divisions lost touch with higher headquarters. An army corps spent most of the day marching back and forth in a manner that would have guaranteed a spate of early retirements had it happened in a maneuver. Yet despite this series of fiascoes the 8th Army's staff began to relax by the end of the afternoon. They did so with a certain relief at having avoided disaster—not all of it in the field.

Both Scholtz and Hermann Hoth, then a lieutenant on the army staff, described Ludendorff as receiving during the morning of August 28 an unsubstantiated report that Rennenkampf was advancing southward. He responded by proclaiming that the battle against Samsonov would have to be broken off and the 8th Army turned against Rennenkampf if anything was to be saved. Hindenburg took his chief of staff by the arm and led him behind a hedge. They talked for a few minutes. When they returned Hindenburg calmly said that operations would be carried out as planned.

For those officers unreassured by Hindenburg's confidence, at 4:10 p.m the governor of Königsberg reported that though "apparently" three Russian corps were marching westward, their main bodies were still well behind the Alle River. This meant the bulk of Rennenkampf's army faced a seventy-kilometer march to the battle zone. As for Samsonov's forces, according to the best information available to the 8th Army, their left flank, I Corps, was fleeing south. The 2nd Army's center, two and a half corps, was pinned in the woods between Allenstein and Neidenburg. On the Russian right, VI Corps had retreated beyond Ortelsburg. The army staff nevertheless took discretion as valor's better part, and decided to leave only I and XX Corps and the 3rd Reserve Division to continue the pursuit of the 2nd Army on August 29. Goltz's *Landwehr* and Unger's garrison troops, who had fought better than anyone expected, were ordered to move into reserve. The I Reserve Corps and XVII Corps would remain in the north, deployed behind Allenstein to meet the 1st Army should it appear unexpectedly. This proposed disposition contradicted the orders given Mackensen at 2:35 p.m. to drive south as fast as possible. But since no one at army headquarters had any real idea of the situation of either Bülow or Mackensen's corps, the new orders were initially not sent to *Ostgruppe*.[11]

At 5:30 p.m. on August 28, Ludendorff started to dictate the text. He began, according to Hoffmann, with the words, "Frögenau—leave the exact time open." Hoffmann instead suggested that Ludendorff should use as the place the name of the historic village in front of them— Tannenberg.[12] Five centuries earlier, in 1410, a Polish-Lithuanian army had smashed the forces of the Teutonic Knights in a battle symbolizing the end of Germanic eastward expansion. As the history and mythology of the Teutonic Knights grew to be a major subject of study and popularization in the Second Empire the battle had become correspondingly familiar to Germans.[13] For anyone who might have overlooked it, the five hundredth anniversary had been thoroughly observed, with suitable contemporary allusions, both in Russia and among Germany's Polish community. Scholtz saw the connection as clearly as Hoffmann. Ludendorff, after a few moments' reflection, decided it was a fine idea. The stain of an ancient defeat would be blotted out by a modern victory; the Teutonic Knights would be avenged.

After the christening Hindenburg felt cheerful enough to propose an excursion to the front lines, to the Mühlen sector. He wanted to thank and congratulate Scholtz's men in person. But the headquarters cavalcade had driven scarcely three kilometers when it encountered a roadblock of ambulances and wagons, their drivers shouting that the Russians were coming. The staff officers quickly solved the problem; the teamsters had been frightened by the sight of Russian prisoners moving to the rear under escort. Ludendorff, never remarkable for his equanimity, grumbled at the unpleasant impression made by the spectacle of German soldiers in flight from rumors and shadows. By the time the panic had been explained and its victims turned back towards the front it was too dark to risk the drive to Mühlen. The staff returned to Osterode for dinner in high spirits, its mood almost certainly improved by the ephemeral nature of their earlier fright. For the first time in a week, and however temporarily, Rennenkampf was not an invisible guest at the meal.[14]

Whatever the Russians' next moves, 8th Army would have additional troops to meet them. Reinforcements from the west were on the way. Prewar German planning had stressed the necessity for East Prussia to defend itself with its own resources. Gumbinnen, however, convinced Moltke that the Russian army had been badly, if not fatally, underestimated. A German force of seven divisions had apparently been so mauled in a single day of fighting that the commander, with as was naturally assumed the agreement of his principal staff officers, thought it necessary to retreat behind the Vistula. This suggested a need for complete revision of all calculations of the strength required to defend East Prussia. The effect of defeat on Austria also had to be considered. Given the delay of Conrad's offensive, when the Austrians did attack it might be to relieve pressure on the Germans—a shift in roles likely to have uncomfortable postwar consequences.

Events in the west, on the other hand, were apparently proceeding better than expected. The attack through Belgium was proceeding on schedule. A French offensive on the other flank, in Lorraine, initially generated anxiety at OHL, but by August 23 the situation there had changed as well. Not only did the advance on Paris appear to be in full swing, the 6th and 7th German Armies on the German left had checked the French in a murderous three-day battle and were in hot pursuit of their beaten foe. For Moltke and his staff the war seemed over. The victory in Lorraine opened the door to the kind of decisive battle German officers had been for forty years conditioned to seek—a double envelopment instead of Schlieffen's now apparently modest single version, a Cannae on a continental scale.

Moltke, not previously remarkable for optimism, began developing his own version of "victory disease." Already some of his critics were suggesting that formations initially left behind in Germany to guard against a British amphibious attack would have been more useful in the east than brought forward to support the drive on Paris. According to Groener the kaiser received at least one message from a senior civil servant requesting help for beleaguered East Prussia. Moltke's decision, however, was his own: to reinforce to the eastern front and seek a decision there corresponding to the one expected daily in the west.[15]

From what part of the front could troops best be spared? Groener favored drawing them from the German left wing. His often-expressed postwar fears for the consequences of diluting Schlieffen's planned concentration by weakening the right were exaggerated by hindsight. Arguably at least as important to this railway expert in August, 1914, was the relative ease of moving troops eastward across Germany from Lorraine, instead of additionally straining the already crowded lines and junctions further north. But his recommendation to transfer XXI Corps and I Bavarian Corps found little echo at OHL. Both of these formations, Groener was told, had suffered heavy casualties in the recent fighting. Political considerations also made undesirable the drawing off of a Bavarian corps for service in a secondary theater. The tendency of Prussian officers to treat Bavarians as inferior troops in 1870/71 still rankled south of the Main. In operational terms, moreover, Moltke's emerging hopes for a double envelopment could hardly have been fulfilled by a left wing deprived of two of its best fighting units.[16]

The chief of staff seems still to have been in the process of deciding whom to send when on August 25 the Belgian fortress of Namur surrendered, releasing the besieging force. Second Army Commander Colonel-General Karl von Bülow duly reported XI Corps and the Guard Reserve Corps available for other duties. OHL initially considered sending one corps to reinforce the right wing of the 3rd Army, the other to the left flank of the 2nd. But with the German envelopment growing tighter as it swung east of Paris, the front had contracted to the point where fresh corps-sized units could not be immediately deployed. Retaining them in local reserve was an obvious possibility, but for twenty years German doctrine had emphasized the necessity of shifting forces eastward after the initial, decisive victories in the west. Bülow expressed no sense of urgently requiring the services of the corps in question. At 3:10 a.m. on August 26, they were instructed to prepare for transport to the Eastern Front. The V Corps of the 5th Army was initially ordered to concentrate at Thionville for the same reasons. Moltke, however, subsequently decided against including a formation that had to be withdrawn from the fighting line. Instead he added to the troop list the 8th Cavalry Division from the 3rd Army.[17]

Whatever might be said about Moltke's decision to relieve Prittwitz, his reinforcement of the eastern front was not a hasty measure. The chief of staff had a week to consider the possibilities and to change his mind. There is no evidence that he was under pressure from the kaiser or anyone else to save the property of East Elbian aristocrats. Indeed, according to one account, the kaiser found himself in the unexpected role of calming Moltke's initial excitement at the news of civilian requests for help.[18]

Nor was supreme headquarters responding to appeals from the 8th Army. Moltke's decision came as a complete surprise to that formation. On the night of August 26, Ludendorff received a call from OHL. He asked Max Hoffmann to listen in on another phone, and for the first time the two officers learned of the proposed transfer of three corps and a cavalry division to East Prussia. Ludendorff said they were not essential and would arrive too late for the battle now in progress. He asked that they be sent only if they could easily be spared. If they were at all needed to gain a victory in the west, the 8th Army could manage easily on its own.

Two nights later Hoffmann was once more asked to monitor a phone call from OHL. This one confirmed the dispatch of reinforcements: two corps and a cavalry division, with V Corps now remaining in the west. Again Ludendorff said that they were not necessary and should be kept on the western front if needed there. Providing detraining areas for such a large force would be a particular problem. The only double-track lines into 8th Army's zone of operations ended at Elbing and Allenstein-Osterode. No more than a few detachments of *Landwehr* were available to cover this area against Russian cavalry, which might well be tempted out of its inactivity if offered such a vulnerable target.[19]

Moltke's determination to send troops eastward in the face of these conversations remains unexplained. Partly it reflected a negative: the 2nd and 3rd Armies' commanders and staffs did not protest that they needed additional strength to accomplish their respective missions. On the other hand an intelligence report submitted to OHL on August 28 described a growing body of Russian military opinion as favoring maintaining the offensive against Germany, even at the price of going over to the defensive against Austria. To implement this strategy the Russians could concentrate in East Prussia up to thirteen corps, supported by eight reserve divisions. However, weaknesses in the Russian command should enable the 8th Army, once reinforced by the two corps from the west, to hold its ground until the Austrian offensive's effect became noticeable.[20]

The report, little more than a warmed-over version of prewar information, nevertheless confirmed Moltke's decision to override the commander on the spot. From his first peacetime months as chief of staff Moltke had proven himself a tinkerer, a man unable to leave situations alone. It was fully in character for him to be eager to move troops from a theater where events seemed to be well under German control to a front where war was still the province of uncertainty.

Ludendorff for his part faced what seemed a no-lose situation. Since the reinforcements could not arrive in time to influence the ongoing battle, he could well afford to enhance his budding reputation outside his own headquarters for iron nerves in a crisis by denying any need at all for them. On the other hand if Moltke was in fact determined to begin building German strength in the east, the two corps he proposed to send would be a welcome addition to 8th Army's order of battle. These were no improvised formations of family men, no untested collections of middle-aged reservists. The XI Corps was part of the active army. If its Thuringian regiments had not quite the reputation of their Pomeranian or Brandenburg comrades, they were generally regarded as well up to the Imperial army's average. The Guard Reserve Corps had been formed on mobilization, but one of its divisions included three active regiments plus a fourth raised from cadres and students of the musketry and NCO schools in the Berlin region. It was a crack formation by any standards.

And a second cavalry division would be a welcome relief for 8th Army's overworked horsemen.

Ludendorff maintained his sanguine mood through the evening of the 28th despite the continuing absence of information on the whereabouts and circumstances of Below's and Mackensen's corps. At 9:30 p.m. he cheerfully informed OHL that everything was fine, with at least two Russian corps safely in 8th Army's bag.[21] Thirty minutes later, however, an army liaison officer, Major Drechsel, arrived by auto from I Reserve Corps headquarters. He brought bad news. Ludendorff and Hindenburg learned at first hand that not only had Below's corps still not caught up with Kluyev, but that the Russians in that sector were far from destroyed. If Drechsel's report was accurate, the positions of the two northern corps meant the 2nd Russian Army could retire eastward without much risk of being cut off by François's already overextended troops. Worse yet, to the best of Drechsel's knowledge XVII Corps was still somewhere on the road to Allenstein instead of advancing south. The army staff had the classic bad quarter of an hour assimilating this information—not least because its chief had only minutes earlier informed OHL that everything was rolling on wheels. The orders issued at 5:30 p.m. were cancelled. Instead, at 10:00 p.m. I Reserve Corps was told to continue attacking south and east on the 29th, this time with one division advancing directly on Hohenstein to assist in Kluyev's defeat, and the other towards Jedwabno with the hope that it would be able to cut off the Russian retreat. The exact position of Mackensen's corps was still a mystery, and it received orders accordingly: to remain in its bivouac areas and be ready to move against either Rennenkampf or Samsonov as circumstances demanded.

Hindenburg read the document, then scrawled an addendum at the bottom. "I expect," he said, "my orders to be followed exactly. This is doubly urgent in the present complicated situation." It was the first overt sign of stress this consciously unflappable man had shown since his arrival in East Prussia. Neither Below nor Mackensen had demonstrated the kind of insubordinate independence characteristic of François. Both generals could have argued that the "complicated situation" in *Ostgruppe*'s sector had been caused by their attempts to obey too many orders not fitting the tactical situation. But a man of sixty-seven who saw his battle slipping away from him could be forgiven if his Olympian detachment slipped a bit as well.[22]

An army staff desperately looking for troops to close roads that suddenly yawned open also turned to the cavalry. At midnight Brecht was ordered to send one of his brigades to Ortelsburg as a blocking force, and literally enjoined not to spare the horses.[23] This left only two cavalry brigades directly facing the Russian 1st Army. But the risks of being taken in the rear by Rennenkampf seemed far less certain than the consequences of reporting to OHL that the promised enemy corps would not be delivered after all.

Shortly after midnight 8th Army's chief of staff telephoned OHL to inform them of the changes in the general situation, and to pass the buck.

Ludendorff expressed his disappointment that part of the enemy would now probably escape due to the failures of individual corps commanders. He described 8th Army as "highly nervous" and badly in need of rest.[24] Apart from the question of "loyalty downwards," just whose nerves were by this time on the edge of breaking is a question for debate. Anything less than overwhelming success meant Ludendorff's stock was not likely to be very high among colleagues whose unspoken motto was, "Be more than you seem," and who had not forgotten prewar controversies in which this rising star had been all too prominent.

Eighth Army's chief of staff had another surprise for breakfast next morning. Ludendorff had counted on having XVII Corps ready for immediate service against Rennenkampf. At 6:30 a.m. on August 29, however, he learned that Mackensen had not received the 10:00 p.m. order to halt and camp, that instead his vanguards were in Ortelsburg. Ludendorff made the best of the situation. Ordering Mackensen's men on still another countermarch after their previous exertions might well mean rendering the corps entirely useless from exhaustion. The XVII Corps would therefore continue south—but no farther than Passenheim. To replace it in the blocking role against Rennenkampf, one of Below's divisions was to disengage as rapidly as possible from the fighting around Hohenstein and face front to the north. Unger's troops and elements of Goltz's *Landwehr* were ordered to concentrate in support of the reservists. And the governor of Königsberg was instructed to mount strong sorties to engage as many Russians as possible. Even if he had only second line troops available to open the battle, Ludendorff subsequently declared, he was determined to commence operations as soon as possible against the 1st Army, "whether it advanced or stood still." For the moment he had little choice in his order of battle, and less in whether to accept action if Rennenkampf decided to force the issue by marching south.[25]

II

Ludendorff's immediate opponents had also made some uncomfortable decisions. Samsonov reached XV Corps headquarters around 11:00 a.m. on August 28. He found a disturbed Martos who complained that his corps was fought out. It could not hold its positions much longer, to say nothing of advancing, unless it received reinforcements somewhat more substantial than an army commander and his staff. Throughout the afternoon Samsonov kept encouraging Martos to wait for XIII Corps to arrive from the north. But Kluyev was fighting his own battle, described above, against Below, Goltz, and Morgen. Instead of Russian guns shelling the German flank, instead of flat caps and khaki tunics becoming visible through the trees, instead of victorious shouts of "*Urrah,*" the men of XV Corps only saw individual stragglers, then companies and battalions shaken by the increasing German pressure. Martos, according to his own account, told Samsonov the time had come to expect the worst. Samsonov was less pessimistic. The army commander informed Martos that he intended to fall back on Neidenburg with the XV and XIII Corps and the 2nd Division. Martos was instructed to issue appropriate orders to his divisions, then report to Neidenburg and organize the defense of the town. As long as Neidenburg was in Russian hands, Samsonov declared, it was still possible to avert disaster. As Samsonov expressed his hope, Neidenburg was on the point of falling, undefended, to the Germans.

Unaware of the situation to their rear, Martos's infantry and artillery, with what remained of the 2nd Division, began abandoning their forward positions late on the 28th. Kluyev's predicament was even worse. During the day his corps had engaged Germans coming from north, east, and west. His trains had been overrun and scattered, with only the small consolation that most of the supply wagons were empty. To stand his ground was to invite destruction. Kluyev decided that his best alternative was to pull his corps together and push south in the direction of Martos' guns. Then around midnight on the 28th he received orders from Samsonov. The XIII Corps was to move eastward to Kurken, and expect "further instructions."

Implementing these orders involved significant risks. The locations of Kluyev's regiments by the evening of August 28 condemned them to night marches over sandy secondary roads in order to thread a needle. Kurken was a crossroads—but a crossroads that lay in the midst of a half-dozen lakes. The routes to the village were easily barred, and obvious targets for German artillery. In particular the Schlaga-Mühle causeway, between Little Plautzinger Lake and Stau Lake, was the only way from Grieslienen and Mörken to Kurken. Block it, and the elements of XIII Corps that had performed so well against Goltz and Morgen would be isolated prey for their enemies.

The Russian army never encouraged the kind of initiative among its subordinates that might lead to the creative disobedience of a François. For Kluyev the move to Kurken was the line of least resistance in more ways than one. His original intention to march south would involve fighting his way through the Germans around Hohenstein, while the way to Kurken was as yet unobstructed. But as XIII Corps prepared to retreat, Below's reservists were also on the move.[26]

The revised army order of 10:00 p.m. was late in reaching Below's headquarters. Rather than risk its interception or misunderstanding by using the radio or the telephone, Ludendorff had sent Drechsel back by car. He arrived around 2:00 a.m. on August 29 with the new orders, and almost certainly with the verbal information that Hindenburg and Ludendorff were anything but pleased at the situation in Below's sector. The corps commander had reservations of his own. Below had already ordered both of his divisions to advance toward Hohenstein as early as possible the next morning without regard for straggling. This sharp contrast to Below's usual concern for the condition of his men indicated his desire to complete on the 29th what he had expected, and been expected, to do on the 28th. Now he was supposed to send half his corps away from the fighting, towards Jedwabno, in the middle of nowhere in particular. Despite

Hindenburg's strictures on obedience, Below decided that both his divisions were too far west and too closely engaged with the Russians to be dispatched on this particular excursion. Instead he detached two independent battalions, the 1st and 2nd Reserve *Jäger*, and a machine-gun company, supported by two *Landwehr* squadrons and six guns. The senior officer of this improvised force, a captain, was told to advance not to Jedwabno, but toward Kurken, fifteen kilometers further west and correspondingly closer to the main body of the corps should his detachment need support.[27]

Below's initiatives suggest that he was expecting a harder fight than army headquarters thought likely. Initially he was not mistaken. The I Reserve Corps advanced down the Allenstein-Hohenstein road at first light, the 1st Reserve Division in the lead, picking up enemy stragglers on the way. Around 7:00 a.m., south of Grieslienen, the corps encountered the first serious Russian resistance and stuck fast. Below brought up his artillery—two field regiments and the pride of I Reserve Corps, a nonregulation battalion of heavy howitzers borrowed from the Königsberg garrison. The Germans even managed, for one of the few times in the campaign, to put up a balloon. Below's operations officer, an artilleryman by training, shed rank, years, and dignity to climb an observation ladder and direct fire when he suddenly saw even more lucrative targets coming into range from the west.[28]

Around 5:00 a.m. the battalions of Goltz's *Landwehr* bivouacked south of Mörken had observed columns of Russians moving over the Schlaga-Mühle causeway. Their commander promptly sent his men forward to occupy the road and cut the Russian line of retreat. Shortly afterward the 6th Reserve Brigade also attacked towards Mörken, under orders from Morgen to push across the causeway. Then the 37th Division came on the scene with a commander burning to make good the previous day's fiasco. Its vanguard advanced through Hohenstein, now ablaze from German and Russian shelling, while the *Landwehr* and reservists fought through the woods south of Schlaga-Mühle. Kluyev's riflemen made the Germans pay for every yard of ground. Russian guns firing over open sights broke up advance after advance, defying the best efforts of Staabs's batteries to silence them. Two *Landwehr* battalions finally reached the Schlaga-Mühle causeway, but lost their commanding officers in the process and were too badly disorganized to push further. The XIII Corps, in short, was fighting another model rear-guard action—until the artillery of I Reserve Corps took a hand.

At 10:30 a.m. sixty-six German light guns and sixteen 150-millimeter howitzers opened fire simultaneously. Russians scattered in all directions. Driverless wagons and riderless horses careened through the fields. Gun crews fell around their suddenly silenced pieces. Yet detachments and organized units continued to put up a desperate fight, ignoring or overlooking the surrender tokens raised by their comrades. Would-be German parliamentarians were shot down beneath their flags of truce. In Hohenstein, snipers and stragglers continued to take toll of the careless and the unlucky. Goltz and his staff came under such heavy rifle fire on entering the town that the general personally organized a house-to-house mop-up. As the *Landwehr* and elements of I Reserve Corps cleared out other pockets of resistance, Morgen's division pushed through the tangled mass of guns and wagons on the causeway to open the way for pursuit towards Kurken. By 2:00 p.m. the fighting in this sector was over. Germans who the day before had sworn vengeance for dead comrades were plying Russian prisoners with cigars and sweets. At least one group of Russians feared to eat the chocolate they were given, begging to be shot rather than be poisoned by "that brown stuff."[29]

As German privates enjoyed proof of their cultural superiority, as captains and colonels sorted out their formations, as generals congratulated each other, Ludendorff, accompanied by Max Hoffmann, suddenly appeared on the scene. In the course of the morning his headquarters had grown uncomfortably warm. At 8:40 a.m. the army's telegraph service received a message from the Zeppelin base at Königsberg. It reported that a reconnaissance flight, begun around midnight and ending at 6:00 a.m., had observed Russian bivouac fires as far west as Preussisch-Eylau. Perhaps they had only been made by cavalry patrols. But the Zeppelin's commander declared that his ship had been under heavy infantry and artillery fire during the entire flight, and the gas bag and the gondola had enough holes to sustain his description. Twenty minutes later the signallers reported another dispatch from Königsberg. Sent at 7:35 a.m. but delayed in transmission, it was an intercepted order to Rennenkampf from the Northwest Front. The 2nd Army was hard pressed; Rennenkampf was to send infantry and cavalry to Samsonov's support—just how many, or which units, could not be deciphered from the message.[30]

This information came near to precipitating another crisis at 8th Army headquarters. Opposed to the Russians stood only two brigades of the 1st Cavalry Division and, far to the north, the 6th *Landwehr* Brigade. A half-dozen small towns were garrisoned by small detachments. Against this weak cordon the whole 1st Army could be advancing. Suddenly it seemed that any hour might see at least Russian cavalry in 8th Army's wide-open rear.

What exactly *had* become of the Russian 1st Army? It had spent two days recovering from its victory at Gumbinnen, burying the dead and evacuating the wounded, replenishing ammunition and replacing officer casualties. On August 23 its advance resumed. By the 26th, the Russians had moved no farther than fifty miles against no more than the token resistance offered by scattered patrols and detachments. This slowness was a product of both tactical and operational decisions. Rennenkampf's cavalry remained committed to dismounting in the face of a few rifle shots, despite the fact that the situation prefigured Palestine in 1918 rather than Cambrai in 1917. The Russians faced no complex network of prepared defenses, no impassable concentrations of firepower—only scattered detachments of home guards and rear guards. Opportunities for going around instead of going through were virtually unlimited. But

Barrows, Macandrews, and Light Horse Harry Chauvels are not always available at need. The troopers who might have overtaken the retreating Germans, and who certainly would have given their generals some anxious moments, remained tied to the main body—tied so closely that even junior officers wondered at their superiors' caution.[31]

At command level Rennenkampf was not a simple victim of his own inertia. A school of thought on the American Civil War holds that Union generals in the eastern theater suffered from a massive inferiority complex vis-à-vis their Confederate opposite numbers. This factor is presented as contributing to many southern military successes. Equivalent attitudes were not widespread in the Russian high command at this stage of the war. Like Samsonov, Rennenkampf respected his German counterparts. He did not concede that they were better generals in command of better troops—nor, based on the course of events to date, did he have any convincing reason to believe that. What Rennenkampf *was* doing was attempting to lead from strength. For all its prewar talk of mobility the Russian army of 1914 was not an ideal instrument for a proto-blitzkrieg. Its familiar image as a steamroller reflected structural realities in which haste was indeed likely to make waste. Rennenkampf's attitude after Gumbinnen prefigured to a degree that of Montgomery after El Alamein. Maintaining the initiative did not mean preserving direct contact. Instead of challenging the Germans on their own terms, the process that was proving so costly to Samsonov, the better part of wisdom in Rennenkampf's mind involved positioning 1st Army to deliver a single sledgehammer blow to end the campaign once and for all. Whether the decisive battle took place east or west of the Vistula was less important than its nature.

Then on the morning of August 26, Rennenkampf received new orders from the Northwest Front. Two of his corps were to blockade Königsberg. The rest of the army, two corps and the cavalry, were to pursue the Germans who had not taken refuge in the fortress. Zhilinski and his staff were certain at this point that neither the 1st nor the 2nd Armies had anything to fear from the apparently defeated and demoralized Germans. Dividing Rennenkampf's army in the fashion ordered meant great strains on the already shaky services of supply. More seriously, however, Zhilinski's orders created an attitude loop. They reinforced at Rennenkampf's headquarters an impression largely created at Northwest Front by Rennenkampf's reports from Gumbinnen: the Germans were retreating in disorder. By emphasizing the blockade of Königsberg, Zhilinski proposed to hold the 1st Army back while the 2nd pushed northwest as Samsonov proposed to do, driving the Germans onto Rennenkampf's guns.

Rennenkampf, though less than pleased with the division of his forces, responded by ordering his right-flank corps, III and XX, to prepare to turn north, cross the Deime River, and besiege Königsberg. The IV and II Corps were to continue their advance westward. In his army order number 4, Rennenkampf declared that the army must not be

301

halted for lack of bread. Vegetables and potatoes gathered along the line of march would replace the temporarily missing staple. Victory, declared the commander, is in the legs. More or less responding to the exhortation, IV Corps reached the area of Friedland-Allenburg and II Corps Gerdauen-Rastenburg on August 27. Both formations were still a good distance from Samsonov's operational sector, but close enough, as has been seen, to unnerve the Germans at regular intervals.

Any possibility that the 1st Army might move from the realm of psychological intimidation ended when Rennenkampf received another telegram from Zhilinski on the night of August 27. It declared that the troops defeated on the 1st Army's front on August 20 had been moved south by rail, and were now attacking the 2nd Army. Rennenkampf was ordered to assist Samsonov by advancing his own left wing as far south as possible. The dispatch reflected, however, little substantive anxiety about the 2nd Army's position. Had Zhilinski been really concerned, he could have assigned Rennenkampf specific geographic objectives farther south. He could have ordered his subordinate to advance by forced marches—a method whose shortcomings scarcely deterred its regular employment by subordinate Russian generals in the Tannenberg campaign. Instead Zhilinski merely instructed the advance of the 1st Army's left into the area he also expected the 2nd to reach within the next few days. This was hardly an encouragement for Rennenkampf to move southward with any haste, particularly in the context of a follow-up order from Northwest Front prescribing in great detail the procedures to be followed in besieging Königsberg—still the 1st Army's principal objective in the mind of the Northwest Front's commander.

Rennenkampf and Zhilinski have been so universally excoriated for their lack of insight during the Tannenberg campaign that it seems appropriate to stress the fact that neither general had any reason to assume the 2nd Army faced any problems it would be unable to solve with its own resources. The German order of battle was known, and events on the western front precluded any likelihood of significant reinforcements being stamped out of the ground. In a worst-case scenario, four German corps, at least two of them roughly handled at Gumbinnen, plus a mélange of second-line garrison and fortress troops, faced four Russian active corps. The German army might be good, but to accept it as so much better than one's own that even odds were too great was the kind of mind-set no army can afford at the beginning of a war. Northwest Front's telegram, intercepted by the Germans as noted above and received by 1st Army at 7:00 a.m. on August 29, did not suggest an emergency, much less a disaster. And when it was cancelled four hours later, Rennenkampf received no information no more specific than the bald fact that the 2nd Army had retreated.[32]

Ludendorff responded to the morning's news of Rennenkampf by hedging his bets and taking the field. At 12:20 p.m. he telephoned Koblenz to declare the battle won, with five army corps and three cavalry divisions the victims of German prowess. But, he declared, the predicted encirclement of two Russian corps could not now be expected to succeed. The bag of prisoners was less than it might have been had the extremely "nervous" German corps been properly handled.[33]

After this blast at his subordinates Ludendorff left for Hohenstein. The mere sight of the crowds of demoralized captives was reassuring, and their surrender could not have been more timely. Ludendorff ordered Staabs's 37th Division withdrawn from the fighting line as rapidly as possible to reorganize. Below was to concentrate not one division, as the 6:30 a.m. army order stated, but his whole corps on the Osterode-Allenstein road and dig in against the possibility of any sudden move by Rennenkampf. The Goltz Division, badly disorganized from its two-day fight, would pull itself together and provide support. These four divisions would be available against Rennenkampf by the end of the day.[34]

Below's rewriting of his direct orders had contributed not a little to Ludendorff's anxieties. In the event, the whole of I Reserve Corps was not needed around Hohenstein. A division sent to Jedwabno would almost certainly have cut Kluyev's line of retreat beyond remedy. As it was the two battalions Below actually ordered in that direction got no closer than ten kilometers to the highway, then spent the day destroying captured Russian ammunition—a task safer, if less glorious, than blocking the escape of a presumably desperate enemy.

The I Reserve Corps's failure to perform part of its assigned mission was highlighted by the behavior of the 41st Division. That unfortunate unit had advanced at 7:15 a.m., also with Jedwabno as its objective—the southern half, in other words, of a possible tactical pincers. But its officers and men were a bit too conscious of previous defeats and previous casualties. A weak screening force of XV Corps held them almost on their start lines from 8:45 a.m. to 1:00 p.m. Even after these Russians had retired, Sontag's pursuit was slow and cautious. His division made a total of only fifteen kilometers during the day, getting no further than Orlau by 5:00 p.m.

Below's insubordination and Sontag's slowness meant that Morgen's 3rd Reserve Division found itself pushing the Russians through an open bottleneck. By nightfall Kurken was in German hands, but the men were too tired to advance further. Once again their kitchens had failed to keep pace. Men unable to grub potatoes from abandoned fields or liberate chickens from abandoned farmyards fell asleep with empty stomachs. Some battalions compensated with music, the Leuthen Chorale being an obvious choice for the division's Pomeranian Protestants.[35]

Below was also more pleased with himself than he might have been. Captain Borowski, commanding a battalion of the 1st Reserve Field Artillery, had spent the afternoon and most of the evening inching his guns along the Kurken road through masses of prisoners and wagons. Around 10:00 p.m. he met no less a personage than his corps commander, who asked Borowski what he was doing. "Hunting Russians, your excellency," was the reply. "Not at all necessary. They're in the pot. A great victory. Plenty of prisoners. Find a nice place to bivouac and let your people relax properly." It was not exactly a Napoleonic recommendation, however welcome it might have been to the weary gunners, but it admirably fit the mood of soldiers conditioned to think in terms of wars ending with one decisive victory.[36]

On the German right flank, I Corps faced two problems. Hermann von François was under orders to bar the thirty-five-kilometer gap from Neidenburg to Willenberg. He also had to expect a serious Russian attempt to break through at Neidenburg, since the only major road to the frontier ran through the town. In preparing his orders for August 29, the corps commander decided to send his 1st Division along the Neidenburg-Willenburg road behind Schmettau, while the 2nd took position at Grünfliess to cover Neidenburg against any counterattacks by the 2nd Army's center corps.

When the 2nd Division began its advance on the morning of the 29th, Falk's forward units demonstrated the truth of the adage that there are old soldiers and bold soldiers, but no old and bold soldiers. Its opponents, elements of that same Russian 2nd Division so severely handled on August 26, withdrew slowly towards Orlau. But in the minds of Falk's two-week veterans, every furrow and every rooftop posed a potential threat. Instead of leading gallant and costly rushes, officers waited for the machine guns, using them to blast real or suspected Russian positions. Entire companies and battalions deployed to clear out a few snipers, often demanding help from the artillery. By day's end the 2nd Division was no more than five kilometers north of Neidenburg.[37]

Other detachments of the Russian 2nd Division also delayed François's 1st Division for several hours. Conta had received reports of enemy columns marching on Neidenburg from the north, and his subordinates were sufficiently concerned about the possibility of surprise to deploy their men in the face of anything resembling a threat. The German cavalry was initially more active than their infantry. At 5:00 a.m. the 8th Uhlans, reinforced by three squadrons from XX Corps and a battery of the 16th Field Artillery with a platoon of the 3rd Grenadiers perched on its caissons, rode southward out of Neidenburg towards the Russian border. The countryside seemed empty of life until midafternoon, when the troopers overtook what remained of the trains of XV Corps and the 2nd Division. The escorts were scattered and dispirited. The drivers were middle-aged family men, many of them unarmed. German trumpets shrilled the charge. Amid scenes reminiscent of Tilly, Murat, and Nathan Bedford Forest, the German horsemen rounded up over a thousand wagons and almost five thousand prisoners—including a disconsolate and exhausted pilot routed from his bed in the border village of Roggen by two artillerymen. His aircraft was destroyed on the ground; another Russian machine barely managed to take off in time to avoid a similar fate.[38]

The I Corps' second cavalry regiment, the 10th *Jäger zu Pferde*, also left Neidenburg around 5:00 a.m., but in a different direction, northeast along the high road to Willenberg. On the way they overtook the infantry of Schmettau's Force. That energetic commander had his battalions on the march by 8:00 a.m., most of the men with less than four hours' sleep. Again and again Schmettau's vanguards deployed under rifle and artillery fire, but Russian resistance was light and poorly coordinated. Here and there the main body marched past a gray-uniformed corpse or a man twisting with pain on a litter. A more common scene was a knot of walking wounded glad enough to be out of it, waving to and cheering on their comrades still in the ranks. As they advanced the Germans began overrunning Russian supply trains. Kitchens, wagons, and war chests fell to the East Prussians. Silverware and underwear, top hats and feather beds—the pitiful plunder of the Russian advance was now reclaimed, though contemporary accounts say little about how much of it eventually reached its rightful owners.

Schmettau was not the kind of tidy-minded officer who worried about securing either his rear or his booty. Keeping his columns closed as tightly as possible, he drove them toward Willenberg as fast as the men could march or limp. Enterprising riflemen loaded their packs on liberated horses. Others impressed Russian prisoners to carry their gear. One company converted itself into mounted infantry with the aid of Cossack ponies. At 8:00 p.m. on August 29, after twelve hours on the road, Schmettau's vanguard entered Willenberg. The Russians had done nothing worse than break a few store windows. There was plenty of beer and wine on hand, and Willenberg's citizens were not slow to show appreciation of their liberation.

In a campaign of hard marches, that of Schmettau's Force stands out. Since early morning on August 28 it had covered sixty-five kilometers, most of them under combat conditions in August heat. Willenberg was the last major road junction in the Russian line of retreat. Regimental historians describe it as fitting that these troops, who had fought the 2nd Army from the beginning, should be the ones to close the trap. The rank and file, so exhausted that they fell asleep standing in ranks, may have been less enthusiastic, but they too were catching victory fever. A captain of the III/151st Infantry, the first battalion into Willenberg, received a report that a detachment of Russians was to be found four kilometers outside the town. Inspired by a sense of duty mixed with dreams of the Iron Cross, he called for volunteers. At the head of forty men he marched out and returned with over eight hundred prisoners. Most of them had been glad enough to trade their rifles for a drink of water. The 151st's colonel, not to be outdone, led a lieutenant and twenty men to a farm whose owner declared that his buildings were full of Russians who wanted to surrender. When he ordered them to come out and lie down on the ground, 150 men emerged and stretched out under the German rifles. By the time that column reached Willenberg it had grown to almost two thousand hungry, confused Russians willing to obey anyone willing to give orders in any language.[39]

The human trophies collected by Schmettau's Force indicated growing Russian demoralization. The detachment, however, had been too weak even to consider picketing its route of advance with its own resources. That was Conta's job. By early afternoon the 1st Division had shaken itself loose from its tormentors. Conta drove towards Willenberg as fast as the men could march, scattering detachments along the highway like beads on a string. By midnight I Corps's share of the encirclement was complete, with the 1st Division providing a cordon anchored at one end by Schmettau's Force in Willenberg and at the other by the 2nd Division covering Neidenburg. It remained to be seen how seriously the Russians would test the barrier. Singly and in detachments, Russians sought to break through the slowly tightening cordon. Some were taken prisoner. Others, particularly Cossacks, were shot down by Germans seeking to avenge the devastation of their home province, or seeking easier targets than they had found so far in the war.

Mackensen's XVII Corps formed the other arm of the 8th Army's operational pincers. Initially he proposed to move the 36th Division into position along a north-south axis from Passenheim to Jedwabno. The 35th, less the detachments around Ortelsburg, would continue south, deploying below the 36th's area of operations and cutting the roads through the woods north of Neidenburg. At 11:00 a.m. he informed army headquarters of this decision from his headquarters at Passenheim.

Mackensen's advancing divisions pushed their way through Russian supply columns and past abandoned field hospitals. At Jedwabno the 129th Infantry liberated several hundred prisoners. Most of them were from the battalion of the 59th Infantry that had crossed the Maranse on the 28th and been cut off there. Rearmed and re-equipped, they were a welcome reinforcement for the weakened and exhausted regiment of XVII Corps—not least because of their embarrassment at having surrendered to an enemy now on the verge of collapse. The men of XVII Corps were almost at the end of their strength. Only the encouragement of the officers and the lashing tongues of their NCOs kept them going, but a battalion of the 21st Infantry got almost to Kannweisen, only four kilometers from the Neidenburg-Willenberg road and François's 1st Division, before its legs gave out. Even deeper in the woods, the 5th Hussars dismounted and skirmished into the key road junction of Kaltenborn. The XVII corps had accomplished its mission—if its men could hold the ground they had reached.[40]

Ludendorff's midday pessimism dissipated as the tally of prisoners and booty increased. By the evening of August 29 at least 10,000 Russians had surrendered. Between 20,000 and 30,000 men, individual stragglers and fragments of battalions and companies from XIII and XV Corps, were still in the woods north of Neidenburg, but the army staff no longer considered them a real threat. The 2nd Army seemed for all practical purposes destroyed as a fighting force. The problems for the 30th, Hindenburg and Ludendorff were sure, would involve securing prisoners, collecting those Russians still free, and establishing a front against Rennenkampf.

The army orders for August 30, issued at 10:00 p.m., confirmed

306

that I Reserve Corps and the 37th Division were to form a line facing northwest on both sides of Allenstein and begin constructing field fortifications. The Goltz Division would secure the left of this position; the 1st Cavalry Division would move to Ortelsburg and cover its right. Unger's troops and the 41st and 3rd Reserve Divisions were to withdraw from the front, rest, and reorganize. The XVII Corps would continue barring the 2nd Army's way to the east, while the 5th *Landwehr* Brigade provided security against any attempt to break through to Neidenburg from the south. This last was not considered very likely, as the Russians in this sector were supposed to be in full retreat.[41]

There was also time for boasting. At 7:45 p.m. on August 29, Hindenburg reported to William II the destruction of the Russian 2nd Army. Flags, guns, and machine guns; paymasters' chests and an airplane, over 10,000 prisoners, testified to the magnitude of 8th Army's victory. He received in return imperial thanks in the name of the Fatherland.[42] A subsequent dispatch referred to the "victory at Allenstein." Von Stein's official announcement spoke of a battle "in the area of Gilgenburg and Ortelsburg." Hindenburg, however, asked the kaiser to permit it to be known as the Battle of Tannenberg. Wilhelm was pleased with the idea; Hoffmann's suggestion of the 28th became official.[43]

At 11:30 p.m. Ludendorff telephoned a slightly more sober message to OHL. Bad connections made him difficult to understand, but the thrust of his message was clear: victory. Three and a half Russian corps had been completely defeated; twenty or thirty thousand survivors and hundreds of abandoned cannon were there for the collecting. Eighth Army needed no more than two or three days' rest, then would be ready to repeat its performance against Rennenkampf.[44] Ten minutes later a coded dispatch was on its way to Austrian GHQ from the liaison officer at Hindenburg's headquarters. It too described whole corps surrounded by the Germans, with Russians surrendering in masses.[45]

The Russian center had fought well enough to deserve a better fate. Martos, responding to Samsonov's last orders, spent the night of August 28th/29th trying to reach a Neidenburg that he did not know was in German hands. He learned the truth at dawn, but spent the rest of the day dodging enemy patrols and never regained contact with any of his headquarters. Deprived of central control, the units of XV Corps and the 2nd Division retreated south and east, fighting the previously described series of stubborn but uncoordinated rear-guard actions against I Corps and the 41st Division. By nightfall the bulk of the troops still under command were in the woods north of Muschaken, their surviving officers trying to decide what to do next.

As for XIII Corps, its headquarters reached Kurken at noon on the 29th with what remained of its infantry straggling along behind. At 2:00 p.m. Kluyev's chief of staff returned from Orlau with new orders from Samsonov. Issued at 11:00 a.m., they provided for a "phased withdrawal." XV Corps and the 2nd Division would cover XIII Corps's march to Muschaken; Kluyev would in turn cover the retreat of the latter units across the frontier.

As a staff exercise these orders deserved a failing grade for passing the fighting elements of one corps across the lines of communication of another. But they had been issued almost in the face of the enemy. Kluyev believed—again—that 2nd Army headquarters must know what it was doing. He not only started his men south; for the second consecutive day he ordered a night march. This time the route lay through even denser woods whose few secondary roads were blocked beyond immediate remedy by the trains of XV Corps. Kluyev, his way south cut off, turned his column east.[46] At Kaltenborn it was fired on by German pickets—the men of the 5th Hussars.

The hussars, two and a half squadrons of them, had a paper strength of over 350. Straggling detachments and lame horses had reduced the actual number of men available for the firing line to about seventy. The troopers were accompanied by a field battery, but guns were more a source of weakness than of strength if they could not be properly supported. Too few in numbers to man a perimeter defense, the Germans instead established outposts on the main roads through the village. German cavalrymen were not as completely helpless afoot as their French counterparts, but they had no machine guns, no entrenching tools, and no bayonets. Regulations allowed them only forty rounds per man instead of the 150 carried by the infantry. That ammunition fast ran out as Russian detachments mounted probing attacks on the hussars' positions. Out of touch with higher headquarters, with no support in sight, the troopers faced a choice: either write their regiment's name in the history books with what was likely to be a heroic last stand, or mount, ride out, and live for later fights at better odds. Their commander wasted little time deciding on discretion as valor's better part. Hussars, after all, were supposed to be light cavalry! Leaving a dozen casualties behind them, the 5th evacuated Kaltenborn shortly before 6:00 a.m.—to the scarcely muted curses of their comrades from the artillery, forced to abandon to the Russians two guns whose crews fought to the last round before being overrun.[47]

Elsewhere in the woods, just outside of Kannwiesen, a battalion of the 35th Division's 21st Infantry provided a neat reverse lesson in tactical ambushes. The battalion had spent an uneasy night north of the village, its commander unwilling to involve his bone-tired men in a house-to-house fight that might well attract more Russian attention than he could handle. In his neglected prewar classic, *The Defence of Duffer's Drift*, British author Sir Ernest Swinton had argued that modern firepower offered infantry better ways of controlling a position than physically occupying it. Now Captain Tamms had a chance to prove the point. His four rifle companies counted only half their assigned strength, but were supported by two platoons of the regimental machine gun company. As dawn broke he saw long columns of Russian wagons moving through Kannwiesen on their way east. Within minutes four German machine guns and five hundred rifles turned the village streets into an impassable tangle of wrecked wagons and screaming horses. With every exit under fire, the Russian escort was unable to mount anything like a coordinated counterattack. A thousand of them surrendered on the spot. Eight hundred more fled the scene to fall into the hands of another battalion of the 21st, hurrying to the aid of its presumably desperate sister formation.[48]

The Russian main body, such as it was by then, turned south again, *faute de mieux*. The XIII Corps by this time had covered almost seventy kilometers through thick woods in forty hours, without either rations for the men or fodder for the horses. Water bottles were empty. Most of the men were out of ammunition. Many had abandoned their packs and "lost" their rifles. As the night waned the Russians, all order lost, straggled north towards no particular destination. As for Samsonov, after leaving XV Corps headquarters on the afternoon of the 28th the army commander went to Orlau, where he briefly met, as noted, the chief of staff of XIII Corps. He then decided to ride to Yanov, where the rear echelon of his headquarters was supposed to have gone, but found the road blocked by a mass of carts, wagons, and ambulances. He turned toward Willenburg hoping to contact his VI Corps, only to find the town in German hands. Any lingering hopes of restoring the situation by command decisions had long since vanished. Samsonov ordered his Cossack escort to save themselves while he and his staff tried to continue on foot. Through the night of the 29th/30th the officers blundered through the woods north of the Neidenburg-Willenberg highway. Weight and asthma slowed the general's movements and further lamed his spirit. Again and again Samsonov repeated that the disgrace was more than he could bear: "The Emperor trusted me." Finally he slipped aside in the dark. Minutes later a single pistol shot cracked out of the underbrush. Samsonov would never be called upon to explain the fate of his army.[49]

At 2:40 a.m. on August 30, 8th Army headquarters received further information about Rennenkampf's movements. According to these reports Zhilinski's injunction to move south did not seem to have taken effect. Instead the mass of the 1st Army was turning on Königsberg. Even its IV Corps, according to another intercepted radio dispatch, was apparently under orders to attack the Baltic fortress. Should the new information prove correct, the only threat from the north on August 30 would come from Rennenkampf's cavalry, and this was no threat at all.[50]

The staff felt correspondingly comfortable in turning to matters of interior administration. Hindenburg notified his corps commanders that since his appointment his orders had been frequently protested, ignored, or thwarted— "naturally with the best intentions." Because things had worked out satisfactorily did not mean that such insubordinate behavior was to be institutionalized. A word to the wise should be sufficient to avert sterner measures.

Communications and liaison were also major subjects of Hindenburg's concern. German troops had regularly fired on each other by mistake, and had been shelled by their own artillery. Now Hindenburg ordered the infantry to sew white patches on their knapsacks or the backs of their tunics, and instructed them to mark their forward positions by brightly colored cloths or boards. He accompanied these suggestions with the common-sense reminder that German soldiers wore helmets while Russians wore flat peaked caps—a difference that should assist the least-experienced artillery observer. The army commander's recommendation that the artillery should not allow an excessive distance to develop between its batteries and the infantry they were supporting showed slightly less appreciation of the problems of fire control in 1914. Guns pushed too far forward were frequently guns lost to enemy artillery. Nor did the forests in which so much of 8th Army's fighting took place give many suitable sites for battery positions—especially for the flat-trajectory cannon which still made up over three-fourths of the German field artillery.

Temporary panics might be difficult to avoid in modern war, but their effects could be limited by taking sensible precautions. Supply columns should be kept outside of the battle area. Soldiers spreading rumors of defeat were to be arrested and court-martialed. Men of the telephone detachments were not to discuss the general situation without direct orders from a superior. Hindenburg also reminded corps commanders that they were responsible for maintaining contact with, and thereby control over, their subordinates. Influenced by his memories of events at Scholtz's headquarters on August 27 and 28, he specifically warned against depending on the telephone to the exclusion of the old-fashioned dispatch rider. Some information was preferable to none at all.[51]

III

Apparently all that remained was mopping up. Nevertheless, for all of Samsonov's despair and Ludendorff's confidence, the fighting was far from over. The Russians might no longer be able to win the battle. It was still possible for them to avoid losing it, either directly, by breaking through the thin German cordon and breaking out the survivors of Samsonov's center, or indirectly, by intimidating and confusing a taut-stretched opponent into making mistakes in deployment or concentration. Neither possibility should be dismissed out of hand. German concerns for what their enemy *might* do had been amply evidenced since the beginning of the campaign. As for a breakthrough/breakout, the Russian soldier has time and again demonstrated his capacity to rise to a desperate occasion. What would be remembered of Stalingrad had the beleaguered 6th Army's command been willing to lunge towards Manstein's relief columns—which were no more formidable relative to their opposition than the Russian troops available outside the German cordon.

In particular, François remained concerned for his southern exposure. Ever since his corps had turned away from Soldau he had been expecting a Russian counterattack from that direction. After Artamonov's relief on August 29, General Sirelius of the 3rd Guard Division had assumed tactical command in the Soldau-Mlawa sector. His orders were to concentrate all available forces and attack Neidenburg immediately to relieve the 2nd Army's center. Rather than lose time collecting I Corps, he started his own division towards the objective, and throughout August 29 François received enough reports of the Russian advance to make him uneasy.[52]

The commander of I Corps was almost more disturbed by 8th Army's optimistic orders. They entirely ruled out the possibility of a Russian advance in force from the south. François was supposed to move his whole force north toward Jedwabno, both to complete the circle around the 2nd Army and for possible eventual use against Rennenkampf. François says in his memoirs that it was "lucky" that this document reached him too late to affect the corps orders for the 30th. In reality, it arrived in good time. François, once again going his own way, simply decided he needed more information before taking the risk of leaving his rear wide open.[53]

In this situation, the corps commander turned to his airmen. He was sufficiently assertive and sufficiently unconventional to feel more affinity for the lieutenants of Air Detachment 14 than was perhaps to be expected from one of his rank and responsibilities. A reconnaissance flight made with the last light of August 29 had reported a Russian brigade at Mlawa, and a regiment only fifteen kilometers from Neidenburg. François ordered his airmen to resume patrols at daybreak. At 6:00 a.m. on the 30th an air crew spotted a Russian column on the road from Mlawa to Neidenburg. The pilot tried to land at corps headquarters, but saw no suitably open ground. Rather than risk a crash the two officers agreed to return to their airfield, then drive to Neidenburg and deliver their information in person. They reached the town shortly after 8:30 a.m.

François had spent an anxious night. In an effort to cheer himself up he was inspecting the captured guns and wagons in the marketplace when at 9:15 a.m. another aircraft circled low and dropped another message. Lieutenants Hesse and Körner reported a Russian column of all arms advancing on Neidenburg from Mlawa—about a corps in strength on the basis of the road space it occupied. This confirmed the earlier sighting. Even worse, when observed at 9:10 a.m. the Russian vanguard had been only six kilometers south of Neidenburg itself.[54]

The two reports were an unpleasant shock. François had been expecting a Russian counterattack, but was amazed that such a strong force had come so close to his positions unobserved. The enemy was indeed too close for written orders. François sent an officer by auto to summon Major Schlimm, commanding the Neidenburg garrison. Another of I Corps's staff cars went to the 2nd Division with orders for Falk to turn his men about, advance south, and attack the Russian left. Initially François refused to disturb the 1st Division along the high road. In retrospect, he declared he was never anything but confident that I Corps could check this new attack without abandoning the encirclement. In reality, by the time Conta's strung-out formations could be concentrated, the fighting was likely to be over one way or another.

Just as François finished issuing his orders, Schlimm reported to the marketplace. The two batteries originally assigned to his force had left during the night. But even without artillery, Schlimm proposed to make a stand with his two infantry battalions along a low range of hills south of the town. François ordered the major to hold at all costs—or at least long enough to force the Russians to deploy from line of march into fighting formation. His promise of immediate reinforcements rang slightly hollow to the men on the spot, particularly when corps headquarters drove out of town as the first Russian shells began falling on the marketplace.

As Schlimm's men marched south, François halted at the neighboring village of Gregersdorf. His first act was to find a phone and inform both Falk and 8th Army headquarters of the new situation in more detail.[55] His superiors were taken by surprise. At 9:00 a.m. army command had once more boasted by telephone to OHL of complete success, with the prospect of an even larger bag of prisoners than originally expected.[56] An hour later it learned of Lieutenant Hesse's sighting of Russians outside Neidenburg. And bad news kept coming. An aircraft of Air Detachment 16 returned from a patrol to report Russians—at least a division of them—advancing on Ortelsburg in Mackensen's sector.[57] Given the time the report took to reach army headquarters, the Russians could easily have overrun Ortelsburg and opened an escape route for Kluyev and Martos before Hindenburg and Ludendorff knew of their presence.

Air reconnaissance in 1914 resembled ULTRA in 1942. It simultaneously generated skepticism and was credited with magical accuracy. Both attitudes could and did exist not only side by side, but in the same officers. To date 8th Army's airmen had never been proved wrong enough to be summarily dismissed. Instead of ordering a second mission to confirm the advance on Ortelsburg, 8th Army headquarters combined the single report with the information received from François, and concluded that the Russians were advancing in force from the east and the south in order to break the German ring around the 2nd Army. It was what they would have attempted had the situations been reversed.

In focussing its attention on Rennenkampf, the 8th Army staff had neglected 2nd Army's remaining fighting power. But how best to cope with a threat that seemed all the greater for being unexpected? The I Corps was extended along a day's march worth of roads from Neidenburg to Willenberg. The XVII Corps was even more widely scattered, its men even more exhausted. Army headquarters saw the attack on Neidenburg as the most immediately dangerous. The concentration against Rennenkampf, so carefully developed the night before, was tossed aside as waste paper. Instead Grünert, the coolest head among the junior staff officers, was sent north to deliver orders for Unger's troops and the Goltz Division to march south and support François. Scholtz was ordered to turn the 41st Division, which had been moving northeast as originally ordered, southward once more, with the 3rd Reserve Division following it. The 37th Division was ordered east to reinforce XVII Corps.

It was noon by the time the new instructions were on their way to 8th Army's subordinate commands. In the interval, the phone line to I

Corps had been cut by Russian artillery fire. François compensated by sending the airmen who first saw the Russians to Osterode by car, where they reported personally to Hindenburg and Ludendorff. Their intelligence was by then over six hours old. No further information about the Russian advance on Ortelsburg had reached Osterode. Army headquarters was still almost completely in the dark.[58]

As for the commanders on the spot, by noon François had assembled only a half-dozen battalions on the high ground north of Neidenburg. This force, however, was supported by no fewer than sixteen artillery batteries, including seven of heavy howitzers, drawn from everywhere in the corps sector. With that mass of guns behind them, François was confident his infantry could hold its position against anything up to an army corps. But as the day passed the Russians failed to appear. Major Schlimm's two battalions, reinforced by odd lots of cyclists and gunners, were still—somehow—holding on south of Neidenburg.

Defeat had made their enemy cautious. Long-range artillery fire from François's new positions slowed the attack even more. By 3:45 p.m. the fighting line was three kilometers outside the town. Schlimm's infantry put up a resistance determined enough to deter the Russians from using their superior numbers in one quick, overwhelming rush. Instead they sought a way around, and made no haste in the process. Not until 6:00 p.m. did Schlimm report to François that he was outflanked and in danger of being overrun. Shortly afterwards all communications with him were lost. His small force continued, however, to delay the Russians by making a fighting withdrawal through Neidenburg. Not until 9:00 p.m. did elements of the 3rd Guard Division occupy and secure the town. Schlimm's valiant defense had bought François most of a day.[59]

The bulk of I Corps spent that day rounding up Russian prisoners—a process more easily described than accomplished. Through the night of August 29/30, bursts of rifle and machine gun fire, the screams of terrified horses, and the uglier sounds of men dying had echoed everywhere along the Neidenburg-Willenberg road. In the midst of disaster the Russian artillery lived up to a tradition dating back to Peter the Great. Batteries, sections, and individual crews fought it out to the muzzle until shot to pieces by German guns or overrun by German infantry. In one sector dawn found a silent Russian battery, its cannoneers shot or bayoneted to a man, with fifty German bodies heaped in front of the guns as grim tokens of the last rounds.

Max Hoffmann later declared categorically that German troops would have broken through I Corps's thin cordon, but there was no ammunition, no food, no water, no orders. The Russians were impeded by their own transport as abandoned wagons, mired guns, and dead horses piled up on the paths and trails. To leave the shelter of the forest was to run a withering gauntlet of fire. Nor was it always easy to surrender. German detachments seeking to disarm prospective prisoners found themselves taken under fire by Russians more belligerent or less aware of their situation. In at least one case they responded by mowing down the

Russians to their front with machine guns, white flags or not, until all shooting in the sector stopped.

By the afternoon of August 30, XV Corps dissolved on the road between Ruttkowen and Saddek. Most of its men sat down and waited for the Germans to come and get them. The unfortunate General Martos spent the morning dodging German patrols until he finally took the risk of trying to reach the Russian frontier by car. His driver was promptly shot by a picket of the 43rd Infantry. Martos suffered the supreme indignity of a general: being captured apart from his troops.[60] Taken to Osterode, he was quartered for the night in the same hotel that sheltered the 8th Army staff. Ludendorff, like Eisenhower in Tunisia thirty years later, had no interest in offering the traditional courtesies to a defeated enemy. Hindenburg took pains personally to greet his adversary, praising the bravery of his corps and expressing regret at meeting under such circumstances. As Hindenburg took his hand, Martos burst into tears.[61]

But were the captured guns, the thousands of prisoners, merely Bellona's jest? Shortly after noon on August 30 an aircraft from Osterode brought François a message that reinforcements were on the way.[62] None had appeared by nightfall. Once again the 8th Army suffered from the yawning gap between intelligence information and the practical capacity to respond to that information. Von Staabs for one protested vigorously that the men of his 37th Division were simply too tired to move. By this time Scholtz and his division commanders had acquired a certain reputation as what British Field-Marshal Montgomery would in a later war call "belly-achers," but this was no time to weed out senior command assignments. Grudgingly, army headquarters agreed to Staabs's suggestion that the march be delayed until the next day.

Staabs was at least honest in his reservations. Other commanders simply fudged. Goltz reached the area west of Michalken before stopping. Unger's men bivouacked in Frankenau. The 41st Division halted northeast of that town. The 3rd Reserve Division received its marching orders so late that Morgen postponed its advance entirely until the next day.[63] Nevertheless at 7:30 p.m. on August 30 army command notified François that he would be in tactical command of an attack to be made the next morning against the Russians around Neidenburg. He was authorized to issue any orders he thought necessary, though army headquarters wanted the Goltz Division and the 3rd Reserve Division held as far north of Neidenburg as possible just in case Rennenkampf complicated the situation by a surprise appearance.[64]

Nor were the encircled Russians completely helpless. During the afternoon four battalions of Conta's 1st Brigade, supported by a battalion of the 52nd Field Artillery, had pushed northward into the forest from Muschaken. The operation seemed a walkover. Whole Russian companies led by their officers came in under white flags—so many that the Germans disarmed them and sent them to the rear without escort. Cheering and laughing, the column reached a comfortable-looking meadow just outside the village of Malagofen around 5:00 p.m. The Germans halted, stacked arms, and doffed their equipment. Cooking fires were started, quarter-masters were preparing to issue rations, when a burst of Russian rifle fire ended the idyllic maneuver picture.

Frightened horses dragged guns and wagons in every direction. Riflemen and machine gunners blazed away at random. Officers who had no idea what was happening gave orders anyway. A few company commanders rallied enough men to form a skirmish line and led it into the woods. The brigade commander, Brigadier-General von Trotha, joined the charge with the color party of the I/41st Infantry. The flag was an obvious target and Trotha went down fatally wounded before taking twenty steps. Two battalion commanders were killed trying to rally their men. A battery was temporarily abandoned in the confusion. Colonel Schönfeld of the 41st Infantry finally had his headquarters bugler blow "Rally" again and again. Squad by squad, the Germans straggled into Malagofen and began to sort themselves out. Firing continued until nightfall, with Germans shooting each other more often than Russians. The Russian detachment that had started it all was long since gone, its men never to know what they had done to their conquerors.[65]

The incident at Malagofen suggested the encircled Russians could still fight. François slept with his pistol by his side. Morgen, who normally prided himself on his calm, was awakened during the night by loud shouts that the Russians were attacking. Discovering that a zealous orderly had taken away his clothes, the division commander ran outdoors in his nightshirt, strapping on his Luger as he went.[66]

Mackensen's corps also spent an anxious day wondering what had become of the Russians they had faced and beaten on August 26. Here chronology must be modified in the interests of clarity. Most of the Russian VI Corps reached the Ortelsburg area by the morning of August 29. Regimental commanders urged the necessity for a day's rest. Communications with army headquarters were episodic, and Blagoveschensky was not anxious to report his disaster in detail. He was saved, at least for the moment, by Samsonov's last order to VI Corps, issued on the 28th while the army commander was riding to meet Martos. It was to hold the Ortelsburg area "at all costs." Blagoveschensky seized the chance to remain passive, even when German vanguards occupied Ortelsburg itself.[67]

His army corps faced no more than companies and shadows. The German detachment from the 35th Division that had arrived in Ortelsburg during the night of August 28/29 left the town on the morning of the 29th and took the road to Willenburg. This was a calculated risk on the part of its commander, Brigadier-General von Hahn. The nearest German troops, a half-dozen companies of the 176th Infantry, were still far back on the road. Hahn's superior, Major-General Hennig, was correspondingly and uncomfortably surprised when he and his staff drove into Ortelsburg at 1:00 p.m. on the 29th to find only a cavalry detachment trying to keep control of a town still full of Russian stragglers. Within minutes of Hennig's arrival Russian patrols, elements of the 4th Cavalry Division, gingerly entered Ortelsburg's outskirts. Were they an isolated force or the vanguard of a counterattack? It was no time for heroics. Hennig and his staff officers abandoned Ortelsburg at top speed under Russian fire and drove north looking for reinforcements.

By the time they encountered the vanguards of the 1st Cavalry Brigade, the 176th Infantry had reached the scene. The regiment was a drill sergeant's nightmare. Packs long since abandoned, cartridge belts slung around their necks, the men marched along in a column of flocks, gnawing on chunks of bread obtained from village bakeries and houses by an enterprising reserve lieutenant. But they retained enough energy to clear the Russians out of Ortelsburg by 9:00 p.m.

His cavalry's brief success inspired even the supine Blagoveschensky. During the night of August 29/30 elements of VI Corps, about a division supported by some heavy artillery, began advancing towards Ortelsburg from the east and north. It was this force that was spotted by Air Detachment 16. The Russians were indecisive and hesitant, unwilling to press home an attack. Nevertheless the position of the Germans occupying the town was serious. The cavalry had withdrawn the previous evening rather than risk being surprised in bivouac. Hennig had his headquarters staff and six understrength infantry companies—not a single artillery piece or machine gun. One house after another burst into flames as Russian guns found the range, but Hennig refused to abandon Ortelsburg a second time. Instead he sent messengers in every direction requesting support.[68]

Army headquarters meanwhile had forwarded the air report of Russian troops near Ortelsburg to Mackensen. The commander of XVII Corps received the information at 11:20 a.m. on August 30, and found himself once again at square one. His 35th Division was supposed to be making contact with François's I Corps and rounding up stragglers in the forest around Neidenburg. Instead its commander, at least, was miles north of his assigned sector, playing the hero in a surrounded outpost. The 36th Division was supposed to be acting as a backstop against Russians coming from the north or west. Now Mackensen felt constrained to order that formation to turn eastward, meet the threat from Ortelsburg, and put Hennig back at the head of his own troops where he belonged.[69]

Good intentions at higher levels were no substitute for firepower on the line. Hennig's handful of men were counting their cartridges and eyeing their bayonets when, in a scene more appropriate to a Hollywood battle than an East Prussian one, two squadrons of the 10th *Jäger zu Pferde* rode through heavy Russian fire into Ortelsburg. They had left Willenburg earlier that morning, sent north by Schmettau to find and engage the enemy. The lieutenant-colonel in command heard the guns and marched to their sound as a Prussian officer was supposed to do. His hundred or so carbines were welcome enough on the skirmish line. Even better were the shrapnel rounds of the field battery he brought with him.

By noon slightly more substantial help arrived in the form of Ortelsburg's original conquerors. Von Hahn's detachment had made such slow progress south that one of Hennig's messengers was able to reach it and turn it around. By this time it was a real flying column—a machine-gun company, a squadron of cavalry, and a battalion of field howitzers. The few infantrymen who remained with it were riding captured Cossack horses. At the trot and the gallop, Hahn brought his men the thirteen kilometers to Ortelsburg and took the Russians under fire from positions south of the town. A lieutenant of the 176th led twenty-five men, the remnants of his platoon, in a counterattack just as the shells of eighteen German howitzers began bursting on the Russian positions. And in what seemed like a miracle to the Germans on the spot, the Russians began to retreat east and southeast.[70]

This maneuver was less a response to German boldness than a reaction to the Northwest Front's only direct effort to influence the developing disaster. At 11:00 a.m. Zhilinski's chief of staff had tele-graphed an order to VI Corps. Blagoveschensky was ordered to cooperate with Samsonov by concentrating his corps at Willenberg! He immediately broke off the fighting at Ortelsburg and started his men south, only to be checked during the night of the 30th/31st by another front order—this one to withdraw across the Russian frontier. Once again Blagoveschensy obeyed with alacrity. The surviving Germans were too few to do more than catch their breaths and give thanks to providence.

François, like Mackensen, respected Russian powers of recovery. His orders for August 31, issued at 5:30 a.m. on that day, were for Goltz and Unger's troops, the 3rd Reserve Division, the 41st Division, *and* the 5th *Landwehr* Brigade to advance against the Russians around Neiden-burg. If all went well, he reasoned, this mass of troops should close in on the town from three sides and end the last Russian threat in the south once and for all. But by the time his orders reached their destinations, elements of the 41st Division had reached Neidenburg and found it empty. The Russians occupying the town had retreated during the night.

Sirelius had learned from survivors of the disaster to the Russian center and calculated the approximate strength of the German forces moving against him. His decision, generally condemned, cost him his command. Had Sirelius moved faster on the 29th, had he risked his superior numbers in overrunning Schlimm's battalions when the Russians in the pocket still retained their organization, he might have opened a corridor for some of the trapped men. His critics, however, discounted the lessons taught since the opening of the campaign. Prewar Russian doctrine might stress attacking off the line of march. Wartime Russian experience, however brief, suggested improvisation was a recipe for disas-ter against the Germans. At least Sirelius was able to draw consequences and pull his division out of the German noose. With the Russians in his sector again in flight to the south, François ordered his own corps to continue mopping up while notifying 8th Army that its reserves were free for service as required.[71]

The roundup of the 2nd Army's broken center continued through-out August 31. Skirmish lines and small columns of XVII Corps pushed their way through the forest from the north, collecting stragglers as they went. An Orthodox chaplain negotiated the surrender of several thousand exhausted soldiers to Schmettau just outside Willenberg. At 11:00 a.m. Kluyev himself handed over another thousand men to a detachment of I Corps. Hour by hour the numbers grew. Hundreds, then thousands of men sat glumly under the guard of a few German riflemen. Riderless or unharnessed horses wandered about. The detritus of a broken army, ambulances, supply wagons, telephone carts, piled up on the Neidenburg-Willenberg road. Farm houses filled with captured officers. A village school saw teachers and pupils give way to a half-dozen Russian generals and their staffs. The plunder of a campaign found its way into German knapsacks or pockets. Every Russian officer appeared to carry his own personal hair-clippers somewhere in his baggage. Linen, lingerie, and silverware, looted from houses on the Russian line of march, called forth ironic admiration for the taste of Muscovites who seldom fell prey to *kitsch*. Even Martos's car, carefully searched, turned up a large and expensive silver bowl belonging to the local *Landrat*. Martos denied any knowledge of the object. His chauffeur was not available for interrogation.[72]

Detachments and individual Russians continued to straggle in and surrender or to lay down their arms after a brief exchange of honor-saving shots. Other parties, bolder or luckier, made their way across the border. But the only organized formation that broke through the German cordon was a cavalry brigade reduced to about two hundred riders—all that remained intact of Samsonov's main body.[73]

The Germans seemed almost as disorganized by victory as the Russians by defeat. The I and XVII Corps in particular had companies and battalions scattered everywhere from Neidenburg and Ortelsburg to the Russian frontier, securing booty and guarding prisoners. Cleaning up proved almost as much a challenge as winning the battle. The sandy roads of the region were blocked in every direction by destroyed or abandoned guns, caissons, carts, and wagons. Dead Russians were beginning to bloat in the August heat. Wounded Russians were being combed out of the woods by search parties. Tens of thousands of prisoners had to be evacuated to Germany on a railroad network straining to support a developing two-front war. They had to be fed without drawing on supplies destined for the 8th Army; no one took seriously the kaiser's shocking suggestion that the captives simply be driven into a barren peninsula in the Baltic and left to starve.[74]

On the evening of August 30 Ludendorff tempered his boasts to OHL with praise for the tenacity of the Russians and warnings that the battle in the south might not yet be over. But by the afternoon of the 31st he was reporting the "complete destruction" of the enemy. Sixty thousand prisoners, he declared, were in German hands, with more certain to come as stragglers were rounded up. Three Russian corps had been annihilated; the commanders of two of them, Martos of XV and Kluyev of XIII, were prisoners. The battle, Ludendorff declared, was over. Eighth Army was ready for new operations. As for Rennenkampf's army, it appeared to be going nowhere.

This did not stop Ludendorff from requesting reinforcements. However strongly he may have denied his need for XI Corps and the Guard Reserve Corps while the battle was going on, Ludendorff on the 31st declared that "in spite of the victory" their arrival would now be welcome. He also requested heavy artillery for use against the Russian fortresses in the interior. Next stop—St. Petersburg.[75]

In response the 8th Army shook off its brief victory euphoria. Staff officers began studying maps and charts, their eye on the next moves. Stragglers rejoined their units, or were delivered by the military police. Replacements arrived from provincial depots themselves often disrupted by the invasion. Lightly wounded men showed off their bandages. Talk of Iron Crosses swept the ranks. The dead were buried in those neat little cemeteries that were the German army's pride: fifty here and a hundred there, neatly fenced and marked. Not yet for them the anonymity of Verdun or the Somme, where cynics and realists sang to the tune of *Zapfenstreich*, "Auf Wiedersehen ins Massengrab, wir sehen uns wieder ins Massengrab. . . ." That time was coming.

PART IV

THE BITTER FRUITS
OF VICTORY

10
Opportunities and Illusions

The details of the Russian disaster at Tannenberg remain varied. Eighth Army headquarters was too busy to tally jots and tittles. On the Russian side nobody was left to keep records. The German official history gives a total of 92,000 Russian prisoners, plus approximately 50,000 dead and wounded. These are the figures most frequently cited, and while the Germans could hardly be accused of understatement, their numbers are probably reasonably reliable. In operational terms, the Russian 2nd Army had been annihilated. Its center corps were destroyed. Only two thousand stragglers from XV Corps and the 2nd Division escaped the German noose. The XIII Corps had three thousand men left in its two divisions. The I and VI Corps could muster at most the equivalent of a division each, and both formations were badly demoralized. N. N. Golovine gives an elaborate breakdown of the prisoners taken by each German corps in an attempt to prove that the 2nd Army did not really surrender as a unit. But 90,000 prisoners constituted a self-evident fact.[1]

I

On closer examination, however, the data begins to blur. Two Russian corps had been destroyed, and two more badly mauled. But the Russian army of 1914 mobilized no fewer than thirty-seven active corps, to say nothing of independent brigades, reserve formations, and enough individual replacements to begin reconstituting 2nd Army's decimated formations almost immediately. Losses of guns and equipment, while serious, were not out of proportion to the forces engaged.

323

Tannenberg, in other words, was by no stretch of the imagination a "battle of annihilation" in any material sense relative to Russia's numbers. Nor did the losses represent the kind of cost exacted in a later war at Stalingrad and Kursk, where the cutting edge of an already overmatched army was irreparably dulled. Tannenberg's significance is better sought in the realm of will. At the start of the campaign the Russian Northwest Front was reckoned by its own command as having a two-to-one superiority. The Russians had the further advantage of deploying principally active units, while almost half of the 8th Army was composed of ill-equipped reserve and fortress troops. The stage seemed set for an overwhelming victory, and the effect of Tannenberg was therefore even more crushing. By 1917 the then war minister A. J. Guchkov, testifying before the provisional government's commission of inquiry, said that he had decided the war was lost "as early as August, 1914." He said further that he had been made to feel this way by his "first impressions at the front"—that is, by Samsonov's defeat.[2] If this was the effect of Tannenberg on such a vigorous statesman, what must it have been on weaker spirits?

Tannenberg affected Russia's allies as well—particularly Great Britain. In 1914 the British government realized the necessity of cooperating with its entente partners to avert a German victory. But Britain suspected the long-term objectives of her friends almost as much as the immediate intentions of her enemy. Memories of past imperial rivalries, concerns for the future welfare of Britain's empire and Europe's balance of power generated a significant body of opinion asserting that Britain could best assist her allies by providing money and arms rather than men.

This policy of "business as usual" had enough of perfidious Albion about it to have at best limited appeal on the continent. Its success depended on the ability and the willingness of France and Russia to stand against the German onslaught with no more than nominal direct support from their third partner. After Tannenberg neither the British nor the Russian government entertained that kind of faith in the tsar's empire. Britain's increasing commitment to a land war in Europe during 1915–16 was to a significant degree instrumental—a gesture that allies were not being left to their own resources, and one meant to show abandonment of Britain's original strategy for conducting a great European war.[3]

If victory has many fathers, defeat too is rarely an orphan. Its roots are sought so assiduously that when the critics are finished, every aspect of the vanquished military system and the socio-political order supporting it have been presented in such a negative context that future generations wonder how such a ramshackle society and such a patchwork army ever dared try conclusions in battle. While the most familiar examples remain France in 1870 and 1940, the France of Zola's *La Débacle* and Marc Bloch's *Strange Defeat*, Tsarist Russia takes a strong second place in the literature, and Tannenberg plays a key role in that literature.

Though most of the senior Russian officers involved were re-employed, a number of divisional and regimental commanders had their careers broken early. This gave them ample time to tell their stories with

324

memories sharpened, if not always rendered more accurate, by idleness. The success of the Russian Revolution offered still another reason for concentrating on Tannenberg. A generation of officers forced into exile and poverty found accounts of this great German victory from the other side of the hill were reasonably marketable in central Europe—not exactly best-sellers, but worth a few hundred marks in royalties and publishers' advances. Postwar Russian writers, the most recent and familiar being Alexander Solzhenitsyn, continue to find Tannenberg a convenient metaphor for the collapse of a doomed system.

In such a context the initial German response to their victory seems significantly mundane. The first reports of Tannenberg were almost lost in the excitement of the developing western front. To the men in the headquarters and on the fighting lines in Lorraine or Picardy, tales of a whole army destroyed and tens of thousands of prisoners taken seemed exercises in fantasy—not least because such triumphs had eluded them. At OHL the picture was clearer. As early as August 28, Tappen noted in his diary that "victory in the east appears to be an accomplished fact." By the 31st Wenninger, whose attention had been distracted for several days by an inspection tour of the Bavarian army, was able to write that the results of the victory were growing by the hour, with 60,000 prisoners already counted.[4]

For the 8th Army's staff any desire to relax, whether among the rank and file or on the part of their commanders, was a threat to be fought with every possible moral weapon. The Russian 1st Army was still virtually intact and little more than a day's forced march from the German rear. Max Hoffmann apologized to his wife for being too busy to write, excusing himself by describing a work schedule that kept him from sleeping more than two hours a night.[5] He and Ludendorff were at their professional best during the first days of September in redeploying their weary men to the north against Rennenkampf. Reinforced by the two corps from the western theater, the Germans began their attack on September 7. In many ways it was a reprise of the earlier fighting. Mackensen's corps once again suffered ruinous casualties in frontal attacks against prepared Russian positions around Lötzen. François repeated his flank maneuver at Gumbinnen from the other direction, the south. This time, as I Corps drove deep into the Russian rear, Mackensen's divisions finally broke through their front. With five thousand prisoners and sixty guns in German hands, with two veteran corps poised to roll up the Russian flank, another Tannenberg seemed in the making.

Its failure to materialize indicated once again that great victories depend on the quality of one's enemies. Rennenkampf's right and center corps not only held their positions but mounted a series of local counterattacks fierce enough to alarm XI Corps on the German left wing. This formation had not been heavily engaged in the west. Its regiments were still recovering physically from the march into France and the enervating train ride across Germany. Its commanders had not yet taken the measure of their adversaries. But neither Ludendorff nor Hindenburg were any more willing to take risks than they had been at Tannenberg. On September 11, army headquarters ordered Mackensen and François to close towards the north and provide direct support for XI Corps instead of attempting to envelop the Russian left.

The decision reflected a general belief at 8th Army headquarters that the Russians were preparing to fight it out as Samsonov had done two weeks earlier. Zhilinski, at least, had intended Rennenkampf to stand his ground and deter German pursuit of the 2nd Army's remnants. Rennenkampf for his part was worried about both his flanks. The prospects of a sortie from Königsberg, perhaps reinforced from the sea, initially concerned him almost as much as any threat from 8th Army. Once François's move against the Russian left became clear Rennenkampf acted decisively if unheroically. He ordered a general retreat. In the context of Samsonov's disaster, discretion seemed by far the better part of valor. His corps and division commanders, eager to avoid the German buzz saw, forced the pace. Withdrawing as far as twenty-five miles a day, the Russians literally ran faster than the Germans could chase them. Eighth Army's men, footsore and exhausted, lagged behind on the sandy roads. Periodic efforts to send the army's two cavalry divisions forward in independent pursuit proved vain because of the troopers' inability to get forward along roads blocked for miles by abandoned carts and wagons. No one in the Russian supply services wanted to be the last man on German soil. Instead teamsters cut traces and rode to safety on their draft horses. Others simply took to the forests. Pushing through the mess they left behind was well-nigh impossible even for fresh troops.[6]

By mid-September, only rear guards and stragglers remained of the great Russian invasion. If Rennenkampf's army had managed to escape with its structure intact, it had lost 150 guns and all its transport. Its units would need a good deal of work before they would again amount to much as combat troops. But an indication that this double victory was to be something other than an immediately recognized world-historical event came on September 14, when 8th Army's signal troops opened lines of communication from the new headquarters in Insterburg to OHL and to the Austrian high command. Since arriving in the east, Hindenburg and Ludendorff had been too preoccupied with their own problems to pay systematic attention to developments on other fronts. Now they learned the details of the Schlieffen Plan's failure, of the French counterattacks and the German withdrawal that constituted the Battle of the Marne.[7]

More seriously and more immediately, the German commanders also discovered that the Austrian advance into the Polish salient had been a high road to disaster. Conrad had sent four armies marching into Galicia. Successful small-scale battles along the frontier obscured the fact that the Austrian lines of advance were extrinsic, with their armies actually marching away from each other. On August 23 the Russians counterattacked at Lemberg. Within a week the Austrians were in a retreat that by mid-September turned to a rout bringing the Russians almost to the frontier of Hungary. In the process the Austrian army lost a third of its fighting strength—a quarter-million dead and wounded, over 100,000 prisoners. Included in the casualties were a disproportionate number of career officers and NCOs, the cadres on which a polyglot army depended heavily for its cohesion.[8] While Austria-Hungary was far from the military cipher of legend in the war's later years, Winston Churchill's judgment that Conrad broke his army's heart and used it up in less than a month nevertheless stands as an epitaph for the Habsburg Empire's status as a great power.[9]

The Austrian collapse ended any hope of exploiting the German victories in East Prussia. Instead Hindenburg, Ludendorff, and the bulk of 8th Army—now renumbered the 9th—were transferred south, into Silesia, to support their ally directly and secure their own frontier from invasion. In an operation facilitated by clumsy Russian efforts at redeployment, the Germans drove to the Vistula River by October 6, threatening Warsaw itself. But the Russians were too strong, the Germans too weak, the Austrians too crippled, to sustain the offensive's momentum. By the end of October the Germans had retreated almost to their original start lines. And within days the Russian army in turn mounted its best-coordinated offensive of the war to date, rolling through Poland almost to the Silesian border. Once again Ludendorff used the railroads to shift his Tannenberg veterans, this time northward into Posen on the right flank of the Russian advance. But the German counterthrust into the Russian rear, towards the city of Łodz, provided an object lesson in the risks of consistently underestimating an adversary. This time the Russians held, rallied, and counterattacked, isolating an entire corps. With memories of Tannenberg and fears of a Tannenberg in reverse throbbing at all levels of command, the Germans fought their way out of the encirclement.[10]

As winter set in and fronts stabilized, evaluations began. Tannenberg was the first battle between two great empires in what was expected to be an off-the-shelf, come-as-you-are war. Such a conflict is a corresponding test of professionalism. How well did the adversaries prepare for the contingencies they expected? More importantly, how successful were they in maintaining the initiative? This question is particularly important in a war's first stages. As the Army of Northern Virginia demonstrated after Gettysburg and the Wehrmacht after Kursk, an experienced, worked-in army can damage even a significantly superior adversary to the point of exhaustion by ripostes. An army first taking the field after a long period of peace can put no such trust in either its fighting power or its powers of improvisation. It is impossible to determine precisely which officers and units will perform up to their responsibilities, which will prove hopeless, and which will develop with seasoning—if seasoning is an affordable luxury. This fact enhances the importance of taking a first battle to the enemy, not necessarily by incessant offensive action, but by constraining him to fight your way.[11]

In this context the discrepancies between the German and the Russian armies in East Prussia were by no means as great as myth and history suggest. Both fought about as they expected to fight, and faced no major surprises. Tactically the adversaries were reasonably well matched. The fighting was on terms even enough that the Russians' consistent hopes of turning around the campaign by winning the next day's action were by no means ill-founded, especially since the Germans' flexibility at platoon and company levels was accompanied by a corresponding instability. The Germans' proneness to panic when surprised, or to break unpredictably and all at once after a day's hard fighting, offered significant opportunities for an enemy able to take advantage of them. The repeated successes of German officers in rallying their men and bringing them back into the firing line owed much to their being left undisturbed in their work.

In contrast to the German situation, the Russian soldiers were appreciably better than their officers. In attack they overran positions by weight of numbers; in defense they were likely to die before they ran. But they tended, for good and ill, to stay where they were placed. The men of both Samsonov's and Rennenkampf's armies were easier to outmaneuver than to outfight. And that fact in turn reflected the Russians' essential command failure: commitment to a strategy of maneuver, a strategy that paid more attention to lines on a map than to the enemy's presence in the field.

In making this commitment, the Russian command at all levels was guilty of misunderstanding the essential nature of its tool. The Russian army was a broadsword. It could not be used like a rapier. It could not fight like even a blurred carbon copy of the German. And as a result of the friction generated by false expectations, it sacrificed too many of its concrete advantages. Rennenkampf's often-cited diliatoriness was less significant in this respect than the misplaced focus on operational flexibility of Samsonov and his corps commanders, who consistently gave their German opposite numbers the thing they most needed: time to recover from shocks and surprises.

German performances in the Tannenberg campaign are best described as professional. The 8th Army operated within expected frameworks, and sustained a command structure that in turn made sustainable demands on subordinates' capabilities. At corps and army levels the Germans' reaction time was consistently within the Russians' loop of initiative. The German conduct of operations also showed the importance of will power at a period when the availability of information far outweighed the capacity to act on that information. The real importance of the often-cited radio interceptions was as a security blanket, helping army and corps staffs to execute decisions already made. For the Germans as much as for the Russians, attempts to change plans too often resulted in dangerous levels of confusion. And when a German corps commander was left altogether on his own, like François at Stallupönen or Mackensen at Gumbinnen, the results were not much more impressive than those achieved by their Russian counterparts.

Administratively the Germans were far more successful than the Russians in keeping their troops supplied. Logistics are particularly important to citizen armies in their first weeks of war—and only partly because the men in the ranks have not yet learned to look after themselves. War brings with it a basic uncertainty, an ongoing fear that can be at least be reduced by everyday proof that the system works well enough to deliver the rations.

Tannenberg's significance, however, transcended the operational level. Above all the victory lent domestic credence to Germany's definition of her war as fundamentally defensive. Prewar advocates of militia systems or citizen armies justified them largely on the grounds that citizen soldiers could not be mobilized for participation in aggressive wars as readily as professionals or mercenaries.[12] Their position was partly validated by the deliberate, not to say desperate, efforts of the continental combatants to present the war of 1914 as a defensive measure. The sense of protecting home and hearth was an important element of morale in all of the conscript armies. Its waning or overshadowing prefigured collapse, whether in 1916 Russia, 1917 France, or 1918 Germany.

This was a sense particularly difficult to sustain in a Germany whose main armies stood deep in enemy territory from the war's first days. The letters and diaries of the reservists, draftees, and war volunteers who made up the vast bulk of the fighting forces indicate a significant dichotomy between an intellectual conviction of Germany's righteous cause and the pragmatic reality that it was French and Belgian towns that were being destroyed, French and Belgian civilians coping with the burdens of military occupation.[13] Tannenberg, however, was fought on German soil. The destruction accompanying the Russian invasion, mild enough by the standards of 1632, 1812, or 1945, served as an early warning of what the Fatherland might expect if its defenders faltered.

By September 1, Germany's media began to react. Tannenberg made headlines in every corner of the Reich. It inspired speeches, parades, and votes of thanks. Such a mystique developed about no other battles of World War I. One of the most enduring legends pictured an old general who spent the years of his retirement devising a gigantic trap for a Russian invasion, exploring paths and sounding the bottoms of marshes in which the enemy was to be engulfed and then fulfilling his dream in 1914.[14] Another, this one slightly more plausible, developed as the shadow of Ludendorff grew behind Hindenburg. It described a masterly plan for a second Cannae, improvised and dictated by Ludendorff as the train bore him eastward.[15] Ludendorff, never a man to be modest about his own achievements, himself denied this by recounting in his memoirs a conversation which he had in October 1914 with the Spanish military attaché. That officer asked if Tannenberg had been fought according to a set plan, and was extremely surprised when Ludendorff told him it had not.[16] But the myth defied suppression.

Tannenberg also created heroes. A German military historian once said that it would be possible to fill a room with generals who claimed the credit, particularly after 1918 when there was so little credit to go around.[17] Even Prittwitz suggested that *he* was the real architect of victory by his decision to break off the retreat and turn south against Samsonov.[18]

329

A few candidates stand out from the pack. Winston Churchill's history of the "unknown war" in the east was long a standard English account. He especially admired François as a man who knew how to win battles the wrong way while his superiors were losing them the right way. According to Churchill "the glory of Tannenberg must forever go to François" for his "rare combination" of prudence and audacity in his operations in the south. François showed "true soldierly genius" in twice acting on his justly founded convictions and defying Ludendorff to win a victory against orders.[19] The validity of the conclusion is, however, called into question by substituting "Churchill" for "François" and "Gallipoli" for "Tannenberg." The result is an autobiographical statement influenced by wish-fulfillment, as opposed to a detached historian's analysis.

Max Hoffmann admired himself. He began modestly, proud that some of his ideas had found approval in the new operations plan. On September 9, 1914, he expressed surprise at getting the Iron Cross for his humble role behind a desk. One year later he was affirming that he deserved all the credit for the victory. By 1919 he told the English journalist Sefton Delmer that he was the sole initiator of the battle, and the savior of East Prussia. He was quoted as saying that after hearing people say that Hindenburg had won the battle of Tannenberg, he had ceased believing in the existence of Caesar and Hannibal. Another time, showing Hindenburg's bed to some visitors to army headquarters, he allegedly said, "There is where the Field Marshal slept *before* the battle, that is where he slept *after* the battle, and that, my friends, is where he slept *during* the battle."[20]

Max Hoffmann was always good copy. But his aphorisms do not deny the fact that Tannenberg produced only two real public figures. Ludendorff, with an Iron Cross to add to his Blue Max, reinforced his image as an archetype of the army's "new man." In general staff circles he was regarded from the beginning as the brains and the driving force behind Hindenburg. To junior staff officers like Adolf Tappen and Max Bauer, Ludendorff was something more. He was a man who understood not only modern war but modern society. Given a chance he could run Germany as efficiently as he did the 8th Army, and dispatch the Socialists as easily as the Russians. To many of his supporters Ludendorff's image was of a man destined by intellect, character, and personality to a place outside the spotlight, but as the real wielder of power. Twenty years later his successors in uniform would dream of playing similar roles to Adolf Hitler.[21]

To some historians of Tannenberg, the battle would have been won had Paul von Hindenburg never been born. Critics suggested that his only contributions were the signing of the orders and the announcing of the victory. Because he was the "official" commander, he received an undeserved share of the glory. Hindenburg, not noted for his sharp wit, nevertheless provided the best answer. Since the battle was won, he once declared, many had won it, but "if it had been lost, I would have lost it alone."[22]

Opportunities and Illusions

The German people seemed to agree. Newly promoted to field marshal, decorated with the *Pour le Mérite*, Hindenburg became the subject of a wartime cottage industry. His photo dominated the illustrated press. His moustache was copied in hundreds of barber shops. War loans were promoted by allowing subscribers to drive nails into his wooden statue. The navy named a new battle cruiser after him. The Silesian industrial city of Zabrze was rebaptized in his name, becoming Hindenburg. So much Hindenburg memorabilia found its way onto the market that it remains possible for collectors to specialize in the category.

Hindenburg's role as a public figure in part reflected the frustrations of the empire's war correspondents and the newspapers employing them. The movements of journalists at the front were closely restricted, their reports rigidly and ponderously censored. The army had learned to distrust the press over the previous two decades, but had not yet developed a systematic interest in techniques of manipulating and controlling news. From the chief of staff down, the soldiers' optimal approach to publicity involved telling the civilians when the war began, when it ended, and who won.[23]

As much to the point, World War I proved from its first days at least as confusing to its reporters as to its directors. Since the Crimea, the war correspondent had been an increasingly familiar part of the world's battlefields. Men like William Howard Russell became public figures by virtue of their eyewitness analyses. The battles and campaigns they reported were on a scale small enough to facilitate overview and observation. One person, if energetic and assertive, could conceivably make sense of what was happening. The pace of events, even in South Africa or Manchuria, was slow enough to enable digestion and absorption.[24] In 1914, battles followed each other so rapidly as to be indistinguishable. Casualty lists that would have meant the climax of a campaign became part of the weekly routine. Particularly on the western front, events that would in earlier wars have inspired poets were lost in the shuffle: the heroic and hopeless charge of a Bavarian cavalry brigade in Lorraine, or the hard-won victory of XVIII Reserve Corps over crack French colonial troops at Rossignol.

Tannenberg, on the contrary, was a natural publicity event. It had a suitably-heroic theme: defense of the homeland against heavy odds. It had a central figure who could be fleeted up to public recognition. And since 8th Army headquarters had no correspondents attached to it during the critical days of August, 1914, the process was not handicapped by any direct knowledge of awkward or uncomfortable facts.

For the first time in its history, Imperial Germany had a popular hero independent of the royal house. In any industrialized country the executive performs an important representational role. Individual or collective, president or first secretary, anointed monarch or revolutionary *jefe*, the leaders function as tribal totems, tutelary deities, symbols of what subjects, citizens, and followers wish to be, wish to see, and can be convinced or constrained to accept. Historically this role in the German states had been played by princes—not least because the small size of most of the traditional sovereign territories offered little scope for rival public figures. The foundation of the empire brought no significant change in this respect. Bismarck or Moltke may have symbolized the new Reich in foreign eyes. Domestically, however, that function was performed by William I, whose projected images of homely virtues and grandfatherly attitudes provided welcome relief to good citizens bewildered and often not a little alienated by the complexities of their new existence. William's position was further reinforced, not so much by constitutional guarantees of his authority as by Moltke's and Bismarck's acceptance and internalization of their roles as the emperor's faithful servants.

After 1890 the representational role of the crown grew exponentially. On one hand this was a function of William II's definition of his role, his determination to push his legal and extralegal powers to their limits, his delight in public display. On the other it reflected a Germany too internally divided to generate alternate public symbols acceptable outside a relatively limited circle. Men like Ludwig Windthorst or August Bebel generated more anathemas than hosannas. An increasingly bureaucratized political structure threw off a succession of faceless men in frock coats, distinguishable even to contemporaries more by tastes in facial hair than by deeds or attitudes. The army, for all its self-proclaimed role as an agency of national integration, developed no heroes after the elder Moltke. The military's popularity was collective. Its leaders were seen as part of the institution, not above or outside it. Patterns of ultimate submission to political authority combined with an ethic of "be more than you seem" and a pseudo-aristocratic distaste for the masses to produce military men who, literally and figuratively, took a back seat to their posturing supreme warlord. Nor did an emerging popular culture produce athletes or entertainers with a national following. German editors were as willing as their French or British counterparts to boost circulation by featuring the wardrobes and the behavior of public figures. But in a country of home towns and regional loyalties, it was correspondingly difficult to focus those kinds of interest anywhere but on the numerous royal houses—with the imperial house, of course, at their apex.

This approach had been increasingly difficult to sustain even before the outbreak of war in 1914. William himself was too much a wax figure to sustain the light cast on him by an expanding network of public information. Germany's appetite for sensation was negative as well as positive. The kaiser's public persona and his private personality were virtually identical. On stage or off, he was vain, egotistical, shallow: the kind of man who wore better at a distance, who showed better under softer lights than the new German media provided. The repeated scandals that rocked the imperial entourage further diminished the aura of deference necessary to any successful executive. Nor was William able to compensate for his shortcomings as a representational figure by significant, or even exploitable, triumphs in foreign or domestic policy.[25]

A totem unable to deliver that which is demanded of it risks being sacrificed, or at least displaced. The kaiser's public involvement in World War I peaked with his *Burgfrieden* address of August 4: "From this date I know no parties, only Germans." Once he took the field with his armies as supreme warlord, William's eclipse was as swift as it was inevitable. Had he remained outside the strategic-operational level, as ostensible coordinator of the Reich's military and diplomatic efforts, the kaiser might have sustained his image for a few months or a few years. His grandfather had been a legitimate soldier-king who commanded respect from the professionals who served him. By the time of William II's accession, however, the craft of war had become arcane enough, complex enough, to preclude its mastery by even the most gifted of political amateurs. A quarter-century later, Winston Churchill would be the despair of his chiefs of staff because of his penchant for claiming expertise in operational matters. Adolf Hitler's grand-strategic insights were vitiated by his insistence on acting as an army-group commander. By 1914 the German army had grown significantly intolerant of men from outside the soldiers' guild. Here as in so many areas, William was unable to bridge the gap. His reluctance to apply himself seriously to anything was most pronounced in his approach to military affairs. His was a mind that wavered consistently towards matters of haberdashery: the cut of a tunic or the spacing of buttons. His concern for identifying the new Imperial army with Prussia and Germany's military past, in itself praiseworthy, was no substitute for ongoing, systematic involvement in the strategic, technical, and logistic issues that preoccupied Germany's military planners in the years before war's outbreak.[26]

Added to this was growing resentment within the officer corps at William's constant occupation of the spotlight, his assumption of undeserved credit for the army's progress and development. A rising new breed of technocrats, the generation typified by Ludendorff, regarded William as a positive handicap to the conduct of a modern war. Older officers like Hindenburg sustained respect, almost reverence, for the kaiser as an abstraction but at the same time found it easier and easier to disregard his person and his recommendations in practice. By the end of 1914 Bülow and Tirpitz were discussing the possibility of having William II declared insane and hospitalized. His son would become regent, with Hindenburg holding the emergency post of imperial administrator (*Reichsverweser*). No one doubted who would wield the real power.[27]

Quick victories on the western front might have encouraged papering over the situation, allowing the kaiser to posture at stage center while the generals congratulated each other behind his back. Instead as it became increasingly apparent that the Schlieffen Plan was encountering snags, no one of importance at OHL had time to entertain the kaiser. William's relegation to figurehead status during the first three weeks of August was not a conscious, deliberate process. He was the first to notice what had happened. The kaiser's almost pathetic appreciation of anyone at headquarters willing to spend time with him was commented on by visitors and observers alike.[28] His withdrawal into what amounted to a fantasy world of long lunches and heroic anecdotes fresh from the trenches had begun even before the Battle of the Marne.

In the context of William's shortcomings, Hindenburg's wartime image was psychologically specific. It focussed on mature male virility. This image seems incongruous in a war that demonstrated more clearly with every passing day that combat was a young man's province. The Germans, the French, and to a lesser extent the British learned painfully the risks of having forty-year-olds commanding battalions and men in their fifties riding at the heads of regiments. A high proportion of the men *Limogé* by Joffre in the fall of 1914 were victims not of incompetence, but of fatigue and stress, which sapped their judgment to the point where they made stupid mistakes.[29] While the kaiser's army had no equivalent systematic purge, its front-line units experienced a steady erosion of senior officers rendered dangerous by age. In 1915 the image of youth would be further served by the emergence of the airman as a public, almost a folk, hero. It is worth noting that the *Pour le Mérite*, historically awarded only to senior, aristocratic, and victorious generals, became by war's end increasingly common currency among pilots scarcely out of their teens.[30]

World War I became a conflict between generations. The contrast drawn by so many participants between the old men who made wars and the young men who fought them was rendered even sharper in Germany by the youth movement. Well before 1914 the *Wandervögel* had challenged the verities and the virility of the older generation publicly and systematically. The outburst of enthusiasm that characterized young Germany's response to war's outbreak reflected a desire to establish their generation's own parameters, to have something distinctively theirs, unclaimable and unsharable by their elders. In this context, Hindenburg was the answer to Langemarck. Typical was the cartoon published in *Lustige Blätter* in March, 1915. It featured a powerful field-marshal at the point of throwing a caricatured Russian officer bodily across the frontier. Hindenburg's short-cropped gray hair and prominent stomach suggest not advancing age but a man "in the best years," unaffected by the inroads of time in anything that mattered. The two symbols would coexist uneasily through the Weimar era until officially united in Adolf Hitler's carefully staged 1934 Potsdam extravaganza fusing "the Marshal and the PFC."[31]

Ludendorff and Hindenburg were more than simple media creations. Institutionally the German army badly needed heroes by mid-September. Its commitment to a quick decisive victory made it correspondingly vulnerable to even slight checks in its announced program. Nor were its peacetime stars playing their intended roles very well. Moltke all but collapsed from stress. Kluck, among the darlings of the army's new men, was unable to execute the programmed sweep through Belgium. Crown Prince William bogged his army down in a series of costly encounter battles. Prince Rupprecht of Bavaria checked an invasion of Lorraine, but then sacrificed thousands of men in a vain effort to break through the French frontier defenses. Their respective staff officers proved correspondingly unable to work miracles—a fact highlighted by the fiasco of the Hentsch mission. The spectacle of a mere lieutenant-colonel deciding the movement of whole armies would have been hard enough to swallow in the context of total victory. As German troops fell back from the Marne, as Schlieffen's grand design degenerated into a series of thwarted flanking movements, friction between staff and command, between higher and lower headquarters, flared far beyond the parameters of command accepted since the days of Moltke the Elder.

Ludendorff's contemporaries and Hindenburg's acquaintances knew that these men had not suddenly been apotheosized into military geniuses. Even in mid-September, voices at OHL suggested that the Russians had been easy meat, that the defensive had ever been the strongest form of warfare, even that the victors had slipped into *ein gemachtes Bett*: a "made bed," a situation in which it was impossible to lose. But such comments bore the unmistakable tang of sour grapes—particularly when the booty of Tannenberg was compared with the relatively meager spoils of the French campaign.

Hindenburg and Ludendorff also had the advantages of isolation, of being separated from the tensions and rivalries proliferating in a high command forced in the aftermath of the Marne not merely to replan a campaign, but to rethink its basic views of war.[32] Erich von Falkenhayn, Prussia's war minister, also assumed for all practical purposes the post of chief of staff on September 14. In the next weeks he brought order from the broken-down Schlieffen-Moltke visions for the West. He developed practical, if not necessarily optimal, proposals for the conduct of a war that had suddenly taken on a life of its own. Yet his credibility suffered precisely because he was the symbolic bearer of bad news. Falkenhayn's presence as chief of staff was a reminder of failed hopes and opportunities that would never come again. Hindenburg and Ludendorff correspondingly symbolized both the success of the old military order and the hopes for greater achievements in new contexts.

II

The *fata morgana* of Tannenberg above all strengthened the moral position of Hindenburg and Ludendorff in their arguments for an "eastern" solution to Germany's strategic dilemma in the aftermath of the Marne and First Ypres. In the years before 1914 the idea of concentrating Germany's primary military effort against Russia had virtually no defenders. Its reappearance was a function of personal ambition combined with professional reappraisals. Hindenburg, Ludendorff, and their staff officers had without exception entered the war as committed "Westerners." Yet they could hardly avoid asking what might have been achieved in the east with slightly stronger forces. Ludendorff regarded reinforcements as unnecessary to win an immediate victory at Tannenberg. But add three or four fresh corps to the operational equation at the Masurian Lakes, on the plains of Poland, or in front of Łódz, and was it so far-fetched to speak of decisive victory? Was Russia's surrender, or at least her seeking a negotiated peace, merely the stuff of late-night fantasies?

In 1914–15 the Russian front played a role in German strategy similar to that of the Mediterranean in Wehrmacht planning for a later war. Andreas Hillgruber and Gerhard Schreiber are only two of the distinguished scholars who insist the Middle Sea was ultimately a strategic dead end, that Britain could not be driven from the war as long as the United States underwrote her participation, and that in any case the Axis had neither the logistical system nor the operational resources to achieve anything but the sterile illusions of victory in the Mediterranean and Near East. Their arguments are compelling, yet the irresistible questions also remain in this context: what might the Axis have achieved with two or three more Panzer divisions, a few hundred additional aircraft, and a little bit of grand-strategic vision?[33]

The closing of the western front with the completion of the race to the sea in November, 1914, put the Imperial German army at a sudden disadvantage in its own eyes. The offensive was still regarded as the only form of war that could generate a decision. But the tactical superiority of defense over offense had been a familiar point of departure in German doctrine and planning since the days of the elder Moltke. This was why the German army so favored flanking movements. A continuous front from Switzerland to the English Channel prefigured a series of breakthrough battles against determined and capable foes. The strengths of the German army, argued the emerging Easterners, involved mobility, flexibility, and imagination—not brute force. Germany's soldiers had spent decades insisting that Germany's society could not afford a war of attrition. Further concentration on the western front seemed all too likely to prove them right.

Tannenberg invited interpretation as a case study in vindication. In its only fair test in the east the Imperial German Army's strategic planning, operational doctrine, and institutional preparation had apparently resulted in exactly what the generals promised: a battle of annihilation, a *Vernichtungsschlacht* on a scale unmatched since Napoleon. Given the level of information generally available even to the German military in 1914–15, Tannenberg indicated that the army's approach to war had not been completely mistaken. Under the conditions of the Russian theater, where the balance between numbers and space had not yet created stasis, where "flank" and "rear" were still meaningful strategic concepts, the German army would have the chance to do best what it did well.

Another significant reason for pursuing an eastern option involved the Russian army. If it had shown great shortcomings in the autumn campaigns, it had also shown great potential. The orderly Russian retreat, the new quartermaster-general and future Prussian war minister Wild von Hohenborn declared, was far from "what we need: a catastrophe."[34] The Russian steamroller might well prove even more formidable for being delayed a season. Ludendorff's thinking in December paralleled Conrad's in August. The relative weakness of the Central Powers in the east

336

demanded action, not reaction—both for itself and as the best means of propping up a badly battered Habsburg ally.

Newly appointed chief of staff Erich von Falkenhayn was anything but indifferent to the prospects of an eastern concentration. His images, however, harked back to those of the elder Moltke four decades earlier. Victories in the east could not, must not, be pursued at the cost of weakening the western front. Falkenhayn was even more Moltkean in his underlying conviction of the necessary linkages of force and diplomacy. Even in the heyday of the Schlieffen and post-Schlieffen eras, German planners had never confused a *battle* of annihilation with a *war* of annihilation. Indeed, the success of the great plan itself depended heavily on negotiations. In order to transfer forces to the eastern theater as projected, France must not merely be defeated. She must acknowledge that defeat in a way precluding either a broken-backed *Volkskrieg* in the style of 1871 or a long and comprehensive military occupation. And that in turn meant, if only by implication, a French government willing to make peace and strong enough to enforce authority within its own frontiers. Wilhelm Groener wondered on September 3 if the war in the west was not going a bit too well. France's armies were in full retreat. Its president had fled to Bordeaux. Generals were refusing to obey orders. Paris was demanding a commune. But if the dissolution continued, mused Groener, there would be no government with which peace could be negotiated.[35]

As the prospects for forcing a political decision in the west sank into the mud of Ypres, Falkenhayn increasingly began considering the prospects on Germany's other front. Falkenhayn was aware that the entente powers had pledged themselves by bell, book, and candle never to negotiate a separate peace. He was also aware of the historic weaknesses of such grand coalitions. Even against the overwhelming threats of Louis XIV or Napoleon they had proved significantly unstable. Like most of his counterparts, Falkenhayn was psychologically unable to cast Germany in the role of a hegemony-seeking disturber of Europe's order. This was instead a defensive war, to be fought within parameters set by cabinets and general staffs. Above all it must not be allowed to take on a life of its own. As late as August 1 Falkenhayn had warned against the risks of declaring war on Russia prematurely. Now he began urging Bethmann to consider the possibilities of negotiation.[36]

Bethmann-Hollweg was reluctant to accept a military program with such strong political coloring. His suspicion that the army was seeking to pass the buck for its operational failures to the political authories reflected too many past realities in the Second Reich. Pragmatically, Bethmann was less confident than Falkenhayn that Russia could readily be brought to the peace table after being taught a few salutary lessons in the open field. In his mind Falkenhayn was relying on an outmoded appeal to the solidarity of the conservative eastern monarchies and on a faith in the power of single victories, which experience of the last four months suggested might be equally outdated. Even if successful, moreover, a negotiated peace of the kind projected by Falkenhayn would do nothing to remove the Russian threat that had exercised such an increasing influence on German foreign policy since the days of Bismarck.

In early December, 1914, Bethmann visited Hindenburg's headquarters. The chancellor, like his counterparts everywhere in Europe, was a military amateur. Like most amateurs, he had developed over the years an exaggerated respect for the generals' military competence, combined with certain fears for their political aspirations. The respect at least had been considerably shaken by the events of August, 1914. In one sense Bethmann was in a mood to be convinced when he journeyed east—convinced that the German army could still earn its pay by winning the war. While details of the meeting remain obscure, Bethmann was impressed by the abilities of a new team that seemed to incorporate the old virtues. He came away with glowing opinions of the professional skills of Hindenburg, Ludendorff, and their staff officers—a sharp contrast to what seemed Falkenhayn's growing pessimism. The chief of staff's reiterated description of the German army as a broken weapon unable to conduct decisive operations in existing parameters contrasted sharply with Hindenburg's and Ludendorff's confident appeals for just a little more of everything, and their even more confident assertions of light at the end of a tunnel that already had proved far longer than anyone expected.[37]

Hindenburg and Ludendorff for their part saw Bethmann as a highly desirable ally against a chief of staff who, even more than his unfortunate predecessor, seemed to have no idea of what to do next. At the end of October Falkenhayn had summoned Ludendorff to Berlin in an effort to take the measure of his principal subordinate's attitudes and opinions. The meeting was unfortunate. Falkenhayn shared the widespread prewar opinion that Ludendorff was primarily concerned for his own career—the kind of personally ambitious man whose advancement boded ill for Germany as well as for the army. His suspicions were not alleviated by Ludendorff's proposal to make Hindenburg the supreme commander of German forces in the east. Apart from the likely impact of this move on Falkenhayn's own hopes for a peace with Russia—another cook would be stirring the pot—it would offer new fields for Ludendorff's ambitions, which by this time plainly included Falkenhayn's post as chief of staff.[38]

Ludendorff's visions were still wavering between theater level and grand strategy. Neither he nor Hindenburg seem to have believed at this stage that the war could ultimately be won in the east. Instead they hoped to cripple Russia beyond recovery in order to settle accounts with Britain and France. And what they really wanted was more troops to pursue the victory that seemed so close—the next Tannenberg. The resources to do it seemed at hand. In August the army had begun the raising of thirteen new divisions from a mixture of volunteers, reservists who had not received actual peacetime training, and trained reservists superfluous to requirements in existing units. Nine more divisions with a similar composition would be ready for the field early in the new year.

Of the first thirteen divisions, eleven had been sent west—a decision logical enough given prewar doctrine and the existing operational situation. They had formed a good part of the forces directed against the Channel ports. Their failure at Ypres,Langemarck as it was known in Germany, had already been written into mythos as "the massacre of the innocents"—teenagers, the hope of Germany's future, sent forward without adequate training, leadership, or support, to be mowed down by Godless British mercenaries and their black auxiliaries.[39] The German army was not a nursery for the finer feelings. Nevertheless, for social and political as well as military reasons, no one on the general staff was particularly anxious to risk a repeat performance with the next group of war-raised formations. Technically much had been done to give these nine divisions a better chance. Their cadres were larger and younger, including a number of experienced officers and NCOs who became available as they recovered from wounds suffered in August and September. Their training was better: much less close-order drill and much more practice in field-craft, in open-order tactics, and in working closely with artillery.[40]

Where could these new formations be most profitably used? Falken-hayn initially saw them as necessary reinforcements for a western front that was sure to face a massive allied attack in the spring. For Ludendorff and Hindenburg the eastern theater was a far more logical area of deployment. The inevitable weaknesses of the new formations were unlikely to be as pitilessly exposed by the Russians as by the French, particularly since these young soldiers would be under the genial supervision of Germany's proven best operational brains. A small increment of force in the east promised results disproportionate to anything likely to be obtained in a west already gaining an evil reputation as a corpse factory where generalship had become virtually impossible.

Initially Ludendorff and Hindenburg sought to bring Falkenhayn to their viewpoint by sending a "special liaison officer," Major Hans von Haeften, to Falkenhayn's headquarters. For a man with a delicate assignment Haeften proved remarkably heavy handed. The report he submitted on the previous course of operations in the east praised Ludendorff in such glowing terms that it had a predictably negative effect on Falkenhayn. Haeften then turned to the chancellor, recommending Falkenhayn's relief by Ludendorff—not least, he argued, because the combination of war minister and chief of staff posed disturbing domestic political problems. But this maneuver failed when William, with a flash of his old spunk, said that he would never appoint "a dubious character, devoured by personal ambition" to the post once held by Moltke and Schlieffen.[41]

The German problem was further complicated by alliance politics. In January, 1915, Conrad von Hötzendorf, still convinced of the necessity for the weaker party to maintain the initiative, proposed a grand Austro-Hungarian offensive from the Carpathians—supported, of course, by a parallel German attack further north. Ludendorff had by this time little respect for either Conrad's strategic capacities or the Austrian army's military potential. But he did see Austria's proposed offensive as a way of obtaining at least the new corps, and perhaps many more, for an eastern theater that by this time he regarded as critical. Both Hindenburg and

Ludendorff remained "Westerners" in their belief that the final decision must come against France and Britain. But only decisive victories in the east, victories leaving Russia completely prostrate, would free enough German strength to achieve that kind of triumph in a west stalemated partly by technology, partly by the grim determination of the combatants.

Falkenhayn remained convinced that this proposed combined offensive would achieve no more than the previously rejected prewar plans for a *Grosse Ostaufmarsch*. In his mind Hindenburg and Ludendorff were blinded by the same mirages that had lured Charles XII and Napoleon. Given Russia's objective military potential, an operational victory in the east was a utopia. What was the worth of battles won, no matter how convincingly, if the ultimate goal of peace remained ephemeral? "The East," Falkenhayn declared, "gives nothing back." The other side of the Russian steamroller was the strategic retreat—a maneuver that set any enemy at war with the land itself. Russia was shaped like a fan. The deeper one advanced, the more scattered became one's own forces. The more one occupied, the more there was to occupy. Germany might well conquer itself to death, or at least exhaustion. Falkenhayn's concept of a negotiated peace depended essentially on political strategy. Hold Italy at least neutral. Bring Bulgaria and Rumania into the war on the side of the Central Powers. Eliminate Serbia once and for all. Keep applying maximum pressure on the western front, while using just enough force in the east to show the temper of Germany's steel. Finally, offer terms to a Russian government isolated from any immediate support.

Bethmann was sufficiently conscious of Germany's internal weaknesses to regard attrition as his country's final option. Any possibility of evading total war demanded pursuing. But the first step in executing this grand design was to do something about Ludendorff. Since he was unlikely to be won to Falkenhayn's vision and was too powerful politically simply to be relieved, a compromise must be found. Falkenhayn had a nice sense of irony. Since Ludendorff enthusiastically urged German support for an Austrian offensive, why not make him directly responsible for the operation? On January 8 Falkenhayn appointed Ludendorff chief of staff of the "South Army," a mixed German-Austrian formation in the Carpathian sector. Hindenburg responded by appealing directly to the kaiser that he be allowed to retain Ludendorff as his chief of staff. The field-marshal initially even threatened to resign rather than accept separation from his advisor. Deterred from presenting this challenge officially, Hindenburg spent a long night composing a letter that declared he could no longer cooperate with Falkenhayn, and proposing instead that Moltke be recalled as chief of staff.

Ludendorff too declared the war was lost if Falkenhayn remained in his current post, but Wilhelm remained unwilling to dismiss Falkenhayn, particularly in favor of the thoroughly discredited Moltke. Instead he urged Hindenburg not to desert his post in wartime. Deeply moved, Hindenburg abandoned any talk of resigning. Falkenhayn for his part agreed both to allow Ludendorff to remain as Hindenburg's chief of staff, and to assign the new formations to Hindenburg's theater.[42]

The reasons for this change of mind were complex. Austria's constant appeals for support by now parallelled a lack of obvious opportunities for a successful major offensive on the western front. Perhaps as much to the point, Falkenhayn decided the best way of demonstrating the ultimate sterility of Ludendorff's strategic concepts was to give him the chance to put his ideas to the test. This attitude should not be completely dismissed as a cold-blooded sacrifice of the lives of German soldiers. Since the days of Frederick the Great Prussia's military experience had shown the importance of a common doctrine. Now two schools of thought were contending for mastery, and in Falkenhayn's mind this was a sure recipe for disaster. Perhaps after all Ludendorff might even be right. The only way to prove the point was to give him most of what he requested, and then await results.

The great January offensive in fact achieved no more than tactical successes under terrible weather conditions. The newly raised German units suffered heavy losses in the broken country of the Masurian Lakes. Things were worse farther south. Over three-quarters of a million Austrians were killed or wounded, or simply disappeared in the Carpathian snows. A successful Russian counterattack had the tsar's generals dreaming of a victory parade through Budapest. Falkenhayn felt himself vindicated. The chief of staff had seen his last fresh reserves bled white. Any new maneuver force could be formed only by reducing the strength of existing divisions. He refused to consider further concentration on a sterile theater—particularly as Britain's national mobilization brought more and more divisions of the New Army to the western front.[43]

At the same time, however, Hindenburg and Ludendorff could take comfort from the fact that the political matrix for a Russian peace on Falkenhayn's model was rapidly crumbling. Since the turn of the year Falkenhayn had insisted that Germany could not spare troops to sustain Austria-Hungary should Italy and Rumania join the war against her. But even as Russian troops debouched through the Carpathians, Austria stubbornly refused concessions either to Italy or in the Balkans. German diplomatic efforts to preserve Italian neutrality were being checked and mated by entente promises. At GHQ, Wild von Hohenborn fulminated about the "noodle eaters" in Rome who saw their sacred duty as blackmailing former friends for all the traffic would bear.[44]

In war as in bridge, an effective player leads from strength. Falkenhayn, studying his cards in late March, decided that Germany's least-worst option now involved mounting an offensive in the east. Since the long-term balance of resources between the Central Powers and the entente did not favor the former, it became correspondingly important that in military terms, Austria-Hungary was becoming both an increasing liability for Germany as the war went on, and at the same time an increasingly indispensable ally. Just as Germany prior to August, 1914, had been unable to accept passively Austria's decline into regional power status, so now, eight months later, Germany could not afford to have her principal ally sink into military paralysis. Italy would play a similar role during World War II. Weaker partners in a coalition always have the option of folding their cards. For over thirty years the Federal Republic of Germany's commitment to NATO rested heavily on the success of deterrence *cum* forward defense. Perceptions of West German lives and West German territory being used to buy time for superpower negotiations were a recurring nightmare in Bonn, no matter the nature of the coalition in power. The FRG's probable response to the first nuclear explosion in its territory, or the first of its cities to come under massive conventional attack, was correspondingly less predictable than the U.S. government wished their citizens to acknowledge. Nor, from the other side of the border, was Soviet rhetoric on the eternal solidarity of the Warsaw Pact reflected in Soviet troop dispositions in Eastern Europe.

Apart from its effect on Russia, a Central Powers victory in the eastern theater might deter Italy from entering the war. Nevertheless, any belief Falkenhayn might have had in the effectiveness of wide-ranging strategic penetrations on the Russian front had been destroyed by the January offensives. The new operation must remain limited. Not only was there no time for grand combinations. Were German aid too generous Austria might continue her policy of diplomatic intransigence, blackmailing Germany at will by threatening to collapse. On the other hand, with too little German support the Austrian front might disappear entirely. The best compromise seemed to be direct intervention: inserting German troops into the Austrian sector, where their presence would be immediately felt, and where relatively small forces might achieve disproportinate results. As much to the point, direct intervention would clip Ludendorff's claws. The new sector would be, at least on paper, under Austrian command, not German.[45]

Falkenhayn scraped up eight divisions. Most of them had been organized when existing divisions were reduced from four to three regiments. Falkenhayn's plans accepted the need for a breakthrough, and these troops were as well qualified for the mission as any in Germany's order of battle. Unlike their predecessors, the new formations were composed of case-hardened combat veterans seasoned in the trench warfare of the western front. Their commander too was, at least in Falkenhayn's mind, the right man for the job. August von Mackensen made no secret of his belief that breakthrough battles could be won with enough resources and a capable commander. He had shown since Gumbinnen an aggressive willingness to accept casualties in pursuit of an objective. And he was chafing under Ludendorff's authority. Giving this man an independent opportunity might well diminish Ludendorff's luster by creating a rival. As an insurance policy Falkenhayn assigned as Mackensen's chief of staff one of the army's most brilliant young officers. Hans von Seeckt had gone to war as chief of staff of III Brandenburg Corps, and established his reputation as a planner in the positional warfare of autumn, 1914. The combination seemed both promising in itself and susceptible of control from Berlin.[46]

Beginning on May 2, 1915, Mackensen's troops and guns, organized as XI German Army, tore the Russian front wide open on a forty-kilometer sector between the Galician towns of Gorlice and Tarnow. By the third week of June a quarter-million prisoners crowded Mackensen's cages. Hundreds of thousands more were dead, in hospital, or missing. The Russian army's disposable reserves of ammunition and material were virtually exhausted, its cadres of regular officers and NCOs virtually destroyed.

The relative contributions to this outcome of German material superiority and tactical skill on one hand, Russian "misfortune and mismanagement" on the other, remain subjects of controversy. Ludendorff insisted almost automatically that with a few more troops on the ground and a broader strategic vision on the part of OHL, the Russian army could have been entirely destroyed and the war in the east ended. Falkenhayn and his supporters pointed to grand-strategic restraints: the Franco-British spring offensive against an undermanned western front; Italy's declaration of war on May 23, and its attack on Austria's virtually undefended southern frontier; and the British assault on Gallipoli. Underlying these operational factors, however, was Falkenhayn's belief that Gorlice-Tarnow could be the first, military step to a negotiated peace with Russia.[47]

This was by no means an isolated position. Writing in 1915, Max Weber warned that for all the rhetoric about the dangers posed by England, Russia was the only power that, once victorious, could threaten not only Germany's political independence but her very existence as a nation. Above all the western Slavic peoples must somehow be convinced that escaping Russia's clutches did not mean violation by Germany. An exaggerated policy of annexation would mean no more than German elbows in everyone else's ribs.[48]

Bethmann-Hollweg developed a similar attitude during 1915. His initial proposals to Russia in the summer and early fall of that year were relatively moderate, involving frontier rectifications rather than the drastic changes of sovereignty proposed by the annexationists. They fell on deaf ears. The Russian foreign office, and Tsar Nicholas himself, were not indifferent to the German overtures. But since August Russian war aims, like those of the other belligerents, had grown in proportion to the demands and sacrifices made of the system. Few men in positions of power anywhere in Europe believed their people could withstand the stresses of a long war without corresponding gains. The belligerents depended heavily on hopes and promises. More and more of the empire's vocal pressure groups advanced specific aims and goals, political, cultural, or economic. Sazonov still hoped for a network of Slavic client states in central Europe—including an independent Bohemia, whose creation meant the end of the Habsburg Empire. In the spring of 1915 the British offered to fulfill a dream of centuries: Constantinople. The western allies also guaranteed Russia a share, unspecified but large, of the reparations to be exacted from Germany at war's end. A government confident of its own strength might make peace in defiance of these factors. Russia, which had entered the war largely from a sense of its own weakness, was in no position to take such a perceived risk.[49]

"Russia remains the puzzle," the German chancellor wrote to Progressive Reichstag deputy Conrad Haussman. Reports on her prospective behavior were "uncertain, changing, and contradictory." Bethmann, like Falkenhayn, was a product of that belief in Russia's strength and military potential, which had so influenced Germany's strategy and diplomacy before 1914. The mind-sets that expected Cossacks in Hohenfinow and accepted the impossibility of conquering, as opposed to defeating, Russia in a two-front war found no difficulty in assuming a level of strength and coherence in Russia's diplomatic decision making that did not exist—at least not in the context of the combination of threats and pressures Germany produced in 1915.[50]

Michael Geyer puts the Bethmann-Falkenhayn strategy in the context of modern deterrence theory: balancing limited interests against the risks of general catastrophe.[51] Experience suggests, however, that deterrence is successful not so much from actual positions of strength as from perceptions of strength, whether equivalency or sufficiency.[52] By mid-1915, what remained of Tsar Nicholas's government resembled nothing so much as a novice gambler seeking to recoup an initial loss by the process of doubling the stakes. In such a context the game assumes a life of its own, independent of any initial wagers. As long as her allies would back Russia's bets, even if only with promises, she was likely to remain at the table. Even the first revolutionary government proposed to continue the war.

Does that in turn suggest the validity of the Hindenburg-Ludendorff strategy, of a revived and expanded *Ostaufmarsch*? The answer, demanding an excursion into the world of might-have-been, involves several levels of consideration. On the tactical/operational level, it remains open to speculation whether the armed forces of any great power could have been in fact crushed by the balances of firepower and mobility technically possible between 1914 and 1918. Time and again Russian armies proved able to evade the ultimate consequences of defeat by withdrawing faster than their enemies could pursue them.

Ludendorff throughout his career found it difficult to grasp this point—not least because his early successes, at Liège and Tannenberg, were ultimately tactical. The concept behind his planning for the March offensives of 1918, that victory in the field would generate strategic success, was the product of four years' belief that he never had been given quite enough resources to achieve the triumph glimmering over the horizon.[53] In this sense, for all his native ability and general staff training, Ludendorff never rose beyond the level of an infantry colonel.

Nor must Falkenhayn's concern for the western front be entirely dismissed. The allied offensives of 1915–16 bled, if they did not cripple, a German army already focussed on that theater. A reallocating of force for the benefit of the east generated corresponding risks, particularly given the complex structure of the German state. A Napoleon, a Stalin, even a Churchill or a Roosevelt, could take strategic risks impossible for a Bethmann or a Falkenhayn.

And this in turn suggests Germany's fundamental failure in grand strategy. The German Empire had made no preparations for winning the war, as opposed to fighting it. Both Bethmann and Falkenhayn were sharply critical of what they regarded as Pan-German fantasies. They were also constrained to recognize the increasing domestic problems in concluding peace with Russia on the basis of a *status quo ante bellum*. Austria's weaknesses, demonstrated all too clearly in the first nine months of war, suggested to a broad spectrum of German opinion that Habsburg survival depended on tight German control: not merely a customs union but sweeping Germanization, at least in Cisleithania. This would be accompanied by massive territorial gains for the Dual Alliance—Russian Poland and the Baltic states at a minimum. In this way the Slavic threat would be forever banished and German predominance at the heart of the continent secured.[54]

Germany's diplomats spoke of "freeing Europe from Russian pressure," and of "forming several buffer states" between Russia and her western neighbors.[55] Exactly how this was to be done, no one was quite certain. From the war's beginning the German foreign office was submerged in memoranda from people no one had ever heard of, guaranteeing revolts next week if only the Reich would pay the bills. The German embassy in Stockholm was charged with preparing an uprising in Finland. It replied that to make much impression on the Finns, the German navy must operate extensively in the eastern Baltic.[56] The German consul in Lemberg reported that Ukranian nationalists were ready to set south Russia ablaze. All they needed was Germany's moral and financial support.[57]

In theory the proposals were attractive, particularly in the first heady days of war. In practice they encountered snags. There were no ships available to inspire a Finnish rebellion. The German ambassador to Vienna supported the idea of a Ukranian insurrection. The only problem was that Germany had no direct contacts in that area. Any German initiatives were likely to generate friction with Austria, and the Habsburg government had its own ideas on the matter. The Ukraine, declared Berchtold, was in no way ready for autonomy.[58] Revolution would create only anarchy. As for any Russian territory that might come under direct allied occupation, the Austrians proposed that they take "temporary" responsibility. After all, they had a large number of Polish and Ruthenian officials, and centuries of experience in dealing with touchy nationalities. "Naturally," Germany could claim as much of White Russia and Russian Poland as it wished, but the issue was best settled after the fighting stopped.[59]

The increasing differences of opinion between the allies over what should ultimately be done with Eastern Europe precluded developing a coherent policy of what to do next month. Senior officials of the Prussian civil administration debated the merits of sending food across the prewar frontier to Russians who had worked in the Silesian mines until August. Generals said they "had no objections" to letting "Russian citizens of Polish nationality" continue to mine coal in Germany.[60] It was all a far cry from both the subsequent compulsory mobilizations of labor in France and Belgium, and the cloud-castle dreams of German empires in the east. But precisely that lack of planning made the latter events possible—in the way that hot air ultimately fills a balloon.

The kinds of victories foreseen by German military and civil planners before 1914 demanded an enemy government not only willing to conclude peace, but able to enforce it as well. Lacking that, the Germans in any theater were all too likely to conquer themselves to destruction, dispersing their forces as they occupied and controlled Russian territory. The possibilities of organizing subjected territory to support a war of attrition remained undeveloped by 1918—not least because the Second Reich was not the Third. The general staff's encouragement of revolution in Russia, culminating in the famous "trainload of plague germs," reflected three years of failure to secure any kind of peace in the east, whether by victory or negotiation.

Epilogue

From 1914 to 1918 Tannenberg retained some links to diplomatic and military realities. Thereafter it moved increasingly into the realms of myth. This process reflected decision as well as accident. The Weimar Republic needed heroes; its critics required focal points for nostalgia. Tannenberg was one of the few points of common agreement. Most of the "battles" of 1914–18 had lasted for months, their phases distinguished only by official, artificially determined dates. Tannenberg was the only battle of World War I that could be directly compared with the great victories of history. It had a beginning, a middle, and an end, coming over a relatively short span of time. It was an undisputable victory, the only one of its kind Germany could show for four years of war.

Tannenberg as a rallying point had more practical political aspects as well. It had been won against a safe enemy—the vanished tsarist empire. Its glorification could hardly damage relations with a Soviet Russia that was already doing everything possible to separate itself from its history. Domestically the Versailles Treaty, by creating the Polish Corridor to the Baltic Sea, severed East Prussia from the rest of Germany. The Weimar Republic and the government of Prussia made corresponding efforts to reassure the inhabitants of that province that isolation did not mean abandonment. The East Prussians took pains to stress the continued importance of their roles as guardians of the Reich's eastern border. Tannenberg became symbolic, particularly for the DNVP and the other nationalist groups that dominated postwar East Prussian politics. When Hindenburg, still in retirement, visited the province in 1922, the trip became a tour through the memories of 1914.

The Tannenberg mythology was further enhanced when Hindenburg ran for the presidency of the Weimar Republic in 1925. Whatever his feelings about the new order, his role as a symbol of German grandeur was a key feature of his campaign. The marshal was identified, not with 1915's nameless victories in the middle of Russia, not with 1917's stalemate in the west, or 1918's collapse, but with the glory days of 1914—with Tannenberg.[1]

Such a victory needed a fitting monument. Germany's veterans' associations took the lead in raising funds and mobilizing support for a memorial, which they described as a symbol of defiance, an assertion of Germany's continued presence in the east. Logically, and perhaps unfortunately, the Social Democrats and the trade unions refused to become involved in the project despite the presence on the battlefield of so many men from Social Democratic strongholds. In contrast to 1914, Tannenberg was left to the nationalists.

The design of the memorial itself was impressive. The architects, Johannes and Walter Krüger, took Stonehenge as their model. They envisaged not a monument to be observed from outside, but an enclosed space, an assembly area where rites could be performed. This owed something to ancient Nordic imagery. It also reflected the fact that the numbers involved in national celebrations were growing. The crowds to be expected on great occasions defied contemporary techniques of amplification; too many people at a traditional monument could neither hear nor see.

The Krügers therefore blended myth and acoustics. Eight large towers, placed in a circle large enough to contain 100,000 people, were linked by heavy walls. Each tower had a specific function. One was a youth hostel, one housed battle flags, a third was a chapel, and so on. Together they defined what George L. Mosse calls a "sacred space," with the participants at the center of the festival rather than looking upward and forward at a ritual performer.[2] This significant departure in German national monuments would be replicated time and again during the Third Reich.

There were simpler, homelier memorials as well. Stones and plaques marked individual sites of the battle. Nor were the graves of the fallen collected, as in the west, into huge plots suggesting anonymous mass sacrifice. The region was dotted with little military cemeteries, fenced in birch and carefully tended. Even after the memorial's erection these remained places of pilgrimage. School children from all over the Reich came by train on reduced fare excursions, back-packing from Allenstein or Neidenburg to the villages mentioned in their guidebooks, placing flowers on the graves, completing the trip by standing open-mouthed within the memorial to East Prussia's German identity.[3]

Among Tannenberg's principal figures, Ludendorff's postwar career is only slightly less familiar than Hindenburg's. An open foe of the Weimar Republic, he became a corresponding focal point of nationalist and Right-radical elements. His involvement in the Kapp Putsch of 1920 and Adolf Hitler's Beer Hall Putsch of 1923 was followed by his selection in 1924 as head of the Nazi delegation in the Reichstag. For a time Hitler even considered himself the "drummer" of Ludendorff or someone like him. But the strain of years of war service combined with the influence of his second wife to lead Ludendorff down the path of crackpot religious and political activity. As Hitler moved closer to power, Ludendorff withdrew even further into a shadow world. Alienated from Hindenburg, and from most of his wartime comrades, he emerged in 1934 to warn his old commander that in appointing Hitler chancellor he had delivered Germany to "one of the greatest demagogues of all time."[4]

As Ludendorff and Hindenburg became involved with national issues, Max Hoffmann took over more and more of the operational and strategic planning for the eastern front. When his superiors left for Berlin in 1916, Hoffmann remained in Russia—partly because he had made himself indispensable there, partly because his confidence in his own abilities made him an increasingly uncomfortable subordinate. By denying Hoffman a wider field for the exercise of his talents, Hindenburg and Ludendorff may well have compounded their own problems later in the war.

Hoffmann for his part emerged as the gray eminence of the east, recognized by superiors and subordinates as the brains of the theater. He was largely responsible for the plans that halted the 1916 Brusilov offensive, and for orchestrating the German breakthrough at Riga the next year. He was a key figure in negotiating the armistice at Brest-Litovsk. While as anti-Bolshevik as the rest of the officer corps, Hoffmann favored policies of limited territorial annexation—an attitude earning Ludendorff's wrath. After the collapse, he performed a last service, coordinating the withdrawal of German troops from Russia. The postwar publication of his diaries and memoirs kept him before the public as a controversial figure until his death in 1927.

Of the corps commanders, Mackensen's career continued to flourish after Gorlice-Tarnow. With Seeckt at his elbow, he commanded the army group that overran Serbia in 1915. The next year he spearheaded the conquest of Rumania. By this time age had finally caught up with Mackensen; he spent the rest of the war commanding the occupation forces in Rumania. While evacuating his troops after the armistice, Mackensen was arrested by the Hungarians and turned over to the French.[5] Interned for a year, he returned home a hero symbolizing Germany's victimization. Scholtz rose unobtrusively and competently to army command by 1918. But the real success story among 8th Army's corps commanders was Otto von Below. In November, 1914, he was promoted to army command—one of the most rapid advances in the history of the Second Reich. In Russia and the Balkans he continued to demonstrate the same energy and tactical skill that characterized him at Tannenberg, with fewer of the questionable command decisions. Sent to Italy in 1917, he led an improvised German-Austrian army to the victory of Caporetto. The next year he commanded a field army in Ludendorff's March offensive. But perhaps the greatest tribute to Below's abilities came

Epilogue

at the war's very end, when on November 8 he was assigned to command the expected last stand on Germany's soil.

Hermann von François was less fortunate. As 8th Army's senior corps commander he took over when Hindenburg and Ludendorff were promoted to command of the eastern front. He remained a difficult subordinate. Relieved in November, 1914, for what amounted to persistent refusal to follow orders, François accepted demotion to a corps command on the western front and retired from that post in 1918. Ludendorff's critics later suggested he wished to be rid of a man who knew too much about the shaky foundations of his reputation. But François's personal papers for the war years are replete with complaints of his antagonistic behavior to colleagues and subordinates alike. "You still refuse to fit in," wrote the director of the military cabinet in 1916. It was at once a description and an epitaph.[6]

François was born too late, or too early. He could have commanded a corps under Napoleon, or a division of Stonewall Jackson's foot cavalry. He was the type of man who might have reached distinction in 1940 or 1941 at the head of a panzer group. But a loose cannon like François was an unacceptably high risk in the days before the internal-combustion engine once more made possible the conduct of war from forward command posts.

Conta ended the war as commanding general of the Carpathian Corps, and Heineccius of VII Corps in France. Staabs finished his career as commander of XXIX Reserve Corps, one of the formations raised in 1915. Emil Hell rose to become chief of staff of Army Group Kiev. Schmidt von Schmidtseck survived his ups and downs with François to command the 11th Infantry Division with distinction. Even the panic-stricken major of the 4th Grenadiers learned enough from his experiences to be trusted with an infantry regiment, albeit a wartime reserve formation.

In the course of the war, Tannenberg's rank and file were scattered across the battle fronts of Europe even more thoroughly than their commanders. Easier to trace are the formations. Six active and three reserve divisions bore the brunt of the Tannenberg campaign. They remained on the Eastern Front through 1915, the core of Hindenburg's and Ludendorff's hopes for decisive victory. As the fighting in Russia died down, their destiny lay in the west. First to go were the 35th and 36th Divisions, transferred in September, 1915, in response to the Allies' fall offensive. The 1st Division fought at Verdun in 1916. Most of the others changed fronts in the first months of 1917, with the 41st briefly detoured into Rumania. The cavalry, the *Landwehr*, and the other garrison troops by and large remained in the east, their roles changing from combat to garrison and occupation duties as the war wound down. The strangest odyssey of any of 8th Army's old formations was that of the 146th Infantry. War's end found the regiment, originally part of the 37th Division, in Palestine, part of the forces sent by OHL to stiffen the Turkish defense. The Masurians were a long way from their peacetime

350

Epilogue

garrison of Allenstein when they faced the British, Indian, and Anzac troops of Sir Edmund Allenby. But the regiment fought as well in Asia Minor as it had in East Prussia, sustaining the reputation of German arms in an unlikely setting and earning the ungrudging admiration of its enemies.

In that the 146th was an exception. None of the Tannenberg divisions rose much above mediocrity in the war's later years, being used primarily as sector-holding formations. For this the army's personnel policies was largely responsible. Even before the war Germany's eastern regiments needed recruits and reservists from outside their assigned recruiting districts. The unheard-of casualties of World War I rendered these formations even more dependent on outside sources of replacements. The war ministry and OHL initially provided them by transferring large numbers of men from Alsace-Lorraine, presumed to be less reliable in the west, to the eastern theater. The effect on morale and combat efficiency was obvious, with the *Reichsländer* too often nursing the grievances of second-class citizens and the old hands distrustful or contemptuous of their new comrades in arms. As 8th Army's divisions were transferred westward, the Alsatians were often replaced by Poles whose dependability against the Russian army was challenged, and who responded much like the Alsatians. The effect of these transfers was to leave too many formations with little more than their numbers and their traditions. Of the Tannenberg divisions, only the 37th was rated by allied intelligence as a first-class division in 1918. Its price for the designation was a casualty list so high that by the armistice its regiments counted little more than 300 riflemen apiece. They had marched to war with a strength of over 3,000.[7]

Long after its veterans had retired, Tannenberg continued to influence German military thinking. For the Imperial army's successors, the Reichswehr and the Wehrmacht, Tannenberg was a sign of hope—a sign that professionalism and its accompanying virtues of flexibility, mobility, and will power could bring victory without a wearing down an enemy's resources. Despite its limitations it was the only nonattritional victory achieved in a major theater by any of the major combatants in World War I. The French and British could point to their triumphs in open warfare, but these had come only at the end of hard pounding that had exhausted the winners almost as much as the losers.

Tannenberg became a benchmark of professionalism—proof of what a well-prepared peacetime army with a minimum amount of grit in its machinery might achieve. It was by no means a direct inspiration for the blitzkrieg. One Wehrmacht general, commenting on what he regarded as a casual attitude to orders during the 1938 occupation of Czechoslovakia, even asserted that "unconditional obedience" at Tannenberg had brought about one of Germany's greatest victories![8] Nevertheless, if in the interwar years the Seeckts, the Guderians, and the Ludwig Becks focussed on tactical maneuver and operational art to a greater extent than elswhere in Europe, their energies were to a significant degree inspired by memories of August, 1914, in East Prussia.[9] And in the later years of World War II on the eastern front, the daring ripostes that kept the Russians at bay for so long similarly owed much to the legacy of an earlier war.

Tannenberg epitomized a basic change in the German army's attitude towards Russia. The caution with which generals and general staff alike viewed the eastern colossus before 1914 had long before 1941 been replaced by what amounted to open contempt. This owed something to the Reichswehr's self-definition as Bolshevik Russia's military mentor in the Rapallo years of the 1920s. At a time when the rest of the world was turning to France for inspiration, it was satisfying to have at least one power paying attention to German concepts and doctrines.[10] But it owed even more to the mythology developed on the eastern front during World War I: a mythology stressing the Russian soldier as uniformed protoplasm, unable to respond to the demands of modern war, dangerous only in mass, and even then readily susceptible to defeat at the hands of an enemy that kept his head and used his skills.

This myth focussed on Tannenberg rather than such later victories as Gorlice-Tarnow. Its limited correspondence to the facts tended to go unchallenged because of the relatively small number of German troops involved, and their relative lack of influence in the Reichswehr. The western front was the most common body of German military experience, the place where careers and reputations were made. Anyone presenting the French or British in terms too distant from reality faced prompt challenges from colleagues with different memories. The Russian front had been remote. Units fortunate enough to be transferred there regarded it as a rest cure. Their first encounters with the Russian army usually dispelled that illusion. But it was too comforting for their comrades in the west to abandon. Somewhere there *had* to be an easy enemy.[11]

Recent West German research has established the relationship between Hitler's and the Wehrmacht's approaches to planning conflict with Russia as much closer than the generals wished to accept when they wrote their postwar memoirs. The Wehrmacht high command's involvement in the atrocities accompanying Operation Barbarossa also has been demonstrated beyond question.[12] To some extent this reflected the permeation of the military at all levels with Nazi racial and ideological ideals. But it was also, in its way, a consequence of the Tannenberg mythos—a mythos establishing the Russians as objects of suppression, so easily defeated that there was neither glory nor honor to be won in the process. The mythologizing of what had actually happened in East Prussia in 1914 thus facilitated both the careless planning and the moral indifference with which the Wehrmacht embarked on Operation Barbarossa. Within six months reality would exact the first installments of a bitter revenge.

The Tannenberg myth also proved significantly useful to Adolf Hitler. Despite his bitter contempt for the old Prussian aristocracy, after becoming chancellor the Nazi leader missed no opportunity to link himself with Hindenburg and to appeal to those elements, particularly in the army, which looked to the aging *Reichspräsident* as a symbol of stability and honor in rapidly changing times. On March 21, 1933, the private first class took the hand of the field-marshal at a formal ceremony in the garrison church at Potsdam. On August 1, 1934, Hindenburg died at his country estate. The next day Hitler accepted a personal oath of allegiance from the armed forces. And on August 6, the *Führer* presided over Hindenburg's burial, in the place of honor beneath the Tannenberg monument.

Tannenberg played a wider role as well in National Socialist propaganda. Before 1933, rearmament and revision of the Versailles Treaty were for most Germans abstract concepts—worth another round of drinks as long as someone else paid the bill. Germans were by and large no more willing than the English to die for Danzig. Since World War I had left Germany essentially unscathed, the Nazis found it correspondingly difficult to conjure up emotionally effective threats. Tannenberg became the major exception. Between 1934 and 1939 the German book market was flooded with popular histories of a barbaric horde turned away in confusion by an outraged *Volk*. Unlike equivalent works set on the western front, the material built around Tannenberg was able to stress the defensive nature of German behavior in 1914. Here was no room for doubt about who was on whose territory. From general to private the victors were a band of brothers, and all the brothers were valiant in the defense of their violated Fatherland.[13]

This interpretation, while popular enough, could hardly be said to have contributed directly to the attitudes the Wehrmacht took into Russia in 1941. But its outlines remained. The Tannenberg myth flared one last time in the last months of World War II. As Red Army spearheads drew ever closer to the German frontier, the eastern provinces' frightened inhabitants comforted themselves with the notion that "last time" the Russians had not only been driven out of East Prussia, but eventually defeated. Somehow, everything would be all right again.[14]

The end of that dream came in January, 1945, as the Russians broke out of their positions on the Vistula River and drove for the Oder and the Baltic. It was a final, unintentional irony that the Russian attack in the East Prussian sector resembled in outline that of 1914, with the Third White Russian Front performing Rennenkampf's mission and the Second White Russian Front that of Samsonov. Only this time the pincers bit and closed.

Rape and murder stalked the German east. What remained of the Third Reich's navy evacuated thousands of refugees from the Baltic ports as the remnants of once-proud divisions held the Russians from their prey. Other civilians trekked west afoot, or in farm wagons. Some escaped. Some were shot, or crushed by T-34's. Still others were overtaken by the Russian advance and forced to return, awaiting their conqueror's pleasure in what remained of their homes.

Between 1945 and 1947, East Prussia, already largely depopulated, was partitioned between Poland and Russia. Those Germans not deported to labor camps in the Soviet Union were expelled, making their way as best they might to the new frontiers. A thousand years of history had come to an end.

In January, 1945, as the Red Army drew closer, the coffin of Field-Marshal Paul von Hindenburg was removed from its place in the Tannenberg monument and taken to the port of Königsberg. On a warship packed with refugees, place was made for a symbol. Hindenburg was brought "home to the Reich," buried first in Marburg, ultimately at Burg Hohenzollern. The monument itself was destroyed by German engineers. Goebbels' *Rundfunk* promised it would be rebuilt after the war.

"After the war" the ground over which Tannenberg had been fought became instead part of the People's Republic of Poland. New families, themselves often refugees from lands now part of the Soviet Union, moved into the empty houses and plowed the deserted fields. They gave the land a new identity. Allenstein is now Olsztyn. Neidenburg became Nidzica. Osterode was renamed Ostroda. In 1960 Poland celebrated the 550th anniversary of the Teutonic Order's defeat by dedicating its own newly built monument on the site. Aircraft traced red and white smoke patterns in the sky to symbolize the "unity, strength, and readiness of the Polish people." Anywhere from 50,000 to 200,000 people attended the ceremonies, which continued to be held annually at varying levels of pomp. Poland's victory remained a frequent subject of study in the pre-Solidarity People's Republic.[15] Any celebrations of the Tannenberg of 1914 in either of the German successor states have remained private affairs.

Notes

INTRODUCTION

[1]As in *America's First Battles*, ed. C. E. Heller, W. A. Stofft (Lawrence, Kans., 1986).

[2]Robert E. Doughty, *The Seeds of Disaster: The Development of French Army Doctrine, 1919–39* (Hamden, Conn., 1985).

[3]Sven Ekdahl, *Die Schlacht bei Tannenberg 1410. Quellenkritischer Untersuchungen*, Vol. I (Berlin, 1982), 12 ff.

[4]Cf. inter alia and almost at random, James Joll, *The Origins of the First World War* (New York, 1984), Sean M. Lynn-Jones, "Détente and Deterrence: Anglo-German Relations, 1911–14," *International Security* XI (Fall, 1986), 121–150; M. R. Gordon, "Domestic Conflict and the Origins of the First World War: The Brtitish and the German Cases," *Journal of Modern History* XLVI (1974), 191–226.

[5]Patrick Glynn, "The Sarajevo Fallacy," *The National Interest* IX (Fall, 1987), 3–32; and Donald O. Kagan, "World War I, World War II, World War III," *Commentary* LXXXIII (March, 1987), 21–40, are recent, accessible summaries of the line of argument.

[6]Paul W. Schroeder, "World War I as Galloping Gertie: A Reply to Joachim Remak," *Journal of Modern History* XLIV (1972), 319–345.

[7]Godfather of this thesis remains Fritz Fischer. See most recently, *Juli 1914: Wir sind nicht hineingeschlittert* (Berlin, 1983), a *Streitschrift* whose avowed polemical nature highlights Fischer's essential arguments beyond misunderstanding.

[8]As in Paul Kennedy, *The Rise of the Anglo-German Antagonism, 1860–1914* (London, 1980).

[9]Holger H. Herwig, "Clio Deceived: Patriotic Self-Censorship in Germany After the Great War," *International Security* XII (Fall, 1987), 5–44; and Ulrich Heinemann, *Die Verdrängte Niederlage: Politische Öffentlichkeit und Kriegsschuldfrage in der Weimarer Republik* (Göttingen, 1983).

[10]William C. Wohlforth, "The Perception of Power: Russia in the Pre-1914 Balance," *World Politics* XXXIX (1987), 353–381, is an up-to-date survey of this

Notes

issue. Cf. also Risto Ropponen, *Die Kraft Russlands* (Helsinki, 1968) for the academic side. W. Bruce Lincoln, *Passing through Armageddon: The Russians in War and Revolution, 1914–18* (New York, 1986); and Alexander Solzhenitsyn, *August 1914*, tr. H. Willetts (New York, 1989), are distinguished popular accounts with the same theme.

[11]Cf. *inter alia* and from differing perspectives, John M. Joyce, "The Old Russian Legacy," *Foreign Policy* LV (1984), 132–153; Andrew Cockburn, *The Threat: Inside the Soviet Military Machine* (New York, 1983); and Dimitri K. Simes, "Gorbachev: A New Foreign Policy?" *Foreign Affairs* LXV (1987), 477–500.

1. THE CIRCUS RIDER OF EUROPE

[1]Cf. in particular Marc Raeff, "Seventeenth-Century Europe in Eighteenth-Century Russia?" *Slavic Review* XLIV (1982), 611–619; and *The Well-Ordered Police State: Social and Institutional Changes through Law in the Germanies and Russia, 1660–1800* (New Haven, Conn., 1983). The latter work may be profitably compared to Erich Donnert, *Politische Ideologie der russischen Gesellschaft zu Beginn der Regierungszeit Katharinas II* (Berlin, 1976), which stresses the role of Germans in transmitting ideas from the west to Russia.

[2]This process is described by a participant in Friedrich von Schubert, *Unter dem Doppeladler. Erinnerungen eines Deutschen in russischem Offiziersdienst 1789–1814*, ed. with intro. by E. Ambruger (Stuttgart, 1962), esp. 69 ff.

[3]The most authoritative interpretations of Western influence on Russian ideas in this period are Andrzej Walicki, *The Slavophile Controversy*, tr. H. Andrews-Rusiecka (Oxford, 1975), and, more generally, *A History of Russian Thought from the Enlightenment to Marxism*, tr. H. Andrews-Rusiecka (Stanford, Calif., 1979).

[4]Peter Jahn, *Russophilie und Konservatismus* (Stuttgart, 1980).

[5]See, for example, the report of Guard Corps chief of staff Carl von Reyher on the maneuvers of the Russian Dragoon Corps in 1834 in General der Infanterie Ollech, *Carl Wilhelm Friedrich Reyher*, Vol. IV (Berlin, 1879), 72 ff.

[6]Winfried Baumgart, *The Peace of Paris 1856. Studies in War, Diplomacy, and Peacemaking*, tr. Ann Pottinger Saab (Santa Barbara, Calif., 1981), 153 ff. The older account by Kurt Börries, *Preussen im Krimkrieg (1853–1856)* (Stuttgart, 1930), remains useful for details.

[7]D. Beyrau, *Russlands Orientpolitik und die Entstehung des deutschen Kaiserreiches, 1866–1870/71* (Wiesbaden, 1974), stresses the centrality of Balkan ambitions in Russia's acceptance of German unification. Cf. too Eberhard Kolb, "Russland und die Gründung des Norddeutschen Bundes," in *Europa und der Norddeutscher Bund* (Berlin, 1968), 183–219.

[8]Cf. John A. Armstrong, "Socializing for Modernization in a Multiethnic Elite," *Entrepreneurship in Imperial Russia and the Soviet Union*, ed. G. Guroff, F. V. Carstensen (Princeton, 1983), 98 ff.; and "Mobilized Diaspora in Tsarist Russia: The Case of the Baltic Germans," *Soviet Nationality Policies and Practices*, ed. J. Azrael (New York, 1978), 63–104; and Anders Henriksson, *The Tsar's Loyal Germans. The Riga German Community: Social Change and the Nationality Question, 1855–1905* (New York, 1983).

[9]M. B. Petrovich, *The Emergence of Russian Panslavism 1856–1870* (New York, 1956), remains reliable on the genesis and nature of the movement. Cf. also Franck Fadner, *Seventy Years of Pan-Slavism in Russia: Karamzen to Danielevskii* (Washington, D.C., 1962). On its consequences see particularly Dietrich Geyer, *Der russische Imperialismus. Studien über den Zusammenhang von innerer und auswär-*

Notes

tiger Politik 1860–1914 (Göttingen, 1977), pp. 56 ff. Samarin's work and its impact is discussed in E. C. Thaden, "Samarin's 'Okrainy Rossii' and Official Policy in the Baltic Provinces," *Russian Review* XXXIII (1974), 405–415; and more generally in Gerda Hucke, *Jürij Fedorovic Samarin. Sein geistesgeschichtliche Position und politische Bedeutung* (Munich, 1970).

[10]Paul W. Schroeder, "Containment Nineteenth-Century Style: How Russia Was Restrained," *South Atlantic Quarterly* LXXXII (1983), 7.

[11]George Lichtheim, *A Short History of Socialism* (London, 1975), 222.

[12]Reinhard W. Wittram, "Bismarcks Russlandpolitik nach der Reichsgründung," *Historische Zeitschrift* 186 (1958), 261–284, is a general introduction to Bismarck's approach to Russia. W. V. Medlicott, *The Congress of Berlin and After*, 2nd ed. (London, 1963); and *Bismarck, Gladstone, and the Concert of Europe* (London, 1956); remain useful, as does Alexander Novotny, "Der Berliner Kongress und das Problem einer europäischen Politik," *Historische Zeitschrift* 186 (1958), 285–307. Bruce Waller, *Bismarck at the Crossroads. The Reorientation of German Foreign Policy after the Congress of Berlin 1878–1880* (London, 1974) stresses both the central role of Russia in Bismarck's foreign policy and the activism of the chancellor's approach. Winfried Baumgart, "Bismarck et la crise d'orient de 1875 à 1878," *Revue d'Histoire Moderne et Contemporaine* XXVII (1980), 104–108, exaggerates Bismarck's role. K. O. von Aretin, ed., *Bismarcks Aussenpolitik und der Berliner Kongress* (Wiesbaden, 1978), includes well-done essays by Andreas Hillgruber on Bismarck's foreign policy from 1871 to 1882, and Immanuel Geiss on the conference itself.

[13]Cf. the general discussions by Walter Laqueur, *Russia and Germany: A Century of Conflict* (Boston, Toronto, 1968), 27 ff.; Fritz T. Epstein, "Der Komplex 'Die russische Gefahr' und sein Einfluss auf die deutsch-russischen Beziehungen im 19. Jahrhundert," in *Deutschland in der Weltpolitik des 19. und 20. Jahrhunderts*, ed. I. Geiss, B-J Wendt, 2nd ed. rev. (Düsseldorf, 1974), pp. 149–152; and Othmar Feyl, "Zu den deutsch-russischen Beziehungen von 1861 bis 1917 im Lichte der Buchgeschichte," *Jahrbuch für Geschichte der sozialistischen Länder Europas* XXII (1982), 83–105.

[14]Berthold F. Haselitz and Paul W. Blackstock (eds.), *The Russian Menace to Europe: A Collection of Articles, Letters and News Despatches by Karl Marx and Friedrich Engels* (Glencoe, Ill., 1952), remains a useful compendium despite its cold war origins. Cf. also Helmut Krause, *Marx und Engels und das zeitgenossische Russland* (Giessen, 1958); and Roman Rosdolsky, "Friedrich Engels und das Problem der geschichtslosen Völker (Die Nationalitätenfrage in der Revolution 1848–1849 im Lichte der *Neuen Rheinischen Zeitung*)," *Archiv für Sozialgeschichte* IV (1964), 87–282.

[15]Cf. Claudie Weill, *Marxistes russes et social-democratie allemand 1898–1904* (Paris, 1977); and DDR scholar Botho Brachmann, *Russische Sozialdemokraten in Berlin, 1895–1914* (Berlin, 1964). Peter Lösche, *Der Bolschewismus im Urteil der deutschen Sozialdemokratie 1903–1920* (Berlin, 1967), is good for the later years, as is Dietrich Geyer, "Lenin und der deutsche Sozialismus," in *Deutsch-russische Beziehungen von Bismarck bis zur Gegenwart*, ed. W. Maerkert (Stuttgart, 1964), 80–96.

[16]Leo Stern, *Die Auswirkung der ersten russischen Revolution von 1905–1907 auf Deutschland* (Berlin, 1955), is a detailed DDR account. Cf. also Barbara Vogel, "Die deutsche Regierung und die russische Revolution von 1905," in *Deutschland in der Weltpolitik*, 222–236.

[17]Paul de Lagarde, "Über die gegenwärtigen Aufgaben der deutschen

Notes

Politik," (1853); "Über die gegenwärtige Lage des deutschen Reiches" (1871); and "Die nächsten Pflichten deutscher Politik," (1886); reprinted in *Deutsche Schriften*, ed. W. Rössle (Jena, 1944), 63–93, 157–268, 435–487. See also Richard Breitling's survey, *Paul de Lagarde und der grossdeutsche Gedanke* (Vienna, 1927).

[18]For an analysis of his career see particularly Klaus Meyer, *Theodor Schiemann als politischer Publizist* (Frankfurt, 1956).

[19]Viktor Hehn, *De moribus Ruthenorum. Zur Charakteristik der russischen Volksseele*, ed. T. Schiemann, reprint ed. (Osnabrück, 1966). Cf. Loren Campion. "Behind the Modern 'Drang nach Osten.' Baltic Emigrés and Russophobia in 19th-Century Germany" (Ph.D. Dissertation, University of Indiana, 1967); and more generally Heinrich Stammler, "Wandlungen des deutschen Bildes vom russischen Menschen," *Jahrbücher für die Geschichte Osteuropas* V (1957), 271–305.

[20]Cf. Theodor Scheider, *Das Deutsche Reich von 1871 als Nationalstaat* (Köln, 1961); and James J. Sheehan, "What is German History? Reflections on the Role of the Nation in German History and Historiography," *Journal of Modern History* LIII (1981), 1–23.

[21]Stephen Kern, *The Culture of Time and Space 1880–1918* (Cambridge, Mass., 1983), 235 ff. The quotation is from Alfred von Tirpitz, *My Memoirs*, 2 vols. (New York, 1919), I, 77.

[22]Woodruff D. Smith, *The Ideological Origins of Nazi Imperialism* (New York, 1986), 21 ff., establishes a general ideological framework putting *Mitteleuropa* in the context of *Weltpolitik* and *Drang nach Osten* in the context of *Lebensraum*. Cf. *inter alia* Henry Cord Meyer, *Mitteleuropa in German Thought and Action* (The Hague, 1953); Wolfgang Wippermann, *Der "Deutsche Drang nach Osten." Ideologie und Wirklichkeit eines politischen Schlagwortes* (Darmstadt, 1981); and Dirk Oncken, "Das Problem des Lebensraums in der deutschen Politik von 1914" (Ph.D. Dissertation, University of Freiburg, 1948).

[23]"Alldeutsch," *Grossdeutschland und Mitteleuropa um das Jahr 1950*, 2nd ed. (Berlin, 1895); Friedrich von Bernhardi, *Deutschland und der nächste Krieg* (Stuttgart, 1912), 189 ff.; Daniel Frymann [Heinrich Class], *"Wenn ich der Kaiser wär": Politische Wahrheiten und Notwendigkeiten* (Leipzig, 1912), 168 ff. The quotation is from p. 170. Cf. Roger Chickering, *We Men Who Feel Most German: A Cultural Study of the Pan-German League 1886–1914* (London, 1984); and William W. Hagen, *Germans, Poles and Jews: The Nationality Conflict in the Prussian East, 1772–1914* (Chicago, 1980).

[24]The best presentation of parliament's reponse to the Caprivi tariffs is Helmut Altrichter, *Konstitutionalismus und Imperialismus. Der Reichstag und die deutsch-russischen Beziehungen 1890–1914* (Frankfurt, 1977), 111 ff. Walther Kirchner, "Russian Tariffs and Foreign Industries before 1919: The German Entrepreneur's Perspective," *The Journal of Economic History* XLI (1981), 361–380, stresses their limited effect on German industry.

[25]For the ideological development of German agrarian conservatism cf. Hans-Jürgen Pühle, *Agrarische Interessenpolitik und preussischer Konservatismus* (Hanover, 1967); and Kenneth D. Barkin, *The Controversy over German Industrialization 1890–1902* (Chicago, 1970), 131 ff. For its impact on German politics see particularly Geoff Eley, *Reshaping the German Right: Radical Nationalism and Political Change After Bismarck* (New Haven and London, 1980); and more narrowly Abraham J. Peck, *Radicals and Reactionaries: The Crisis of Conservatism in Wilhelmine Germany* (Washington, D.C., 1978).

[26]For the evolution and ramifications of Bismarck's eastern policies cf. most

Notes

recently the DDR account by Heinz Wolter, *Bismarcks Aussenpolitik 1871–1881* (Berlin, 1983), 191 *passim*; Susanne Zulinski, "Das Dreikaiserbündnis von 1881- Ein Bündnis der Entzweiung?" (Ph.D. Dissertation, University of Vienna, 1983); and Andreas Hillgruber, *Bismarcks Aussenpolitik* (Freiburg, 1972). Still useful for details is Wilhelm Windelband, *Bismarck und die europäischen Grossmächte 1879– 18885*, 2nd ed. (Essen, 1942) Pending the appearance of Ivo Lambi's projected study, the best English accounts remain A. J. P. Taylor, *The Struggle For Mastery in Europe, 1848–1918* (Oxford, 1954), 258 ff.; George F. Kennan, *The Decline of Bismarck's European Order: Franco-Russian Relations 1875–1890* (Princeton, 1979), 60 ff.; and W. N. Medlicott, "Bismarck and the Three Emperors' Alliance, 1881- 1887," *Transactions of the Royal Historical Society*, 4th Series, XXVII (1945), 61– 83. In 1867 the Habsburg Empire of Austria officially became the Dual Monarchy of Austria-Hungary. Its halves retained a common foreign office and in principle sustained a common foreign policy. Contemporary diplomats tended to use "Austria" as a shorthand, much as "Russia" presently stands for "USSR." The following text similarly uses "Austria" instead of "Austria-Hungary" except when the dual character of the Habsburg state is of primary importance to the point under discussion.

[27]For the evolution of Moltke's official views and their implications, cf. his memoranda of April 27, 1871, and January, 1880, in Helmuth von Moltke, *Die deutschen Aufmarschpläne 1871–1890*, ed. by F. von Schmerfeld, pub. as *Forschungen und Darstellungen aus dem Reichsarchiv* VII (Berlin, 1929), 4 ff.; Eberhard Kessel, *Moltke* (Stuttgart, 1957), 622 *passim*, and Graydon A. Tunstall, "The Schlieffen Plan: The Diplomacy and Military Strategy of the Central Powers in the East, 1905–1914," (Ph.D. Dissertation, Rutgers University, 1975), 12 ff.

[28]"Generalstabsreisen (Reise 1885)," in *General-feldmarschall Alfred Graf Waldersee in seinem militärischen Wirken*, ed. H. Mohs, Vol. II, *1882–1904* (Berlin, 1929), 147 ff.

[29]For Moltke's 1887 memoranda on the military advantages of a first strike, see *Die deutschen Aufmarschpläne*, 137 *passim*. Cf. also "Generalstabsreisen (Reise 1886)," in Mohs, *Waldersee* II, 168 ff.; and Gerhard Ritter, "Die Zusammenarbeit der Generalstäbe Deutschlands und Österreich-Ungarns vor dem Ersten Weltkrieg," in *Zur Geschichte und Problematik der Demokratie. Festgabe für Hans Herzfeld* (Berlin, 1958), 523–549.

[30]Cf. F. C. Bridge, *From Sadowa to Sarajevo: The Foreign Policy of Austria-Hungary, 1866–1914* (London, 1972), 34 ff.; and Lothar Hobelt, "Österreich-Ungarn und das Deutsche Reich als Zweibundpartner," in *Österreich und die deutsche Frage im 19. und 20. Jahrhundert*, ed. H. Lutz and H. Rumpler (Munich, 1982), 256-281.

[31]Kennan, *Bismarck's European Order*, 103 ff., is comprehensive on Russia's reaction to the Bulgarian crisis. On the issue of public opinion cf. Geyer, *Der russische Imperialismus*, 93 ff.; and the older and more detailed work of Irene Grünig, *Die russische öffentliche Meinung und ihre Stellung zu den Grossmächten 1878–1894* (Berlin, 1929), 86 ff.

[32]The general patterns of Russo-German economic relations are summarized in the brief essay by Helmut Böhme, "Die deutsch-russischen Wirtschaftsbeziehungen unter dem Gesichtspunkt der deutschen Handelspolitik (1878–1894)," in *Deutschland und Russland im Zeitalter des Kapitalismus*, ed. K. O. von Aretin and Werner Conze (Wiesbaden, 1977), 173–190, and the accompanying discussion, 191-206. H. Müller-Link, *Industrialisierung und Aussenpolitik. Preussen-Deutschland und das Zarenreich, 1860–1890* (Göttingen, 1977), is a detailed account, best

Notes

read in company with Theodore H. von Laue, *Sergei Witte and the Industrialization of Russia* (New York, 1963). Bleichröder's role is presented in Fritz Stern, *Gold and Iron: Bismarck, Bleichröder, and the Building of the German Empire* (New York, 1977), 434 ff.

[33]Holstein's views are reflected in the diary entries of Feb. 7, 1884, Oct. 13, 1885, Sept. 14 and Dec. 1, 1886, in *The Holstein Papers*, ed. N. Rich and M. H. Fisher, 4 vols. (Cambridge, 1955–63), II, 75, 253, 298–300, 315–316. Cf. Norman Rich, *Friedrich von Holstein: Politics and Diplomacy in the Era of Bismarck and Wilhelm II*, 2 vols. (Cambridge, 1965), I, 183 ff. Relevant models of Russian imperialism include Reinhard Wittram, "Das Russische Imperium und sein Gestaltwandel," *Historische Zeitschrift* 187 (1959), 568–593; Donald W. Treadgold, "Russian Expansion in the Light of Turner's Study of the American Frontier, *Agricultural History* XXVI (1952), 147–152; and J. L. Wieczynski, "Toward a Frontier Theory of Early Russian History," *Russian Review* XXIII (1974), 284–295.

[34]Diary entry of Jan. 8, 1887; and letter to Max von Thielmann, Mar. 22, 1887, *Holstein Papers* II, 330–331, 336–338.

[35]For the context of the Reinsurance Treaty cf. particularly Hans-Ulrich Wehler, "Bismarcks späte Russlandpolitik 1879–1890," in *Krisenherde des Kaiserreiches 1871–1918. Studien zur deutschen Sozial-und Verfassungsgeschichte* (Göttingen, 1970), 163–180; and Peter Rassow, "Die Stellung Deutschlands im Kreise der Grossen Mächte 1887–1890," in *Mainzer Akademie der Wissenschaft und der Literatur, Abhandlungen . . . 1959*, 179-231. H. Hallmann, ed. *Geschichte und Problematik des deutsch-russischen Rückversicherungsvertrags von 1887* (Darmstadt, 1968), incorporates the key documents, as well as excerpts from most major German interpretations.

[36]Cf. Heide W. Whelan, *Alexander III and the State Council: Bureaucracy and Counter-Reform in Late Imperial Russia* (New Brunswick, N.J., 1982); and more generally Jacob W. Kipp and W. Bruce Lincoln, "Autocracy and Reform: Bureaucratic Absolutism and Political Modernization in Nineteenth-Century Russia," *Russian History* VI (1979), 1–21. The most detailed accounts of Russo-German economic and financial relations are from the DDR: Sigrid Kumpf-Korfes, *Bismarcks "Draht nach Russland." Zum Problem der sozialökonomischen Hintergründe der russisch-deutschen Entfremdung im Zeitraum von 1878 bis 1894* (Berlin 1968), and more generally, Joachim Mai, *Das deutsche Kapital in Russland 1850–1894* (Berlin, 1970).

[37]Waldersee's view of events is summarized in his *Denkwürdigkeiten*, ed. H. O. Meisner, 3 vols. (Stuttgart, 1923–25), I, 334 ff., especially the entries for Nov. 17 and Dec. 4. Moltke's recommendation of Nov. 30 is in the Politisches Archiv des Auswärtigen Amtes (hereafter cited as PAAA), Deutschland 121, Geheim 12a/1. General analyses of the preventive war issue in 1887 include Karl-Ernst Jeismann, *Das Problem des Präventivkrieges im europäischen Staatensystem* (Munich, 1957), esp. 116 ff.; and R. Koop, "Das Problem des Präventivkrieges in der Politik Bismarcks" (Ph.D. Dissertation, University of Freiburg, 1953). DDR scholar Konrad Canis goes to another extreme in asserting an essential identity of ends and interests between the chancellor and the general in *Bismarck und Waldersee* (Berlin, 1980). J. Alden Nichols, *The Year of the Three Kaisers* (Urbana Ill., 1987) integrates Germany's foreign and domestic politics in 1887/88.

[38]Bülow to Holstein, Dec. 10, 1887 and Jan. 5, 1888, in *Holstein Papers* III, 236 ff., 246 ff. Allegations that Bülow supported a preventive war during this period are strongly disproved by his letter of Dec. 25 to Philipp Eulenburg, in

Notes

which he states that from a political perspective, war with Russia is not very promising, "and our politics must do everything consistent with our security and honor to avoid this 'unproductive' war." *Philipp Eulenburgs Politische Korrespondenz*, ed. J. C. G. Röhl, 3 vols. (Boppard, 1976–83), I, 257–258.

[39]"Bemerkungen Graf Ws zu einer Denkschrift des Generalleutnants v. Brandenstein vom November 1883, Jänuar 1884"; and comments of Oct. 14, 1885, on the *Aufmarschplan* of 1884/85, in Mohs, *Waldersee* II, 256–257, 277.

[40]Gordon Martel, *Imperial Diplomacy: Rosebery and the Failure of Foreign Policy* (Kingston, Montreal, 1986), 96–97.

[41]"Offensive gegen Russland," April 15, 1889; and "Krieg gegen Russland," Feb. 1890, in Mohs, *Waldersee* II, 323 ff., 327 ff. Cf. Wolfgang Foerster, *Aus der Gedankenwerkstaat des deutschen Generalstabes* (Berlin, 1931), 42ff.

[42]On the French army's low self-image in this period see Alan Mitchell, "A Situation of Inferiority: French Military Reorganization after the Defeat of 1870," *American Historical Review* LXXXVI (1981), 49–62.

[43]On the failure to renew the Reinsurance Treaty see the documents in Hallmann, *Deutsch-russischen Rückversicherungsvertrages*. Rich, *Holstein* I, 307 ff., is the most detailed treatment in English.

[44]The chief of staff explained himself in detail to, among others, the French deputy chief of staff in July, 1891; and to Giers in May, 1892. Cf. General Raoul de Boisdeffre's report of July 16, 1891, in France, Ministère des Affaires Étrangères, *Documents Diplomatiques Français (1871–1914)*, 41 vols. (Paris, 1929–59), 1st Series, VIII, Nr. 424 (hereafter cited as *DDF*); and Obruchev to Giers, May 19, 1892, reproduced in George F. Kennan, *The Fateful Alliance: France, Russia, and the Coming of the First World War* (New York, 1984), 264 ff. Giers's conversation with Alexander is noted in V. N. Lamsdorf, *Dnevik, 1891–1892* (Moscow, 1934), 311–312.

[45]The position of Andreas Hillgruber, "Die deutsch-russischen politischen Beziehungen (1887–1917)," in *Deutschland und Russland im Zeitalter des Kapitalismus*, 213.

[46]Rich, *Holstein* II, 356 ff., presents the evolution of Holstein's attitudes towards Russia.

[47]William C. Fuller, *Civil-Military Conflict in Imperial Russia, 1881–1914* (Princeton, N.J.: 1985), 52 *passim*; Edward R. Goldstein, "Military Aspects of Russian Industrialization: The Defense Industries, 1890–1917" (Ph.D. Dissertation, Case/Western Reserve University, 1977).

[48]G. S. Holzer, "German Electrical Industry in Russia: From Economic Entrepreneurship to Political Activism" (Ph.D. Dissertation, University of Nebraska, 1970), is a good case study of economic relations between the two states. Cf. also B. Bonwetsch, "Handelspolitik und Industrialisierung. Zur aussenwirtschaftlichen Abhängigkeit Russlands," in *Wirtschaft und Gesellschaft im vorrevolutionären Russland*, ed. D. Geyer (Koln, 1975), 277–299.

[49]Holstein to Radolin, July 2, 1895, *Holstein Papers* III, Nr. 541.

[50]Paul M. Kennedy, *The Rise of the Anglo-German Antagonism 1860–1914* (London, 1980). Gregor Schollgen, *Imperialismus und Gleichgewicht. Deutschland, England und die orientalische Frage 1871–1914* (Munich, 1984); and Peter Winzen, "Die Englandpolitik Friedrich von Holsteins 1895–1901" (Ph.D. Dissertation, University of Köln, 1975), focus on the English question; Winzen adds a general dimension in *Bülows Weltmachtkonzept* (Boppard, 1977).

[51]Cf. *inter alia* Aaron L. Friedberg, *The Weary Titan, Great Britain and the Experience of Relative Decline, 1895–1905* (Princeton, N.J., 1988); H. W. Koch,

"The Anglo-German Alliance Negotiations: Missed Opportunity or Myth?" *History* LIV (1969), 378–392; and Paul M. Kennedy, *The Realities behind Diplomacy: Background Influences on British External Policy, 1865–1980* (London, 1981); and "The Tradition of Appeasement in British Foreign Policy, 1865–1939, in *Strategy and Diplomacy, 1870–1945* (London, 1983), 15–39.

[52]Keith Wilson, "The Invention of Germany," in *The Policy of the Entente. Essays on the Determinants of British Foreign Policy 1904–1914* (Cambridge, 1985), 100–120.

[53]The German naval threat was almost welcome as the one challenge Britain was on the whole confident of meeting successfully. For the diplomacy of appeasement at the turn of the century, cf. *inter alia* Christopher Andrew, *Théophile Delcassé and the Making of the Entente Cordiale* (New York, 1968); P. J. V. Rolo, *Entente Cordiale: The Origins and Negotiations of the Anglo-French Agreements of 8 April, 1904* (London, 1969); F. R. Bridge, *Great Britain and Austria-Hungary, 1906–1914: A Diplomatic History* (London, 1972); Horst Jaeckel, *Die Nordwestgrenze in der Verteidigung Indiens 1900–1908 und der Weg Englands zum russischen-britischen Abkommen von 1907* (Köln, 1968); and F. Kazemzadeh, *Russia and Britain in Persia 1864–1914: A Study in Imperialism* (New Haven, Conn., 1968), 447 *passim*.

[54]Geyer, *Der russische Imperialismus*, 71 ff., 143 ff., summarizes Russia's Asian expansion. Otto Hoetzsch, *Russland in Asien* (Stuttgart, 1966), and A. M. Malozemoff, *Russian Far Eastern Policy, 1881-1904* (Berkeley, 1958), provide the details. Ian Nish, *The Origins of the Russo-Japanese War* (London, 1985), stresses that conflict's "Russian dimension," as opposed to external factors.

[55]Bülow to Holstein, 16.1.04, in *GP* XIX, 1, Nr. 5943; and *Holstein Papers* IV, Nr. 818. Winzen, *Bülows Weltmachtkonzept*, argues strongly and convincingly for the primacy of foreign policy in determining the chancellor's approach to international relations. Barbara Vogel, *Deutsche Russlandpolitik. Das Scheitern des deutschen Weltpolitik unter Bülow 1900–1906 (Düsseldorf, 1973)*, stresses economic factors. For German policies toward France cf. H. Raulff, *Zwischen Machtpolitik und Imperialismus. Die deutsche Frankreichpolitik 1904–05* (Düsseldorf, 1976); and P. Guillen, *L'allemagne et le Maroc 1870–1905* (Paris, 1967).

[56]James W. Long, "The Economics of the Franco-Russian Alliance, 1904–06" (Ph.D. Dissertation, University of Wisconsin, 1968) is a mine of information on the financial underpinning of Russian diplomacy in this period. For Russia's behavior at Algeciras see Bernard F. Oppel, "The Waning of a Traditional Alliance. Russia and Germany after the Portsmouth Peace Conference," *Central European History* V (1972), 318–329. For Austria's, see F. Fellner, "Die Haltung Oesterreich-Ungarns während der Konferenz von Algeciras 1906," *Mitteilung des Instituts für Österreichische Geschichtsforschung* LXXI (1963), 462–477.

[57]On the process of decision making in 1905, Albrecht Moritz, *Das Problem des Präventivkrieges in der deutschen Politik während der ersten Marokkokrise* (Bern, 1974); and Raulff, *Machtpolitik*, 127 ff., are the most recent treatments. For German military thought cf. *inter alia* Jack Snyder, *The Ideology of the Offensive: Military Decision-Making and the Disasters of 1914* (Ithaca, N.Y., 1984), pp. 107 *passim*; and more generally Stephen Van Evera, "The Cult of the Offensive and the Origins of the First World War," *International Security* IX (1984), 58–107.

[58]The evolution of German military intentions towards the Low Countries can be traced in Bundesarchiv-Militärarchiv, RM 5/1666, "Angriffspläne gegen Holland und Belgien von 19.Juni 1885 bis Jan. 1902," and RM 5/1667, "Angriffspläne gegen Holland und Belgien vom Mai 1905 bis Dez. 1912." For Schlieffen's

Notes

concern with Belgium as an invasion route see his memoranda of May 1 and June 7, 1905, RM 5/1667. The general staff request of Nov. 27, 1909, is in *ibid*. General accounts include Ivo N. Lambi, *The Navy and German Power Politics, 1862–1914* (Boston, 1984), esp. 90 *passim*; Folkert Krieger, "Deutsch-dänische Beziehungen 1901–1914" (Ph.D. Dissertation, University of Bonn, 1974), 157 *passim*; and Horst Lademacher, *Die belgische Neutralität als Problem der europäischen Politik 1830–1914* (Bonn, 1971), esp. 427 ff.

[59]"Der Aufmarsch gegen Russland," Jan., 1894, Mohs, *Waldersee* II, 343 ff.

[60]Lothar Höbelt, "Schlieffen, Beck, Potiorek und das Ende der gemeinsamen deutsch-österreichischen-ungarischen Aufmarschpläne im Osten," *Militärgeschichtliche Mitteilungen* XXXVI (1984), 7–30, demonstrates that this anxiety was shared by the Austrians, and was a major factor in their ready acceptance of the revised German strategy.

[61]Gerhard Ritter, *The Schlieffen Plan: Critique of a Myth*, tr. E. Wilson (London, 1958); and Jehuda Wallach, *The Dogma of the Battle of Annihilation* (Westport Conn.: 1986). Both minimize Schlieffen's concern for the east as a factor in his planning. Cf. L. C. F. Turner, "The Significance of the Schlieffen Plan," *Australian Journal of Politics and History* XIII (1967), 49–66.

[62]Allan Mitchell, *Victors and Vanquished: The German Influence on Army and Church in France after 1870* (Chapel Hill, N.C., 1984), presents this process in detail.

[63]The Anglo-French entente of 1904 also generated the "hostage theory," by which in case of war with England, decisive pressure was to be exerted on an otherwise inaccessible enemy by overrunning France, and arguably the Low Countries as well. Cf. Einem to Bülow, Oct. 17, 1904, with Schlieffen's enclosure of Oct. 7, in PAAA, Deutschland 138, Geheim/6; and Bülow to Holstein, Dec. 15, 1904, in *Holstein Papers* IV, Nr. 869.

[64]Schlieffen to his sister Marie, November 13, 1892, in Eberhard Kessel, ed., *Generalfeldmarschall Graf Alfred Schlieffen. Briefe* (Göttingen, 1958), 295–298.

[65]The evolution of Schlieffen's thought can be traced in the *Aufgaben* for 1903 and 1904 in Generalstab des Heeres, Kriegswissenschaftliche Abteilung (ed.), *Dienstschriften des Chefs des Generalstabes der Armee Generalfeldmarschalls Graf von Schlieffen*, Vol. I, *Die taktisch-strategischen Aufgaben aus den Jahren 1891–1905* (Berlin, 1937), 103 *passim*; and the "Staff Rides East" for 1901 and 1903, in *ibid.*, Vol. II, *Die Grossen Generalstabsreisen-Ost aus den Jahren 1891–1905* (Berlin, 1937), 222 ff. and 300 ff.

[66]"Operationsstudie gegen Russland," Mar. 1898, Mohs, *Waldersee* II, 348 ff.

[67]Cf. in particular *Aufgaben* of 1891, 1898, 1899 and 1904; and the Staff Rides East for 1897, 1899, 1901, and 1903, in *Dienstschriften* I and II. The anecdote is from Hermann von François, *Marneschlacht und Tannenberg* (Berlin, 1920), 126.

[68]Schlieffen's growing pessimism is described in Gerhard Ritter, *Sword and Scepter*, tr. Heinz Norden, 4 vols. (Coral Gables, Fla., 1969–73), II, 199 ff. Hans Delbrück's 1896 critique of Bloch, "Zukunftskriege und Zukunftsfriede," is reprinted in *Erinnerungen, Aufsätze und Reden* (Berlin, 1902), 498–525. Cf. for purposes of comparison T. E. H. Travers, "Technology, Tactics, and Morale: Jean de Bloch, the Boer War, and British Military Theory 1900–1914," *Journal of Modern History* LI (1979) 264–286.

Notes

[69]John Lewis Gaddis, *Strategies of Containment: A Critical Appraisal of Postwar American National Security Policy* (New York, 1982), 273.

[70]Holstein to Brauer, Dec. 23, 1905, *Holstein Papers* IV, 376 ff.

[71]For the entente see particularly J. J. Williams, "The Strategic Background to the Anglo-Russian Entente of August, 1907," *Historical Journal* IX (1966), 360–373; and G. Monge, *Ursachen und Entstehung der englisch-französischen-russischen Entente 1900–1907* (Seeheim, 1969). Barbara Jelavich, "British Means of Offense against Russia in the Nineteenth Century," *Russian History* I (1974), 119–135, legitimates Russia's strategic concerns. Keith Neilson, "Wishful Thinking: The Foreign Office and Russia, 1907–1917," in *Shadow and Substance in British Foreign Policy 1895–1939. Memorial Essays Honouring C. V. Lowe* (Edmonton, Alberta, 1984), 151–180, stresses Britain's need for an arrangement with Russia.

[72]Nicolson to Grey, Jan. 2, 1907 and Jan. 29, 1908, *British Documents on Foreign Affairs: Reports and Papers from the Foreign Office Confidential Print*, Series A, *Russia, 1859–1914*, ed. D. Lieven, 6 vols. (Washington, D.C., 1983), IV, Nr. 187; V, Nr. 20.

[73]Immanuel Geiss, *German Foreign Policy, 1871–1914* (London, Boston, 1976), 107; Fritz Fischer, *War of Illusions*, tr. M. Jackson (New York, 1975), 51.

2. THE CENTER FAILS TO HOLD

[1]Wilhelm M. Carlgren, *Iswolsky und Aehrenthal vor der bosnischen Annexionskrise: Russische und österreichisch-ungarische Balkanpolitik 1906–1908* (Uppsala, 1955), presents the background of the annexation. Bernadotte Schmitt, *The Annexation of Bosnia, 1908–1909* (Cambridge, 1937), and M. Nintchitch, *La Crise bosniaque et les puissances européenes*, 2 vols. (Paris, 1937), cover the annexation itself. For the developing role and belligerent nature of public opinion in Russia cf. Manfred Hagen, *Die Entfaltung politischer Öffentlichkeit in Russland 1906–1914* (Wiesbaden, 1982); and Caspar Ferenczi, *Aussenpolitik und Öffentlichkeit in Russland, 1906–1912* (Husum, 1982). For the Central Powers cf. H. A. Gemeinhardt, *Deutsche und österreichische Pressepolitik während der Bosnischen Krise 1908/09* (Husum, 1980).

[2]For tension between Austria and Germany at this period see Michael Belinen, *Rüstung-Bündnis-Sicherheit. Dreibund und informeller Imperialismus 1900–1908* (Tübingen, 1985).

[3]Roger Chickering, *Imperial Germany and a World without War* (Princeton, 1975); Wolfgang J. Mommsen, "The Topos of Inevitable War in Germany in the Decade before 1914," in *Germany in the Age of Total War*, ed. V. R. Berghahn and M. Kitchen (London, 1981), 23–45.

[4]Holstein to Bülow, Oct. 13, 1908, in *The Holstein Papers*, 4 vols., ed. Norman Rich (Cambridge, 1959–63), IV, Nr. 1142; Bülow to Holstein, Dec. 27, 1908, *ibid.*, Nr. 1173; Szögeny to foreign office, Dec. 16, 1908, in Ludwig Bittner, et al., *Oesterreich-Ungarns Aussenpolitik von der bosnischen Krise 1908 bis zum Kriegsausbruch 1914* , 8 vols. (Vienna, 1930), I, Nr. 752. Hintze to William, Oct. 23, 1908; Monts to Bülow, Oct. 25, 1908; Pourtalès to Bülow, Oct. 30, 1908, in Politisches Archiv des Auswärtigen Amtes, Deutschland 121/30 (hereafter cited as PAAA).

[5]Bülow's memorandum of Oct. 27, 1908, *ibid.*; Bülow to Aehrenthal, Jan. 8, 1909, in J. Lepsius, A. Mendelsohn-Bartholdy, F. Thimme, eds., *Die Grosse Politik der europäischen Kabinette 1871–1914*, 40 vols. (Berlin, 1922–27), XXV, Nr. 9173 (hereafter cited as *GP*).

[6]Aehrenthal to Bülow, Feb. 20, 1909; and Kaegenich's report of Feb. 23, 1909, in *GP* XXVI, 2, Nrs. 9386, 9390; Cartwright to Grey, Mar. 6, 1909, in

Notes

British Documents on the Origins of the War, 1878–1914, ed. G. P. Gooch and H. W. V. Temperley, 11 vols. (London, 1926–1938), V, Nr. 657 (hereafter cited as *BD*).

[7]Miquel to Bülow, Nov. 27, 1908; Pourtalès to Bülow, Dec. 11, 1908 and Jan. 30, 1909; Moscow Consulate to Bülow, Dec. 4, 1908; PAAA, Deutschland 131/30.

[8]Nicolson to Grey, Feb. 8, 1909, *British Documents on Foreign Affairs: Reports and Papers from the Foreign Office Confidential Print,* Series A, *Russia, 1859–1914,* ed. D. Lieven, 6 vols. (Washington, D.C., 1983), V, Nr. 61 (hereafter cited as *BDFA*).

[9]Hintze to William, Feb. 24, 1909, PAAA, Russland 98, Geheim.

[10]Bülow to Pourtalès, Mar. 14 and 29, 1909, *GP* XXVI, 2, Nrs. 9437, 9460; Hintze to Bülow, Mar. 20, 1909, PAAA, Deutschland 131/30; Pourtalès to foreign office, Mar. 22, 1909; *GP*, XXVI, 2, Nr. 9464.

[11]Nicolson to Grey, May 1, 1909, *BDFA* V, Nr. 67. Detailed analyses sympathetic to the German position are Heinz-Günther Sasse, *War das deutsche Eingreifen in die Bosnische Krise im März 1909 ein Ultimatum?* (Stuttgart, 1936); and Heinz Gerhardt, *War in der bosnischen Annexationskrise die deutsche Démarche vom 22.März ein Ultimatum?* (Berlin, 1965).

[12]Nicolson to Grey, May 7, 1909, *BDFA* V, Nr. 70.

[13]D. W. Sweet, "The Bosnian Crisis," in *British Foreign Policy under Sir Edward Grey,* ed. F. R. Hinsley (Cambridge, 1977), 190 ff.

[14]A good overview of this process is Peter F. Sugar, "External and Domestic Roots of Eastern European Nationalism," in *Nationalism in Eastern Europe,* ed. P. F. Sugar, I. J. Lederer (Seattle, London, 1969), 3–54.

[15]Pourtalès to Bülow, Mar. 19 and Apr. 1, 1909, PAAA, Deutschland 131/30. Hintze to William, Apr. 3 and May 29, 1909; GP, XXVI, 2, 9505, 9545; and Mar. 24, 1910, PAAA, Russland 98, Geheim.

[16]Pourtalès to Bethmann, Feb. 9, 1910, PAAA, Deutschland 131/32; Posadowsky-Wehner to war ministry, Aug. 12, 1910, GP XXVI, 2, Nr. 9950; Hintze to William, Aug. 19, 1910, PAAA, Russland 98, Geheim. For anti-German attitudes in Russia at this period Cf. D. C. B. Lieven, *Russia and the Origins of the First World War* (New York, 1983), p. 37; and Uwe Liszkowski, "Zur Aktualisierung der Stereotype 'Die Deutsche Gefahr' im russischen Neoslawismus," in *Russland und Deutschland. Festschrift für G. v. Rauch,* ed. U. Liszkowski (Stuttgart, 1974), 278–294.

[17]The outlines of Moltke's approach can be found in Moltke to Bülow, Jan. 19, 1909, "Militärische Leistungsfähigkeit der wichtigsten Staaten Europas zu Beginn dieses Jahren," PAAA, Deutschland 121/31, Geheim; Adolf Tappen's comments on strategic planning for a two-front war of Oct. 22, 1919, Bundesarchiv-Militärarchiv, Nachlass Tappen, N56/4; and the *Immediatvortrag* of Nov. 4, 1909, in BA-MA, RM 5/1607.

[18]*Immediatvortrag* to William, Oct. 24, 1908, *ibid.*; memorandum from the chief of the admiralty staff, Mar. 19, 1909, and report of a conference between the chief of the admiralty staff and Moltke on March 18, 1909, *ibid.*, RM5/1633.

[19]Colonel Wyndham to Nicolson, Nov. 19, 1908, BDFA V, Nr. 53.

[20]A report of the *Schlussaufgabe* for 1907 is in BA-MA, Nachlass Groener, N46/111. Moltke's comment on the navy is in his reply of Apr. 2, 1909, to an admiralty questionnaire in BA-MA, RM5/1633.

[21]Moltke's general reasoning on the prospects of an offensive against Russia is developed in his 1909 correspondence with Conrad, most of it reprinted in Franz Conrad von Hötzendorf, *Aus meiner Dienstzeit,* 5 vols. (Vienna, 1921–25),

Notes

II, 633 *passim*. Cf. also the analyses by Norman Stone, "Moltke-Conrad: Relations between the Austro-Hungarian and German General Staffs, 1909–1914," *Historical Journal* IX (1966), 201–228; and "Die Mobilmachung der österreichischen-ungarischen Armee 1914," *Militärgeschichtliche Mitteilungen* XVI (1974), 67–95 and Dennis E. Showalter, "The Eastern Front and German Military Planning, 1871–1914: Some Observations," *East European Quarterly* XV (1981), 163–180.

[22]Bethmann made his intentions plain in his conferences of Oct. 14 and Nov. 4, 1909, with the British Ambassador. Cf. Yale University, Kiderlin-Wächter Papers, Box 16, Folder 173; with Goschen to Grey, Oct. 15 and Nov. 4, 1909, in *BD* VI, Nrs. 200, 204. Fritz Fischer, "Die Neutralität Englands als Ziel deutscher Politik 1908/09–1914," in *Von der freien Gemeinde zum föderativen Europa*, ed. F. Esterbauer *et al.* (Berlin, 1983), pp. 261–282, insists this was no more than an effort to clear the ground for a general war. For more balanced interpretations of Bethmann's policies cf. Oswald Hauser, *Deutschland und der englisch-russische Gegensatz, 1900–1914* (Göttingen, 1958); Hansjoachim Henning, *Deutschlands Verhältnis zu England in Bethmann-Hollwegs Aussenpolitik 1909–1914* (Köln, 1962), and more generally and very perceptively, Konrad Jarausch, *The Enigmatic Chancellor. Bethmann Hollweg and the Hubris of Imperial Germany* (New Haven, Conn., 1973), pp. 108 ff.

[23]Bethmann to Metternich, Nov. 10, 1909, Kiderlin Papers 10/173.

[24]Bethmann's memorandum of Feb. 20, 1910, PAAA, Orientalia Generalia 5/17.

[25]Mirbach to Bethmann, Oct. 4 and Oct. 20, 1910, PAAA, Deutschland 131/32; Pourtalès to Bethmann, Apr. 22, 1910, *ibid.*, 30; Hugh O'Bierne to Grey, Oct. 5, 1910, *BDFA* VI, Nr. 40.

[26]A useful recent treatment of the Potsdam Conference is Robert E. Simmons, "German Balkan Diplomacy, 1906–1913. The Genesis and Implementation of a War-Risk Policy" (Ph.D. Dissertation, Auburn University, 1982), 320 ff. Key documents include Bethmann to William, Nov. 1 and Nov. 6, 1910, GP XXVI, 2, Nrs. 10152, 10153; Bethmann to Pourtalès, Nov. 8 and Nov. 15, 1910, *ibid.*, Nrs. 10155 and 10159; Bethmann to Aehrenthal, Nov. 14, 1910, PAAA, Orientalia Generalia 5/17; and Tschirsky to Bethmann, Nov. 6 and Nov. 20, 1910, PAAA, Deutschland 131/32. Germany's problem in generating investment capital is described in Raymond Poidevin, "Weltpolitik allemand et capitaux français 1898–1914," in *Deutschland in der Weltpolitik des 19. und 20. Jahrhunderts*, ed. I. Geiss, B-J Wendt (Düsseldorf, 1973), 237–249.

[27]"Die wichtigsten Veränderungen im Heerwesen Russlands im Jahre 1910," BA/MA, RM5/1486; Military attaché's report to war ministry of Sept. 13, 1911, PAAA, Russland 72/92.

[28]Kiderlin to Lichnowsky, Dec. 6, 1912, PAAA, Deutschland 131/34; letter of Mar. 20, 1909, in E. Jäckh, *Kiderlin-Wächter, der Staatsmann und Mensch*, Vol. II (Stuttgart, 1924), 26–27.

[29]V. N. Kokovtsov, *Out of My Past*, ed. H. H. Fischer, M. L. Malveev (Stanford, 1935), 334 ff.; Mary S. Conroy, *Peter Arkad'evich Stolypin: Practical Politics in Late Tsarist Russia* (Boulder, Colo., 1976); Ferenczi, *Aussenpolitik und Öffentlicheit*, 259 ff.

[30]Hans Uebersberger, *Österreich zwischen Russland und Serbien* (Köln, Graz, 1958), highlights on the other hand the objective threat these Russian initiatives posed to vital Habsburg interests.

[31]For Russia's Balkan policy generally cf. Andrew Rossos, *Russia and the Balkans: Inter-Balkan Rivalries and Russian Foreign Policy, 1908–1914* (Toronto,

Notes

1981); and E. C. Thaden, *Russia and the Balkan Alliance of 1912* (University Park, Penn., 1965).

[32]At the conference of the general staffs, held on August 31. France, Ministère des Affaires Étrangères, *Documents Diplomatiques Français 1871–1914*, 41 vols. (Paris, 1929–59), 3rd Series, II, Nr. 90 (hereafter cited as *DDF*).

[33]Cf. D. W. Spring, "Russia and the Franco-Russian Alliance, 1905–14: Dependence or Interdependence?" *Slavonic and East European Review* LXVI (1988), 564–592; and Douglas Porch, "The Marne and After: A Reappraisal of French Strategy in the First World War," *The Journal of Military History*, LIII (1989), 363-386. Donald R. Mathieu, "The Role of Russia in French Foreign Policy, 1908–1914" (Ph.D. Dissertation, Stanford University, 1968); and Carol H. Wilcox, "The Franco-Russian Alliance, 1908–1911" (Ph.D. Dissertation, Clark University, 1968), survey this subject in detail from a diplomatic perspective.

[34]Report of the German consulate at Tiflis, Dec. 25, 1912, in PAAA, Russland 72/94. On the Turkish rearmament after 1908 see particularly Jehuda L. Wallach, *Anatomie einer Militärhilfe. Die preussisch-deutsche Militärmissionen in der Türkei, 1835–1919* (Düsseldorf, 1976).

[35]Geoffrey Barraclough, *From Agadir to Armageddon* (New York, 1982), is a strong recent argument for the Second Moroccan Crisis as a decisive event in the origins of World War I. Douglas Porch, *The Conquest of Morocco* (New York, 1983), focusses on the local and regional factors inspiring the French action. J. C. Allain, *Agadir 1911* (Paris, 1976), is a detailed analysis from a French perspective. Emily Oncken, *Panthersprung nach Agadir: Die deutsche Politik während der zweiten Marokkokrise 1911* (Düsseldorf, 1981), is excellent for the German side.

[36]Cf. T. W. Childs, "Mediterranean Imbroglio: The Diplomatic Origins of Modern Libya (The Diplomacy of the Belligerents during the Italo-Turkish War, 1911–1912)" (Ph.D. Dissertation, Georgetown University, 1982); and R. J. B. Bosworth, *Italy, the Least of the Great Powers. Italian Foreign Policy before the First World War* (Cambridge, 1979), 127 *passim*.

[37]Sazonov expressed himself in those terms to his ambassador to Bulgaria in October, 1911. A. Nekliudov, *Diplomatic Reminiscences 1911–1917* (London, 1920), 45–46. Hartwig was quoted by the German ambassador to Serbia a year later. Griesinger to Bethmann, Oct. 28, 1912, PAAA, Serbien 17/8.

[38]Pourtalès to Bethmann, Feb. 5, 1912; and Bethmann's report of July 6/7, 1912, PAAA, Orientalia Generalia 5/17.

[39]Memorandum of Oct. 9, 1912, PAAA, Russland 72/93.

[40]For Austria's preparations, cf. Samuel R. Williamson, Jr., "Military Dimensions of Habsburg-Romanov Relations During the Era of the Balkan Wars," in *East Central European Society and the Balkan Wars*, ed. B. Király, D. Djordjevic (New York, 1987), 328–345.

[41]Reports from Germany's Warsaw consulate of Oct. 19, 1912, and the Moscow consulate of Oct. 6, Nov. 11, and Nov. 28, 1912, PAAA, Russland 72/93.

[42]Kiderlin to Tschirsky, Nov. 26, 1912, PAAA, Deutschland 143.

[43]Pourtalès to Bethmann, Nov. 19 and Nov. 20, 1912, PAAA, Russland 72/93; Kagenech to foreign office, Nov. 27, 1912, PAAA, Deutschland 143. Cf. also E. Tuiczynski, "Österreich-Ungarn und Südosteuropa während der Balkankriege," *Balkan Studies* V (1964), 11–46.; Luigi Albertini, *The Origins of the War of 1914*, tr. and ed. I. M. Massey, 3 vols. (London, 1952–57), I, 379 ff.; and L. C. F. Turner, *Origins of the First World War* (New York, 1970), pp. 40 ff.

[44]Kokovtsov, *Out of My Past*, 344 ff.; Ernest R. May, "Cabinet, Tsar,

Notes

Kaiser: Three Approaches to Assessment," in *Knowing One's Enemies. Intelligence Assessment before the Two World Wars*, ed. E. R. May, (Princeton, 1984), 17–26.

[45]Raymond Poidevin and Jacques Bariety, *Les relations franco-allemandes 1815–1975* (Paris, 1977), 191 ff., is a brief general survey. John Keiger, *France and the Origins of the First World War* (New York, 1983); and "Jules Cambon and Franco-German Détente, 1907–1914," *Historical Journal* XXVI (1983), 641–659, cover the relationship's diplomatic aspects; Poidevin, "Wirtschaftlicher und finanzieller Nationalismus in Frankreich und Deutschland, 1907–1914," *Geschichte in Wissenschaft und Unterricht* (1974), incorporates a useful bibliography.

[46]Cf. the general staff reports of July 13 and Sept. 2, 1912 in *DDF*, 3rd Series, III, Nrs. 200, 359. Samuel R. Williamson, *The Politics of Grand Strategy: Britain and France Prepare for War, 1904–1914* (Cambridge, Mass., 1969), 205 *passim*, develops the British influence on French planning.

[47]Izvolsky to Sazonov, Sept. 12, 1912, in *Un Livre Noir. Diplomatie d'avant-guerre d'apres les documents des archives russes, 1910–1917*, 3 vols. in 6 (Paris, 1922–34), I, 323 ff. Robert H. Allshouse, "Aleksander Izvolskii and Russian Foreign Policy, 1910–1914" (Ph.D. Dissertation, Case Western Reserve University, 1977) presents Izvolsky's ambassadorial career without exaggerating its impact.

[48]Louis Garros, "En Marge de l'Alliance Franco-Russe," *Revue Historique de e'Armee* VI (June, 1950), pp. 29–30, 36.

[49]Raymond Poincaré, *Au service de la France. Neuf années de souvenirs*, 10 vols. (Paris, 1926–33), II, 336 ff.

[50]Pourtalès to Bethmann, Dec. 1, 1912, PAAA, Deutschland 131/34.

[51]Kiderlin to Bethmann, Sept. 2, 1912, *ibid.*

[52]R. J. Crampton, *The Hollow Détente: Anglo-German Relations in the Balkans, 1911–1914* (London, 1979), *passim*.

[53]Minute by Sir Edward Grey, Apr. 18, 1910, *BD* VI, Nr. 344. Cf. Keith M. Wilson, "The British *Démarche* of 3 and 4 December, 1912: H.A. Gwynne's Note on Britain, Russia and the First Balkan War," in *Empire and Continent* (London, 1987), 141-148.

[54]For Bethmann's speech see *Verhandlungen des Reichstages, Stenografische Berichte*, Vol. 286, 2471–2472. A copy of Kiderlin's is in Kiderlin Papers 10/185.

[55] Grey to Bertie, Dec. 3, 1912; and Nicholson to Buchanan, Dec. 3, 1912, in *BD*, IX, 2, Nos. 321, 322; and Prince Karl Max von Lichnowsky, *Heading for the Abyss*, tr. S. Delmer (London, 1928), *passim*.

[56]William's comments, on an article of Oct. 1, 1912, in the *Täglichen Rundschau*, are in Kiderlin Papers 10/176.

[57]The best examples of the first approach in John G. Röhl, whose most recent version of his case is "Der Militärpolitische Entscheidungsprozess in Deutschland am Vorabend des Ersten Weltkrieges," *Kaiser, Hof und Staat. Wilhelm II und die deutsche Politik.* (Munich, 1987), pp. 175–202. For the second, cf. especially Wolfgang J. Mommsen, "Domestic Factors in German Foreign Policy before 1914," *Central European History* VI (1973), 12–14; and Egmont Zechlin, "Die Adriakrise und der 'Kriegsrat' von 8. Dezember 1912," in *Krieg und Kriegsrisiko* (Düsseldorf, 1979), 115–159.

[58]Kiderlin to Lichnowski, Dec. 6, 1912, PAAA, Deutschland 131/34.

[59]Immanuel Geiss, *German Foreign Policy, 1871–1914* (London, 1976), 123–124; and Fritz Fischer, *Germany's Aims in the First World War* (New York, 1967), 19, are familiar statements of this position.

[60]Ann Taylor Allen, *Satire and Society in Wilhelmine Germany. Kladderadatsch and Simplicissimus, 1890–1914* (Lexington, Ky., 1984), pp. 131–132; Moltke to

Notes

Bethmann, June 19, 1914, in *Die Deutschen Dokumente zum Kriegsausbruch*, ed. W. Schücking, M. Montgelas, rev. ed., 5 vols. (Berlin, 1927), II, Nr. 349.

[61]Michael R. Marrus, *The Unwanted: European Refugees in the Twentieth Century* (New York, 1985), 45–46. The quotation is from Carnegie Endowment for International Peace, *Report of the International Commission to Inquire into the Causes and the Conduct of the Balkan Wars* (Washington, D.C., 1914), 151.

[62]Djordje Mikić "The Albanians and Serbia During the Balkan Wars," in *East Central European Society and the Balkan Wars*, 165-196.

[63]Joachim Remak, "1914—The Third Balkan War: Origins Reconsidered," *Journal of Modern History* XLIII (1971), 353–366; Barbara Jelavich, *History of the Balkans*, 2 vols (Cambridge, 1983), II, 108 ff.

[64]Benedict Anderson, *Imagined Communities* (London, 1986).

[65]Alfred Cobban, *National Self-Determination* (London, 1945), 45–46; and Anthony Hartley, "The 'Cold War' for Beginners," *Encounter* LXXII (Feb. 1988), 13; H. R. Trevor-Roper and George Urban, "Aftermaths of Empire: The Lessons of Upheavals and Destabilisation," *ibid.*, LXXIII (Dec. 1989), 13; On the evolution of self-determination as a political concept during World War I see particularly Harold Nelson, *Land and Power: British and Allied Policy on Germany's Frontiers, 1916–1919* (Toronto, 1963).

[66]Crampton, *Hollow Détente*, stresses the short-term aspects of the German initiative. J. M. Miller, Jr., "The Concert of Europe in the First Balkan War, 1912–1913" (Ph.D. Dissertation, Clark University, 1969), is a more general treatment.

[67]Klaus Schwabe, *Woodrow Wilson, Revolutionary Germany and Peacemaking, 1918–1919. Missionary Diplomacy and the Realities of Power*, tr. M. R. and R. Kimber (Chapel Hill, N.C., 1985), p. 69.

[68]Cf. Roland Stromberg, *Redemption by War: The Intellectuals and 1914* (Lawrence, Kans., 1982); and Michael Howard, "Men Against Fire: Expectations of War in 1914," *International Security* IX (Summer, 1984), 41–57.

[69]The respect accorded these men in German military circles reflected their status as experts on tactical and operational issues—a fact giving their opinions on broader questions a more polite hearing than might otherwise have been the case. Cf. Dennis E. Showalter, "Goltz and Bernhardi: The Institutionalization of Originality in the Imperial German Army," *Defense Analysis* III (1987), 305–318.

[70]"Memorandum of December 28, 1912, on a War with France and Russia," in Gerhard Ritter, *The Schlieffen Plan: Critique of a Myth*, M. A. and E. Wilson (New York, 1958), 168 ff.; and A. Böhm-Tettelbach, *Der Böhmische Feldzug Friedrichs des Grossen 1757 im Lichte Schlieffensche Kritik* (Berlin, 1934).

[71]"Die Militärpolitische Lage Deutschlands," Dec. 2, 1911, in *Kriegsrüstung und Kriegswirtschaft*, ed. Reichsarchiv, *Anlageband* (Berlin, 1930), 126 ff.; "Die wichtigste Veränderungen im Heerwesen Russlands im Jahre 1911," BA-MA, RM5/1946, Russland Militärisches, Apr. 1892-Apr. 1914.

[72]Paul M. Kennedy, "The First World War and the International Power System," in *International Security* IX (Summer, 1984), 28–29. Parallel critiques of the Russian army are John Bushnell, "The Tsarist Army after the Russo-Japanese War: The View from the Field," and W. C. Fuller, "The Tsarist Army after the Russo-Japanese War: The View from the War Ministry," in *The Impact of Unsuccessful Military Campaigns on Military Institutions, 1860–1980*, ed. Lt.-Col. C. E. Shrader (Washington, D.C., 1984), 77–99, 100–119. Walter T. Wilfong, "Rebuilding the Russian Army, 1905–1914: The Question of a Comprehensive

Notes

Plan for National Defense" (Ph.D. Dissertation, Indiana University, 1977), is a bit more optimistic, but remains negative.

[73]Modris Eksteins, "When Death Was Young . . . : Germany, Modernism, and the Great War," in *Ideas into Politics: Aspects of European History 1880–1950*, ed. R. J. Bullen *et al*. (London, 1984), pp. 25–35, is an eloquent brief presentation of Germany in the modern era as "more modern than we have had the courage to admit" (p. 33). Frank J. Ward, "The Center Party and the German Election of 1907" (Ph.D. Dissertation, University of California, Los Angeles, 1984) is a convincing case study showing that the Reich by 1907 had moved much closer to parliamentary responsibility than is generally accepted.

[74]For Russia's new cultural position see Camilla Gray, *Die russische Avant-garde der modernen Kunst 1863–1922* (Köln, 1962). German responses are presented in Brigitte Löhr, *Die "Zukunft Russlands": Prospektiven russischer Wirtschaftsentwicklung und deutsch-russische Wirtschaftsbeziehungen vor dem Ersten Weltkrieg* (Wiesbaden, 1985); Werner Markert, "Die deutsch-russischen Beziehungen am Vorabend des ersten Weltkrieges," in *Deutsch-russische Beziehungen von Bismarck bis zur Gegenwart*, ed. W. Markert (Stuttgart, 1964), 40–79; and Robert C. Williams, "Russians in Germany: 1900–1914," in *1914: The Coming of the First World War*, ed. W. Laqueur, G. L. Mosse (New York, 1966), 254–282.

[75]For the history and significance of German intelligence operations cf. Fritz Gempp, "Geheimer Nachrichtendienst und Spionageabwehr des Heeres," National Archives T-77, rolls 1,438–1,440, 1,442, 1,507–1,509, Part I, *passim*; and the excellent analysis by Holger Herwig, "Imperial Germany," in *Knowing One's Enemies*, 62–97.

[76]Keith Neilson, "Watching the 'Steamroller': British Observers and the Russian Army before 1914," *The Journal of Strategic Studies* VIII (1985), 199–217.

[77]Moscow consulate to Bethmann, Feb. 8, 1913; PAAA, Russland 72/92; Warsaw consulate to Bethmann, PAAA, Russland 72/95; reports of Feb. 23, 1913, *ibid*.

[78]Eggeling to Bethmann, Feb. 2, 1913; PAAA, Russland 72/94; Russian ambassador to Jagow, Aug. 18, 1913; *ibid*., 72/95; Warsaw consulate to Bethmann, Oct. 26, 1913, PAAA, Deutschland 131/35.

[79]Memorandum of Oct. 16, 1912; and attaché's report of June 19, 1912, BA/MA, RM 5/1633.

[80]Eggeling to war ministry, Dec. 6, 1912; PAAA, Russland 72/94; Moltke to Bethmann, May 5, 1913, PAAA, Russland 72/95.

[81]Moltke to Bethmann, "Nachrichten über die militärische Lage in Russland," Nov. 21, 1912; and Jan. 28, 1913; and Moltke to Kiderlin, Nov. 12, 1912, PAAA, Russland 72-93.

[82]Eggeling to war ministry, Aug. 28, 1913; Moscow consulate to Bethmann, July 4, 1913; Adolf Frank Export-Gesellschaft to foreign ministry, Dec. 12, 1913, PAAA, Russland 72/95; Knox to Buchanan, Nov. 10, 1912, *BDFA* VI, Nr. 126.

[83]"Die wichtigste Veränderungen im Heerwesen Russlands im Jahre 1913," BA-MA, RM5/1486; Moltke to Bethmann, Jan. 7, 1914, PAAA, Russland 72/96.

[84]Germany, Reichsarchiv. *Der Weltkrieg 1914 bis 1918*, Vol. II (Berlin, 1925), 16–17.

[85]Beck's defense of the *Grosse Ostaufmarsch*, "West-oder Ost-Offensive 1914?" is in *Studien*, ed. Hans Speidel (Stuttgart, 1955), 143–189. Cf. Adolf Gasser, "Deutschlands Entschluss zum Präventivkrieg 1913/1914," *Discordia Concors: Festgabe für Edgar Bonjour*, Vol. I (Basel and Stuttgart, 1968), 171–224, esp.

Notes

175 ff.; and "Der deutsche Hegemonialkrieg von 1914," in Immanuel Geiss and B. J. Wendt (eds.), *Deutschland in der Weltpolitik des 19. und 20. Jahrhunderts*, 2nd ed., rev. (Düsseldorf, 1974)), 307–339.

[86]Tappen's comments of Oct. 22, 1919, in BA-MA, Nachlass Tappen, N 56/2.

[87]H. von Staabs, *Aufmarsch nach zwei Fronten: Auf Grund der Operationsplane von 1871–1914* (Berlin, 1925).

[88]The war game is described in Jack Snyder, *The Ideology of the Offensive: Military Decision-Making and the Disasters of 1914* (Ithaca, N.Y., 1984), 117; and Garros, "En Marge de l'Alliance," 38.

[89]Tappen to H. H. von Pertz, July 20, 1928, BA-MA, Nachlass Tappen, N 56/4.

[90]For German evaluations of Russia's military potential, cf. Bernd F. Schulte, *Vor dem Kriegsausbruch 1914. Deutschland, die Türkei und der Balkan* (Düsseldorf, 1980); and Risto Ropponen, *Die Kraft Russlands. Wie Beurteilte die politische und militärische Führung der Europäischen Grossmächte in der Zeit von 1905 bis 1914 die Kraft Russlands* (Helsinki, 1968). The evolution of military plans for the east is described in Graydon A. Tunstall, "The Schlieffen Plan: The Diplomacy and Military Strategy of the Central Powers in the East, 1905–1914" (Ph.D. Dissertation, Rutgers University, 1974); Ivo Lambi, *The Navy and German Power Politics, 1862–1914* (Boston, 1984), 398 *passim*, covers the naval aspects.

[91]See, for example, Conrad's recommendation of Mar. 25, 1913, that Austria must establish a reserve army. Conrad III, 187–188. Cf. Norman Stone, *The Eastern Front, 1914–1917* (New York, 1975), 226 ff.; and Oskar Regele, *Feldmarschall Conrad. Auftrag und Erfüllung 1906–1918* (Vienna, 1955), 169.

[92]On Italy's changing military policies, cf. Ludendorff's report of Jan. 3, 1913; Moltke to Kleist, Jan. 1913; and the naval attaché's report of Oct. 15, 1913, in BA-MA, RM5/2670. Michael Palumbo, "German-Italian Military Relations on the Eve of World War I," *Central European History* XII (1979), 343–371, stresses the German military's continued faith that Italy would honor her commitments. But cf. Alberto Monticone, *Deutschland und die Neutralität Italiens 1914–1915*, (Wiesbaden, 1982); and Risto Ropponen, *Italien als Verbündeter: Die Einstellung der politischen und militärischen Führung Deutschlands und Österreich-Ungarns zu Italien von der Niederlage von Adua bis zum Ausbruch des Weltkrieges 1914*, tr. C. Krotzl (Helsinki, 1986).

[93]Eugen Bircher and Walter Bode, *Schlieffen: Mann und Idee* (Zurich, 1957), 144.

[94]Conrad III, 669–670.

3. WAR FINDS A WAY

[1]Konrad Jarausch, *The Enigmatic Chancellor: Bethmann-Hollweg and the Hubris of Imperial Germany* (New Haven, Conn., 1973), 118–119.

[2]Riezler's views are best expressed in his *Die Erforderlichkeit des Unmöglichen* (Munich, 1913). For evaluations of his career and influence cf. Karl-Dietrich Erdmann's introduction to Kurt Riezler, *Tagebücher, Aufsätze, Dokumente* (Göttingen, 1972), pp. 19 ff.; Wayne C. Thompson, *The Eye of the Storm: Kurt Riezler and the Crisis of Modern Germany* (Iowa City, Iowa, 1980); and Andreas Hillgruber, "Riezlers Theorie des kalkulierten Risikos und Bethmann-Hollwegs politische Konzeption in der Julikrise 1914," *Historische Zeitschrift* 202 (1966), 333–351.

[3]Jack Dukes' article, "Militarism and Arms Policy Revisited: The Origins of the German Army Law of 1913" in *Another Germany: A Reconsideration of the*

Notes

Imperial Era, ed. J. R. Dukes, J. Remak (Boulder, Colo., 1987), 19–39, is an introduction to a major work in progress on the military bill. Michael Geyer, *Deutsche Rüstungspolitik 1860–1980* (Frankfurt, 1984), 83 ff., highlights the quantity versus quality issue. For the debates on the bill itself see Stig Förster, *Der doppelte Militärismus. Die deutsche Heeresrüstungspolitik zwischen Status-Quo-Sicherung und Aggression 1890–1913* (Stuttgart, 1983), 274 ff.; Helmut Altrichter, *Konstitutionalismus und Imperialismus. Der Reichstag und die deutsch-russischen Beziehungen 1890–1914* (Frankfurt, 1977), 68 ff. The mobilization of public opinion is presented in Roger Chickering, "Der 'Deutsche Wehrverein' und die Reform der deutschen Armee 1912–1914," *Militärgeschichtliche Mitteilung* XXV (1979), 7–33. The Socialist position is evaluated in Dieter Groh, *Negative Integration und revolutionärer Attentismus: Die deutsche Sozialdemokratie am vorabend des Ersten Weltkrieges* (Frankfurt, 1973); Bernstein's and Eisner's reactions are described in Roger Fletcher, *Revisionism and Empire. Socialist Imperialism in Germany 1897–1914* (London, 1984), 116, 148.

[4]Cf. G. A. Hosking, *The Russian Constitutional Experiment. Government and Duma, 1906–1914* (Oxford, 1973); A. Levin, *The Third Duma. Election and Profile* (Hamden, Conn., 1973); and D. R. Costello, "Prime Minister Kokovtsov and the Duma: A Study in the Disintegration of the Tsarist Regime, 1911–1914" (Ph.D. Dissertation, University of Virginia, 1970).

[5]France, Ministère des Affaires Étrangères, *Documents Diplomatiques Français (1871–1914)*, 41 vols. (Paris, 1929–59), 3rd Series, VIII, Nr. 79 (hereafter cited as *DDF*); Louis Garros, "En Marge de l'Alliance Franco-Russe, 1902–1914," *Revue Historique de l'Armee* VI (June, 1950), 40.

[6]For the attenuation of Russia's Balkan position after 1912 cf. Andrew Rossos, *Russia and the Balkans: Inter-Balkan Rivalries and Russian Foreign Policy, 1908–1914* (Toronto, 1981); and more specifically Henryk Batowski, "The Failure of the Balkan Alliance of 1912," *Balkan Studies* VII (1966), 111–122; and L. A. Pejković, "La Serbie et les rapports entre les Puissances de l'Entente (1908–1913)," *ibid.*, VI (1965), 305–344.

[7]Scharfenberg to Bethmann, Jan. 30, 1914, Politisches Archiv des Auswärtigen Amtes, Serbien 17/8 (hereafter cited as PAAA).

[8]The role of Serbia's journalists is detailed in Dragon Gasić, "Die Presse Serbiens 1903–1914 und Österreich-Ungarn" (Ph.D. Dissertation, University of Vienna, 1971).

[9]Alan Badger, "Russia and the End of the Ottoman Empire," in *The Great Powers and the End of the Ottoman Empire*, ed. M. Kent (London, 1984), 76–110, is a useful survey of Russia's Turkish policies despite a tendency to exaggerate Russia's harmlessness. M. Hiller, "Die politischen, militärischen und wirtschaftlichen Interessen Russlands im Nahen und Mittleren Osten 1905–1914" (Ph.D. Dissertation, University of Tübingen, 1978), is better balanced and more comprehensive.

[10]Pourtalès to Bethmann, Dec. 4, Dec.12, 1913, PAAA, Deutschland 131/35; O'Bierne to Grey, Dec. 9, 1913; and O'Bierne to Nicholson, Dec. 11, 1913, *British Documents on the Origins of the War, 1898–1914*, ed. G. P. Gooch, H. W. V. Temperley, 11 vols. (London, 1926–38), X, Nrs. 413, 418 (hereafter cited as *BD*).

[11]Bompard to Pichon, Nov. 19, 29, 30, 1913, *DDF* 3rd Series, VIII, Nrs. 500, 550, 554; O'Bierne to Grey, Dec. 18, 1913; Buchanan to Grey, Dec. 19, 1913, in *BD* X, 1, Nrs. 412, 440.

[12]The protocol is in M. N. Pokrovsky, *Drei Konferenzen. Zur Vorgeschichte des Krieges* (Berlin, 1920), 32 ff. Bethmann had presented Germany's position in

detail during Kokovtsov's visit to Berlin in Nov. Memoranda of Nov. 18 and Nov. 19, 1913; *Die Grosse Politik der Europäischen Kabinette, 1871–1914*, ed. J. Lipsius, A. Mendelsohn-Bartholdy, F. Thimme, 40 vols. (Berlin, 1922–27), XXXVIII, Nrs. 15 450, 15 451 (hereafter cited as *GP*).

[13]Andreas Hillgruber, *Germany and the Two World Wars*, tr. W. C. Kirby (Cambridge, Mass., 1981), 20–21; and Fritz Fischer, "Weltpolitik, Weltmachtstreben und deutsche Kriegsziele," *Historische Zeitschrift* 199 (1964), 265–346.

[14]Wangenheim to Bethmann, PAAA, Orientalia Generalia 5/17. Jehuda Wallach, *Anatomie einer Militärhilfe. Die preussisch-deutsche Militärmissionen in der Türkei 1835–1919* (Düsseldorf, 1976), 136 ff., show Liman's shortcomings as a diplomat in uniform. Ulrich Trumpener, "Germany and the End of the Ottoman Empire," in *Great Powers and the End of the Ottoman Empire*, 117–140; and H. S. W. Carrigan, "German-Turkish Relations and the Outbreak of War in 1914: A Reassessment," *Past and Present* (1967), establish Turkey's essential independence from Germany in 1914. David B. King, "Marschall von Biberstein and the New Course" (Ph.D. Dissertation, Cornell University, 1962) describes the positive role of the German ambassador in furthering his country's Turkish policies. Charles D. Sullivan, "Stamboul Crossings: German Diplomacy in Turkey, 1908 to 1914" (Ph.D. Dissertation, Vanderbilt University, 1977); and Wilhelm van Kampen, "Studien zur deutschen Türkeipolitik in der Zeit Wilhelms II" (Ph.D. Dissertation, University of Kiel, 1968), put the Reich's Ottoman frustrations in a broader context. Both stress the absence of a comprehensive, coherent German policy towards Turkey.

[15]Engellbrecht to Bethmann, Jan. 3, 1914; Tiflis consulate to Bethmann, Apr. 8, 1914, PAAA, Russland 72/96; Cf. Roderic H. Davidson, "The Armenian Crisis, 1912–1914," *American Historical Review* LIII (1948), 481–505. I. Klein, "The Anglo-Russian Convention and the Problem of Central Asia, 1907–1914," *Journal of British Studies* XI (1971), 126–147; and Keith M. Wilson, "Imperial Interests in the British Decision for War: The Defence of India in Central Asia," *Review of International Studies* IX (1984), 189–203.

[16]D. C. B. Lieven, *Russia and the Origins of the First World War* (New York, 1983), 47.

[17]Pourtalès to Bethmann, Feb. 25, 1914, PAAA, Deutschland 131/35; and Mar. 21, 1914, PAAA, Deutschland 131/36; report of the conversation between S. Lienow, editor of the *Grenzboten*, and Sazonov on Apr. 8, 1914, PAAA, Deutschland 131/36.

[18]For Austro-German tension at this period, see Dörte Löding, *Deutschlands und Oesterreich-Ungarns Balkanpolitik von 1912 bis 1914 under besonderer Berücksichtigung ihrer Wirtschaftsinteresse* (Hamburg, 1969), which includes an excellent bibliography. Cf. also Willibald Gutsche, "Mitteleuropaplanung in der Aussenpolitik des deutschen Imperialismus vor 1918," *Zeitschrift für Geschichtswissenschaft* XX (1972), 533–549; F. R. Bridge, "Tarde venietibus ossa: Austro-Hungarian Colonial Aspirations in Asia Minor," *Middle Eastern Studies* IX (1970), 319–330, and Andrej Mitrovic, "Germany's Attitude toward the Balkans, 1912–1914," in *East Central European Society and the Balkan Wars*, ed. B. Kiraly, D. Djordievic (New York, 1987), 295-316.

[19]For France's approach to the Austrian and Balkan questions cf. John Keiger, *France and the Origins of the First World War* (New York, 1983), 82–83; David Dutton, "The Balkan Campaign and French War Arms in the Great War," *English Historical Review* XCIV (1979), 97–113; and A. S. Mitrakos, *France in Greece during World War I* (New York, 1982). British policies are discussed in F. R

Notes

Bridge, *Great Britain and Austria-Hungary, 1906–14* (London, 1972); and Keith M. Wilson, "Isolating the Isolator: Cartwright, Grey and the Seduction of Austria-Hungary, 1908–1912," *Mitteilungen des Österreichischen Staatsarchivs* XXV (1982), 169–198. H. Hanak, *Great Britain and Austria-Hungary during the First World War: A Study in the Formation of Public Opinion* (Oxford, 1962); and P. Schuster, *Henry Wickham Steed und die Habsburgermonarchie* (Vienna, 1970), cover the growing intellectual hostility to the Habsburg system in Britain.

[20]Pertti Luntinen, *French Information on the Russian War Plans* (Helsinki, 1984), 69 ff.

[21]Buchanan to Grey, Apr. 14, 1913, *BD* IX, 2, Nr. 849. Buchanan has no biography, but see the brief recent evaluation in Keith Neilson, *Strategy and Supply. The Anglo-Russian Alliance, 1914–1917* (London, 1984), 24 ff., and the accompanying references.

[22]Buchanan to Grey, Mar. 19, Mar. 31, 1914, *BD* X, 2, Nrs. 530, 536; Sukhomlinov's second comment is cited in F. N. Bradley, "Quelques aspects de la politique étrangère de Russe avant 1914 a travers les archives françaises," *Études slaves et est-européennes* VII (1967), 100–101.

[23]Paul W. Schroeder, "World War I as Galloping Gertie: A Reply to Joachim Remak," *Journal of Modern History* XLIV (1972), 345.

[24]Durnovo's memorandum of Feb., 1914 to Tsar Nicholas is reprinted in F. Golder, *Documents on Russian History, 1914–1917* (New York, 1927), 3 ff.; cf. D. C. B. Lieven, "Bureaucratic Authoritarianism in Late Imperial Russia: The Personality, Career, and Opinions of P. N. Durnovo," *Historical Journal* XXVI (1983), 391–402. The activity of the "pro-Germans" in 1914 is generally discussed in M. Taube, *La Politique Russe d'avant-guerre* (Paris, 1928), 331 ff.

[25]German naval attaché's report to Marineamt, Mar. 30, 1914; Krupp to Bethmann, Apr. 21, 1914, PAAA, Deutschland 131/36; and Pourtalès to Bethmann, Feb. 25, 1914, PAAA, Russland 72/96. Ruth Ann E. Roosa, "The Association of Industry and Trade, 1906–1914: An Examination of the Economic Views of Organized Industrialists in Pre-Revolutionary Russia" (Ph.D. Dissertation, Columbia University, 1907); and Gregory Guroff, "The State and Industrialization in Russian Economic Thought" (Ph.D. Dissertation, Princeton University, 1970), integrate analyses of the business community's attitude to Germany into the general question of economic development in Russia.

[26]Report of Mar. 19, 1914, PAAA, Deutschland 131/36.

[27]W. Bruce Lincoln, *In War's Dark Shadow: The Russians Before the Great War* (New York, 1983) brilliantly evokes the mood of prewar Russia. Judith Head, "Russian Attitudes toward Germany and Austria" (Ph.D. Dissertation, North Texas State University, 1981), and Lieven, *Russia and the Origins of the First World War*, 83 ff., discuss the growing spectrum of anti-German attitudes. For the political aspects cf. Marguerite Wolters, *Aussenpolitische Fragen vor der vierten Duma* (Hamburg, 1969), and M. Jablonowski, "Die Stellungnahme der russischen Parteien zur Aussenpolitik der Regierung von der russisch-englischen Verständigung bis zum Ersten Weltkrieg," *Forschungen zur Osteuropäschen Geschichte* V (1957), 60–92. On the press war in general, cf. Klaus Wernecke, *Der Wille zur Weltgeltung. Aussenpolitik und Öffentlichkeit am Vorabend des Ersten Weltkrieges* (Düsseldorf, 1969), 249 ff.; and A. Jux, *Der Kriegsschrecken des Frühjahrs 1914 in der europäischen Presse* (Berlin, 1929). The latter work remains particularly useful for its many quotations from contemporary newspapers.

[28]For example Engelbrecht to Bethmann, Jan. 1, 1914, PAAA, Russland 72/96, specifically mentions the five-year lead time.

Notes

[29]W. A. Sukhomlinov, *Erinnerungen* (Berlin, 1924), p. 252; cf. Buchanan to Grey, Mar. 15, 1914, in *British Documents on Foreign Affairs: Reports and Papers from the Foreign Office Confidential Print*, Series A, *Russia 1859–1914*, ed. O. Lieven, 6 vols. (Washington, D.C., 1983), VI, Nr. 173.

[30]Louis Hirsch to Jagow, Mar. 12, 1914; Pourtalès to Bethmann, Mar. 13 and Mar. 16, 1914, PAAA, Deutschland 131/36; and Mar. 31, 1914, in PAAA, Russland 72/96.

[31]Fritz Fischer, *War of Illusions*, tr. M. Jackson (New York, 1975), 384 ff.; and Wernecke, *Wille*, 249 ff., tend to exaggerate the degree of government control over the press. Cf. Kurt Koszyk, *Geschichte der deutschen Presse*, Vol. II (Berlin, 1966), *passim*.

[32]Paul Rohrbach, *Zum Weltvolk hindurch* (Stuttgart, 1914). Rohrbach was also one of the founders of *Das grössere Deutschland*.

[33]Bethmann to foreign office, Apr. 22, 1914 and reply of Apr. 23, PAAA, Russland 72/96.

[34]Pourtalès to Bethmann, Mar. 16 and Apr. 14, 1914, PAAA, Deutschland 121/36, and Mar. 11, PAAA, Russland 72/96.

[35]Circular of the Friedrich Wilhelm Lebensversicherungs-Aktiengesellschaft zu Berlin, PAAA, Deutschland 131/36; report of the Italian embassy, Apr. 10, 1914, PAAA, Russland 72/96.

[36]Moltke to Jagow, Feb. 24, 1914, *GP*, XXXIX, Nr. 15839; General Staff report, Mar. 1914, in Bundesarchiv-Militärarchiv, RM5/1487.

[37]Conrad recorded Moltke's observation to him in *Aus meiner Dienstzeit*, 5 vols. (Vienna, 1921–25), III, 670. Jagow's account of the later conversation, written down only after the war, was published in Egmont Zechlin, "Motive und Taktik der Reichsleitung 1914. Ein Nachtrag," *Der Monat* 209 (Feb., 1966), 91–95. His letter to Lichnowski of July 18, 1914, is in *Die Deutschen Dokumente zum Kriegsausbruch*, ed. W. Schücking, M. Montgelas, rev. ed. 5 vols. (Berlin, 1927), I, Nr. 72 (hereafter cited as *DD*). The kaiser's opinion is from Max Warburg, *Aus meinen Aufzeichnungen* (Glückstadt, 1952), 29.

[38]Wilson's comment is in Egmont Zechlin, "Cabinet versus Economic Warfare in Germany: Policy and Strategy During the Early Month of the First World War," in *The Origins of the First World War*, ed. H. W. Koch (London, 1971), 150. Cf. Buchanan to Grey, Mar. 18, 1914, and Buchanan to Nicholson, Mar. 18, 1914, *BD* X, 2, Nrs. 528, 529; Grey to Bertie, May 1, 1914, *BD* X, 2, Nr. 541.

[39]Yale University, Edward M. House Papers, Diary, Vol. IV, Jan. 1-July 3, 1914, entries of May 10, May 23, and June 1; House to Wilson, May 28, 1914, in Edward M. House Papers, Select Correspondence, 119a/4232.

[40]House Papers, Diary, Vol. V, July 4, 1914-Jan. 1, 1915, entry of Aug. 30. House did add China to the President's list.

[41]Sazonov to Beneckendorff, Feb. 19, 1914, in *Die internationalen Beziehungen im Zeitalter des Imperialismus. Dokumente aus den Archiven der Zarischen und der Provisorischen Regierung*, ed. O. Hoetzsch, Series I, 5 vols. (Berlin, 1931), Series I, Vol. 1, Nr. 289 (hereafter cited as *Int.Bez*); Nicolson to Bunsen, Apr. 27, 1914; and Grey to Bertie, May 1, 1914, *BD* X, 2, Nrs. 540, 541.

[42]The conversation is quoted in Georges Michon, *The Franco-Russian Alliance, 1891–1917*, tr. N. Thomas (Paris, 1929), 274 ff. For the Three Years' Law see most recently Gerd Krumeich, *Armaments and Politics in France on the Eve of the First World War*, tr. S. Conn (Dover, N.H.: 1984).

[43]Cf. Jagow's comments of June 15 to the British Ambassador; and Goschen

Notes

to Grey, June 16, 1914, in *BD* X, 2, Nr. 550. The *Novoye Vremya* article is also extensively discussed in *DDF*, 3rd Series, X, Nr. 369. The quotation evaluating Sukhomlinov's character is from Bernhard von Eggeling, *Die russische Mobilmachung und der Kriegsausbruch* (Oldenburg, 1919), 9.

⁴⁴Alex N. Dragnich, *Serbia, Nicola Pašić, and Yugoslavia* (New Brunswick, N.J., 1974), 92.

⁴⁵For the diplomats' perspective cf. Tschirsky to Bethmann, Feb. 13, 1914, PAAA, Russland 72/96; Treutler to Bethmann, Mar. 4, 1914, PAAA, Deutschland 131/36; Berchtold to Franz Josef, July 14, 1914, in Ludwig Bittner, *et. al.* *Oesterreich-Ungarns Aussenpolitik von der bosnische Krise 1908 bis zum Kriegsausbruch 1914*, 8 vols. (Vienna, 1930), VIII, Nr. 1072. (Hereafter cited as *Oe-U*). For the soldiers cf. the German military attaché's reports to the foreign ministry of Feb. 11, 1914, PAAA, Russland 72/96; Mar. 3 and 17, 1914, PAAA, Deutschland 131/36; May 30, 1914, PAAA, Russland 72/97; and July 13, 1914, in Immanuel Geiss, ed., *Julikrise und Kriegsausbruch 1914*, 2 vols. (Hanover, 1963–64), I, Nr. 84. General treatments of the decision making climate in Vienna at the time of Sarajevo include M. B. A. Peterson, "Das österreichisch-ungarische Memorandum an Deutschland vom 5. Juli 1914,"*Scandia* XXX (1964), 138–190; Hugo Hantsch, *Leopold Graf Berchtold*, 2 vols. (Graz, 1963), II, 608 *passim*; and Gary W. Shanafelt, *The Secret Enemy: Austria-Hungary and the German Alliance, 1914–1918* (Boulder, Colo.: 1985), 7 ff.

⁴⁶Cf. *inter alia* Alan N. Sabrosky, "From Bosnia to Sarajevo," *Journal of Conflict Resolution* XIX (1975), 3–24; William Jannen, Jr., "The Austro-Hungarian Decision for War in July, 1914," *Essays on World War I*, ed. S. R. Williamson, P. Pastor (New York, 1983), 55–81; Remak, "Third Balkan War," 363.

⁴⁷Samuel R. Williamson, Jr., "Vienna and July 1914: The Origins of the Great War Once More," in *Essays on World War I*, 9–36.

⁴⁸Waldhausen to Bethmann, Apr. 19, 1914, PAAA, Deutschland 143.

⁴⁹On the changing military balance in the Balkans cf. Gunther Rothenberg, *The Army of Francis Joseph* (Lafayette, Ind., 1976), 170 ff.; and Horst Brettner-Messler, "Die Balkanpolitik Conrad von Hötzendorfs von seiner Wiederernennung zum Chef des Generalstabes bis zum Oktober-Ultimatum 1913," *Mitteilungen des Österreichischen Staatsarchivs* XX (1967), 180 ff.

⁵⁰John R. Lampe, "Financial Structure and the Economic Development of Serbia, 1878–1912," (Ph.D. Dissertation, University of Wisconsin, 1971).

⁵¹Berchtold to Czernin, Nov. 26, 1913, *Oe-U*, VII, 592. For a more general example of this attitude see the diaries of Josef Redlich, *Schicksalsjahre Österreich, 1908-1919. Das politische Tagebuch Joseph Redlichs*, ed. F. Fellner, Vol. I (Graz, 1953), 209 *passim*.

⁵²Cf. D. C. Watt, "The British Reactions to the Assassination at Sarajevo," *European Studies Review* I (1971), 233–247; and A. J. A. Morris, *The Scaremongers: The Advocacy of War and Rearmament 1896–1914* (London, 1984), 354 ff.

⁵³Grey to Bunsen, *BD* XI, Nr. 91.

⁵⁴Anthony Di Ionic, "Italy, Austria-Hungary, and the Balkans, 1904–1914: Italy's Appraisal" (Ph.D. Dissertation, University of Illinois, 1980), documents this process from the perspective of another regional power.

⁵⁵Cf. David Mackenzie, "Serbian Nationalist and Military Organization and the Piedmont Idea, 1844–1914," *East European Quarterly* XVI (1982), 323–344; and *Ilja Garasanin: Balkan Bismarck* (Boulder, Colo., 1985).

⁵⁶The process of decision making in Serbia in 1914 remains controversial. The most complete collection of Serbian diplomatic documents from the period is

Notes

Dokumenti o spoljnoj politici Krajelvine Srbije, 1903–1914, Vol. VII, Part 2, *1/14 maj - 22. juli/4. avgust 1914*, ed. V. Dedijer, Z. Amic (Belgrade, 1980). Samuel R. Williamson, Jr., "The Origins of World War I," *The Journal of Interdisciplinary History* XVIII (1988), 810–811; and Gale Stokes, "The Serbian Documents from 1914: A Preview," *Journal of Modern History* XLVIII, Supplement (1976), both exaggerate Russia's importance. The best secondary accounts in English remain Joachim Remak, *Sarajevo: The Story of a Political Murder* (New York, 1959); and Vladimir Dedijer, *The Road to Sarajevo*, (New York, 1966). Friedrich Würthle, *Die Spur fuhr nach Belgrade* (Vienna, 1975), expresses its approach in its title. Willibald Gutsche, *Sarajevo 1914* (Berlin, 1984) is a recent East German work denying any significant importance to the question of Serbia's role in the assassination.

[57]To the seemingly endless literature on Germany's behavior in the July Crisis have recently been added Hartmut Pogge von Strandmann, "Germany and the Coming of War," in *The Coming of the First World War*, ed. R. J. W. Evans and H. Pogge von Strandmann, (Oxford, 1988), 87–123; Fritz Fischer, *Juli 1914: Wir sind nicht hineingeschlittert* (Hamburg, 1983); Egmont Zechlin, "Julikrise und Kriegsausbruch 1914," in *Politik und Geschichte: Europa 1914: Krieg oder Frieden*, ed. Landeszentrale für politische Bildung (Kiel, 1985), 49–96; and Klaus Hildebrand, "Julikrise 1914. Das europäische Sicherheitsdilemma," *Geschichte in Wissenschaft und Unterricht*, XXXVI (1985), 469–502.

[58]Leichenfeld to Hertling, June 4, 1914, in *Bayerische Dokumente zum Kriegsausbruch und zum Versailler Schuldspruch*, ed. Pius Dirr (Munich, 1928), 110 ff.

[59]A. J. P. Taylor, *The Struggle for Mastery in Europe, 1848–1918* (Oxford, 1954), 518 ff.

[60] Wilhelm Groener, *Der Weltkrieg und seine Probleme* (Berlin, 1920), 51.

[61]Germany's preparations, or lack of them, are discussed in Lothar Burchardt, *Friedenswirtschaft und Kriegsvorsorge. Deutschlands wirtschaftliche Bestrebungen vor 1914* (Boppard, 1968), and Gerhard Hehr, *Walther Rathenau und sein Verhältnis zu Militär und Krieg* (Boppard, 1983), 146 passim.

[62]For Moltke cf. especially Correlli Barnett, *The Swordbearers* (London, 1963), 15 ff.; and Isabel Hull, *The Entourage of Kaiser Wilhelm II, 1888–1918* (Cambridge, 1982), 239 ff.

[63]Sean M. Lynn-Jones, "Détente and Deterrence: Anglo-German Relations, 1911–1914," *International Security* XI (Fall, 1986), 121–150.

[64]Cf. Manfred Rauh, "Die 'deutsche Frage' von 1914: Weltmachtstreben und Obrigkeitsstaat?" in *Die Deutsche Frage im 19. und 20. Jahrhundert*, ed. J. Becker, A. Hillgruber (Munich, 1983), 109–166; James M. McPherson, *Battle Cry of Freedom: The Civil War Era* (New York, 1988) 272 n.78; and Richard N. Current, *Lincoln and the First Shot* (Philadelphia, 1963).

[65]E. G. Tschirsky to Bethmann, July 2, 1914, and Berchtold's note of a July 2 conversation with Tschirsky in Geiss, *Julikrise* I, Nrs. 11, 14. Cf. also F. Fellner, "Die 'Mission Hoyos' " in *Deutschlands Sonderung von Europa, 1862–1945* (Frankfurt, 1984), 283–316.

[66]For Sazonov's Serbian dilemma cf. in particular Strandtmann to Sazonov and Sazonov to Strandtmann, July 24, 1914, *Int. Bez* I, 5, Nrs. 22, 36. The protocol of the Crown Council is most readily available in Geiss I, Nr. 286. Lieven, *Russia and the Origins of the First World War*, 141 ff., includes a summary, based on the unpublished memoirs of Finance Minister P. A. Bark, that modifies details without altering substance.

Notes

[67]Cf. Friedrich Graf Pourtalès, *Meine letzten Verhandlungen in St. Petersburg, ende Juli 1914* (Berlin, 1927), 22–23; Pourtalès to Jagow, July 26, 1914, *DD* I, 217; Pourtalès to Bethmann July 25 (sent July 26, 12:20 a.m.), July 26, 3:25 p.m., and July 27, 1:00 p.m., in PAAA, Russland 72/97. and Szapary to Berchtold, July 26, 1914, *Oe-U* VIII, 10835. The assigned date of the latter document, July 27, is corrected following Geiss, *Julikrise* II, Nr. 397.

[68]Leichardt to Carlowitz, July 3, 1914, in *ibid.*, I, Nr. 15.

[69]"Die Wachsende Macht Russland," PAAA, Deutschland 121/31, Geheim 2. I am indebted to Ivo Lambi for sharing his detailed notes on this document.

[70]Entry of July 7, 1914 in Riezler, *Tagebücher*. The damage done by the Riezler diaries to the more extreme assertions of German responsibility for the war's outbreak is best attested to by the recent attempts to deny their authenticity. The most extreme of these is Bernd F. Schulte, *Die Verfälschung der Riezler Tagebücher* (Frankfurt, 1985). Their failure is documented in Agnes A. Blänsdorf, "Der Weg der Riezler-Tagebücher. Zur Kontroverse über die Echtheit der Tagebücher Kurt Riezlers," *Geschichte in Wissenschaft und Unterricht* XXXV (1984), 651–684.

[71]Entries of July 20 and 23, 1914, in Riezler, *Tagebücher*, 186 ff: and Bethman's conversations of Feb. 9 and July 30, 1915, with journalist Theodor Wolff in *Theodor Wolff: Tagebücher 1914–1919*, ed. B. Sösemann, 2 vols. (Boppard, 1984), I, 156–157, 265 ff. Cf. D. W. Sweet, "The Baltic in British Diplomacy before the First World War," *Historical Journal* XIII (1970), 451–490; Manfred Rauh, "Die britisch-russische Marinekonvention von 1914 und der Ausbruch des Ersten Weltkrieges, *MGM*, XLI (1987), 37–62.

[72]Sazonov to Beneckendorff, June 28, 1914, *Int. Bez.* I, 5, Nr. 164; entry of July 23, 1914, in Riezler, *Tagebücher*, 190.

[73]Lichnowsky's January, 1915 memorandum and Eulenberg's 1919 correspondence with Professor Kurt Breysig are reprinted in *1914: Delusion or Design?* ed. with intro. by John Röhl (New York, 1973).

[74]Goschen to Grey, July 29, 1914, *BD* XI, Nr. 293. Cf. Volker Ullrich, "Das deutsche Kalkül in der Julikrise 1914 und die Frage der Englischen Neutralität," *Geschichte in Wissenschaft und Unterricht* XXXIV (1983), 73–97.

[75]Waldersee to Jagow, July 8, 1914, *DD* I, Nr. 74.

[76]Ulrich Trumpener, "War Premeditated? German Intelligence Operations in July 1914," *Central European History* IX (1976), 58–85, based heavily on Fritz Gempp, "Geheimer Nachrichtendienst und Spionageabwehr des Heeres," National Archives T-77, Rolls 1,438–1,440, 1,422, 1,507–1,509, accurately stresses the lack of urgency in the German military response. Cf. particularly Gempp, "Nachrichtendienst" II, 1, 2 ff. For the French-Russian radio link see Luntinen, *French Information on Russian War Plans*, 167 ff.

[77]Sazonov's comments on Austria's behavior are in Szapary to Berchtold, July 24, 1914, *Oe-U* VIII, Nr. 10616; and in the Russian foreign ministry's memorandum of July 18, 1914 in *Int. Bez.* I, 4, Nr. 272. The most detailed secondary reconstruction in a Western language of Sazonov's decision to order partial mobilization remains Luigi Albertini, *The Origins of the War of 1914*, 3 Vols., tr. and ed. I. M. Massey (London, 1952–57), II, 528 ff. Cf. Serge Doborolski, *Die Mobilmachung der russischen Armee 1914* (Berlin, 1922), for the specifically military aspects.

[78]L. C. F. Turner, "The Russian Mobilization in 1914," *Journal of Contemporary History* I (1968), 65–88, is significantly modified by Lieven, *Russia and the Origins of the First World War*, 148 ff.

Notes

[79]Cf. Paléologue's dispatch of July 26, 1914, in *DDF*, 3rd Series, XI, Nr. 80; Messimy's statement in Raymond Recouly, *Les Heures Tragiques d'avant-guerre* (Paris, 1922), pp. 61 ff.; Joffre's account in his *Memories*, 2 vols., tr. T. B. Mott (London, 1932), I, 117–118; and Krumeich, *Armaments and Politics*, 215 ff.

[80]Gempp, "Nachrichtendienst" II, 1, 18 ff., 70 ff.

[81]Moltke to Bethmann, July 29, 1914, *DD* II, Nr. 349.

[82]Gempp, "Nachrichtendienst" II, 1, 31–32. The report is in *DD* II, Nr. 372.

[83]Bethmann to Wilhelm, July 26, PAAA, Preussen, 1a/23. Egmont Zechlin, "Bethmann-Hollweg, Kriegsrisiko und SPD/1914," in *Krieg und Kriegsrisiko*, 64–93, stresses the importance in Bethmann's mind of maximizing domestic support by waiting as long as possible to order mobilization.

[84]Sazonov's itinerary and behavior are reconstructed primarily from the "daily report" of the Russian foreign ministry for July 29, 1914, in *Int. Bez.* I, 5, Nr. 224; and Pourtalès's dispatches of 4:30 and 9:30 a.m. and 1:01 p.m. July 30, to Jagow in *DD* II, Nrs. 401, 412, and 421. Albertini, *Origins* II, 563-564, analyzes the discrepancies between the two accounts. I have followed the Russian version in placing Sazonov's final proposal during the night, rather than on the morning of the 30th, as described by Pourtalès.

[85]Buchanan to Grey, Aug. 30, *BD* XI, Nr. 302. Sazonov had used the same comparison to Pourtalès the previous day. *DD* II, Nr. 412.

[86]Cf. the daily report of July 30, 1914, in *Int. Bez.* I, 5, Nr. 284; and Sazonov's own memoir, *Fateful Years, 1909–1916* (London, 1928), 201 ff.

[87]Stephen Kern, *The Culture of Time and Space, 1880–1918* (Cambridge, Mass., 1983), 259 ff.

[88]Entry of July 25, 1914, in Wolff, *Tagebücher* I, 63 ff; entry of Aug. 15, 1914, in Riezler, *Tägebücher*, 194.

[89]Bethmann to Tschirsky, 3:00 a.m., 9:00 p.m., July 30, 1914, *DD* II, Nrs. 396, 441.

[90]Berchtold to Szapary, July 30, 1914; Berchtold to Szogyeni, July 31, 1914, in *Oe-U* VIII, Nrs. 11092, 11155.

[91]Albertini, *Origins* III, 24 ff., remains the best analysis of the still-controversial issue of exactly when the German leaders first learned of Russia's mobilization.

[92]First Lieutenant Hermann Hoth, who was to become one of the Wehrmacht's most distinguished panzer commanders, was the duty officer in Berlin that morning. His account is in Gempp, "Nachrichtendienst" III, 2, 34 ff. For the phone call to XX Corps see F. von Notz, *General von Scholtz: Ein deutsches Soldatenleben in Grosser Zeit* (Berlin, 1937), 37.

[93]Nicolai observed that the advantages of Jewish agents were their "unscrupulous greed, slyness, and persistence." Disadvantages were insolence, cowardice, vengefulness, and excessive imagination. He graciously commented, however, that the better elements among Russia's oppressed Jews repaid decent treatment with gratitude and loyalty. Gempp, "Nachrichtendienst," I, 149.

[94]Gert Buchheit, *Der deutsche Geheimdienst* (Munich, 1966), 22.

[95]Bethmann to Pourtalès, 3:30 p.m., July 31, 1914, *DD* III, Nr. 490.

4. THE VIRGIN SOLDIERS

[1]For military life in Germany's eastern provinces, regimental histories are a mine of direct and indirect information. I found particularly useful Erich Balla's history of the 1st *Jäger*, *Im Yorkschen Geist: Der Deutsche Frontsoldat und seine*

Notes

Seele (Berlin, 1926), 1 ff.; Kurt Hennig, *Das Infanterie-Regiment (8.Ostpreussisches) Nr. 45* (Oldenburg, Berlin, 1928), 15 ff.; Alfred Dieterich, *Geschichte des Grenadierregiments König Friedrich der Grosse (3.Ostpreussischen) Nr. 4* (Berlin, 1928), 590 ff. (hereafter cited as *4.Grenadiere*); and Konrad Marschall, "Die 5.Grenadiere in Danzig," *Zeitschrift für Heeresführung und Truppenkunde* XXXII (1968), 64–75. Economic conditions are best summarized in Frank B. Tipton, Jr., *Regional Variations in the Economic Development of Germany during the Nineteenth Century* (Middletown, Conn., 1976), 112 ff.; and Heinz Rogmann, *Die Bevölkerungsentwicktung im preussischen Osten in den letzten hundert Jahren* (Berlin, 1937).

[2]Geoff Eley, "German Politics and Polish Nationality: The Dialectic of Nation-Forming in the East of Prussia," *East European Quarterly* XVIII (1984), 335–364, is at once an excellent analysis of the question and a perceptive survey of the relevant literature. Eric A. Johnson, "The Roots of Crime in Imperial Germany," *Central European History* XV (1982), 351–376, presents the relationship between ethnic makeup and criminal activity in the *Kreise* mentioned. For the emergence of ethnic politics in the east see Stanley Suval, *Electoral Politics in Wilhelmine Germany* (Chapel Hill, N.C., 1985), 180 ff.

[3]Quoted in Daniel Hughes, "The Social Composition of the Prussian Generalcy, 1871–1914" (Ph.D. Dissertation, University of North Carolina, 1979), 215.

[4]Martin Kitchen, *The German Officer Corps, 1890–1914* (Oxford, 1968), especially 99 ff., 115 ff., is a familiar summary of the case against the officers. For the Bilse scandal, the 1904 translation of *Aus einer kleinen Garnison*, published by John Lane, incorporates a summary of the court-martial. Cf. also Ernst Arnold, *Aus allerlei Garnisonen . . . Zugleich Lehren und Forderungen des Falles Bilse* (Leipzig, 1904), *passim*.

[5]The anecdotes are from Bundesarchiv-Militärarchiv, Nachlass Below, N87/44, 572, 626. The problems of balancing professional and social requirements are presented in such contemporary works as Rudolf Krafft, *Glänzendes Elend* (Stuttgart, 1895); *Das moderne Landsknechtsthum. Streiflichter über die sociale Stellung der Officiercorps* (Leipzig, 1898); and Eduard Preuss, *Die höheren Aufgaben des jungen Offiziers für Armee und Volk* (Munich, 1906).

[6]The changed living conditions are described in Traugott Hoffmann and Ernst Hahn, *Geschichte des Infanterie-Regiments Graf Dönhoff (7.Ostpreussischen) Nr. 44 1860–1918* (Berlin, 1930), 72 ff.; and Dieterich, *4.Grenadiere*, 622. The anecdote of the major is from BA-MA, Nachlass Below, N87/45, 573.

[7]Balla, *Yorkschen Geist*, 2–3.

[8]For justifications and explanations of the negatives cf. Ann Taylor Allen, *Satire and Society in Wilhelmine Germany. Kladderadatsch and Simplicissimus 1890–1914* (Lexington, Ky., 1984), 103 ff.; and Alex Hall, *Scandal, Sensation, and Social Democracy; The SPD Press and Wilhelmine Germany, 1890–1914* (Cambridge, 1977), 116 ff.

[9]Jürgen Kocka, *Facing Total War. German Society 1914–1918*, tr. B. Weinberger (Cambridge, Mass., 1984), supports this interpretation against the intention of its author.

[10]Cf. particularly Manfred Messerschmidt, "Die Armee in Staat und Gesellschaft," *Das kaiserliche Deutschland*, ed. M. Stürmer (Düsseldorf, 1970), 89–118; and Wilhelm Deist, "Die Armee in Staat und Gesellschaft, 1890–1914," *ibid.*, 312–329.

[11]As in most recently Hartmut John, *Das Reserveoffizierkorps im Deutschen*

Notes

Kaiserreich 1890–1914. Ein sozialgeschichtlicher Beitrag zur Untersuchung der gesellschaftlichen Militärisierung im Wilhelminischen Deutschland (Frankfurt, 1981).

[12]Günther Martin, *Die bürgerlichen Exellenzen. Zur Sozialgeschichte der preussischen Generalität 1812–1918* (Düsseldorf, 1979). Hughes, "Prussian Generalcy," challenges the concept of an open-access elite, but nevertheless stresses government service, as opposed to birth, as the primary social matrix of even general officers.

[13]Gerhard Hecker, *Walther Rathenau und sein Verhältnis zu Militär und Krieg* (Boppard, 1983), 32 *passim*.

[14]Hoffmann and Hahn, *Infanterie-Regiment 44*, 76–77.

[15]Paul Frh. v. Schoenaich, *Mein Damaskus. Erlebnisse und Bekenntnisse* (Berlin, 1926), 48–49.

[16]Nicolaus Sombart, "The Kaiser in His Epoch: Some Reflections on Wilhelmine Society, Sexuality, and Culture," in *Kaiser Wilhelm II. New Interpretations*, ed. J. G. C. Röhl (Cambridge, 1982), 287–311.

[17]Hartmut Kaelble, *Industrialization and Social Inequality in 19th-Century Europe*, tr. B. Little (New York, 1986) is a sound recent overview.

[18]Nachlass Below MA-BA, N87/44, 581–582.

[19]Dennis E. Showalter, "Army and Society in Imperial Germany: The Pains of Modernization," *Journal of Contemporary History* XVIII (1983), 583–618.

[20]"Wie man als Reservist behandelt wird," *Dresdner Volkszeitung*, Aug. 8, 1911, in Politisches Archiv des Auswärtigen Amtes, Deutschland 121/16 (hereafter cited as PAAA). The same file includes a number of clippings from other Socialist papers on the theme of mistreatment. Hans Rau, *Der Sadismus in der Armee* (Berlin, 1904), incorporates a cross-section of contemporary case studies in a psychological framework.

[21] Karl von Einem to the Lübeck prosecutor, Oct. 8, 1908, in PAAA, Deutschland 121/14. Representative public admonitions include "Soldatenmisshandlungen und öffentliches Gerichtsverfahren," *Militär-Wochenblatt* 1892, 6; von Kessling, "Massnahmen für Hintanhaltung von Misshandlungen sowie vorschriftswidriger Behandlungen überhaupt," *Jahrbücher für die deutsche Armee und Marine* 125 (1903), 623–630; Pelet-Narbonne, "Die Einfluss von Offizierinspektionen bzw. Offizierberichte auf die Misshandlungen," *ibid.* 130 (1906), 188–191.

[22]The most extreme statement of this thesis remains Bernd F. Schulte, *Die deutsche Armee 1900–1914. Zwischen Beharren und Verändern* (Düsseldorf, 1977). But cf. Manfred Messerschmidt, "Preussens Militär in seinem gesellschaftlichen Umfeld," *Geschichte und Gesellschaft, Sonderheft 6, Preussen im Rückblick*, ed. H-J Pühle, H-U Wehler (Göttingen, 1980), 43–88.

[23]Von Tschischwitz, "Die dreigliedrige Division als taktischer Körper," E. V. Eisenhardt-Rothe, *Deutsche Infanterie. Das Ehrenmal der vordersten Front* (Zeulenroda, 1929), 200–201, is a good summary. But cf. W. Balck, *Development of Tactics—World War*, tr. M. H. Bell (Ft. Leavenworth, Kans., 1922), 21–22. Details of the German organization in 1914 can be found in *Der Weltkrieg 1914 bis 1918. Kriegsrüstung und Kriegswirtschaft, Anlageband*, ed. Reichsarchiv (Berlin, 1930).

[24]Jenö von Egon-Krieger, *Die deutsche Kavallerie im Krieg und Frieden* (Karlsruhe, 1928), surveys prewar doctrine and training. Cf. *inter alia* Friedrich von Bernhardi, *Reiterdienst* (Berlin, 1910); G. von Pelet-Narbonne, "Die Massenattacken der Kavallerie bei unseren grossen Uebungen gegen die anderen Waffen," *JAM* 123 (1902), 476–483; and "Mehr Kavallerie," *ibid.*, 124 (1903), 137–164.

[25]For a more detailed treatment see Dennis E. Showalter, "Prussia, Tech-

nology and War: Artillery from 1815 to 1918," *Men, Machines and War*, ed. R. Haycock, K. Nelson (Waterloo, Ontario, 1988), 113–151.

[26]Bruce I. Gudmundsson, *Stormtroop Tactics: Innovation in the German Army, 1914–1918* (New York, 1989).

[27]Cf. *inter alia* "Prüfungsschiessen und Königsabzeichen," *MW* 1896, 102–103; and Reisner Frh. v. Lilienstern, "Kriegsmässiges Schiessen," *JAM* 125 (1903), 325–338.

[28]Cf. Beckmann, "Zur Maschinengewehrfrage," *JAM* 134 (1908), 384–407, 463–473, 571–587; "Zur Frage der Verteilung und Verwendung der Maschinengewehr," *Kriegstechnische Zeitschrift* VIII (1905), 26–35; "Die Notwendigkeit der Maschinengewehre," *ibid.*, VII (1904), 530–537; A. Fleck, *Maschinengewehre, ihre Technik und Taktik* (Berlin, 1914); and Krieger, *Das Gefecht der Maschinengewehr-Kompagnien* (Oldenburg, 1913).

[29]Cf. Steven T. Ross, *From Flintlock to Rifle: Infantry Tactics 1740–1866* (Rutherford, N.J., 1979); and Dennis E. Showalter, *Railroads and Rifles: Soldiers, Technology and the Unification of Germany* (Hamden, Conn., 1975).

[30]Peter Stearns, *Lives of Labor: Work in a Maturing Industrial Society* (New York: 1975), is a useful survey of this development. His *Be a Man! Males in Modern Society* (New York, 1979), 59 ff., focusses more sharply on the development of new male bonding and coping patterns in industrial Europe.

[31]Hermann Müller, *Die Erziehung der Truppe zum moralischen Wert in Deutschland, Russland und Japan* (Berlin, n.d.); "Zum Infanterieangriff," *JAM* 130 (1906), 170–188; *Exerzier-Reglement für die Infanterie von 29 Mai 1906*, rev. ed. Berlin (1909), esp. pars. 265, 327, 347; Balck, "Das Exerzierreglement für die Infanterie von 29. May 1906," *JAM* 131 (1906), 111–135; Wold, "Die Infanterie der Zukunft," *ibid.*, 136 (1909), 35–38.

[32]Schlieffen's 1912 recommendation of amalgamating reserve and active units in the same corps owed less to his faith in reservists than his conviction that active corps were too weak in infantry and reserve corps too weak in artillery to be balanced fighting units. Schlieffen to Freytag-Loringhoven, Aug. 14, 1912, in *Generalfeldmarschall Graf Alfred Schlieffen. Briefe*, ed. E. Kessel (Göttingen, 1958), 317–318.

[33]Cf. Eric Leed, *No Man's Land* (New York, 1979); Robert Wohl, *The Generation of 1914* (Cambridge, Mass., 1979); and Roland N. Stromberg, *Redemption by War: The Intellectuals and 1914* (Lawrence, Kans., 1982).

[34]The Russian army's problems of professionalism and integration are presented in Dietrich Beyrau, *Militär und Gesellschaft im vorrevolutionären Russland* (Cologne, 1984), which focusses on the period before 1870; William C. Fuller, Jr., *Civil-Military Conflict in Imperial Russia, 1881–1914* (Princeton, N.J., 1985); and Hans-Peter Stein, "Der Offizier des Russischen Heeres im Zeitabschnitt zwischen Reform und Revolution (1861–1905)," *Forschungen zur Osteuropäischen Geschichte*, N. F., XIII (1967), 346–504.

[35]The most detailed presentation of Russian war plans remains A. M. Zaionchovski, *Plany voiny* (Moscow, 1926). This may be supplemented by Pertti Luntinen, *French Information on the Russian War Plans 1880–1914* (Helsinki, 1984); and Jack Snyder, *The Ideology of the Offensive. Military Decision-Making and the Disasters of 1914* (Ithaca, N.Y., 1984), 157 ff. Peter von Wahlde, "Military Thought in Imperial Russia" (Ph.D. Dissertation, Indiana University, 1966); and Walter T. Wilfong, "Rebuilding the Russian Army, 1905–1914: The Question of a Comprehensive Plan for National Defense" (Ph.D. Dissertation, Indiana University, 1977); incorporate excellent bibliographies. William C. Fuller, Jr., "The

Notes

Russian Empire," in *Knowing One's Enemies: Intelligence Assessment Before the Two World Wars*, (Princeton, N.J., 1984), 98–126, focuses on intelligence aspects of Russian planning.

[36]Mikhnevich's concepts are best expressed in *Strategia*, 3rd ed. (St. Petersburg, 1911). Their impact is summarized in Jacob W. Kipp, "The Beginning: Imperial Russia and Soviet Mobile Warfare to 1920," in *Historical Analysis of the Use of Mobile Forces by Russia and the USSR*, ed. J. W. Kipp *et. al.* (College Station, Tex., 1985), 50–51.

[37]Col. Wyndham to Nicolson, May 31, 1909 and Apr. 6, 1910, in *British Documents in Foreign Affairs: Reports and Papers from the Foreign Office Confidential Print*, Series A, *Russia, 1851–1914*, ed. D. Lieven, 6 vols. (Washington, D.C., 1983), V, Nr. 78; VI, Nr. 14; Matton to ministry of war, Mar. 1909, in France, Ministère des Affaires Étrangerès, *Documents Diplomatiques Français* (1871–1914), 41 vols. (Paris, 1929–59), 2nd series, XII, Nr. 88 (hereafter cited as *DDF*); Pelle to Buirn, Mar. 6 and 24, 1910, *ibid.*, Nrs. 453, 467.

[38]N. N. Sukhotin, *Voina v istorii russkogo mira* (St. Petersburg, 1989), 13–14; cit. Richard Pipes, "How to Cope with the Soviet Threat," *Commentary* LXXVIII (Aug., 1985, 13).

[39]"Procès-verbal des entretiens du mois août 1913 entre les chefs d'état-major des armées française et russe," *DDF* 3, VIII, Nr. 79. Recent analyses of Russian prewar planning include Bruce Menning's forthcoming *Bayonets before Bullets*, Chapter 7; and Jacob W. Kipp, *Fromm Foresight to Forecasting: The Russian and Soviet Military Experience* (College Station, Tex., 1988), 31 ff.

[40]D. W. Spring, "Russia and the Franco-Russian Alliance, 1905–1914: Dependence or Interdependence?" *Slavonic and East European Review* LXVI (1988), 564–592; and the older account by Donald R. Mathieu, "The Role of Russia in French Foreign Policy, 1908–1914" (Ph.D. Dissertation, Stanford University, 1968), highlight the growing importance to France of the Russian connection.

[41]Jean Savant, *Épopée russe. Campagne de l'Armée Rennenkampf en Prusse-Orientale* (Paris, 1945), 174; Norman Stone, *The Eastern Front, 1914–1917* (New York, 1975), 55–56.

[42]In the event, the Russians faced no significant hostile action in their rear until policies of repression generated such response. Daniel Graf, "The Reign of the Generals: Military Government in Western Russia, 1914–1915" (Ph.D. Dissertation, University of Nebraska, 1972), *passim.*

[43]Yanushkevitch's Instruction of Aug. 10 to Northwest Front and Zhilinski's of Aug. 13 to the 1st and 2nd Armies are translated in Edmund Ironside, *Tannenberg*, 42 ff. See also the summary in Yuri Danilov, *Russland im Weltkrieg*, tr. R. v. Campenhausen (Jena, 1925), 194 ff. Dean W. Lambert, "The Deterioration of the Imperial Russian Army in the First World War, August 1914–March 1917" (Ph.D. Dissertation, University of Kentucky, 1975), is useful for its pedestrian, common-sense approach to the question of the army's fighting power.

[44]For German evaluations of the Russian command see Eggeling to war ministry, Feb. 2, 1914, in PAAA, Russland 72, Nr. 96; and BA-MA, Nachlass Below, N 87/45, 602. Cf. Snyder, *Offensive*, 179 *passim*. Savant, *Épopée russe*, 94 ff., is a laudatory description of Rennenkampf's prewar career.

[45]Max Hoffmann, *War of Lost Opportunities* in *War Diaries and Other Papers*, 2 vols., M. E. Sutton (London, 1929), II, 40–41; Savant, *Épopée russe*, 261 ff.

[46]Maurice Paléologue, *An Ambassador's Memoirs*, Vol. I, tr. F. A. Holt (London, 1923), 71.

Notes

[47]For an extreme statement of the balance thesis of staff and command assignments see Stone, *Eastern Front*, 18 *passim*; von Wahlde, "Military Thought in Imperial Russia," 182 ff., offers a more judicious interpretation.

[48a]Jeffrey Brooks, *When Russia Learned to Read. Literacy and Popular Literature 1861–1917* (Princeton, N.J., 1985), 18 ff.; John S. Brown, *Draftee Division. The 88th Infantry Division in World War II* (Lexington, Ky., 1986), 13 ff.

[49]Cf. N. N. Golovine, *The Russian Campaign of 1914*, tr. A. G. S. Muntz (Ft. Leavenworth, Kans., 1933), 101 *passim*; and *The Russian Army in the World War* (New Haven, Conn., 1931); with most recently Stone, *Eastern Front*.

[50]Gempp, "Nachrichtendienst" II, 2, 223.

[51]Yanushkevich to Zhilinski, Aug. 7 and Aug. 10, 1914, in *Sbornik dokumentov mirovoy voyni na russkom fronte. Manevrenni period 1914 goda: Vostochvo-Prusskaya operasya*, ed. Generalny Shtab RKKA (Moscow, 1939), 81, 85–86; and the general accounts in Danilov, *Russland*, 194–195; Golovine, *1914*, 93 ff.; and Savant, *Épopée russe*, 150–151, 165 ff.

5. TAKING THE MEASURE OF DANGER

[1]Familiar evaluation of Prittwitz include Max Hoffmann, *War of Lost Opportunities*, in *War Diaries and Other Papers*, 2 vols., tr. E. Sutton (London, 1929), I, 21; E. Kabisch, *Streitfragen des Weltkrieges 1914–1918* (Stuttgart, 1924), 65; and Walter Elze, *Tannenberg. Das Deutsche Heer von 1914* (Breslau, 1928), 93.

[2]Bundesarchiv-Militärarchiv, Nachlass Below, NL 87/45, 684.

[3]Hoffmann, *War of Lost Opportunities*, 22; Walter Goerlitz, *Hindenburg: Ein Lebensbild* (Bonn, 1953), 55.

[4]There is a brief survey of his career in Holger Herwig and Neil Heyman, *Biographical Dictionary of World War I* (Westport, Conn., 1987), 188–189.

[5]A familiar example from the western front is von Kluck's negative reaction to the "Hentsch mission." Alexander von Kluck, *The March on Paris and the Battle of the Marne 1914* (London, 1920), 137 ff.

[6]Cf. Germany, Reichsarchiv, *Der Weltkrieg 1914 bis 1918*, Vol. II (Berlin, 1925), 46ff.; and Hermann von François, *Marneschlacht und Tannenberg* (Berlin, 1920), 130–131.

[7]Reichsarchiv to Tappen, July 4, 1921, BA-MA, Nachlass Tappen, NL 56/2; *Weltkrieg* II, 45.

[8]Quoted in "Besass Deutschland 1914 einen Kriegsplan?" Ludwig Beck, *Studien*, ed. H. Speidel (Stuttgart, 1955), 102.

[9]Norman Stone, "Austria-Hungary," in *Knowing One's Enemies. Intelligence Assessment Before the Two World Wars*, ed. E. R. May (Princeton, 1984), 49–50. Robert Asprey, *The Panther's Feast* (New York, 1959), is a sultry popular narrative of the Redl affair with a reasonable archival basis.

[10]Interwar descriptions of Austria's plan include Rudolf Kiszling, "Feldmarschall Konrads Kriegsplan gegen Russland," *Militärwissenschaftliche und technische Mitteilungen* (1925), 469–475; Max Freiherr von Petreich, *1914: Die militärischen Probleme unseres Kriegsbeginnes* (Vienna, 1934); and Josef Metzger, "Der Krieg 1914 gegen Russland," in *Der Grosse Krieg*, ed. M. Schwarte, Vol. V (Leipzig, 1922), 22–53. Graydon A. Tunstall, "The Schlieffen Plan: The Diplomacy and Military Strategy of the Central Powers in the East, 1905–1914" (Ph.D. Dissertation, Rutgers University, 1974), 353 *passim*, is a detailed modern analysis. Cf. also Georg von Waldersee, "Über die Beziehungen des deutschen zum österreichische-ungarischen Generalstab von dem Weltkrieg," *Berliner Monatshefte* VIII (1930), 103–142.

Notes

[11]"Aufmarschanweisung 1914/15 für Oberkommando der 8. Armee," Elze, *Tannenberg*, 185–196. The destruction of German military archives for this period during World War II is partly compensated for by Elze's work, which includes a large number of the relevant documents.

[12]Hoffmann, *War of Lost Opportunities*, 21.

[13]"Allgemeinen Direktiven für die kommandierenden Herrn Generale," Aug. 6, 1914, Elze, *Tannenberg*, 201–202.

[14]This description of the East Prussian terrain is based on Edmund Ironside, *Tannenberg* (Edinburgh, 1925), 12 ff.; and the Cook's-tourist account in BA-MA, Nachlass Below, NL 87/45, 571 ff. For the nature of the road and railway network see Frank B. Tipton, *Regional Variations in the Economic Development of Germany During the Nineteenth Century* (Middletown, Conn., 1976), 113.

[15]Fritz Gempp, "Geheimer Nachrichtendienst und Spionageabwehr des Heeres," National Archives T-77 (rolls 1,438–1,440, 1,442, 1,507, 1,509), Part II, Section 2, 15 ff.

[16]David R. Jones, "The Advanced Guard and Mobility in Russian Military Thought and Practice," SAFRA Papers, No. 1 (*Soviet Armed Forces Review Annual*) (Gulf Breeze, Fla., 1985), 57–59.

[17]Hoover Institution Archives, Adam Pavlovich Bennigsen, Papers 1914–1919, diary entries, July 27 [Aug. 9] and July 31 [Aug. 13], 1914; Jean Savant, *L'Épopée russe* (Paris, 1945), 152 ff., 197 ff.; and Basil Gourko's more favorable *War and Revolution in Russia, 1914–1917* (New York, 1919), 12–13. Gourko commanded the 1st Cavalry Division of Rennenkampf's army.

[18]The standard work on uniform and equipment is Richard Knötel, Herbert Knötel, and Herbert Sieg, *Uniforms of the World*, tr. R. G. Ball (New York, 1980), 129 *passim*.

[19]Buchholz, "Die Coca und ihre Anwendung bei Mängel an Nährungsmitteln für die Verpflegung der Truppen im Felde," *Jahrbücher für die deutsche Armee und Marine* II (1872), 211–216; Dr. Vogeler, "Bemerkungen zur Cocafrage," *ibid.*, III (1872), 260–265.

[20]The anecdote of the doctor is from Walter Richter, *Das Danziger Infanterie-Regiment Nr. 128*, Vol. I (Zeulenroda, 1930), 8.

[21]Gempp, "Nachrichtendienst" II, 3 *passim*; and II, 115 ff.

[22]M. von Poseck, *Die deutsche Kavallerie 1914 in Belgien und Frankreich* (Berlin, 1924), *passim*.

[23]For German cavalry operations in this sector see particularly Osterroht and Hermann, *Dragoner-Regiment Prinz Albrecht von Preussen (Litthauisches) Nr. 1, 1917–1919* (Berlin, 1930), 40 ff.; the anecdote of the wounded Cossack is in Alexis Wrangel, *The End of Chivalry. The Last Great Cavalry Battles 1914–1918* (New York, 1982), 13 ff.

[24]BA-MA, Nachlass Below, N87/45, 577; John H. Morrow, Jr., *Building German Air Power 1909–1914* (Knoxville, Tenn., 1976), 48 ff.

[25]Germany, Kriegswissenschaftliche Abteilungen der Luftwaffe, *Kriegsgeschichtliche Einzelschriften der Luftwaffe*, Vol. III, *Mobilmachung, Aufmarsch und erster Einsatz der deutschen Luftstreitkräfte im August 1914* (Berlin, 1939), 85–86 (hereafter cited as *Luftstreitkräfte*).

[26]Waldersee to Moltke, Aug. 18, 1914, Elze, *Tannenberg*, 202–204.

[27]*Luftstreitkräfte*, 87.

[28]Colmar Freiherr von der Goltz, *Denkwürdigkeiten*, ed. F. Freiherr von der Goltz, W. Foerster (Berlin, 1929), 305–306.

Notes

[29]Hoffmann, *War Diaries* I, 37; and the letter to his wife of 13.8.14 in BA-MA, Nachlass Hoffmann, N 37.

[30]Cf. BA-MA, Nachlass Below, N 87/45, 687, 700–701; William to François, Feb. 17, 1914, BA-MA, Nachlass François, N 274/16.

[31]Tappen to Reichsarchiv, Jan. 5, 1929, BA-MA, Nachlass Tappen, N 56/16.

[32]Hoffmann, *War of Lost Opportunities*, 24–25; *Weltkrieg*, II, 56–57.

[33]Norman Stone, "Die mobilmachung der österreichisch-ungarischen Armee 1914," *Militärgeschichtliche Mitteilung* (1974), 67–95, both establishes Conrad's fixation on Serbia and his ultimate indecisiveness, and forms the basis for Stone's numerous subsequent evaluations of Austrian strategy. Emil Ratzenhofer, "Österreich-Ungarns Mobilisierung, Transport und Versammlung Sommer 1914," Hoover Institution Archives, Ratzenhofer Deposit, demonstrates that strategic decisions rather than technical considerations ultimately determined troop movements in 1914. Conrad's justifications and the correspondence supporting them are in *Aus meiner Dienstzeit* 5 vols. (Vienna, 1921–25), IV, 161 *passim*. Cf. Helmuth von Moltke, *Erinnerungen. Briefe. Dokumente 1877–1916* (Stuttgart, 1922), 19–20.

[34]Waldersee to Freytag (liaison officer at Austrian GHQ), Aug. 11, 1914; Conrad to 8th Army HQ, 14.8.14, and to Prittwitz, 15.8.14, in Elze, *Tannenberg*, 205, 265, 266–267; cf. Conrad, *Aus meiner Dienstzeit* IV, 388 ff.; and Theobald von Schäfer, "Deutsche Offensive aus Ostpreussen über den Narew auf Siedlice," *Militärwissenschaftliche und technische Mitteilungen* (1930), 961–976.

[35]*Luftstreitkräfte*, 88–89.

[36]One critique of this kind, delivered in 1910 by then-Lt.-Gen. Paul von Hindenburg, made such an impression on a young subaltern that he repeated it word for word in his memoirs over seventy years later. Erich Hampe, . . . *als Alles in Scherben fiel* (Osnabruück, 1980), 10–11.

[37]François, *Marneschlacht und Tannenberg*, 174–175.

[38]As in Franz von Gottberg, *Das Grenadier-Regiment Kronprinz (1. Ostpreussischen) Nr. 1 im Weltkriege* (Berlin, 1927), 19 ff.; Alfred Dieterich, *Geschichte des Grenadierregiments König Friedrich der Grosse (3. Ostpreussischen) Nr. 4* (Berlin, 1928), 651.

[39]Lerchenfeld to Hertling, Oct. 9, 1914, in Ernst Deuerlein, ed., *Briefwechsel Hertling-Lerchenfeld 1912–1917*, Vol. I (Boppard, 1973), 341–342; Immanuel Geiss, *Das deutsche Reich und der Ersten Weltkrieg* (Munich, 1978), 62 ff.

[40]Hoover Institution, Bennigsen Diaries, July 29 (Aug. 11), Aug. 3 (Aug. 16), Aug. 10 (Aug. 17), Aug. 10 (Aug. 23); Gourko, *War and Revolution*, 42 ff.; Graf, "Military Government," 123. John Bushnell, "Peasants in Uniform: The Tsarist Army as a Peasant Society," *Journal of Social History* XIII (1980), 565–576; makes the case that that army's real internal structure was a network of *artels*, which the average junior leader had neither the will nor the competence to dominate. This in turn suggests the structural pattern of command by consensus described above. On the general issue of requisitions see Martin van Creveld, *Supplying War* (Cambridge, 1977), 190 *passim*.

[41]*Grenadier-Regiment Nr. 1*, 22, 24; Fritz Rohde, *2. Ostpreussisches Feldartillerie-Regiment Nr. 52* (Oldenburg, Berlin, 1928), 9–10.

[42]Reichsarchiv, *Weltkrieg* II, 59 ff.; François, *Marneschlacht und Tannenberg*, 167.

[43]Gerhard Lapp, *Das 1. Ostpreussische Feldartillerie-Regiment Nr. 16* (Oldenburg, Berlin, 1928), 13; *Grenadier-Regiment Nr. 1*, 24.

[44]François, *Marneschlacht und Tannenberg*, 170. Cf. the general account of

Notes

Stallupönen in Reichsarchiv, *Weltkrieg* II, 73 ff., with the major regimental histories: Alfred Bülowius and Bruno Hippler, *Das Infanterie-Regiment v. Boyen (5. Ostpreussisches) Nr. 41 im Weltkriege 1914–1918* (Berlin, 1929), 9 ff.; Fritz Schillmann, *Grenadier-Regiment König Friedrich Wilhelm I (2. Ostpreussisches) Nr. 3 im Weltkriege 1914–1918* (Berlin, 1924), 22–23; Georg Dorndorf, *Das Infanterie-Regiment Nr. 43* (Berlin, 1923), 13 ff.; *Grenadier-Regiment Nr. 1*, 26 ff.

[45]David Landes, *Revolution in Time: Clocks and the Making of the Modern World* (Cambridge, Mass., 1983), 51–52, 95 ff.

[46]Comments on Schäfer to Conta, Mar. 15, 1929, in BA-MA, Nachlass François, N 274/18.

[47]Bülowius and Hippler, *IR 41*, 13–14.

[48]Elze, *Tannenberg*, 101; record of phone conversation, 3:30 p.m., *ibid.*, 215; and François, *Marneschlacht und Tannenberg*, 170 ff. François blamed his chief of staff for the incident, and demanded that officer's immediate relief for disloyalty. Not until after the battle did he seek to withdraw his complaints. Telegram of Aug. 31, 1914, in BA-MA, Nachlass François, N 274/16.

[49]Prittwitz to François, 6:50 p.m.; record of phone conversation, François to Prittwitz, 8:00 p.m.; and report of 11:15 p.m. Aug. 17, 1914, in Elze, *Tannenberg*, 215–216.

[50]Bülowius and Hippler, *IR 41*, 14–15.

[51]General accounts critical of Rennenkampf's behavior include Ironside, *Tannenberg*, 85 ff.; Golovine, *1914*, 114 ff.

[52]Army orders of Aug. 17 and Aug. 18; communication of Aug. 18 to OHL; order of Aug. 18 to I Corps, in Elze, *Tannenberg*, 215 ff.

[53]François, *Marneschlacht und Tannenberg*, 179.

[54]Reichsarchiv, *Weltkrieg* II, 79 ff.

[55]*Luftstreitkräfte*, 90–91.

[56]Gemmp, *Nachrichtendienst* II, 1, 30; 1st Lt. Randewig, "Deutsche Funkaufklärung in der Schlacht bei Tannenberg," *Wissen und Wehr* XII (1932), 129–130, 139. Not until the end of Sept., 1914, did the Germans break the Russian field code.

[57]Record of telephone conversation between I Corps and AOK, 4:10 p.m. Aug. 19, Elze, *Tannenberg*, 218–219; François, *Marneschlacht und Tannenberg*, 180.

[58]Orders to XVII Corps and I Corps, Aug. 19, in Elze, *Tannenberg*, 219; François, *Marneschlacht und Tannenberg*, 181–182.

[59]"Bei Gumbinnen findet heute grosses Gefecht statt," Order to Air Detachment 16, 2:45 a.m., Aug. 20, in Elze, *Tannenberg*, 221.

[60]Order to 3rd Reserve Division, 4:50 p.m. Aug. 19, in *ibid.*, 220; and Reichsarchiv, *Weltkrieg* II, 83–84.

6. FIRST CONTACT: GUMBINNEN

[1]Hermann von François, *Marneschlacht und Tannenberg* (Berlin, 1920), 182–183; N. N. Golovine, *The Russian Campaign of 1914*, tr. A. G. S. Muntz (Leavenworth, Kans., 1933), 123.

[2]E. G. "Der Kampf um Dörfer," *Militär-Wochenblatt*, 1881, 30–31; "Gedanken über den Angriff auf befestigte Feldstellungen," *Jahrbücher für die deutsche Armee und Marine*, 119 (1899), 295–309.

[3]For the attack of Falk's division cf. Traugott Hoffmann and Ernst Hahn, *Geschichte des Infanterie-Regiments Graf Dönhoff (7. Ostpreussischen) Nr. 44 1860–1918* (Berlin, 1930), 108–109; Alfred Dieterich, *Geschichte des Grenadierregiments König Friedrich der Grosse (3. Ostpreussischen) Nr. 4* (Berlin, 1928), 653–654; and

Notes

the detailed account in Kurt Hennig, *Das Infanterie-Regiment (8. Ostpreussischen)*
Nr. 45 (Berlin, 1928), 20 ff. The Russian artillery's role in this sector is presented
in General V. Chernavin, "28th Artillery Brigade in the Vicinity of Gumbinnen,
Aug. 6–7 (19–20), 1914," Hoover Institution Archives, Nikolai N. Golovin
Collection, Box 13.

[4]Franz von Gottberg, *Das Grenadier-Regiment Kronprinz (1. Ostpreussischen)*
Nr. 1 im Weltkriege, Vol. I (Berlin, 1927) 31 ff; Alfred Bülowius and Bruno
Hippler, *Das Infanterie-Regiment von Boyen (5. Ostpreussischen) Nr. 41 im Welt-*
kriege 1914–1918 (Berlin, 1929), 16–17; and Germany, Reichsarchiv, *Der Weltkrieg*
1914 bis 1918, Vol II (Berlin, 1925), 87–88.

[5]Gerhard Lapp, *Das 1. Ostpreussische Feldartillerie-Regiment Nr. 16* (Berlin,
1928), 15–16; and *Grenadier-Regiment Nr.1*, 35–37, are the fullest accounts of this
mix-up.

[6]For Mackensen's peacetime career see his *Briefe und Aufzeichnungen*, ed.
Wolfgang Foerster (Leipzig, 1938), and Rüdt von Collenberg's *völkisch*-popular
Mackensen (Berlin, 1935).

[7]William Clive, *Fighting Mac. The Climb to Disaster of Sir Hector Macdonald*
(London, 1977), 300.

[8]A vivid account of XVII Corps's night march is Kurt Hesse, *Der Feldherr*
Psychologos (Berlin, 1922), 3 ff. Hesse was a company officer in the 5th Grenadiers,
whose regimental history, Alfred Seydel, *Das Grenadier-Regiment König Friedrich*
I (4. Ostpreussisches) Nr. 5 im Weltkriege (Berlin, 1926), 35 ff., is also evocative. Cf.
Walter Richter, *Das Danziger Infanterie-Regiment Nr. 128*, Vol. I (Zeulenroda,
1930), 12–13.

[9]Hesse, *Feldherr Psychologos*, 14–15.

[10]*Ibid.*, 16.

[11]Mackensen, *Briefe und Aufzeichnungen*, 36–37; Reichsarchiv, *Weltkrieg* II,
90.

[12]Ernst Zipfel, *Geschichte des Königlich Preussischen Husaren-Regiment Fürst*
Blücher von Wahlstätt (Pommersches) Nr. 5 (Zeulenroda, 1930), 21 ff.

[13]Mackensen, *Briefe und Aufzeichnungen*, 38; Reichsarchiv, *Weltkrieg* II, 90;
von Keiser, *Geschichte des Inf.-Regts. v.d. Marwitz (8. Pomm.) Nr. 61 im Weltkriege*
1914–1918 (Oldenburg, 1928), 11 ff.; Wilhelm Preusser, *Das 9. Infanterie-Regi-*
ment Nr. 176 im Weltkrieg (Berlin, 1931), 35 ff.; Edmund Schulemann, *Das Kulmer*
Infanterie-Regiment Nr. 141 im Weltkriege (Oldenburg, 1926), 14 ff. General
Ardaridi, "Die 27. russische Infanterie-Division in den Kämpfen bei Stallupönen
und Gumbinnen am 17. und 20. August, 1914," *Schweizer Monatshefte für Offiziere*
(Apr.-May 1928) 113–123, 153–163, is an account from the perspective of the
formation that bore the brunt of Mackensen's attack.

[14]Richter, *IR 128*, 13–14.

[15]Cf. *inter alia* the *Exerzier-Reglement für die Infanterie von 29. Mai 1906*,
rev. ed. (Berlin, 1909); Balck, "Das Exerzierreglement für die Infanterie von 29.
Mai 1906," *Jahrbücher für die deutsche Armee und Marine*, 131 (1906), 111–135;
and Otto Schulz, "Gruppenkolonne und Kompagniekolonne," *ibid.*, 136 (1909),
35–38.

[16]See, for example, the description of the death of Major Haupt, commanding I/128, from the diary of one of his officers, quoted in Richter, *IR 128*, 15–16.

[17]Von Beseler, "Ingenieurkunst und Offensive," *Vierteljahresheft für Truppen-*
führung und Heereskunde VII (1910), 362–384; Immanuel, "Der Infanteriepionier
im Feldkriege," *Kriegstechnische Zeitschrift* XV (1912), 145–157.

[18]Seydel, *5. Grenadiere*, 38–39.

Notes

[19]Undated letter of Lt. Wartze, quoted in Schulemann, *IR 141*, 15–16.

[20]Hesse, *Feldherr Psychologos*, 28–29.

[21]Richter, *IR 128*, 17–18.

[22]Joseph Steuer, *Das Infanterie-Regiment Generalfeldmarschall von Mackensen (3. Westpreussisches) Nr. 129 im Weltkriege* (Oldenburg, 1929), 20 ff.

[23]John Ellis, *A Social History of the Machine Gun* (New York, 1975) is a brief treatment of the human dynamics of the weapon. Cf. also Balck, "Maschinengewehre und ihre Verwendung," *JAM*, 132 (1907), 269–288, 393–411.

[24]Seydel, *Grenadier-Regiment Nr. 5*, 40–41; Hesse, *Feldherr Psychologos*, 33–34.

[25]"Bis zur letzten Kartusche," in *Das Ehrenbuch der deutschen Feldartillerie*, ed. A. Benary (Berlin, 1930), 251–252, is a vivid account of the fight and fate of 2./36.

[26]Oberstabsarzt Leopold, "Der Sanitätsdienst in der ersten Linie," *MW* 1903, 26–27.

[27]It is worth noting that the "Neumann" of jest and song ultimately evolved from a pathetic figure to a combination of Kilroy and Joe the Grinder. With his rank upgraded and his title changed to fit the times, *Sanitätsgefreiter* Neumann was credited by the end of World War II with the ability to beat the army system and the watchful gaze of chaperones in a thousand ingenious ways—even to inventing the sofa pillow as an aid to spontaneous coitus.

[28]Diary entry of Aug. 23 by Staff Surgeon Krägel of II/141, quoted in Schulemann, *IR 141*, 16–17.

[29]Elmar Dinter, *Hero or Coward? Pressures Facing the Soldier in Battle* (London, 1985), is typical of many works on this theme in focussing on formations with extensive combat experience or with a high number of professional soldiers in the ranks.

[30]Narrative of Lt. Wendland, 5./141, in Schulemann, *IR 141*, 19.

[31]Mackensen, *Briefe und Aufzeichnungen*, 40–41.

[32]Report of Lt. Gittermann, 3./71st Field Artillery, in Schulemann, *IR 141*, 21–22.

[33]Preusser, *IR 176*, 23.

[34]*Reserve-Infanterie Regiment Nr. 3*, ed. by Regimental Officers' Association (Berlin, 1926), 9 ff.; Max Gengelbach, *Das Reserve-Feldartillerie-Regiment Nr. 36 im Weltkrieg*, Part I (Berlin, 1929), 1 ff.; Max Meyhöfer, *Das Reserve-Feldartillerie-Regiment Nr. 1 im Weltkriege (1914–1918)* (Oldenburg, 1926), 12 ff.

[35]Below presents his peacetime career in stupefying but useful detail in his memoirs, held in Bundesarchiv-Militärarchiv, Nachlass Below, N87.

[36]The proposed support, the 3rd Reserve Division on the extreme right of the army, was in fact not ordered to advance until 4:30 p.m., and did not reach its assigned position until nightfall. It took no part in the day's fighting.

[37]The march and fight of I Reserve Corps has been reconstructed from the summary in Reichsarchiv, *Weltkrieg* II, 91 ff.; and the more complete and evocative treatments in Hellmuth Neumann, *Die Geschichte des Reserve-Infanterie-Regiments Nr. 59 im Weltkriege* (Oldenburg, 1927), 12 ff.; Alfred Rothe, *Das Reserve-Infanterie-Regiment Nr. 61 im Weltkriege* (Berlin, 1929), 13 ff.; *RIR Nr. 3*, 14 ff.; Gengelbach, *RFAR Nr. 1*, 17 ff.; and Meyhöfer, *RFAR Nr. 36*, 6 ff.

[38]"The Point of View," in *The Green Curve and Other Stories*, by 'Ole-Luk-Oie' (New York, 1911), 251–276.

[39]Germany: Kriegswissenschaftliche Abteilung der Luftwaffe, *Kriegsgeschichtliche Einzelschriften der Luftwaffe*, Vol. III, *Mobilmachung, Aufmarsch und*

Notes

erster Einsatz der deutschen Luftstreitkräfte im August 1914 (Berlin, 1939), 94 (hereafter cited as *Luftstreitkräfte*); extract from XX Corps war diary in Walter Elze, *Tannenberg. Das Deutsche Heer von 1914* (Breslau, 1928), 226.

[40]François, *Marneschlacht und Tannenberg*, 187.

[41]Unger to 8th Army, Aug. 20, 1914, in Elze, *Tannenberg*, 226.

[42]*Luftstreitkräfte*, 94; extract from XX Corps war diary in Elze, *Tannenberg*, 226.

[43]Max Hoffmann, *War of Lost Opportunities*, in *War Diaries and Other Papers*, 2 vols., tr. E. Sutton (London, 1929), II, 28.

[44]*Ibid.*, 28–29.

[45]Reichsarchiv, *Weltkrieg* II, 102.

[46]Hoffmann to his wife, Aug. 21, 1914, in BA-MA, Nachlass Hoffmann, NL 37; and *War of Lost Opportunities*, 29–30; Elze, *Tannenberg*, 368.

[47]Orders to XVII Corps and I Reserve Corps, timed at 9:00 a.m.; and to I Corps, timed at 9:30 a.m., are in *ibid.*, 253–254. Cf. Elze's comment on p. 216.

[48]Prittwitz's reports of Aug. 17 and 18, OHL's requests of Aug. 18 and 19, and OHL's record of the noon conversation are in *ibid.*, 216–217, 220, 233.

[49]Moltke's "Comments on the Change of Command of the 8th Army," dated Aug. 26, is in *ibid.*, 242 ff.

[50]Mackensen's report, "dictated from memory" on Aug. 25, is in *ibid.*, 227.

[51]François to Hoffmann, Apr. 5, 1925, and to Col. Emil Seelinger of the *Neues Wiener Journal*, in BA-MA, Nachlass François, NL 274/15, 19; François, *Marneschlacht und Tannenberg*, 190 ff.

[52]Hoffmann, "The Truth About Tannenberg," in *War Diaries and Other Papers* II, 250–251.

[53]This dispatch, printed in Elze, *Tannenberg*, 233, was not received in Koblenz until 2:20 a.m. on Aug. 21. The governors of the fortresses of Königsberg, Thorn, Posen, and Graudenz were informed that the army was retreating into West Prussia in messages sent at 10:45 p.m.

[54]Report of Stellvertretendes Generalkommando I, Aug. 20, 1914, received by OHL at 7:00 p.m., in *ibid.*, 233.

[55]Wenninger's reports of Aug. 21 and 22 and an excerpt from his diary entry of Aug. 22 are reprinted in Bernd F. Schulte, "Neue Dokumente zu Kriegsausbruch und Kriegsverlauf," *Militärgeschichtliche Mitteilungen* XV (1979), 154–156.

[56]OHL's records of the phone conversations are in Elze, *Tannenberg*, 233–244. Cf. Reichsarchiv, *Weltkrieg* II, 104–105; and François to Hoffmann, Apr. 5, 1925, BA-MA, Nachlass François, NL 274/15. A corps commander's right of direct access to the sovereign lapsed on the outbreak of war.

[57]Hoffmann to his wife, Aug. 22, 1914, BA-MA, Nachlass Hoffmann, NL 37; Hoffmann to François, Apr. 10, 1925, Nachlass François, NL 274/15; Waldersee to Scholtz, Aug. 22, 1914, Nachlass Groener, NL 46/38. The latter conversation follows Prittwitz's description of his intentions in his report of Aug. 25, which he described as having been composed before his relief from command. Elze, *Tannenberg*, 237 ff.

[58]OHL's conversations with I Corps (9:30 a.m.), XX Corps (1:50 p.m. and 11:30 p.m.), I Reserve Corps (2:30 p.m.) and XVII Corps (4:30 p.m.) are in Elze, *Tannenberg*, 236, 245–246.

[59]Stein's record of the conversation is in *ibid.*, 235. OHL learned of the move of 8th Army headquarters only at 11:00 p.m., *ibid.*, 236. The impact of the information is discussed in Reichsarchiv, *Weltkrieg* II, 105–106.

Notes

[60]Helmuth von Moltke, *Militärische Werke*, ed. Grossen Generalstab, 13 vols. in 4 (Berlin, 1892–1912), Part 3, Vol. III, 11.

[61]8th Army received this news from I Corps at 6:00 p.m.; it was noted by OHL at 7:15–7:30 p.m. as part of the conversation between Prittwitz and Moltke. Reports in Elze, *Tannenberg*, 258, 236. Max Hoffmann also refers to the 1st Cavalry Division's triumphant return in his letter of Aug. 22. BA-MA, Nachlass Hoffmann, NL 37.

[62]Schäfer, "Wollte Generaloberst von Prittwitz im August 1914 hinter die Weichsel zurückgehen?" *MW*, 1921, 45 Reichsarchiv, *Weltkrieg* II, 106–107; Elze, *Tannenberg*, 112–113.

[63]Reitzenstein, "Generaloberst von Prittwitz nach der Schlacht bei Gumbinnen am 20. August 1914," *MW*, 1921, 43.

[64]Report of Aug. 21 in Schulte, "Dokumente," 154–155.

[65]Wenninger's diary entry of Aug. 22, *ibid.*, 156.

[66]Erich Ludendorff, *Ludendorff's Own Story*, Vol. I (New York, 1926), 49–50.

[67]Among the major English-language indictments of Ludendorff are Martin Kitchen, *The Silent Dictatorship. The Politics of the German High Command under Hindenburg and Ludendorff, 1916–1918* (New York, 1976); and Norman Stone, "Ludendorff," in *The War Lords. Military Commanders of the Twentieth Century*, ed. M. Carver (London, 1976), 73–83. D. J. Goodspeed, *Ludendorff: Genius of World War I* (Boston, 1966), establishes its tone in its title. Roger Parkinson, *Tormented Warrior: Ludendorff and the Supreme Command* (London, 1978), tries without success to establish Ludendorff's humane and human aspects. The most balanced brief treatment remains Corelli Barnett, *The Swordbearers: Studies in Supreme Command in the First World War* (London, 1963), 15–106.

[68]Ludendorff, *Ludendorff's Own Story*, 52 ff.

[69]See particularly his *Denkwürdigkeiten*, ed. F. Freiherr von der Goltz and W. Foerster (Berlin, 1932); and Hermann Teske, *Colmar Freiherr von der Goltz. Ein Kämpfer für den militärischen Fortschritt* (Göttingen, 1957), 66–67.

[70]Wilhelm Groener, *Lebenserinnerungen* (Göttingen, 1957), 164–165.

[71]Verdy to Waldersee, Jan., 1884, in *General-feldmarschall Alfred Graf von Waldersee in seinem militärischen Wirken*, ed. H. Mohs, Vol. II, *1882–1904* (Berlin, 1929), 180.

[72]The story was probably apocryphal. August Lindner, in a letter to F. W. Foerster dated Mar. 23, 1957, said that a similar tale had earlier been linked with August Lentze of I Corps. BA-MA, Nachlass Foerster, NL 121/18.

[73]For summaries of Hindenburg's peacetime career see Walter Görlitz, *Hindenburg: Ein Lebensbild* (Bonn, 1953), esp. 41 *passim*; Andreas Dorpalen, *Hindenburg and the Weimar Republic* (Princeton, 1964), 7–8; and Walther Hubatsch, *Hindenburg und der Staat* (Göttingen, 1966), 12 ff.

[74]Paul von Hindenburg, *Out of My Life*, tr. F. A. Holt, (London, 1933), 60.

[75]Wilhelm Deist in *Kaiser Wilhelm II: New Interpretations*, ed. J. C. G. Röhl and N. Sombart (Cambridge, 1982), 169–192.

[76]Isabel Hull, *The Entourage of Kaiser Wilhelm II, 1888–1918* (Cambridge, 1982), 266 *passim*; Georg Alexander von Müller, *The Kaiser and His Court*, ed. W. Görlitz, tr. M. Savill (London, 1961), 22–23.

[77]Hindenburg, *Out of My Life*, 61; Ludendorff, *Ludendorff's Own Story*, 55.

[78]Winston Churchill, *The Unknown War* (New York, 1931), *passim*; Ludendorff, *Ludendorff's Own Story*, 14; Hindenburg, *Out of My Life*, 62.

[79]*Ibid.*, 63.

Notes

[80]Lyncker's telegram of 4:45 p.m., Aug. 22, in BA-MA, Nachlass François, NL 274/16.

[81]Hoffmann, "Tannenberg," 252–253; and *War of Lost Opportunities*, 33–34; letter of Aug. 23 in BA-MA, Nachlass Hoffmann, NL 37.

[82]Franz Conrad von Hötzendorf, *Aus meiner Dienstzeit*, 5 vols. (Vienna, 1921–25), IV, 455–458.

[83]Hoffmann, "Tannenberg," 252; Reichsarchiv, *Weltkrieg* II, 115.

[84]Ludendorff, *Ludendorff's Own Story*, 55–56; Hoffmann, "Tannenberg," 251.

[85]Hermann Büschleb, *Die Verzögerung: Das schwerste Gefecht* (Osnabrück, 1978), 32 ff.

[86]J. W. Wheeler-Bennett, *Hindenburg: Wooden Titan* (New York, 1936), 20–21; Hoffmann, *War Diaries* I, 18–19.

[87]Holger H. Herwig and Neil M. Heyman, *Biographical Dictionary of World War I* (Westport, Conn., 1982), 88.

[88]Jean Savant, *Épopée Russe, Campagne de l' ármée Rennenkampf en Prusse-Orientale* (Paris, 1945), 249 *passim*, eloquently defends Rennenkampf's behavior. Churchill, *Unknown War*, 187–185, is an imaginative reconstruction of possibilities. Cf. also Norman Stone, *The Eastern Front, 1914–1917* (New York, 1975), 62. The anecdote of the staff officer encouraged to retire is from Alfred Knox, *With the Russian Army, 1914–1917* (London, 1921), I, 89; the interrogator's experiences are quoted in Savant, 428.

[89]François, *Marneschlacht und Tannenberg*, 198.

[90]Curt von Morgen, *Meiner Truppen Heldenkämpfe* (Berlin, 1918), 6–7.

[91]Mackensen, *Briefe und Aufzeichnugen*, 46–47.

[92]*Richter, IR 128*, 24 ff.; Steuer, *IR 129*, 30–31; Seydel, *Grenadier-Regiment Nr. 5*, 45 ff.

[93]Edmund Ironside, *Tannenberg* (Edinburgh, 1925), 154; *RIR Nr. 3*, 22 ff.; Meyhöfer, *RFAR Nr. 36*, 11 ff.

[94]A detailed account of the cavalry's movements and condition is in Lt.-Col. Osterroht and Major Herrmann, *Geschichte des Dragoner-Regiments Prinz Albrecht von Preussen (Litthauisches) Nr. 1, 1717–1919* (Berlin, 1930), 53 ff. Cf. Savant, *Épopée russe*, 219 ff.

7. THE PROVINCE OF UNCERTAINTY

[1]For the movements of the Russian 2nd Army, cf. the general staff history, *La Grande Guerre. Concentration des armées. Premières operations en Prusse Orientale, en Galicie et en Pologne (1er âout–24 novembre 1914)*, tr. E. Chapouilly (Paris, 1926), 32 ff, 89 ff.; N. N. Golovine, *The Russian Campaign of 1914*, tr. A. G. S. Muntz (Ft. Leavenworth, Kans., 1933), 178 ff.; Edmund Ironside, *Tannenberg* (Edinburgh, 1925), 42 ff.; 117 ff.

[2]David R. Jones, "The Advanced Guard and Mobility in Russian Military Thought and Practice," SAFRA Papers, No. 1 (*Soviet Armed Forces Review Annual*) (Gulf Breeze, Fla., 1985); Ironside, *Tannenberg*, 120–121.

[3]Yanushkevich to Zhilinski, Aug. 10, 1914; Zhilinski to Samsonov, Aug. 13, 1914; 2nd Army's Directive No. 1, Aug. 16, 1914, in *Sbornik dokumentov mirovoy voyni na russkom fronte. Manevrenni period 1914 goda: Vostochno-Prusskaya operasiya*, ed. Generalny Shtab RKKA (Moscow, 1939), 85–86, 157–158, 245–246. Golovine, *1914*, 166 *passim*; and Alfred Knox, *With the Russian Army, 1914–1917*, Vol. I (London, 1921), 59 ff., remain the most vivid descriptions of the 2nd Army's situation. The Russian use of radio in 1904/05 is mentioned in Mario de

Notes

Arcangelis, *Electronic Warfare from the Battle of Tsushima to the Falklands and Lebanon Conflicts* (Poole, Dorset, 1985), 11 ff.

[4]Golovine, *1914*, 184–185.

[5]Andreas Kuhn, *Das Tannenberg-Nationaldenkmal* (Allenstein, 1932), 22 passim. This account is essentially a reprint of Kuhn's earlier pamphlet, *Die Schreckenstage von Neidenburg in Ostpreussen. Kriegserinnerungen aus dem Jahre 1914* (Minden, 1915). Cf. Heinrich Plickert, *Das 2. Ermländische Infanterie-Regiment Nr. 151 im Weltkriege* (Berlin, 1929), 27 ff. Gerhard Kneiss, *Der Kreis Neidenburg/ Ostpreussen im Ersten Weltkrieg und die Tannenberg-Schlacht 1914* (Bremerhaven, 1981), is local history in the old style, but useful for its anecdotes.

[6]Knox, *With the Russian Army*, 62; Kuhn, *Tannenberg*, 30 ff.

[7]2nd Army Directive Nr. 4, Aug. 23, 1914, *Sbornik*, 263–264; *Grande Guerre*, 96–97; Ironside, *Tannenberg*, 132–133.

[8]For Scholtz's peacetime career and his approach to corps command, see Ferdinand von Notz, *General von Scholtz. Ein deutsches Soldatenleben in grosser Zeit* (Berlin, 1937), 11 ff. For the problems faced by artillerymen aspiring to high command cf. Hermann von François, "Kriegslage bei der 8. Armee zur Zeit des Kommandowechsels," 7, Bundesarchiv-Militärarchiv, Nachlass François, NL 274/17; and more generally Daniel J. Hughes, "The Social Composition of the Prussian Generalcy" (Ph.D. Dissertation, University of North Carolina, 1979), 139 ff.

[9]Dr. Ernst Zipfel, *Geschichte des Dragoner-Regiments König Albert von Sachsen (Ostpr.) Nr. 10* (Zeulenroda, 1933), 16 ff.; Reichsarchiv, *Der Weltkrieg 1914 bis 1918*, Vol. II (Berlin, 1925), 115, 125–126.

[10]Erich Balla, *Im Yorckschen Geist. Der deutsche Frontsoldat und seine Seele* (Berlin, 1926), 16 ff.; Plickert, *IR 151*, 30 ff.; Theobald von Schäfer, *Tannenberg* (Oldenburg, 1927), 35.

[11]Balla, *Im Yorckschen Geist*, 22 ff.

[12]*Ibid.*, 24–25; Plickert, *IR 151*, 40 *passim*; Heinrich Siebert, *Geschichte des Infanterie-Regiments Generalfeldmarschall von Hindenburg (2. Masurisches) Nr. 147 im Weltkriege* (Oldenburg, 1927), 35 ff.; Schäfer, *Tannenberg*, 36–37.

[13]Reichsarchiv, *Weltkrieg* II, 126 ff.; Schäfer, *Tannenberg*, 37 ff.; *Geschichte des 1. Ermländischen Infanterie-Regiments Nr. 150*, ed. Regimental Officers' Association (Zeulenroda, 1931), 17 ff.

[14]Telegram from Königsberg to 8th Army, Aug. 24, 8:55 a.m.; XX Corps to 8th Army, Aug. 24, 11:10 a.m., Walter Elze, *Tannenberg* (Breslau, 1928), 282–283.

[15]*IR 150*, 20; Balla, *Im Yorckschen Geist*, 30.

[16]Max Hoffmann, "Tannenberg," in *War Diaries and Other Papers*, tr. Eric Sutton, Vol. I (London, 1929), 261–262; Paul von Hindenburg, *Out of My Life* (London, 1933), 68; Reichsarchiv, *Weltkrieg* II, 131 ff.; W. von Stephani, *Mit Hindenburg bei Tannenberg* (Berlin, 1919), 16.

[17]Hermann von François, *Marneschlacht und Tannenberg* (Berlin, 1920), 199 *passim*.

[18]Army order for Aug. 25, Aug. 24, 8:40 p.m., and telegrams to I Reserve Corps and XVII Corps, Aug. 24, 9:50 p.m., Elze, *Tannenberg*, 285–286; *Weltkrieg* II, 133–134.

[19]Record of phone conversation between Ludendorff and Capt. Geyer, Aug. 24, 6:30 p.m., Elze, *Tannenberg*, 284–285.

[20]Königsberg to 8th Army, Aug. 25, 5:30 a.m., Elze, *Tannenberg*, 289.

Notes

[21]OHL to 8th Army, Aug. 25, 3:52 a.m.; army command to Field Railway Commander II, Aug. 25, 10:00 a.m., Elze, *Tannenberg*, 291–292.

[22]François, *Marneschlacht und Tannenberg*, 201–202.

[23]Hoffman, "Tannenberg," 265 ff.; Walter Görlitz, *Hindenburg: Ein Lebensbild* (Bonn, 1953), 66, 68; Reichsarchiv, *Weltkrieg* II, 139; François, *Marneschlacht und Tannenberg*, 202–203.

[24]Hoffmann, "Tannenberg," 267–268; radio message intercepted by 8th Army headquarters, Aug. 25, 6:00 a.m., Elze, *Tannenberg*, 289–290.

[25]Knox, *With the Russian Army* I, 65–66.

[26]*Ibid.*, 72; Ironside, *Tannenberg*, 139 ff.; Golovine, *1914*, 205 ff.; *La Grande Guerre*, 98–99.

[27]Reichsarchiv, *Weltkrieg* II, 140 ff.; *Infanterie-Regiment 151*, 49; Wilhelm Reichert, *Das Infanterie-Regiment Frh. Hiller von Gaertringen (4. Posensches) Nr. 59 im Weltkriege 1914–1918*, Vol. I, *1914/15* (Berlin, 1930), 43–44.

[28]Reichsarchiv, *Weltkrieg* II, 142.

[29]Army order for Aug. 26 in Elze, *Tannenberg*, 293.

[30]Golovine, *1914*, 205; Ironside, *Tannenberg*, 142 ff.

[31]François, *Marneschlacht und Tannenberg*, 203–205; Hoffmann, "Tannenberg," 272; Reichsarchiv, *Weltkrieg* II, 141, 148.

[32]Telephone message I Corps to 8th Army, Aug. 26, 5:30 a.m., Elze, *Tannenberg*; Hoffmann, "Tannenberg," 273.

[33]I Corps to 8th Army, Aug. 26, 8:40 a.m., 11:15 a.m., and 11:35 a.m.; 8th Army to I Corps, 11:25 a.m., Elze, *Tannenberg*, 299–300; François, *Marneschlacht und Tannenberg*, 206–207; Hoffmann, "Tannenberg," 275.

[34]8th Army to I Corps, Aug. 26, 11:45 a.m., Elze, *Tannenberg*, 300.

[35]I Corps to 8th Army, Aug. 26, *ibid.*, 301; François, *Marneschlacht und Tannenberg*, 207–208.

[36]Stephani, *Mit Hindenburg bei Tannenberg*, 20–21.

[37]Fritz Rohde, *2. Ostpreussisches Feldartillerie-Regiment Nr. 52* (Oldenburg, 1928), 15; Schäfer, *Tannenberg*, 54 ff.; François, *Marneschlacht und Tannenberg*, 207–208.

[38]Kurt Hennig, *Das Infanterie-Regiment (8. Ostpreussisches) Nr. 45 im Weltkrieg 1914–1918* (Oldenburg, 1928), 25; Alfred Dieterich, *Geschichte des Grenadierregiments König Friedrich der Grosse (3. Ostpreussisches) Nr. 4*, (Berlin, 1928), 655.

[39]B. H. Liddell-Hart, *The Real War, 1914–1918* (Boston, 1931), 126.

[40]Hoffmann, "Tannenberg," 274.

[41]This conversation, mentioned in François's message to 8th Army of Aug. 26, 5:30 a.m. in Elze, *Tannenberg*, 299, is corroborated in Hoffmann, "Tannenberg," 273.

[42]Erich Ludendorff, *Ludendorff's Own Story*, Vol. II (New York, 1929), 60; Hoffmann, "Tannenberg," 275.

[43]Schäfer to François, Mar. 16, 1927; François to Schäfer, Mar. 18, 1927, BA-MA, Nachlass François, NL 274/18.

[44]Notz, *Scholtz*, 49; Balla, *Im Yorkschen Geist*, 31–32.

[45]8th Army to XX Corps, Aug. 26, 1:05 p.m., Elze, *Tannenberg*, 302.

[46]Schäfer, *Tannenberg*, 61 ff.; Werner Meyer, *Das Infanterie-Regiment von Grolman (1. Posensches) Nr. 18 im Weltkriege* (Oldenburg, 1929), 16–17; Reichert, *IR 59*, 47 ff.; Plickert, *IR 151*, 23 ff.

[47]Curt von Morgen, *Meiner Truppen Heldenkämpfe* (Berlin, 1920), 9; Hoffmann, "Tannenberg," 274, 276; Elze, *Tannenberg*, 129.

Notes

[48]Ironside, *Tannenberg*, 172.

[49] Report of Air Detachment 16 to 8th Army, Aug 26, 12:05 p.m. Elze, *Tannenberg*, 301; Reichsarchiv, *Weltkrieg* II, 155–156.

[50]Hoffmann, "Tannenberg," 282; Hindenburg, *Out of My Life*, 68, 70; Goerlitz, *Hindenburg*, 79 ff.

[51]Elze, *Tannenberg*, 132–133; and statement of Dec. 6, 1934, in BA-MA, Nachlass Foerster, NL 121/17.

[52]Ludendorff to Foerster, Nov. 30 and Dec. 20, 1934; Foerster to Ludendorff, Dec. 6 and Dec. 18, 1934, in *ibid.*

[53]XVII Corps to 8th Army, Aug. 25, 1:22 p.m. [arrival time]; 8th Army to XVII Corps Aug. 28, 5:15 p.m. [erroneously written 8:15] in Elze, *Tannenberg*, 294. Cf. *ibid.*, 129; and August von Mackensen, *Briefe und Aufzeichnugen*, ed. F. W. Foerster (Leipzig, 1938), 47.

[54]Reichsarchiv, *Weltkrieg* II, 169; Schäfer, *Tannenberg*, 95 ff.

[55]XVII Corps Order, Aug. 25, 11:45 p.m., Elze, *Tannenberg*, 298; Mackensen, *Briefe und Aufzeichnugen*, 47–49. The army order in question, issued at noon, took twelve hours and fifteen minutes to reach Mackensen. Elze, *Tannenberg*, 295.

[56]Below's comments on Hoffmann's "Tannenberg wie es wirklich war," in BA-MA, Nachlass Below, NL 87/21; I Reserve Corps to XVII Corps, Aug. 25, 9:50 p.m., Elze, *Tannenberg*, 297; Hoffmann, "Tannenberg," 279.

[57]Ironside, *Tannenberg*, 154–156.

[58]Cf. Mackensen, *Briefe und Aufzeichnungen*, 49; Schäfer, *Tannenberg*, 99 ff.; Alfred Seydel, *Das Grenadier-Regiment König Friedrich I (4. Ostpreussisches) Nr. 5 im Weltkrieg* (Oldenburg, 1926), 48 ff.

[59]Schäfer, *Tannenberg*, 105 ff.; Alfred Rothe, *Das Reserve-Infanterie Regiment Nr. 61 im Weltkriege* (Berlin, 1929), 20 ff.; Max Gengelbach, *Das Reserve-Feldartillerie-Regiment Nr. 36 im Weltkrieg* (Berlin, 1929), 13–14.

[60]Ironside, *Tannenberg*, 178–179; *La Grande Guerre*, 118–119.

[61]I Reserve Corps to 8th Army, Aug. 26, 8:30 p.m., Elze, *Tannenberg*, 304; François, *Marneschlacht und Tannenberg*, 246; Hoffmann, "Tannenberg," 281.

[62]Intercept made Aug. 26 at 1:00 p.m. by Signal Station Richthofen, to 8th Army 1:48 p.m., in Elze, *Tannenberg*, 302.

[63]Schäfer, *Tannenberg*, 98–99; Mackensen, *Briefe und Aufzeichnungen*, 51; Reichsarchiv, *Weltkrieg* II, 174.

8. THE PROVINCE OF CHANCE

[1]8th Army to I Corps, Aug. 26, 9:00 p.m., Walter Elze, *Tannenberg* (Breslau, 1928), 304–305.

[2]8th Army to OHL, Aug. 26, 10:50 p.m., *ibid.*, 305; Reichsarchiv, *Der Weltkrieg 1914 bis 1918*, Vol. II (Berlin, 1925), 157–158.

[3]The text of the order is given in Theobald von Schäfer, *Tannenberg* (Oldenburg, 1927), 70. The task force from XX Corps, drawn from both its active divisions, included the 1st *Jäger* Battalion, I and II/18, III/141, III/147, and III/151, with the 82nd Field Artillery's 1st Battalion providing fire support. Its commander, Maj.-Gen. von Schmettau, had been without a job since the two *Landwehr* brigades of his 35th Reserve Division had been detached to other commands. For convenience, it will be referred to as Schmettau's Force.

[4]Hermann von François, *Marneschlacht und Tannenberg* (Berlin, 1920), 211; Reichsarchiv, *Weltkrieg* II, 159.

[5]Edmund Ironside, *Tannenberg* (Edinburgh, 1925), 164–165.

[6]Schäfer, *Tannenberg*, 79 ff.; Reichsarchiv, *Weltkrieg* II, 159 ff.; Alfred

Notes

Dieterich, *Geschichte des Grenadierregiments König Friedrich der Grosse (3. Ostpreussischen) Nr. 4* (Berlin, 1928), 656; Traugott Hoffmann and Ernst Hahn, *Geschichte des Infanterie-Regiments Graf Dönhoff (7. Ostpreussischen) Nr. 44, 1860–1918* (Berlin, 1930), 112; Kurt Hennig, *Das Infanterie-Regiment (8. Ostpreussisches) Nr. 45 im Weltkriege 1914–1918* (Oldenburg, 1928), 25; and Dr. Zinzow, *Königlich Preussisches Landwehr-Infanterie-Regiment Nr. 9* (Berlin, 1930), 17–18.

[7]Jeffrey Greenhut, "The Imperial Reserve: The Indian Infantry on the Western Front, 1914–15" (Ph.D. Dissertation, Kansas State University, 1978); and Dennis E. Showalter, "Tactics and Recruitment in Eighteenth Century Prussia," *Studies in History and Politics/Études d'Histoire et de Politique* III (1983/84), 26–32.

[8]Franz von Gottberg, *Das Grenadier-Regiment Kronprinz (1.Ostpreussisches) Nr. 1 im Weltkriege*, Vol. I (Berlin, 1927), 43–44; Alfred Bülowius and Bruno Hippler, *Das Infanterie-Regiment v. Boyen (5. Ostpreussisches) Nr. 41 im Weltkriege 1914–1918* (Berlin, 1929), 19–20; François, *Marneschlacht und Tannenberg*, 211–212; Heinrich Siebert, *Geschichte des Infanterie-Regiments Generalfeldmarschall von Hindenburg (1. Masurisches) Nr. 147* (Berlin, 1927), 43–44.

[9]I Corps to 8th Army, Aug. 26, 11:20 a.m.; and 8th Army to I Corps, Aug. 26, 11:30 a.m., Elze, *Tannenberg*, 306–307.

[10]François, *Marneschlacht und Tannenberg*, 213.

[11]Ironside, *Tannenberg*, 168–169.

[12]Reichsarchiv, *Weltkrieg* II, 163 ff.; Schäfer, *Tannenberg*, 84 ff.; Wilhelm Reichert, *Das Infanterie-Regiment Frh. Hiller von Gaertringen (4. Posensches) Nr. 59 im Weltkriege 1914/18*, Vol. I (Berlin, 1930), 52.

[13]Ironside, *Tannenberg*, 176.

[14]Reichsarchiv, *Weltkrieg* II, 165.

[15]Erich Ludendorff, *Ludendorff's Own Story*, Vol. I (New York, 1929), 62; Walter Goerlitz, *Hindenburg. Ein Lebensbild* (Bonn, 1953), 70; 8th Army to I Corps, Aug. 26, 1:30 a.m., Elze, *Tannenberg*, 306.

[16]Schäfer, *Tannenberg*, 88 ff.; Reichsarchiv, *Weltkrieg* II, 166 ff.; Ernst Zipfel, *Geschichte des Dragoner-Regiments König Albert von Sachsen (Ostpr.) Nr. 10* (Zeulenroda, 1933), 41.

[17]Schäfer, *Tannenberg*, 90–91.

[18]Golovine, *1914*, 218–220.

[19]Oberbürgermeister Zülch, "Aus meiner Kriegsmappe," in *Tannenberg*, 10th anniversary special issue of the *Allensteiner Zeitung*, copy in Bundesarchiv-Militärarchiv, Nachlass Bülow, NL 87/45.

[20]W. von Stephani, *Mit Hindenburg bei Tannenberg* (Berlin, 1919), 23 ff.

[21]Schäfer, *Tannenberg*, 92–93; Heinrich Plickert, *Das 2. Ermländische Infanterie-Regiment Nr. 151 im Weltkriege* (Oldenburg, 1929), 50–51.

[22]8th Army to XVII Corps and I Reserve Corps, Aug. 17, 7:30 a.m., Elze, *Tannenberg*, 306.

[23]I Reserve Corps to 8th Army, Aug. 27, 12:45 p.m., *ibid.*; Schäfer, *Tannenberg*, 112 ff.

[24]8th Army to I Reserve Corps, Aug. 27, 12:15 p.m., Elze, *Tannenberg*, 307. The time given is almost certainly an error, since the order's contents directly reply to Below's questions. The document was written in pencil on a plain sheet of paper, suggesting a degree of haste that explains the mistake.

[25]Hoffmann, "Tannenberg," 295 ff.; army order for Aug. 28, dated Aug. 27, "evening," Elze, *Tannenberg*, 312.

Notes

[26]Max Hoffmann, *War of Lost Opportunities*, in *War Diaries and Other Papers*, tr. E. Sutton, Vol. II (London, 1929), 37–38.

[27]François, *Marneschlacht und Tannenberg*, 213–214; Schäfer, *Tannenberg*, 73, 80 fn. 2. The 4th Grenadiers' regimental history is predictably silent on the subject.

[28]Alfred Seydel, *Das Grenadier-Regiment König Friedrich I. (4. Ostpreussisches) Nr. 5 im Weltkriege* (Oldenburg, 1926), 51; Ernst Zipfel, *Geschichte des Königlich Preussischen Husaren-Regiments Fürst Blücher von Wahlstatt (Pommersches) Nr. 5* (Zeulenroda, 1930), 37; Schäfer, *Tannenberg*, 112 ff.; Reichsarchiv, *Weltkrieg II*, 175–176.

[29]Schäfer, *Tannenberg*, 113–114; Wilhelm Preusser, *Das 9. Westpreussische Infanterie-Regiment Nr. 176 im Weltkrieg* (Berlin, 1931), 26–27.

[30]Record of telephone conversation between I Reserve Corps and 8th Army, Aug. 27, 9:00 p.m.; 8th Army order to I Reserve Corps, received by telephone Aug. 27, 9:30 p.m.; 8th Army to I Reserve Corps, Aug. 27, 10:00 p.m., Elze, *Tannenberg*, 308–309.

[31]The war diaries of 8th Army and XVII Corps, lost during World War II, are excerpted on this issue in Elze, *Tannenberg*, 310. Cf. Mackensen, *Briefe und Aufzeichnungen*, 53.

[32]Army order for Aug. 28, Aug. 27, 10:00 p.m., Elze, *Tannenberg*, 312.

[33]Golovine, *1914*, 285 ff.

[34]Elze, *Tannenberg*, 136.

[35]Mackensen, *Briefe und Aufzeichnungen*, 63; and his report to Kaiser William of Aug. 28 in Elze, *Tannenberg*, 311.

[36]Samsonov's order is in *Sbornik dokumentov mirovoy voyni na russkom fronte. Manovrenni period 1914 goda: Vostochno-Prusskaya operasiya*, ed. Generalny Shtab RKKA (Moscow, 1939), 296. Cf. Golovine, *1914*, 223 ff., 252; Ironside, *Tannenberg*, 178 ff.

[37]Hoffmann, "Tannenberg," 285.

[38]Ironside, *Tannenberg*, 175 ff.; Schäfer, *Tannenberg*, 115.

[39]Golovine, *1914*, p. 255 *passim*; Ironside, *Tannenberg*, 179 *passim*; Knox, 73–74.

[40]XX Corps to 8th Army, Aug. 28, 5:50 a.m., Elze, *Tannenberg*, 315; Reichsarchiv, *Weltkrieg* II, 184–185; Ludendorff, *Ludendorff's Own Story*, 64.

[41]Hoffmann, *Tannenberg*, 298–299; Schäfer, *Tannenberg*, 124 ff.; Reichert and Claer, *IR 59*, 54 ff.

[42]Cf. Keller, "Vergleich der Schiessverfahren der deutschen, fränzosischen, und russischen Feldartillerie," *Vierteljahrshefte für Truppenführung und Heereskunde* I (1904), 73–79; and Richter, "Die Schiessvorschrift für die Feldartillerie vom 15. Mai 1907," *Jahrbücher für die deutsche Armee und Marine* 133 (1907), 111–119.

[43]3rd Reserve Division to XX Corps, Aug. 28, 8:10 a.m.; XX Corps to 8th Army, reporting telephone message of Aug. 28, 8:00 a.m., Elze, *Tannenberg*, 316.

[44]Curt von Morgen, *Meiner Truppen Heldenkämpfe* (Berlin, 1920), pp. 11–12; Schäfer, *Tannenberg*, 135 ff.; Reichsarchiv, *Weltkrieg* II, 188; Arthur Maas, *Das Reserve-Infanterie-Regiment Nr. 9 im Weltkrieg* (Zeulenroda, 1933), 9.

[45]Moritz Holzmann, *Hanseatische Landwehr im Felde (Geschichte des L-I-R 75)* Vol. I (Oldenburg, 1928), 9 ff.; Wilhelm Suhrmann, *Geschichte des Landwehr-Infanterie-Regiments Nr. 31 im Weltkriege* (Oldenburg, 1928), 23 ff.; Landwehr Division to 8th Army, Aug. 28, 3:30 a.m., in Elze, *Tannenberg* 135; Schäfer, *Tannenberg*, 142 ff.

[46]Schäfer, *Tannenberg*, 144; Golovine, *1914*, 221–222.

Notes

[47]Schäfer, *Tannenberg*, 144–145, 161 ff.; Morgen, *Meiner Truppen Helden-kämpfe*, 12.

[48]Governor of Thorn to 8th Army, Aug. 28, 8:15 a.m., Elze, *Tannenberg*, 316; Hoffmann, "Tannenberg," 303–304; Reichsarchiv, *Weltkrieg* II, 190–191.

[49]41st Division to XX Corps, Aug. 28, 8:00 a.m. Elze, *Tannenberg*, 317; Ludendorff, *Ludendorff's Own Story*, 65; Görlitz, *Hindenburg*, 72–73.

[50]François, *Marneschlacht und Tannenberg*, 213 ff.; Fortress Graudenz to 8th Army, received Aug. 28, 1:30 a.m., Elze, *Tannenberg*, 314; I Corps to 8th Army, received Aug. 28, 7:45 a.m., *ibid.*,315–316; Schäfer, *Tannenberg*, 148 ff.

[51]I Corps to 8th Army and reply, Aug. 28, 8:00 a.m.; 8th Army to I Corps, Aug. 28, 9:40 a.m.; report of I Corps, Aug. 28, 10:10 a.m., Elze, *Tannenberg*, 316 ff.

[52]41st Division to XX Corps, Aug. 28, 10:15 a.m., telephone message from 41st Division to XX Corps, Aug. 18, 11:15 a.m., *ibid.*, 317.

[53]I Corps to 8th Army, Aug. 28, 11:45 a.m.; 8th Army to I Corps, Aug. 28, 11:45 a.m.; telephone message, 8th Army to I Corps, Aug. 28, 12:15 p.m., Elze, *Tannenberg*, 319.

[54]François to Schäfer, Mar. 18, 1927, BA-MA, Nachlass François, N 274/18; François, *Marneschlacht und Tannenberg*, 218–219.

[55]Eliot A. Cohen and John Gooch, *Military Misfortunes: Anatomy of Failure in War* (New York, 1989).

[56]8th Army to I Corps, Aug. 28, 1:30 p.m., Elze, *Tannenberg*, 319; Reichsarchiv, *Weltkrieg* II, 193–194.

[57]I Corps to 8th Army, arrived Aug. 28, 4:00 p.m., Elze, *Tannenberg*, 320; François, *Marneschlacht und Tannenberg*, 219–220; Balla, *Im Yorkschen Geist*, 34–35.

[58]Andreas Kuhn, *Das Tannenberg-Nationaldenkmal* (Allenstein, 1922), 57 ff.; Balla, *Im Yorkschen Geist*, 35; François, *Marneschlacht und Tannenberg*, 223.

[59]Golovine, *1914*, 267; Hoffmann and Hahn, *IR 44*, 112–113; Dieterich, *Grenadier-Regiment Nr. 4*, 656–657.

[60]Schäfer, *Tannenberg*, 159 ff.; Reichsarchiv, *Weltkrieg* II, 195–196; Morgen, *Meiner Truppen Heldenkämpfe*, 12; Hans Martens, "Geschichte des Schweren Reserve-Reiter-Regiments Nr. 3," Appendix to Ernst Zipfel, *Geschichte des Küras-sier-Regiments . . . Nr. 5* (Berlin, 1930), 372 passim.

[61]Schäfer, *Tannenberg*, 164 ff.; *Geschichte des 1. Ermländischen Infanterie-Regiments Nr. 150*, ed. Regimental Officers' Association (Zeulenroda, 1932), 27 ff.

9. THE PROVINCE OF VICTORY

[1]XVII Corps to 8th Army, Aug. 28, 1:20 a.m., Walter Elze, *Tannenberg* (Leipzig, 1925), 312–313; Reichsarchiv, *Weltkrieg 1914 bis 1918*, Vol. II (Berlin, 1925), 198–199.

[2]I Reserve Corps to 8th Army, Aug. 18, 1:30 a.m., and 8th Army to I Reserve Corps, Aug. 28, 9:45 a.m., Elze, *Tannenberg*, 317, 318; Bundesarchiv-Militärarchiv, Nachlass Below, NL 87/21; Theobald von Schäfer, *Tannenberg* (Old-enberg, 1927), 170 ff.; Max Meyhöfer, *Das Reserve-Feldartillerie-Regiment Nr. 1 im Weltkriege* (Oldenburg, 1926), 23–24.

[3]Max Hoffmann, "The Truth About Tannenberg," in *War Diaries and Other Papers*, tr. E. Sutton, Vol. I (London, 1929), 309; Reichsarchiv, *Weltkrieg* II, 199.

[4]*Ibid.*, 199 ff.; Schäfer, *Tannenberg*, 172; 8th Army to I Reserve Corps, Aug. 18, 2:45 p.m., Elze, *Tannenberg*, 245.

Notes

[5]Hoffmann, "Tannenberg," 310; August von Mackensen, *Briefe und Aufzeichnungen*, ed. F. W. Foerster (Leipzig, 1938), 55; Reichsarchiv, *Weltkrieg* II, 201.

[6]8th Army to I Reserve Corps, Aug. 28, 4:30 p.m., BA-MA, *Nachlass Below*, N 87/21.

[7]For the fight of Below's corps cf. *Reserve-Infanterie Regiment Nr. 3*, ed. by Regimental Officers' Association (Oldenburg, 1926), 25 ff.; Alfred Rothe, *Das Reserve-Infanterie-Regiment Nr. 61 im Weltkriege* (Berlin, 1929), 26 ff.; Max Gengelbach, *Das Reserve-Feldartillerie-Regiment Nr. 36 im Weltkrieg*, Vol. I (Berlin, 1925), 15–16; Meyhöfer, *RFAR Nr. 1*, 24; and Schäfer, *Tannenberg*, 172 ff.

[8]Mackensen, *Briefe und Aufzeichnugen*, 55; Schäfer, *Tannenberg*, 172.

[9]Alfred Seydel, *Das Grenadier-Regiment König Friedrich I. (4. Ostpreussisches) Nr. 5 im Weltkriege* (Oldenburg, 1926), 52.

[10]Edmund Schulenmann, *Das Kulmer Infanterie-Regiment Nr. 141 im Weltkriege* (Oldenburg, 1926), 25–26; Schäfer, *Tannenberg*, 198–199.

[11]Fortress Königsberg to 8th Army, Aug. 28, 4:10 p.m., Elze, *Tannenberg*, 320; Walther Hubatsch, *Hindenburg und der Staat. Aus den Papieren des Generalfeldmarschalls und Reichspräsidenten von 1878 bis 1934* (Göttingen, 1966), 14; Walter Görlitz, *Hindenburg, Ein Lebensbild* (Bonn, 1953), pp. 72–73; Hoffmann, "Tannenberg," 313–314; Reichsarchiv, *Weltkrieg* II, 204 ff.

[12]8th Army order, Aug. 28, 5:30 p.m.; Elze, *Tannenberg*, 321; Hoffmann, "Tannenberg," 211–212.

[13]Sven Ekdahl, *Die Schlacht bei Tannenberg 1410. Quellenkritische Untersuchungen*, Vol. I (Berlin, 1982), 12 ff.

[14]W. Von Stephani, *Mit Hindenburg bei Tannenberg* (Berlin, 1919), pp. 30–31; Schäfer, *Tannenberg*, 178–179.

[15]Cf. BA-MA, Nachlass Tappen, NL 56/1, Kriegstagebuch entries Aug. 20, 21, 24, 25; Adolf Tappen, *Bis zur Marne 1914* (Oldenburg, 1920), 16–178; Karl Ritter von Wenniger's reports of Aug. 23 and 24, excerpted in Bernd F. Schulte, "Neue Dokumente zu Kriegsausbruch und Kriegsverlauf," *Militärgeschichtliche Mitteilungen* XV (1979), 156–157; and Reichsarchiv to Tappen, Mar. 20, 1922, Nachlass Tappen, NL 56/2.

[16]Wilhelm Groener, *Lebenserinnerungen*, ed. F. Frh. Hiller von Gaertringen (Göttingen, 1957), 163; E. Kabisch, *Streitfragen des Weltkrieges 1914–1918* (Stuttgard, 1924), 116; Wenniger's diary entries of Aug. 20 and 21 in Schulte, "Dokumente," 151, 155, also reflect the enduring tension between the Prussian and Bavarian contingents.

[17]BA-MA, Nachlass Tappen, NL 56/1, Kriegstagebuch, Aug. 25; Max von Gallwitz, *Meine Führertätigkeit im Weltkriege* (Berlin, 1921), 21; Karl von Bülow, *Mein Bericht zur Marneschlacht* (Berlin, 1919), 30. Jehuda Wallach, *The Dogma of the Battle of Annihilation* (Westport, Conn., 1985), 102 ff.; is the best general analysis of the transfer.

[18]Reichsarchiv to Tappen, Mar. 20, 1922, BA-MA, Nachlass Tappen, NL 56/2.

[19]Hoffmann, "Tannenberg," 315 ff.; and *War of Lost Opportunities*, 42; Reichsarchiv, *Weltkrieg* II, 207.

[20]Intelligence Section to Operations Section of OHL, Aug. 28, 1914; telephoned to 8th Army Aug. 29, Elze, *Tannenberg*, 322–323.

[21]8th Army's response to telephoned inquiry from OHL, Aug. 28, 9:30 p.m., Elze, *Tannenberg*, 321. This was probably the same conversation in which Ludendorff denied any immediate need for reinforcements.

²²Hoffmann, "Tannenberg," 316–317; 8th Army to Mackensen, Aug. 28, 10:00 p.m., Elze, *Tannenberg*, 322.

²³8th Army to 1st Cavalry Division, Aug. 28, midnight, Elze, *Tannenberg*, 322.

²⁴8th Army to OHL, Aug. 29, 12:20 a.m., Elze, *Tannenberg*, 323.

²⁵I Reserve Corps to 8th Army, Aug. 29, 6:30 a.m., and army orders issued at the same time to Major Drechsel; and 8th Army to Königsberg, Aug. 29, 8:30 a.m. Elze, *Tannenberg*, 324–325; Hoffmann, "Tannenberg," 318–319; Reichsarchiv, *Weltkrieg* II, 207–208; Erich Ludendorff, *Ludendorff's Own Story*, Vol. I (New York, 1929), 66.

²⁶8*La Grande Guerre. Concentration des armées. Premières operations en Prusse Orientale, en Galicie et en Pologne*, tr. E. Chapouilly (Paris, 1926), 106 ff.; N. N. Golovine, *The Russian Campaign of 1914*, tr. A. G. S. Muntz (Ft. Leavenworth, Kans., 1933), 259 ff.

²⁷Schäfer, *Tannenberg*, 181–182.

²⁸*Ibid.*, 182 ff.; Gengelbach, *RFAR 36*, 16 ff.; *RFAR 1*, 25–26.

²⁹Schäfer, *Tannenberg*, 184 ff.; *Geschichte des 1. Ermländischen Infanterie-Regiments Nr. 150*, ed. Officers' Association (Zeulenroda, 1929), 28–29. Wilhelm Suhrmann, *Geschichte des Landwehr-Infanterie-Regiments Nr. 31 im Weltkriege* (Oldenburg, 1928), 33.

³⁰Report of Zeppelin Z4, Aug. 29, 8:40 a.m.; Königsberg to army headquarters, Aug. 29, 9:00 a.m., Elze, *Tannenberg*, 326.

³¹Hoover Institution Archives, Adam Pavlovich Bennigsen, Papers, 1914–1919, diary entry Aug. 14 [27], 1914.

³²Cf. Jean Savant, *Épopeé russe* (Paris, 1945), 269 ff.; Edmund Ironside, *Tannenberg* (Edinburgh, 1925), 201 ff.; *La Grande Guerre*, 93 ff. The relevant army orders and correspondence are available in *Sbornik dokumentov mirovoy voyny na russkom fronte. Manevrenni period 1914 Goda: Vostochno-Prusskaya operasiya*, ed. Generalny Shtab RKKA (Moscow, 1939), 210 ff.

³³8th Army to OHL, Aug. 28, 12:20 p.m., Elze, *Tannenberg*, , 323.

³⁴Ludendorff, *Ludendorff's Own Story*, 69; Reichsarchiv, *Weltkrieg* II, 218; Goltz to 8th Army, Aug. 29, 2:40 p.m., Elze, *Tannenberg*, 327.

³⁵Schäfer, *Tannenberg*, 189 ff.; Reichsarchiv, *Weltkrieg* II, 213–214; Wilhelm Reichert, *Das Infanterie-Regiment Frh. Hiller von Gaertringen (4. Posensches) Nr. 59 im Weltkriege 1914/18*, Vol. I (Berlin, 1930), 68; Ernst Zipfel, *Geschichte des Dragoner-Regiments König Albert von Sachsen (Ostpr.) Nr. 10* (Zeulenroda, 1933), 42–43.

³⁶*RFAR 1*, 26.

³⁷Schäfer, *Tannenberg*, 192 ff.; Alfred Dieterich, *Geschichte des Grenadierregiments König Friedrich der Grosse (3. Ostpreussischen) Nr. 4* (Berlin, 1928), 657; Fritz Schillmann, *Grenadier-Regiment König Friedrich Wilhelm I (2. Ostpreussisches) Nr. 3* (Oldenburg, 1924), 27–28.

³⁸Schäfer, *Tannenberg*, 196–197; Gerhard Lapp, *Das 1. Ostpr. Feldartillerie-Regiment Nr. 16* (Oldenburg, 1928), 20 ff.

³⁹Schäfer, *Tannenberg*, 194–195; Reichsarchiv, *Weltkrieg* II, 214–215; Heinrich Plickert, *Das 2. Ermländische Infanterie-Regiment Nr. 151 im Weltkriege* (Oldenburg, 1929), 57.

⁴⁰Mackensen, *Briefe und Aufzeichnungen*, 57; Reichsarchiv, *Weltkrieg* II, 215–216; Schäfer, *Tannenberg*, 115 ff.; Joseph Steuer, *Das Infanterie-Regiment Generalfeldmarschall von Mackensen (3. Westpreussisches) Nr. 129 im Weltkriege* (Oldenburg,

Notes

1925), 34–35; Ernst Zipfel, *Geschichte des Königlich Preussischen Husaren-Regiments Fürst Blücher von Wahlstatt (Pommersches) Nr. 5* (Zeulenroda, 1930), 30 ff.

[41]Army order Aug. 29, 10:00 p.m., Elze, *Tannenberg*, 328–329; Reichsarchiv, *Weltkrieg* II, 218–219.

[42]Hindenburg to William, Aug. 29, 7:45 p.m.; William to 8th Army, Aug. 29, in Elze, *Tannenberg*, 330; Hindenburg to Frau Hindenburg, Aug. 30, 1914, in Hubatsch, *Hindenburg*, 152.

[43]*Der Kriegsverlauf. Zwölf Monate im amtlichen Nachrichten, Noten, und Urkunden, August 1914-Juli 1915* (Berlin, 1915), 30; Görlitz, *Hindenburg*, 75.

[44]Ludendorff to OHL, Aug.29, 11:30 p.m., Elze, *Tannenberg*, 330.

[45]Captain Fleischmann to Austro-Hungarian high command, Aug. 29, 11:40 p.m., *ibid.*, 331.

[46]Golovine, *1914*, 290 ff.; Ironside, *Tannenberg*, 183 ff.

[47]Zipfel, *Husaren-Regiment Nr. 5*, 32–33.

[48]Schäfer, *Tannenberg*, 225.

[49]Knox, *With the Russian Army*, 82; Golovine, *1914*, 300–301.

[50]Königsberg to 8th Army, Aug. 30, 2:40 a.m., Elze, *Tannenberg*, 333.

[51]8th Army to corps commanders, Aug. 29; 8th Army general order, Aug. 29, 1914, *ibid.*, 332–333.

[52]Ironside, *Tannenberg*, 189; Reichsarchiv, *Weltkrieg* II, 222–223.

[53]Golovine, *1914*, 312 ff.; François, *Marneschlacht und Tannenberg*, 225 ff.

[54]François, *Marneschlacht und Tannenberg*, 228; John R. Cuneo, *Winged Mars*, Vol. II, *The Air Weapon 1914–1916* (Harrisburg, Penn., 1947). The text of the Hesse/Körner report in Elze, *Tannenberg*, 336, has incorrect times of delivery, and is apparently a copy of the version telephoned to 8th Army.

[55]François, *Marneschlacht und Tannenberg*, 229–230; Reichsarchiv, *Weltkrieg* II, 223–224.

[56]Ludendorff to OHL, Aug. 30, 9:00 a.m., Elze, *Tannenberg*, 335.

[57]Reconnaissance report, Aug. 30, 10:30 a.m., *ibid.*, 336–337.

[58]8th Army to I Corps, Aug. 30, 11:55 a.m., *ibid.*, 337; Reichsarchiv, *Weltkrieg* II, 221 ff.

[59]François, *Marneschlacht und Tannenberg*, 231; Schäfer, *Tannenberg*, 270–271.

[60]*Ibid.*, 220 ff.; Franz von Gottberg, *Das Grenadier-Regiment Kronprinz (1. Ostpreussisches) Nr. 1 im Weltkriege*, Vol. I (Berlin, 1927), 48 ff.; Dieterich, *Grenadierregiment Nr. 4*, 657–658; Hoffmann, "Tannenberg," 328.

[61]Hindenburg to Frau Hindenburg, Aug. 31, 1914, Hubatsch, *Hindenburg*, 152.

[62]8th Army to I Corps, Aug. 30, 12:35 p.m., Elze, *Tannenberg*, 337.

[63]Reichsarchiv, *Weltkrieg* II, 221 ff.

[64]Army order, Aug. 30, 7:30 p.m., Elze, *Tannenberg*, 339.

[65]Alfred Bülowius and Bruno Hippler, *Das Infanterie-Regiment v. Boyen (5. Ostpreussisches) Nr. 41 im Weltkriege 1914–1918* (Berlin, 1929), 22 ff.; *Grenadier-Regiment Nr. 1*, 50–51; Fritz Rohde, *2. Ostpreussisches Feldartillerie-Regiment Nr. 52* (Oldenburg, 1928), 18 ff.

[66]François, *Marneschlacht und Tannenberg*, 232; Curt von Morgen, *Meiner Truppen Heldenkämpfe* (Berlin, 1920), 13–14.

[67]Golovine, *1914*, 306 ff.

[68]Schäfer, *Tannenberg*, 213 ff.; Wilhelm Preusser, *Das 9. Westpreussische Infanterie-Regiment Nr. 176 im Weltkrieg* (Berlin, 1931), 28 ff.

Notes

[69]8th Army to XVII Corps, Aug. 30, 11:20 a.m., Elze, *Tannenberg*, 337; Reichsarchiv, *Weltkrieg* II, 226.

[70]Schäfer, *Tannenberg*, 215 ff.; Preusser, *IR 176*, 30 ff.

[71]François, *Marneschlacht und Tannenberg*, 234 ff.; Reichsarchiv, *Weltkrieg* II, 225–226; Hoffmann, "Tannenberg," 326–327; Ironside, *Tannenberg*, 191–192.

[72]For details of the roundup, cf. Schäfer, *Tannenberg*, 221 ff; and François, *Marneschlacht und Tannenberg*, 240.

[73]Reichsarchiv, *Weltkrieg* II, 228–230.

[74]Manuscript diary entry of Sept. 4 by Admiral Georg von Müller, chief of the naval cabinet, cited in Isabel V. Hull, *The Entourage of Kaiser Wilhelm II 1888–1918* (Cambridge, 1982), 267.

[75]Ludendorff to OHL, Aug. 30, 8:40 p.m., Aug. 31, 3:00 p.m., Elze, *Tannenberg*, 340, 341, 342; Bronsart to 8th Army, Aug. 31, 3:30 p.m., *ibid.*, 342; Hindenburg to William, Aug. 31, 7:15 p.m., *ibid.*, 343.

10. OPPORTUNITIES AND ILLUSIONS

[1]Germany, Reichsarchiv, *Der Weltkrieg 1914 bis 1918*, Vol. II (Berlin, 1925), 230; N. N. Golovine, *The Russian Campaign of 1914* (Leavenworth, Kans., 1933), 324.

[2]N. N. Golovine, *The Russian Army in the World War* (New Haven Conn., 1931), 214 ff.

[3]David French, *British Strategy and War Aims, 1914–1916* (London, 1986); Keuh Nielsen, *Strategy and Supply: The Anglo-Russian Alliance, 1914–1917* (London, 1984).

[4]Diary entry of Aug. 28 and 29, 1914 and report of Aug. 31, 1914 in Bernd F. Schulte, "Neue Dokumente zu Kriegsausbuch und Kriegsverlauf 1914," *Militärgeschichtliche Mitteilungen* XXV (1979), 158, 162.

[5]Bundesarchiv-Militärarchiv, Nachlass Hoffmann, NL37, letter of Aug. 30, 1914.

[6]Reichsarchiv, *Weltkrieg* II, 268 ff; Savant, *L'Épopée Russe. Campagne de l'Armee Rennenkampf en Prusse-Orientale* (Paris, 1945), 313 ff.

[7]Erich Ludendorff, *Ludendorff's Own Story*, 2 vols. (New York, 1929), I, 82 ff.

[8]Norman Stone, *The Eastern Front, 1914–1917* (New York, 1975), pp. 70 ff., is the best account in English. Cf. as well M. von Pitreich, *Lemberg* (Vienna, 1924); and *1914. Die Militärgeschichtliche Probleme unseres Kriegsbeginnes* (Vienna, 1934); and for the general consequences Gunther Rothenberg, *The Army of Francis Joseph* (Lafayette, Ind., 1976), 180–181.

[9]Winston Churchill, *The Unknown War* (London, 1931), 231.

[10]Ludendorff, *Ludendorff's Own Story* I, 90 ff.; Germany, Reichsarchiv, *Der Weltkrieg 1914 bis 1918*, Vol. V (Berlin, 1929), 402 ff.; Vol VI (Berlin, 1929), 98 passim.

[11]C. E. Heller and W. A. Stofft, eds., *America's First Battles, 1776–1965* (Lawrence, Kans., 1986), offers a comprehensive overview of this subject.

[12]Cf. *inter alia* Wolfram Wette, *Kriegstheorien deutschen Sozialisten* (Stuttgart, 1971); and Gerd Krumeich, *Armaments and Politics in France on the Eve of the First World War*, tr. S. Conn (Dover, N.H., 1984).

[13]Eric Leed, *No Man's Land* (New York, 1979).

[14]As in John Buchan, *Nelson's History of the War*, Vol. II (London, n.d.), 108–122.

Notes

[15]This story is incorporated even in critical accounts such as Karl Tschuppik, *Ludendorff: The Tragedy of a Specialist* (London, 1932).

[16]Ludendorff, *Ludendorff's Own Story* I, 56.

[17]Walter Görlitz, *Hindenburg: Ein Lebensbild* (Bern, 1953), 77.

[18]Cf. Reitzenstein, "Generaloberst von Prittwitz nach der Schlacht bei Gumbinnen," *Militär-Wochenblatt*, 1921, 43; and Schäfer, "Wollte Generaloberst von Prittwitz im August 1914 hinter die Weichsel zurückgehen?" *ibid.*, 1921, 45.

[19]Churchill, *Unknown War*, 213–214.

[20]BA-MA, Nachlass Hoffmann, NL37, letters of Sept. 4 and 9, 1914; Görlitz, *Hindenburg*, 69–69; Emil Ludwig, *Hindenburg* (Philadelphia, 1935), 98; H. A. de Weerd, *Great Soldiers of Two World Wars* (New York, 1941), 79–80.

[21]Cf. Martin Kitchen, "Militarism and the Development of Fascist Ideology: The Political Ideas of Colonel Max Bauer, 1916–1918," *Central European History* VIII (1975), 199–220; *The Silent Dictatorship. The Politics of the German High Command under Hindenburg and Ludendorff, 1916–1918* (New York, 1976); and Richard Piazza, "Ludendorff: The Totalitarian and Völkisch Politics of a Military Specialist" (Ph.D. Dissertation, Northwestern University, 1969).

[22]Görlitz, *Hindenburg*, 78.

[23]K. Koszyk, *Deutsche Pressepolitik im Ersten Weltkrieg* (Düsseldorf, 1968).

[24]Philip Knightely, *The First Casualty. From the Crimea to Vietnam: The War Correspondent as Hero, Propagandist, and Mythmaker* (New York, 1975).

[25]Cf. Elisabeth Fehrenbach, *Wandlungen des deutschen Kaisergedankens* (Munich, Vienna, 1969); and Isabel Hull, *The Entourage of Kaiser Wilhelm II, 1888–1918* (Cambridge, 1982).

[26]Wilhelm Deist, "Kaiser Wilhelm II in the Context of his Military Entourage," in *Kaiser Wilhelm II: New Interpretations*, ed. J. C. G. Röhl and N. Sombart (Cambridge, 1982), 169–192.

[27]Egmont Zechlin, "Friedensbestrebungen und Revolutionierungsversuche im Ersten Weltkrieg," *Das Parlament*, B, May 15, 1963, 36–40.

[28]Georg Alexander von Müller, *The Kaiser and His Court*, ed. W. Görlitz, tr. M. Savill (London, 1961), 22–23.

[29]Pierre Paul Rocolle, *L'Hécatombe des generaux* (Paris, 1980).

[30]Jürgen Brinkeman, *Die Ritter des Ordens 'Pour le Mérite 1914–1918'* (Hanover, 1982).

[31]Cf. Robert Wohl, *The Generation of 1914* (Cambridge, Mass., 1979); and Walter Laqueur, *Young Germany: A History of the Youth Movement* (New York, 1962).

[32]Wenninger's diary entries, Sept. 14 and 15, 1914; and his reports of Sept. 9, 1914 in Schulte, "Neue Dokumente," 173 ff.

[33]Cf. *inter alia* Andreas Hillgruber, "Politik und Strategie Hitlers im Mittelmeerraum," in *Deutsche Grossmacht-und Weltpolitik im 19. und 20. Jahrhundert* (Düsseldorf, 1977), 276–295; and Gerhard Schreiber, "Der Mittelmeerraum in Hitlers Strategie 1940. 'Programm' und militärische Planung," *Militärgeschichtliche Mitteilungen* XXVIII (1980), 69–99.

[34]Wild von Hohenborn to his wife, Dec. 23, 1914, in *Adolf Wild von Hohenborn: Briefe und Tagebuchaufzeichnungen . . .*, ed. H. Reichold, G. Granier (Boppard, 1986), 46.

[35]Wilhelm Groener, *Lebenserinnerungen*, ed. F. Frh. v. Gärtringen (Göttingen, 1957), 526.

[36]Falkenhayn's memoirs, *The German General Staff and Its Decisions, 1914–1916* (New York, 1970) are best supplemented by Heinz Krafft, *Staatsraison und*

Notes

Kriegführung im kaiserlichen Deutschland 1914–1916 (Göttingen, 1980). L. L. Farrar, *Divide and Conquer: German Efforts to Conclude a Separate Peace, 1914–1918* (New York, 1978), is an unsympathetic survey of the subject.

[37]Karl-Heinz Janssen, *Der Kanzler und der General* (Göttingen, 1967), 49 ff.; Konrad Jarausch, *The Enigmatic Chancellor: Bethmann-Hollweg and the Hubris of Imperial Germany* (New Haven, Conn., 1973), 266 ff. Gerhard Ritter, *The Sword and the Scepter*, Vol. III, *The Tragedy of Statesmanship. Bethmann-Hollweg as War Chancellor (1914–1917)*, tr. H. Norden (Coral Gables, Fla., 1972), 47 ff.

[38]Ludendorff, *Ludendorff's Own Story* I, 95–96.

[39]Karl Unruh, *Langemarck. Legende und Wirklichkeit* (Koblenz, 1986).

[40]Ludendorff, *Ludendorff's Own Story* I, 134; Adolf von Schell, *Battle Leadership*, reprint ed. (Quantico, 1982), 40 ff.

[41]Wild von Hohenborn to his wife, Jan. 3 and Jan. 4, 1915, in *Wild von Hohenborn*, 48 ff; Ekkehard P. Guth, "Der Gegensatz zwischen dem Oberbefehlshaber Ost und dem Chef des Generalstabes des Feldheeres 1914/15. Die Rolle des Majors v. Haeften im Spannungsfeld zwischen Hindenburg, Ludendorff und Falkenhayn," *Militärgeschichtliche Mitteilungen* XXXV (1984), 75–111; Ritter, *Sword and Scepter* III, 48 ff.

[42]Guth, "Gegensatz," 82 ff; Janssen, *Kanzler*, 71 ff.; Kraft, *Staatsraison und Kriegführung*, 55 ff.; Ludendorff, *Ludendorff's Own Story* I, 134 passim; Falkenhayn, *German General Staff*, 61 ff.

[43]Stone, *Eastern Front*, 112 ff.; Falkenhayn, *German General Staff*, 67; Ludendorff, *Ludendorff's Own Story* I, 135 ff.

[44]Wild von Hohenborn to his wife, Apr. 3, 1915, in *Wild von Hohenborn*, 56. Cf.; Alberto Monticone, *Deutschland und die Neutralität Italiens 1914–1915* (Wiesbaden, 1982); and Gary W. Shanafelt, *The Secret Enemy: Austria-Hungary and the German Alliance, 1914–1918* (Boulder, Colo., 1985), 46 ff.

[45]Adolf Tappen to Reichsarchiv, Nov. 11, 1927, BA-MA, Nachlass Tappen, N56/4; Wild von Hohenborn to his wife, June 7, 1915, in *Wild von Hohenborn*, 64 ff; Kraft, *Staatsraison und Kriegführung*, 63 ff.; Ritter, *Sword and Scepter* III, 66 ff.; Falkenhayn, *German General Staff*, 82 ff.

[46]August von Mackensen, *Briefe und Aufzeichnungen*, ed. F. W. Foerster (Leipzig, 1938), 137 passim; Hans Meier-Welcker, *Seeckt* (Frankfurt A.M., 1967), 39 passim.

[47]Ludendorff, *Ludendorff's Own Story* I, 171 ff.; and Falkenhayn, *German General Staff*, 155 ff., present the views of the principal adversaries. An excellent recent survey of Germany's eastern policies in 1915 is Volker Ullrich, "Entscheidung im Osten oder Sicherung der Dardanellen: das Ringen um den Serbienfeldzug 1915," *Militärgeschichtliche Mitterilungen* XXXII (1982), 45–63.

[48]Max Weber, *Gesammelte politische Schriften*, 2nd ed. (Tübingen, 1958), 120 passim.

[49]Horst-Günther Linke, *Das zarische Russland und der Erste Weltkrieg. Diplomatie und Kriegsziel 1914–1917* (Munich, 1982), is the best recent overview of this subject.

[50]Volker Ullrich, "Zwischen Verhandlungsfrieden und Erschöpfungskrieg. Die Friedensfrage in der deutschen Reichsleitung Ende 1915," *Geschichte in Wissenschaft und Unterricht* XXXVII (1986), 397–419. The quotation is from 403.

[51]Michael Geyer, "German Strategy in the Age of Machine Warfare, 1914–1945," in *Makers of Modern Strategy from Machiavelli to the Nuclear Age*, ed. Peter Paret (Princeton, N.J., 1986), 534 ff.

[52]Cf. *inter alia* Jack Snyder, "Perceptions of the Security Dilemma in 1914,"

Notes

in *Psychology and Deterrence*, ed. R. Jervis, R. N. Lebow, and J. G. Stein (Baltimore, 1985), 153–179; and Stephen Van Evera, "Why Cooperation Failed in 1914," *World Politics* XXXVIII (1985), 80–117.

[53]Ludendorff, *Ludendorff's Own Story* II, 583 *passim*.

[54]Cf. Woodruff D. Smith, *The Ideological Origins of Nazi Imperialism* (New York, 1986), 166 ff.; and Shanafelt, *Secret Enemy*, 67 ff.

[55]Fritz Fischer, *Juli 1914: Wir sind nicht hineingeschlittert* (Berlin, 1983), 20–21.

[56]Reichenau to foreign office, Aug. 20, 1914, in Politisches Archiv des Auswärtigen Amtes, Krieg 1914, Unternehmungen und Aufweigelung gegen unsere Feinde, WK 11 c Geheim (hereafter cited as PAAA).

[57]Lemberg Consulate to Tschirsky; Tschirsky to foreign office, Aug. 11, 1914, PAAA, Krieg 1914, WK 11 a, Ukraine.

[58]Tschirsky to foreign office, Oct. 11, Oct. 13, 1914; Jagow to Zimmermann, Aug. 31, 1914, *ibid.*

[59]Szogeny to Jagow, Aug. 15, 1914; Tschirsky to foreign office, Aug. 21, 1914, PAAA. Krieg 1914, WK 14 a, Verwaltung besetzten Gebiet in Russland.

[60]Steenbiss to Prussian ministry of public works, Aug. 11, 1914; Worysch to 8th Army command, Aug. 12, 1914, *ibid.*

EPILOGUE

[1]Dietrich Orlow, *Weimar Prussia, 1918–1925: The Unlikely Rock of Democracy* (Pittsburgh, 1986), 241; Andreas Dorpalen, *Hindenburg and the Weimar Republic* (Princeton, N.J., 1964).

[2]The design and its history are summarized in George L. Mosse, *The Nationalization of the Masses* (New York, 1975), 69 ff. Cf. also Erich Maschke, "Die Geschichte des Reichsehrenmals Tannenberg," and Johannes Kruger, "Bauliche Gedanken um das Reichsehrenmal Tannenberg und seine Einfügung in die Landschaft," in *Tannenberg. Deutsches Schicksal, deutsche Aufgabe*, ed. Kuratorium für das Reichsehrenmal (Oldenburg, 1935), 199–247.

[3]Konrad Wagner, ed., *Tannenberg und seine Heldengräber. Ein Lesebuch von deutscher Grösse*, 2nd ed. rev. (Osterode, 1936).

[4]For Ludendorff's postwar career see particularly Richard Piazza, "Ludendorff: The Totalitarian and Völkisch Politics of a Military Specialist" (Ph.D. Dissertation, Northwestern University, 1969).

[5]August von Mackensen, *Briefe und Aufzeichnungen*, ed. W. Foerster (Leipzig, 1938), 363 *passim*.

[6]Lyncker to François, Jan. 1, 1916; letters of Aug. 7 and Aug. 10, 1917, by two of VII Corps' regimental commanders, in Bundesarchiv-Militärarchiv, Nachlass François, NL 274/16.

[7]Information on the wartime experiences of the Tannenberg divisions is drawn from the specific entries in *Histories of the Two Hundred and Fifty-One Divisions of the German Army which Participated in the War (1914–1918)*, ed. by General Staff, AEF (Washington, D.C., 1920), supplemented from regimental histories.

[8]Quoted in Williamson Murray, *The Change in the European Balance of Power, 1918–1939* (Princeton, 1984), 149.

[9]Cf. *inter alia* Klaus-Jürgen Müller, *General Ludwig Beck* (Boppard, 1980); Robert J. O'Neill, "Doctrine and Training in the German Army, 1918–1939," in *The Theory and Practice of War*, ed. M. Howard (New York, 1965), 143–165; and Charles Messenger, *The Art of Blitzkrieg* (London, 1976).

Notes

[10]Hans Gatzke, "Russo-German Military Collaboration During the Weimar Republic," *American Historical Review* LXIII (1958), 565–597.

[11]Erich Wagner, "Gedanken über den Wort von Kriegserfahrung," *Militär-wissenschaftliche Rundschau* II (1937), 231–245.

[12]Most particularly in the work of Jürgen Förster. Typical is "New Wine in Old Skins? The Wehrmacht and the War of 'Weltauschaungen,' 1941," in *The German Military in the Age of Total War*, ed. W. Deist (Dover, N.H., 1985), 304–322. Cf. also Omer Bartov, *The Eastern Front, 1941–45: German Troops and the Barbarization of Warfare* (New York, 1986).

[13]Cf. Heinz Bürger, *Bei Tannenberg zwei Schlachten. Ritter und Feldherren auf Wacht im Osten* (Stuttgart, 1935); Rudolf van Wehrt, *Tannenberg* (Berlin, 1934); Rolf Bathe, *Tannenberg. Der Einsatz des letzten Mannes* (Berlin, 1935).

[14]Andreas Hillgruber, *Der Zusammenbruch im Osten 1944/45 als Problem der deutschen Nationalgeschichte und der Europäischen Geschichte* (Wiesbaden, 1985), 13; Michael Salewski, "Der Erste Weltkrieg-ein deutsches Trauma," *Revue International d'Histoire Militaire* LXII (1985), 184.

[15]Cf. *inter alia* Stefan Kuczynski, *Wielka wojna z Zakonem Krzyzackim w latach 1409–1411* (Warsaw, 1955; rev. ed. 1960); and *Spor o Grunwald rozpiawy polemiczne* (Warsaw, 1972).

Bibliographical Essay

The nature of the chapter references in this volume make a full bibliography redundant. My principal archival sources were the holdings of the German foreign office in Bonn and the *Bundesarvhiv-Militärarchiv* in Freiburg. From Bonn, the *Deutschland*, *Russland*, and *Krieg 1914* files were particularly valuable. The BA-MA collection of private papers includes the *Nachlässe* of Max Hoffmann, Hermann von François, and Otto von Below. The latter is also a rich source of information on the prewar army. The *Nachlässe* of Wilhelm Gröner and Adolf Tappen helped reconstruct prewar planning for the defense of East Prussia, while the *Nachlass* of F. W. Foerster contains correspondence clarifying—or attempting to clarify—several controversial points of the campaign. The records of the *Admiralstab der Marine* in the German Navy Archive include a good deal of significant correspondence with the general staff, as well as the navy's own analyses of German strategic and geographical positions.

The exhaustive and exhausting literature on specific aspects of the contributions of Russo-German hostility to the outbreak of World War I is best traced through the footnotes. Paul Kennedy, *The Rise and Fall of the Great Powers* (New York, 1987), incorporates the most recent, and by far the most familiar, statement of Russia's relative weakness. James Joll, *The Origins of the First World War* (New York, 1984), emphasizes Europe's structural weaknesses; Volker Berghahn, *Germany and the Approach of War in 1914* (New York, 1973), differs from its companion volumes in the St. Martin series, *The Making of the 20th Century*, (Zara Steiner on Britain, D. C. B. Lieven on Russia, and John Keiger on France) in stressing the aggressive intentions of his subject. Walter Laqueur, *Russia and Germany: A Century of Conflict* (Boston, Toronto, 1965), deserves renewed attention, particularly in a current context stressing the possibilities of long-term German-Soviet rapprochement. The new translation of Dietrich Geyer, *Russian Imperialism: The Interaction of Domestic and Foreign Policy, 1860–1914* (Leamington Spa, 1987), establishes for an English-speaking audience the fence-moving nature of Russian expansionism prior to World War I, and how it differed essentially from imperialism's more familiar forms, colonialism and economic penetration.

On the opposing armies, Bernd Schulte, *Die deutsche Armee 1900–1914. Zwischen Beharren und Verändern* (Düsseldorf, 1977); and Manfred Messerschmidt, "Preussens Militär in seinem gesellschaftlichen Umfeld," *Geschichte und Gesellschaft, Sonderheft 6, Preussen im Rückblick*, ed. H-J Pühle, H-U Wehler (Göttingen, 1980), pp. 43–88; are the best examples of a currently dominant school of thought sharply critical of the German army's social role and fighting power. David R. Jones, "Imperial Russia's Forces at War," in *Military Effectiveness*, Vol. I, *The First World War*, ed. A. R. Millett, W. Murray (Boston, 1988), 249–328, is the best readily-available survey of a subject treated at greater length in "Russia's Armed Forces at War: 1914–1918: An Analysis of Military Effectiveness" (Ph.D. Dissertation, Dalhousie University, 1986). Bruce Menning's forthcoming *Bayonets Before Bullets* is a definitive analyses of doctrine, training, and tactics in the Russian army of 1914. Allan Wildman's two volumes on *The End of the Russian Imperial Army* (Princeton, 1979) stresses the impact of war on the army's structure.

Operationally Tannenberg is most familiar to English-language readers from its Russian perspective. Alexander Solzhenitsyn's *August 1914*, especially its revised and enlarged edition (New York, 1989), incorporates an historical dimension that makes its case more by weight than by scholarship. W. Bruce Lincoln, *Passage through Armageddon* (New York, 1986), and Norman Stone, *The Eastern Front, 1914–17* (New York, 1975), include up-to-date summary accounts of Tannenberg. Lincoln focusses on the command aspects of Russia's disaster; Stone emphasizes the army's structural weaknesses. Of the older secondary accounts, N. N. Golovine, *The Russian Campaign of 1914*, tr. A. G. S. Muntz (Ft. Leavenworth, Kans., 1933) remains valuable for its copious excerpts from unpublished or obscure Russian accounts. British general Sir Edmund Ironside's *Tannenberg: The First Thirty Days in East Prussia* (Edinburgh, 1933), is a professional soldier's account containing translations of many of the Russian orders whose original texts are in *Sbornik dokumentov mirovay voyni na russkom fronte. Manevrenni period 1914 goda: Vostochno-Prusskaya operasiya*, ed. Generalny Shtab RKKA (Moscow, 1939), Alfred Knox, *With the Russian Army, 1914–1917*, Vol. I (London, 1921), incorporates the most familiar description of the 2nd Army's situation. Jean Savant, *Épopée Russe* (Paris, 1945), is an emigré apologia for Rennenkampf, nevertheless helpful in explaining the 1st Army commander's behavior during the Tannenberg campaign.

Material from the German side of the battle line is at least as ample, though less accessible. Hindenburg and Ludendorff both left memoirs, published in English as *Out of My Life* (London, 1933) and *Ludendorff's Own Story* (New York, 1929). Max Hoffmann's *War Diaries and Other Papers* (London, 1929); and Hermann von François's *Marneschlacht und Tannenberg* (Berlin, 1920), give their respective authors the best of every situation, but are useful retrospectives. Walther von Stephani, *Mit Hindenburg bei Tannenberg* (Berlin, 1919) offers a junior staff officer's perspective.

Of the secondary accounts, the German official history, *Die Befreiung Ostpreussens*, Volume II of *Der Weltkrieg* (Berlin, 1925), is detailed and reliable on everything that can be verified, but glosses over the problems of command that played such a major role in the campaign. Walter Elze, *Das Deutsche Heer von 1914* (Breslau, 1928), despite its title, is a sound analysis of Tannenberg by one of interwar Germany's finest civilian military historians. The volume is particularly valuable because it reprints many orders whose originals were lost during World

War II. Elze's distaste for what he considers Ludendorff's unjustified postwar pretensions are as clear as his admiration for Hindenburg.

Theobald von Schäfer, the archivist responsible for Volume II of the official history, used the anecdotal and descriptive material excluded from the larger work as a basis for *Tannenberg* (Berlin, 1927), a volume in the *Reichsarchiv's* series *Schlachten des Weltkrieges*. This drum-and-trumpet narrative account, constantly contrasting German heroism with Russian incompetence, invites dismissal as Weimar revisionism at its worst. Its extensive citations of sources, since lost, nevertheless make it a rough equivalent of Golovine, at least for the operations against the Russian 2nd Army.

Almost every regiment of the kaiser's army produced its own history of World War I. These range from simple précis of war diaries and stupefying lists of dates to well-researched, sophisticated accounts by academically trained historians who made full use of diaries, letters, and interviews. Given the extensive destruction of German military archives for the period, these volumes are the best remaining source of information on the wartime army's domestic economy. Their authors on the whole strove for honesty. In their pages not all the comrades are valiant and not all the officers are above average. The most senior and socially acceptable regiments, those with the largest funds and the richest old comrades' associations, tended to produce the most detailed, and correspondingly useful, works. For the 8th Army, Franz von Gottberg, *Das Grenadier-Regiment Kronprinz (1. Ostpreussische) Nr. 1 im Weltkriege*, Vol. I, *Die Ereignisse von Kriegsbeginn bis zum 31.Juli 1916* (Berlin 1927); Alfred Bülowius and Bruno Hippler, *Das Infanterie-Regiment v. Boyen (5. Ostpreussisches) Nr. 41 im Weltkriege 1914–1918* (Berlin, 1929); and Wilhelm Reichert, *Das Infanterie-Regiment Frhr. Hiller von Gaertringen (4. Posensches) Nr. 59 im Weltkriege 1914/18*, Vol. I, *1914/15* (Berlin, 1930) stand out. Moritz Holzmann, *Hanseatische Landwehr im Felde (Geschichte des L.I.R. 75)*, Vol. I, *Bewegungskrieg* (Hamburg, 1928), casts useful light on the fight of the Goltz Division; and Ernst Zipfel, *Geschichte des Dragoner-Regiments König Albert von Sachsen (Ostpr.) Nr. 10* (Zeulenroda, 1933), gives a comprehensive picture of the patrols and skirmishes that made up the cavalry's still-vital contribution.

Index

Aehrenthal, Alois Lexa, 36, 38, 42, 47

Air reconnaissance, 152–53, 169, 189, 192, 267, 300, 311–12

Alexander III, Tsar of Russia, 19

Alieuv, Eris Khan, 137, 189

Army Bill of 1913 (German), 70–71

Army, French, compared with Germany, 31–32; strategy and tactics, 52–53

Army, German: and strategic planning, 20–22, 25–26, 30–35, 43–46, 59–60, 98, 335–46; and views on war, 58–59; military intelligence, 61–63, 95–98; officer corps, 108–11, 272–73; socialists and, 109–10; regimental system, 111–12, 113–14; as socializing institution, 112–13, 116–17; doctrine and training, 114–15, 124, 164–65; mistreatment in, 115–16; structure of, in 1914, 117–20; tactics, 121–23, 174; reservists in, 123–24, 142–43, 149–50; uniforms and equipment, 148–49; intelligence, 150–51; morale, 252–54; pioneers in, 272–73

Army, Russian: deployment, 25; and economy, 27; effectiveness, 62–63, 64–65; and possible Baltic invasion, 64; mobilization of, in 1914, 97–99; officer corps, 126, 134–35; doctrine, 126–27; strategic planning, 127–31; organization, 135; supply system, 215–16; communications, 216–17

Artamonov, Lt.-Gen., 233, 250, 252

Artillery, German: organization, 119–20; material, 119–20; communications, 176–77; tactics, 185

Artillery, Russian, 136, 151–60, 313

Austria-Hungary, foreign relations of, 20–21, 24, 36, 41, 54; new sick man of Europe, 75–76; and Serbia, 85–87; war plans, 143–44, 156–57; disaster of, in 1914, 326–27

Bakunin, Michael, 13

Balkan League, 48–51

Balkan Wars, 51–52, 56

Bartenwerfer, Capt., 287–88, 290

Bauer, Max, 330

Beck, Ludwig, 65

Below, Otto von, 108; commands I Reserve Corps, 188, 209–10; at Gumbinnen, 188–90; at Bischofsburg, 240–48; and advance on Allenstein, 265, 286–90, 298–99,

411

Index

303–04; subsequent career, 349–50

Benecke, Capt., 271–73

Bennigsen, Adam, 147, 148, 160

Berchtold, Leopold von, 84, 86

Bernstein, Eduard, 16, 71

Bethmann-Hollweg, Theobald von: and Britain, 46–47; and Russia, 46, 69; and Balkans, 56–57; and Concert of Europe, 58–59; and military budget of 1913, 70–71; and Austria, 75–76; and July Crisis, 88–94; and prospects for a separate Russian peace, 337–44

Bismarck, Otto von, 2, 10; Russian policies, 16, 20–22; and *Lombardverbot*, 23–24; and Reinsurance Treaty, 23; resignation of, 26

Blagoveschensky, Lt.-Gen., 243–47, 315–17

Bloch, I. S., 34

Bosnian Crisis, 36–42

Brecht, Maj.-Gen., 151, 296

Brusilov, Alexei, 64

Buchanan, Sir George, 77

Bülow, Bernhard von, 333; on Russia, 24–25, 29–30; and Weltpolitik, 29; and Bosnian crisis, 38–42

Bülow, Karl von, 67, 294

Cambon, Jules, 52

Caprivi, Leo von, 26, 32

Cavalry, German: doctrine, 151–52; at Gumbinnen, 180, 189, 210

Cavalry, Russian: organization, 136; doctrine, 146–48; and reconnaissance, 217

Congress of Berlin, 16

Conrad von Hötzendorf, Franz, 45, 67–68, 84, 327, 339

Conta, Richard von, 162–66, 174, 176, 234–37, 250–55, 279–80, 304–06

Crown Council (1912), 55

Danilov, Yuri, 129

De moribus Ruthenorum (Hehn), 17

Drechsel, Maj., 296

Durnovo, Pavel, 78

East Prussia: strategic geography of, 32–33, 145–46; ethnic tensions in, 106–07; Russian behavior in, 159–60

Einem, Karl von, 61

Elze, Walter, 240–41

Fabeck, Col. von, 201

Falk, Maj.-Gen. von, 165–66, 167, 172–73, 237, 250–55, 282

Falkenhayn, Erich von, 98, 138, 335; and eastern front, 337–45

Franco-Russian alliance, 26, 28, 49–50, 52–54, 71–72, 127–28

François, Hermann von: proposals for defense of East Prussia, 155–56; initial deployment of I Corps, 158–59, 161–62; at Stallupönen, 162–67; convinces Prittwitz to attack, 170–71; at Gumbinnen, 172–77; and proposed retreat, 191–92, 194, 156–202; concentration of I Corps against Samsonov, 229–31; conflict with Hindenburg and Ludendorff, 233–38; and attack on Usdau, 250–55; advance on Neidenburg, 278; concern for southern flank, 310–13, 315, 317; after Tannenberg, 325, 330, 350

Frantz, Capt., 151

Franz, Josef, Emperor of Austria-Hungary, 77, 84

Freiherr von Marschall, Col., 201

Giers, N. I., 20, 26–27

Goltz, Colmar Freiherr von der, 154

Goltz, Maj.-Gen. Freiherr von der, 207, 275–77, 284–85, 299–300

Great Britain: and German rivalry, 3, 28–29; naval negotiations with Russia, 92–94; in July Crisis, 89–90, 93–94

Grey, Sir Edward, 54, 55, 76, 86

Groener, Wilhelm, 88, 94–95, 201, 293–94

Grosse Ostaufmarsch, 65–66

Grünert, Col., 140, 192–94, 257

Guchkov, A. J., 324

Haeften, Hans von, 339

Hahn, Brig.-Gen. von, 181, 316–17

Hahndorff, Brig.-Gen., 185

Haldane, Richard, 55

Hartwig, Nicholas, 51

Index

Hausmann, Conrad von, 344
Heeringen, Josias von, 70
Hehn, Viktor, 17
Heineccius, Maj.-Gen. von, 181, 244–45, 350
Hell, Emil, 191, 205–06, 222, 227–28, 232, 238
Hennig, Maj.-Gen., 186, 315–16
Hesse, Lt., 371–72
Hindenburg, Paul von: character and career, 201–02; commander 8th Army, 202; relationship to Ludendorff, 204–05, 241–42, 291–92; and concentration against Samsonov, 228, 233; reactions on August 27, 261–62; and advance on Allenstein, 286–88, 296–97; tactical conclusions, 309–10; and Tannenberg mythos, 329–31; as symbol, 334–35, 347–48; and eastern front, 338–41
Hintze, Paul von, 39, 40, 41, 42, 43
Hitler, Adolf, 333–34, 352–53
Hoffmann, Max, 140–41, 154, 192–94, 195, 196, 205, 206–07, 262–63, 276, 290, 292, 294–95, 300, 313, 330, 349
Holstein, Friedrich von, 22–24, 27–28, 35
Hoth, Hermann, 291
House, Edward, 82–83

Izvolsky, A. P., 37–42, 53

Jagow, Gottlieb von, 75, 82
Joffre, Joseph, 52–53

Kiderlin-Wächter, Alfred von, 48, 54, 55
Kluck, Alexander von, 139–40, 155, 178
Kluyev, Maj.-Gen., 258–59, 266–67, 277, 297–98, 299, 308–09
Knox, Alfred, 216, 231–32, 269
Körner, Lt., 311
Kokovtsov, V. N., 42, 48, 52, 73, 79, 83
Kruger, Johannes and Walter, 348
Kühl, Hermann von, 66
Kuhn, Andreas, 218, 220–21, 281

Lagarde, Paul de, 17
Liman von Sanders, 72–74
Ludendorff, Erich: early career, 199; at Liège, 199–200; 8th Army chief of staff, 200; relationship to Hindenburg, 204–05; and army staff, 206–07; and concentration against Samsonov, 228–33; reaction to François's delays, 235–36; anxiety of, on August 26, 240–41; plans for August 27, 249–50; and Rennenkampf's threat, 261–62, 264–66; orders I Corps to Lahna, 279–80; and advance on Allenstein, 286–88, 296–97, 300; gives battle its name, 292–93; and reinforcements, 293–96; plans operations against Rennenkampf, 302–03, 306–07, 318–19; reinforces François, 312–13; career after Tannenberg, 329–30, 334–44
Lyncker, Maj.-Gen. von, 201

Mackensen, August von: early career, 177–78; at Gumbinnen, 180–88, 194; at Bischofsburg, 240–48; concern for Rennenkampf's advance, 247–48; advance on Allenstein, 264, 286–88, 290–91; and pursuit south, 306, 316; later career, 325, 342–43, 349
Martos, Lt.-Gen., 297–98, 307, 314
Mediterranean Agreements, 23
Messimy, Adolphe, 97
Mikhnevich, N. P., 128–29
Miliutin, D. I., 127
Moltke, Helmuth von (the elder), 20, 24–25
Moltke, Helmuth von (the younger), 43–45, 64, 65–67, 81–82, 94; views on war, 1911, 59–60; character, 88; in July crisis, 97–101; and eastern front, 144; and Conrad, 45–46, 157; and Prittwitz's relief, 194–200; and decision to reinforce eastern theater, 293–96
Morgen, Curt von, 208, 227, 239–40, 274–75, 282–83, 303, 305
Macdonald, Hector, 178

Nakhitchevanski, Hussein Khan, 147
Nationalism: German, 16–18, 55–56,

Index

60–61; Russian, 15, 22, 55–56, 71; Serbian, 56–57; Slavic, 36–37, 42, 51

Nesselrode, K. R., 14

Nicholas I, Tsar of Russia, 13

Nicholas II, Tsar of Russia, 28, 38, 52, 77–78, 90

Nicolai, Walter, 62

Nicolson, Sir Arthur, 35, 40

Pašić, Nikola, 84, 87

Poincaré, Raymond, 53–54

Posadowsky, Col., 264–65

Postovsky, Gen., 216, 266

Pourtalès, Friedrich von, 38, 42

Prittwitz und Gaffron, Max von, 139–40, 143–44, 153, 154, 156, 158, 201, 329; and François, 161, 165–67; plans for Gumbinnen, 168–77; concern for advance of Russian 2nd Army, 191; proposes to retreat, 192–96; relief of, 196–99

Radio intelligence, 95, 169–70, 191, 196, 227–30, 277–78, 287, 300

Reinsurance Treaty, 23, 26

Riezler, Kurt, 69–70, 92, 100

Rennenkampf, Pavel, 133–34; at Stallupönen, 167–68; relations with Samsonov, 134, 206–07; pursuit after Gumbinnen, 207–08, 291, 300–02; and Masurian Lakes, 325–26, 328

Reusteck, Otto, 173

Ritter von Wenninger, Karl, 196–99, 325

Russia: Germanophobia in, 14–15; foreign policy of, 15–16; commercial relations with Germany, 18–19, 22, 27–28; internal crisis of, 79–81, 83–84; decision for war, 96–100

Saher zum Weissenstein, Burscher von, 219

Schlimm, Maj., 311–12, 313

Samarin, Yuri, 14

Samsonov, A. V., 134; alleged feud with Rennenkampf, 134, 206–07; advance into East Prussia, 213–18; extends areas of advance westward,

221, 231–34; tries to concentrate center corps, 243, 258–59, 266–67; leaves headquarters, 268–69; with XV Corps, 297–98; suicide of, 309

Sarajevo assassination, 84–85

Sazonov, Sergei, 46–47, 49, 51, 52, 54, 63, 72–73, 79, 81, 83, 90–91, 92, 96–99, 100

Schaffer von Bernstein, Lt.-Col., 278

Schiemann, Theodor, 17

Schlieffen, Alfred von: east versus west, 31–32; and eastern theater, 32–33, 59, 65; on war, 33–34; Schlieffen Plan, 34–35

Schmettau, Maj.-Gen., 281, 305

Schmidt von Schmidtseck, Col., 158, 205

Scholtz, Lt.-Gen., 221–23, 228, 232–33, 238–39, 255–57

Schwerin, Maj., 290

Second Moroccan Conference, 50

Seeckt, Hans von, 342, 349

Serbia: regional ambitions, 55, 56–57; in aftermath of Balkan Wars, 72; relations with Austria, 85–88

Seton-Watson, R. W., 75

Sirelius, Maj.-Gen., 310, 317

Smirnov, Lt.-Gen., 137

Sontag, Maj.-Gen., 256–58, 269–74, 303

Staabs, Maj.-Gen. von, 66, 256, 283–84, 299, 314

Stein, Hermann von, 196–98

Stephani, Walther von, 259–60

Stolypin, P. A., 37, 42, 48

Sukhomlinov, V. A., 53, 63, 80, 81, 83, 133

Tamms, Capt., 308

Tannenberg: named, 292–93, 307; military results, 323–24, 327–29; moral effect on Russia, 324–25; psychological impact, 328–32; postwar legacy, 347, 351; monument, 348, 354; and World War II, 353–54

Tappen, Adolf, 66, 325, 330

Three Emperors' League (1873), 16; (1881), 20, 23, 224; possible revival of, 36

Tirpitz, Alfred von, 30, 333

Index

Treutler, Georg von, 84
Trotha, Brig.-Gen., 314–15

Unger, Brig.-Gen. von, 192, 258, 282
Urwicz, Pincus, 101–02

Verdy du Vernois, Julius, 201

Waldersee, Alfred von, 24–26, 31
Waldersee, Georg von, 91, 94; 8th
   Army chief of staff, 140, 153, 156,
   171, 193–94, 196–97, 199–200
"War in sight" crisis, 1914, 79–80
Wickham Steed, Henry, 75, 86

Wild von Hohenborn, Adolf, 336,
   341
William II, Emperor of Germany, 2,
   26, 55, 74, 177, 202–04, 294;
   eclipse of, 331–33, 339, 340
Wilson, Sir Henry, 82
Wilson, Woodrow, 57, 58
Witte, Sergei, 19

Yanushkevich, N. N., 96
Yepantschin, Lt.-Gen., 137, 167

Zhilinski, Yahou, 132–33, 207, 213–
   14, 221, 231–32, 301–02, 326

Index to
Military Formations

German formations engaged in the Tannenberg campaign

OHL: and 8th Army Command, 194–204; campaign in west, 195–96; reinforces 8th Army, 293–96

8th Army: formation of, 139–43; mission of, 143–45; concentrates on Angerapp, 157–58; effect of Stallupönen on, 164–70; decision to retreat after Gumbinnen, 190–99; change of command, 199–204; concentrates against 2nd Army, 205–07, 228–33; concerns of on August 26, 240–42, 249–50; and threat from Rennenkampf, 261–62, 263–66, 277–78; and I Corps's advance on Neidenburg, 279–80; unsure of positions of XVII Corps and I Reserve Corps, 286–87, 296; plans for August 29, 292, 296–97; renewed concern for Rennenkampf's movements, 291–93, 302–03; orders for August 30, 306–07; and Russian counterattack, 312–14; and aftermath of Tannenberg, 325–27.

I Corps, 139, 142–43, 146; and fron-tier operations, 155–56, 158–59, 161–62; at Stallupönen, 162–68; at Gumbinnen, 172–77, 191–92; re-deploys south, 206, 229–31, 233–36; at Seeben-Usdau, 234–38, 250–55, 261; advance of Neiden-burg, 278–82; closes ring around 2nd Army, 304–06; and counterat-tack from south, 310–13, 317–18

XVII Corps, 142, 146, 170, 177, 191; advance to Gumbinnen, 178–80; attack of, 180–86; rout of, 186–88; advances south, 208–09, 229, 242; at Bischofsburg, 242–48; pursues Russians, 261–65; confusion in or-ders to, 265–66, 286–87, 290–91; pursuit on August 29, 306; and Russian counterattack, 315–16, 317–18

XX Corps, 142, 146, 153, 170, 191–93, 196, 205–06, 222, 237; at Lahna-Orlau, 223–28, 232–33; ad-vance of on August 26, 237–40; detachment of, with I Corps, 250, 255; on August 27, 255–60; on Au-gust 28, 269–74, 282

I Reserve Corps, 142, 146; at Gum-

Index to Military formations

binnen, 188–90; redeploys, 209; at Bischofsburg, 243–48, 255, 261, 264; advance on Allenstein, 286–90; pursuit to Hohenstein, 298–300, 303–04

1st Division: at Stallupönen, 162–66; at Gumbinnen, 172–77; at Seeben-Usdau, 234–37, 250–55; advance on Neidenburg, 278–82; pursues Russians, 304–06; and Russian counterattack, 311–14

2nd Division: at Stallupönen, 162, 165–66; at Gumbinnen, 172–77; at Seeben-Usdau, 234–37, 250–55; advance on Neidenburg, 278–82; and Russian counterattack, 311–14

35th Division: at Gumbinnen, 180–86; move south, 242; at Bischofsburg, 244–46; and pursuit of Russians, 306, 316

36th Division: at Gumbinnen, 180–86; move south, 242; at Bischofsburg, 244–46; and pursuit of Russians, 306, 316

37th Division: at Lahna-Orlau, 223–28, 233; movements of, on August 26, 239; on August 27, 256–57, 260; advance on Hohenstein, 283–84, 299–300; redeploy, 312, 314

41st Division: at Lahna-Orlau, 223–27, 233; attacks on August 26, 239; on August 27, 256–58; attacks Waplitz, 269–74, 281; on August 29, 303

1st Reserve Division, 189–90, 245, 288–90

3rd Reserve Division, 142, 146, 208–10, 227, 233, 239–40, 249–50, 255–56, 260, 274–75, 283, 303

36th Reserve Division, 189–90, 245–46, 288, 290

Goltz Landwehr Division, 230, 259, 275–77, 283–85, 299–301

1st Cavalry Division, 151, 210

5th Landwehr Brigade, 250, 252, 278, 307

6th Landwehr Brigade, 245, 247, 300

70th Landwehr Brigade, 223, 233, 274, 282

69th Garrison Brigade, 258, 274

Schmettau's Force, 250, 255, 256, 270, 278, 280–82, 304–06

1st Grenadiers, 161, 174–76

3rd Grenadiers, 143, 166, 173, 304

4th Grenadiers, 109, 253, 262–63, 281

5th Grenadiers, 143, 182, 185–86, 290–91

18th Infantry, 223

21st Infantry, 306, 308–09

33rd Fusiliers, 166, 252

41st Infantry, 164, 167, 315

43rd Infantry, 163, 278

44th Infantry, 111, 253

45th Infantry, 166, 173–74, 252–53

59th Infantry, 223, 239, 271–73, 306

128th Infantry, 183

129th Infantry, 180, 183

141st Infantry, 109, 182, 188

148th Infantry, 271, 272, 273

150th Infantry, 227, 228, 239, 273, 283

151st Infantry, 219, 224, 225, 305

152nd Infantry, 271, 273

175th Infantry, 242

176th Infantry, 315–17

1st Jäger Battalion, 109, 223, 225–26, 238

26th Pioneer Battalion, 272–73

3rd Reserve Infantry, 143, 188, 290

16th Field Artillery, 161, 304

35th Field Artillery, 274

36th Field Artillery, 185

37th Field Artillery, 253

52nd Field Artillery, 161, 314

71st Field Artillery, 188

81st Field Artillery, 185

1st Reserve Field Artillery, 188

36th Reserve Field Artillery, 143, 303–04

1st Dragoons, 152

10th Dragoons, 223

11th Dragoons, 223

5th Hussars, 263, 306, 308

4th Mounted Rifles, 263, 291

10th Mounted Rifles, 280, 304, 316

8th Uhlans, 278, 280, 304

1st Reserve Uhlans, 245, 290

Air Battalion 2, 152

Air Detachment 14, 153–54, 311

Air Detachment 16, 158, 287, 312

Index to Military formations

Other German formations

2nd Army, 294
3rd Army, 294–95
5th Army, 294–95
V Corps, 132, 294
XI Corps, 294, 295, 326
XXI Corps, 294
I Bavarian Corps, 294
Guard Reserve Corps, 294, 295–96
8th Cavalry Division, 294

Russian formations

Stavka, 132
Northwest Front, 132–33, 231–32, 301–02
1st Army: formation, 132–34, 137–38; at Stallupönen, 163–70; Gumbinnen, 173–90; failure to pursue, 207–08, 229–30, 300–02
2nd Army: formation, 132–35; initial advance of, 158, 169–70; lines of march changed, 213–14, 221, 231–32; difficulties of, 215–18; orders to continue attack on August 27, 266–69; collapse of, 297–98, 307–09

I Corps, 213–14, 218, 221, 231–32, 233–34, 250–52, 255
II Corps, 213, 247, 301
III Corps, 137, 301
IV Corps, 137, 189, 247, 301
VI Corps, 213, 218, 221, 231–32, 242–48, 258, 266–69, 315–17
XIII Corps, 213, 218, 221, 231–32, 258–59, 266–69, 275, 277, 297, 300, 307–08, 309
XV Corps, 213, 217, 218, 221, 223, 231–32, 258–59, 266–69, 307–08, 314, 315–17
XX Corps, 137, 173, 301
XXIII Corps, 213, 218
3rd Guard Division, 218, 234, 310, 313
2nd Division, 218, 221, 232, 239, 251, 256
4th Division, 243, 244, 246–47
8th Division, 223
16th Division, 245, 246
27th Division, 166
28th Division, 176
30th Division, 189
4th Cavalry Division, 243, 315–17
6th Cavalry Division, 234
15th Cavalry Division, 234